THE CHOCOLATE
AND COFFEE BIBLE

THE CHOCOLATE
AND COFFEE BIBLE

Over 300 delicious, easy-to-make recipes for total indulgence, from
bakes to desserts, shown step by step in 1300 glorious photographs

Catherine Atkinson, Mary Banks,
Christine France & Christine McFadden

HERMES
HOUSE

This edition is published by Hermes House, an imprint of Anness Publishing Ltd,
Hermes House, 88–89 Blackfriars Road,
London SE1 8HA; tel. 020 7401 2077; fax 020 7633 9499

www.hermeshouse.com; www.annesspublishing.com

If you like the images in this book and would like to investigate using them for publishing, promotions or
advertising, please visit our website www.practicalpictures.com for more information.

© Anness Publishing Ltd 2002, 2008

Publisher: Joanna Lorenz
Editorial Director: Judith Simons
Project Editor: Mariano F.X.P. Kälfors
Designers: Nigel Partridge, Ian Hunt, Jane Felstead and Ian Sandom
Photography: Don Last (chocolate section), William Lingwood (coffee recipes),
Louisa Dare (coffee steps and equipment) and Janine Hosegood (coffee bean samples)
Editorial Reader: Jonathan Marshall
Production Controller: Ben Worley

ETHICAL TRADING POLICY
At Anness Publishing we believe that business should be conducted in an ethical and ecologically sustainable way, with respect for the environment and a proper regard
to the replacement of the natural resources we employ.
As a publisher, we use a lot of wood pulp to make high-quality paper for printing, and that wood commonly comes from spruce trees. We are therefore currently
growing more than 750,000 trees in three Scottish forest plantations: Berrymoss (130 hectares/320 acres), West Touxhill (125 hectares/305 acres) and Deveron Forest
(75 hectares/185 acres). The forests we manage contain more than 3.5 times the number of trees employed each year in making paper for the books we manufacture.
Because of this ongoing ecological investment programme, you, as our customer, can have the pleasure and reassurance of knowing that a tree is being cultivated on
your behalf to naturally replace the materials used to make the book you are holding.
Our forestry programme is run in accordance with the UK Woodland Assurance Scheme (UKWAS) and will be certified by the internationally recognized Forest
Stewardship Council (FSC). The FSC is a non-government organization dedicated to promoting responsible management of the world's forests. Certification ensures
forests are managed in an environmentally sustainable and socially responsible way. For further information about this scheme, go to www.annesspublishing.com/trees

A CIP catalogue record for this book is available from the British Library.

Previously published as *Chocolate & Coffee*

NOTES

Bracketed terms are intended for American readers.

For all recipes, quantities are given in both metric and imperial measures and, where appropriate, in standard cups
and spoons. Follow one set of measures, but not a mixture, because they are not interchangeable.

Standard spoon and cup measures are level. 1 tsp = 5ml, 1 tbsp = 15ml, 1 cup = 250ml/8fl oz.

Australian standard tablespoons are 20ml. Australian readers should use 3 tsp in place of 1 tbsp
for measuring small quantities.

American pints are 16fl oz/2 cups. American readers should use 20fl oz/2.5 cups in place
of 1 pint when measuring liquids.

Electric oven temperatures in this book are for conventional ovens. When using a fan oven, the temperature will probably
need to be reduced by about 10–20°C/20–40°F. Since ovens vary, you should check with your manufacturer's
instruction book for guidance.

Medium (US large) eggs are used unless otherwise stated.

Main front cover image shows Mocha Viennese Swirls – for recipe, see page 212

Contents

Introduction 6

INTRODUCTION

It's almost unthinkable to imagine modern day life without the pleasures of chocolate and coffee. Hardly a day goes by in most of our lives without sipping a mood-lifting cup of coffee, or nibbling on an indulgent, comforting chocolate treat. Yet these two ancient, exotic flavours, now such a familiar part of our everyday lives, were virtually unknown throughout Europe and Asia until just a few centuries ago.

This indispensable book covers just about everything you need to know about coffee and chocolate, tracing their respective journeys from early discovery, cultivation and the development of trading right up to present day, looking at modern production and their place in society. It tracks the intricate and interwoven histories of these two legendary foods, how they have over centuries woven their way into almost every aspect of society, establishing vital roles in religion, medicine, politics, economics and culture, crossing continents and spreading throughout the world. They have known conflict, fuelled armies, made fortunes, nourished many nations, caused political unrest and encouraged much social interaction.

Although chocolate has its origins in South America and the birthplace of coffee was on the other side of the world in Africa, it's surprising how many aspects of their history run parallel. The chapters on history begin by showing how ancient civilizations attributed both these foods with god-given powers. The Aztecs believed that chocolate was food of the gods and brought spiritual wisdom, energy and sexual power; coffee was thought by the Muslims to be a gift from Allah and it was used not only as a stimulant but to treat an astonishing variety of ailments.

Originally highly prized and expensive, both chocolate and coffee were an exotic luxury reserved only for kings and noblemen, priests and warriors, but in more recent times cultivation has made them widely available to all. The proliferation of trendy coffee shops we know today is

a shadow of the chocolate and coffee houses that became fashionable throughout Europe and the Middle East in centuries past. Then, they were a vital centre for socializing and debate, popular meeting places which enticed people from all walks of life. Patronized by politicians, poets, musicians, professionals and artisans, the coffee house played an important role in social and cultural change in many nations.

Other chapters look at the actual chocolate and coffee plants, discussing characteristics of the different types of beans, countries of production and how they are harvested and processed. We investigate the medicinal powers and sensual pleasures of these fascinating foods and their stimulating effects. Chocolate and coffee alike arouse all our senses – smell, touch, sight, sound and taste, which explains why they play such an important role in our lives. Chocolate, for instance, has long been attributed with aphrodisiac powers, and even Casanova reputedly used it to great effect.

You'll learn the importance of quality chocolate, how to identify different types and tips on handling this sensitive product. The coffee chapters guide you through the huge variety of coffee types and blends and the language of professional coffee tasters. The intricacies and traditions of roasting, grinding and brewing coffee in the home can be daunting, but the section on the art of coffee drinking will help you to avoid the pitfalls in the quest for that perfect cup of coffee.

No book about these two irresistible foods would be complete without recipes. For chocoholics, there's a wide selection of indulgent chocolate recipes, from classic Sachertorte to the more unusual Mango and Chocolate Crème Brûlées. Or, if your passion is for coffee flavours, you will find a varied collection of cakes, desserts and cookies which illustrate the versatility of coffee in the kitchen, including – of course – coffee drinks.

CHOCOLATE

This section provides a definitive reference guide to chocolate. It starts
by examining the intricate links woven by chocolate through history
among people on every imaginable level — national, cultural, political,
economical and spiritual. It traces the evolution of the cacao bean to
beverage, and from beverage to the much loved confectionery of today.
We take a look at the specialist world of quality chocolate,
followed by a tour of chocolate makers around the world.
Lastly and most importantly, Chocolate takes us into the kitchen.
The recipe section contains over 200 mouthwatering creations
waiting to be explored, from Chocolate Zabaglione and Hot Mocha
Rum Soufflés to Chocolate Pecan Pie and Death by Chocolate!

THE HISTORY
OF CHOCOLATE

This chapter traces the journey of the cacao bean, the original source of chocolate, from the land of the Maya in Central America to Spain and the rest of Europe, and then back across the Atlantic to the United States. The transformation of the bean to beverage and, ultimately, confectionery is looked at as well as how the pioneers of the chocolate industry, such as Cadburys and Rowntrees of Britain, Ghirardelli of San Francisco and Van Houten of Holland among others, all contributed towards realizing its immense commercial potential. We also discover how chocolate has never failed to make an impact on all levels of society, initiating comments from the church, the medical profession, scientists, social reformers and royalty.

DRINK OF THE GODS

The origins of the solid, sensuous and, to some, addictive substance we know as chocolate are rooted in New World prehistory in the mysterious realm of the Olmec and the Maya. It was these ancient Mesoamerican civilizations living in the heart of equatorial Central America who were responsible for cultivating the tree from which chocolate is derived.

The Olmec

Three thousand years ago the Olmec people, one of the earliest Mesoamerican civilizations, occupied an area of tropical forests south of modern-day Veracruz on the Gulf of Mexico. In recent times linguists have managed to reconstruct the ancient Olmec vocabulary and during their research they have discovered that it includes the word "cacao". This took a lot of people by surprise, but given the cacao tree's requirement for hot, humid and shady conditions, such as were to be found in the land of the Olmecs, many historians are now convinced that the first civilization to cultivate the cacao tree (*Theobroma cacao*) was the Olmecs, and not the Aztecs, as had been commonly believed.

The Maya

Around the fourth century AD, several centuries after the demise of the Olmecs, the Maya had established themselves in a large region just south of present-day Mexico, stretching from the Yucatán peninsula in Central America across to the Chiapas and the Pacific coast of Guatemala. The humid climate there was perfect for the cacao tree, and it flourished happily in the shade of the tropical forest.

The Maya called the tree *cacahuaquchtl*, meaning "tree" because as far as they were concerned, there was no other tree worth naming. They believed that the tree belonged to the gods and that the pods growing from its trunk were an offering from the gods to man.

The period around AD 300, known as the Classic Mayan civilization, was a time of great artistic, intellectual and spiritual development. The Maya built magnificent stone palaces and temples, carving into the sacred walls images of cacao pods – for them the symbol of life and fertility.

Known as "the people of the book", the Maya were gifted astronomers and mathematicians and had extremely accurate

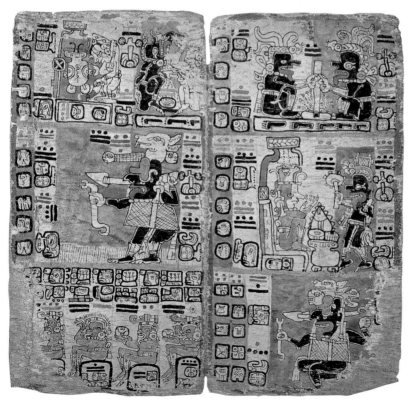

Left: The Maya wrote their books on folding screens of bark paper. These two pages show a black-faced merchant god with cacao growers.

Below: Fifteenth-century Aztec stone figure holding a cacao pod.

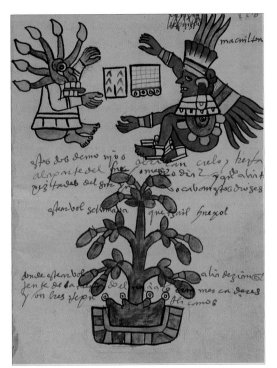

Above: This pre-Columbian codex shows Theobroma cacao, *with its pods, growing in a soil-filled sink-hole.*

calenders. They also devised a system of hieroglyphics, or picture-writing, so they were able to keep records that were written down on fragile sheets of bark paper. Unfortunately today only four of the Maya's books survive, and these are all from the post-Classic period. The books are full of drawings of gods who are depicted performing various religious rituals in which cacao pods frequently feature prominently, and the texts often refer to cacao as the gods' food.

Theobroma cacao

The eighteenth-century Swedish botanist Linnaeus, who invented the binomial system of classification for all living things, later named the tree *Theobroma cacao*, meaning "drink of the gods", from the Greek *theos* (god) and *broma* (beverage). He felt it deserved a name that reflected the Mayan belief that the tree belonged to the gods, rather than the New World name of cacao or chocolate tree.

The Maya were the originators of a bitter brew made from cacao beans. This was considered to be a luxury drink which was enjoyed by kings and noblemen, and also used to solemnize sacred rituals. In their books the Maya describe several ways of making and flavouring the brew. It could be anything from porridge thickened with ground maize meal, to a thinner concoction for drinking. An early picture shows the dark brown liquid being poured from one vessel to another to produce an all-important froth. Various spices were used as flavourings, the favourite being hot chilli.

More evidence of Mayan use of cacao survives on the many painted vessels that have been unearthed from their burial grounds. For example, a tomb excavated in Guatemala in 1984 contained several vessels that were obviously used for chocolate drinking. One exotic and beautiful specimen bears the Mayan symbol for chocolate on its lid and was found still to contain residues of the drink.

The Toltecs and Aztecs

After the mysterious fall of the Mayan empire around AD 900, the gifted and supremely civilized Toltecs, later followed by the Aztecs who came from Mexico, settled in the former Mayan territory. Quetzalcoatl, the Toltec king, was also believed by his people to be the god of air, whose mission was to bring the seeds of the cacao tree from the Garden of Eden to man and to teach mortals how to cultivate various crops.

Because of political uprisings, Quetzalcoatl and his followers left the capital of Tenochtitlán and fled south to the Yucatán. During a period of ill health he was persuaded to drink a mysterious cure, which in fact drove him insane. Convinced he must leave his kingdom, Quetzalcoatl sailed away on a small raft, promising to return in a pre-ordained year to reclaim his kingdom. The legend of Quetzalcoatl's exile became part of Aztec mythology, and astrologers predicted that in 1519 a white-faced king would return to release his people. This prediction was to influence the whole future of the New World when Hernan Cortés arrived from Spain in that same year.

Right: Aztecs greeting the white-skinned explorers landing on the coast of Tabasco. The Aztecs believed they were gods returning to recover their kingdom.

THE SPANISH ADVENTURERS

Although the Spanish explorer Hernán Cortés is generally considered to be the first European to recognize the potential of Aztec chocolate, the initial discovery must be attributed to Christopher Columbus. In 1502, on his fourth and final voyage to the Caribbean, Columbus reached the island of Guanaja off the Honduran coast. The story goes that he was greeted by Aztecs who offered him a sackful of what looked like large almonds in exchange for some of his own merchandise. Noticing his puzzlement, the Aztecs explained that a very special drink, *tchocolatl* (or *xocolatl*), could be made with these beans. Their chief demonstrated by having his servants prepare some on the spot. Columbus and his crew found the resulting dark and bitter concoction repellent but nevertheless took some cacao beans back to Spain for curiosity value, little realizing their future economic worth.

Above: Hernán Cortés, the Conquistador.

Cacao as Currency

When Hernán Cortés arrived in the New World seventeen years later, Montezuma II, the then Aztec emperor, believed Cortés to be a reincarnation of Quetzalcoatl, the exiled Toltec god-king whose return had been predicted to take place in the same year. This confusion made it easy for Cortés to gain access to Tenochtitlán, the Aztec capital, where Montezuma received him and his men with a royal welcome. The emperor offered them numerous gifts, including a cacao plantation, and an extravagant banquet was prepared in their honour.

Despite the overwhelming welcome, Montezuma eventually realized that he had made a mistake and had wrongly identified the Spaniard. Immediately recognizing the insecurity of his position, Cortés enlisted the help of sympathetic natives and managed to take Montezuma prisoner. Within the space of two or three years he brought about the downfall of the Aztec kingdom. Unlike Columbus, Cortés quickly realized the enormous economic value of the cacao bean, both as food and a form of currency.

A contemporary of Cortés reported that a slave could be bought for one hundred cacao beans, the services of a prostitute for ten, and a rabbit for four. The Jesuit, Pedro Martyre de Angleria, called the beans "pecuniary almonds" and described them as "blessed money, which exempts its possessors from

Above: A painting showing Montezuma giving a royal welcome to Cortés.

Right: Aztecs greeting Columbus and his fleet with welcoming gifts as he lands on Guanaja.

avarice, since it cannot be hoarded or hidden underground". It is presumed that he was referring to the fact that the beans could not be stored for long without rotting.

The writings of Thomas Gage, a seventeenth-century English Dominican friar, are a rich source of information on chocolate. Visiting the City of Mexico, Gage describes how the cacao bean is used as "both meat and current money". Basing the exchange rate on the Spanish real, which at that time (1625) was worth sixpence (2½p), he explained that two hundred small cacao beans were worth one Spanish real, and "with these the Indians buy what they list, for five, nay for two cacaos, which is a very small part of a real, they do buy fruits and the like".

The Cacao Plantations

When Cortés set out on his voyage to the New World, his primary goal was to find El Dorado – Aztec gold. When he failed to unearth the dreamed-of riches, his attention turned to cacao beans. Having seen them used as currency, and noticing the importance attached to them, Cortés soon realized that money could literally be made to grow on trees. He devoted the next few years to exploiting the commercial potential of this "liquid gold" by setting up cacao plantations around the Caribbean.

Cacao was cheap to cultivate and reasonably profitable, and the prospect of easy riches attracted plenty of Spanish colonists. Before long, the Spanish had established plantations in Mexico, Ecuador, Venezuela, Peru, and the islands of Jamaica and Hispaniola (now called Haiti and the Dominican Republic). Cacao production has since spread all over the world, but the plantations in these original regions still produce the most highly prized varieties of bean.

The Spanish Secret

The Spanish colonists had tried to keep the secret of cultivating and preparing cacao to themselves, and with good reason – they were making fat profits out of processing the beans in Latin America before shipping them to Europe. However, the colonists did not remain in sole possession of their secret forever. In 1580, the first-ever chocolate-processing plant was set up in Spain.

From that time on, the popularity of chocolate spread to other European countries.

Left: An early illustration showing cacao pods drying and a cacao tree growing under a shade-creating "mother" tree.

Above: This lithograph, produced by the Empire Marketing Board, shows cacao pods being gathered.

These, in turn, established their own plantations, trade routes and processing facilities.

The Dutch transplanted the tree to their East Indian states of Java and Sumatra in the early seventeenth century, and from there it spread to the Philippines, New Guinea, Samoa and Indonesia with a degree of financial success made possible by the exploitation of hundreds of thousands of African slaves. The French settled in Martinique in 1660, and in Brazil in 1677, along with the Portuguese. Trinidad was fought over by the Dutch, the French and the British for years; it eventually went to the British in 1802. In the early nineteenth century, the Portuguese successfully transplanted Brazilian cacao saplings to the island of São Tomé off the African coast, and later to the island of Fernando Póo (now called Bioko) and West Africa. By the end of the nineteenth century, the Germans had settled in the Cameroons and the British in Sri Lanka. Plantations have since spread to South-East Asia, and Malaysia is now one of the world's leading producers.

Cacao Fever

It was no easy job for the early planters to clear the jungle, but their fierce determination spurred them on. A Brazilian writer, Jorge Amado, described the vision of those early planters gripped by "cacao fever": "He does not see the forest ... choked with dense creepers and century-old trees, inhabited by wild animals and apparitions. He sees fields planted with cacao trees, straight rows of trees bearing golden fruit, ripe and yellow. He sees plantations pushing the forest back and stretching as far as the horizon."

THE POWER OF CHOCOLATE

To the Aztecs, chocolate was a source of spiritual wisdom, tremendous energy and enhanced sexual powers. The drink was highly prized as a nuptial aid, and, predictably, was the favourite beverage at wedding ceremonies. The Emperor Montezuma was reputed to get through fifty flagons of chocolate a day, always fortifying himself with a cup before entering his harem.

Although drunk on a daily basis, chocolate was still considered an exotic luxury and consumed primarily by kings, noblemen and the upper ranks of the priesthood. (Some historians say that priests would not have drunk chocolate, arguing that it would have been the equivalent of a priest quaffing champagne every day.)

Because of its renowned energy-boosting properties, chocolate was also given to Aztec warriors to fortify them on military campaigns, compressed into conveniently travel-sized tablets and wafers. Perhaps as a kind of incentive scheme, a special law was instated declaring that unless a warrior went to war, he was forbidden to drink chocolate or eat luxury meats, or wear cotton, flowers or feathers – even if he was a royal prince or nobleman.

The Spanish colonists, too, became infatuated by the chocolate mystique. Once they had become accustomed to the strangeness of the drink, they took to it with enthusiasm. The Jesuit José de Acosta, wrote: "The Spaniards, both men and women, that are accustomed to the country, are very greedy of this chocolaté. They say they make diverse sortes of it, some hote, some colde, and put therein much of that chili."

Increasingly aware of its restorative values, Cortés convinced Carlos I of Spain of the enormous potential of this New World health food: "... the divine drink which builds up resistance and fights fatigue. A cup of this precious drink enables a man to walk for a whole day without food".

The Midas Touch

Chocolate has always been associated with gold, possibly originating from Montezuma's ritual of drinking chocolate from a golden goblet, which, immediately after use, was thrown into the lake beside his palace. The lake turned out to be quite literally a gold mine for the Spanish after the conquest of the Aztecs. Evidence of the association with gold can still be seen today with chocolate manufacturers, especially the Swiss, selling fake gold bars and chocolate coins encased in gold wrapping.

Thomas Gage was heavily reliant on it too. He wrote: "Two or three hours after a good meal of three or four dishes of mutton, veal or beef, kid, turkeys or other fowles, our stomackes would bee ready to faint, and so wee were fain to support them with a cup of chocolatte."

Rites, Rituals and Ceremonies

The writings of New World travellers give us some fascinating insights into the strange and sometimes barbaric rites, rituals and ceremonies that are attached to the cacao bean and the drinking of chocolate.

Religious rituals took place at different stages during cultivation. The Maya always held a planting festival in honour of the gods during which they sacrificed a dog with a cacao-coloured spot in its hair. Another practice, calling for a certain amount of commitment, required the planters to remain celibate for thirteen nights. They were allowed to return to their wives on the fourteenth night, and then the beans were sown. Another somewhat gory planting ceremony involved placing the seeds in small bowls before performing secret rites

Left: Chocolate was drunk by Aztec warriors in military campaigns, but it did not win them victory over the Spanish.

Right: An Aztec with his chocolate pot and molinillo. The molinillo has shaped paddles for making the drink frothy.

Chocolate and Cuisine

Contrary to what some cookery writers would have us believe, the Aztecs did not use chocolate as an ingredient in cooking. To do so would have been considered sacrilegious – rather like devout Christians using communion wine to make gravy. What possibly causes confusion is a classic Mexican recipe called Mole Poblano, turkey or chicken in a chilli sauce flavoured with chocolate. The recipe is often assumed to have Aztec origins, but the ingredients include several items – onions, tomatoes and garlic, for instance – that would not have been available then. This is a recipe for Mole Poblano:

8 dried mulato chillies; 4 dried ancho chillies; 4 dried pasilla chillies; 2 dried chipotle chillies; 1 small turkey; 50g/2oz/4 tbsp lard (or vegetable oil); 60ml/4 tbsp sesame seeds; 115g/4oz/1 cup blanched almonds; 1 corn tortilla; 2 crushed garlic cloves; 1 chopped onion; 1.5ml/¼ tsp each of ground cloves, cinnamon and anise; 6 black peppercorns; 50g/2oz/⅓ cup raisins; 3 peeled tomatoes; 5ml/1 tsp salt; 50g/2oz/2 squares unsweetened chocolate; chicken or turkey stock

1 Arrange the dried chillies in a single layer in a roasting pan and soften in a hot oven for 2–3 minutes, taking care not to let them burn. Discard the stems and seeds and put the chillies in a bowl. Cover with barely boiling water. Leave to soak for 20–30 minutes.
2 Divide the turkey into portions. Heat the lard or oil in a heavy flameproof casserole and fry the turkey until golden brown.

Using a slotted spoon, remove the turkey portions from the casserole and set aside.
3 Roast the sesame seeds and almonds in a dry frying pan over a medium heat until golden. Remove from the pan. Cut the tortilla into strips and heat in the pan until brittle.
4 Put the almonds, tortilla and all but 5ml/1 tsp sesame seeds into a food processor. Add the garlic, onion, spices, raisins, tomatoes and salt. Drain the chillies, reserving the soaking water, add them to the processor and purée until smooth, adding some of the chilli soaking water if necessary. Add this purée to the fat remaining in the casserole. Fry gently for about 5 minutes, stirring constantly.
5 Return the turkey to the casserole, with the chocolate and enough stock to just cover. Bring to the boil, then lower the heat, cover and simmer gently for 45–60 minutes until the turkey is tender and cooked through and the sauce has thickened. Garnish with the reserved sesame seeds and serve with rice and tortillas.

Note: If you have difficulty in finding Mexican dried chillies, use 115g/4oz fresh green chillies and 2 small dried red chillies, and do not preheat them in the oven. Simply remove the seeds, tear the chillies into shreds and soak as above.

Left: A Mexican metate was used for grinding cacao beans to a paste.

Left: A mosaic of Quetzalcoatl, the Toltec godking who, according to legend, brought the cacao bean as a gift to humankind.

in the presence of an idol. Blood was then drawn from different parts of the human body and used to anoint the idol. Other practices include sprinkling "the blood of slain fowls" over the land to be sown. There were also tales of frenzied dancing, orgiastic rituals and bloody sacrifices. The sixteenth-century Italian historian and traveller, Girolamo Benzoni, recorded that during festivals "they used to spend all the day and half the night in dancing with only cacao for nourishment". Another legend tells of how, as a prize, the winner of a type of ball game would be offered as a sacrifice. The unfortunate man was first fed vast quantities of chocolate in order "to colour his blood" before his heart was cut out and presented to the gods, who, it was believed, would be honoured by the chocolate-rich blood.

Another use of chocolate was as a face paint with which the Aztecs adorned themselves in religious ceremonies. Even the early Spanish planters believed that secret rites were necessary for a successful crop and performed planting ceremonies. From its earliest days, then, chocolate was regarded as a substance of power, a gift from the gods, a source of vitality and life.

Below: Cacao beans laid out to dry on plantain leaves.

FROM BEAN TO BEVERAGE

Above: A seventeenth-century lithograph showing Aztecs on a plantation harvesting, preparing and cooking chocolate.

The Aztec drink bore little resemblance to the deliciously smooth, rich and creamy beverage that we know today; it was bitter, greasy, and served cold. Early travellers give differing accounts of how the drink was made. Giramolo Benzoni, a sixteenth-century Italian botanist, described the method that was used in rural areas: "They take as many fruits as they need and put them in an earthenware pot and dry them over the fire. Then they break them between two stones and reduce them to flour just as they do when they make bread. They then transfer this flour into vessels made of gourd halves ... moisten the flour gradually with water, often adding their 'long pepper' [chilli]."

Still on the subject of ingredients, Thomas Gage described additions other than chilli: "But the meaner set of people, as Blackamoors and Indians, commonly put nothing in it, but Cacao, Achiotte, Maize, and a few Chillies with a little Aniseed." Maize was used to blot up the cacao butter which floated to the top, and also to bind and thicken the drink.

It seems that the grinding stone, or metate, was an important part of the production process. One writer describes the process in some detail: "For this purpose they have a broad, smooth stone, well polished and glazed very hard, and being made fit in all respects for their use, they grind the cacaos thereon very small, and when they have so done, they have another broad stone ready, under which they keep a gentle fire." Because of the crude manual processing, all sorts of undesirable bits and pieces – shells, husks and pith – were allowed to remain

Right: Aztec chocolate-making equipment: chocolate pot, drinking goblet, whisk and rolling pin.

in the resulting liquor. In Benzoni's opinion: "This mixture looks more fit for the pigs than like a beverage for human beings."

A Frothy Brew

The Jesuit José de Acosta wrote: "The chief use of this cacao is in a drincke which they call chocolaté, whereof they make great account, foolishly and without reason: for it is loathsome to such as are not acquainted with it, having a skumme or frothe that is very unpleasant to taste, if they be not well conceited thereof."

For the Maya and Aztecs the froth was an all-important and most delicious part of the drink. One historian pointed out the importance "of opening the mouth wide, in order to facilitate deglutition, that the foam may dissolve gradually and descend imperceptibly, as it were, into the stomach". The Maya made the drink frothy by pouring it from one bowl to another from a height. Later, the Aztecs invented a device that the Spanish called a molinillo – a wooden swizzle stick with specially shaped paddles at one end, which fitted into the hole in the lid of the chocolate pot.

The eighteenth-century missionary Father Jean-Baptiste Labat, described this indispensable item in one of his books: "A stick is about ten inches longer than the chocolate pot, thus enabling it to be freely twirled between the palms of the hand." The molinillo is still in use today and can be found in Latin American shops and markets. The design of the basic wooden stick remains unchanged, but there are also beautiful antique pots and swizzle sticks in silver and other decorative materials, which have now become collectors' items.

There is evidence of yet more ingredients than those mentioned by Thomas Gage. The Spanish historian, Sahagún,

Champurrado (Chocolate *Atole*)

The addition of maize would have turned the Aztec drink into a thin gruel or porridge known as *atole*. This is a type of fortified drink, not necessarily flavoured with chocolate, still served at meals or used as a pick-me-up by workers in the fields in Latin America today. The chocolate-flavoured version is always referred to as *champurrado*, from *champurrar*, meaning to mix one drink with another:

Put 65g/2½oz/½ cup masa harina (treated maize flour) or finely ground tortillas in a large pan with 750ml/1¼ pints/3 cups water. Stir over a low heat until thickened. Remove from the heat and stir in 175g/6oz/1 cup soft light brown sugar (or to taste), and 750ml/1¼ pints/3 cups milk. Grate 75g/3oz/3 squares unsweetened chocolate and add to the pan. Beat well with a molinillo and serve steaming hot and frothing.

A Mexican Recipe for Hand-made Chocolate

1 Take 2.75kg/6lb good quality cacao beans, at least three different types, in equal quantities. Roast in a metal pan studded with holes until they begin to give off their oil. Do not to remove from the heat too soon, or the resulting chocolate will be discoloured and indigestible. If allowed to burn, the chocolate will be bitter and acrid.

2 Rub the roasted beans through a fine hair sieve to remove the husks. Next, place your *metate* (grinding stone) on a flat pan containing hot coals. Once the stone is warm, begin to grind the chocolate. Grind the chocolate with 1.75–2.75kg/ 4–6lb sugar, depending on the desired sweetness, pounding it with a large mallet.

3 Shape the resulting paste into tablets as preferred – round, hexagonal or oblong – and place on a rack to air. If you wish, make dividing lines on the surface of the chocolate with the tip of a sharp knife.

describing a menu of chocolate drinks to be served to lords, tells us that there were "ruddy cacao; brilliant red cacao; orange cacao; black cacao; and white cacao". Many of the very early recipes for chocolate share common ingredients, and from these we can tell that the likely flavourings for the lords' impressive choice of cacao were chilli, allspice, cloves, vanilla, a type of black pepper, various flower petals, nuts and annatto.

Below: A modern chocolate pot, whisk and chocolate from Colombia. The design of the whisk has not changed since the days of the Aztecs.

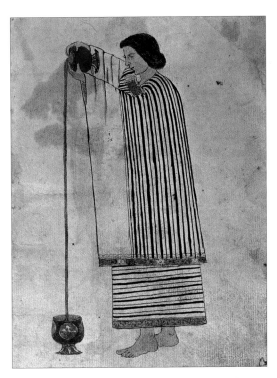

Above: Aztecs poured chocolate from a height to make it frothy.

Sugar was not added until much later. There is a story that the nuns of Oaxaca, an Aztec town occupied by the Spanish until 1522, developed new recipes in deference to the Spanish sweet tooth. They added sugar and sweet spices such as cinnamon and aniseed, and so the bitter beverage of the Aztecs began its transformation to the delicious drink that we know today.

The Spanish Version

In 1701 an Englishman travelling in Spain gave a detailed and lengthy account of the manufacturing process developed by the Spanish. After the preliminary roasting, dehusking and grinding, the cacao mass was ground again to a fine paste with plenty of sugar, cinnamon, vanilla, musk and annatto. The chocolate was formed into blocks, along the lines of modern block chocolate, but even so, these were still used only for making the beverage, rather than as confectionery.

As far as we know, this is the recipe that was used throughout Spain and the rest of Europe until the process was revolutionized in the nineteenth century by the technological achievements of the Dutchman Van Houten.

FROM BEVERAGE TO CONFECTIONERY

*Above: A 1893 poster
with a background of
cacao pods and leaves.*

Van Houten's Press

In its early days chocolate was an extremely rich beverage. It contained a fatty substance known as cacao butter, which tended to rise to the top, where it would float in unappetizing greasy pools. Manufacturers overcame this to some extent by adding starchy substances to absorb the fat – a process similar to the Aztec tradition of adding ground maize.

Manufacturers had also tried unsuccessfully for years to devise a way of separating out the greasy cacao butter. The breakthrough came in 1828 when, after years of trial and error, a Dutch chemist named Coenraad Van Houten patented a new and extremely efficient hydraulic press. His machine was able to extract about fifty per cent of the cacao butter present in the "liquor" (the paste produced after grinding the beans), leaving behind a refined, brittle, cake-like residue that could then be pulverized to a fine powder.

Not satisfied, Van Houten went one step further. He treated the powder with alkaline salts in order to improve the ease with which it could be mixed with water. The process, which came to be known as "Dutching", also darkened the colour of the chocolate and lightened the flavour – a curious anomaly because plain chocolate is usually assumed to have a stronger flavour. Today, many people believe they prefer Dutch chocolate because of its strong flavour, but it may simply be the colour of the chocolate that attracts them.

Van Houten's inexhaustible patience and skill revolutionized the chocolate industry. It led to the manufacture of what we now know as cocoa powder, which in Van Houten's time was called "cocoa essence". It also led to an all-round improvement within the industry. Van Houten sold his rights ten years after he took out the patent, and the machine came into general use. Among the first customers were the Frys and the Cadburys, ever eager to outdo each other.

*Right: Modern packaging based on the art
nouveau style.*

*Above: An early advertisement for Van Houten's cocoa powder –
"the best liquid drinking chocolate".*

Both firms were quick to enter the cocoa essence market, actively promoting the product's purity and ease of preparation. The old-style starch-based products were classified as adulterated, resulting in several fierce legal battles between rival firms. Van Houten's press also initiated the industry's next step in gearing up – the large-scale production of chocolate as confectionery.

Eating Chocolate

Having separated out the butter from the bean, the industry was left with the question of what to do with it – it was certainly too good to waste. What happened was that somehow one of the cocoa manufacturers – and there are conflicting claims as to who was the first – hit upon the idea of melting the cacao butter and combining it with a blend of ground cacao beans and sugar. The resulting mixture was a smooth and malleable paste that tolerated the added sugar without becoming gritty; the fat helped to

Above: A charming poster for Bovril's nourishing new chocolate bars, or cakes. The lettering on the box refers to them as "the perfect food".

dissolve it. The paste was also thin enough to be poured into a mould and cast, and it is from this concept that "eating chocolate" was developed.

The Fry family claim to have been the first to market the new product. Reflecting the current popularity of French-style products, they named the bars "*Chocolat Délicieux à Manger*" and exhibited them at a trade fair in Birmingham in 1849. The bars were an immediate success, and eating

Right: Hershey's famous little Kisses were introduced in 1907.

chocolate caught on in a big way. Not to be outdone, Cadbury's introduced the first box of small individual chocolates, followed by a Valentine's Day presentation box. Other companies, such as Bovril, began producing eating chocolate, and thus the new confectionery was firmly established.

As a result of the new craze the price of cacao butter rocketed and, predictably, eating chocolate became an expensive sought-after product popular with society's élite. Meanwhile, cocoa was relegated to the masses.

The United States developed their version of chocolate bars a little later on. After experimenting with cream and chocolate – time and time again the mixture scorched or failed to set – Milton Hershey's milk chocolate bars finally appeared on the market in 1900. His world-famous Kisses followed in 1907. Over on the west coast, Ghirardelli was making use of new chocolate-moulding technology, and soon added chocolate bars to their lines, too.

Above: Modern packaging with old-fashioned appeal.

Specialist chocolate shops began to spring up all over the country and most towns had at least one well-respected establishment producing hand-made chocolates. The early chocolatiers were too small to import cacao beans or invest in expensive processing machinery. Instead, they bought industrial-sized blocks of coating chocolate from large companies such as Guittard and melted them down to use as "couverture" for their own hand-dipped fillings. Alice Bradley's 1917 *Candy Cook Book*, published in America, devoted a whole chapter to "Assorted Chocolates" with over sixty recipes for fillings. Bradley stated: "More than one hundred different

Above: Ghirardelli's first chocolate bars were "full of toasted almonds".

chocolates may be found in the price lists of some manufacturers." The American chocolate industry got its biggest boost during the Second World War, when millions of chocolate bars were issued to the American armed forces in Europe. By this time both Ghirardelli and Hershey were well-equipped for the challenge of supplying the demand.

CHOCOLATE TRAVELS THE WORLD

During the sixteenth century chocolate began its journey into the countries of Europe as colonialists exploited their New World discoveries. Reaching Spain first, then following trade routes to Northern Europe and Great Britain, chocolate eventually made its way back across the Atlantic to North America.

Spain

It was probably through merchants, and also through contact between New World convents and monasteries and their Spanish counterparts, that chocolate found its way to Spain.

Once the first commercial cargo of beans from Veracruz had been unloaded in 1585 and the official trade routes established, chocolate quickly became part of the Spanish way of life, especially among society's élite. However, a French noblewoman visiting Spain was unimpressed. She says of the drink: "They take it with so much pepper and so many spices, that it is impossible they don't burn themselves up." Nor was she impressed by their dental care and personal habits: "Their teeth are good, and would be white if they took care of them, but they neglect them. Besides the sugar and the chocolate which spoil them, they have the bad habit, men and women alike, of cleaning them with a toothpick, in whatever company they are."

Chocolaterías, chocolate houses, sprang up in cities all over the country, and it became the fashion for people to to visit them in the afternoons to drink a cup of the foaming fragrant brew, accompanied by *picatoste*, fried bread, to dip in it. Today, the chocolate drinking habit remains strong in Spain, and there are still many *chocolaterías*. A traditional time to take the beverage is

Right: The chambermaid model for "The Beautiful Chocolate Girl" married a wealthy aristocrat and so got to drink chocolate herself.

Below: This early eighteenth-century Spanish tiled panel shows gentlemen serving chocolate to their ladies.

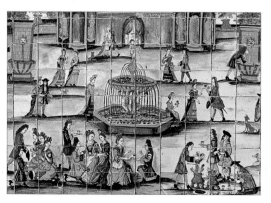

Spanish Egg Chocolate

The Spanish like their chocolate thick – so thick that a spoon will stand up in it, and it can almost be classified as a food rather than a drink. Cornflour (cornstarch) is used as a thickener, or sometimes eggs, which practically turn the drink into chocolate mousse.

In a double boiler, melt 50g/2oz/2 squares unsweetened chocolate in 475ml/16fl oz/2 cups milk until thick and smooth. Keep stirring and add 115g/4oz/½ cup sugar, a pinch of salt, 10ml/2 tsp ground cinnamon and 5ml/1 tsp vanilla essence (extract). Beat 1 egg in a jug (pitcher) with a molinillo, pour over the hot chocolate mixture, whisk until frothy and serve immediately.

*Above: The pleasures of taking chocolate are captured in this
seventeenth-century still life by Philippe Rousseau.*

in the morning with freshly cooked *churros* (piped strips of deep-
fried choux pastry), which replaced the *picatoste.*

In Spain, as in other parts of Europe, chocolate was always
associated with stimulating foods such as spices, coffee and tea;
it was a long while before chocolate was used as an ingredient for
confectionery and desserts. Although its first use was as a
beverage, chocolate was also a flavouring ingredient in savoury
dishes. Both the Spanish and the Mexicans traditionally add
chocolate to sauces for meat and game, and even fish.

The Netherlands

The Netherlands became part of the Spanish territories in the
fourteenth century. Because of this, the Dutch were familiar with
chocolate from an early stage.

The Dutch West India Company eventually defied the Spanish
ban on foreign traders and started shipping cacao beans in bulk
to Amsterdam during the seventeenth century. They then re-
exported the beans in small lots to foreign buyers, as well as
setting up their own processing plants in The Netherlands.
Until the end of the eighteenth century, production was limited
and chocolate was seen only in the homes of a few wealthy
merchants and financiers.

Italy

There are conflicting theories as to how and when chocolate
reached Italy. Some historians believe it was around the middle of
the sixteenth century when the exiled duke Emmanuel-Philibert
returned to power, having experienced the delights of chocolate in
Spain. The popular theory is that chocolate was imported by a
Florentine merchant, Antonio Carletti, who discovered it while
travelling the world in search of new products to sell. The most
likely theory is that chocolate was brought in as a medicine
through the convents and monasteries.

By the seventeenth century a growing number of chocolate
companies had become established in northern Italy, particularly
around the towns of Perugia and Turin. These companies in turn
began to export their newly developed products to other
European countries.

Italian Chocolate Recipes

A collection of recipes by an eighteenth-century priest
shows the imagination of the Italians in their use of
chocolate. Recipes included such dishes as liver dipped in
chocolate and fried, chocolate soup, chocolate pudding
with veal, marrow and candied fruit, and chocolate polenta.

France

France was also quick to fall under chocolate's spell. As with Spain and Italy, there are conflicting theories about the circumstances surrounding its first appearance. Some say it was a result of networking between Spanish and French monasteries. Another theory states that chocolate entered France as a medicine. There is certainly some evidence from the French historian Bonaventure d'Argonne that the Cardinal of Lyons drank chocolate "to calm his spleen and appease his rage and foul temper", and that he may have "had the secret from some Spanish monks who brought it to France". However, there is also no doubt that the trend was largely set by nobility and the royal court, as it was in other European countries.

Above: Cardinal Mazarin had his own chocolate-maker.

The most popular theory is that the drink made its first appearance in 1615 when Louis XIII married Anne of Austria, the young daughter of Philip II of Spain. The new queen loved her chocolate with a passion and introduced it to members of the court. There were plenty of devotees: the king's personal adviser, the formidable Cardinal Mazarin, absolutely refused to travel anywhere without his personal chocolate-maker; and later Marie

Below: A tapestry depicting the marriage of princess María Teresa to Louis XIV. Chocolate and the king were her only passions.

Antoinette, also very fond of chocolate, created the prestigious "Charge of chocolate-maker of the Queen". Chocolate parties held by royalty, *chocolat du roi*, became a fashionable social ritual to which it was the ultimate in chic to be invited.

The many anecdotes include the story of the Spanish princess María Theresa, who married Louis XIV in 1660. She is said to have declared: "Chocolate and the King are my only passions." (Note the order.) The princess brought with her a Spanish maid, who prepared chocolate each morning for her queen. The ladies of the French court were intrigued by this new drink, especially as word had got round that it was an aphrodisiac. Chocolate sales in France apparently sky-rocketed around that time. Another often-repeated story about the princess is that her passion for chocolate was so excessive that she developed a horrendous complexion, and that her teeth were black and riddled with cavities.

Throughout France, chocolate never failed to evoke strong feelings. In 1664 learned academics praised its food value, presumably because of the fat content, but at the same time it was violently attacked by other writers, who accused those who drank it of moral depravity. Even Madame de Sévigné, a French courtesan and a great devotee of chocolate, turned against it for a while. In one of her letters to her daughter she wrote: "Chocolate is no longer for me what it was, fashion has led me astray, as it always does ... it is the source of vapors and palpitations; it flatters you for a while, and then suddenly lights a continuous fever in you that leads to death ... In the name of God, don't keep it up ..." In another letter she told a horrendous tale of the Marquise de Coëtlogon who "took so

Above: Chocolate consumption was often depicted as being rather risqué.

much chocolate during her pregnancy last year that she produced a small boy as black as the devil, who died". Eventually Madame de Sévigné regained her enthusiasm, and in a wonderful letter she neatly got round the issue of fasting and chocolate: "I took some chocolate night before last to digest my dinner, in order to have a good supper. I had some yesterday for sustenance so that I could fast until the evening. What I find most pleasant about chocolate is that it acts according to one's wishes."

Switzerland

After the mid-seventeenth century, chocolate was making an appearance in all the principal cities of Europe. Although

Above: The elegant refreshment room where chocolate was served at Confiserie Sprüngli in Zurich.

Switzerland was later to become a major producer of chocolate as confectionery, chocolate as a beverage was relatively late in arriving. It was first noticed in Zurich in 1697 after the mayor had enjoyed drinking chocolate on a trip to Brussels. By the mid-eighteenth century, chocolate was more widely available and was often brought into the country by travelling Italian merchants, known as *cioccolatieri*, who sold it at fairs and markets.

Germany and Austria

Like Switzerland, Germany was also relatively late to take up chocolate. For years the Germans regarded it as medicine, and it was sold only by apothecaries. But by the middle of the seventeenth century, chocolate had become accepted among fashionable society, although enthusiasm varied from city to city. Berliners still looked on it as an unpleasant tonic, but the drink was a hit in Dresden and in Leipzig, where the city's *glitterati* took

to drinking it at the fashionable Felsche café, one of the earliest German *schokoladestuben* (chocolate houses).

Among Germany's confirmed chocoholics were the famous poets Goethe (1749–1832) and Schiller (1759–1805). Goethe was reputed to have found the beverage a deep source of inspiration and drank it well into ripe old age. During his travels he often wrote to his wife asking her to send supplies from his favourite chocolate-maker, Riquet, in Leipzig.

Germany started producing its own chocolate on a large scale in 1756 when Prince Wilhelm von der Lippe erected a factory at Steinhude and brought over Portuguese workers especially skilled in the art of chocolate-making.

In Austria, Viennese aristocracy were quick to take up the new drink, especially after the Emperor Charles VI had moved his court and his chocolate from Madrid to Vienna in 1711. Since Austria did not impose such punishing taxes on chocolate as Germany, it was drunk not just by the aristocracy but also by lesser mortals who could afford it. There is a story of a German traveller in Vienna who was horrified to see someone as common as a tailor drinking a cup of best quality chocolate.

Both the Germans and the Austrians were accomplished pastry cooks. Indeed, in the Austrian imperial court it seemed that the head pâtisserie chef was on a par with the most senior general. Like the Italians, the German and Austrian pastry cooks took a while to start using chocolate as an ingredient in their baking rather than just as a beverage. It was worth the wait – their most wickedly delicious creations, the rich Black Forest Cake from Germany and the Viennese Sachertorte, are now celebrated forms of indulgence the world over.

Below: Goethe in the Campagna (1787) by German painter Johann Tischbein. Goethe was a lifelong drinker of chocolate.

Chocolate and China

The popularity of chocolate spawned a whole new industry for the famous china factories in Austria, Germany and France. At the beginning of the eighteenth century, European factories started producing the most exquisite chocolate services in porcelain; before that earthenware or metal, including gold and silver, were the materials used. As well as the traditionally shaped serving pots, the new range included elegant cups known as *trembleuse*. These new porcelain wares were specially designed to protect the aristocracy from the embarrassment of accidental spills. They featured double-handled cups which fitted into a holder or a very deep saucer.

Above: The interior of a typical seventeenth-century London chocolate house. These were hotbeds of gossip, frequented by politicians and the literary set.

Great Britain

In the sixteenth century, when the Spanish were shifting cacao as if there were no tomorrow, the British couldn't have cared less about it. Even the pirates who plagued the Spanish ports and shipping routes seemed unaware of its economic and cultural importance, for they showed no interest in the valuable cargo. Like their Dutch counterparts, they are reputed to have thrown boatloads of it overboard in disgust.

When chocolate finally arrived in Britain, it did so more or less simultaneously with two other stimulants, tea from Asia and coffee from Africa. Coffee was the first to catch on in British society – it was relatively cheaper – but chocolate soon followed.

Documentary evidence of the first chocolate house in London appeared in *The Public Advertiser* in 1657, followed two years later by a paragraph in *Needham's Mercurius Politicus* that drew attention to "an excellent West India drink, sold in Queen's-Head alley, in Bishopsgate-street, by a Frenchman".

The most famous establishment was White's Chocolate House, near St James's Palace, opened by an Italian immigrant. A rival

Left: Cacao beans from the tropics arriving at an English warehouse.

Right: A Cup of Chocolate by Sir John Lavery. Drinking chocolate in the new chocolate houses was a fashionable pastime for ladies of society.

establishment was The Cocoa Tree in St James's Street. By chance rather than design the two establishments catered to different political loyalties – The Cocoa Tree was the favourite haunt of members of the Tory party, while the Whig aristocrats and the literary set frequented White's. White's was the inspiration for some of the scenes from William Hogarth's famous series of paintings, *The Rake's Progress*.

For the wealthy upper classes, both the coffee and chocolate houses were the place to be seen. They were hotbeds of vicious gossip and political intrigue, as well as popular gambling venues where vast fortunes were won and lost. In 1675, Charles II tried in vain to have both types of establishment closed down on the grounds that politicians and businessmen were frequenting them too often and were in danger of neglecting their families. It is also possible that he was trying to suppress the kind of talk that could potentially lead to a rebellion similar to the one that caused his father's execution in 1649.

The diarist Samuel Pepys (1633–1703) was an ardent fan of chocolate, or "jocolatte", and a regular frequenter of the chocolate houses. One entry in his diary records a horrendous hangover the morning after the king's coronation: "Waked in the morning with my head in a sad taking through last night's drink, which I am very sorry for; so rose, and went with Mr Creed to drink our morning draught, which he did give me in Chocolate to settle my stomach."

In England, as in other countries, the government seized on chocolate as a potential source of revenue. Importers were obliged

Left: Examples of early packaging for Ghirardelli's revolutionary instant cocoa powder.

to pay a hefty duty on every sack of cacao beans brought into the country, and in 1660 a tax of 8d (about 3p) a gallon was imposed on all chocolate made and sold in England.

These penalties led to an inevitable increase in smuggling cacao beans, as well as adulteration of the chocolate, for which anything from brick dust to red lead was used. Brandon Head in *The Food of the Gods* refers to "the reprehensible practice (strongly condemned)" of padding out chocolate with husks and shells. He goes on: "To prevent this practice it was enacted in 1770 that the shells or husks should be seized or destroyed." Some of these husks did not go to waste, however. Head tells us: "From these a light, but not unpalatable, table decoction is still prepared in Ireland and elsewhere, under the designation of 'miserables'."

By the mid-1800s, the high levels of taxation had come down, thanks to the vast volume of imports, as well as the influence of respected Quaker industrialists who had convinced the government of chocolate's nourishing virtues. Chocolate was now affordable by all and had become big business.

United States of America

The first chocolate found its way back across the Atlantic to North America in around 1765, probably in the pockets of high-ranking English officials going to their posts in the east coast colonies. We also know that Domingo Ghirardelli, an Italian confectioner then trading in Lima in Peru, exported cacao beans and other essential commodities from South America to San Francisco to supply the needs of the gold rush hordes. Another possible route for cacao beans was directly from Jamaica after the Spanish had given up control there.

Thomas Jefferson (1743–1826), third president of the United States, is quoted as saying: "The superiority of chocolate, both for health and nourishment, will soon give it the preference over tea and coffee in America which it has in Spain." Because of the pioneering nature of North American society, chocolate was given a somewhat different reception from the one it had received in Europe. Although the wealthy east coast society enjoyed chocolate, they drank it at home – chocolate houses did not exist. Another difference was that chocolate was generally marketed to the masses rather than to the élite (as in Europe), with the emphasis on wholesomeness rather than sophistication, so it consequently reached a far broader segment of society than it had in Spain, France and England.

The first American chocolate factory was set up in 1765 in Massachusetts by Dr James Baker and John Hannon. The Walter Baker Company was established in 1780 by Baker's grandson and is still synonymous with quality chocolate. By 1884, Milton Hershey, of the Hershey Chocolate Company, was producing baking chocolate, cocoa and sweet chocolate coatings for his famous caramels; and by 1885, Domingo Ghirardelli had set up his California Chocolate Manufactory in San Francisco. Right from the start, chocolate was big business in North America.

Below: Nineteenth-century advertising poster for curious chocolate products from the Walter Baker Company.

CHOCOLATE AND THE CHURCH

The Church played an important role, directly and indirectly, in the early history of chocolate. The bitter and bloody religious wars raging between Catholics and Protestants in the sixteenth and seventeenth centuries were, in a way, the cause of chocolate's appearance and gradual dispersal through Europe. The Jesuits, actively involved in the religious wars and fiercely committed to empowering the Catholic Church, were a driving political force both in Europe and Latin America. It was almost certainly the Jesuit missionaries, rather than New World explorers, who were responsible for bringing the first chocolate into Spain, Italy and France; it would have passed through an international network of monasteries and convents. It was also thanks to the pressure of Jesuit missionaries that raw, rather than processed, cacao beans were eventually shipped to Europe. Before this, the Spanish colonists had had a monopoly on processing the beans in Latin America, making fat profits from it.

In Italy, the religious wars resulted in a great many high-level marriages between aristocratic families and the ruling powers. Until its unification in 1879, Italy was a collection of self-governing

Above: Friar Drinking Chocolate *by Jose M. Oropeza.*

states, and it was felt that marriages of this kind were the best way of cementing diplomatic relationships and consolidating the states' collective power. The aristocratic brides liked to take their maids, cooks and favourite foods with them when they moved from one Italian state or foreign country to another, and so through them chocolate began to appear in all sorts of places.

Until the eighteenth century, chocolate was made by monks and nuns, both in Europe and Latin America, using the methods handed down from the Aztecs. Thomas Gage, in his book *The English-American, His Travail by Sea and Land, or a New Survey of the West Indies* (published 1648), wrote of "cloister churches" run by nuns and friars. He said these were "talked of far and near, not for their religious practices, but for their skill in making drinkes which are used in those parts, the one called chocolatte, another atolle. Chocolatte

Below: Part of Columbus's mission was to conquer new lands in the name of the Catholic Church. This picture illustrates that religious fervour.

Above: This seventeenth-century Spanish still life shows tablets of chocolate, which were often made by monks and nuns.

worth repeating. The upper-class white ladies of Chiapa Real claimed "much weakness and squeamishness of stomacke, which they say is so great that they are not able to continue in church ... unless they drinke a cup of hot chocolatte ... For this purpose it was much used by them to make their maids bring them to church ... a cup of chocolatte, which could not be done to all without a great confusion and interrupting both mass and sermon".

Driven to distraction by the endless disturbances, the Bishop posted a notice stating that anyone who ate or drank in church would be excommunicated. The scornful women carried on their chocolate drinking regardless, and eventually the situation exploded into an uproar in which swords were drawn against the priests as they tried to remove the cups of chocolate from the women's maids.

The women retaliated by refusing to attend the Bishop's services and attending mass at the convents instead. The local priest warned the Bishop that if the women "cannot have their wills, they will surely work revenge either by chocolate or conserves, or some fair present, which shall surely carry death along with it!" Lo and behold, the Bishop fell ill and died a most unpleasant death eight days later. Gage wrote: "His head and face did so swell that the least touch upon any part of him caused the skin to break and cast out white matter, which had corrupted and overflown all his body." Rumour had it that a gentlewoman "noted to be somewhat too familiar with one of the Bishop's pages" had persuaded the innocent young man to administer a cup of poisoned chocolate to "him who so rigorously had forbidden chocolate to be drunk in Church". A popular proverb in the region thereafter was "Beware of the chocolate of Chiapa".

Dangerous Stimulants

At the time that chocolate was becoming all the rage in Europe, there was a similar rise in the consumption of other tropical commodities such as coffee, tea, tobacco, rum and sugar; it seems that the Europeans were developing a taste for stimulants. The Church took a strong position and, with the exception of sugar, denounced the new foods as potentially dangerous. Even so, there was a certain amount of rule-bending when it came to chocolate.

Right: Detail from a diorama based on a seventeenth-century engraving of monks drinking chocolate.

is (also) made up in boxes, and sent not only to Mexico, but much of it yearly transported into Spain".

In the New World, the Church generally took a pragmatic view of chocolate. It was popular with nuns and monks because it sustained them through the lengthy fasts they had to endure, and they were convinced of its health-promoting properties. There was an occasional difference of opinion in the Old World, however. A Spanish monk was said to have declared the drink diabolical, claiming its invigorating properties were the work of evil spirits, but his views went unheard. In 1650 the Society of Jesus (the Jesuit school) issued an act outlawing the drink to Jesuits, but this was impossible to enforce, especially when students started to abandon the school because of it.

The Chocolate of Chiapa

One major objection to chocolate appears to have been raised by the Bishop of Chiapa, whose mass was continually disturbed by its use. A famous and rather lengthy story told by Thomas Gage is

CHOCOLATE AS MEDICINE

Chocolate was used therapeutically as long ago as the fourth century, when the Maya first started cultivating the cacao tree. Sorcerers, the predecessors of priests and doctors, prescribed cacao both as a stimulant and as a soothing balm. Warriors took it as an energy-boosting drink, and cacao butter was used as a dressing for wounds.

Later on, the Aztecs prescribed a potion of cacao mixed with the ground exhumed bones of their ancestors as a cure for diarrhoea. The Spanish colonists, too, were aware of cacao's healing properties. A traveller reported of his countrymen: "They make paste thereof, the which they say is good for the stomacke, and against the catarre."

However, chocolate was given a mixed reception by the scientific and medical community, who were just as vociferous as the Church when it came to debating the rights and wrongs of this mysterious new substance. In the sixteenth century, when medicine was in its infancy, many of the theories were based on the principle of "hot" and "cold" humours, or body energies, which, if not kept in balance, would cause illness. The Spanish classified chocolate as "cold" and tried to neutralize its effect by drinking it hot, flavoured with "hot" spices. They found it hard to

Above: Utensils needed "to make cocoa to perfection".

understand why the Aztecs had drunk unheated chocolate when it was already a "cold" food.

By the seventeenth century, chocolate had been given the seal of approval by several botanists and medical men, who discovered that it contained all kinds of beneficial substances. Henry Stubbe (1632–72), the English court physician, even visited the West Indies to investigate the physical effects of chocolate. On his return, he published *The Indian Nectar*, in which he had nothing but praise for the beverage, with the proviso that adding too much sugar or spice was unwise.

Among the many others who sang the praises of chocolate was Stephani Blancardi (1650–1702), an Italian physician. He commented: "Chocolate is not only pleasant of taste, but it is also a veritable balm of the mouth, for the maintaining of all glands and humours in a good state of health. Thus it is, that all who drink it, possess a sweet breath."

The French faculty of medicine officially approved its use in 1661. The magistrate and gastronome Brillat-Savarin (1755–1826), summed up in *Physiologie du Goût*: "Chocolate, when carefully prepared, is a wholesome and agreeable form of food ... is very suitable for persons of great mental exertion, preachers, lawyers, and above all travellers ... it agrees with the feeblest stomachs, has proved beneficial in cases of chronic illness and remains the last resource in the diseases of the pylorus." Some of his contemporaries claimed that chocolate cured tuberculosis. A French doctor, probably sensing chocolate's ability to lift the spirits, was convinced of its merits as an antidote to a broken heart. He wrote: "Those who love, and are unfortunate enough to suffer from the most universal of all gallant illnesses, will find [in chocolate] the most enlightening consolation."

Praise was by no means universal. An eighteenth-century physician to the Tuscan court threw a spanner in the works by declaring that chocolate was "hot" and that it was madness to add "hot drugs" to it. He obviously noticed the effects of caffeine for he lists as ill effects incessant chatter, insomnia, irritability and hyperactivity in children. The French, too, became disenamoured for a short period, blaming chocolate for "vapours", palpitations, wind and constipation.

In general, however, the medicinal and nutritional benefits of chocolate were well accepted. An early English writer described it

Below: French doctors believed chocolate was beneficial for chronic illnesses and broken hearts.

A Mexican Recipe for Lip Salve

Take 2.5ml/ ½ tsp cocoa butter from freshly roasted beans and mix to an ointment with sweet almond oil.

Right: This eighteenth-century painting shows how chocolate was adopted by well-to-do households as a nutritious breakfast drink.

Below: This engraving from Physiologie du Goût ou Méditations de Gastronomie Transcendante (1848) depicts chocolate being served to uplift the spirits.

Below: This nineteenth-century advertisement shows British children enjoying cocoa. Medical experts in Britain proclaimed cocoa as "the drink par excellence for children, with whom it is a universal favourite".

as "incomparable as a family drink for breakfast or supper, when both tea and coffee are really out of place unless the latter is nearly all milk". Brillat-Savarin commented on digestion: "When you have breakfasted well and copiously, if you swallow a generous cup of good chocolate at the end of the meal, you will have digested everything perfectly three hours later."

By the 1800s charlatans were beginning to cash in on chocolate's seal of approval by the medical profession. Various forms of "medicinal" chocolate started to appear including sinister-sounding products such as "pectoral chocolate" made with Indian tapioca, recommended for people suffering from consumption, and "analeptic" chocolate made with a mysterious "Persian tonic".

By the end of the century, the genuine article was approved of by hospitals and sanatoria, as well as by the navy, army and various public institutions.

THE FOUNDING FATHERS

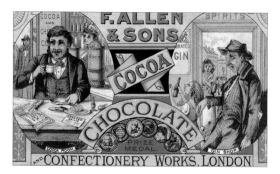

Above: Nineteenth-century British cocoa manufacturers were keen to wean the poor off their favourite tipple of gin.

Great Britain

The manufacture of drinking chocolate in Britain was transformed by the Industrial Revolution and the cultural, social and economic changes that followed in its wake. During the eighteenth century the pioneering chocolate manufacturers were still using primitive manufacturing methods, similar to those used by the Aztecs. Technology gradually entered the scene, bringing with it two key developments: a hydraulic grinding press, invented in 1728 by Walter Churchman, and, in 1765, James Watt's steam engine, which changed the food industry overnight. Another crucial development in chocolate manufacture was a revolutionary type of chocolate press invented in 1828 by the Dutch chemist, Coenraad Van Houten.

In 1853 the taxes on drinking chocolate were reduced because the volume of imports had grown enormously. By then the new railways had made transport easier, and power-driven machinery had largely replaced the old slow method of making chocolate by hand. These changes radically brought down the price, meaning that drinking chocolate could potentially be enjoyed by all.

Right: Cadbury's printed endorsements from the medical press on their packaging.

It was during this era that several eminent Quaker families – the Frys, the Cadburys, the Rowntrees and the Terrys – became involved in chocolate manufacturing. These families established themselves as the main producers in Britain and succeeded in transforming chocolate from the drink of the aristocracy to the drink of the people.

It was undoubtedly the Quakers' evangelical outlook that was behind their decision to choose chocolate as a commercial venture. Because the beverage was so wholesome, the Quakers hoped it would provide a means of weaning the poor off beer and gin, their favourite tipples, and improving the quality of their lives in general. The Quakers were also concerned for their employees' welfare. They created exemplary working conditions and built model villages where education, healthcare and community services were provided for the workers, both active and retired, without charge. Cadbury's Bournville village near Birmingham and Rowntree in York are famous examples.

The Frys were the sole suppliers of chocolate to the navy, making them the largest chocolate manufacturer in the world. Not to be outdone, the rival Cadbury family gained the privileged title of purveyors of chocolate to Queen Victoria.

Italy

The Italians have always been accomplished sweet-makers. They started using chocolate as an ingredient very early on and thus established themselves as leading experts in the art of making fine chocolates. In 1884, when the Russian Czar commissioned from the jeweller Fabergé his first golden egg with its surprise filling of precious stones, Italian

Above: Military-style packaging.

producers introduced what may have been the first chocolate Easter eggs containing a surprise gift.

The Italian chocolate industry is centred around Turin in Piedmont and Perugia in Umbria. Production on a commercial scale developed in the early nineteenth century when Bozelli, an engineer from Genoa, designed a machine capable of producing over 300kg/660lb of chocolate per day. By the end of the century the industry was booming.

There are several long-established firms in northern Italy. These include Caffarel from whom the Italians learned to make chocolate, and Baratti & Milano, from the Turin area; Perugina (now owned by Nestlé) from Perugia, makers of the famous "Baci" (kisses) chocolates with the memorable pack; and Majani in Bologna, who now produce the ultimate in designer chocolates.

Switzerland

Unsurprisingly, Switzerland boasts an incredible list of founding fathers. The first, an enterprising young man named François Cailler, travelled to Turin in 1815, learned the tricks of the trade from Caffarel, then opened the first Swiss chocolate factory four years later. Next to set up was Philippe Suchard, inventor of the world's first chocolate mixing machine. In 1845 Richard Sprüngli opened his world-famous shop in Zurich, followed by a factory in 1900. Henri Nestlé, a chemist, invented a type of evaporated milk powder, which was used by Daniel Peter, a chocolate-maker, to produce the first milk chocolate bars in 1879.

In the same year Rodolphe Lindt invented the "conching" process, which revolutionized forever the texture and flavour of solid chocolate bars. Richard Sprüngli's grandson, David, bought out Lindt in 1899; five generations later, Lindt-Sprüngli is Switzerland's largest independent chocolate manufacturer. Finally, in 1908 Jean Tobler produced the famous "Toblerone" bar, now marketed by Suchard. Its distinctive triangular shape was designed to represent the Swiss Alps.

France

The first chocolate factories appeared in the mid-seventeenth century, and, as in England, production was a slow and primitive process. Life became easier in 1732, when a Frenchman named Dubuisson invented a grinding table. This allowed the workers to grind the beans standing up, instead of kneeling in front of a floor-level stone, which they had done until then.

France's most famous mass producers were Auguste Poulain and Jean-Antoine Menier. Poulain set up shop in Blois in 1848, making chocolate in a back room. By 1878 he was producing chocolate by the ton from five different factories. In 1884 his son Albert developed a chocolate breakfast drink, now known as Grand Arôme and still loved by French children. Meanwhile, Menier, a pharmacist famous for his "medicinal powders", bought a small chocolate factory near the River Marne, intending simply to produce chocolate to coat his pills. When he died in 1853, his son Émile-Justin stepped in, concentrating on full-scale chocolate manufacture. A man of capitalist vision,

Left: Menier cooking chocolate is widely used today.

Right: As this 1893 poster shows, Menier chocolate has always been popular with French children.

Left: Established for over a hundred years, Weiss still produces quality drinking chocolate.

Émile built a new factory in France, opened a factory in London, a warehouse in New York, bought cacao plantations in Nicaragua, and built a Bournville-like model village for his workers. When he died Émile's son, Henri, continued in the same expansionary spirit. In 1889 he arranged for electricity lines and telephones to be installed in the workers' homes and, many years before the rest of the French working population, gave them the right to retire at sixty.

France's chocolatiers also include a strong contingent of smaller specialist firms that played an important role in forming the character of France's present-day chocolate industry. Debauve & Gallais was established in Paris in 1800 and are the oldest producers of hand-made chocolates in the city today. Another prestigious company is Weiss, based in Saint-Étienne for over a hundred years, and famous for its delicious drinking chocolate and hefty foil-wrapped chocolate drops.

Above: The electronic automobile bought by Hershey in 1900.

United States of America

Chocolate arrived relatively late in North America, around the middle of the eighteenth century. The first industrial producers were Dr James Baker and his partner John Hannon, who built a chocolate factory in 1765 on the banks of the River Neponset in Massachusetts. In 1780 the company was renamed the Walter Baker Company, after John Hannon's grandson, and is still a household name today, producing bakers' (a confusing generic term) chocolate as well as better quality varieties under their own name of Baker's.

Over a century later Milton Hershey, a successful caramel manufacturer from Pennsylvania, visited the 1893 Chicago World Fair and was overwhelmingly impressed by German chocolate production machinery on display. With a shrewd sense of timing, he decided that chocolate was going to be a runaway success and his company has never looked back. Hershey sold his first milk chocolate bar in 1895, and since then Hershey Bars and Hershey Kisses have become part of the American way of life – just as he predicted.

Like his Quaker counterparts in Britain, Hershey had a strong social conscience. He enlisted nutritionists to vouch for the sanctity of his product, set up a squeaky-clean working environment and built the factory town of Hershey in Pennsylvania. The main thoroughfares are called East Chocolate Avenue and Cocoa Avenue, while the tree-lined side streets are named after places where cacao is grown, or by types of bean – Java, Caracas, Arriba and so on.

Hershey went one better than the Quaker factory villages in England and provided very generous out-of-town facilities for his employees such as an amusement park, a zoo, sporting facilities and a theatre. Hershey also made it clear that no "taverns, piggeries, glue, soap, candle, lamp-black factories" were allowed, making sure that his model working communities stayed as wholesome as possible.

It is interesting that the early North American and British manufacturers of a product that was, and still is, associated with sensory enjoyment and indulgence, should have had quite a puritanical outlook. A cynical view might be that their social philanthropy was a clever marketing ploy, but these businessmen did have a genuine social conscience, and it is perhaps another illustration that chocolate is all things to all people – both a luxurious treat and a wholesome daily food.

Milton Hershey was not the only American producer pushing the wholesomeness of chocolate. Like-minded but rather more extreme companies included the Taylor Brothers, who entered the market with their Natural Hygienist Practitioners, and Dr William Hay, of the still-popular Hay System of food-combining. Taylor's selling point was the curative, homeopathic nature of chocolate. This shows a continuity with the earliest European marketeers, who sold their chocolate through the apothecaries, monasteries and convents of the sixteenth and seventeenth centuries, and had much to say on the beneficial properties of the cacao bean and its products.

Above: Street signs to the main thoroughfares in Hershey.

Below: Publicity for Taylor Brothers demonstrating their social conscience, while promoting the nourishing powers of chocolate.

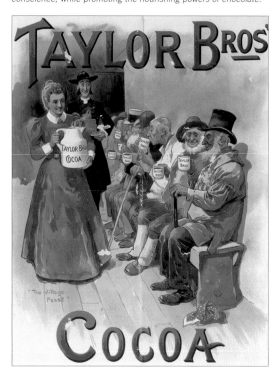

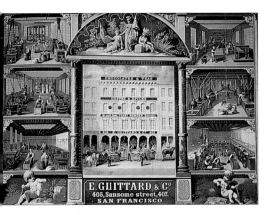

Above: A picture of the original Guittard building surrounded by scenes showing early chocolate manufacture.

A much more colourful American chocolate producer was Domingo Ghirardelli, an Italian confectioner with South American links who was originally in business in Lima, Peru. He befriended an American cabinetmaker named James Lick, who, in 1847 just before the discovery of gold at Sutter's Mill, moved from Lima to San Francisco, taking with him a large quantity of Ghirardelli's chocolate. Lured by reports of a lucrative market, Ghirardelli followed Lick to California. As astute and entrepreneurial as his

Below: The Ghirardelli company was the first in America to make easily dissolvable powdered cocoa.

fellow chocolate producers, both in the United States and worldwide, Ghirardelli foresaw the potential in satisfying the day-to-day needs of the goldrush pioneers, who by then were arriving in hordes. He set up a business in San Francisco importing and selling sugar, coffee and, of course, chocolate.

There were various disasters over the years, including devastating bankruptcy and a serious fire, but business continued despite the inevitable setbacks in a volatile period of American history. By 1856 the company was known as Ghirardelli's California Chocolate Manufactory. The company was to make its mark on the chocolate industry in the 1860s when, by sheer accident, a way of making a low-fat powdered cocoa was discovered. The new product was known as Sweet Ground Chocolate and Cocoa and is still sold today.

The original factory buildings have become a well-known San Francisco landmark in Ghirardelli Square, and the company continues to flourish. It was bought by the Golden Grain Macaroni Company in 1963, which in turn was acquired as a subsidiary of the Quaker Oats Company in 1983.

Another chocolate maker, Etienne Guittard from France, set off for the gold-fields of San Francisco in 1860. After three years, he hadn't found any gold, but the supply of fine chocolate he had brought with him to barter for prospecting gear had been enthusiastically received. The shopkeepers he traded with assured him that there was a future for him and his wonderful chocolate in San Francisco. Guittard went back to France, where he worked and saved to buy the equipment he would need. In 1868 he returned to San Francisco and opened the business that developed into one of the important American manufacturers of top-grade chocolate for wholesale customers. Some of the country's best confectioners, bakers and ice-cream makers (Baskin-Robbins, for one) use Guittard.

Ghirardelli's Accident

Cacao beans have a high fat content and because of this do not combine easily with liquids when ground to a powder. Ghirardelli's most important contribution to the chocolate industry was the accidental discovery of a way of making a virtually fat-free powder.

A worker left some ground cacao beans hanging from a hook in a cloth bag overnight. By the morning, the floor was covered in cacao butter that had dripped from the bag. The ground chocolate left behind was almost fat-free and was found to combine with liquids much more smoothly. Ghirardelli's ever-popular Sweet Ground Chocolate and Cocoa was developed from this.

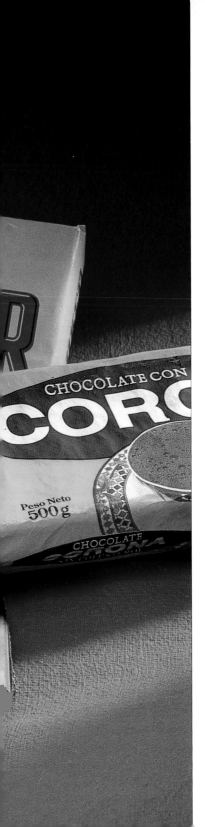

THE WORLD OF CHOCOLATE

This chapter examines how the cacao bean is cultivated and processed,

where and how it is grown and harvested, and describes the different

types of bean. We look at the specialist world of quality chocolate,

demistifying terms such as couverture and cacao solids, praline and

ganache. There is also a guide to the different types of chocolate and

how to taste it properly, in the same way that tasters evaluate a fine

wine. The psychology behind our chocolate cravings and addiction is

explored, and its various connotations with romance and pleasure.

There is a country by country look at today's leading chocolate makers

and their creations and lastly a handy reference section devoted to the

various techniques used in cooking with chocolate.

GROWING AND HARVESTING

There are many stages in the processing of chocolate and there has been a corresponding amount of development in its history as it has grown from a cold drink to the complex and adaptable substance it is today. This section traces the most important steps in the production of chocolate.

Above: Cacao tree and seedling.

Growing

The cacao bean grows in large pods on the cacao tree, *Theobroma cacao*, an evergreen that thrives in tropical areas lying between 20° north and 20° south of the equator. It grows in altitudes of up to 700m/2300ft. The tree is an exacting specimen, for it refuses to grow where it is too high, too cold or too dry, and it demands shelter from wind and sun. It also needs protection from wild animals, which delight in picking its pods, and it easily succumbs to various rots, wilts and fungal diseases.

It is traditional for the cacao tree to be grown under the protection of taller, shade-creating trees, the conditions resembling its natural jungle habitat. In areas such as Grenada and parts of Jamaica, cacao trees grow successfully without additional shade, as long as there are sufficient moisture and nutrients in the soil. The cacao tree grows to about the size of an apple tree and starts bearing fruit in its third year. It matures at six years and, with luck, it will continue to bear fruit until at least its twentieth year. It is not unknown for a tree to live to be a hundred years old. The glossy, dark green leaves, similar to those of the

Below: A shady cacao plantation in the garden island of Grenada, where cacao production is a staple industry.

laurel, grow to nearly 30cm/12in long. The small pale pink flowers grow in dense clusters straight out of the trunk and main branches on little raised cushions, a feature technically known as "cauliflory". Only flowers that have been fertilized, either by insects or manually by the farmers, turn into fruits or pods.

Cacao is essentially the botanical name and refers to the tree, the pods and, at one time, the unfermented beans from the pods. The term is now also used for beans that have been fermented.

Cocoa refers to the manufactured powder sold for drinking or for food manufacturing purposes.

The fertilized flowers take about five months to develop into cacao pods. It is a colourful crop – the pods range from bright red, green, purple or yellow, changing hue as they ripen. Ripe pods are about 20cm/8in long, and weigh around 380g/13oz. They are oval and pointed, each containing 20 to 40 beans, embedded in a soft white pulp, which is called mucilage.

Fifty-five per cent of the mass of cacao beans is taken up by two cotyledons, which give them a high fat content. They also contain polyphenols (a group of chemicals that include antioxidants), theobromine (a stimulant), tannins, caffeine, carbohydrates, proteins, fibre and mineral salts.

Harvesting

It is by assessing the colour of the pod and the sound it makes when tapped that the picker can be sure it is ready for picking. To be absolutely certain that the pod is ripe enough requires years of practice, and experienced pickers are highly valued.

The pods are removed from the tree by cutting through their stalks, those within reach with a cutlass, and those on higher branches with a curved knife fixed to a long pole. Cutting must be done with extreme care so as not to damage the cauliflory, as this continually produces the flowers and therefore the fruit. In some countries, harvesting takes place all year round, although most heavily from May to December. In other parts of the world, West Africa for instance, the main crop of pods is harvested from September to February.

Fermenting

The next stage is to split the pods with a cutlass, taking care not to damage the precious beans. These are scooped out, together with their surrounding pulp, and formed into a conical heap on a carefully arranged mat of banana leaves. When the heap is complete the leaves are folded over, and yet more of these giant

Above: Early lithograph issued by the Empire Marketing Board in Britain showing cacao beans being scooped from the pods.

Types of Cacao Bean

There are two distinct species of cacao bean used in the manufacture of chocolate: the criollo (meaning "native") and the forastero (meaning "foreign").

The criollo, the Rolls Royce of beans and the most delicate, is in a way a "limited edition", representing only 10 to 15 per cent of the world's production. It is cultivated mainly in the countries where cacao originated, namely Nicaragua, Guatemala, Mexico, Venezuela and Colombia, as well as Trinidad, Jamaica and Grenada. The criollo's exceptional flavour and aroma are prized by chocolate manufacturers the world over. Not surprisingly, the bean is always used in combination with other varieties.

The much hardier and higher-yielding forastero bean is grown mainly in Brazil and Africa, and it accounts for about 80 per cent of the world's production. It has a stronger, more bitter flavour than the criollo and is mainly used for blending.

The one exception that is not used for blending is the amenolado variety, known as the "Arriba" bean. It is grown in Ecuador. Its delicate flavour and fine aroma are considered equal to the world's best beans.

Finally, there are also several hybrid beans, of which the trinitario is the best known. As the name suggests, it began life in Trinidad where, following a hurricane in 1727 that all but destroyed the plantations, it was a result of cross-breeding. It has inherited the robustness of the forastero and the delicate flavour of the criollo, and it is used mainly for blending.

---

eaves are added to enclose the heap completely. This is the start of the fermentation process, which lasts for up to six days.

The chemical processes involved are complicated, but basically bacteria and yeasts present in the air multiply on the sugary pulp surrounding the beans, causing it to decompose to an acidic juice. The process raises the temperature of the heap and under these conditions magical changes take place within the bean itself. The colour changes from purple to chocolate brown and the familiar cacao smell begins to emerge – the first crucial stage in developing beans of superior quality. That said, the fermentation process is sometimes omitted, with planters and manufacturers arguing both for and against.

Drying

After fermentation, the beans are spread out on bamboo mats or wooden drying floors. During the ten to twenty days needed for drying, the beans are regularly turned to keep them well aired and to prevent moulds forming. In some places, where rainfall and humidity are high, the beans are dried in commercial drying plants. However, the best quality cacao comes from beans that have been dried naturally in the warm tropical sun.

Below: The large and beautiful cacao pods grow directly from the tree branches and change colour as they ripen.

MODERN MANUFACTURING

Above: A chocolate manufacturer inspects a shipment of beans.

Cleaning and Grading

Cacao beans arrive at a chocolate factory in the condition in which they leave the plantations in cacao-growing countries. They have been fermented and dried but are still a raw material with the edible part enclosed inside the hard skin, which is dusty with the remains of the dried pulp.

The beans are given a preliminary cleaning, during which any stones or other objects that may have arrived in the sacks are removed by sieving. The beans pass on a moving belt to storage hoppers, and from there they travel on another conveyor belt to the cleaning and grading machines. The beans are carefully inspected, and any shrivelled or double beans are discarded, as is any undesirable material still clinging to the beans. Next, the cleaned and graded beans are collected either in containers or passed on another continuous conveyor belt to the roasting machines.

Roasting for Flavour

Roasting is a crucial part of the process and serves several functions. First, it develops the flavour and aroma, and it enriches the colour. Roasting also dries the husk surrounding the "nib", or edible inner part of the bean, making its removal easier, and dries the nib itself so that it is ready for grinding.

The degree of roasting is extremely important. Overdoing it

Below: The beans are cleaned and sifted through a mesh to get rid of small or shrivelled beans and foreign bodies.

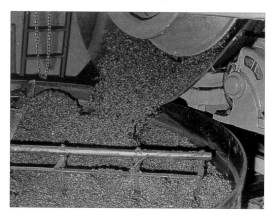

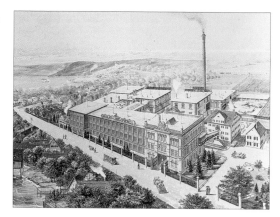

Above: A contemporaneous picture of Richard Sprüngli's famous factory, which opened in Switzerland in 1900.

destroys the natural flavour of the bean and produces a bitter product, while under-roasting makes the removal of the husk more difficult and also fails to eradicate the natural bitterness of the raw bean. Some manufacturers who want their chocolate to have a strong flavour, but who are not prepared to increase the cacao content, attempt to achieve the required intensity by roasting the beans longer.

Different types of bean need different roasting temperatures, depending on their texture and flavour; the mild varieties are usually roasted at lower temperatures than the stronger types.

After roasting, the beans are cooled as quickly as possible to prevent further internal roasting.

Below: The beans are gently roasted to develop the aroma, enrich the colour and to dehydrate them prior to grinding.

Winnowing

During the next stage the beans are passed through the husking and winnowing machine, which cracks open the roasted beans, and blows the lighter husks away from the heavier pieces of nib. Manufacturers send the husks off for recycling as garden mulch, or use them to make low-quality soft "shell" butter.

The Crucial Blend

During the blending process, specified quantities of different varieties of cacao nibs are weighed and transferred to a cylindrical blender before they are fed into the grinding machines. The blending of beans for cocoa powder is generally less exacting than for eating chocolate. The latter requires the utmost skill from the chocolatier as knowledge of the characteristic flavours imparted by different beans is acquired only by years of experience. There are subtle differences of flavour in each type of bean, and the final flavour is obtained by blending two, three or more types of bean after roasting. In the same way that the winemaker blends his grapes, the chocolatier needs to determine the proportion of strong and mild cacao beans necessary to

Above: A picture of the grinding hall in the Sprüngli factory. The rollers can be seen on the left.

produce a blend that will result in a satisfying chocolate, and the formulae are jealously guarded secrets.

Grinding

Once in the grinding mill, the nibs pass through a series of rollers, resulting in coarse particles that eventually turn into a warm paste because of the frictional heat of the grinding action. Then follows a second grinding to bring the particles down to the required size, usually between 25 and 50 microns (about 0.001in). Large particles result in coarse grainy chocolate, while very finely ground particles will produce a pasty and slightly sticky chocolate. After grinding, the cacao mass or "liquor" flows out of the machine into shallow metal containers.

The Parting of the Ways

At this stage, further treatment of the liquor depends on whether it is to be made into cocoa powder or eating chocolate. For cocoa powder the next step is the extraction of a large proportion of the cacao butter. This is pressed out of the liquor, and the residue is formed into cakes, which go through one more grinding. Some cocoa is "dutched", which helps to make cocoa powder easier to mix with water. It also improves the colour and lightens the flavour. Sometimes a wetting agent is added, especially to the "instant" varieties of cocoa intended for use as a cold drink; it makes the powder easier to mix with cold water or milk. The wetting agent is usually lecithin, a vegetable fat found in egg yolks and soy beans. Chocolate destined for eating is treated very differently from cocoa powder.

Right: Two types of instant drinking chocolate.

Bean Blends

The final flavour of chocolate depends largely on the chocolatier's skill and experience in selecting and blending various types of beans. Availability of supplies and cost also have to be taken into account.

Types of cacao beans may be divided into strong and mild varieties:

Strong varieties	Mild varieties
Accra	Caracas
St Lucia	Mauritius
Para	Sri Lanka
Trinidad	Arriba
Grenada	Java
Surinam	Madras
Cuba	Jamaica
Dominica	Seychelles

If made only with Accra beans, for example, chocolate will have a very strong, harsh flavour, whereas Caracas beans make mild but excellently flavoured chocolate. Superb chocolate can be made with a blend of 42 per cent Trinidad beans (strong), 21 per cent Accra beans (strong) and 37 per cent Caracas (mild).

THE MANUFACTURE OF EATING CHOCOLATE

Above: Rolls of ground chocolate paste (foreground) are moulded into bars and various shapes in the moulding hall.

Above: Prolonged conching transforms the chocolate paste into velvety smoothness.

Mixing

Cacao beans used for manufacturing eating chocolate are processed in a different way from beans used in cocoa manufacture. First, a carefully selected blend of roasted and ground nibs, the edible centre of the bean, is mixed with pulverized sugar and enriched with cacao butter, not necessarily extracted from the same batch of nibs. The mass producers in the chocolate industry are very keen on adding lecithin, a vegetable fat, to replace some or all of the cacao butter. This means they can sell the valuable butter at a profit.

The mixture then goes to the *mélangeur*, a round machine with a horizontal rotating base on which run heavy rollers. After mixing, the chocolate paste that is discharged from the *mélangeur* resembles well-kneaded dough.

When manufacturing milk chocolate, powdered milk or evaporated sweetened milk is added to the rest of the ingredients in the mixer.

Refining

Next, the chocolate paste is ground between a series of five rollers, each succeeding roller rotating faster than the previous one. The paste enters the first pair of rollers as a thin film, which is then taken up by the next pair, through a carefully adjusted gap – rather like making pasta with a machine.

By the time the paste emerges from the fifth roller it is wafer thin. As far as some mass-producers are concerned, this is the end of the process, but the finest quality chocolate needs further treatment known as "conching".

Conching

The conching machine was invented in 1880 by the Swiss chocolatier, Rodolfe Lindt. The name comes from the French (*conche*, meaning "shell") and is derived from the shape of the machine, a large shell-shaped container.

The function of the machine is to agitate the liquid chocolate gently over a period that may be as long as seven days. It is a vital process in which the flavour of the chocolate is developed and mellowed, any residual bitterness is removed, and the texture reaches that essential stage of velvety smoothness.

Manufacturers of cheaper chocolate give as little as twelve hours to the process. Quality producers will continue conching for up to a week, sometimes adding extra cacao butter to make the chocolate smoother still.

During conching, various flavours are added, such as vanilla, cloves or cinnamon.

Left: Luscious slices of crystallized fruit are enrobed with smooth, dark chocolate.

Vanilla is almost always used and dates back to the days of the Aztecs. Our palates have become so accustomed to its flavour in chocolate that leaving it out would be like making bread without adding salt. Pure vanilla extract is used for the best quality chocolate, but cheaper varieties are likely to contain vanillin, an inferior and synthetic substitute.

Tempering

Once the conching stage is complete, the chocolate is fed into tempering kettles, where it is stirred and carefully cooled but still remains liquid. This is a tricky process since cacao butter contains various types of fat, all with different melting and setting points. If the chocolate mass is cooled too slowly, some fats will remain liquid and separate from the mass, creating a bloom on the surface when the chocolate finally solidifies. Tempering causes rapid cooling, resulting in a more even distribution of the various fats.

After tempering, chocolate to be made into bars is pumped into moulding machines, while chocolate to be used as coating is pumped into enrobing machines.

Below: Hollow Easter eggs, filled with small chocolates, are a classic example of chocolate moulding.

Chocolate misses

In *Cocoa and Chocolate* (1921), R. Whymper tells of how, in the early 1900s, the popularity of milk chocolate "raised hopes in the breasts of manufacturers that a similar demand might be created among the masses for such articles as Date Chocolate, Egg Chocolate, Malt Chocolate". A number of patents were taken out, one of which was for mixing cacao beans and dates to a pulp, and covered the use of apples, pears and apricots for the same purpose. There was apparently a shortage of cane sugar at the time, and the fruit pulp was intended to be a sweetener.

Another patent was for "dietetic and laxative" chocolate. As Mr Whymper pointed out: "Such preparations must have only a very limited sale, so long as the chocolate consuming public does not seek to find cures in its confections."

Moulding

Liquid chocolate is also moulded into hollowed-out shapes that are sometimes filled with small chocolates. These products are often marketed as gifts for children, and specialist chocolate-makers give full rein to their creativity here, producing not simply exquisite Easter eggs, bunnies and hearts, but also pigs, fish, lions, hippos, crocodiles and cars. Because of the contact

Above: 1930s' metal moulds for producing novelty chocolates.

with the smooth tinned surfaces of the mould, good quality hollow chocolate has a high degree of gloss, which adds to its attraction.

Enrobing

Enrobing is the tricky process of coating confectionery centres. Liquid chocolate of a slightly "thin" consistency is pumped into the enrobing machine, where it is agitated once more and maintained at a temperature just high enough to keep it liquid. The centres themselves have to be warm when they enter the coating chamber, but not so warm that they lose their shape. The danger of a cold centre is that it is likely to expand when it comes in contact with the warm coating, resulting in burst chocolates. Enrobing is the process used not only for top quality chocolates in their luxury packaging, but also for the mass-produced candy bars that are bought as snacks around the world.

TYPES OF EATING CHOCOLATE

There is a wealth of wonderful chocolate products available, with an often confusing array of types, qualities, fillings and added flavourings. Here is a brief guide on what you should look for and how to enjoy chocolate at its best.

Plain Chocolate (also known as Bittersweet)

Plain or bittersweet (or semisweet as it's called in the US) chocolate must contain a minimum of 34 per cent cacao solids, however generally speaking, the higher the proportion the better the chocolate. Not so very long ago, plain chocolate that contained just 30 per cent cacao solids was considered high quality. Today, as our taste and awareness of chocolate grows, 60 per cent is the preferred minimum, while for chocoholics 70–80 per cent is even more desirable.

High-quality dark chocolate contains a correspondingly small proportion of sugar. Adding sugar to chocolate has been compared with adding salt to food. You need just enough to enhance the flavour, but not so much that the flavour is destroyed. Quality chocolate contains pure vanilla, an expensive flavouring sometimes called bourbon vanilla, extracted from a type of orchid grown in Madagascar. It also contains the minutest amount of lecithin, which is a harmless vegetable stabilizer. In unsweetened chocolate, which can be found only in specialist shops, cacao solids can be as high as 98 per cent.

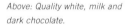

Above: Quality white, milk and dark chocolate.

Couverture

This is high-quality chocolate in the professional league, used mainly for coating and in baking. To make couverture chocolate, cocoa butter and sugar are added to cocoa mass. The mixture is kneaded and then ground to reduce the size of the granules. To develop the chocolate aroma and make the chocolate into a liquid, the cocoa mass then undergoes the process called conching. Before it takes on its final form it is tempered, during which the temperature is lowered until the desired consistency is reached.

Left: Couverture chocolate, which has a very high proportion of cacao solids.

Right: Best quality couverture with a good sheen. Blocks of this size are supplied to chocolatiers.

Milk Chocolate

Milk chocolate was first produced successfully in 1875 by the Swiss chocolate-maker Daniel Peter after eight years of experimenting. He used condensed milk instead of fresh milk so that the cocoa would not be affected by the acidity.

Formula for Quality Chocolate

56–70% cacao solids, to include 31% cacao butter
29–43% finely ground sugar
1% lecithin and pure vanilla extract

Formula for Mass-produced Milk Chocolate

11% cacao solids
3% vegetable fat
20% milk solids
65% sugar
1% lecithin and synthetic vanillin

To some aficionados, milk chocolate is not really chocolate, but increasingly there are some good brands around, even though they may be difficult to find. A good brand will have a cacao solid content of around 40 per cent, but most mass-produced milk chocolate contains only 20 per cent. Mass-produced milk chocolate has a high sugar content, often up to 50 per cent. It can also contain up to 5 per cent vegetable fat, used as a substitute for expensive cacao butter, and artificial flavouring.

White Chocolate

This is basically cacao butter without any cacao solids, with some added sugar, flavouring and milk. White chocolate does not have the same depth of flavour as plain chocolate. It is mainly sold for its novelty value, or to provide an attractive colour contrast in

Left: A layered bar of plain, white and milk chocolate.

chocolates and chocolate desserts. The best quality brands tend to be French and Swiss. British brands usually contain vegetable oil instead of cacao butter, as well as synthetic flavourings.

Assessing Quality

All our senses – sight, smell, sound, touch and taste – come into play when assessing the quality of plain chocolate. There are several points to watch out for:

Appearance The chocolate should be smooth, brilliantly shiny and pure mahogany-black in colour.

Smell The chocolate should not smell excessively sweet.

Sound The chocolate should be crisp and make a distinct "snap" when broken in two. If the chocolate splinters, it is too dry; if it resists breaking, it is too waxy.

Touch Chocolate with a high cacao butter content should quickly start to melt when held in the hand – this is a good sign. In the mouth, it should feel ultra smooth with no hint of graininess, and it should melt instantly.

Taste Chocolate contains a kaleidoscope of flavours and aromas that continue to develop in the mouth. The basic flavours are bitterness with a hint of acidity, sweetness with a suggestion of sourness, and just a touch of saltiness, which helps release the aromas of cocoa, pineapple, banana, vanilla and cinnamon.

Storage

Humidity and heat are chocolate's greatest enemies; both can cause a "bloom" to appear on the surface. Heat-induced bloom is

What to Drink with Chocolate

Generally speaking, chocolate and wine do not mix. The lingering intensity of the chocolate competes with the aroma of the wine, and chocolate's bitterness can mask the tannins essential to the wine's flavour. White wine or champagne drunk with chocolate is a particularly uneasy combination. At the end of a meal, coffee, perhaps accompanied by a fine cognac, whisky or bourbon, is the best choice. Professional chocolate tasters swear by a glass of cold, fresh water, as it not only quenches the thirst but also cleanses the palate.

Tasting Techniques

It is best to taste chocolate on an empty stomach. If your chocolate is correctly stored, you will need to allow an hour or so for it to reach the recommended temperature of 19–25°C/66–77°F.

Plain chocolate Allow the chocolate to sit in your mouth for a few moments to release its primary flavours and aromas. Then chew it five to ten times to release the secondary aromas. Let it rest lightly against the roof of your mouth so that you experience the full range of flavours. Finally, enjoy the lingering tastes in your mouth.

Filled chocolate Allow the chocolate to sit in your mouth for a few moments to release its primary flavours and aromas. Then chew it three to five times to mix the chocolate and the filling. Let the mixture melt slowly in your mouth so that you experience a new range of flavours. Enjoy the lingering tastes.

Left: The perfect bar of chocolate has a glossy sheen and a rich dark colour.

the result of cacao butter crystals rising to the surface and recrystallizing. The flavour is unaffected but the appearance is spoiled.

Humidity-induced bloom is more damaging. It is a result of sugar crystals being drawn to the surface, where they dissolve in the moist atmosphere and eventually recrystallize to form an unpleasant grey coating. As the texture and taste of the chocolate deteriorate, too, the dustbin is the best place for chocolate that has suffered in this way. The ideal temperature for storage is 10–15°C (50–60°F), slightly warmer than the refrigerator, and the humidity should be 60–70 per cent. Chocolate also absorbs surrounding odours easily and should be kept in an airtight container.

Below: A bloom has formed on the surface of the chocolate on the right. The unaffected piece shows the difference in appearance.

Couverture (left)
The professionals' choice, this is a fine-quality pure chocolate with a high percentage of cocoa butter. It is suitable for decorative use and for making hand-made chocolates. It must generally be tempered.

Plain Dark (Bittersweet) Chocolate (below)
Often called "luxury", "bitter" or "Continental" chocolate, this has a high percentage of cocoa solids – around 75 per cent – with little or no added sugar. Its rich, intense flavour and dark colour makes it ideal for desserts and cakes.

Milk Chocolate (right)
This contains powdered or condensed milk and generally around 20 per cent cocoa solids. The flavour is mild and sweet. Although this is the most popular eating chocolate, it is not as suitable as plain (semisweet) chocolate for melting and cooking.

Plain (Semisweet) Chocolate (above)
Ordinary plain chocolate is the most widely available chocolate to use in cooking. It contains anywhere between 30 per cent and 70 per cent cocoa solids. The higher the cocoa solids, the better the chocolate flavour will be.

Cocoa (left)
This is made from the pure cocoa mass after most of the cocoa butter has been extracted. The mass is roasted, then ground to make a powder. It is an economical way of giving puddings and baked goods a chocolate flavour.

Organic Chocolate (above)

This is slightly more expensive than other types of chocolate but it is a quality product, high in cocoa solids. Organic chocolate is produced without pesticides and with consideration for the environment.

Chocolate Chips (above)

These are small pieces of chocolate of uniform size. They contain fewer cocoa solids than ordinary chocolate and are available in plain dark (bitter-sweet), milk and white flavours.

Chocolate-flavoured Cake Covering (left)

This is a blend of sugar, vegetable oil, cocoa and flavourings. The flavour is poor, but the high fat content makes it suitable for chocolate curls. To improve the flavour, add some plain (semisweet) chocolate.

Chocolate Powder (below)

Chocolate powder is used in baking and for making drinks. It has lower cocoa solids than pure cocoa and has a much milder, sweeter taste.

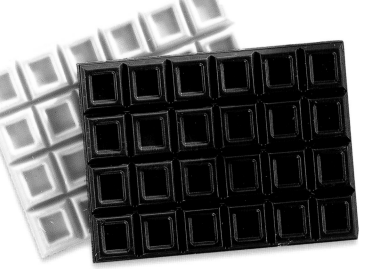

White Chocolate (below left)

This does not contain any cocoa solids but gets its flavour from cocoa butter. It is sweet, and the better quality white chocolate is quite rich and smooth. White chocolate must be melted with care, as it does not withstand heat as well as plain chocolate.

FLAVOURINGS AND FILLINGS

Every chocolate manufacturer has a secret condiment or blend of flavourings that he or she claims gives their product a unique character. Fillings and flavourings from the same tropical latitude as the cacao bean itself – vanilla, cinnamon, cardamom, coffee, rum, ginger, even pepper and chilli – are the ones most commonly used. Even in this age of "culinary fusion", when we happily mix and match cuisines in our never-ending quest for novelty, flavouring chocolate with spices from a more northerly latitude simply seems wrong – it is hard to imagine fennel or caraway-flavoured chocolate, for instance – but perhaps it is merely a matter of time before it happens.

Secret Flavours

Every chocolate-consuming country has its favourite flavourings. Italy prefers its chocolate mixed with hazelnuts, almonds or chestnuts. France likes a nutty flavour too, but strongly flavoured dark bitter chocolate is also a popular favourite. Spain likes spiced chocolate, and fillings such as almonds and dried fruits. The United States consumes mostly milk chocolate, often with whole peanuts or almonds embedded in it, while Britain likes vanilla. Not only that, every

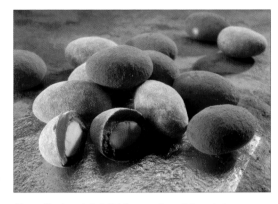

Above: Hand-made tartufini *from southern Italy – whole almonds coated in praline and dusted with dark cocoa and powdered sugar.*

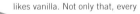

Left: Spanish chocolate packed with plump almonds.

country uses different blends of beans, and, as already mentioned, the subtle variations in the flavour of different bean varieties play their part in determining the final flavour of the chocolate. If we also take into account different processing methods used by individual factories, the number of flavour combinations is almost endless.

Within the scientific community, the complexity of chocolate's flavour is a source of enormous fascination to the many flavour scientists who are regularly producing learned papers on the subject. Daniel Querici, speaking at the 1992 Oxford Symposium on Food & Cookery, summed up the subject of chocolate's flavour in a delightful way: "Its complex flavour profile looks like a royal peacock tail, although not fully deployed, as food scientists keep discovering new components."

Below: Plump and glistening, these unusual, luscious chocolate-covered figs come from Italy.

Fillings

Boiled Based on sugar and glucose and including caramels, butterscotch and fudge.

Creams and fondants A mixture of sugar crystals in a sugar syrup, with fruit or other flavourings, coated with tempered chocolate.

Croquet (or brittle) Molten sugar with crushed nuts.

Ganache A mixture of chocolate, cream and butter, either rolled in cocoa powder to make a truffle or enrobed in tempered chocolate.

Gianduja Finely ground nuts and sugar mixed with plain or milk chocolate.

Marzipan Molten sugar mixed with ground almonds, coated with plain or milk chocolate.

Nougat A mixture of beaten egg white, boiled sugar, nuts and/or candied fruit. Known as *Montélimar* in France (after the town where it is made), *torrone* in Italy, and *turrón* in Spain.

Praline Similar to gianduja but with a coarser texture and usually coated with plain or milk chocolate.

Above: Italian chocolates from Maglio, with succulent fillings of walnuts, dried fruit and pistachio marzipan.

Fantastic Fillings

Chocolate has been used as a coating for anything from almonds and dried fruit to bizarre ingredients such as ants, and a look at the contents of a global box of chocolates will reveal many more.

In the United States, chillies and chocolate come together once more in the whacky confectionery range created by two chocolatiers from Oregon. Their products, which won an award at the Fiery Foods Show at Albuquerque, New Mexico, include Mexican Zingers, a creamy, green jalapeño salsa encased in a white chocolate shell, and Southwest Coyote Kickers, a red jalapeño salsa cream covered in light milk chocolate.

Although chilli-filled chocolates are legal in the United States, alcoholic fillings are not universally acceptable. As recently as 1986, only one American state permitted the manufacture of alcoholic chocolates, only eleven states permitted their sale, and

Below: Hand-made British chocolates with melt-in-the-mouth fondant fillings, delicately flavoured with violet and rose.

A Filling Story

In 1987 Ethel M. Chocolates, owned by 82-year-old Forrest Mars and named after his mother, attempted to introduce liqueur-filled chocolates to Las Vegas, Nevada. The chocolates were spiked with crème de menthe, brandy, Scotch and bourbon.

Mr Mars found that the sale and/or manufacture of alcoholic chocolates was illegal in most American states. Things were not looking good, especially as an appeal to legalize alcoholic chocolates had recently been rejected in Pennsylvania, home of Hersheyville. As was to be expected, the squeaky-clean Hershey Company added their support to the rejection on the grounds that "liquor-laced chocolates are inconsistent with values emphasized by religious and medical communities".

Not one to give up easily, the determined Mr Mars successfully petitioned the sale and manufacture of alcoholic chocolates in his home state of Nevada. This meant he could sell his chocolates there but not across the border, and so he had to content himself with selling to the twenty million tourists who visit Las Vegas each year. Ethel M. Chocolates are still to be found at Las Vegas airport and in many of the city's luxury hotels.

even then the permitted alcohol levels were severely restricted. Move on to Europe, however, and it is a different story. In Italy smooth dark chocolates are filled with decadent liqueur-soaked fruits – cherries, kumquats, slices of dried peach, pear, apricots and oranges. There are also plump prunes, dates and walnuts filled with marzipan and covered with dark chocolate.

In Britain, chocolate lovers can enjoy delicate fondant fillings such as violet and rose creams or marzipan; truffle fillings laced with champagne, Cointreau or Drambuie; or chunks of preserved stem ginger, and whole Brazil nuts. France is the birthplace of the dusky chocolate truffle created in the late nineteenth century by the Duc de Praslin, one of Louis XIV's ministers. At that time it was considered amusing to create a food resembling something totally unrelated. *Truffes au chocolat* were deeply rich, buttery chocolate balls that were then rolled in dark cocoa powder to resemble the savoury black fungi from Périgord.

The dragée is a French confectionery classic that in its original form, almonds coated with sugar and honey, dates back to the thirteenth century. The dragée adapted well to the introduction of chocolate and now consists of praline or nuts covered in chocolate and with a hard sugar coating.

CHOCOLATE WRAPPERS AND BOXES

Wrapping and packaging tell a great deal about what kind of chocolate is inside. Much can be learnt from the nutritional information on a bar, while the style of its presentation says much about who is expected to buy it.

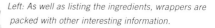

Wording on Wrappers

As with the label on a bottle of fine wine or virgin olive oil, the wording on a chocolate wrapper can provide some significant clues as to the quality of the product, so for a chocolate lover it is worth becoming familiar with the terminology.

An area of confusion arises over the terms "cacao liquor" and "cacao solids". Liquor is the term used in the United States, while Europe favours solids, but both refer to the same thing – the entire cacao content including the butter. This is usually expressed as a percentage of the net weight of the end product. Cacao content ranges from 15 per cent, which hardly comes into the category of chocolate, to an incredible 99 per cent, which is an almost inedible but interesting experience.

Above: A wrapper that makes a feature of the cacao content.

Since the setting up of the European Union, legislation on the labelling of food has become much more regulated, and the classification of chocolate has become an issue. Some chocolate-producing countries feel that Britain's product should be classified as "vegolate" because of its use of vegetable fat and low cacao content. Happily for British chocolate producers, this has as yet remained a discussion point only.

What to Look For

The key indicator of quality is the cacao content – the combined total of cacao solids (liquor) and cacao butter. In some cases, couverture for instance, the

Left: As well as listing the ingredients, wrappers are packed with other interesting information.

cacao butter content is itemized separately. In the case of plain chocolate, a minimum of 50 per cent total cacao is an indicator of quality. Quality milk chocolate should have a minimum of 30 per cent. Since sugar makes up the balance of the ingredients, a high sugar content is a warning of a correspondingly low cacao content.

Unlike wine labels, which mention the grape variety, chocolate wrappers rarely divulge the type of cacao bean used and are not obliged to do so. An exception is in France, where the words "fine cocoa" mean that the superior varieties of bean, such as the criollo, have been used.

Vegetable or animal fats are used as a cheap substitute for some or all of the cacao butter, so if either is listed as an ingredient, the chocolate is not going to come up to scratch. The fact that they are not listed, however, does not necessarily always mean they are not present. In Britain, for example, up to 5 per cent cacao butter substitutes can be included without mentioning them on the wrapper.

Lecithin, an emulsifier derived from egg yolk and soya beans, is used in all types of chocolate, and at 1 per cent or less is not an indicator of inferior quality. Its function is to stabilize the chocolate and to absorb any moisture.

As far as flavourings are concerned, look for the words "pure vanilla extract". If "vanillin", a synthetic substitute, or simply the word "flavouring" is listed, then the chocolate is likely to be of an inferior quality.

The Americans outdo any other nation in the world when it comes to providing information on the ingredients that go into their chocolate; the wrappers and packaging often read like a book. There are very

Left and Below: Early chocolate boxes often featured inlaid metal decorations and intricate decorative painting.

Left: The ultimate in kitsch packaging, this opulent white plastic "grand piano" chocolate box comes from Germany.

precise specifications for the quantity of cacao solids in different types of chocolate; all flavouring ingredients must be fully declared; there are additional lists of sugars, such as dextrose and glucose, which all have maximum permitted levels; and there is always a detailed panel of nutritional information.

Chocolate Boxes

Chocolate-makers have been strongly aware of the value of shelf-appeal since the industry's early days. In France the most exquisitely designed chocolate boxes came into vogue as early as 1780, featuring beautiful paintings, intricately embossed plaques and inlaid semi-precious stones. Britain's chocolate boxes were not so ostentatious; they featured sentimental images that were

very much the fashion when boxed chocolates came on the market. The first was produced in 1868 by Cadbury and featured a painting of a young girl cuddling a kitten; the model was Richard Cadbury's daughter Jessica.

Also part of the appeal are the beautiful papers used to line boxes and separate layers of chocolate. Although grease-resistant, the types of paper used have always had a special quality. They may be elaborately padded or embossed with gold or silver, or mysteriously translucent, like crisp tracing paper, with a swirly hammered finish. Another type of paper is known as glasine. It has a waxy feel and comes in wonderfully glossy, dark colours, almost smelling of chocolate in its own right.

Today, packaging design veers from one extreme of style to another. Reminiscent of the glamourous thirties, there are some amazingly lavish, fabric-covered boxes trimmed with satiny ribbons and roses. In the kitsch category there is a large, white, grand-piano-shaped box from Germany with chocolates hidden beneath the lid, and at the other end of the spectrum there is the ultimate in modern minimalist designer chocolates and packaging with slim chocolates wrapped in gold leaf.

Below: Espresso-infused dark chocolate truffle fingers from the United States, end-wrapped with delicate gold foil.

Below: The packaging room at Cadbury's factory in 1932. Cadbury were the first manufacturer in Britain to produce boxed chocolates.

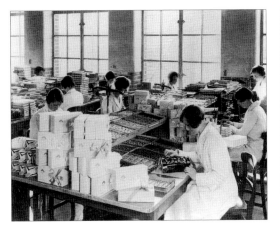

CHOCOLATE'S THERAPEUTIC POWERS

The therapeutic properties of chocolate were much written about in the seventeenth and eighteenth centuries. Agreement had not yet been reached on the beneficial effects of chocolate on health. Opinion was divided, and there were claims and counter-claims. Physician and chocolate-maker Sir Hans Sloane was firmly in favour and marketed his drinking chocolate as an aid to digestion as a result of his findings in Jamaica: "Chocolate is here us'd by all People, at all times. The common use of this ... proves sufficiently its being a wholesome Food."

The Aztec beliefs in the power of chocolate travelled with it, and great claims were made by manufacturers and converts alike for its powers as an antidote to exhaustion and weakness. Cadbury's aimed their cocoa advertising at athletes, captioning one of their posters with the words: "Sustains against fatigue. Increases muscular strength. Gives physical endurance and staying power." As well as athletes, soldiers, scholars and clerics used it to keep them going during prolonged periods of physical, intellectual or spiritual endurance.

We now know that the fat and carbohydrate in chocolate provide fuel for the body, and the fat content means that chocolate is digested slowly, thus maintaining a feeling of fullness. Even the iron content, which helps transport oxygen to the brain, may result in greater mental alertness, although this has yet to be proven.

(per 100g)	Plain (semisweet) chocolate	Milk chocolate	White chocolate
Protein (g)	4.7	8.4	8.0
Fat (g)	29.2	30.3	30.9
Calories	525	529	529
Carbohydrate (g)	64.8	59.4	58.3
Calcium (mg)	38	220	270
Magnesium (mg)	100	55	26
Iron (mg)	2.4	1.6	0.2
Zinc (mg)	0.2	0.2	0.9
Carotene (vitamin A) (mcg)	40	40	75
Vitamin E (mg)	0.85	0.74	1.14
Thiamin (vitamin B1) (mg)	0.07	0.10	0.08
Riboflavin (vitamin B2) (mg)	0.08	0.23	0.49
Niacin (vitamin B3) (mg)	0.4	0.2	0.2
Vitamin B6 (mg)	0.07	0.07	0.07
Vitamin B12 (mcg)	—	trace	trace
Folate (mcg)	10	10	10
Vitamin C	0	0	0

Source: McCance and Widdowson's The Composition of Foods, *fifth edition.*

Nutritional Analysis

Although the relevance of nutritional analysis is questionable if the level of cacao solids or brand of chocolate used is not known, we can see from the comparative table above that plain (semisweet) chocolate, considered by the chocolate fraternity as infinitely superior, does not fare as well as might be expected.

Containing no milk, plain chocolate provides roughly half the protein of white and milk chocolate, and much less calcium. Protein is vital for the growth, repair and maintenance of the body; calcium is essential for muscle contraction, including the muscles that make the heart beat, and for healthy nerve function, enzyme activity and clotting of blood. Plain

Left: Early publicity material depicted cocoa as wholesome. Right: Chocolate fortified the army in the First World War.

Above: Carbohydrate in chocolate provides energy.

chocolate contains slightly less fat, something we are advised to cut down on, and comes out on top in terms of carbohydrate, magnesium (an essential constituent of our body cells and involved with releasing energy from the food we eat), iron (essential for the production of red blood cells and for transporting oxygen around the body), and niacin (also involved in energy release from food). Plain chocolate also contains slightly fewer calories. White chocolate, sometimes dismissed by chocolate experts, contains more calcium, zinc, carotene and riboflavin (vitamin B2) than plain chocolate.

A Natural Stimulant

As well as the more well-known nutrients, chocolate contains certain alkaloids – organic substances found in plants – which have a potent effect on the body. The most important is theobromine, which stimulates the kidneys as a mild diuretic. Chocolate is also a stimulant of the central nervous system, with an effect similar to caffeine, which is also present in chocolate. Theobromine makes up about 2 per cent of the cacao bean and about 200 mg finds its way into an average-sized bar. The caffeine content is much smaller – about 25 mg per bar, roughly one quarter the amount found in a fresh cup of coffee.

Below right: Many manufacturers depicted chocolate as providing growing children with plenty of energy for healthy activity.

Myths and Prejudices

Claims that chocolate is bad for you are almost certainly based on the excess sugar and added vegetable fat in poor grade, mass-produced chocolate. Quality chocolate contains pure cacao butter with no added fat, as well as a high percentage of cacao solids and correspondingly less sugar – in some cases hardly any. Specific claims that chocolate causes migraine, obesity, acne, tooth decay and allergies have also been refuted by several medical experts:

Migraine Cheese and chocolate have been cited as the cause of migraine, which can be set off by large doses of tyramine. Chocolate, however, contains only a very small quantity of tyramine, far less than cheese.

Obesity Good-quality plain (semisweet) chocolate is unlikely to be the cause of obesity because it contains far less sugar than junk chocolate and, because it is more expensive, is less likely to be eaten to excess.

Acne American surveys show no correlation between chocolate consumption and acne in teenagers. Likely culprits are hormonal imbalances and a lack of fresh fruit and vegetables in the diet.

Tooth decay Chocolate melts in the mouth and is therefore in contact with the teeth for a relatively short time. While the sugar content will contribute to tooth decay, the risk is far less than that associated with sticky sweets or toffee, which remain in the mouth for longer.

Allergy Less than 2 per cent of the population have a genuine food allergy, and an allergy to chocolate is extremely rare. It is more likely to be the nuts and milk in chocolate that are the cause, so check the ingredients.

Homeopathic "Proving" of Chocolate

Experimental "provings" of chocolate by homeopaths clearly indicate its stimulating effect. One experiment conducted with a decoction of roasted ground cacao beans in boiling water produced "an excitement of the nervous system similar to that caused by a strong infusion of black coffee" and "an excited state of the circulation, shown by an accelerated pulse". Interestingly, when the same decoction was made with unroasted beans neither effect was noticeable, leading the provers to conclude that the physiological changes were caused by a number of aromatic substances released during roasting.

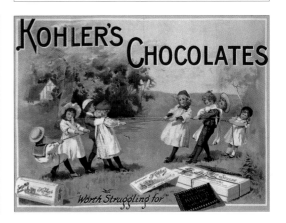

CHOCOLATE AND THE MIND

The question of whether or not chocolate is an addictive substance always raises spirited discussion. Some social historians have even reported tales of chocolate addiction and associated crimes committed in order to satisfy an ever-increasing need. And as recently as 1991, the French dietary expert Michel Montignac advised in his book *Dine Out and Lose Weight*: "Be sure to limit yourself, since chocolate is of an addictive nature. To control your 'chocoholism', drink a tall glass of water."

Above: A deeply indulgent chocolate experience.

Linda Henly, a contemporary American writer, positively recommends that addictive personalities should use chocolate to satisfy their needs, stating that its advantages vastly outweigh those of other substances: "Chocolate doesn't make you stupid and clumsy. It doesn't render you incapable of operating heavy machinery ... You don't have to smuggle chocolate across the border ... Possession, even possession with intent to sell, is perfectly legal."

Some medical experts believe that the theobromine and caffeine in chocolate are the cause of its so-called addictive properties, but it may well be the presence of another substance called phenylethylamine. This is one of a group of chemicals known as endorphins, which have an effect on the body similar to amphetamine, to which phenylethylamine is related. When released into the bloodstream, endorphins lift the mood, creating positive energy and feelings ranging from happiness to euphoria, as can be experienced in the runner's "high" or the aerobic exerciser's "burn". Phenylethylamine is also naturally present in the human body. Levels in the brain have even been found to increase when we experience the state we refer to as "falling in love", which is no doubt why we experience that heady feeling when we eat good chocolate.

Craving and Addiction

Chocolate lovers would do well to be aware of the wealth of difference there is between craving and addiction. Craving is an unmet desire for a pleasurable substance, whether it be chocolate, hot buttered toast, or a cup of coffee. The craving is usually brought on by stress, and the desired substance usually diffuses the stress more effectively than any other means. It may actually, as a result, enhance a person's performance by increasing concentration and reducing fatigue.

Addiction, on the other hand, is defined as the habitual use of a substance, such as alcohol or drugs, which becomes less and less effective at satisfying the need and results in unpleasant withdrawal symptoms should any attempt be made to give up the substance in question.

Chocolate hardly comes into the addictive category, although it has been said that the glucose in chocolate triggers a release in the production of endorphins – the body's natural opiates – which in turn can lead to a cycle of craving.

Left: A silver platter of gorgeous, high-quality, hand-made chocolates is every chocolate lover's fantasy.

Below: An advertisement showing two French ladies sharing a bottle of chocolate as if it were wine. The initial effect can be very similar.

Right: Dark, rich and irresistible, a slice of moist chocolate cake is both pleasure and temptation.

Below: French courtesan and famous chocolyte, Madame Du Barry, was well aware of the stimulating effect chocolate had on her lovers.

Women's Craving and Chocolate

Women are the greatest consumers of chocolate, and several studies have sought to explain why. Although some women may enjoy chocolate as a guilt-free treat or as an energy-boost, others seem almost obsessed by it. While researching her 1995 book *Why Women Need Chocolate*, Debra Waterhouse conducted a survey which revealed that of the women surveyed:

• 97 per cent had cravings, 68 per cent of which are for chocolate
• 50 per cent would choose chocolate in preference to sex
• 22 per cent were more likely than men to choose chocolate as a mood elevator

Psychiatrists have suggested that the mechanism that regulates body levels of phenylethylamine may be faulty in some women. This may explain a tendency to binge on chocolate after an emotional upset – it is an instinctive form of self-medication to treat the imbalance of mood-controlling chemicals.

Waterhouse states that the foods we crave are defined by a multitude of factors that may include cultural influences, emotional attachments, taste and habit, as well as biological, chemical and physiological factors. In the case of chocolate, the "prozac of plants", Waterhouse adds to its mood-changing components a substance called seratonin, known for its calming properties.

It must be said, however, that although statistically it may be the case that more women buy chocolate than men, it is also true that for both sexes, and for people of all ages, chocolate can be many things. There are probably many women who could instantly name a man whose chocolate consumption is more regular and compulsive than hers, and it is perhaps one of the many cultural myths that women are more addicted to it than men. What we can say is that the seduction of chocolate, and its comforting allure, is as strong in the present as it was for the Maya warrior princes and princesses of the fourth century.

CHOCOLATE AND LOVE

Chocolate has long been associated with passion and its reputation as an aphrodisiac can be traced back to the days of the Aztecs and the Spanish conquistadors. Conclusions were obviously drawn from the Emperor Montezuma's liking for copious flagons of chocolate before retiring to his harem. However, as observer Bernal Díaz del Castillo was careful to point out in his memoirs: "It [chocolate] was said to have aphrodisiac properties, but we did not pay any attention to this detail."

In *The True History of Chocolate*, authors Sophie and Michael Coe state that the idea that Montezuma needed sexual stimulants was a Spanish obsession for which there was no factual basis. The conquistadors apparently suffered from constipation and "searched for native Mexican laxatives as avidly as they did for aphrodisiacs". However, once the rumour that chocolate was an aphrodisiac had taken root, there was no stopping it. When chocolate eventually appeared in Europe, eighteenth-century society took to it with suspicious enthusiasm.

Historical sources abound with tales of chocolate being used as an aphrodisiac. Casanova thought that hot chocolate was "the elixir of love", and drank it instead of champagne! It may well be that the unshakeable belief of the Spanish had something to do with chocolate being an ingredient in that notorious aphrodisiac "Spanish Fly". In the following tale, the Marquis de Sade uses

both chocolate and Spanish fly to amuse his guests at a ball: "Into the dessert he slipped chocolate pastilles so good that a number of people devoured them ... but he had mixed in some Spanish fly ... those who ate the pastilles began to burn with unchaste ardor ... Even the most respectable of women were unable to resist the uterine rage that stirred within them. And so it was that M. de Sade enjoyed the favors of his sister-in-law."

Left and Right: The images may not be as explicit as today, but advertising has always used chocolate's link with sensuality to sell its products.

Right: An early Cadbury chocolate tin uses sensual imagery.

The Great Inflamer

Brandon Head, in *The Food of the Gods*, reported that even after chocolate had become widely accepted as a nourishing beverage, it was still regarded by some "as a violent inflamer of passions, which should be prohibited to the monks". In 1905 a journalist writing in the British *Spectator* magazine issued dire warnings: "I shall also advise my fair readers to be in a particular manner careful how they meddle with romances, chocolates, novels, and the like inflamers, which I look upon as very dangerous to be made use of ... "

Sensual Associations

Although contemporary scientific research suggests that chocolate does not contain substances of a directly aphrodisiac nature, modern advertising clearly links chocolate with sensuality and sexuality. With the exception of chunky "macho" chocolate products, or situations in which the product is being used as a healthy, energy-boosting snack, chocolate is invariably depicted as a "naughty" indulgence, appearing in scenes that are heavy with sexual innuendo.

Advertising also demonstrates a definite gender bias by specifically targeting women as the primary users. Most

Above: A poster illustrating the link between lovers and chocolate.

nourishing mugs of chocolate to young children, and advertising made much of the wholesomeness of chocolate with posters of healthy, lively children enjoying cups of chocolate in the fresh air. The first chocolate boxes showed sentimental images of pretty young girls, flowers and kittens. Chocolate plays a large part in childhood the world over. Christmas treats, Easter eggs, birthday presents, party gifts, rewards or bribes from parents coaxing their offspring to behave well. Encouraged as most of us are to be passionate about chocolate from an early age, it is no wonder we carry that ardour with us through childhood and beyond.

Right: The famous Rowntree advertisement.

Below: A loving mother offers chocolate to her daughter.

advertisements show chocolate being enjoyed by beautiful women, or gifts of chocolate being offered to them by a man.

The association between women, sensuality and chocolate was reinforced by the cinema, too. A common image in the 1930s was the glamorous *femme fatale*, usually blonde and usually draped on satin sheets, languorously working her way through a lavish box of chocolates.

This association between chocolate and women perpetuated the association between chocolate and romantic love, as shown on Perugina's classic Baci box. Baci means "kisses" in Italian, and since the chocolates first appeared in 1922 they have been exchanged as gifts between lovers who look for the romantic message hidden beneath the foil wrapper of each chocolate.

Chocolate and Childhood

This association with love and nurture, but not necessarily passion, was also exploited by manufacturers. Chocolate cake mix packets carry homely scenes of mother in the kitchen; the earliest cocoa tins portrayed nursemaids or even parents serving

THE PLEASURE OF CHOCOLATE

Research carried out by ARISE (Associates for Research Into the Science of Enjoyment) suggests that pleasure, far from being an emotion of indeterminate nature, is a distinct neurochemical process with its own pathway through the nervous system. Laboratory tests have shown that when we are experiencing pleasure, the body's defence system is more effective; and when we are unhappy, depressed or stressed, the system becomes less efficient, leaving us less resistant to infection.

So it seems that pleasure is good for us even if it means we indulge in "forbidden fruits" such as chocolate. The secret, it would seem, is to indulge in our "naughty" craving without feeling guilty or anxious. That said, ARISE make it clear that they are not advocating orgies of over-indulgence; the secret is to eat better chocolate, not more chocolate.

Sensory Pleasure

One of the reasons we love chocolate so much is the pure unmatched physical pleasure we get not just from eating it, but also from unwrapping it, smelling it, looking at it and feeling it. When we slip the wrapper off a slim bar of dark chocolate or open up the softly padded papers of a luxury box, our sense of anticipation is already at work. The pure chocolatey smell is like perfume and the chocolate looks so smooth and glossy we want to stroke it. Breaking off a piece, it snaps cleanly with a pleasing crack. When it finally passes the lips, chocolate melts instantly in the mouth – an exquisitely pleasurable sensation. Then the flavours come flooding through – overwhelming our taste buds with over five hundred of them, two-and-a-half times more than any other food. With such a wealth of sensory pleasure in store, no wonder chocolate should be eaten slowly.

Whether or not we choose to share our pleasure with others by attempting to describe the complex flavours is another matter. The current passion for chocolate indicates that perhaps a tasting language will evolve along the same lines as that used for wine and, more recently, olive oil. At the moment, fellow chocolate lovers get by without a specialized vocabulary – they just know when it is good and a roll of the eyes or a deep sigh is enough to communicate this.

Elaine Sherman, a twentieth-century American writer, more than adequately sums up: "Chocolate is heavenly, mellow, sensual, deep, dark, sumptuous, gratifying, potent, dense,

Below: Unmatched sensory pleasure – a delight to look at, a pleasure to touch, wonderful to smell and pleasurable to eat.

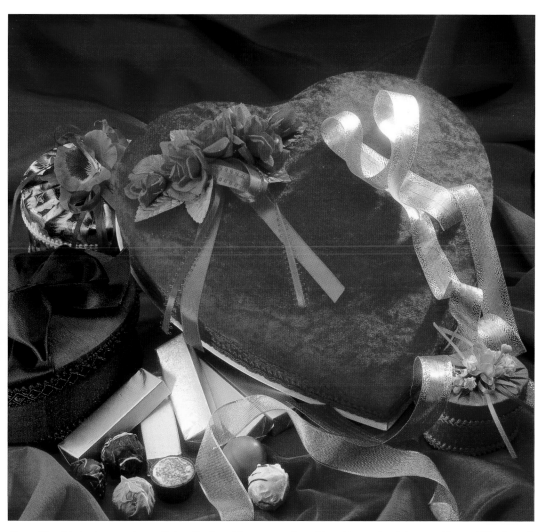

Above: Chocolate has been used as a gift since the days of the Aztecs. It speaks a thousand words and feelings.

creamy, seductive, suggestive, rich, excessive, silky, smooth, luxurious, celestial. Chocolate is downfall, happiness, pleasure, love, ecstasy, fantasy ... chocolate makes us wicked, guilty, sinful, healthy, chic, happy."

A Cultural and Social Lubricant

Chocolate has always been used as a gift. As Michel Richart, an inspired chocolate-maker in Lyon, rightly states, when we share good quality chocolate it weaves links between people on many, many levels. Chocolate also creates valuable cultural, social and even spiritual awareness.

A small box of luxury chocolates says a thousand "thank yous" to a hostess, a mother or a lover. Chocolate also says "good luck", "congratulations", "*bon voyage*" and "sorry". Queen Victoria symbolically sent 2,268kg/5,000lbs chocolate to her loyal troops at Christmas. Sales of chocolate rocket on Mother's Day and Valentine's Day. We use it in one form or another to celebrate Easter, Christmas and weddings.

There is hardly a country in the Western world that does not have chocolate as part of its culinary culture, whether it be a moist chocolate brownie from America, a chocolate-covered pancake from Hungary, a velvety square of Swiss milk fondant chocolate, or a foaming cup of thick Spanish drinking chocolate. It is chocolate "experiences" such as these that unite chocolate lovers throughout the world in celebration of the food of the gods.

THE CHOCOLATE-MAKERS

In the next few pages of the book we survey some of the world's highest quality chocolate products. This is not a comprehensive selection, and it includes some of the most familiar quality brands, as well as the more exclusive. Some products, such as the famous Toblerone bars, are internationally popular and universally available, and others, such as the exquisite chocolates made by the small specialist companies in America, are known to a much smaller market, but their first-class products are available by mail order and their market will increase as our appreciation of chocolate becomes more discerning.

BELGIUM

Belgium is renowned for its *ballotins*, chocolate-covered pralines, invented by Jean Neuhaus who, in 1912, developed coating chocolate capable of containing liquid fillings. Today **Neuhaus** is well-known for its flavoured Côte d'Or bars: immortalized by the elephant logo on the wrapper, it is a classic Belgian chocolate with a rich flavour. Belgians enjoy chocolate in bars, among them the filled bars of chocolate introduced by Jean Galler of the **Jacques** chocolate house in the 1930s.

Of all Belgian chocolate companies, **Godiva** must be the most recognized internationally. Established in 1929 by the Drap family, the company has 14-year-old Joseph Drap to thank for its success. Realizing that people needed a little luxury in the austere post-war years, Joseph created the chocolate truffle. They were marketed under the name of Godiva and they were an instant success. Another classic creation from Godiva, and from **Léonidas**, is the Manon, made from whipped mocha-flavoured butter cream and crushed nuts enveloped in a sugar coating.

Above: A selection of Kim's Cachet chocolates, exported worldwide.

Belgium also boasts many smaller specialists producing their own excellent chocolates. **Charlemagne** produces superior quality thin squares of plain (semisweet) and white chocolate with exotic flavours such as spiced ginger, cardamom and coffee, and spiced Earl Grey tea.

Kim's, which was established in 1987 and is the manufacturer of the widely available luxury Cachet brand, specializes in hand-made fillings. Kim's range includes white, milk and plain chocolate bars with luscious cream fillings such as hazelnut, coconut truffle, mocha and vanilla.

Pierre Colas specializes in unusual bars of plain and milk chocolate that are set in antique moulds and flavoured with esoteric combinations of cardamom, juniper, pink peppercorns and lavender. The company supplies specialist retailers in Belgium, Spain, France and the London chocolate shop Rococo.

Wittamer probably ranks highest with connoisseurs. The range includes unusual seasonal specialities and Wittamer's famous Samba cake made with two contrasting chocolate mousses.

THE NETHERLANDS

The Netherlands is the birthplace of Coenraad Van Houten, who revolutionized the chocolate industry with his cocoa press. With this background, it is not surprising that the Dutch chocolate industry today concentrates largely on cocoa rather than eating chocolate. The four biggest companies, **Van Houten**, **Bensdorp**, **De Zaan** and **Gerkens**, were all set up in the nineteenth century and continue to supply the world with fine-quality unsweetened cocoa powder. Van Houten is now based in Germany, having undergone several takeovers and mergers,

and trades in Europe, the United States, Hong Kong and Singapore.

The Netherlands do produce a certain amount of eating chocolate, however, and enthusiasts enjoy Dutch chocolate for its dark colour and distinctive flavour. **Droste**, of the distinctive "Droste man" logotype, makes delicious chocolate discs, or pastilles, from which the logotype is derived. Bensdorp and Van Houten also make quality chocolate.

Left: Droste are famous for their chocolate pastilles.

GERMANY

The Germans are one of the largest consumers of chocolate in Europe. Faced with this demanding clientèle, German chocolate manufacturers pride themselves on producing fresh, quality chocolates made with the very best ingredients.

Confiserie Heinemann, based in München-Gladbach and run by master chocolatier Heinz Heinemann, makes over sixty varieties of freshly made chocolates every day, including their exceptional champagne truffles. Heinemann also offers an interesting range of moulded chocolate-filled seasonal specialities.

Dreimeister is a long-established family enterprise set up by the father of Hans Wilhelm Schröder, the present owner, and originally known as Café Schröder. Although the company has a large turnover and supplies to hotels, restaurants and airlines, Dreimeister produces the freshest of chocolates and truffles, made only with top-quality ingredients.

Below: Feodora's elegant range produced for the international market.

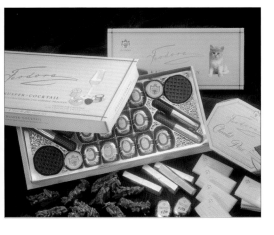

Right: Leysieffer's freshly made seasonal chocolate.

Feodora is probably Germany's best-known brand internationally. Their chocolate is wonderfully smooth due to lengthy conching. The elegantly packaged quality chocolates include champagne truffles, bitter milk chocolate wafers, espresso Brazil chocolates and luxury pralines.

Hachez, based in Bremen since 1890, makes chocolates exclusively with rare cacao beans from Venezuela and Ecuador. Loved by generations of chocolate connoisseurs, the range includes melt-in-the-mouth cat's tongues, gold-covered nut sticks, ginger sticks, chocolate leaves and fruit cream-filled chocolate pastilles.

Leysieffer has produced hand-made chocolates in its Osnabrück bakery since 1909. In order to guarantee their absolute freshness, the company starts manufacture only on receipt of an order. Its products include good-quality white and milk chocolate, flavoured with a tempting range of ingredients – cinnamon, ginger, orange, pistachio and a mouthwatering combination of mocca and Jamaica rum.

Stollwerck in Cologne began as a bakery in 1839 and is now an international group with impressive headquarters on the banks of the River Elbe. The Imhoff-Stollwerck Museum boasts a fascinating collection of chocolate-related exhibits, including a collection of vending machines resembling grandfather clocks, porcelain chocolate services and printed ephemera, as well as a tropical greenhouse planted with young cacao trees. The company produces a wide range of chocolates for all levels of the market.

AUSTRIA

Austria's chocolate delicacies include both pâtisserie and confectionery. Among the world-famous pâtisserie establishments are the palatial **Hotel Imperial**, Vienna's grandest, and home of Imperial Torte, an unbelievably rich, layered, square chocolate cake. The **Hotel Sacher** is famous for its delectable Sachertorte, a moist apricot-glazed rich chocolate cake. **Demel**, the celebrated Viennese pâtisserie, produces a rival version of Sachertorte based on a recipe said to have been given to Anna Demel by Franz Sacher's son. Demel also produces whole roasted cacao beans

coated with fine chocolate.

Altmann & Kühne, established in Vienna for more than eighty years, produce exquisite hand-dipped miniature chocolates, appropriately called *Liliputconfekte*, in the most unusual shapes. The chocolates are beautifully packaged in miniature chests of drawers and treasure chests.

Mirabell in Salzburg produces traditional *Mozartkugeln*, an Austrian speciality consisting of creamy marzipan and hazelnut-nougat balls with a delicate chocolate coating.

ITALY

Above: Gianduja are Italy's favourite chocolate.
Right: Italians prefer chocolate in bite-sized pieces.

Hazelnuts, chestnuts, almonds and honey
have always been an integral part of
Italian cuisine. It comes as no
surprise, therefore, that Italians like
their chocolate nutty and sweet. They
also like their chocolate small, so bars are often sold
in single serving sizes – handy for a quick fix, should
the need arise. Neapolitans, which look exactly like
miniature chocolate bars, complete with individual wrappers, are
well-known throughout Europe.

The Italians are creative chocolate-makers, and they excel at
presentation, too; Italian packaging is stunning, whether the
design is traditionally ornate or 1990s' minimalist.

Caffarel in Turin is one of Italy's oldest chocolate-makers.
Established in 1826, the company purchased a chocolate-making
machine designed by Bozelli, a Genoese engineer, and so became
the pioneers in setting out on the route to industrialization. In
1865 Caffarel developed Italy's favourite confection, *gianduja*,
a rectangle of luscious chocolate and hazelnut paste, instantly
recognizable by its triangular profile and rounded ends.
Nowadays most Italian chocolate-makers produce their own
special version of *gianduja* using jealously guarded recipes.
There is a glorious giant-sized version, *grangianduja*, as well as
miniature *gianduiotti*.

An ancient culture of confectionery lives on in Italy's far south,
and it was here in Salantino, in Italy's heel, that Maglio opened
their factory in 1875. The business has passed from father to son
and is now run by brothers Massimo and Maurizio. The **Maglio**
range is based on plump, dark chocolates with inspirational
fillings, including liqueur-infused dried kumquats, peaches, pears
and oranges, marzipan-stuffed dates and prunes, and lemon-zest-
coated figs stuffed with a whole almond.

Founded in 1796, **Majani** in Bologna is one of Italy's most
creative chocolate-makers. Their specialities are *scorze*,
deliciously bittersweet chocolate sticks still made to the same
ancient recipe, and *"Fiat" Cremino*, launched in 1911 as a
publicity stunt to celebrate the Fiat Tipo 4 car. The car has since
gone out of production but *"Fiat" Cremino* live on. These stunning
miniature squares are made with four types of layered chocolate,
something like a brown striped liquorice allsort.

Perugina, based in the medieval city of Perugia, Umbria, was
set up in 1907 by Francesco Buitoni, a descendant of the well-
known pasta-making family. From humble beginnings making
sugared almonds, Perugina is now one of Italy's largest chocolate
manufacturers. The most popular brand in their extensive range is
Baci (kisses), introduced in 1922 and still going strong. Lovers
still like to discover the romantic messages
hidden under the wrapper.

Peyrano, an exclusive chocolatier in Turin,
is almost unique in grinding their own cacao
beans – very, very few chocolatiers do so.
The chocolates are superb, especially
their *gianduja*. Peyrano also sell *bicerin*, a
very rare paste of bitter chocolate, cocoa,
hazelnuts and honey used for sweetening coffee.

Below: Baci with amorous messages under wrap.

SWITZERLAND

Above: The Confiserie Sprüngli in Zurich, around 1895.

Three key developments undoubtedly contribute to Switzerland's preference for its very delicate, melt-in-the-mouth milk chocolate. Switzerland is the birth- place of Rodolphe Lindt, inventor of the conching machine that transforms chocolate from a rough gritty paste to a state of silky-smooth perfection. Lindt also created soft, creamy fondant chocolate by adding cacao butter to the paste before conching. We have the Swiss to thank, too, for the invention of milk chocolate.

Sprüngli in Zurich is one of the most famous chocolate establishments in the world. The shop in Bahnhofstrasse is renowned for its freshest of fresh *Truffes du Jour*, a heart-stopping mixture of finest chocolate, cream and butter, made to the highest possible standards. The company operates a worldwide delivery service that guarantees that the longed-for parcel will arrive within 24 hours of despatch.

Set up by master confectioner Rudolf Sprüngli in 1845, the company has been handed down through six generations of Sprünglis. When Rudolf retired, he divided his empire between his two sons. The younger, David, received the confectionery shops. The elder brother, Johann, became the owner of the chocolate factory. In the same year he retired, Rudolf Sprüngli also decided to purchase Rodolphe Lindt's chocolate factory in Berne. Overnight, the company acquired all Lindt's manufacturing secrets, and it was this transaction that was the foundation for the success of the now world-famous Lindt & Sprüngli company.

Lindt & Sprüngli operates entirely independently from Sprüngli. The company produces an enormous range of excellent quality chocolates sold in supermarkets and specialist shops worldwide. One of their best products is the tastefully thin Excellence bar, a sublime blend of finest cacao beans with a hint of pure vanilla,

Above: A 1935 street poster.

Above: Lindt's mini chocolate bars.

and a cacao solid content of 70 per cent. This is closely followed in quality by Excellence Milk, possibly one of the best milk chocolate bars available. Another Lindt bar, called Swiss Bittersweet Chocolate, which is easily recognized by its traditional wrapper design, is also good.

Suchard in Berne is another long-established and respected company, now owned by the American multinational Philip Morris. Suchard was a gold medallist several times over at the 1855 Exposition Universelle in Paris, and their milk chocolate bar, Milka, produced in 1901, is well-known all over Europe. Since 1970, Suchard have been the manufacturer of the famous Toblerone bars, although these were originally produced by their inventor Jean Tobler. The bars were designed with a triangular profile representing the Swiss Alps. The name is derived from merging that of the inventor, Tobler, together with the word *torrone*, the Italian word for nougat. Toblerone is made with a blend of chocolate, nougat, almonds and egg white, and the bar is one of Switzerland's most popular products – outside the country at least.

Enthusiasts can enjoy giant bars weighing more than 4kg/8.8lb, miniature bars and a whole range in between.

Above: Superior chocolate bars.

Above: The famous Toblerone bars.

FRANCE

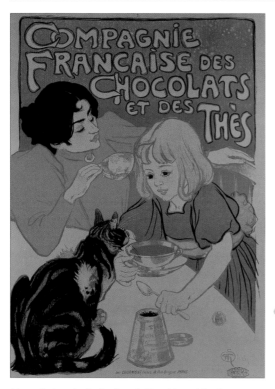

Above: Early poster for the French Chocolate and Tea Company.

A large part of the French chocolate industry is made up of small, independent firms making ever more innovative *grand cru* chocolates to jealously guarded recipes. The French, who prefer dark, intensely flavoured chocolate, have a wide choice at their disposal.

Bernachon, a greatly respected family of artisan chocolatiers, set up in 1955 in Lyon. Sharing the caring attitude of the Quakers,

Above: One of Bonnat's superb grand cru bars.

Right: The ultimate dark chocolate.

the company provides daily lunch for the workers and, until recently, housed them in dormitories above the workshop. The Bernachons travel the world in search of the rarest cacao beans and the best nuts and fruit. Their chocolates are the very best. The range includes unusually flavoured chocolate bars, truffles, pralines, *giandujas* and marzipans.

Bonnat in Voiron near Grenoble is one of the few companies that roasts its own beans. A purist at heart, master chocolatier Raymond Bonnat uses a single *grand cru* bean, rather than a blend, for each of the chocolates in his range. Bonnat's choice of seven *crus*, which consist of Côte d'Ivoire, Madagascar, Ceylon, Trinité, Chuao, Maragnan and Puerto Cabellois, is selected from the world's finest cacao plantations. Bonnat chocolates are available from specialist outlets in France, and from Mortimer and Bennett's shop in London, which is the sole British importer.

Above: Chocolate almonds.

Cluizel, in Paris, is a family-run business set up in 1947, producing excellent chocolate with rare South American and African beans ground and roasted on the premises. It is perhaps best known for a small and rather sinister chocolate bar containing 99 per cent cacao solids. Cluizel's chocolates are available throughout Europe.

Christian Constant, set up in 1970 in Paris, produces matchless ganache-filled chocolates. The flavourings read like an exotic travel brochure: Malabar cardamom, Yemeni jasmine, Chinese ginger and Tahitian vanilla.

The famous **Fauchon** shop in Paris was established in 1925 by August Fauchon, whose passion was for collecting unusual merchandise. The company was taken over after his death by Joseph Pilosoff, whose granddaughter runs the business today. Fauchon specialities are the very best quality chocolate marrons glacés, truffles, pralines and ganaches, all exquisitely packaged.

La Maison du Chocolat in Paris was opened in 1977 by Robert Linxe, master chocolate-maker *extraordinaire*. Linxe's rigorous training and deep understanding of chocolate's complexities have played a major part in furthering the reputation of France's chocolate-makers. It was Linxe's collaboration with Valrhona that set the quality of their *grand cru* couvertures, which they in turn supply to smaller chocolate-makers. Linxe's specialities are exquisitely shaped squares, pyramids and lozenges of the very best plain (semisweet) and milk chocolate, filled with praline, buttery caramel or the lightest and creamiest ganache. The chocolates are sold in Paris and by leading specialist outlets in New York, Houston and Dallas.

Le Roux, founded in 1977 in Quiberon, Brittany, is renowned for *Caramel au Beurre Salé* (salted butter caramel), and for rare chocolate truffles containing fragments of Périgord truffle.

Michel Chaudun set up shop in Paris in 1986. His award-winning work includes not only the highest quality chocolates but ambitious chocolate sculptures. Only the rarest cacao beans are used together with top-quality fruit and nuts. His chocolates are available in Paris and Tokyo.

Richart Design et Chocolat started life in 1925 in the laboratory of Lyon-based master chocolatier Joseph Richart. Using only the

Above: Elegance from Richart Design et Chocolat.

Below: A Chocolat Carpentier poster from 1895.

finest cacao beans, Richart produces exquisite, smoother than smooth, miniature chocolate squares silk-screened with designs in cacao butter. Fillings and flavourings are equally inspired. The choice includes pure malt Scotch, green tea, blackcurrants, pineapple, clementines, the very best Andalucian almonds, chestnuts from the Ardèche, and pralines and ganaches flavoured with thyme, curry, bergamot, anise or nutmeg. Beautifully packaged in slim trays, Richart's chocolates are sold in boutiques in Paris, Lyon and New York.

Valrhona, set up in 1922 and based in the Rhône valley, is the leading supplier of couverture chocolate for smaller chocolate-makers. The beans are all of superior quality and include guanaja, pur caraibe, manjari and jivara. Each shipment is tested by a panel of experts. Its products include *Carré*, small chocolate squares made from individual bean varieties, packed in beautiful tins; *BonBons de Chocolat*, individual chocolates packed in gift boxes with a guide recommending the order in which they should be eaten; and the well-known Valrhona bars in their distinctive black wrappers. The cacao content of the bars ranges from 71 per cent for *Noir Amer* (bitter) to a relatively high 40 per cent for *Le Lacté* (milk).

Right: Valrhona Lacté has a high cacao content.

SPAIN

As recently as 1920, chocolate-makers in Spain were still using the curved granite metate for grinding cacao beans. The *chocolateros* would travel around with the *metate* strapped to their backs and bags of cacao beans under their arms. They would kneel on a little cushion in front of the stone and grind the beans in full public view so that the buyer could be sure he was getting unadulterated stone-ground chocolate. Today chocolate-making in Spain is a fully industrialized process, but, even so, the tradition of quality craftsmanship is very much alive and well.

In some ways Spanish chocolate is indistinguishable from quality chocolate made in the rest of Europe. What sets it apart is the creativity and imagination of the chocolate-makers, and their use of the very best quality Mediterranean fruits and nuts. Spain grows some of the best nuts in the world, so there is no shortage of supply. Plump almonds, hazelnuts, pine nuts and mouth-puckeringly bitter Seville oranges are all used by the chocolate-makers with excellent results.

Blanxart, set up in 1954 in Barcelona, is one of Spain's smaller specialist firms, producing hand-made, high-quality chocolates from the very best cacao beans. The company prides itself on roasting and grinding the beans itself to achieve the desired perfection of flavour and aroma. The mouthwatering range includes a delicate curl of candied Seville orange dipped in bitter chocolate, clusters of chocolate-covered pine nuts, as well as liqueur-filled chocolates and several types of praline.

Ludomar, in Barcelona, specializes in superior, made-to-order chocolates, which they sell to pâtisserie shops in Spain, France, Germany and Britain. Specialities are plump, chocolate-smothered cherries; *postre de músico*, a chocolate-covered cluster of fresh almonds, hazelnuts and raisins; and *grageas*, almonds or hazelnuts drenched in dark (bittersweet) chocolate, white chocolate or toffee.

Ramón Roca is a large company set up in Gerona in 1928 by the Roca family. Roca chocolates are said to be a favourite of former US Secretary of State Henry Kissinger, and they certainly grace the tables of Spain's society élite, as well as finding their way on to first class intercontinental flights and the pillows of Spain's grandest hotels. Roca has always been imaginative in an ostentatious type of way, producing masterpieces such as a 500g/1¼lb chocolate sculpture of the Statue of Liberty, and a hand-painted chocolate reproduction of the twelfth-century tapestry that hangs in Gerona cathedral. The company also produces a

Above: The Spanish love chocolate "a la taza" (in the cup).

unique range of edible board games, particularly popular with the Japanese market, which includes a draughts set in luxury dark and white chocolate. Their Victoria Bonbons (named after the mother of Ramón Roca) – elegant wafers of dark chocolate decorated with a perfectly positioned almond, a hazelnut, a walnut and four raisins – won first prize at the 1988 Chicago Fancy Food Fair.

Right: The Valor range of chocolates.
Left: Chocolate croquettes from Roca.

Valor in Villajoyosa, Alicante, was founded in 1881 by López Lloret, one of Spain's itinerant *chocolateros*. The fledgling enterprise has been handed down through three generations and is now one of Spain's largest and most technologically advanced chocolate companies, with a gleaming stainless-steel fully computerized factory. Even though Valor has an enormous turnover and a vast range of products, the company prides itself on maintaining traditional quality, creativity and attention to detail. Drinking chocolate is still widely enjoyed in Spain, and Valor is the country's leading producer. It is sold both in powdered form and, more commonly, as a solid bar to be broken off as required and dissolved in foaming hot milk.

On the confectionery side, Valor's specialities are Chocolate Pearls – chocolate-covered almonds gathered from local almond groves; *doblones* – individually wrapped chocolate wafers; foil-wrapped hazelnut pralines; exquisite miniature four-piece gift boxes of chocolates; and luxury chocolate bars filled with toffee, cream caramel or tiramisu. Eye-catching and attractive packaging is a crucial part of the presentation, particularly as Valor's luxury chocolates are exported to speciality shops all over the world.

Right: Chunks of chocolate in tablet form, used in Spain for making thick, dark drinking chocolate.

MEXICO

Chocolate as confectionery never really caught on in Mexico. The most important use of chocolate is still as a beverage, and as a flavouring in some of the special *moles* – rich, savoury sauces thickened with ground nuts and seeds. Chocolate is sold in rough, grainy tablets made with cacao, sugar, ground almonds and cinnamon – not so very different from the tablets made by the Spanish in the days of the conquistadors.

The most widely available brand outside Mexico is Ibarra, manufactured by **Chocolatera de Jalisco** in Guadalajara, and packaged in a striking red and yellow striped hexagonal box. The individually wrapped tablets are delicious whipped to a froth in hot milk and served with freshly baked *churros* (fried pastries). They can be used in baking to give a unique spicy flavour to chocolate cake. The tablets can also be melted to make a wonderfully fudgy chocolate sauce that goes particularly well with good quality vanilla ice cream.

Right: Coarse, grainy tablets of Ibarra chocolate.
Below: The melted tablets are delicious with vanilla ice cream.

GREAT BRITAIN

Above: Ackermans chocolates, a favourite of the Royal family.

During the last few years British taste in chocolate has been undergoing a quiet revolution. Following the establishment of The Chocolate Society, a sort of sub-culture of chocolytes has emerged. Perhaps as a result of this new-found fervour, superior varieties of chocolate are increasingly finding their way into supermarkets, where they provide much-needed competition for the old-style sweet British milk chocolate.

Below: Bendicks, premier supplier of superior mint chocolates.

Ackermans, a small family firm founded fifty years ago by German-born Werner Ackerman and his wife, is one of the major producers of hand-made chocolates in Britain. Ackermans has a shop in north London, and also supplies leading supermarkets and specialist outlets in Britain, mainland Europe and the United States. Its chocolates are a favourite with the Queen Mother, who awarded the firm her royal warrant in 1969. Ackermans offers a range of fresh cream truffles, chocolate-coated whole nuts, ginger wafers, hand-dipped crystallized fruits, and rose and violet fondant creams. It also produces a wonderful chocolate menagerie of hollow moulded hippos, crocodiles, bears and bunnies.

Bendicks of Mayfair, founded in the late 1920s by Colonel Benson and Mr Dickson, was granted a royal warrant by Queen Elizabeth II in 1962. Bendicks are famous for their excellent peppermint chocolates – an essentially British taste not shared by other European countries. Best-loved by connoisseurs are Bendicks Bittermints, a powerful mint fondant disc drenched with smooth, dark unsweetened chocolate – a devastating combination. As well as the mint collection, Bendicks produces delicious truffles, chocolate-coated preserved stem ginger, and the delightfully named Sporting & Military Chocolate.

Charbonnel et Walker, founded in 1825, is one of Britain's earliest producers of chocolates. With the encouragement of

Below: Exquisite chocolates from the Charbonnel et Walker range.

Left: Organic chocolate made with Maya beans.

Edward VII, the company began life as a partnership between Mrs Walker and Madame Charbonnel from the Maison Boissier chocolate house in Paris. Tempting items from the magnificent range include truffles flavoured with Chartreuse, muscat or port, and cranberry; chocolate-covered espresso beans; and Cointreau-flavoured marzipan. The packaging is superb and caters for styles ranging from elegant navy-trimmed white boxes, nostalgic boxes with a faded pink floral pattern, and outrageously lavish, ruched red satin boxes.

Gerard Ronay is one of Britain's most highly respected private chocolatiers. A former psychiatric nurse, Ronay set up in 1989 having trained with the very best teachers – Linxe, Constant and Bernachon in France, Wittamer in Belgium and Charbonnel et Walker in Britain. His highly secretive recipes include geranium chocolate and superb hand-painted eggs.

Green and Black's, set up in the 1980s by Josephine Fairly, sells organic chocolate endorsed by The Soil Association. The company launched with its Organic Dark (bittersweet) Chocolate, soon followed by its latest brainchild, the "ethically correct" Maya Gold Organic Dark Chocolate, made with beans grown by the Kechi Maya in Belize. This product was the first in Britain to be awarded the Fairtrade mark, which guarantees that small farmers are not exploited. Maya Gold contains 70 per cent cacao solids, but no cacao butter, and is described on the wrapper as having "the authentic Maya taste of rainforest spices and orange". Even

Below: Rococo's grand cru single bean bars speciality with distinctive wrappers.

Above: A tempting, imaginative range from The Chocolate Society.

though oranges were unknown to the Maya in pre-Conquest days, the chocolate still tastes pretty good.

Rococo, in London's King's Road, is an Aladdin's cave of a shop founded in 1983 by chocolate enthusiast Chantal Coady. Using cacao from the world's finest plantations, Rococo specializes in *grand cru* single bean bars; artisan bars with exotic flavourings such as pink pepper and juniper, lavender, petitgrain and cardamom; stunning chocolate dragées – try the dark green *Olives de Nyons*; and hand-made boxed chocolates moulded into the most beautiful shapes.

Sara Jayne, a London-based private chocolate-maker, is also public relations manager of the Académie Culinaire de France. She learnt her chocolate-making skills first-hand from leading experts, including the Roux brothers. Blackberry and Calvados, ginger and spice, and champagne are among the tempting flavourings used in her celebrated hand-made truffles.

Terrys of York, founded in 1797, is perhaps alone among the mass-producers in manufacturing plain (semisweet) chocolate with a reasonable flavour. Their famous chocolate orange has been tucked in the toe of British children's Christmas stockings for generations, while their individually wrapped miniature Neapolitans have always been a welcome gift.

The Chocolate Society was formed in 1990 to promote the consumption of the finest chocolate. The society manufactures a range of products under its own label, as well as selling quality brands made by other companies. Its own range includes the most delicious chocolate-dipped candied citrus fruits; imaginative moulded items such as pigs, egg-filled nests, fish, hens and hearts; fresh hand-made truffles with luscious flavourings such as raspberry, whisky or champagne; and elegant tins of drinking-chocolate flakes, cocoa powder and cooking chocolate.

THE UNITED STATES OF AMERICA

Chocolate consumers in the United States share the British liking for sweet milk chocolate, and the American chocolate industry is therefore dominated by a small number of very large mass-producers who satisfy this national need. However, in the same way that British consumers have become aware of and learned to appreciate quality hand-made plain (semisweet) chocolate, American taste has been changing, too. A number of small but sophisticated chocolate-makers have appeared on the scene and are taking advantage of the increasing popularity of European-style chocolate.

Above and Right: Ghirardelli, new and old.

Above: Glossy sugar-coated dragées from Dilettante.

Dilettante, in Seattle, was established in 1976 by Dana Davenport, a third-generation chocolatier and descendant of Hungarian master chocolatier Julius Franzen. Franzen emigrated to the USA in 1910, after studying in Paris, and won prestigious appointments in Vienna as Master Pâtissier to Emperor Franz Joseph, and later in St Petersburg as Master Chocolatier to Czar Nicholas II. Franzen passed on his skills to his brother-in-law Earl Remington Davenport, whose grandson Dana carries on the business today. Dilettante's signature product is its Aristocrat range of chocolate truffles, flavoured with ginger, raspberries, hazelnuts, pecan nuts or coffee. Dilettante also makes intensely rich buttercream fondant, beautiful chocolate dragées with various coatings, and slim bars of good quality milk or dark (bittersweet) chocolate.

Fran's, set up in Seattle by ex-accountant Fran Bigelow, is at the forefront of America's new generation of chocolatiers. She trained in cookery under Josephine Araldo, a 1921 graduate of the Cordon Bleu school in Paris, and later enrolled at the California Culinary Academy, where desserts became her passion. Bigelow opened a tiny dessert shop in 1982, supplying local restaurants with speciality cakes. Her reputation went from strength to strength, and, soon after, she started making the European-style chocolates on which her business is now founded. An award-winning speciality are Fran's baton-shaped Fixations – individual sticks of Belgian chocolate with soft, creamy centres, flavoured with espresso, peanut butter, orange or mint. Her range also includes rich dark truffles, hand-dipped fruit and nuts covered in smooth dark Belgian chocolate, GoldBars studded with macadamia nuts, and the smaller GoldBites with almonds, as well as chocolate and caramel sauces, and various seasonal items.

Ghirardelli, founded in 1856 in San Francisco and one of America's

Above: Irresistible luxury from Fran's.

Right: Joseph Schmidt's stunning truffles.

pioneering chocolate-makers, produces quality eating chocolate, chocolate products for use in baking, and powdered drinking chocolate. Ghirardelli's Sweet Ground Chocolate with Cocoa has been a signature product for over a century. Although a mass producer, Ghirardelli uses methods based on European traditions, producing bittersweet eating chocolate as well as the popular sweet milk varieties. Ghirardelli still grinds and roasts its own cacao beans, which are shipped from quality plantations in Central and South America, and West Africa as well. Its range includes milk, white and plain chocolate squares and attractively wrapped bars with various tempting flavours such as raspberry, white mocha and biscotti, and double chocolate mocha.

Joseph Schmidt Confections was opened in San Francisco in 1983 by master chocolatier Joseph Schmidt and partner Audrey Ryan. Born in 1939 and raised in what was formerly known as Palestine, Schmidt looks to his Austrian roots for his skills. He was trained as a baker, but his supremely imaginative and sometimes outrageous creations show no evidence of this conventional background. Unusual in the chocolate world for his bold use of colour, and the large size of the individual chocolates, Schmidt's truffles gleam with perfect hand-painted spots of bright red or green, and his Slicks, thin chocolate discs, are beautifully painted in various colours. Special commissions include amazingly opulent sculpted creations for visiting dignitaries from abroad – including a giant panda for Prince Philip and a white dove for Nelson

Mandela. Schmidt's chocolates are available from department stores in the United States and Harrods in London.

Richard Donnelly, in Santa Cruz, California, is another of America's new breed of young, inspired artisan chocolate-makers. Donnelly trained with several renowned chocolatiers both in Europe and the United States before setting up on his own in 1988. Donnelly uses French couverture chocolate to which he adds flavourings and fillings geared to the American market – coffee buttercream, and roasted salted macadamia nuts, for instance. His speciality is very slim, smooth chocolate bars which, in terms of quality, are among the very best chocolate in the world. The bars are beautifully wrapped in hand-made Japanese papers.

Moonstruck Chocolatier in Portland, Oregon, is a young company set up by an impressive consortium of live-wire marketing experts. With more then a hundred outlets in the United States and a thriving mail-order business they look set to make their name in the world of chocolate.

Moonstruck's chocolates are inspired creations from master chocolatier Robert Hammond, who served his apprenticeship in America and France, and who is now thought to be one of the leading experts in modern chocolate-making. Moonstruck's signature product is a moon-shaped, metallic blue box containing a stunning selection of beautifully designed chocolates. Flavourings include wine, brandy, coffee, *sake* and various fruits, often using award-winning local products. Favourites are wild huckleberry truffles made with white chocolate ganache and Clear Creek apple brandy truffles. There is also an impressive *gianduja* almond praline tower of crisp buttery toffee and toasted almonds.

Right: Elegance from Richard Donnelly.

TECHNIQUES

MELTING CHOCOLATE

If chocolate is being melted on its own, all the equipment must be completely dry, as water may cause the chocolate to thicken and become a stiff paste. For this reason, do not cover chocolate during or after melting it, as condensation could form. If the chocolate does thicken, add a little pure white vegetable fat (not butter or margarine) and mix well. If this does not work, start again. Do not discard the thickened chocolate; melt it with cream to make a delicious sauce.

With or without liquid, chocolate should be melted very slowly. It is easily burned or scorched, and then develops a bad flavour. If any steam gets into the chocolate, it can turn into a solid mass. If this happens, stir in a little pure white vegetable fat. Dark (bittersweet) chocolate should not be heated above 50°C/120°F. Milk and white chocolate should not be heated above 45°C/110°F. Take particular care when melting white chocolate, which clogs very easily when subjected to heat.

Melting Chocolate Over Simmering Water

1 Chop or cut the chocolate into small pieces with a sharp knife to enable it to melt quickly and evenly.

2 Put the chocolate in the top of a double boiler or in a heatproof bowl over a pan of barely simmering water. The bowl should not touch the water.

3 Heat gently until the chocolate is melted and smooth, stirring occasionally. Remove from the heat and stir.

Melting Chocolate Over Direct Heat

When a recipe recommends melting chocolate with a liquid such as milk, cream or even butter, this can be done over direct heat in a pan.

1 Choose a heavy pan. Add the chocolate and liquid and melt over a low heat, stirring frequently, until the chocolate is melted and the mixture is smooth. Remove from the heat at once. This method is also used for making sauces, icings and some sweets.

2 Chocolate can also be melted in a very low oven. Preheat the oven to 110°C/225°F/Gas ¼. Put the chocolate in an ovenproof bowl and place in the oven for a few minutes. Remove the chocolate before it is completely melted and stir until absolutely smooth.

Melting Chocolate in the Microwave

Check the chocolate at frequent intervals during the cooking time. These times are for a 650–700W oven and are approximate, as microwave ovens vary.

1 Place 115g/4oz chopped or broken dark (bittersweet) or plain (semisweet) chocolate in a microwave-safe bowl and microwave on Medium for about 2 minutes. The same quantity of milk or white chocolate should be melted on Low for about 2 minutes.

2 Check the chocolate frequently during the cooking time. The chocolate will not change shape, but will start to look shiny. It must then be removed from the microwave and stirred until completely melted and smooth.

TEMPERING CHOCOLATE

Key factors

Tempering is the process of gently heating and cooling chocolate to stabilize the emulsification of cocoa solids and butterfat. This technique is generally used by professionals handling couverture chocolate. It allows the chocolate to shrink quickly (to allow easy release from a mould, for example with Easter eggs) or to be kept at room temperature for several weeks or months without losing its crispness and shiny surface. All solid chocolate is tempered in production, but once melted loses its "temper" and must be tempered again unless it is to be used immediately. Untempered chocolate tends to "bloom" or becomes dull and streaky, or takes on a cloudy appearance. This can be avoided if the melted chocolate is put in the refrigerator immediately: chilling the chocolate solidifies the cocoa butter and prevents it from rising to the surface and "blooming". General baking and dessert-making do not require tempering, which is a fussy procedure and takes practice. However, it is useful to be aware of the technique when preparing sophisticated decorations, moulded chocolates or coatings. Most shapes can be made without tempering if they are chilled immediately.

Equipment

To temper chocolate successfully, you will need a marble slab or similar cool, smooth surface, such as an upturned baking sheet. A flexible plastic scraper is ideal for spreading the chocolate, but you can use a metal spatula. As the temperature is crucial, you will need a chocolate thermometer. Look for this at a specialist kitchen supply shop, where you may also find blocks of tempered chocolate, ready for immediate use.

1 Break up the chocolate into small pieces and place it in the top of a double boiler or a heatproof bowl over a pan of hot water. Heat gently until just melted.

2 Remove from the heat. Spoon about three-quarters of the melted chocolate on to a marble slab or other cool, smooth, non-porous work surface.

3 With a flexible plastic scraper or metal spatula, spread the chocolate thinly, then scoop it up before spreading it again. Repeat the sequence, keeping the chocolate constantly on the move, for about 5 minutes.

4 Using a chocolate thermometer, check the temperature of the chocolate as you work it. As soon as the temperature registers 28°C/82°F, tip the chocolate back into the bowl and stir into the remaining chocolate.

5 With the addition of the hot chocolate, the temperature should now be 32°C/90°F, making the chocolate ready for use. To test, drop a little of the chocolate from a spoon on to the marble; it should set very quickly.

Storing Chocolate

Chocolate can be stored successfully for up to a year if the conditions are favourable. This means a dry place with a temperature of around 20°C/68°F. At higher temperatures, the chocolate may develop white streaks as the fat comes to the surface. Although this will not spoil the flavour, it will mar the appearance of the chocolate, making it unsuitable for use as a decoration. When storing chocolate, keep it cool and dry. Place inside an airtight container, away from strong-smelling foods. Check the "use by" dates on the pack regularly.

PIPING WITH CHOCOLATE

Key factors

Pipe chocolate directly on to a cake, or on to baking parchment to make run-outs, small outlined shapes or irregular designs. After melting the chocolate, allow it to cool slightly so it just coats the back of a spoon. If it still flows freely it will be too runny to hold its shape when piped. When it is the right consistency, you then need to work fast as the chocolate will set quickly. Use a paper piping (pastry) bag and keep the pressure very tight, as the chocolate will flow readily without encouragement.

Making a Paper Piping Bag

A non-stick paper cone is ideal for piping small amounts of messy liquids like chocolate as it is small, easy to handle and disposable, unlike a conventional piping bag, which will need cleaning.

1 Fold a square of baking parchment in half to form a triangle. With the triangle point facing you, fold the left corner down to the centre.

2 Fold the right corner down and wrap it around the folded left corner to form a cone. Fold the ends into the cone.

3 Spoon the melted chocolate into the cone and fold the top edges over. When ready to pipe, snip off the end of the point neatly to make a tiny hole, about 3mm/⅛in in diameter.

4 Another method is to use a small heavy-duty freezer or plastic bag. Place a piping nozzle in one corner of the bag, so that it is in the correct position for piping. Fill as above, squeezing the filling into one corner and twisting the top to seal. Snip off the corner of the bag, if necessary, so that the tip of the nozzle emerges, and squeeze gently to pipe the design.

Chocolate Drizzles

You can have great fun making random shapes or, with a steady hand, special designs that will look great on either cakes or biscuits (cookies).

1 Melt the chocolate and pour it into a paper cone or small piping bag fitted with a very small plain nozzle. Drizzle the chocolate on to a baking sheet lined with baking parchment to make small, self-contained lattice shapes, such as circles or squares. Allow these to set for 30 minutes then peel off the paper.

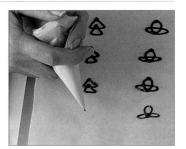

2 Chocolate can be used in many designs, such as flowers or butterflies. Use baking parchment as tracing paper and pipe the chocolate over the chosen design or decorative shape.

3 For butterflies, pipe chocolate on to individually cut squares and leave until just beginning to set. Use a long, thin box (such as an egg carton) and place the butterfly shape in the box or between the cups so it is bent in the centre, creating the butterfly shape. Chill until needed.

Piping on to Cakes

This looks effective on top of a cake iced with coffee glacé icing.

1 Melt 50g/2oz each of white and plain (semisweet) chocolate in separate bowls, and allow to cool slightly. Place in separate paper piping bags. Cut a small piece off the pointed end of each bag.

2 Hold each piping bag in turn above the surface of the cake and pipe the chocolates all over, as shown in the picture. Alternatively, pipe a freehand design in one continuous curvy line, first with one bag of chocolate, then the other.

Piping Curls

Make lots of these curly shapes and store them in a cool place ready for using as cake decorations. Try piping the lines in contrasting colours of chocolate to achieve a different effect.

1 Melt 115g/4oz chocolate and allow to cool slightly. Cover a rolling pin with baking parchment and attach it with tape. Fill a paper piping (pastry) bag with the chocolate and cut a small piece off the pointed end in a straight line.

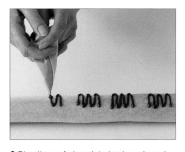

2 Pipe lines of chocolate backwards and forwards over the baking parchment.

3 Leave the piped curls to set in a cool place, then carefully peel off the baking parchment. Use a metal spatula to lift the curls on to the cake.

Feathering or Marbling Chocolate

These two related techniques provide some of the easiest and most effective ways of decorating the top of a cake, and they are also used when making a swirled mixture for cut-outs. Chocolate sauce and double cream can also be feathered or marbled to decorate a dessert.

1 Melt two contrasting colours of chocolate and spread one over the cake or surface to be decorated.

2 Spoon the contrasting chocolate into a piping (pastry) bag and pipe lines or swirls over the chocolate base.

3 Working quickly before the chocolate sets, draw a skewer or cocktail stick (toothpick) through the swirls to create a feathered or marbled effect.

Chocolate Run-outs

Try piping the outline in one colour of chocolate and filling in the middle with another. The effect can be dramatic.

1 Tape a piece of baking parchment to a baking sheet or flat board. Draw around a shaped biscuit (cookie) cutter on to the paper several times. Secure a piece of baking parchment over the top.

2 Using a piping (pastry) bag, pipe over the outlines in a continuous thread.

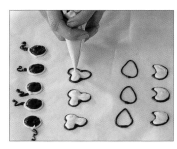

3 Cut the end off the other bag, making the hole slightly wider than before, and pipe the chocolate to fill in the outline so it looks slightly rounded. Leave the shapes to set in a cool place, then carefully lift them off the baking parchment using a metal spatula.

CHOCOLATE DECORATIONS

Grated Chocolate

Chocolate can be grated by hand or in a food processor. Make sure you grate it at the correct temperature.

1 Chill the chocolate and hold it with a piece of folded foil or kitchen paper to prevent the heat of your hand melting it. Hold a hand- or box-grater over a large plate and grate with an even pressure.

2 A food processor fitted with the metal blade can also be used to grate chocolate, but be sure the chocolate is soft enough to be pierced with a sharp knife. Cut the chocolate into small pieces and, with the machine running, drop the chocolate pieces through the feeder tube until very fine shavings are produced. Use the grater attachment and pusher to feed the chocolate through the processor for larger shavings.

> **Cook's Tips**
> The chocolate you use for decorating should not be too cold or it will splinter; warm chocolate will give a softer, looser curl, but do not allow it to become too soft or warm or it will be difficult to handle and may bloom. You should use tempered chocolate for the best results.

> **Cook's Tips**
> If using a metal grater for grating chocolate, chill it in the freezer before use and the chocolate will be less likely to melt.
>   Experiment with different utensils when making chocolate curls. Metal spatulas, paint scrapers, tablespoons and even wide, straight pastry scrapers can be used.

Mini Chocolate Curls

Chocolate curls make an ideal decoration for many desserts and cakes, whether these are made from plain(semisweet), bittersweet or white chocolate. These curls can be made very quickly using a vegetable peeler, and can be stored for several weeks in an airtight container in a cool, dry place.

1 Bring a thick piece or bar of chocolate to room temperature. (Chocolate that is too cold will "grate", or if too warm will slice.) With a swivel-bladed peeler held over a plate or baking sheet, pull the blade firmly along the edge of the chocolate and allow curls to fall on to the plate or baking sheet in a single layer.

2 Use a cocktail stick (toothpick) or similar to pick up the curls.

Chunky Chocolate Curls

These curls are best made with dark (bittersweet) chocolate that has been melted with pure white vegetable fat (about 5ml/1tsp per 25g/1oz of chocolate), which keeps the chocolate from hardening completely.

1 Melt 175g/6oz plain (semisweet) or dark chocolate with 30ml/2tbsp pure white vegetable fat, stirring until smooth. Pour into a small rectangular or square tin lined with foil or baking parchment to produce a block about 2.5cm/1in thick. Chill until set.

2 Allow the block to come to room temperature, remove it from the tin, then hold it with a piece of folded foil or kitchen paper (to stop it melting) and use a swivel-bladed peeler to produce short chunky curls. The block of chocolate can also be grated.

> **Cook's Tips**
> The decorations on this page are useful for all kinds of cakes and desserts. When you have mastered the techniques, try marbling dark and white chocolate together for a special effect.

Chocolate Scrolls or Short Round Curls

Temper dark (bittersweet) or white chocolate, or use chocolate prepared for Chunky Chocolate Curls.

1 Pour the prepared chocolate evenly on to a marble slab or the back of a baking sheet. Using a palette knife (metal spatula), spread to about 3mm/⅛in thick and allow to set for about 30 minutes until just firm.

2 To make long scrolls, use the blade of a long, sharp knife on the surface of the chocolate, and, with both hands, push away from your body at a 25–45° angle to scrape off a thin layer of chocolate. Twist the handle of the knife about a quarter of a circle to make a slightly wider scroll. Use a teaspoon to make cup-shaped curls.

3 A variety of shapes and sizes can be produced, depending on the temperature of the chocolate and the tool used.

Chocolate Squiggles

Melt a quantity of chocolate and spread fairly thinly over a cool, smooth surface, leave until just set, then draw a citrus zester firmly across the surface to remove curls or "squiggles" of the chocolate.

Chocolate Cut-outs

You can make abstract shapes, or circles, squares and diamonds, by cutting them out freehand with a sharp knife.

1 Cover a baking sheet with baking parchment and tape down at each corner. Melt 115g/4oz dark (bittersweet), milk or white chocolate. Pour the chocolate on to the baking parchment.

2 Spread the chocolate evenly with a palette knife (metal spatula). Allow to stand until the surface of the chocolate is firm enough to cut, but is not too hard. The chocolate should not feel sticky when it is touched.

3 Press the cutter firmly through the chocolate and lift off the paper with a palette knife. Try not to touch the surface of the chocolate or you will leave marks on it and spoil its appearance.

4 The finished shapes can be left plain or piped with a contrasting chocolate for a decorative effect.

5 Abstract shapes can be cut with a knife freehand. They look particularly effective pressed on to the sides of a cake iced with plain or chocolate buttercream.

Cook's Tips

If you do not feel confident about cutting chocolate cut-outs freehand, use biscuit (cookie) or aspic cutters. Cut-outs look good around the sides of cakes or gâteaux. Space them regularly or overlap them.

Chocolate Leaves

You can use any fresh, non-toxic leaf with distinct veins to make these decorations. Rose, bay or lemon leaves work well. If small leaves are required, for decorating petits fours, for instance, use mint or lemon balm leaves.

1 Wash and dry the leaves. Melt plain (semisweet) or white chocolate. Use a pastry brush or spoon to coat the veined side of each leaf completely.

2 Place the coated leaves chocolate-side up on a baking sheet lined with baking parchment to set.

3 Starting at the stem end, gently peel away each leaf in turn. Store the chocolate leaves in a cool place until needed.

Chocolate Baskets

These impressive baskets make pretty, edible containers for desserts.

MAKES 6
  175g/6oz plain (semisweet), milk or
    white chocolate
  25g/1oz/2 tbsp butter

1 Cut out six 15cm/6in rounds from baking parchment.

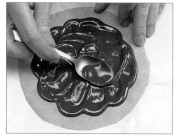

2 Melt the chocolate with the butter in a heatproof bowl over barely simmering water. Stir until smooth. Spoon one-sixth of the chocolate over each round, using a teaspoon to spread it to within 2cm/¾in of the edge.

Below: Chocolate baskets can be used to hold many kinds of delicious desserts, such as mousse, ice cream and tiramisu.

3 Carefully lift each covered paper round and drape it over an upturned cup or ramekin, curving the edges to create a frilled effect.

4 Leave until completely set, then carefully turn over and peel the paper away from the chocolate shape.

5 For a different effect, brush the chocolate over, leaving the edges jagged. Invert chocolate baskets on individual dessert plates and gently peel off the paper. Add your chosen filling, taking care not to break the chocolate.

6 For a simple filling, whip cream with a little orange-flavoured liqueur, pipe the mixture in swirls in the chocolate cups and top with mandarin segments.

Chocolate Cups

Large or small cupcake papers or sweet cases can be used to make chocolate cups to fill with ice cream, mousse or liqueur. Use double liners inside each other for extra support.

1 Melt the chocolate. Using a paintbrush or pastry brush, completely coat the base and sides of the paper cases. Allow to set, then repeat once or twice to build up the layers. Allow to set for several hours or overnight.

2 Carefully peel off the paper case, set the chocolate cups on a baking sheet and fill as desired.

Chocolate Shortcrust Pastry (1)

Suitable for sweet flans and tarts, this quantity will line a 23cm/9in flan tin.

> 115g/4oz plain (semisweet) chocolate, broken into squares
> 225g/8oz/2 cups plain (all-purpose) flour
> 115g/4oz/½ cup unsalted (sweet) butter
> 15–30ml/1–2 tbsp cold water

1 Melt the chocolate in a bowl over hot water. Remove from heat, but do not set.

2 In a mixing bowl, rub together the flour and butter until the mixture resembles fine breadcrumbs.

3 Make a well in the centre. Add the cooled chocolate and mix in with just enough cold water to make a firm dough. Knead lightly, then wrap in clear film (plastic wrap) and chill before rolling out. Once you have chilled the flan tin, chill again before baking.

Left: These tiny chocolate cups are ideal as a container for sweets. You can also fill them with nuts and fruit for petits fours. Look out for different sizes of cases for these little cups.

Chocolate Shortcrust Pastry (2)

An alternative sweet chocolate pastry, made with cocoa. Use a 23cm/9in flan tin.

> 175g/6oz/1½ cups plain (all-purpose) flour
> 30ml/2 tbsp cocoa powder
> 30ml/2 tbsp icing (confectioners') sugar
> 115g/4oz/½ cup butter
> 15–30ml/1–2 tbsp cold water

1 Sift the flour, cocoa powder and icing sugar into a mixing bowl.
2 Place the butter in a pan with the water and heat gently until just melted. Cool.
3 Stir into the flour to make a smooth dough. Chill until firm, then roll out and use as required.

Tips for Cooking with Chocolate

• Melt chocolate slowly, as over-heating will spoil both the flavour and texture.
• Avoid overheating – dark (bittersweet) chocolate should not be heated above 49°C/120°F; milk and white chocolate should not be heated above 43°C/110°F.
• Never allow water or steam to come into contact with melting chocolate, or it might form a solid mass. If the chocolate does come into contact with the steam and form a solid mass, add a small amount of pure vegetable oil and mix in. If this does not work, start again. Don't discard spoiled chocolate, it can be used to make a cream sauce.
• Remember to use high quality chocolate for the best results. Look for the cocoa solid content on the back of the wrapper. It should be between 30 and 70 per cent.
• Do not cover chocolate after melting, as condensation could cause it to stiffen.

THE
RECIPES

Few foods are as rich, sensuous and wickedly tempting as chocolate.
Whether you nibble it, savour it or simply surrender to its charms,
chocolate is pure pleasure. There's something almost addictive about
this gift of the gods, as anyone who has ever tried to give it up,
however briefly, will testify.

CAKES AND GATEAUX

Any special celebration is a good excuse for indulgence and nothing could be more indulgent than a luxuriously rich chocolate gâteau or a lavish Sachertorte, or try out your skills on a more unusual, impressive Rich Chocolate Leaf Gâteau. Alternatively, you could disregard everyone's diet and go totally overboard with the richest chocolate cake ever — Death by Chocolate!

SIMPLE CHOCOLATE CAKE

This cake is no less delicious because it is simple to make. It has a rich filling, so there is no need for icing. Dust the top with a little icing sugar and cocoa, if you like.

2 Cream the butter or margarine with the sugar in a mixing bowl until pale and fluffy. Add the eggs one at a time, beating well after each addition. Stir in the chocolate mixture until well combined.

3 Sift the flour and cocoa over the mixture and fold in with a metal spoon until evenly mixed. Scrape into the prepared tins, smooth level and bake for 35–40 minutes or until well risen and firm. Turn out on to wire racks to cool.

4 Sandwich the cake layers together with a thick layer of chocolate buttercream. Dust with icing (confectioners') sugar and cocoa just before serving, if liked.

SERVES 6–8

115g/4oz plain (semisweet) chocolate, chopped into small pieces
45ml/3 tbsp milk
150g/5oz/⅔ cup unsalted (sweet) butter or margarine, softened
150g/5oz/scant 1 cup light muscovado (brown) sugar
3 eggs
200g/7oz/1¾ cups self-raising (self-rising) flour
15ml/1 tbsp cocoa powder
1 quantity Chocolate Buttercream

1 Preheat oven to 180°C/350°F/Gas 4. Grease two 18cm/7in round sandwich cake tins (pans) and line the bases with baking parchment. Select a small pan and a heatproof bowl that will fit over it. Place the chocolate and the milk in the bowl. In the pan bring some water to just below simmering point. Place the bowl containing the chocolate mixture on top. Leave for about 5 minutes, until the chocolate softens, then stir until smooth. Leave the bowl set over the pan, but remove from the heat.

ONE-MIX CHOCOLATE SPONGE

SERVES 8–10

175g/6oz/¾ cup soft margarine

115g/4oz/½ cup caster
(superfine) sugar

60ml/4 tbsp golden (light corn) syrup

175g/6oz/1½ cups self-raising
(self-rising) flour, sifted

30ml/2 tbsp cocoa powder, sifted

2.5ml/½ tsp salt

3 eggs, beaten

150ml/¼ pint/⅔ cup whipping cream

15–30ml/1–2 tbsp marmalade

icing (confectioners') sugar, to decorate

1 Preheat the oven to 180°C/350°F/Gas 4. Grease two 18cm/7in sandwich cake tins (pans). Cream the margarine, sugar, syrup, flour, cocoa, salt and eggs in a bowl.

2 If the mixture seems a little thick, stir in enough milk to give a soft dropping consistency. Spoon the mixture into the prepared tins, and bake for about 30 minutes, changing shelves if necessary after 15 minutes, until just firm and springy to the touch.

3 Leave the cakes to cool for 5 minutes, then remove from the tins and leave to cool completely on a wire rack.

4 Whip the cream and fold in the marmalade. Use the mixture to sandwich the two cakes together. Sprinkle the top with sifted icing sugar, if liked.

CHOCOLATE <u>AND</u> BEETROOT LAYER CAKE

SERVES 10–12

cocoa powder, for dusting

225g/8oz can cooked whole beetroot
(beets), drained and juice reserved

115g/4oz/½ cup unsalted (sweet)
butter, softened

425g/15oz/2½ cups soft light brown sugar

3 eggs

15ml/1 tbsp vanilla essence (extract)

75g/3oz dark (bittersweet)
chocolate, melted

225g/8oz/2 cups plain (all-purpose) flour

10ml/2 tsp baking powder

2.5ml/½ tsp salt

120ml/4fl oz/½ cup buttermilk

chocolate curls (optional)

For the Chocolate Ganache Frosting

475ml/16fl oz/2 cups whipping cream

500g/1¼lb dark (bittersweet) or plain
(semisweet) chocolate, chopped

15ml/1 tbsp vanilla essence (extract)

1 Preheat the oven to 180°C/350°F/Gas 4. Grease two 23cm/9in cake tins (pans) and dust the base and sides with cocoa. Grate the beetroot and add to the juice. Set aside. With a hand-held electric mixer, beat the butter, brown sugar, eggs and vanilla essence in a mixing bowl until pale. Reduce the speed and beat in the melted chocolate. Sift the flour, baking powder and salt into a bowl.

2 With the mixer on low speed, gradually beat the flour mixture into the butter mixture, alternately with the buttermilk. Add the beetroot and juice and beat for 1 minute. Divide between the tins and bake for 30–35 minutes, or until a cake tester inserted in the centre of each cake comes out clean. Cool for 10 minutes, then turn the cakes out onto a wire rack and cool completely.

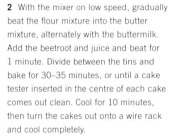

3 To make the ganache frosting, heat the cream in a heavy pan over medium heat, until it just begins to boil, stirring occasionally to prevent it from scorching. Remove from the heat and stir in the chocolate, stirring constantly until melted and smooth. Stir in the vanilla essence. Strain into a bowl. Cool, then chill, stirring every 10 minutes for 1 hour, until spreadable.

4 Assemble the cake. Place one layer on a serving plate and spread with one-third of the ganache frosting. Place the second layer on top and spread the remaining ganache over the cake, taking it down the sides. Decorate with the chocolate curls, if using. Allow the ganache frosting to set for 20–30 minutes, then chill the cake in the refrigerator before serving.

CHOCOLATE <u>AND</u> ORANGE ANGEL CAKE

SERVES 10

25g/1oz/¼ cup plain (all-purpose) flour

30ml/2 tbsp cocoa powder

30ml/2 tbsp cornflour (cornstarch)

pinch of salt

5 egg whites

2.5ml/½ tsp cream of tartar

115g/4oz/½ cup caster (superfine) sugar

blanched and shredded rind of

1 orange, to decorate

For the Icing

200g/7oz/scant 1 cup caster sugar

75ml/5 tbsp cold water

1 egg white

1 Preheat the oven to 180°C/350°F/Gas 4. Sift the flour, cocoa, cornflour and salt together three times. Beat the egg whites in a large bowl until foamy. Add the cream of tartar to the egg whites and whisk until soft peaks form.

2 Add the caster sugar to the egg whites a spoonful at a time, whisking after each addition. Sift in a third of the flour and cocoa mixture, and gently fold in. Repeat sifting and folding in of flour and cocoa mixture two more times. Spoon the mixture into a 20cm/8in non-stick ring tin (pan) and level the top. Bake for 35 minutes or until springy when lightly pressed. When slightly cooled, invert on to a wire rack and leave to cool further in the tin.

3 Make the icing. Put the sugar in a pan with the water. Stir over a low heat until dissolved. Boil until the syrup reaches a temperature of 120°C/250°F on a sugar thermometer, or when a teaspoonful of the syrup makes a soft ball when dropped into a cup of cold water. Remove the pan from the heat. Ease the cake out of the tin.

4 Whisk the egg white until stiff. Add the syrup in a thin stream, whisking all the time. Continue to whisk until the mixture is very thick and fluffy. Spread the icing over the top and sides of the cooled cake. Sprinkle the shredded orange rind over the top of the cake and transfer to a platter before serving.

CHOCOLATE AND CHERRY POLENTA CAKE

SERVES 8

50g/2oz/⅓ cup quick-cook polenta
200g/7oz plain (semisweet) chocolate,
  chopped
5 eggs, separated
175g/6oz/¾ cup caster
  (superfine) sugar
115g/4oz/1 cup ground almonds
75ml/5 tbsp plain (all-purpose) flour
finely grated rind of 1 orange
115g/4oz/1 cup glacé (candied)
  cherries, halved
icing (confectioners') sugar, for dusting

1 Place the polenta in a heatproof bowl and pour over boiling water to cover. Stir well, cover the bowl and leave to stand for about 30 minutes, until all the water has been absorbed.

2 Preheat the oven to 190°C/375°F/Gas 5. Grease a deep 22cm/8½in round cake tin (pan) and line the base with baking parchment. Melt the chocolate.

3 Whisk the egg yolks with the sugar in a bowl until thick and pale. Beat in the chocolate, then fold in the polenta, ground almonds, flour and orange rind.

4 Whisk the egg whites in a grease-free bowl until stiff. Stir about 15ml/1 tbsp of the whites into the chocolate mixture to lighten, then fold in the rest. Finally, fold in the cherries. Scrape the mixture into the prepared tin and bake for 45–55 minutes or until well risen and firm. Turn out and cool on a wire rack, then dust with icing sugar to serve.

MARBLED CHOCOLATE-PEANUT BUTTER CAKE

<u>SERVES 12–14</u>

115g/4oz dark (bittersweet) chocolate

225g/8oz/1 cup unsalted (sweet)
  butter, softened

225g/8oz/⅔ cup smooth or chunky
  peanut butter

200g/7oz/scant 1 cup granulated sugar

225g/8 oz/1¼ cups soft light brown sugar

5 eggs

225g/8 oz/2 cups plain
  (all-purpose) flour

10ml/2 tsp baking powder

2.5ml/½ tsp salt

120ml/4fl oz/½ cup milk

50g/2oz/⅓ cup chocolate chips

For the Chocolate Peanut Butter Glaze

25g/1oz/2 tbsp butter, cut up

30ml/2 tbsp smooth peanut butter

45ml/3 tbsp golden (light corn) syrup

5ml/1 tsp vanilla essence (extract)

175g/6oz plain (semisweet) chocolate

15ml/1 tbsp water

1 Preheat the oven to 180°C/350°F/Gas 4. Generously grease and flour a 3 litre/ 5 pint/12 cup tube or ring tin (pan). Chop the dark chocolate into small pieces and melt. In a large mixing bowl beat the butter, peanut butter and sugars until light and creamy. Add the eggs one at a time, beating well after each addition.

2 Sift together the flour, baking powder and salt. Add to the butter mixture alternately with the milk until just blended. Pour half the mixture into another bowl. Stir the chocolate into one bowl until well blended. Stir the chocolate chips into the other bowl.

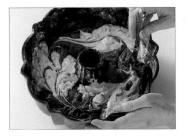

3 Using a large spoon, drop alternate spoonfuls of chocolate mixture and peanut butter mixture into the prepared tin. Using a knife, pull through the batters to create a swirled marbled effect. Bake for 50–60 minutes, until the top springs back when touched. Cool the cake in the tin for about 10 minutes. Turn out on to a rack to cool completely.

4 Make the glaze. Chop the plain chocolate into small pieces and combine with the rest of the ingredients in a small pan. Melt over a low heat, stirring until well blended and smooth. Cool slightly. When slightly thickened, drizzle the glaze over the cake, allowing it to run down the sides.

FRENCH CHOCOLATE CAKE

SERVES 10

250g/9oz dark (bittersweet) chocolate,
  chopped into small pieces
225g/8oz/1 cup unsalted (sweet) butter,
  cut into small pieces
90g/3½oz/scant ½ cup granulated sugar
30ml/2 tbsp brandy or orange-
  flavoured liqueur
5 eggs
15ml/1tbsp plain (all-purpose) flour
icing (confectioners') sugar,
  for dusting
whipped or sour cream, to serve

1 Preheat the oven to 180°C/350°F/Gas 4.
Generously grease a 23 x 5cm/9 x 2in
springform tin (pan). Line the base with
baking parchment and grease. Wrap the
base and sides in foil to prevent water
from seeping through.

2 In a pan, over a low heat, melt the
chocolate, butter and sugar, stirring.
Remove from the heat, cool slightly and
stir in the brandy or liqueur.

3 In a large bowl, beat the eggs lightly for
1 minute. Beat in the flour, then the
chocolate mixture. Pour into the tin.

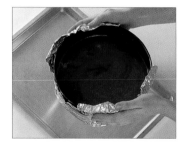

4 Place the springform tin in a large
roasting pan. Add enough boiling water to
come 2cm/¾in up the side of the
springform tin. Bake for 25–30 minutes,
until the edge of the cake is set but the
centre is still soft. Remove the springform
tin from the roasting pan and remove the
foil. Cool on a wire rack. The cake will sink
in the centre and become its classic slim
shape as it cools. Don't worry if the cake
surface cracks slightly.

5 Remove the side of the springform tin
and turn the cake on to a wire rack. Lift off
the springform tin base and then carefully
peel back the paper, so the base of the
cake is now the top. Leave the cake on the
rack until it is quite cold.

6 Cut 6–8 strips of baking parchment
2.5cm/1in wide and place randomly
over the cake. Dust the cake with icing
sugar, then carefully remove the paper.
Slide the cake on to a plate and serve
with whipped or sour cream.

CHOCOLATE CHIP WALNUT LOAF

MAKES 1 LOAF

115g/4oz/½ cup caster (superfine) sugar
115g/4oz/1 cup plain (all-purpose) flour
5ml/1 tsp baking powder
60ml/4 tbsp cornflour (cornstarch)
115g/4oz/½ cup butter, softened
2 eggs, beaten
5ml/1 tsp vanilla essence (extract)
30ml/2 tbsp currants or raisins
25g/1oz/¼ cup walnuts, chopped
grated rind of ½ lemon
45ml/3 tbsp plain (semisweet)
    chocolate chips
icing (confectioners') sugar, for dusting

1 Preheat the oven to 180°C/350°F/Gas 4. Grease and line a 22 x 12cm/8½ x 4½in loaf tin (pan). Sprinkle 25ml/1½ tbsp of the sugar into the pan and tilt to distribute. Shake out any excess sugar.

2 Sift the flour, baking powder and cornflour together three times.

3 With an electric mixer, cream the butter until soft. Add the remaining sugar and continue beating until light and fluffy. Add the eggs, one at a time, beating.

4 Gently fold the dry ingredients into the butter mixture, in three batches, being careful not to overmix.

5 Fold in the vanilla essence, currants or raisins, walnuts, lemon rind and chocolate chips until just blended.

6 Pour the mixture into the prepared tin and bake for 45–50 minutes. Cool in the tin for 5 minutes before transferring to a wire rack to cool. Place on a serving plate and dust with icing sugar before serving. Alternatively, top with glacé icing and decorate with walnut halves.

BITTER MARMALADE CHOCOLATE LOAF

SERVES 8

- 115g/4oz plain (semisweet) chocolate
- 3 eggs
- 200g/7oz/scant 1 cup caster
  (superfine) sugar
- 175ml/6fl oz/¾ cup sour cream
- 200g/7oz/1¾ cups self-raising
  (self-rising) flour

For the Filling and Glaze

- 175g/6oz/⅔ cup bitter orange marmalade
- 115g/4oz plain (semisweet)
  chocolate, chopped
- 60ml/4 tbsp sour cream
- shredded orange rind, to decorate

1 Preheat the oven to 180°C/350°F/Gas 4. Grease and line a 900g/2lb loaf tin (pan). Chop and melt the chocolate.

2 Combine the eggs and sugar in a mixing bowl. Using a hand-held electric mixer, whisk the mixture until it is thick and creamy, then stir in the sour cream and chocolate. Fold in the self-raising flour evenly, using a metal spoon and a figure-of-eight action.

3 Scrape the mixture into the prepared tin and bake for about 1 hour or until well risen and firm to the touch. Cool for a few minutes in the tin, then turn out on to a wire rack and leave the loaf to cool.

4 Make the filling. Melt two-thirds of the marmalade over a gentle heat. Chop and melt the chocolate. Stir into the marmalade with the cream.

5 Slice the cake across into three layers and sandwich back together with about half the marmalade filling. Spread the rest over the top of the cake and leave to set. Spoon the remaining marmalade over the cake and scatter with shredded orange rind, to decorate.

CHOCOLATE CHIP MARZIPAN LOAF

MAKES 1 LOAF

115g/4oz/½ cup unsalted (sweet)
   butter, softened
150g/5oz/scant 1 cup light muscovado
   (brown) sugar
2 eggs, beaten
45ml/3 tbsp cocoa powder
150g/5oz/1¼ cups self-raising
   (self-rising) flour
130g/3½oz marzipan, chopped
60ml/4 tbsp plain (semisweet)
   chocolate chips

1 Preheat the oven to 180°C/350°F/Gas 4.
Cream the butter and sugar until light and
fluffy. Add the eggs one at a time, beating
well after each addition to combine.

2 Sift the cocoa and flour over the mixture
and fold in evenly. Mix the marzipan with
the chocolate chips. Set aside about 60ml/
4 tbsp and fold the rest evenly into the
cake mixture. Grease and base-line a
900g/2lb loaf tin (pan).

3 Scrape the mixture into the prepared
tin, level the top and scatter with the
reserved marzipan and chocolate chips.

4 Bake for 45–50 minutes or until the loaf
is risen and firm. Cool for a few minutes in
the tin, then turn out on to a wire rack.

CHOCOLATE COCONUT ROULADE

4 Scrape the mixture into the prepared tin, taking it right into the corners. Smooth the surface with a palette knife (metal spatula), then bake for 20–25 minutes, or until well risen and springy to the touch.

5 Turn out on to the sugar-dusted paper and carefully peel off the lining paper. Cover with a clean, damp dishtowel and leave to cool completely.

6 Make the filling. Whisk the cream with the whisky in a bowl until the mixture just holds it shape, grate the creamed coconut and stir in with the sugar.

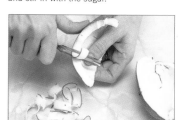

7 Uncover the sponge and spread about three-quarters of the cream mixture to the edges. Roll up carefully from a long side. Transfer to a plate, and pipe or spoon the remaining cream mixture on top. Use a vegetable peeler to make coconut and chocolate curls and pile on the cake.

SERVES 8

  115g/4oz/½ cup caster (superfine)
    sugar
  5 eggs, separated
  50g/2oz/½ cup cocoa powder
For the Filling
  300ml/½ pint/1¼ cups double
    (heavy) cream
  45ml/3 tbsp whisky or brandy
  50g/2oz creamed coconut
  30ml/2 tbsp caster (superfine) sugar
For the Topping
  a piece of fresh coconut and dark
    (bittersweet) chocolate, for curls

1 Preheat the oven to 180°C/350°F/Gas 4. Grease a 33 x 23cm/13 x 9in Swiss roll tin (jelly roll pan). Lay a large sheet of baking parchment on the work surface and dust evenly with 30ml/2 tbsp of the caster sugar.

2 Place the egg yolks in a heatproof bowl. Add the remaining caster sugar and whisk with a hand-held electric mixer until the mixture is thick enough to leave a trail. Sift the cocoa over, then fold in carefully and evenly with a metal spoon.

3 Whisk the egg whites in a clean, grease-free bowl until they form soft peaks. Fold about 15ml/1 tbsp into the chocolate mixture to lighten it, then fold in the rest.

CHOCOLATE CHESTNUT ROULADE

SERVES 10–12

175g/6oz dark (bittersweet) chocolate
30ml/2 tbsp cocoa powder, sifted
60ml/4 tbsp hot strong coffee
6 eggs, separated
75g/3oz/6 tbsp caster (superfine) sugar
pinch of cream of tartar
5ml/1 tsp pure vanilla essence (extract)
cocoa powder, for dusting
glacé (candied) chestnuts, to decorate
For the Chestnut Cream Filling
475ml/16fl oz/2 cups double
  (heavy) cream
30ml/2 tbsp rum
350g/12oz/1½ cups canned sweetened
  chestnut purée
115g/4oz dark chocolate, grated

4 Dust a dishtowel with cocoa. Turn the cake out on to the towel immediately and remove the paper. Trim off any crisp edges. Starting at a narrow end, roll the cake and towel together Swiss-roll fashion. Leave to cool completely.

5 Make the filling. Whip the cream and rum until soft peaks form. Beat a little cream into the chestnut purée to lighten it, then fold in the remaining cream and grated chocolate. Set aside a quarter of this mixture for the decoration. Unroll the cake and spread chestnut cream to within 2.5cm/1in of the edge.

6 Using a dishtowel to lift the cake, carefully roll it up again. Place seam-side down on a serving plate. Spread some of the reserved chestnut cream over the top and use the rest for piped rosettes. Decorate the roulade with the glacé chestnuts.

1 Preheat the oven to 180°C/350°F/Gas 4. Grease and line with a 2.5cm/1in overhang a 39 x 27 x 2.5cm/15½ x 10½ x 1in Swiss roll tin (jelly roll pan). Chop the chocolate into small pieces and melt. Dissolve the cocoa in the hot coffee to make a paste. Set aside.

2 In a mixing bowl, beat the egg yolks with half the sugar until pale and thick. Slowly beat in the melted chocolate and cocoa-coffee paste. In a separate bowl, beat the egg whites and cream of tartar until stiff peaks form. Sprinkle the remaining sugar over the whites in two batches and beat until stiff and glossy, then beat in the vanilla.

3 Stir a spoonful of the egg whites into the chocolate mixture to lighten it, then fold in the remainder. Spoon the mixture into the tin. Bake for 20–25 minutes, or until the cake springs back when touched with a fingertip.

MARBLED SWISS ROLL

SERVES 6–8

90g/3½oz/scant 1 cup plain
    (all-purpose) flour
15ml/1 tbsp cocoa powder
25g/1oz plain (semisweet) chocolate, grated
25g/1oz white chocolate, grated
3 eggs
115g/4oz/½ cup caster (superfine) sugar
30ml/2 tbsp boiling water

For the Filling

1 quantity Chocolate Buttercream
45ml/3 tbsp chopped walnuts

1 Preheat the oven to 200°C/400°F/Gas 6. Grease and line a 30 x 20cm/12 x 8in Swiss roll tin (jelly roll pan). Sift half the flour with the cocoa and stir in the plain chocolate. Sift the remaining flour into another bowl. Add the white chocolate.

2 Whisk the eggs and sugar in a bowl set over a pan of hot water until a ribbon trail remains when the whisk is lifted.

3 Remove the bowl from the heat and tip half the mixture into a separate bowl. Fold the plain chocolate mixture into one portion, then fold the white chocolate mixture into the other. Stir 15ml/1 tbsp boiling water into each half to soften.

BAKED ALASKA

For a truly delicious dessert that takes only minutes to prepare try making individual Baked Alaskas. Top slices of the roll with chocolate ice cream, cover both cake and ice cream thickly with meringue mixture and bake at 230°C/450°F/Gas 8 for 2–3 minutes, watching carefully, until the meringue is tinged with brown.

4 Place alternate spoonfuls of mixture in the prepared tin and swirl lightly together with a knife or slim metal skewer for a marbled effect. Bake for about 12–15 minutes, or until the cake is firm and the surface springs back when touched with a fingertip. Turn the cake out on to a sheet of baking parchment placed on the work surface.

5 Trim the edges to neaten and cover with a clean, damp dishtowel. Leave to cool.

6 For the filling, mix the chocolate buttercream and walnuts in a bowl. Uncover the sponge, lift off the lining paper and spread with the buttercream. Roll up from a long side and place on a serving plate to serve. Store in an airtight container.

CHOCOLATE CHRISTMAS LOG

SERVES 12-14

1 chocolate Swiss roll (*see* Chocolate
    Chestnut Roulade)
1 quantity Chocolate Ganache or
    Buttercream

For the White Chocolate Cream Filling
    200g/7oz fine quality white chocolate,
    chopped into small pieces
    475ml/16fl oz/2 cups double
    (heavy) cream
    30ml/2 tbsp brandy or chocolate-
    flavoured liqueur (optional)

For the Cranberry Sauce
    450g/1lb fresh or frozen cranberries,
    rinsed and picked over
    275g/10oz/1 cup seedless raspberry
    preserve, melted
    115g/4oz/½ cup granulated sugar,
    or to taste

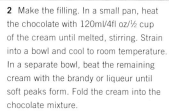

1 Make the cranberry sauce. Process the
cranberries in a food processor fitted with
a metal blade, until liquid. Press through a
sieve into a small bowl, and discard the
pulp. Stir in the melted raspberry preserve
and the sugar to taste. If the sauce is too
thick, add a little water to thin. Cover and
place in the refrigerator.

2 Make the filling. In a small pan, heat
the chocolate with 120ml/4fl oz/½ cup
of the cream until melted, stirring. Strain
into a bowl and cool to room temperature.
In a separate bowl, beat the remaining
cream with the brandy or liqueur until
soft peaks form. Fold the cream into the
chocolate mixture.

3 Unroll the Swiss roll, spread with the
mixture and roll up again from a long end.
Cut off a quarter of the roll at an angle and
arrange both pieces on a cake board to
resemble a log.

4 If using chocolate ganache for the
topping, allow it to soften to room
temperature, then beat to a soft, spreading
consistency. Cover the log with ganache
or buttercream and mark it with a fork to
resemble bark. Dust lightly with icing
(confectioners') sugar and top with a sprig
of holly or similar Christmas decoration.
Serve with the cranberry sauce.

MERINGUE MUSHROOMS
Small, decorative mushrooms are
traditionally used to decorate the yule
log. Using meringue mix, pipe the
"caps" and "stems" separately, dry
out in a low oven, then sandwich
together with ganache or chocolate
buttercream. Dust with cocoa, if
liked. Alternatively, shape mushrooms
from marzipan.

CHOCOLATE DATE TORTE

SERVES 8

4 egg whites

115g/4oz/½ cup caster (superfine) sugar

200g/7oz plain (semisweet) chocolate

175g/6oz/scant 1 cup Medjool dates, pitted and finely chopped

175g/6oz/1½ cups walnuts or pecan nuts, chopped

5ml/1 tsp vanilla essence (extract)

For the Frosting

200g/7oz/scant 1 cup fromage frais or ricotta cheese

200g/7oz/scant 1 cup mascarpone

a few drops of vanilla essence (extract)

icing (confectioners') sugar, to taste

1 Preheat the oven to 180°C/350°F/ Gas 4. Grease a round 20cm/8in springform cake tin (pan). Line the base of the tin with baking parchment and set aside.

2 To make the frosting, mix the fromage frais or ricotta cheese with the mascarpone in a bowl. Add a few drops of vanilla essence while mixing, enough to give a delicate flavour, and icing sugar to taste. Set aside when thoroughly mixed.

3 Whisk the egg whites in a bowl until they form stiff peaks. Whisk in 30ml/ 2 tbsp of the caster sugar until the meringue is thick and glossy, then fold in the remainder.

4 Chop 175g/6oz of the chocolate, then carefully fold into the meringue with the dates, nuts and vanilla essence. Pour into the prepared tin, spread level and bake for about 45 minutes, until risen around the edges of the tin.

5 Allow the cake to cool in the tin for 10 minutes, then invert onto a wire rack. Peel off the lining paper and leave until completely cold.

6 Swirl the frosting over the top of the torte. Melt the remaining chocolate. Use a small paper piping (pastry) bag to drizzle the chocolate over the torte. Work quickly and keep an even pressure on the piping bag. Chill the torte before serving, then cut into wedges. This torte is best eaten on the day that it is made.

CHOCOLATE REDCURRANT TORTE

SERVES 8–10

115g/4oz/½ cup unsalted (sweet)
   butter, softened

115g/4oz/⅔ cup dark muscovado
   (molasses) sugar

2 eggs

150ml/¼ pint/⅔ cup sour cream

150g/5oz/1¼ cups self-raising flour

5ml/1 tsp baking powder

50g/2oz/½ cup cocoa powder

75g/3oz/¾ cup stemmed redcurrants,
   plus 115g/4oz/1 cup redcurrant sprigs

For the Icing

150g/5oz plain (semisweet) chocolate

45ml/3 tbsp redcurrant jelly

30ml/2 tbsp dark rum

120ml/4fl oz/½ cup double (heavy) cream

1 Preheat the oven to 180°C/350°F/Gas 4. Grease a 1.2 litre/2 pint/5 cup ring tin (pan) and dust lightly with flour. Cream the butter with the sugar in a mixing bowl until pale and fluffy. Beat in the eggs and sour cream until thoroughly mixed.

2 Sift the flour, baking powder and cocoa over the mixture, then fold in lightly and evenly. Fold in the stemmed redcurrants. Spoon the mixture into the prepared tin and smooth the surface level. Bake for 40–50 minutes, or until well risen and firm. Turn out on to a wire rack and leave to cool completely.

3 Make the icing. Chop the chocolate into small pieces and mix with the redcurrant jelly and rum in a bowl. Set the bowl over simmering water and heat gently, stirring occasionally, until melted. Remove from the heat and cool to room temperature, then add the cream, a little at a time.

4 Transfer the cake to a serving plate. Spoon the icing evenly over the cake, letting it drizzle down the sides. Decorate with redcurrant sprigs just before serving.

COOK'S TIP

Use a decorative gugelhupf tin or mould, if you have one. When preparing it, add a little cocoa powder to the flour used for dusting the greased tin, as this will prevent the cooked chocolate cake from being streaked with white.

SACHERTORTE

SERVES 10–12

225g/8oz dark (bittersweet) chocolate
150g/5oz/⅔ cup butter, softened
115g/4oz/½ cup caster (superfine) sugar
8 eggs, separated
115g/4oz/1 cup plain (all-purpose) flour

For the Glaze
225g/8oz/scant 1 cup apricot jam
15ml/1 tbsp lemon juice

For the Icing
225g/8oz dark (bittersweet) chocolate
200g/7oz/scant 1 cup caster
  (superfine) sugar
15ml/1 tbsp golden (light corn) syrup
250ml/8fl oz/1 cup double
  (heavy) cream
5ml/1 tsp vanilla essence (extract)
plain chocolate leaves, to decorate

1 Preheat the oven to 180°C/350°F/Gas 4. Grease a 23cm/9in round springform tin (pan) and line with baking parchment. Melt the chocolate in a bowl over a pan of barely simmering water, then set aside.

2 Using a hand-held electric mixer, cream the butter with the sugar in a mixing bowl until pale and fluffy, then add the egg yolks, one at a time, beating well after each addition. Beat in the melted chocolate, then sift the flour over the mixture and fold in evenly. Whisk the egg whites in a clean, grease-free bowl until stiff, then stir about one-quarter of the whites into the chocolate mixture to lighten it. Fold in the remaining whites.

3 Tip the chocolate mixture into the prepared tin and smooth level. Bake for 50–55 minutes, or until firm. Cool in the tin for 5 minutes, then turn out carefully on to a wire rack to cool completely.

4 Make the glaze. Heat the apricot jam with the lemon juice in a small pan until melted, then strain through a sieve into a bowl. Once the cake is completely cold, slice in half across the middle to make two even-sized layers.

5 Brush the top and sides of each layer with the apricot glaze, then sandwich them together. Place on a wire rack.

6 Make the icing. Mix the chocolate, sugar, golden syrup, cream and vanilla essence in a heavy pan. Heat gently, stirring constantly, until the mixture is thick and smooth. Simmer gently for 3–5 minutes, without stirring, until the mixture registers 95°C/200°F on a sugar thermometer. Pour the icing quickly over the cake, spreading to cover the top and sides completely. Leave to set, decorate with chocolate leaves, then serve with whipped cream, if you like.

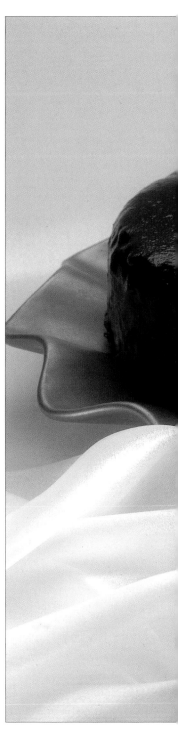

QUEEN <u>OF</u> SHEBA CAKE

SERVES 8–10

100g/3½oz/scant 1 cup whole blanched almonds, lightly toasted

115g/4oz/½ cup caster (superfine) sugar

40g/1½oz/⅓ cup plain (all-purpose) flour

115g/4oz/½ cup unsalted (sweet) butter, softened

150g/5oz plain (semisweet) chocolate, melted

3 eggs, separated

30ml/2 tbsp almond liqueur (optional)

chopped toasted almonds, to decorate

For the Chocolate Glaze

175ml/6fl oz/¾ cup whipping cream

225g/8oz plain (semisweet) chocolate, chopped

25g/1oz/2 tbsp unsalted (sweet) butter

30ml/2 tbsp almond liqueur (optional)

1 Preheat the oven to 180°C/350°F/Gas 4. Carefully grease a 20–23cm/8–9in springform tin (pan). Line the base with baking parchment. Dust the tin lightly with flour.

2 In the bowl of a food processor fitted with a metal blade, process the almonds and 30ml/2 tbsp of the sugar until very fine. Transfer to a bowl and sift over the flour. Stir to mix, then set aside.

3 Beat the butter until creamy, then add half of the remaining sugar and beat for about 1–2 minutes until very light. Gradually beat in the melted chocolate, then add the egg yolks one at a time, beating well after each addition. Beat in the liqueur, if using.

4 In another bowl, beat the egg whites until soft peaks form. Add the remaining sugar and beat until the whites are stiff and glossy, but not dry. Fold a quarter of the whites into the chocolate mixture to lighten it, then alternately fold in the almond mixture and the remaining whites in three batches. Spoon into the tin.

5 Bake for 30–35 minutes, until the edges are puffed but the centre is still soft. Cool in the tin for 15 minutes, then remove the sides and invert the cake onto a wire rack. When quite cold, lift off the base of the tin and the paper.

6 To make the chocolate glaze, bring the cream to the boil in a pan. Remove from the heat and add the chocolate, stirring gently until it has melted and the mixture is smooth. Beat in the butter and almond liqueur, if using. Then cool for about 20–30 minutes, until slightly thickened, stirring occasionally.

7 Place the cake on the wire rack over a baking sheet and pour over most of the warm glaze to cover completely. Cool slightly, then press the nuts on to the sides of the cake. Use the remaining glaze for a piped decoration. Transfer to a plate and chill until ready to serve.

CHOCOLATE, MAPLE AND WALNUT SWIRLS

SERVES 12

450g/1lb/4 cups strong white
   bread flour
2.5ml/½ tsp ground cinnamon
50g/2oz/¼ cup unsalted (sweet) butter,
   cut into small pieces
50g/2oz/¼ cup caster (superfine) sugar
1 sachet easy-blend (rapid rise)
   dried yeast
1 egg yolk
120ml/4fl oz/½ cup water
60ml/4 tbsp milk
45ml/3 tbsp maple syrup, to finish

For the Filling

40g/1½oz/3 tbsp unsalted (sweet)
   butter, melted
50g/2oz/⅓ cup light muscovado
   (brown) sugar
175g/6oz/1 cup plain (semisweet)
   chocolate chips
75g/3oz/¾ cup chopped walnuts

1 Grease a deep 23cm/9in springform tin (pan). Sift the flour and cinnamon into a bowl, then rub in the butter with your fingertips until the mixture resembles coarse breadcrumbs.

2 Stir in the sugar and yeast. In a jug or bowl, beat the egg yolk with the water and milk, then gradually stir into the dry ingredients, using a round-bladed knife, to make a soft dough.

3 Knead the dough on a lightly floured surface until smooth, then roll out to a rectangle measuring about 40 x 30cm/ 16 x 12in.

4 For the filling, brush the dough all over with the melted butter and then sprinkle evenly with the sugar, chocolate chips and chopped nuts.

5 Roll up the dough from one long side, then cut into 12 slices. Pack close together in the tin, cut sides up. Cover and leave in a warm place for about 1½ hours, until well risen and springy. Preheat the oven to 220°C/425°F/Gas 7.

6 Bake for 30–35 minutes, until golden brown. Remove from the tin and cool on a wire rack. Brush with maple syrup while still warm. Pull swirls apart to serve.

WHITE CHOCOLATE MOUSSE AND STRAWBERRY LAYER CAKE

4 Make the mousse filling. In a medium pan over a low heat, melt the white chocolate and cream until smooth, stirring frequently. Stir in the rum or strawberr-flavoured liqueur and pour into a bowl. Chill until just set. With a wire whisk, whip lightly.

SERVES 10

115g/4oz fine white chocolate, chopped
120ml/4fl oz/½ cup double (heavy) cream
120ml/4fl oz/½ cup milk
15ml/1 tbsp rum or vanilla essence (extract)
115g/4oz/½ cup unsalted (sweet) butter, softened
175g/6oz/¾ cup granulated sugar
3 eggs
225g/8oz/2 cups plain (all-purpose) flour
10ml/2 tsp baking powder
a pinch of salt
675g/1½lb fresh strawberries, sliced, plus extra for decoration
750ml/1¼ pints/3 cups whipping cream
30ml/2 tbsp rum
For the White Chocolate Mousse Filling
250g/9oz white chocolate, chopped
350ml/12fl oz/1½ cups double (heavy) cream
30ml/2 tbsp rum or strawberry-flavoured liqueur

1 Preheat the oven to 180°C/350°F/Gas 4. Grease and flour two 23 x 5cm/9 x 2in cake tins (pans). Line the base of the tins with baking parchment. Melt the chocolate and cream in a double boiler over a low heat, stirring until smooth. Stir in the milk and rum or vanilla. Set aside.

2 In a large mixing bowl, beat the butter and sugar with a hand-held electric mixer for 3–5 minutes, until light and creamy. Add the eggs one at a time, beating well after each addition. In a small bowl, stir together the flour, baking powder and salt. Alternately add flour and chocolate to the egg mixture in batches, until just blended. Pour the mixture into the tins and spread evenly with a metal spatula.

3 Bake for 20–25 minutes, until a skewer inserted in the cake comes out clean. Cool in the tin for 10 minutes, then turn the cakes out on to a wire rack, peel off the paper and cool completely.

5 Assemble the cake. With a serrated knife, slice both cake layers in half, making four layers. Place one layer on a plate and spread one-third of the mousse on top. Arrange one-third of the sliced strawberries over the mousse. Place the second layer on top and spread with another third of the mousse. Arrange another third of the sliced strawberries over the mousse. Place the third layer on top and spread with the remaining mousse. Cover with the remaining sliced strawberries. Top with the last cake layer.

6 Whip the cream with the rum or liqueur until firm peaks form. Spread about half the whipped cream over the top and the sides of the cake. Spoon the remaining cream into a piping bag fitted with a medium star nozzle and pipe scrolls on top of the cake. Decorate with the remaining sliced strawberries, pressing half of them into the cream on the side of the cake and arranging the rest on top.

CHOCOLATE GINGER CRUNCH CAKE

SERVES 6

150g/5oz plain (semisweet) chocolate, chopped
50g/2oz/¼ cup unsalted (sweet) butter
115g/4oz ginger nut biscuits (gingersnaps)
4 pieces of preserved stem ginger
30ml/2 tbsp stem ginger syrup
45ml/3 tbsp desiccated (dry unsweetened shredded) coconut
To Decorate
25g/1oz milk chocolate, chopped into small pieces
pieces of crystallized (candied) ginger

1 Grease a 15cm/6in flan ring and place on a board covered with baking parchment. Melt the chocolate and butter in a bowl set over a pan of simmering water. Set aside.

2 Crush the biscuits and tip into a bowl.

3 Chop the stem ginger fairly finely and mix with the crushed biscuits. Stir the biscuit mixture, syrup and coconut into the chocolate and butter, mixing well. Press into the flan ring and chill until set.

4 Remove the flan ring and slide the cake on to a plate. Melt the milk chocolate, drizzle it over the top and decorate with ginger.

FROSTED CHOCOLATE FUDGE CAKE

SERVES 6–8

115g/4oz plain (semisweet) chocolate, chopped
175g/6oz/¾ cup unsalted (sweet) butter, softened
200g/7oz/generous 1 cup light muscovado (brown) sugar
5ml/1 tsp vanilla essence (extract)
3 eggs, beaten
150ml/¼ pint/⅔ cup Greek (US strained plain) yogurt
150g/5oz/1¼ cups self-raising (self-rising) flour
icing (confectioners') sugar and chocolate curls, to decorate
For the Frosting
115g/4 oz dark (bittersweet) chocolate, chopped
50g/2oz/¼ cup unsalted (sweet) butter
350g/12oz/2¼ cups icing (confectioners') sugar
90ml/6 tbsp Greek (US strained plain) yogurt

1 Preheat the oven to 190°C/375°F/Gas 5. Grease and base-line two 20cm/8in sandwich tins (pans). Melt the chocolate.

2 Cream the butter with the sugar until light and fluffy. Beat in the vanilla, then gradually add the beaten eggs. Stir in the chocolate and yogurt evenly. Fold in the flour with a metal spoon.

3 Divide the mixture between the prepared tins. Bake for 25–30 minutes or until the cakes are firm to the touch. Turn out and cool on a wire rack.

4 Make the frosting. Melt the chocolate and butter in a pan. Off the heat, stir in the icing sugar and yogurt. Mix until smooth, then beat until cool and slightly thickened. Use a third to sandwich the cakes together.

5 Working quickly, spread the remainder over the top and sides. Sprinkle with icing sugar and decorate with chocolate curls.

RICH CHOCOLATE LEAF GATEAU

75g/3oz dark (bittersweet) chocolate,
   broken into squares
150ml/¼ pint/⅔ cup milk
175g/6oz/¾ cup unsalted (sweet)
   butter, softened
250g/9oz/1⅓ cups light muscovado
   (brown) sugar
3 eggs
250g/9oz/2¼ cups plain
   (all-purpose) flour
10ml/2 tsp baking powder
75ml/5 tbsp single (light) cream
For the Filling and Topping
   60ml/4 tbsp raspberry conserve
   1 quantity Chocolate Ganache
   dark (bittersweet) and white
   chocolate leaves

1 Preheat the oven to 190°C/375°F/Gas 5. Grease two 22cm/8½in sandwich tins (pans). Line the bases with baking parchment. Melt the chocolate with the milk over a low heat and allow it to cool slightly.

2 Cream the butter with the light muscovado sugar in a mixing bowl until light and fluffy. Add the eggs, one at a time, beating well after each addition, until completely incorporated.

3 Sift the flour and baking powder over the egg mixture and fold in gently but thoroughly. Stir in the chocolate and milk mixture and the single cream, mixing until smooth. Divide between the prepared tins and level the tops using a metal spatula.

4 Bake the cakes for 30–35 minutes, or until they are well risen and firm to the touch. Cool in the tins for a few minutes, then turn out on to wire racks.

5 Sandwich the cake layers together with the raspberry conserve. Spread the chocolate ganache over the cake and swirl with a knife. Place the cake on a serving plate, then decorate with the chocolate leaves.

CHOCOLATE ALMOND MOUSSE CAKE

SERVES 8

50g/2oz dark (bittersweet) chocolate,
   broken into squares
200g/7oz marzipan, grated or chopped
200ml/7fl oz/scant 1 cup milk
115g/4oz/1 cup self-raising
   (self-rising) flour
2 eggs, separated
75g/3oz/½ cup light muscovado
   (brown) sugar

For the Mousse Filling

115g/4oz plain (semisweet) chocolate,
   chopped into small pieces
50g/2oz/¼ cup unsalted (sweet) butter
2 eggs, separated
30ml/2 tbsp Amaretto di Saronno liqueur

For the Topping

1 quantity Chocolate Ganache
toasted flaked (sliced) almonds

1 Preheat the oven to 190°C/375°F/Gas 5. Grease a deep 17cm/6½in square cake tin (pan) and line with baking parchment. Combine the chocolate, marzipan and milk in a pan and heat gently without boiling, stirring until smooth.

2 Sift the flour into a bowl and add the chocolate mixture and egg yolks, beating until evenly mixed.

3 Whisk the egg whites in a grease-free bowl until firmly peaking. Gradually whisk in the sugar. Stir about 15ml/1 tbsp of the whites into the chocolate mixture to lighten it, then fold in the rest.

4 Spoon the mixture into the cake tin, spreading it evenly. Bake for 45–50 minutes, until well risen, firm and springy to the touch. Leave to cool on a wire rack.

5 Make the mousse filling. Melt the chocolate with the butter in a small pan over a low heat, then remove from the heat and beat in the egg yolks and Amaretto. Whisk the egg whites in a clean, grease-free bowl until stiff, then fold into the chocolate mixture.

6 Slice the cold cake horizontally to make two even-size layers. Return one half to the clean cake tin and pour over the chocolate mousse. Top with the second layer of cake and press down lightly. Chill until set.

7 Turn the cake out on to a serving plate. Allow the chocolate ganache to soften to room temperature, then beat to a soft, spreading consistency. Spread the chocolate ganache over the top and sides of the cake, then press toasted flaked almonds over the sides. Serve chilled.

DEATH BY CHOCOLATE

SERVES 16–20

225g/8oz dark (bittersweet) chocolate, chopped into small pieces
115g/4 oz/½ cup unsalted (sweet) butter
150ml/¼ pint/⅔ cup milk
225g/8oz/1¼ cups light muscovado (brown) sugar
10ml/2 tsp vanilla essence (extract)
2 eggs, separated
150ml/¼ pint/⅔ cup sour cream
225g/8oz/2 cups self-raising (self-rising) flour
5ml/1 tsp baking powder

For the Filling and Topping

60ml/4 tbsp seedless raspberry jam
60ml/4 tbsp brandy
400g/14oz dark (bittersweet) chocolate, chopped into small pieces
200g/7oz/scant 1 cup unsalted (sweet) butter
1 quantity Chocolate Ganache
plain (semisweet) chocolate curls, to decorate

1 Preheat the oven to 180°C/350°F/Gas 4. Grease and base-line a deep 23cm/9in springform tin (pan). Place the chocolate, butter and milk in a pan. Stir over a low heat until smooth. Remove from the heat, beat in the sugar and vanilla essence, then leave to cool slightly.

2 Beat the egg yolks and cream in a bowl, then beat into the chocolate mixture. Sift the flour and baking powder over the surface and fold in.

3 Whisk the egg whites in a grease-free bowl until stiff. Stir about 30ml/2 tbsp of the whites into the chocolate cake mixture, to lighten it. Fold in the remaining whites, using a metal spoon.

4 Scrape the mixture into the prepared tin and bake for about 45–55 minutes, or until firm to the touch. Then cool in the tin for 15 minutes. Invert the cake on to a wire rack, remove the tin and set aside until completely cold.

5 Slice the cold cake across the middle to make three even-sized layers. Make the filling. In a small pan, warm the raspberry jam with 15ml/1 tbsp of the brandy, then brush over two of the layers. Leave to set.

6 Place the remaining brandy in a pan with the chocolate and butter. Heat gently, stirring all the time, until smooth. Pour into a bowl and cool until it begins to thicken.

7 Spread the bottom layer of the cake with half the chocolate filling, taking care not to disturb the jam. Top with a second layer, jam side up, and spread with the remaining filling. Top with the final layer and press lightly.

8 Leave to set, then spread the top and sides of the cake with the chocolate ganache. Decorate with chocolate curls, then dust the top of the cake with cocoa powder, if you wish.

VEGAN CHOCOLATE GATEAU

SERVES 8–10

275g/10oz/2½ cups self-raising
  wholemeal (self-rising
  whole-wheat) flour
50g/2oz/½ cup cocoa powder
45ml/3 tbsp baking powder
225g/8oz/1¼ cups caster
  (superfine) sugar
few drops of vanilla essence (extract)
135ml/9 tbsp sunflower oil
350ml/12fl oz/1½ cups water
sifted cocoa powder, for sprinkling
25g/1oz/¼ cup chopped nuts,
  to decorate

For the Chocolate Fudge

50g/2oz/¼ cup vegan (soya) margarine
45ml/3 tbsp water
250g/9oz/2 cups icing (confectioners')
  sugar, sifted
30ml/2 tbsp cocoa powder, sifted
15–30ml/1–2 tbsp hot water

1 Preheat the oven to 160°C/325°F/Gas 3. Grease and line a deep 20cm/8in round cake tin (pan). Grease again with sunflower oil.

2 Sift the flour, cocoa and baking powder into a large bowl. Add the sugar and vanilla, then gradually beat in the sunflower oil, then the water to produce a smooth, thick batter. Pour into the tin and smooth the surface.

3 Bake the cake for about 45 minutes, or until a cake tester or fine metal skewer inserted in the centre comes out clean. Remove from the oven but leave in the tin for about 5 minutes, before turning out on to a wire rack. Peel off the lining paper and leave to cool. Cut the cake in half to make two equal layers.

4 Make the chocolate fudge. Place the margarine and water in a pan and heat gently until the margarine has melted. Remove from the heat and add the sifted icing sugar and cocoa powder, beating until shiny, adding more hot water if needed. Pour into a bowl and cool until firm enough to spread and pipe.

5 Place the bottom layer of the cake on a serving plate and spread over two-thirds of the chocolate fudge mixture. Top with the other layer. Fit a piping (pastry) bag with a star nozzle, fill with the remaining chocolate fudge and pipe stars over the cake. Sprinkle with cocoa powder and decorate with the chopped nuts.

BLACK FOREST GATEAU

4 Prick each layer all over with a skewer or fork, then sprinkle with kirsch. Using a hand-held electric mixer, whip the cream in a bowl until it starts to thicken, then gradually beat in the icing sugar and vanilla essence until the mixture begins to hold its shape.

5 To assemble, spread one cake layer with a thick layer of flavoured cream and top with about half the cherries. Spread a second cake layer with cream, top with the remaining cherries, then place it on top of the first layer. Then place the final cake layer on top.

6 Spread the remaining cream all over the cake. Dust a plate with icing sugar, and position the cake carefully in the centre. Press grated chocolate over the sides and decorate the cake with the chocolate curls and fresh or drained morello cherries.

SERVES 8–10

6 eggs
200g/7oz/scant 1 cup caster
    (superfine) sugar
5ml/1 tsp vanilla essence (extract)
50g/2oz/½ cup plain
    (all-purpose) flour
50g/2oz/½ cup cocoa powder
115g/4oz/½ cup unsalted (sweet)
    butter, melted
For the Filling and Topping
60ml/4 tbsp kirsch
600ml/1 pint/2½ cups double
    (heavy) cream
30ml/2 tbsp icing (confectioners') sugar
2.5ml/½ tsp vanilla essence (extract)
675g/1½lb jar pitted morello cherries
icing (confectioners') sugar, grated
chocolate curls and fresh or drained and
    canned morello cherries, to decorate

1 Preheat the oven to 180°C/350°F/Gas 4. Grease three 19cm/7½in sandwich tins (pans). Line the base of each with baking parchment. Combine the eggs with the sugar and vanilla essence in a bowl and beat with a hand-held electric mixer until pale and very thick.

2 Sift the flour and cocoa powder over the mixture and fold in lightly and evenly with a metal spoon. Gently stir in the butter.

3 Divide the mixture among the prepared cake tins, smoothing them level. Bake for 15–18 minutes, until the cakes have risen and are springy to the touch. Leave to cool in the tins for about 5 minutes, then turn out on to wire racks and leave to cool completely. Remove the lining paper from each cake layer.

WHITE CHOCOLATE CAPPUCCINO GATEAU

SERVES 8

4 eggs

115g/4oz/½ cup caster
   (superfine) sugar

15ml/1 tbsp strong black coffee

2.5ml/½ tsp vanilla essence (extract)

115g/4oz/1 cup plain
   (all-purpose) flour

75g/3oz white chocolate, grated

For the Filling

120ml/4fl oz/½ cup whipping cream

15ml/1 tbsp coffee liqueur

For the Frosting and Topping

15ml/1 tbsp coffee liqueur

1 quantity White Chocolate Frosting

white chocolate curls

cocoa powder or ground cinnamon

1 Preheat the oven to 180°C/350°F/Gas 4. Grease two 18cm/7in round sandwich tins (pans) and line the base of each with baking parchment.

2 Put the eggs, sugar, coffee and vanilla in a heatproof bowl. Set over a pan of hot water and whisk until pale and thick.

3 Sift half the flour over the mixture and fold in gently and evenly. Fold in the remaining flour with the grated chocolate.

4 Spoon into the tins and level. Bake for 20–25 minutes, until firm and golden brown, then turn out on wire racks and leave to cool completely.

5 Make the filling. Whip the cream with the coffee liqueur in a bowl until it holds its shape. Spread over one of the cakes, then place the second layer on top.

6 Stir the coffee liqueur into the frosting. Spread, swirling, over the top and sides of the cake. Top with curls of white chocolate and dust with cocoa or cinnamon. Transfer the cake to a serving plate and set aside until the frosting has set. Serve the gâteau on the day it was made, if possible.

CHOCOLATE BRANDY SNAP GATEAU

SERVES 8

225g/8oz dark (bittersweet)
chocolate, chopped
225g/8oz/1 cup unsalted (sweet)
butter, softened
200g/7oz/generous 1 cup dark
muscovado (brown) sugar
6 eggs, separated
5ml/1 tsp vanilla essence (extract)
150g/5oz/1¼ cups ground hazelnuts
60ml/4 tbsp fresh white breadcrumbs
finely grated rind of 1 large orange
1 quantity Chocolate Ganache, for
filling and frosting
icing sugar, for dusting

For the Brandy Snaps
50g/2oz/¼ cup unsalted (sweet) butter
50g/2oz/¼ cup caster (superfine) sugar
75g/3oz/⅓ cup golden (light corn) syrup
50g/2oz/½ cup plain (all-purpose) flour
5ml/1 tsp brandy

1 Preheat the oven to 180°C/350°F/Gas 4. Grease and base-line two 20cm/8in sandwich tins (pans). Melt the chocolate and set aside to cool slightly.

2 Cream the butter and sugar until pale and fluffy. Beat in the egg yolks and vanilla. Mix in the chocolate.

3 Whisk the egg whites to soft peaks, then fold into the chocolate mixture with the hazelnuts, breadcrumbs and orange rind.

4 Divide the cake mixture between the tins. Bake for 25–30 minutes, or until well risen and firm. Turn out on to wire racks. Leave the oven on.

5 Make the brandy snaps. Line two baking sheets with baking parchment. Melt the butter, sugar and syrup together. Stir until smooth. Off the heat, stir in the flour and brandy.

6 Place small spoonfuls of the mixture well apart on the baking sheets and bake for 8–10 minutes, until golden. Cool for a few seconds until they are firm enough to be picked up.

7 Immediately pinch the edges of each snap to create a frilled effect. If they become too firm, soften briefly in the oven.

8 Sandwich the cake layers together with half the chocolate ganache, transfer to a plate and spread the remaining ganache on the top. Arrange the brandy snaps over the gâteau and dust with icing sugar.

COOK'S TIP
To save time, you could use ready-made brandy snaps. Simply warm them for a few minutes in the oven until they are pliable enough to shape. Or you could use them as they are, filling them with cream, and arranging them so that they fan out from the centre of the gâteau.

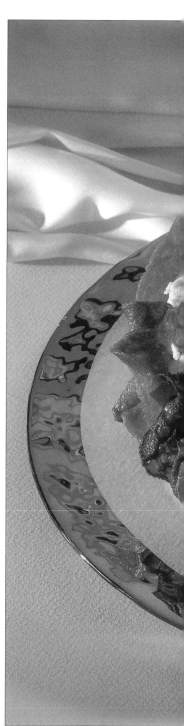

MERINGUE GATEAU WITH CHOCOLATE MASCARPONE

SERVES ABOUT 10

4 egg whites

a pinch of salt

175g/6oz/¾ cup caster
(superfine) sugar

5ml/1 tsp ground cinnamon

75g/3oz dark (bittersweet)
chocolate, grated

icing (confectioners') sugar and rose
petals, to decorate

For the Filling

115g/4oz plain (semisweet) chocolate,
chopped into small pieces

5ml/1 tsp vanilla essence (extract) or
rose water

115g/4oz/½ cup mascarpone cheese

1 Preheat the oven to 150°C/300°F/Gas 2.
Line two large baking sheets with baking
parchment. Whisk the egg whites with the
salt in a clean, grease-free bowl until they
form stiff peaks.

2 Gradually whisk in half the sugar,
then add the rest and whisk until the
meringue is very stiff and glossy. Add the
cinnamon and grated chocolate and
whisk lightly to mix.

3 Draw a 20cm/8in circle on the lining
paper on one of the baking sheets, replace
it upside-down and spread the marked
circle evenly with about half the meringue.
Spoon the remaining meringue in 28–30
even-sized, small neat heaps on both
baking sheets. Then bake in the oven for
1½ hours, until crisp.

4 Make the filling. Melt the chocolate in a
heatproof bowl set over a pan of hot water.
Cool slightly, then add the vanilla essence
or rose water and the mascarpone cheese.
Mix well until thoroughly combined. Cool
the mixture until its holds it shape.

5 Spoon the chocolate mixture into a large
piping bag and sandwich the meringues
together in pairs, reserving a small amount
of filling for assembling the gâteau.

6 Arrange the filled meringues on a
serving platter, piling them up in a
pyramid. Keep them in position with a few
well-placed dabs of the reserved filling.
Dust the pyramid with icing sugar, sprinkle
with the rose petals and serve at once,
while the meringues are crisp.

CARIBBEAN CHOCOLATE RING <u>WITH</u> RUM SYRUP

SERVES 8–10

- 115g/4oz/½ cup unsalted (sweet) butter
- 115g/4oz/¾ cup light muscovado (brown) sugar
- 2 eggs, beaten
- 2 ripe bananas, mashed
- 30ml/2 tbsp desiccated (dry unsweetened shredded) coconut
- 30ml/2 tbsp sour cream
- 115g/4oz/1 cup self-raising (self-rising) flour
- 45ml/3 tbsp cocoa powder
- 2.5ml/½ tsp bicarbonate of soda (baking soda)

For the Syrup

- 115g/4oz/½ cup caster (superfine) sugar
- 30ml/2 tbsp dark rum
- 50g/2oz plain (semisweet) chocolate, chopped

To Decorate

- a mixture of tropical fruits
- chocolate shapes or curls

1 Preheat the oven to 180°C/350°F/Gas 4. Grease a 1.5 litre/2½ pint/6¼ cup ring tin (pan) with butter.

2 Cream the butter and muscovado sugar in a bowl until light and fluffy. Add the eggs gradually, beating well, then mix in the mashed bananas, desiccated coconut and sour cream.

3 Sift the flour, cocoa powder and bicarbonate of soda gradually over the mixture until thoroughly and evenly folded in.

4 Tip the mixture into the prepared tin and spread evenly. Place in the preheated oven and bake for 45–50 minutes, until firm to the touch. Remove from the oven and allow to cool for 10 minutes in the tin, then turn out onto a wire rack and leave to cool completely.

5 For the syrup, place the sugar in a small pan. Add 60ml/4 tbsp water and heat gently, stirring until dissolved. Bring to the boil and boil rapidly, without stirring, for 2 minutes. Remove from the heat.

6 Add the rum and chocolate to the syrup and stir until the mixture is melted and smooth, then spoon evenly over the top and sides of the cake.

7 Decorate the ring with tropical fruits and chocolate shapes or curls.

STRAWBERRY CHOCOLATE VALENTINE GATEAU

SERVES 8

175g/6oz/1½ cups self-raising
  (self-rising) flour
10ml/2 tsp baking powder
75ml/5 tbsp cocoa powder
115g/4oz/½ cup caster
  (superfine) sugar
2 eggs, beaten
15ml/1 tbsp black treacle (molasses)
150ml/¼ pint/⅔ cup sunflower oil
150ml/¼ pint/⅔ cup milk

For the Filling

45ml/3 tbsp strawberry jam
150ml/¼ pint/⅔ cup
  whipping cream
115g/4oz strawberries, sliced

To Decorate

1 quantity Chocolate Fondant
chocolate hearts
icing (confectioners') sugar,
  for dusting

1 Preheat the oven to 160°C/325°F/Gas 3. Grease a deep 20cm/8in heart-shaped cake tin (pan) and line the base with baking parchment. Sift the self-raising flour, baking powder and cocoa powder into a large mixing bowl. Stir in the sugar, and then make a good-sized well in the centre of the dry ingredients.

2 Add the beaten eggs, treacle (molasses), sunflower oil and milk to the well. Mix with a spoon to incorporate the dry ingredients, then beat with a hand-held electric mixer until the mixture is smooth and creamy.

3 Spoon the mixture into the prepared cake tin and spread evenly. Place in the preheated oven and bake for about 45 minutes, until well risen and firm to the touch. Remove from the oven and cool in the tin for a few minutes' then turn out on to a wire rack to cool completely.

4 Using a sharp knife, slice the cake neatly into two layers. Place the bottom layer on a board or plate. Spread with the strawberry jam.

5 Whip the cream in a bowl. Stir in the strawberries, then spread over the jam. Top with the remaining cake layer. Roll out the chocolate fondant and cover the cake. Decorate with chocolate hearts and dust with icing sugar.

COOK'S TIP

If you do not have a heart-shaped cake tin, consider hiring one from a kitchen shop. All sorts of sizes are available, often for a modest fee.

DOUBLE HEART ENGAGEMENT CAKE

SERVES 20

double quantity One-mix Chocolate
Sponge mixture
double quantity Vanilla Buttercream
icing (confectioners') sugar, for sifting
chocolate curls and fresh raspberries,
to decorate

VARIATIONS

Use plain buttercream, tinted to a
delicate shade of rose. Decorate with
strawberries, half-dipped in melted
chocolate.

Cover the cakes with Chocolate
Ganache and drizzle melted chocolate
over the top. Arrange chocolate-dipped
fruit on top.

Cover both the cakes with Chocolate
Fondant and top with pale apricot or
cream sugar roses and chocolate
leaves. Trim each cake with a narrow
apricot or cream ribbon.

1 Preheat the oven to 160°C/325°F/Gas 3.
Grease and base-line two 20cm/8in heart-
shaped cake tins (pans). Divide the one-
mix chocolate sponge cake mixture evenly
between the tins and smooth the surfaces.
Bake for 30 minutes, or until firm to the
touch. Turn on to a wire rack, peel off the
lining paper and leave to cool.

2 Cut each cake in half horizontally. Use
about one-third of the buttercream to fill
both cakes, then sandwich them together
to make two. Cover the tops of the cakes
with buttercream.

3 Arrange on a cake board. Use the
remaining icing to coat the sides of the
cakes. Ensure they are thickly covered.

4 Generously cover the tops and sides
of both the cakes with the chocolate curls,
beginning from the top of the heart and
arranging them as shown, and pressing
them gently into the buttercream.

5 Dust a little icing sugar over the top of
each cake and decorate with raspberries.
Chill until ready to serve.

WHITE CHOCOLATE CELEBRATION CAKE

SERVES 40–50

900g/2lb/8 cups plain (all-purpose) flour
2.5ml/½ tsp salt
20ml/4 tsp bicarbonate of soda
  (baking soda)
450g/1lb white chocolate, chopped
475ml/16fl oz/2 cups whipping cream
450g/1lb/2 cups unsalted (sweet)
  butter, softened
900g/2lb/4 cups caster
  (superfine) sugar
12 eggs
20ml/4 tsp lemon essence (extract)
grated rind of 2 lemons
335ml/11fl oz/1⅓ cups buttermilk
lemon curd, for filling
chocolate leaves, to decorate
For the Lemon Syrup
200g/7oz/scant 1 cup granulated sugar
250ml/8fl oz/1 cup water
60ml/4 tbsp lemon juice
For the Buttercream
675g/1½lb white chocolate, chopped
1kg/2¼lb cream cheese, softened
500g/1¼lb/2½ cups unsalted (sweet)
  butter, at room temperature
60ml/4 tbsp lemon juice
5ml/1 tsp lemon essence (extract)

1 Divide all the ingredients into two equal batches. Use each batch to make one cake. Preheat the oven to 180°C/350°F/Gas 4. Grease and base-line a 30cm/12in round cake tin (pan). Sift the flour, salt and bicarbonate of soda into a bowl and set aside. Melt the chocolate and cream in a pan over a medium heat, stirring until smooth. Set aside to cool.

> **VARIATION**
>
> For a summer celebration, decorate the cake with raspberries and white chocolate petals. To make the petals, you will need about 20 x 7.5cm/3in foil squares. Spread melted white chocolate thinly over each square, like a rose petal. Before it sets, bend the foil up to emphasize the petal shape. When set, peel away the foil.

2 Beat the butter until creamy, then add the sugar and beat for 2–3 minutes. Beat in the eggs, then slowly beat in the melted chocolate, lemon essence and rind. Gradually add the flour mixture, alternately with the buttermilk, to make a smooth pouring mixture. Pour into the tin and bake for 1 hour or until a skewer inserted in the cake comes out clean.

3 Cool in the tin for 10 minutes, then invert the cake onto a wire rack to cool. Wrap in clear film (plastic wrap) until ready to assemble. Make another cake with the second batch.

4 Make the lemon syrup. In a small pan, combine the sugar and water, bring to the boil, stirring until the sugar dissolves. Remove from the heat, stir in the lemon juice and cool. Store in an airtight container until required.

5 For the buttercream, melt then cool the chocolate. Beat the cream cheese. Beat in the chocolate, then the butter, lemon juice and essence. Chill.

6 Split each cake in half. Spoon syrup over each layer, let it soak in, then repeat. Spread the bottom half of each cake with lemon curd and replace the tops.

7 Gently beat the buttercream in a bowl until creamy. Spread a quarter over the top of one of the filled cakes. Place the second filled cake on top. Spread a small amount of softened butter over the top and sides of the cake to create a smooth, crumb-free surface. Chill for 15 minutes, so that the buttercream sets a little.

8 Place the cake on a serving plate. Set aside a quarter of the remaining buttercream for piping, then spread the rest evenly over the top and sides of the filled cake.

9 Spoon the reserved buttercream into a large icing bag fitted with a small star tip. Pipe a shell pattern around the rim of the cake. Decorate with chocolate leaves, made with dark (bittersweet) or white chocolate and fresh flowers.

CHOCOLATE BOX WITH CARAMEL MOUSSE AND BERRIES

SERVES 8–10

275g/10oz plain (semisweet) chocolate, chopped into small pieces

For the Caramel Mousse

4 x 50g/2oz chocolate-coated caramel bars, coarsely chopped

25ml/1½ tbsp milk or water

350ml/12fl oz/1½ cups double (heavy) cream

1 egg white

For the Caramel Shards

115g/4oz/½ cup granulated sugar

60ml/4 tbsp water

For the Topping

115g/4oz fine quality white chocolate, chopped into small pieces

350ml/12fl oz/1½ cups double (heavy) cream

450g/1lb mixed berries or cut up fruits such as raspberries, strawberries, blackberries, nectarines or oranges

1 Prepare the chocolate box. Turn a 23cm/9in square baking tin (pan) bottom-side up. Mould a piece of foil around the tin, then turn it right side up and line it with the foil, pressing against the edges to make the foil as smooth as possible.

2 Place the plain chocolate in a heatproof bowl over a pan of simmering water. Stir until melted. Immediately pour the chocolate into the tin. Tilt to coat the base and sides evenly, keeping the top edges of the sides as straight as possible. Chill until firm.

3 Place the caramel bars and milk or water in a heatproof bowl. Place over a pan of simmering water and stir until melted. Remove from the heat and cool for 10 minutes, stirring occasionally.

4 Using a hand-held electric mixer, whip the cream in a bowl until soft peaks form. Stir a spoonful of the whipped cream into the caramel mixture to lighten it, then fold in the remaining cream. In another bowl, beat the egg white until just stiff. Fold the egg white into the mousse mixture. Pour into the box. Chill for several hours or overnight, until set.

5 Meanwhile, make the caramel shards. Lightly oil a baking sheet. In a small pan over a low heat, dissolve the sugar in the water, swirling the pan gently. Increase the heat and boil the mixture for 4–5 minutes, until the sugar begins to turn a pale golden colour. Protecting your hand with an oven glove, immediately pour the mixture on to the oiled sheet. Tilt the sheet to distribute the caramel in an even layer. (Do not touch – caramel is dangerously hot.) Cool completely, then using a palette knife (metal spatula), lift the caramel off the baking sheet and break into pieces.

6 Make the topping. Combine the white chocolate and 120ml/4fl oz/½ cup of the cream in a small pan and melt over a low heat until smooth, stirring frequently. Strain into a medium bowl and cool to room temperature, stirring occasionally. In another bowl, beat the remaining cream with a hand-held electric mixer, until firm peaks form. Stir a spoonful of cream into the white chocolate mixture, then gently fold in the remaining whipped cream.

7 Remove the mousse-filled box from the tin and peel the foil carefully from the sides, then the base. Slide the box gently on to a serving plate.

8 Spoon the chocolate-cream mixture into a piping (pastry) bag fitted with a medium star tip. Pipe a decorative design of rosettes or shells over the surface of the set mousse. Decorate the chocolate box with the mixed berries or cut up fruits and the caramel shards.

PORCUPINE

SERVES 15

1 quantity One-mix Chocolate Sponge
  Cake
1½ quantity Chocolate Buttercream
5–6 chocolate flake bars
60g/2oz white marzipan
cream, black, green, red and brown
  food colourings
9 cocktail sticks

1 Preheat the oven to 180°C/350°F/Gas 4. Grease and line the bases of a 900ml/ 1½ pint/3¾ cup and a 600ml/1 pint/ 2½ cup ovenproof bowl. Spoon the cake mixture into both bowls to two-thirds full. Bake in the oven, allowing 55–60 minutes for the larger bowl and 35–40 minutes for the smaller bowl. Turn out on to a wire rack to cool.

2 When they are completely cool, place both cakes on a surface so the widest ends are underneath. Take the smaller cake and, holding a sharp knife at an angle, slice off a piece from one side, cutting down towards the middle of the cake. Then make a corresponding cut on the other side to make a pointed nose shape at one end.

3 Place the larger cake on a cake board behind the smaller one. Cut one of the cut-off slices in half and position either side, between the larger and smaller cake, to fill in the side gaps. Place the other cut-off piece on top to fill in the top gap, securing it all with a little buttercream.

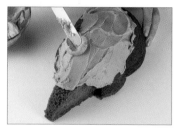

4 Spread the remaining buttercream over the cake. On the pointed face part, make markings with a cocktail stick (toothpick).

5 Break the flake bars into thin strips and stick into the buttercream over the body to represent spikes.

6 Reserve a small portion of marzipan. Divide the remainder into three and colour black, green and cream. Colour a tiny portion of the reserved marzipan brown for the apple stems.

7 Shape the ears and feet from cream marzipan. Make black and white eyes, and black nose and claws. With the green marzipan make the apples, painting on red markings with a fine paintbrush. Position the stems. Place everything except the apples in its proper place on the porcupine cake. Finally, place the apples on the board by the front of the porcupine.

HOT
DESSERTS

Hot chocolate desserts appeal to everyone who
craves comforting food — the sweet smell of
warm chocolate from a Peachy Chocolate Bake
as it cooks is hard to resist, and just the sight
of proper desserts like Chocolate Chip and
Banana Pudding will warm a winter's day.
But if you're looking for something a little
special for a dinner party, offer slices of crisp,
spiced Chocolate, Date and Almond Filo Coil
or luscious poached pears swathed in Chocolate
Fudge Blankets.

CHOCOLATE CINNAMON CAKE <u>WITH</u> BANANA SAUCE

A SPICY CHOCOLATE CAKE IS SERVED WITH WITH A WARM BANANA SAUCE TO COMBINE TWO FLAVOURS THAT COMPLIMENT EACH OTHER TO PERFECTION.

5 Fold a dollop of egg whites into the chocolate mixture to lighten it. Fold in the remaining whites in three batches, alternating with the sifted flour mixture.

6 Pour the mixture into the tin. Bake for 40–50 minutes, or until a skewer inserted in the centre comes out clean. Turn out on to a wire rack. Preheat the grill (broiler).

7 Make the sauce. Slice the bananas into a shallow, flameproof dish. Stir in the brown sugar and lemon juice. Place under the grill for 8 minutes, stirring occasionally, until caramelized. Mash the banana mixture until almost smooth. Tip into a bowl and stir in the cream and rum, if using. Slice the cake and serve with the sauce.

SERVES 6
  25g/1oz plain (semisweet) chocolate, chopped into small pieces
  115g/4oz/½ cup unsalted (sweet) butter, at room temperature
  15ml/1 tbsp instant coffee powder
  5 eggs, separated
  225g/8oz/1 cup granulated sugar
  115g/4oz/1 cup plain (all-purpose) flour
  10ml/2 tsp ground cinnamon
For the Sauce
  4 ripe bananas
  45ml/3 tbsp soft light brown sugar
  15ml/8oz/1 tbsp fresh lemon juice
  175ml/6fl oz/¾ cup whipping cream
  15ml/1 tbsp rum (optional)

1 Preheat the oven to 180°C/350°F/Gas 4. Grease a 20cm/8in round cake tin (pan).

2 Melt the chocolate with the butter in a double boiler or heatproof bowl over a pan of simmering water. Remove from the heat, stir in the coffee and set aside.

3 Beat the egg yolks with the granulated sugar until thick and lemon-coloured. Add the chocolate mixture and beat on low speed until just blended.

4 Stir the flour and cinnamon together in a bowl. In another bowl, beat the egg whites until they hold stiff peaks.

RICH CHOCOLATE AND COFFEE PUDDING

SERVES 6

75g/3oz/¾ cup plain (all-purpose) flour
10ml/2 tsp baking powder
a pinch of salt
50g/2oz/¼ cup butter
25g/1oz plain (semisweet) chocolate,
 chopped into small pieces
115g/4oz/½ cup caster (superfine) sugar
75ml/3fl oz/5 tbsp milk
1.5ml/¼ tsp vanilla essence (extract)
whipped cream, to serve

For the Topping

30ml/2 tbsp instant coffee powder
325ml/11fl oz/generous ½ pint hot water
90g/3½oz/7 tbsp soft dark brown sugar
65g/2½oz/5 tbsp caster (superfine) sugar
30ml/2 tbsp unsweetened cocoa powder

1 Preheat the oven to 180°C/350°F/Gas 4. Grease a 23cm/9in square non-stick baking tin (pan).

2 Sift the flour, baking powder and salt into a bowl. Set aside.

3 Melt the butter, chocolate and sugar in a double boiler or in a bowl set over a pan of simmering water, stirring occasionally. Remove the bowl from the heat.

4 Add the flour mixture and stir well. Stir in the milk and vanilla essence. Mix with a wooden spoon, then pour the mixture into the prepared baking tin.

5 Make the topping. Dissolve the coffee in the water in a bowl. Allow to cool.

5 Mix the sugars and cocoa in a bowl then sprinkle over the pudding mixture.

6 Pour the coffee evenly over the surface. Bake for 40 minutes, or until the pudding is risen and set on top. The coffee mixture will have formed a delicious creamy sauce underneath. Serve immediately with whipped cream.

HOT CHOCOLATE CAKE

MAKES 10–12 SLICES

200g/7oz/1¾ cups self-raising
   wholemeal (self-rising whole-wheat) flour
25g/1oz/¼ cup cocoa powder
a pinch of salt
175g/6oz/¾ cup soft margarine
175g/6oz/1 cup soft light brown sugar
a few drops of vanilla essence (extract)
4 eggs
75g/3oz white chocolate,
   roughly chopped
chocolate leaves and curls, to decorate
For the White Chocolate Sauce
75g/3oz white chocolate, chopped
150ml/¼ pint/⅔ cup single (light) cream
30–45ml/2–3 tbsp milk

1 Preheat the oven to 160°C/325°F/Gas 3. Sift the flour, cocoa and salt into a bowl, then tip in the bran remaining in the sieve. Cream the margarine, sugar and vanilla essence until light and fluffy, then gently beat in 1 egg.

2 Gradually stir in the remaining eggs, one at a time, alternately with the flour mixture, to make a smooth mixture.

3 Stir in the white chocolate and spoon into a 675–900g/1½–2lb loaf tin (pan) or an 18cm/7in greased cake tin (pan). Bake for 30–40 minutes or until just firm to the touch.

4 To make the sauce, heat the chocolate and cream very gently in a pan until the chocolate is melted. Off the heat, add the milk and stir until cool. Spoon a little sauce on to each plate and add a slice of cake. Decorate with chocolate leaves and curls. Do this just before you are ready to serve.

STEAMED CHOCOLATE <u>AND</u> FRUIT PUDDINGS <u>WITH</u> CHOCOLATE SYRUP

SERVES 4

115g/4oz/⅔ cup muscovado (molasses) sugar
1 eating apple
75g/3oz/¾ cup cranberries
115g/4oz/½ cup soft margarine
2 eggs
115g/4oz/½ cup self-raising flour
45ml/3 tbsp cocoa powder

For the Chocolate Syrup

115g/4oz plain (semisweet) chocolate
30ml/2 tbsp clear honey
15ml/½oz/1 tbsp unsalted butter
2.5ml/½ tsp vanilla essence (extract)

1 Prepare a steamer or half-fill a pan with water and bring it to the boil. Grease four individual ovenproof bowls and sprinkle each one with a little of the muscovado sugar to coat well all over.

2 Peel and core the apple. Dice it into a bowl, add the cranberries and mix well. Divide the fruit among the prepared bowls.

3 Place the remaining muscovado sugar in a mixing bowl. Add the margarine, eggs, flour and cocoa. Beat mixture until smooth.

4 Spoon the mixture into the bowls and cover each with a double thickness of foil. Steam for about 45 minutes until the puddings are well risen and firm.

5 Make the syrup. Chop and mix the chocolate with the honey, butter and vanilla essence in a small saucepan. Heat gently, stirring until melted and smooth.

6 Run a knife around the edge of each pudding to loosen, then turn each out on to a plate. Serve at once, with the syrup.

CHOCOLATE, DATE <u>AND</u> WALNUT PUDDING

SERVES 4

25g/1oz/¼ cup chopped walnuts
25g/1oz/2 tbsp chopped dates
2 eggs, separated
5ml/1 tsp vanilla essence (extract)
30ml/2 tbsp caster (superfine) sugar
45ml/3 tbsp plain wholemeal
  (all-purpose whole-wheat) flour
15ml/1 tbsp cocoa powder
30ml/2 tbsp skimmed milk

1 Preheat the oven to 180°C/350°F/Gas 4. Grease and base-line a 1.2 litre/2 pint/ 5 cup ovenproof bowl with baking parchment. Spoon in the chopped walnuts and dates.

2 Combine the egg yolks, vanilla essence and golden caster sugar in a heatproof bowl. Place the bowl over a pan of hot water, making sure that the water is not touching the base of the bowl.

3 Whisk the egg whites until softly peaking. Using a hand-held electric whisk, whisk the egg yolk mixture until it is thick and pale, then remove the bowl from the heat. Sift the flour and cocoa over the mixture and fold them in with a metal spoon. Stir in the milk, to soften the mixture, then fold in the egg whites.

4 Spoon the mixture over the walnuts and dates in the ovenproof bowl and bake for 40–45 minutes, or until the pudding is well risen and firm to the touch. Run a knife around the pudding to loosen it from the bowl, and then turn it out on to a plate and serve immediately.

MAGIC CHOCOLATE MUD PUDDING

SERVES 4

50g/2oz/4 tbsp butter, plus extra
  for greasing
90g/3½oz/scant 1 cup self-raising
  (self-rising) flour
5ml/1 tsp ground cinnamon
75ml/5 tbsp cocoa powder
200g/7oz/generous 1 cup light
  muscovado (brown) sugar
475ml/16fl oz/2 cups milk

1 Preheat the oven to 180°C/350°F/Gas 4. Prepare the dish: use the extra butter to grease a 1.5 litre/2½ pint/6¼ cup ovenproof dish. Place the dish on a baking sheet and set aside.

2 Sift together the flour and cinnamon with 15ml/1 tbsp of the cocoa. Mix well.

3 Gently heat the butter, 115g/4oz/½ cup of the sugar and 150ml/¼ pint/⅔ cup of the milk. When the butter has melted and all the sugar has dissolved, remove the pan from the heat.

4 Stir in the flour mixture, mixing evenly. Pour the mixture into the prepared dish and level the surface.

5 Mix the remaining sugar and cocoa in a bowl, then sprinkle over the pudding mixture.

6 Pour the remaining milk evenly over the pudding.

7 Bake for 45–50 minutes or until risen and firm. Serve hot, with crème fraîche, yogurt or ice cream, if liked.

CHOCOLATE CHIP <u>AND</u> BANANA PUDDING

SERVES 4

200g/7oz/1¾ cups self-raising
(self-rising) flour
75g/3oz/6 tbsp unsalted margarine
2 ripe bananas
75g/3oz/6 tbsp caster (superfine) sugar
60ml/4 tbsp milk
1 egg, beaten
60ml/4 tbsp plain (semisweet)
chocolate chips or chopped chocolate
Glossy Chocolate Sauce, to serve

1 Half-fill a pan with water and bring to
the boil. Grease a 1 litre/1¾ pint/4 cup
ovenproof bowl. Sift the flour and rub in
the margarine until the mixture resembles
coarse breadcrumbs.

2 Mash the bananas. Stir into the flour
mixture. Stir in the sugar.

3 Whisk the milk with the egg in a jug
(pitcher) or small bowl, then beat into the
pudding mixture. Stir in the chocolate
chips or chopped chocolate.

4 Spoon into the bowl, cover with a
double thickness of foil, and steam for
2 hours. Top up the water if needed.

5 Run a knife around the top of the
pudding to loosen it, then turn it out on to
a serving dish. Serve hot, with the sauce.

DARK CHOCOLATE RAVIOLI <u>WITH</u> WHITE CHOCOLATE <u>AND</u> CREAM CHEESE FILLING

SERVES 4

175g/6oz/1½ cups plain (all-purpose) flour
25g/1oz/¼ cup cocoa powder
salt
30ml/2 tbsp icing (confectioners') sugar
2 large eggs, beaten
15ml/1tbsp olive oil
single (light) cream and grated
    chocolate, to serve

For the Filling

175g/6oz white chocolate, chopped
350g/12oz/3 cups cream cheese
1 egg, plus 1 beaten egg to seal

1 Make the pasta. Sift the flour with the cocoa, salt and icing sugar on to a work surface. Make a well in the centre and pour the eggs and oil in. Mix with your fingers, then knead until smooth. Cover and rest for at least 30 minutes.

2 For the filling, melt the white chocolate in a bowl set over a pan of simmering water. Cool slightly. Beat the cream cheese in a separate bowl, then beat in the chocolate and egg. Spoon into a piping bag fitted with a plain nozzle.

3 Cut the pasta dough in half and wrap one portion in clear film (plastic wrap). Roll the it out thinly to a rectangle on a lightly floured surface, or use a pasta machine. Cover with a clean damp dishtowel. Repeat.

4 Pipe small mounds (about 5ml/1 tsp) of filling in rows, spaced at 4cm/1½in intervals across one piece of the dough. Brush the spaces of dough between the mounds with the beaten egg.

5 Using a rolling pin, lift the remaining sheet of pasta over the dough with the filling. Press down firmly between the pockets of filling, pushing out any trapped air. Cut the filled chocolate pasta into rounds with a serrated ravioli cutter or sharp knife, then transfer to a floured dishtowel. Leave for 1 hour to dry out, ready for cooking.

6 Bring a frying pan of water to the boil and add the ravioli a few at a time, stirring to prevent them sticking together. (Adding a few drops of a bland cooking oil to the water will help, too.) Simmer gently for 3–5 minutes, remove with a slotted spoon and keep warm while you cook the rest. Serve with a generous splash of single cream and grated chocolate.

HOT MOCHA RUM SOUFFLES

SERVES 6

25g/1oz/2 tbsp unsalted (sweet) butter, melted
65g/2½oz/generous ½ cup cocoa powder
75g/3oz/6 tbsp caster (superfine) sugar
60ml/4 tbsp strong black coffee
30ml/2 tbsp dark rum
6 egg whites
icing (confectioners') sugar, for dusting

1 Preheat the oven to 190°C/375°F/Gas 5 and heat a baking sheet. Butter six 250ml/8fl oz/1 cup soufflé dishes. Mix 15ml/ 1 tbsp of the cocoa powder with 15ml/1 tbsp of the caster sugar. Tip into each dish to coat evenly.

2 Mix the remaining cocoa powder with the coffee and rum. Whisk the egg whites in a clean, grease-free bowl until they form firm peaks. Whisk in the remaining caster sugar. Stir a generous spoonful of the whites into the cocoa mixture to lighten it, then fold in the remaining whites.

3 Spoon the mixture into the prepared dishes, smoothing the tops. Place on the hot baking sheet and bake for 12–15 minutes, or until well risen. Serve immediately, dusted with icing sugar.

EASY CHOCOLATE ᴬᴺᴰ ORANGE SOUFFLES

SERVES 4

600ml/1 pint/2½ cups milk
50g/2oz/generous ¼ cup semolina
50g/2oz/⅓ cup soft light brown sugar
grated rind of 1 orange
90ml/6 tbsp fresh orange juice
3 eggs, separated
65g/2½oz plain (semisweet) chocolate, grated
icing (confectioners') sugar, for dusting
single (light) cream, to serve

1 Preheat the oven to 200°C/400°F/Gas 6. Butter a shallow 1.75 litre/3 pint/7½ cup ovenproof dish.

2 Pour the milk into a heavy pan, sprinkle over the semolina and sugar, then heat, stirring, until boiling and thickened. Cool slightly, then beat in the orange rind and juice, egg yolks and all but 15ml/1 tbsp of the grated chocolate.

3 In a clean, grease-free bowl, whisk the egg whites until stiff but not dry, then lightly fold into the semolina mixture in three batches. Spoon the mixture into the dish. Place the dish on the baking sheet and bake for about 30 minutes, until just set in the centre and risen. Dust the top with icing sugar and sprinkle over the reserved chocolate. Serve with cream.

CHOCOLATE AMARETTI PEACHES

SERVES 4

115g/4oz amaretti biscuits, crushed
50g/2oz plain (semisweet)
  chocolate, chopped
grated rind of ½ orange
15ml/1 tbsp clear honey
1.5ml/¼ tsp ground cinnamon
1 egg white, lightly beaten
4 firm ripe peaches
150ml/¼ pint/⅔ cup white wine
15ml/1 tbsp caster (superfine) sugar
whipped cream, to serve

1 Preheat the oven to 190°C/375°F/Gas 5.
Mix together the biscuits (cookies),
chocolate, orange rind, honey and
cinnamon. Add the egg white and mix well.

2 Halve and stone (pit) the peaches. Fill
the cavities with the chocolate mixture.

3 Arrange the stuffed peaches in a lightly
buttered, shallow ovenproof dish, which
will just hold the peaches comfortably. Mix
the wine and sugar in a jug (pitcher).

4 Pour the wine mixture around the
peaches. Bake for 30–40 minutes, until
the peaches are tender when tested with a
slim metal skewer and the filling is golden.
Serve at once with a little of the cooking
juices spooned over. Offer the whipped
cream separately.

PEACHY CHOCOLATE BAKE

SERVES 6

200g/7oz dark (bittersweet) chocolate,
chopped into small pieces
115g/4oz/½ cup unsalted (sweet) butter
4 eggs, separated
115g/4oz/½ cup caster
(superfine) sugar
425g/15oz can peach slices, drained
whipped cream, to serve

1 Preheat the oven to 160°C/325°F/Gas 3.
Butter a wide ovenproof dish. Melt the
chocolate with the butter in a heatproof
bowl set over barely simmering water.

2 Whisk the egg yolks with the sugar until
thick and pale. In a clean, grease-free
bowl, whisk the whites until stiff.

3 Beat the chocolate into the egg yolk
mixture. Lightly fold in the whites.

4 Fold the peach slices into the mixture,
then tip into the prepared dish. Bake for
35–40 minutes, or until risen and just firm
to the touch. Serve while still hot, with
whipped cream.

PUFFY PEARS

SERVES 4

225g/8oz puff pastry, thawed if frozen

2 pears, peeled

2 squares plain (semisweet) chocolate, roughly chopped

15ml/1 tbsp lemon juice

1 egg, beaten

15ml/1 tbsp caster (superfine) sugar

1 Roll the pastry into a 25cm/10in square on a lightly floured surface. Trim the edges, then cut it into four equal smaller squares. Cover with clear film (plastic wrap) and set aside.

2 Remove the core from each pear half and pack the cavity with the chopped chocolate. Place a pear half, cut-side down, on each piece of pastry and brush them with the lemon juice.

3 Preheat the oven to 190°C/375°F/Gas 5. Cut the pastry into a pear shape, leaving a 2.5cm/1in border. Use the trimmings to make leaves and brush the pastry border with the beaten egg. Arrange the pastry and pears on a baking sheet. Make deep cuts in the pears, taking care not to cut right through the fruit, and sprinkle them with the sugar. Bake for 20–25 minutes, until lightly browned. Serve hot or cold.

> **VARIATION**
> Use apples instead of pears, if preferred. Cut the pastry into 10cm/4in rounds. Slice 2 peeled and cored eating apples. Toss with a little lemon juice, drain and arrange on the pastry. Dot with 25g/1oz/2 tbsp butter and chopped milk chocolate. Bake as for Puffy Pears. Brush the apple slices with warmed redcurrant jelly while they are still hot, and serve hot or leave to cool before serving.

PEARS IN CHOCOLATE FUDGE BLANKETS

SERVES 6

6 ripe pears

30ml/2 tbsp lemon juice

75g/3oz/6 tbsp caster (superfine) sugar

300ml/½ pint/1¼ cups water

1 cinnamon stick

For the Sauce

200ml/7fl oz/scant 1 cup double (heavy) cream

150g/5oz/scant 1 cup light muscovado (brown) sugar

25g/1oz/2tbsp unsalted (sweet) butter

25g/1oz/2 tbsp golden (light corn) syrup

120ml/4fl oz/½ cup milk

200g/7oz dark (bittersweet) chocolate, broken into squares

1 Peel the pears thinly, leaving the stalks on. Scoop out the cores from the base. Brush the cut surfaces with the lemon juice to prevent them from browning.

2 Place the sugar and water in a large pan. Heat gently until the sugar dissolves. Add the pears and cinnamon. Add more water, if needed, so the pears are almost covered.

3 Bring to the boil, lower the heat, cover and simmer the pears gently for 15–20 minutes, or until they are just tender.

4 Meanwhile, make the sauce. Place the cream, sugar, butter, syrup and milk in a heavy pan. Heat gently until the sugar has dissolved and the butter and syrup have melted, then boil, stirring, for 5 minutes or until the sauce is thick. Off the heat gradually stir in the chocolate until melted.

5 Using a slotted spoon, transfer the poached pears to a dish. Keep hot. Boil the syrup rapidly to reduce to about 45–60ml/3–4 tbsp. Remove the cinnamon stick and stir the syrup into the chocolate sauce. Serve poured over the pears in individual bowls.

PRURE BEIGNETS <u>IN</u> CHOCOLATE ARMAGNAC SAUCE

<u>SERVES 4</u>

75g/3oz/¾ cup plain
(all-purpose) flour
45ml/3 tbsp ground almonds
45ml/3 tbsp oil or melted butter
1 egg white
60ml/4 tbsp water
oil, for deep frying
175g/6oz/1 cup ready-to-eat stoned
(pitted) prunes
45ml/3 tbsp vanilla sugar
15ml/1 tbsp cocoa powder

For the Sauce

200g/7oz milk chocolate, chopped
120ml/4fl oz/½ cup crème fraîche
30ml/2 tbsp Armagnac or brandy

1 Start by making the sauce. Melt the chocolate, remove from the heat, stir in the crème fraîche until smooth, then add the Armagnac or brandy. Replace the bowl over the water, off the heat, so that the sauce stays warm.

2 Beat the flour, almonds, oil or butter and egg white in a bowl, then beat in enough of the water to make a smooth thick batter.

3 Heat the oil for deep frying to 180°C/350°F, or until a cube of dried bread browns in 30–45 seconds. Dip the prunes into the batter and fry a few at a time until the beignets rise to the surface of the oil and are golden brown and crisp.

4 Remove each successive batch of beignets with a slotted spoon, drain on kitchen paper and keep hot. Mix the vanilla sugar and cocoa in a bowl or stout paper bag, add the drained beignets and toss well to coat. Serve in individual bowls, with the chocolate sauce poured over the top of each serving.

COOK'S TIPS

Vanilla sugar is sold commercially in many European countries but is very easy to make. Simply store a vanilla pod in a jar of granulated or caster sugar for a few weeks, until the sugar has taken on the vanilla flavour. Shake the jar occasionally. Used in cakes, biscuits (cookies) and puddings, vanilla sugar imparts a delicate flavour. If you do not have any vanilla sugar for tossing the beignets, use plain granulated or caster (superfine) sugar and add a pinch of ground cinnamon, if you like.

Serve the beignets soon after cooking, as they do not keep well.

Use stoned dates or dried apricots as a substitute for the prunes.

CHOCOLATE, DATE AND ALMOND FILO COIL

SERVES 6

275g/10oz pack filo pastry,
  thawed if frozen
50g/2oz/4 tbsp unsalted (sweet)
  butter, melted
icing (confectioners') sugar, cocoa powder
  and ground cinnamon, for dusting
For the Filling
75g/3oz/6 tbsp unsalted butter
115g/4oz dark (bittersweet) chocolate,
  chopped into small pieces
115g/4oz/1 cup ground almonds
115g/4oz/⅔ cup chopped dates
75g/3oz/½ cup icing
  (confectioners') sugar
10ml/2 tsp rose water
2.5ml/½ tsp ground cinnamon

1 Preheat the oven to 180°C/350°F/Gas 4.
Grease a 22cm/8½in round cake tin (pan).

2 Make the filling. Melt the butter with the
chocolate, then stir in the other ingredients
to make a paste. Leave to cool.

3 Lay 1 filo sheet on a work surface. Brush
with melted butter, then lay a second sheet
on top and brush with melted butter. Roll
some filling into a sausage and place on a
long edge of the filo. Roll the pastry tightly
around the filling.

4 Coil the roll into the tin. Make enough
rolls to fill the tin and fit them in place.

5 Brush the coil with melted butter. Bake
for 30–35 minutes, until the pastry is
golden brown and crisp.

6 Remove the coil from the tin and place
it on a plate. Serve warm, dusted with
icing sugar, cocoa and cinnamon.

CHOCOLATE ALMOND MERINGUE PIE

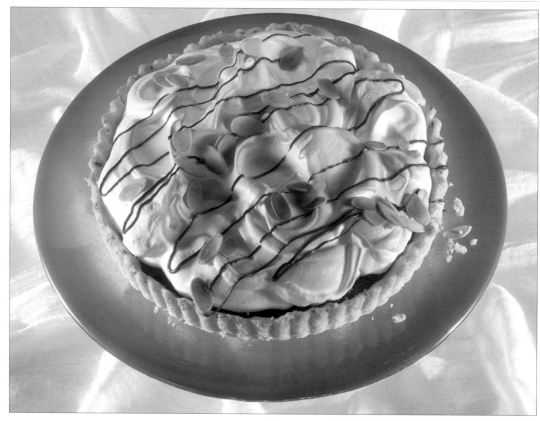

SERVES 6

175g/6oz/1½ cups plain (all-purpose) flour
50g/2oz/½ cup ground rice
150g/5oz/⅔ cup unsalted (sweet) butter
finely grated rind of 1 orange
1 egg yolk
flaked (sliced) almonds and melted dark
   (bittersweet) chocolate, to decorate
For the Filling
150g/5oz dark (bittersweet)
   chocolate, chopped
50g/2oz/4 tbsp unsalted (sweet)
   butter, softened
75g/3oz/6 tbsp caster (superfine) sugar
10ml/2 tsp cornflour (cornstarch)
4 egg yolks
75g/3oz/¾ cup ground almonds
For the Meringue
3 egg whites
150g/5oz/⅔ cup caster (superfine) sugar

1 Sift the flour and ground rice into a bowl. Rub in the butter until the mixture resembles breadcrumbs. Stir in the orange rind. Add the egg yolks and bring the dough together. Roll out and use to line a 23cm/9in round flan tin (tart pan). Chill.

2 Preheat the oven to 190°C/375°F/Gas 5. Prick the pastry case (pie shell), cover with baking parchment weighed down with baking beans and bake blind for 10 minutes.

3 Make the filling. Melt the chocolate, then cream the butter with the sugar in a bowl, and beat in the cornflour and egg yolks. Fold in the almonds, then the melted chocolate. Remove the paper and beans from the pastry case and add the filling. Bake for a further 10 minutes.

4 Make the meringue. Whisk the egg whites until stiff, then gradually whisk in half the sugar. Fold in the rest with a metal spoon.

5 Spoon the meringue over the filling, peaking it with the back of the spoon. Lower the oven to 180°C/350°F/Gas 4 and bake the pie for 15–20 minutes, or until the topping is pale gold. Serve warm, scattered with the almonds and drizzled with the melted chocolate.

CHOCOLATE PECAN PIE

SERVES 6

200g/7oz/1¾ cups plain
(all-purpose) flour
75ml/5 tbsp caster (superfine) sugar
90g/3½oz/scant ½ cup unsalted (sweet)
butter, softened
1 egg, beaten
finely grated rind of 1 orange

For the Filling

200g/7oz/¾ cup golden
(light corn) syrup
45ml/3 tbsp soft light muscovado
(brown) sugar
150g/5oz plain (semisweet) chocolate,
chopped into small pieces
50g/2oz/¼ cup butter
3 eggs, beaten
5ml/1 tsp vanilla essence
175g/6oz/1½ cups pecan nuts

1 Sift the flour and sugar into a bowl.
Work in the butter with your fingertips.
Beat the egg and orange rind and stir into
the flour mixture to make a firm dough.
Add water if needed. Knead, then roll out
the pastry. Line a deep, 20cm/8in loose-
based flan tin (pie pan). Chill.

2 Preheat the oven to 180°C/350°F/Gas 4.
Make the filling. Melt the syrup, sugar,
chocolate and butter in a small pan.

3 Off the heat, beat in the eggs and
vanilla. Sprinkle the pecan nuts into the
pastry case (pie shell), then pour over the
chocolate mixture.

4 Place the tin on a baking sheet and
bake the pie for 50–60 minutes, or until
the filling is set. Leave the pie in the tin
for 10 minutes, then remove the sides
to serve.

CHOCOLATE AND ORANGE SCOTCH PANCAKES

<u>SERVES 4</u>

115g/4oz/1 cup self-raising
  (self-rising) flour
30ml/2 tbsp cocoa powder
2 eggs
50g/2oz plain (semisweet) chocolate,
  chopped into small pieces
200ml/7fl oz/scant 1 cup milk
finely grated rind of 1 orange
30ml/2 tbsp orange juice
butter or oil, for frying
chocolate curls, to decorate

For the Sauce
2 large oranges
25g/1oz/2 tbsp unsalted (sweet) butter
45ml/3 tbsp light muscovado
  (brown) sugar
250ml/8fl oz/1 cup crème fraîche
30ml/2 tbsp Grand Marnier

1 Sift the flour and cocoa into a bowl and make a well in the centre. Add the eggs and beat well, gradually incorporating the dry ingredients until smooth.

2 Mix the chocolate and milk in a pan. Heat gently until the chocolate has melted, then beat into the mixture until smooth and bubbly. Stir in the orange rind and juice to make a batter.

3 Heat a large heavy frying pan or griddle. Grease with a little butter or oil. Drop large spoonfuls of batter on to the hot surface, leaving room for spreading. Cook over a moderate heat. When the pancakes are lightly browned underneath and bubbly on top, flip over to cook the other side. Slide on to a plate and keep hot, then make more in the same way.

4 For the sauce, finely grate the rind of 1 orange into a bowl and set aside. Peel both oranges, then slice fairly thinly.

5 Heat the butter and sugar in a wide, shallow pan over a low heat, stirring until the sugar dissolves. Stir in the crème fraîche and heat gently.

6 Add the pancakes and orange slices to the sauce, heat gently for 1–2 minutes, then spoon over the liqueur. Sprinkle with the reserved orange rind. Scatter over the chocolate curls and serve at once.

CHOCOLATE CHIP BANANA PANCAKES

MAKES 16

2 ripe bananas

2 eggs

200ml/7fl oz/scant 1 cup milk

150g/5oz/1¼ cups self-raising (self-rising) flour, sifted

25g/1oz/⅓ cup ground almonds

15ml/1tbsp caster (superfine) sugar

a pinch of salt

15ml/1tbsp plain (semisweet) chocolate chips

butter, for frying

150ml/¼ pint/⅔ cup double (heavy) cream

50g/2oz/½ cup toasted flaked almonds

1 Mash the bananas in a bowl. Beat in the eggs and half the milk. Mix in the flour, ground almonds, sugar and salt. Add the remaining milk and the chocolate chips.

2 Stir the mixture well until it makes a thick batter. Heat a knob (pat) of butter in a non-stick frying pan. Spoon the pancake mixture into heaps, allowing room for them to spread. When the pancakes are lightly browned underneath, flip them over to cook the other side. Slide on to a plate and keep hot, then make more pancakes.

3 For the topping whip the double (heavy) cream to soft peaks in a bowl. Spoon the cream on to the pancakes and decorate the cream topping with the flaked (sliced) almonds. Serve at once.

CHOCOLATE CREPES WITH PLUMS AND PORT

2 Meanwhile, make the filling. Halve and stone (pit) the plums. Place in a pan and add the sugar and water. Bring to the boil, then lower the heat, cover, and simmer for about 10 minutes or until the plums are tender. Stir in the port, taking care not to break up the plums, then simmer for a further 30 seconds. Remove from the heat and keep warm.

3 Have ready a sheet of baking parchment. Heat a crêpe pan, grease with a little oil, then pour in just enough batter to cover the base of the pan, swirling to coat the pan evenly. Cook until the crêpe has set, then flip it over to cook the other side. Slide the crêpe out on to the parchment, then cook more crêpes in the same way. It should not be necessary to add more oil to the pan, unless the crêpes start to stick.

SERVES 6

50g/2oz plain (semisweet) chocolate
200ml/7fl oz/scant 1 cup milk
120ml/4fl oz/½ cup single (light) cream
30ml/2 tbsp cocoa powder
115g/4oz/1 cup plain
  (all-purpose) flour
2 eggs
oil, for frying
For the Filling
500g/1¼lb red or golden plums
50g/2oz/¼ cup caster
  (superfine) sugar
30ml/2 tbsp water
30ml/2 tbsp port
150g/5oz/¾ cup crème fraîche
For the Sauce
150g/5oz plain (semisweet) chocolate
175ml/6fl oz/¾ cup double
  (heavy) cream
15ml/1 tbsp port

1 Make the crêpe batter. First chop the chocolate, then put it in a pan with the milk. Heat gently, stirring occasionally, until the chocolate has dissolved. Then pour the chocolate and milk mixture into a blender or food processor and add the cream, cocoa, flour and eggs. (If the blender or food processor is a small model, it may be necessary to do this in batches.) Process until completely smooth, then tip into a jug (pitcher) and chill in the refrigerator for at least 30 minutes.

4 For the sauce, chop the chocolate and heat with the cream, stirring until smooth. Add the port and stir in well.

5 Divide the plum filling equally among the crêpes, add a dollop of crème fraîche to each crêpe, then roll them up carefully. Serve in individual bowls, with the chocolate sauce spooned over the top of each portion.

RICH CHOCOLATE BRIOCHE BAKE

SERVES 4

40g/1½oz/3 tbsp unsalted (sweet)
butter, plus extra for greasing
200g/7oz plain (semisweet) chocolate,
chopped into small pieces
60ml/4 tbsp bitter marmalade
4 individual brioches, cut into halves,
or 1 large brioche loaf, cut into
thick slices
3 eggs
300ml/½ pint/1¼ cups milk
300ml/½ pint/1¼ cups single
(light) cream
30ml/2 tbsp demerara (raw) sugar

1 Preheat the oven to 180°C/350°F/Gas 4.
Butter a shallow ovenproof dish.

2 Melt the chocolate with the marmalade
and butter in a bowl set over just
simmering water. Stir until smooth.

3 Spread the melted chocolate mixture
over the brioche slices. Arrange them in
the dish so that the slices overlap.

4 Beat the eggs in a large bowl, then add
the milk and cream and mix well. Transfer
to a jug and pour evenly over the slices.
Sprinkle with the demerara sugar and
bake for 40–50 minutes, until the custard
has set lightly and the brioche slices are
golden brown. Serve hot.

CHOCOLATE SOUFFLE CREPES

MAKES 12 CREPES

75g/3oz/¾ cup plain (all-purpose) flour
15ml/1 tbsp cocoa powder
5ml/1 tsp caster (superfine) sugar
a pinch of salt
5ml/1 tsp ground cinnamon
2 eggs
175ml/6fl oz/¾ cup milk
5ml/1 tsp vanilla essence (extract)
50g/2oz/4 tbsp unsalted (sweet)
   butter, melted
raspberries, pineapple and mint sprigs,
   to decorate

For the Pineapple Syrup
½ pineapple, peeled, cored and
   finely chopped
120ml/4fl oz/½ cup water
30ml/2 tbsp natural maple syrup
5ml/1 tsp cornflour (cornstarch)
½ cinnamon stick
30ml/2 tbsp rum

For the Soufflé Filling
250g/9oz dark (bittersweet) chocolate,
   chopped into small pieces
75ml/3fl oz/⅓ cup double (heavy) cream
3 eggs, separated
25g/1oz/2 tbsp caster (superfine) sugar

1 Prepare the syrup. Put the pineapple, water, syrup, cornflour and cinnamon in a pan. Bring to the boil. Simmer until the sauce thickens, whisking frequently (this should take about 3 minutes). Remove from the heat and discard the cinnamon. Pour into a bowl, and stir in the rum. Cool, then chill.

CHOCOLATE FONDUE
Some gourmet shops sell ready-made crêpes, which will save time.

2 Prepare the crêpes. Sift the flour, cocoa, sugar, salt and cinnamon into a bowl. Make a well in the centre. Beat together the eggs, milk and vanilla, and gradually pour into the well, whisking in the dry ingredients from the side of the bowl to form a smooth batter. Stir in half the melted butter and pour into a jug (pitcher). Allow to stand for 1 hour.

3 Heat an 18–20cm/7–8in crêpe pan. Brush with butter. Stir the batter. Pour 45ml/3 tbsp batter into the pan, swirling the pan to cover the base. Cook over a medium-high heat for 1–2 minutes until the base is golden. Turn over and cook for 30–45 seconds, then turn on to a plate. Stack between sheets of baking parchment and set aside.

4 Prepare the filling. In a pan set over a medium heat, melt the chocolate and cream until smooth, stirring frequently.

5 In a bowl, using a hand-held electric mixer, beat the yolks with half the sugar for 3–5 minutes, until light and creamy. Gradually beat in the chocolate mixture. Allow to cool. In a separate bowl with cleaned beaters, beat the egg whites until soft peaks form. Gradually beat in the remaining sugar until stiff peaks form. Beat a large spoonful of whites into the chocolate mixture to lighten it, then fold in the remaining whites.

6 Preheat the oven to 200°C/400°F/Gas 6. Lay a crêpe on a plate. Spoon a little soufflé mixture on to the crêpe, spreading it to the edge. Fold the bottom half over the soufflé mixture, then fold in half again to form a filled triangle. Place on a buttered baking sheet using a fish slice (spatula). Repeat with the remaining crêpes. Brush the tops with melted butter and bake for 15–20 minutes, until the filling has souffléd. Decorate with raspberries, pineapple pieces and mint, and serve with the syrup.

VARIATION
For a simpler version of the crêpes, just serve with a spoonful of maple syrup rather than making the pineapple syrup.

CHOCOLATE ORANGE MARQUISE

SERVES 6–8

200g/7oz/scant 1 cup caster
  (superfine) sugar
60ml/4 tbsp fresh orange juice
350g/12oz dark (bittersweet) dark
  chocolate, chopped
225g/8oz/1 cup unsalted (sweet)
  butter, cubed
5 eggs
finely grated rind of 1 orange
45ml/3 tbsp plain (all-purpose) flour
icing (confectioners') sugar and
  strips of orange rind, to decorate

1 Preheat the oven to 180°C/350°F/Gas 4.
Grease and base-line a 23cm/9in round
cake tin (pan), 6cm/2½in deep. Place
115g/4oz/½ cup of the sugar in a pan. Add
the orange juice and stir over a gentle heat
until the sugar has dissolved.

2 Remove from the heat and stir in the
chocolate until melted. Add the butter,
cube by cube, until melted.

3 Whisk the eggs with the remaining
sugar in a large bowl until pale and very
thick. Add the orange rind. Then, using a
metal spoon, fold the chocolate mixture
lightly and evenly into the egg mixture.
Sift the flour over the top and fold in.

4 Scrape the mixture into the tin. Place in
a roasting pan, put in the oven, then pour
hot water into the roasting pan to halfway
up the sides of the cake tin.

5 Bake for about 1 hour or until the cake
is firm to the touch. Remove the cake tin
from the water bath and place on a wire
rack to cool for 15–20 minutes. To turn
out, invert the cake on to a baking sheet,
place a serving plate upside down on top,
then turn plate and baking sheet over to
transfer the cake to the plate.

6 Dust with icing sugar, decorate with
strips of pared orange rind and serve still
warm. This cake is wonderfully rich and
moist and really doesn't need an
accompaniment, but you could offer single
(light) cream, if you wish.

HOT CHOCOLATE ZABAGLIONE

SERVES 6

6 egg yolks
150g/5oz/⅔ cup caster (superfine) sugar
45ml/3 tbsp cocoa powder
200ml/7fl oz/scant 1 cup Marsala
cocoa powder, for dusting

2 Add the cocoa and Marsala, then place the bowl over the simmering water. Whisk with a hand-held electric mixer until the mixture is thick and foamy.

3 Pour quickly into tall heatproof glasses, dust lightly with cocoa and serve immediately with chocolate cinnamon tuiles or amaretti.

1 Half-fill a medium sized pan with water and bring to simmering point. Select a heatproof bowl that will fit over the pan and whisk the egg yolks and sugar in it until the mixture is pale and all the sugar has dissolved.

CHOCOLATE FONDUE

SERVES 4–6

225g/8oz plain (semisweet)
   chocolate, chopped
300ml/½ pint/1¼ cups double
   (heavy) cream
30ml/2 tbsp Grand Marnier
25g/1oz/2 tbsp butter, diced
cherries, strawberries, sliced
   bananas, mandarin segments and
   cubes of sponge cake, for dipping

1 Combine the chocolate, cream and Grand Marnier in a fondue pan or small heavy pan. Heat gently until melted, stirring frequently.

2 Arrange the fruit and cake for dipping on a large platter. Stir the butter into the fondue until melted. Place the fondue pot or pan over a lighted spirit burner.

3 Guests spear the items of their choice on fondue forks and swirl them in the dip until coated. Whoever loses a dipper has to pay a forfeit.

TARTS, PIES AND CHEESECAKES

Here you will find every sort of filling for
the most memorable pies, tarts, tortes and
cheesecakes; from orchard fruits to autumn
nuts, tangy citrus to a variety of dessert cheese
and, of course, luscious chocolate.
There can be few families who wouldn't leap
enthusiastically upon a rich Chocolate Pecan
Torte, or drool at the sight of a dripping slice of
Chocolate, Banana and Toffee Pie.
If cheesecakes are a family favourite, making
Raspberry, Mascarpone and White Chocolate
Cheesecake is well worth it for all the praise
you'll get!

GREEK CHOCOLATE MOUSSE TARTLETS

SERVES 6

1 quantity Chocolate Shortcrust Pastry
chocolate shapes, to decorate

For the Filling

200g/7oz white chocolate, chopped into
small pieces
120ml/4fl oz/½ cup milk
10ml/2 tsp powdered gelatine
30ml/2 tbsp caster (superfine) sugar
5ml/1 tsp vanilla essence (extract)
2 eggs, separated
250ml/8fl oz/1 cup Greek (US strained
plain) yogurt

1 Preheat the oven to 190°C/375°F/
Gas 5. Roll out the pastry and carefully
line six deep 10cm/4in loose-based flan
tins (tart pans).

2 Prick the pastry all over with a fork,
cover with baking parchment and weigh
down with baking beans. Bake blind for
10 minutes. Remove the baking beans and
parchment, return to the oven and bake
for a further 15 minutes. Cool in the tins.

3 Make the filling. Melt the chocolate.
Pour the milk into a pan, sprinkle over
the powdered gelatine and heat gently,
stirring until the gelatine has dissolved
completely. Remove from the heat and stir
in the chocolate.

4 Whisk the sugar, vanilla essence and
egg yolks in a large bowl, then beat in the
chocolate mixture. Beat in the yogurt until
evenly mixed.

5 Whisk the egg whites in a clean,
grease-free bowl until stiff, then fold into
the mixture. Divide among the pastry
cases (pie shells) and chill for 2–3 hours,
until set. Decorate with chocolate shapes
and dust with icing (confectioners') sugar,
if wished.

CHOCOLATE AND PINE NUT TART

SERVES 8

200g/7oz/1¾ cups plain
(all-purpose) flour
50g/2oz/¼ cup caster (superfine) sugar
a pinch of salt
grated rind of ½ orange
115g/4oz/½ cup unsalted (sweet)
butter, cut into small pieces
3 egg yolks, lightly beaten
15–30 ml/1–2 tbsp iced water

For the Filling

2 eggs
45ml/3 tbsp caster (superfine) sugar
grated rind of 1 orange
15ml/1 tbsp orange-flavoured liqueur
250ml/8fl oz/1 cup whipping cream
115g/4oz plain (semisweet) chocolate,
chopped into small pieces
75g/3oz/1 cup pine nuts, toasted

For the Decoration

1 orange
50g/2oz/¼ cup granulated sugar
120ml/4fl oz/½ cup water

1 In a food processor, process the flour, sugar, salt and orange rind. Add the butter and process for 20–30 seconds, until the mixture looks like coarse crumbs. Add the yolks and pulse until the dough begins to stick together. If the dough appears dry, add a little iced water until it just holds together. Knead gently, then wrap in clear film (plastic wrap). Chill for 2–3 hours or overnight.

2 Lightly grease a 23cm/9in loose-based tart tin (pan). Let the dough soften briefly, then roll out on a floured surface to a 28cm/11in round. Ease the dough into the tin and press the overhang down slightly with floured fingers to thicken the top edge.

3 Roll a rolling pin over the top edge to cut off the excess dough. Press the top edge against the tin to form a raised rim. Prick the base with a fork. Chill for 1 hour. Preheat the oven to 200°C/400°F/Gas 6. Line the pastry case (pie shell) with greaseproof (waxed) paper. Fill with baking beans, put in the oven and bake blind for 5 minutes. Lift out the paper and beans, then bake for 5 minutes more. Cool in the tin on a wire rack. Lower the oven to 180°C/350°F/Gas 4.

4 Prepare the filling. Beat the eggs, sugar, orange rind and liqueur in a bowl. Stir in the cream. Sprinkle the chocolate evenly over the base of the pastry case, then sprinkle with the pine nuts.

5 Gently pour the filling into the tart shell. Bake for 20–30 minutes, until the pastry is golden and the custard set. Cool slightly in the tin on a wire rack.

6 Prepare the decoration. Peel the orange thinly, avoiding the pith, then cut the rind into thin strips. Dissolve the sugar in the water in a pan over a medium heat, then add the orange rind. Boil for 5 minutes, until the syrup begins to caramelize. Off the heat, stir in 15ml/1 tbsp cold water to stop further cooking.

7 Brush the orange syrup over the tart and decorate with the caramelized strips. Remove the side of the tin and slide the tart on to a plate. Serve warm.

CHOCOLATE TRUFFLE TART

SERVES 12

115g/4oz/1 cup plain (all-purpose) flour
30g/1¼oz/⅓ cup cocoa powder
50g/2oz/¼ cup caster (superfine) sugar
2.5ml/½ tsp salt
115g/4oz/½ cup unsalted (sweet)
  butter, cut into pieces
1 egg yolk
15–30ml/1–2 tbsp iced water
25g/1oz fine quality white or milk
  chocolate, melted
whipped cream, to serve (optional)
For the Truffle Filling
350ml/12fl oz/1½ cups double
  (heavy) cream
350g/12oz couverture or fine quality
  dark (bittersweet) chocolate, chopped
50g/2oz/4 tbsp unsalted (sweet) butter,
  cut into small pieces
30ml/2 tbsp brandy or liqueur

1 Prepare the pastry. Sift the flour and cocoa into a bowl. In a food processor fitted with a metal blade, process the flour mixture with the sugar and salt. Add the butter and process for another 15–20 seconds, until the mixture resembles coarse breadcrumbs.

2 In a bowl, lightly beat the egg yolk with the iced water. Add to the flour mixture and pulse until the dough begins to stick together. Turn out on to clear film (plastic wrap) and shape the dough into a flat disc. Wrap, and then chill for 1–2 hours.

3 Grease a 23cm/9in loose-based tart tin (pan). Let the dough soften, then roll out between sheets of cling film (plastic wrap) to a 28cm/11in round, 5mm/¼in thick. Peel off the top sheet and invert the dough into a tart tin. Remove the base sheet. Ease the dough into the tin. Prick with a fork. Chill.

4 Preheat the oven to 180°C/350°F/Gas 4. Line the tart with foil and fill with baking beans. Bake blind for 5–7 minutes. Lift out the foil with the beans, return to the oven and bake for a further 5–7 minutes, until just set. Cool in the tin on a wire rack.

5 Prepare the filling. In a medium pan over a medium heat, bring the cream to the boil. Remove the pan from the heat and stir in the chocolate until melted and smooth. Stir in the butter and brandy or liqueur. Strain into the prepared pastry case (pie shell), tilting the tin to level the surface. Do not touch the surface of the filling or it will spoil the glossy finish.

6 Spoon the melted chocolate into a paper piping (pastry) bag and cut off the tip. Drop rounds of chocolate over the surface of the tart and use a skewer or cocktail stick (toothpick) to draw a point gently through the chocolate to produce a marbled effect. Chill for 2–3 hours, until set. To serve, first allow the tart to soften slightly at room temperature.

CHOCOLATE TIRAMISU TART

SERVES 12–16

115g/4oz/½ cup unsalted (sweet) butter
15ml/1 tbsp coffee-flavoured liqueur
175g/6oz/1½ cups plain
   (all-purpose) flour
25g/1oz/¼ cup cocoa powder
25g/1oz/¼ cup icing
   (confectioners') sugar
pinch of salt
2.5ml/½ tsp vanilla essence (extract)
cocoa powder, for dusting

For the Chocolate Layer
350ml/12fl oz/1½ cups double
   (heavy) cream
15ml/1 tbsp golden (light corn) syrup
115g/4oz dark (bittersweet) chocolate,
   chopped into small pieces
25g/1oz/2 tbsp unsalted (sweet) butter,
   cut into small pieces
30ml/2 tbsp coffee-flavoured liqueur

For the Filling
250ml/8fl oz/1 cup whipping cream
350g/12oz/1½ cups mascarpone cheese
45ml/3 tbsp icing (confectioners') sugar
45ml/3 tbsp cold black coffee
45ml/3 tbsp coffee-flavoured liqueur
90g/3½oz plain (semisweet)
   chocolate, grated

1 Make the pastry. Grease a 23cm/9in springform tin (pan). In a pan, melt the butter with the liqueur. Sift the flour, cocoa, icing sugar and salt into a bowl. Remove the butter mixture from the heat, add the vanilla essence and gradually stir into the flour mixture until a soft dough forms.

2 Knead lightly until smooth, then press into the tin and up the sides to within 2cm/¾in of the top. Prick the dough. Chill well. Preheat the oven to 190°C/375°F/ Gas 5. Bake the pastry case (pie shell) for 8–10 minutes to set.

3 Prepare the chocolate layer. Bring the cream and syrup to the boil in a pan over a medium heat. Off the heat, add the chocolate, stirring until melted. Beat in the butter and liqueur and pour into the pastry case. Cool completely, then chill.

4 Prepare the filling. Using a hand-held electric mixer, whip the cream in a bowl until soft peaks form. In another bowl, beat the cheese until soft, then beat in the icing sugar until smooth and creamy. Gradually beat in the cold coffee and liqueur. Gently fold in the whipped cream and chocolate. Spoon the filling into the pastry case, on top of the chocolate layer. Level the surface. Chill until ready to serve.

5 To serve, run a sharp knife around the side of the tin to loosen the pastry case. Remove the side of the tin and slide the tart on to a plate. Sift a layer of cocoa powder over the tart to decorate, or pipe rosettes of whipped cream around the rim and top each with a chocolate-coated coffee bean. Chocolate Tiramisu Tart is very rich, so serve it in small wedges, with cups of espresso.

CHOCOLATE PECAN TORTE

SERVES 16

200g/7oz dark (bittersweet) or plain
  chocolate, chopped into small pieces
150g/5oz/10 tbsp unsalted (sweet) butter
4 eggs
90g/3½oz/scant ½ cup caster
  (superfine) sugar
10ml/2 tsp vanilla essence (extract)
115g/4oz/1 cup ground pecan nuts
10ml/2 tsp ground cinnamon
24 toasted pecan halves, to decorate

For the Chocolate Honey Glaze

115g/4oz dark (bittersweet) chocolate,
  chopped into small pieces
50g/2oz/¼ cup unsalted (sweet) butter,
  cut into pieces
30ml/2 tbsp clear honey
pinch of ground cinnamon

1 Preheat the oven to 180°C/350°F/Gas 4.
Grease a 20 x 5cm/8 x 2in springform tin
(pan) and line with baking parchment.
Wrap the tin in foil to prevent water
seeping in. Melt the chopped chocolate,
and butter, cut into pieces, together,
stirring until smooth. Beat the eggs, sugar
and vanilla essence in a mixing bowl until
the mixture is frothy. Stir in the melted
chocolate, ground nuts and cinnamon and
mix well. Pour into the tin.

2 Place the tin in a roasting pan. Pour in
boiling water to come 2cm/¾in up the
side of the springform tin. Bake for about
25–30 minutes, until the edge of the
cake is set but the centre is still soft.
Remove the tin from the water bath and
lift off the foil. Cool the cake in the tin
on a wire rack.

3 Prepare the glaze. Heat all the glaze
ingredients in a small pan until melted,
stirring until smooth. Off the heat, half-dip
the toasted pecan halves in the glaze and
place on a baking sheet lined with baking
parchment until set.

4 Remove the cake from the tin, place it
on the rack and pour the remaining glaze
over. Decorate the edge of the torte with
the chocolate-dipped pecans and leave to
set. Transfer to a plate when ready to
serve, and slice in thin wedges.

CHOCOLATE LEMON TART

SERVES 8–10

175g/6oz/1½ cups plain (all-purpose) flour

10ml/2 tsp cocoa powder

25g/1oz/¼ cup icing
(confectioners') sugar

2.5ml/½ tsp salt

115g/4oz/½ cup unsalted (sweet) butter

15ml/1 tbsp water

For the Filling

225g/8oz/1 cup caster (superfine) sugar

6 eggs

grated rind of 2 lemons

175ml/6fl oz/¾ cup fresh lemon juice

175ml/6fl oz/¾ cup double (heavy) or
whipping cream

chocolate curls, to decorate

1 Lightly grease a 25cm/10in flan tin (tart pan). Sift the flour, cocoa, icing sugar and salt into a bowl and set aside. Melt the butter with the water in a pan over a low heat. When melted, pour over the flour mixture and stir until the flour has absorbed all the liquid and is smooth.

2 Press the dough evenly over the base and side of the prepared tin. Chill the pastry case (pie shell).

3 Preheat the oven to 190°C/375°F/Gas 5. Place a baking sheet inside to heat up. Prepare the filling. Whisk the sugar and eggs in a bowl until the sugar has dissolved. Add the lemon rind and juice and mix well. Stir in the cream. Taste and add more lemon juice or sugar, if needed.

4 Pour the filling into the pastry case. Place the tin on the hot baking sheet. Bake for 20–25 minutes, or until the filling is set. Cool, then decorate with the curls.

CHOCOLATE APRICOT LINZER TART

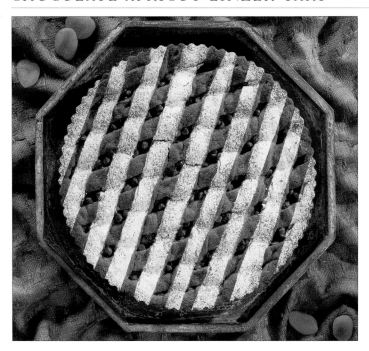

3 Turn the dough on to a lightly floured work surface and knead lightly until just blended. Divide the dough in half. With floured fingers, press half the dough on to the base and sides of the tin. Prick the base of the dough with a fork. Chill for 20 minutes. Roll out the rest of the dough between two sheets of baking parchment or clear film (plastic wrap) to a 28cm/11in round. Slide on to a baking sheet and chill for 30 minutes.

4 Preheat the oven to 180°C/350°F/Gas 4. Spread the filling on to the base of the pastry-lined tin. Sprinkle with chocolate chips. Set aside. Slide the dough round on to a lightly floured surface and cut into 1cm/½in strips. Allow the strips to soften for 3–5 minutes.

SERVES 10–12

50g/2oz/½ cup whole blanched almonds
115g/4oz/½ cup caster (superfine) sugar
175g/6oz/1½ cups plain (all-purpose) flour
30ml/2 tbsp cocoa powder
5ml/1 tsp ground cinnamon
2.5ml/½ tsp salt
5ml/1 tsp grated orange rind
225g/8oz/1 cup unsalted (sweet) butter
45–60ml/3–4 tbsp iced water
75g/3oz/½ cup plain (semisweet) mini
  chocolate chips
icing (confectioners') sugar, for dusting
For the Apricot Filling
350g/12oz/1½ cups dried apricots
120ml/4fl oz/½ cup orange juice
175ml/6fl oz/¾ cup water
45ml/3 tbsp granulated sugar
50g/2oz/2 tbsp apricot jam
2.5ml/½ tsp almond essence (extract)

1 Prepare the filling. In a pan, simmer the apricots, orange juice and water until the liquid is absorbed, stirring often. Stir in the sugar, jam and almond essence. Strain into a bowl, cool, cover and chill.

2 Prepare the pastry. Lightly grease a loose-based 28cm/11in flan tin (tart pan). In a food processor fitted with a metal blade, process the almonds with half the sugar until finely ground. Sift the flour, cocoa, cinnamon and salt into a bowl. Stir in the remaining caster sugar. Add to the food processor and process to blend. Add the orange rind and butter, cut into small pieces, and process for 15–20 seconds until the mixture resembles coarse crumbs. Add about 30ml/2 tbsp iced water and pulse until the dough just begins to stick together. If it appears too dry, add 15–30ml/1–2 tbsp more iced water, little by little, until the dough holds together.

5 Place half the dough strips over the filling, spacing them about 1cm/½in apart. Place the rest at an angle. Then with your fingertips, press down on both sides of each crossing to stress the lattice effect. Press the ends on to the side of the tart and trim. Bake for 35–40 minutes, until the strips are golden and the filling bubbling. Cool on a wire rack. To serve, remove the side of the tin, then dust icing sugar over the top pastry strips using paper templates.

RICH CHOCOLATE BERRY TART <u>WITH</u> BLACKBERRY SAUCE

SERVES 10

- 115g/4oz/½ cup unsalted (sweet) butter, softened
- 115g/4oz/½ cup caster (superfine) sugar
- 2.5ml/½ tsp salt
- 15ml/1 tbsp vanilla essence (extract)
- 50g/2oz/½ cup cocoa powder
- 175g/6oz/1½ cups plain (all-purpose) flour
- 450g/1lb fresh berries, for topping

For the Chocolate Ganache Filling
- 475ml/16fl oz/2 cups double (heavy) cream
- 150g/5oz/½ cup blackberry jelly
- 225g/8oz dark (bittersweet) chocolate, chopped into small pieces
- 25g/1oz/2 tbsp unsalted (sweet) butter, cut into small pieces

For the Blackberry Sauce
- 225g/8oz fresh or frozen blackberries
- 15ml/1 tbsp lemon juice
- 30ml/2 tbsp caster (superfine) sugar
- 30ml/2 tbsp blackberry- or raspberry-flavoured liqueur

1 In a food processor, mix the butter, sugar, salt and vanilla until creamy. Add the cocoa and mix for 1 minute. Add the flour, then pulse for 15 seconds. Turn the dough out on to clear film (plastic wrap) and shape into a flat disc. Wrap and chill for 1 hour.

2 Lightly grease a loose-based 23cm/9in flan tin (tart pan). Let the dough soften for 5–10 minutes, then roll out between two sheets of clear film to a 28cm/11in round, about 5mm/¼in thick. Peel off the top sheet of clear film and invert the dough into the prepared tin. Ease the dough into the tin and when in position lift off the clear film.

3 With floured fingers, press the dough into the base and sides of the tin. Cut off any excess dough using a rolling pin. Prick the base with a fork. Chill for 1 hour. Preheat the oven to 180°C/350°F/Gas 4. Line the pastry case (pie shell) with baking parchment, fill with baking beans and bake blind for 10 minutes. Remove the paper and beans and bake for 5 minutes more. Cool in the tin on a wire rack.

4 Prepare the ganache filling. In a pan over a medium heat, bring the cream and jelly to the boil. Remove from the heat and add the chocolate, stirring until melted and smooth. Stir in the butter until melted, then strain into the cooled pastry case, smoothing the top. Cool the tart completely.

5 Prepare the sauce. Process the berries, lemon juice and sugar in a food processor until smooth. Strain into a small bowl and add the liqueur.

6 To serve, transfer the tart to a serving plate and arrange the berries on top of the tart. Brush the berries with some blackberry sauce. Serve the remaining sauce separately.

HAZELNUT CHOCOLATE MERINGUE TORTE <u>WITH</u> PEARS

SERVES 8–10

175g/6oz/¾ cup granulated sugar
1 vanilla pod (bean), split
475ml/6fl oz/2 cups water
4 ripe pears, peeled, halved and cored
30ml/2 tbsp hazelnut- or pear-
   flavoured liqueur
150g/5oz/1¼ cups hazelnuts, toasted
6 egg whites
a pinch of salt
350g/12oz/2¼ cups icing
   (confectioners') sugar
5ml/1 tsp vanilla essence (extract)
50g/2oz plain (semisweet)
   chocolate, melted
For the Chocolate Cream
275g/10oz fine quality dark (bittersweet)
   or plain (semisweet) chocolate,
   chopped into small pieces
475ml/16fl oz/2 cups whipping cream
60ml/4 tbsp hazelnut- or pear-
   flavoured liqueur

1 In a pan large enough to hold the pears in a single layer, combine the sugar, vanilla pod and water. Over a high heat, bring to the boil, stirring until the sugar dissolves. Lower the heat, add the pears, cover and simmer gently for 12–15 minutes until tender. Set the pan aside and let the pears cool in the pan. Drain on kitchen paper, transfer to a plate, sprinkle over the liqueur, cover and chill overnight.

2 Preheat the oven to 180°C/350°F/Gas 4. With a pencil, draw a 23cm/9in circle on each of two sheets of baking parchment. Turn the paper over on to two baking sheets so that the pencil marks are underneath. Crumb the toasted hazelnuts in a food processor fitted with a metal blade.

3 In a large bowl, beat the whites with a hand-held electric mixer until frothy. Add the salt and beat on high speed until soft peaks form. Reduce the mixer speed and gradually add the icing sugar, beating well until all the sugar has been added and the whites are stiff and glossy; this will take 12–15 minutes. Gently fold in the nuts and vanilla essence and spoon the meringue on to the circles on the baking sheets, smoothing the top and sides.

4 Bake for 1 hour until the tops are dry and firm. Turn off the oven and allow to cool in the oven for 2–3 hours, or overnight, until completely dry.

5 Prepare the chocolate cream. Melt the chocolate in a bowl set over a pan of simmering water. Cool to room temperature. Using a hand-held electric mixer, beat the cream to form soft peaks. Quickly fold the cream into the melted chocolate. Fold in the liqueur. Spoon one-third of the chocolate cream into a piping (pastry) bag with a star nozzle. Set aside.

6 Thinly slice each pear half lengthways with a sharp knife. Place one meringue layer on a serving plate. Spread the meringue with half the chocolate cream and arrange half the sliced pears on top. Pipe a border of rosettes.

7 Top with the second meringue and spread with the remaining chocolate cream. Arrange the remaining pear slices in an attractive pattern over the chocolate. Pipe a border of rosettes. Spoon the melted chocolate into a small paper cone and drizzle the chocolate over the pears. Chill for 1 hour before serving. Decorate with chocolate curls, if wished.

CHILLED CHOCOLATE AND DATE SLICE

SERVES 6–8

115g/4oz/½ cup unsalted (sweet)
  butter, melted
225g/8oz ginger biscuits (cookies),
  finely crushed
50g/2oz/⅔ cup stale sponge
  cake crumbs
75ml/5 tbsp orange juice
115g/4oz/⅔ cup stoned (pitted) dates
25g/1oz/¼ cup finely chopped nuts
175g/6oz dark (bittersweet) chocolate
300ml/½ pint/1¼ cups whipping cream
grated chocolate, icing (confectioners')
  sugar and orange segments, to decorate

1 Mix the butter and ginger biscuit (cookie) crumbs in a bowl, then press the mixture on to the sides and base of an 18cm/7in loose-based flan tin (tart pan). Chill the crust while making the filling.

2 Put the sponge cake crumbs into a bowl. Pour over 60ml/4 tbsp of the orange juice, stir well with a wooden spoon and leave to soak.

3 Put the dates in a pan and add the remaining orange juice. Warm the mixture over a low heat. Mash the warm dates thoroughly and stir in the cake crumbs, with the finely chopped nuts, until evenly blended.

4 Mix the chocolate with 60ml/4 tbsp of the cream in a heatproof bowl. Place the bowl over a pan of barely simmering water and stir occasionally until melted. In a separate bowl, whip the rest of the cream to soft peaks, then fold in the melted chocolate.

5 Add the cooled date, crumb and nut mixture to the cream and chocolate, and mix lightly but thoroughly. Pour into the crumb crust. Using a palette knife (metal spatula), level the mixture. Chill until just set, then mark into portions, using a sharp knife dipped in hot water. Return the tart to the refrigerator and chill until firm. To decorate, scatter the grated chocolate over the surface and dust with icing sugar. Fresh orange segments make an excellent accompaniment. Serve in wedges, with single (light) cream, if wished.

CHOCOLATE MARSHMALLOW PIE
Make the crumb crust in the same way as for the main recipe, but add a delicious marshmallow filling.

Melt 275g/10oz/3 cups white marshmallows with 30ml/2 tbsp milk or single cream in the top of a double boiler over simmering water. Alternatively, use a deep bowl and microwave the mixture on High for about 4 minutes, stirring often. Take the boiler off the heat and stir in 90g/3½oz grated chocolate until melted, then add 30ml/2 tbsp brandy. Tip the mixture into a clean bowl, leave to cool, then chill until just starting to set. Fold in 250ml/8fl oz/ 1 cup whipped cream, pour into the crumb crust and return to the refrigerator until completely set. Decorate with chocolate curls.

BAKED CHOCOLATE CHEESECAKE

SERVES 10–12

275g/10oz plain (semisweet) chocolate, chopped into small pieces

1.2kg/2½lb/5 cups cream cheese, at room temperature

200g/7oz/scant 1 cup granulated sugar

10ml/2 tsp vanilla essence (extract)

4 eggs, at room temperature

175ml/6fl oz/¾ cup sour cream

15ml/1 tbsp cocoa powder

For the Base

200g/7oz chocolate biscuits (cookies)

75g/3oz/6 tbsp butter, melted

2.5ml/½ tsp ground cinnamon

1 Preheat the oven to 180°C/350°F/Gas 4. Lightly grease the base and sides of a 23 x 7.5cm/9 x 3in springform tin (pan).

2 To make the base, crush the biscuits and mix with the butter and cinnamon. Press on to the base of the tin to make a crust. Melt the chocolate and set aside.

3 Beat the cream cheese until smooth, then beat in the sugar and vanilla essence. Add the eggs, one at a time.

4 Stir the sour cream into the cocoa powder to form a paste. Add to the cream cheese mixture. Stir in the melted chocolate and mix until smooth.

5 Pour the filling on to the biscuit crust. Bake for 1 hour. Cool in the tin, then remove the sides of the tin and slide the cheesecake on to a plate. Serve chilled.

MARBLED CHOCOLATE CHEESECAKE

SERVES 6

50g/2oz/½ cup cocoa powder
75ml/5 tbsp hot water
900g/2lb cream cheese, at
 room temperature
200g/7oz/scant 1 cup caster
 (superfine) sugar
4 eggs
5ml/1 tsp vanilla essence (extract)
75g/3oz digestive biscuits (graham
 crackers), crushed

1 Preheat the oven to 180°C/350°F/Gas 4. Line a 20 x 8cm/8 x 3in cake tin (pan) with baking parchment. Grease.

2 Sift the cocoa. Dissolve in the hot water. Beat the cheese until smooth. Beat in the sugar, then the eggs. Divide the mixture into two. Add the chocolate mixture to one half, the vanilla to the other.

3 Pour a ladleful of the plain mixture into the centre of the tin; it will spread out. Slowly pour over a ladleful of chocolate mixture in the centre. Continue in this way until both are used up. Draw a thin metal skewer through the cake mixture for a marbled effect.

4 Set the tin in a roasting pan and pour in hot water to come 4cm/1½in up the sides of the cake tin.

5 Bake the cheesecake for 1½ hours, until the top is golden. Cool in the tin on a wire rack.

6 Run a knife around the inside edge of the cake. Invert a flat plate over the tin and turn out the cake.

7 Sprinkle the crushed biscuits evenly over the cake, gently invert a plate on top, and turn over. Cover and chill for at least 3 hours, but preferably overnight.

RASPBERRY, MASCARPONE <u>AND</u> WHITE CHOCOLATE CHEESECAKE

SERVES 8

50g/2oz/¼ cup unsalted (sweet) butter
225g/8oz ginger biscuits (cookies)
50g/2oz/½ cup chopped pecan nuts

For the Filling

275g/10oz/1¼ cups mascarpone cheese
175g/6oz/¾ cup fromage frais
   (ricotta cheese)
2 eggs, beaten
45ml/3 tbsp caster (superfine) sugar
250g/9oz white chocolate
225g/8oz/1½ cups fresh raspberries

For the Topping

115g/4oz/½ cup mascarpone cheese
75g/3oz/⅓ cup fromage frais
   (ricotta cheese)
white chocolate curls and fresh
   raspberries, to decorate

1 Preheat the oven to 150°C/300°F/Gas 2. Crush the biscuits. Melt the butter in a pan, then stir in the biscuits and nuts. Press into the base of a 23cm/9in springform tin (pan). Level the surface.

2 Make the filling. Using a wooden spoon, beat the mascarpone and fromage frais in a large mixing bowl, then beat in the eggs, a little at a time. Add the caster sugar. Beat until the sugar has dissolved and the mixture is smooth and creamy.

3 Chop and melt the white chocolate gently in a heatproof bowl over a pan of simmering water, then stir into the cheese mixture. Add the fresh or frozen raspberries and mix lightly.

4 Tip into the prepared tin and spread evenly. Bake for 1 hour until just set. Switch off the oven and leave the cheesecake inside until cold.

5 Remove the sides of the tin and carefully lift the cheesecake on to a serving plate. Make the topping by mixing the mascarpone and fromage frais in a bowl and spreading the mixture over the cheesecake. Decorate with chocolate curls and raspberries.

APRICOT AND WHITE CHOCOLATE CHEESECAKE

Use 225g/8oz/1 cup ready-to-eat dried apricots instead of the fresh or frozen raspberries in the cheesecake mixture. Slice the apricots thinly or dice them. Omit the mascarpone and fromage frais topping and serve the cheesecake with an apricot sauce, made by poaching 225g/8oz stoned (pitted) fresh apricots in 120ml/4fl oz/½ cup water until tender, then rubbing the fruit and liquid through a sieve placed over a bowl. Sweeten the apricot purée with caster sugar to taste, and add enough lemon juice to sharpen the flavour. Alternatively, purée drained canned apricots with a little of their syrup, then stir in lemon juice to taste.

BAKED CHOCOLATE AND RAISIN CHEESECAKE

SERVES 8–10

75g/3oz/¾ cup plain (all-purpose) flour
45ml/3 tbsp cocoa powder
75g/3oz/½ cup semolina
50g/2oz/¼ cup caster (superfine) sugar
115g/4oz/½ cup unsalted (sweet) butter

For the Filling

225g/8oz/1 cup cream cheese
120ml/4fl oz/½ cup natural (plain) yogurt
2 eggs, beaten
75g/3oz/6 tbsp caster (superfine) sugar
finely grated rind of 1 lemon
75g/3oz/½ cup raisins
45ml/3 tbsp plain (semisweet)
   chocolate chips

For the Topping

75g/3oz plain (semisweet) chocolate
30ml/2 tbsp golden (light corn) syrup
40g/1½oz/3 tbsp butter

1 Preheat the oven to 150°C/300°F/Gas 2. Sift the flour and cocoa into a mixing bowl and stir in the semolina and sugar. Using fingertips, work the butter into the flour mixture until it makes a firm dough.

2 Press the dough into the base of a 22cm/8½in springform tin (pan). Prick all over with a fork and bake in the oven for 15 minutes. Remove the tin but leave the oven on.

RUM AND RICOTTA CHEESECAKE
Use ricotta instead of cream cheese in the filling. Omit the lemon rind. Soak the raisins in 30ml/2 tbsp rum before stirring them in with the chocolate chips. Add 5ml/1 tsp rum to the topping for a decadent result.

3 Make the filling. In a large bowl, beat the cream cheese with the yogurt, eggs and sugar until evenly mixed. Stir in the lemon rind, raisins and chocolate chips.

4 Smooth the cream cheese mixture over the chocolate shortbread base and bake for a further 35–45 minutes, or until the filling is pale gold and just set. Cool in the tin on a wire rack.

5 To make the topping, combine the chocolate, syrup and butter in a heatproof bowl. Set over a pan of simmering water and heat gently, stirring occasionally, until melted. Pour the topping over the cheesecake and leave until set. Remove the sides of the tin and carefully slide the chocolate and raisin cheesecake on to a serving plate. Serve sliced, with single (light) cream, if wished.

LUXURY WHITE CHOCOLATE CHEESECAKE

SERVES 16–20

150g/5oz (about 16–18) digestive
biscuits (graham crackers)

50g/2oz/½ cup blanched
hazelnuts, toasted

50g/2oz/¼ cup unsalted (sweet)
butter, melted

2.5ml/½ tsp ground cinnamon

white chocolate curls, to decorate

cocoa powder, for dusting (optional)

For the Filling

350g/12oz fine quality white chocolate,
chopped into small pieces

120ml/4fl oz/½ cup whipping cream

675g/1½lb/3 x 8oz packets cream
cheese, softened

50g/2oz/¼ cup granulated sugar

4 eggs

30ml/2 tbsp hazelnut-flavoured liqueur

For the Topping

450ml/¾ pint/1¾ cups sour cream

50g/2oz/¼ cup granulated sugar

15ml/1 tbsp hazelnut-flavoured liqueur

3 Using a hand-held electric mixer, beat the cream cheese and sugar in a large bowl until smooth. Add the eggs one at a time, beating well. Slowly beat in the white chocolate mixture along with the liqueur. Pour the filling into the baked crust. Place the tin on the hot baking sheet. Bake for 45–55 minutes, and do not allow the top to brown. Transfer the cheesecake to a wire rack while preparing the topping. Increase the oven temperature to 200°C/400°F/Gas 6.

4 Prepare the topping. In a mixing bowl, whisk the sour cream, granulated sugar and liqueur until thoroughly mixed. Pour the topping mixture over the cheesecake, spreading it evenly with a metal spatula, and return to the oven. Bake for a further 5–7 minutes. Turn off the oven, but do not open the door for 1 hour. Serve the cheesecake at room temperature, decorated with the white chocolate curls. Dust the surface lightly with cocoa powder, if wished.

1 Preheat the oven to 180°C/350°F/Gas 4. Grease a 23 x 7.5cm/9 x 3in springform tin (pan). In a food processor, process the biscuits and hazelnuts until fine crumbs form. Pour in the butter and cinnamon. Process just until blended. Press into the base of the tin and up the sides to within 1cm/½in of the top. Bake the crumb crust for 5–7 minutes, until just set. Cool in the tin on a wire rack. Lower the oven temperature to 150°C/300°F/Gas 2 and place a baking sheet inside to heat.

2 Prepare the filling. In a small pan over a low heat, melt the white chocolate and cream until smooth, stirring quite frequently. Set aside to cool slightly.

ITALIAN CHOCOLATE RICOTTA PIE

SERVES 6

225g/8oz/2 cups plain (all-purpose) flour
30ml/2 tbsp cocoa powder
60ml/4 tbsp caster (superfine) sugar
115g/4oz/½ cup unsalted (sweet) butter
60ml/4 tbsp dry sherry

For the Filling

2 egg yolks
115g/4oz/½ cup caster (superfine) sugar
500g/1¼lb/2½ cups ricotta cheese
finely grated rind of 1 lemon
90ml/6 tbsp dark (bittersweet)
 chocolate chips
75ml/5 tbsp chopped mixed (candied) peel
45ml/3 tbsp chopped angelica

1 Sift the flour and cocoa into a bowl. Stir in the sugar. Rub the butter in with your fingers, then work in the sherry to make a firm dough.

2 Preheat the oven to 200°C/400°F/Gas 6. Roll out three-quarters of the pastry on a lightly floured surface and line a 24cm/9½in loose-based flan tin (tart pan).

3 Make the filling. Beat the egg yolks and sugar in a bowl, then beat in the ricotta to mix thoroughly. Stir in the lemon rind, chocolate chips, mixed peel and angelica.

4 Scrape the ricotta mixture into the pastry case (pie shell) and level. Cut the remaining pastry into strips. Arrange these in a lattice over the pie.

5 Bake for 15 minutes. Lower the oven to 180°C/350°F/Gas 4 and cook for a further 30–35 minutes, until golden brown and firm. Cool in the tin.

BLACK BOTTOM PIE

SERVES 6–8

250g/9oz/2¼ cups plain
   (all-purpose) flour
150g/5oz/⅔ cup unsalted (sweet) butter
2 egg yolks
15–30ml/1–2 tbsp iced water
For the Filling
3 eggs, separated
20ml/4 tsp cornflour (cornstarch)
75g/3oz/6 tbsp golden caster
   (superfine) sugar
400ml/14fl oz/1⅔ cups milk
150g/5oz plain (semisweet)
   chocolate, chopped
5ml/1 tsp vanilla essence (extract)
1 sachet powdered gelatine
45ml/3 tbsp water
30ml/2 tbsp dark rum
For the Topping
175ml/6 fl oz/¾ cup whipping cream
chocolate curls, to decorate

1 Sift the flour into a bowl and rub in the
butter until the mixture resembles coarse
breadcrumbs. Stir in the egg yolks with
just enough iced water to bind the mixture
to a soft dough. Roll out on a floured
surface and line a deep 23cm/9in flan tin
(tart pan). Chill for 30 minutes.

2 Preheat the oven to 190°C/375°F/Gas 5.
Prick the pastry all over with a fork, cover
with baking parchment and fill with baking
beans. Bake blind for 10 minutes. Remove
the baking beans and paper, and return
to the oven. Bake for a further 10 minutes,
until the pastry is crisp and golden.
Cool in the tin.

POTS AU CHOCOLAT

The chocolate and chestnut mixture
(minus the pastry) also makes
delicious individual *pots au
chocolat*. Make the fillings as
described above, then simply pour
the mixture into small, lightly
buttered ramekins. Decorate with a
blob of whipped cream and grated
chocolate and serve with *langues
de chat*.

CHOCOLATE AND CHESTNUT PIE

23cm/9in pastry case
   (pie shell), cooked
For the Filling
115g/4oz/½ cup butter,
   softened
115g/4oz/¼ cup caster
   (superfine) sugar
425g/15oz can unsweetened
   chestnut purée
225g/8oz plain (semisweet)
   chocolate, broken into
   small pieces
30ml/2 tbsp brandy

1 Make the filling. Cream the butter
with the sugar until pale and fluffy.
Add the chestnut purée, about 30ml/
2 tbsp at a time, beating well after
each addition.

2 Melt the chocolate in a heatproof
bowl placed over a pan of barely
simmering water, stirring from time
to time. Stir the chocolate into the
chestnut mixture until combined,
then add the brandy.

3 Pour the filling into the cold pastry
case. Using a metal spatula, level the
surface. Chill until set. Decorate with
whipped cream and chocolate leaves,
or dust with sifted cocoa.

3 Make the filling. Mix the egg yolks,
cornflour and 30ml/2 tbsp of the sugar in
a bowl. Heat the milk in a pan until almost
boiling, then beat into the egg mixture.
Return to the clean pan and stir over a
low heat until the custard has thickened
and is smooth. Pour half the custard
into a bowl.

4 Put the chocolate in a heatproof bowl
set over a pan of barely simmering water
until the chocolate has melted, stirring
occasionally until smooth. Stir the melted
chocolate into the custard in the bowl,
with the vanilla essence. Spread the
filling in the pastry case (pie shell) and
cover closely with dampened clear film
(plastic wrap) to prevent the formation
of a skin. Allow to cool, then chill
until set.

5 Sprinkle the gelatine over the water in a
bowl and leave until spongy. Place the bowl
over a pan of simmering water until all the
gelatine has dissolved. Stir into the
remaining custard, then add the rum.
Whisk the egg whites in a clean, grease-
free bowl until peaks form. Whisk in the
remaining sugar, a little at a time, until
stiff, then fold the egg whites quickly but
evenly into the rum-flavoured custard.

6 Spoon the rum-flavoured custard over the
chocolate layer in the pastry case. Using a
spatula, level the mixture, making sure that
none of the chocolate custard is visible.
Return the pie to the refrigerator until the top
layer has set, then remove from the tin and
place on a serving plate. Whip the cream,
spread it over the pie and sprinkle with
chocolate curls to decorate before serving.

MISSISSIPPI MUD PIE

SERVES 8

175g/6oz/1½ cups plain
(all-purpose) flour
2.5ml/½ tsp salt
115g/4oz/½ cup butter
30–45ml/2–3 tbsp iced water
For the Filling
75g/3oz plain (semisweet)
chocolate, broken
50g/2oz/¼ cup butter or margarine
45ml/3 tbsp golden (light corn) syrup
3 eggs, beaten
150g/5oz/⅔ cup soft light brown sugar
5ml/1 tsp vanilla essence (extract)
To Decorate
115g/4oz chocolate bar
300ml/½ pint/1¼ cups whipping cream

1 Preheat the oven to 220°C/425°F/Gas 7. Sift the flour and salt into a mixing bowl. Rub in the butter until the mixture resembles coarse breadcrumbs. Sprinkle in the water, about 15ml/1 tbsp at a time, and toss the mixture lightly with your fingers or a fork until the dough forms into a ball.

2 On a lightly floured surface, roll out the pastry and line a 23cm/9in flan tin (tart pan). Ease in the pastry and do not stretch it. With your thumbs, make a fluted edge.

3 Using a fork, prick the base and sides of the pastry case. Bake in the oven for 10–15 minutes, until lightly browned. Leave to cool in the tin on a wire rack.

4 Make the filling. In a heatproof bowl set over a pan of barely simmering water, melt the plain chocolate with the butter or margarine and the golden syrup. Remove the bowl from the heat and stir in the eggs, sugar and vanilla essence. Mix well.

5 Lower the oven temperature to 180°C/350°F/Gas 4. Pour the chocolate mixture into the pastry case (pie shell). Bake for 35–40 minutes, until the filling is set. Leave to cool in the tin on a wire rack.

6 Make the decoration. Use the heat of your hands to soften the chocolate bar slightly. Working over a sheet of baking parchment, draw the blade of a swivel-bladed vegetable peeler across the side of the chocolate bar to shave off short, wide curls. Chill the curls until you are ready to serve.

7 Before serving the pie, pour the cream into a bowl and whip to soft peaks. Spread over the top of the pie, making sure the chocolate filling is completely hidden. Decorate with the chocolate curls, arranging them carefully to cover the pie.

CHOCOLATE, BANANA <u>AND</u> TOFFEE PIE

SERVES 6

65g/2½oz/5 tbsp unsalted (sweet)
  butter, melted
250g/9oz milk chocolate digestive
  biscuits (graham crackers), crushed
chocolate curls, to decorate
For the Filling
397g/13oz can sweetened
  condensed milk
150g/5oz plain (semisweet)
  chocolate, chopped
120ml/4fl oz/½ cup crème fraîche
15ml/1 tbsp golden (light corn) syrup
For the Topping
2 bananas
250ml/8fl oz/1 cup crème fraîche
10ml/2 tsp strong black coffee

1 Mix the butter with the biscuit crumbs. Press into a 23cm/9in loose-based flan tin (tart pan). Chill.

2 Make the filling. Completely submerge the unopened condensed milk can in a pan of boiling water. Simmer for 2 hours, topping up the water as necessary so the can remains under water at all times. Set aside, submerged, until completely cooled. Only then is it safe to open.

3 Gently melt the chocolate with the crème fraîche and golden syrup in a heatproof bowl over a pan of simmering water. Stir in the caramelized condensed milk and beat until evenly mixed. Pour the filling into the biscuit crust and spread evenly.

4 Slice the bananas evenly and arrange them over the chocolate filling.

5 Stir the crème fraîche and coffee together in a bowl, then spoon the mixture over the bananas. Sprinkle the chocolate curls on top. Alternatively, omit the crème fraîche topping and decorate with whipped cream and extra banana slices.

CHILLED
AND
ICED
DESSERTS

Cold desserts mean easy entertaining as they
can mostly be prepared ahead. A rich, dark
Chocolate Sorbet with Red Fruits can be made
days in advance, ready to scoop and serve with
fresh fruits, while a White Chocolate Vanilla
Mousse will keep in the refrigerator for the
next day. But don't stop at mousses and ices —
if your sweet tooth craves a really lavish treat,
how about Devilish Chocolate Roulade, or, for
more formal meals, an elegant Chocolate
Hazelnut Galette?

DOUBLE CHOCOLATE SNOWBALL

THIS IS A SERIOUSLY RICH CHILLED DESSERT MIXING WHITE AND DARK CHOCOLATE, WITH JUST A HINT OF ORANGE LIQUEUR FLAVOUR.

3 Bake for 1¼–1½ hours until the surface is firm and slightly risen, but cracked. The centre will still be wobbly, but will set on cooling. Remove the bowl to a rack to cool to room temperature; the top will sink. Cover the surface of the cake with a dinner plate (to make an even surface for unmoulding); then wrap completely with foil and chill overnight.

4 To unmould, remove the foil, lift off the plate, and place an upturned serving plate over the top of the mould. Invert the mould on to the plate and shake to release the cake. Peel off the foil lining. Cover until ready to decorate.

5 In a food processor, process the white chocolate finely. Heat 120ml/4fl oz/½ cup of the cream until just beginning to simmer. With the food processor running, pour the hot cream through the feeder tube and process until the chocolate has melted completely. Strain into a bowl and cool the mixture to room temperature, stirring occasionally.

6 In another bowl, beat the remaining cream with the electric mixer until soft peaks form. Add the liqueur, if using, and beat until the cream holds its shape, but is not stiff. Fold a spoonful of cream into the chocolate mixture, then fold in the rest. Spoon into a piping (pastry) bag with a star nozzle and pipe rosettes over the cake. Dust lightly with cocoa powder to finish.

<u>SERVES 12–14</u>

350g/12oz dark (bittersweet) or plain (semisweet) chocolate, chopped
350g/12oz/1¾ cups caster (superfine) sugar
275g/10oz/1¼ cups unsalted (sweet) butter, cut into small pieces
8 eggs
60ml/4 tbsp orange-flavoured liqueur
cocoa powder, for dusting
For the White Chocolate Cream
200g/7oz fine quality white chocolate, chopped into small pieces
475ml/16fl oz/2 cups double (heavy) or whipping cream
15ml/1 tbsp orange-flavoured liqueur (optional)

1 Preheat the oven to 180°C/350°F/Gas 4. Carefully line a 1.75 litre/3 pint/7½ cup round ovenproof bowl with aluminium foil, smoothing the sides. Melt the dark chocolate in a heatproof bowl over a pan of barely simmering water. Add the caster sugar and stir until the chocolate has melted and the sugar has dissolved. Strain the mixture into a bowl.

2 With a hand-held electric mixer set at low speed, beat in the butter, then the eggs, one at a time, beating well after each addition. Stir in the liqueur and pour into the prepared foil-lined bowl. Tap the sides of the bowl gently to release any large air bubbles.

CHOCOLATE AMARETTO MARQUISE

SERVES 10–12

- 15ml/1 tbsp sunflower oil
- 75g/3oz/7–8 amaretti, finely crushed
- 25g/1oz/¼ cup unblanched almonds, toasted and finely chopped
- 450g/1lb dark (bittersweet) or plain (semisweet) chocolate, chopped into small pieces
- 75ml/5 tbsp amaretto liqueur
- 75ml/5 tbsp golden (light corn) syrup
- 475ml/16fl oz/2 cups double (heavy) cream
- cocoa powder, for dusting

For the Amaretto Cream

- 350ml/12fl oz/1½ cups whipping cream or double (heavy) cream
- 30–45ml/2–3 tbsp Amaretto di Sarone

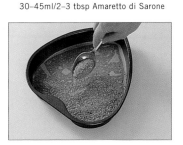

1 Lightly oil a 23cm/9in heart-shaped or springform tin (pan). Line the base with baking parchment, then oil the parchment as well. Combine the crushed amaretti biscuits (cookies) and the chopped almonds in a bowl and mix well. Sprinkle evenly on to the base of the tin.

2 Place the chocolate, amaretto liqueur and golden syrup in a pan over a very low heat. Stir frequently until the chocolate is melted and the mixture is smooth. Remove from the heat and allow it to cool for about 6–8 minutes, until the mixture feels just warm to the touch.

3 Pour the cream into a bowl. Whip with a hand-held electric mixer, until just beginning to hold its shape. Stir a large spoonful into the chocolate mixture, to lighten it, then quickly add the remaining cream and gently fold into the chocolate mixture. Pour into the prepared tin, on top of the amaretti and almond mixture. Level the surface. Cover the tin with clear film (plastic wrap) and chill overnight.

4 To unmould, run a thin-bladed sharp knife under hot water and dry. Run the knife around the tin edge to loosen the dessert. Place a serving plate over the tin and invert to unmould. Peel off the paper, replacing any crust that sticks to it, and dust with cocoa powder. Whip the cream and Amaretto di Sarone to soft peaks. Serve separately. Decorate with sugar-dipped fresh cherries, if wished.

CHOCOLATE PUFFS

SERVES 4–6

- 65g/2½oz/½ cup plain (all-purpose) flour
- 150ml/¼ pint/⅔ cup water
- 50g/2oz/¼ cup butter
- 2 eggs, beaten

For the Filling and Icing

- 150ml/¼ pint/⅔ cup double (heavy) cream
- 225g/8oz/1½ cups icing (confectioners') sugar
- 15ml/1 tbsp cocoa powder
- 30–60ml/2–4 tbsp water

1 Preheat the oven to 220°C/425°F/Gas 7. Sift the flour into a bowl. Place the water in a pan over a medium heat, add the butter and heat gently until it melts. Increase the heat and bring to the boil, then remove from the heat. Add all the flour immediately and beat quickly until the mixture sticks together and becomes thick and glossy while leaving the side of the pan clean. Leave the mixture to cool slightly.

2 Gradually add the eggs to the mixture and beat with a wooden spoon or an electric whisk, until the mixture, called choux pastry, is thick and glossy and drops reluctantly from a spoon. (You may not need all the egg.) Spoon the choux pastry into a piping (pastry) bag with a 2cm/¾in nozzle. Dampen two baking sheets with a little cold water.

3 Pipe walnut-size spoonfuls of choux pastry on to the dampened baking sheets. Leave some space for them to rise. Bake for 25–30 minutes, until golden brown and well risen. Use a metal spatula to lift the puffs on to a wire rack, and make a small hole in each one with the handle of a wooden spoon to allow the steam to escape. Leave to cool.

4 Make the filling and icing. Whip the cream until thick. Put it into a piping bag with a plain or star nozzle. Push the nozzle into the hole in each puff and squirt a little cream inside. Mix the icing sugar and cocoa in a small bowl. Add enough water to make a thick glossy icing. Spread a little icing on each puff and serve when set.

CHOCOLATE HAZELNUT GALETTES

SERVES 4

175g/6oz plain (semisweet) chocolate,
  chopped into small pieces
45ml/3 tbsp single (light) cream
30ml/2 tbsp flaked (sliced) hazelnuts
115g/4oz white chocolate, chopped into
  small pieces
175g/6oz/¾ cup fromage frais
  or mascarpone
15ml/1 tbsp dry sherry
60ml/4 tbsp finely chopped
  toasted hazelnuts
physalis, dipped in white chocolate,
  to decorate

1 Melt the plain chocolate in a heatproof bowl over a pan of barely simmering water, then remove from the heat. Stir the cream into the melted chocolate. Draw 12 x 7.5cm/3in circles on baking parchment.

2 Turn the parchment over and spread the plain chocolate in a thin, even layer over each circle. Scatter flaked hazelnuts over four of the circles. Leave to set.

3 Melt the white chocolate in a heatproof bowl over hot water, then stir in the fromage frais or mascarpone and sherry. Fold in the toasted hazelnuts. Leave to cool until the mixture holds its shape.

4 Remove the plain chocolate rounds from the paper and sandwich together in stacks of three, spooning the white chocolate hazelnut cream between the layers and using the hazelnut-covered rounds on top. Chill before serving.

5 To serve, place the galettes on individual plates and decorate with chocolate-dipped physalis.

CHOCOLATE PAVLOVA <u>WITH</u> PASSION FRUIT CREAM

SERVES 6

4 egg whites

200g/7oz/1 cup caster (superfine) sugar

20ml/4 tsp cornflour (cornstarch)

45ml/3 tbsp cocoa powder

5ml/1 tsp white wine vinegar

chocolate leaves, to decorate

For the Filling

150g/5oz plain (semisweet) chocolate

250ml/8fl oz/1 cup double (heavy) cream

150g/5oz/⅔ cup Greek (US strained
   plain) yogurt

2.5ml/½ tsp vanilla essence (extract)

4 passion fruit

1 Preheat the oven to 140°C/275°F/Gas 1. Cut a piece of baking parchment to fit a baking sheet. Draw a 23cm/9in circle on the parchment.

2 Whisk the egg whites in a bowl until stiff. Gradually whisk in the caster sugar until the mixture becomes stiff again. Then whisk in the cornflour, cocoa powder and white wine vinegar.

3 Place the parchment upside-down on the baking sheet. Spread the mixture over the marked circle, making a slight dip in the centre. Bake for 1½–2 hours.

4 Make the filling. Chop and melt the chocolate in a heatproof bowl set over barely simmering water, then remove from the heat and cool slightly. In a separate bowl, whip the cream with the yogurt and vanilla essence until thick. Fold 60ml/4 tbsp of the cream mixture into the chocolate, then set both mixtures aside.

5 Halve all the passion fruit and scoop out the pulp. Stir half the pulp into the plain cream mixture. Place the meringue shell on a large serving plate. Fill with the passion fruit cream, then spoon over the chocolate mixture and finally the remaining passion fruit pulp.

6 Decorate with chocolate leaves and serve immediately.

CHOCOLATE <u>AND</u> CHESTNUT POTS

SERVES 6

250g/9oz plain (semisweet) chocolate, broken into squares
60ml/4 tbsp Madeira
25g/1oz/2 tbsp butter, diced
2 eggs, separated
225g/8oz/1 cup unsweetened chestnut purée
crème fraîche and chocolate curls, to decorate

1 Melt the chocolate with the Madeira in a heatproof bowl set over a pan of simmering water. Off the heat, gradually add the butter, stirring until melted.

2 Beat the egg yolks quickly into the mixture, then beat in the chestnut purée, a little at a time, making sure that each addition is absorbed before you add the next. Mix until smooth.

3 Whisk the egg whites in a clean, grease-free bowl until stiff. Stir a little into the chestnut mixture, then fold in the rest evenly.

4 Spoon the mixture into six small ramekin dishes or custard cups and chill until set. Serve the pots topped with a generous spoonful of crème fraîche with some chocolate curls positioned on top.

MOCHA VELVET CREAM POTS

SERVES 8

15ml/1 tbsp instant coffee powder
475ml/16fl oz/2 cups milk
75g/3oz/6 tbsp caster (superfine) sugar
225g/8oz plain (semisweet) chocolate, chopped
10ml/2 tsp vanilla essence (extract)
30ml/2 tbsp coffee liqueur (optional)
7 egg yolks
whipped cream and crystallized mimosa balls, to decorate

1 Preheat the oven to 160°C/325°F/Gas 3. Place 8 x 120ml/ 4fl oz/½ cup custard cups or ramekins in a roasting pan.

2 Put the coffee into a pan. Stir in the milk and sugar, and set over a medium heat. Bring to the boil, stirring constantly, until both coffee and sugar have dissolved.

3 Off the heat, add the chocolate. Stir until melted and smooth. Stir in the vanilla and coffee liqueur, if using.

4 Whisk the egg yolks lightly. Slowly whisk in the chocolate mixture, then strain into a large jug (pitcher) and divide equally among the cups or ramekins. Pour enough boiling water into the roasting pan to come halfway up the sides of the cups or ramekins. Carefully place the roasting pan in the oven.

5 Bake for 30–35 minutes, until the custard is just set and a knife inserted into the custard comes out clean. Remove the cups or ramekins from the roasting pan and allow to cool. Place on a baking sheet, cover and chill completely. Decorate with whipped cream and crystallized mimosa balls.

CHOCOLATE VANILLA TIMBALES

<u>SERVES 6</u>

350ml/12fl oz/1½ cups semi-skimmed
   (low-fat) milk
30ml/2 tbsp cocoa powder
2 eggs, separated
10ml/2 tsp vanilla essence (extract)
45ml/3 tbsp granulated sugar
15ml/1 tbsp/1 sachet powdered gelatine
45ml/3 tbsp hot water
extra cocoa powder, for dusting

For the Sauce

115g/4oz/½ cup light Greek
   (US strained plain) yogurt
25ml/1½ tbsp vanilla essence (extract)

1 Heat the milk and cocoa powder until
the milk is boiling. Beat the egg yolks with
the vanilla and sweetener until pale and
smooth. Gradually add the chocolate milk,
beating well.

2 Return the mixture to the pan and stir
constantly over a gentle heat, without
boiling, until thickened and smooth.

3 Remove the pan from the heat. Pour
the gelatine into a bowl with the hot water
and stir until completely dissolved, then
quickly stir into the milk mixture. Set this
mixture aside and allow to cool until
almost setting.

4 Whisk the egg whites until they hold soft
peaks. Fold the egg whites quickly into the
milk mixture. Spoon the timbale mixture
into six individual moulds and chill in the
refrigerator until set.

5 To serve, run a knife around the edge,
dip the moulds quickly into hot water and
turn out. Dust with cocoa. For the sauce,
stir together the yogurt and vanilla and
spoon on to the plates.

TIRAMISU IN CHOCOLATE CUPS

SERVES 6

1 egg yolk

30ml/2 tbsp caster (superfine) sugar

2.5ml/½ tsp vanilla essence (extract)

250g/9oz/generous 1 cup mascarpone

120ml/4fl oz/½ cup strong black coffee

15ml/1 tbsp cocoa powder

30ml/2 tbsp coffee liqueur

16 amaretti biscuits (cookies)

cocoa powder, for dusting

For the Chocolate Cups

175g/6oz plain (semisweet)
    chocolate, chopped

25g/1oz/2 tbsp unsalted (sweet) butter

1 For the cups, cut out 6 x 15cm/6in rounds of baking parchment. Melt the chocolate with the butter in a bowl set over a pan of simmering water. Stir until the mixture is smooth, then spread a spoonful over each circle to within 2cm/¾in of the edge.

2 Lift each paper round and drape it over an upturned teacup so that the edges curve into frills. Leave until set, then lift off and peel away the paper to reveal the chocolate cups.

3 Make the filling. Using a hand-held electric mixer, beat the egg yolk and sugar in a bowl until smooth, then stir in the vanilla essence. Soften the mascarpone if necessary, then stir it into the egg yolk mixture. Beat until smooth. Set aside.

4 Mix the coffee, cocoa and liqueur. Break up the amaretti roughly then stir into the mixture.

5 Place the chocolate cups on individual plates. Divide half the amaretti mixture among them, then spoon over half the mascarpone mixture. Spoon over the remaining amaretti mixture, top with the rest of the mascarpone mixture and dust with cocoa powder. Chill for 30 minutes before serving.

DEVILISH CHOCOLATE ROULADE

SERVES 6–8

175g/6oz dark (bittersweet) chocolate, chopped into small pieces

4 eggs, separated

115g/4oz/½ cup caster (superfine) sugar

cocoa powder, for dusting

chocolate-dipped strawberries, to decorate

For the Filling

225g/8oz plain (semisweet) chocolate, chopped into small pieces

45ml/3 tbsp brandy

2 eggs, separated

250g/9oz/generous 1 cup mascarpone cheese

1 Preheat the oven to 180°C/350°F/Gas 4. Grease and line a 33 × 23cm/13 × 9in Swiss roll tin (jelly roll pan). Melt the chocolate.

2 Whisk the egg yolks and sugar in a bowl until pale and thick, then stir in the melted chocolate. Place the egg whites in a clean, grease-free bowl. Whisk to soft peaks, then fold lightly and evenly into the egg and chocolate mixture.

3 Scrape into the tin and spread to the corners. Bake for 15–20 minutes, until well risen and firm to the touch. Dust a sheet of baking parchment with cocoa powder. Turn the sponge out on to the paper, cover with a clean dishtowel and leave to cool.

4 Make the filling. Melt the chocolate with the brandy in a heatproof bowl over a pan of simmering water. Remove from the heat. Beat the egg yolks together, then beat into the chocolate mixture. In a separate bowl, whisk the egg whites to soft peaks, then fold lightly and evenly into the filling.

5 Uncover the roulade, remove the lining paper and spread with the mascarpone. Spread the chocolate mixture over the top, then roll up carefully from a long side to enclose the filling. Transfer to a serving plate with the join underneath, decorate with fresh chocolate-dipped strawberries and chill before serving.

COOK'S TIP

Chocolate-dipped strawberries make a marvellous edible decoration for cakes and desserts. Break plain, milk or white chocolate into small pieces and place in a small deep heatproof bowl over a pan of barely simmering water. While the chocolate melts, line a baking sheet with baking parchment and set aside.

Stir the melted chocolate until it is completely smooth. Holding a strawberry by its stalk or stalk end, dip it partially or fully into the melted chocolate, allowing any excess chocolate to drip back into the bowl, then place the fruit on the lined baking sheet. Repeat with the rest of the fruit. Leave until the chocolate has set and use the strawberries on the day of making.

The same technique can be applied to other relatively firm fruits, such as cherries and orange segments.

CHOCOLATE CONES WITH APRICOT SAUCE

SERVES 6

250g/9oz plain (semisweet) chocolate,
   chopped into small pieces
350g/12oz/1½ cups ricotta cheese
45ml/3 tbsp double (heavy) cream
30ml/2 tbsp brandy
30ml/2 tbsp icing (confectioners') sugar
finely grated rind of 1 lemon
pared strips of lemon rind, to decorate
For the Sauce
175g/6oz/⅔ cup apricot jam
45ml/3 tbsp lemon juice

1 Cut 12 10cm/4in double thickness
rounds from baking parchment and
shape each into a cone. Secure with
masking tape.

2 Melt the chocolate. Cool slightly, then
spoon a little into each cone, swirling and
brushing to coat the paper evenly.

3 Support each cone point downwards in
a cup or glass held on its side, to keep it
level. Leave in a cool place until the cones
are completely set. Only chill them if it is
a very hot day.

4 Make the sauce. Combine the apricot
jam and lemon juice in a small pan. Melt
over a gentle heat, stirring occasionally,
then press through a sieve into a small
bowl. Set aside to cool.

5 Beat the ricotta cheese until softened,
then beat in the cream, brandy and icing
sugar. Stir in the lemon rind. Spoon the
mixture into a piping (pastry) bag. Fill the
cones, then peel off the paper.

6 Spoon a pool of apricot sauce on to six
dessert plates. Arrange the cones in pairs
on the plates. Decorate with a sprinkling
of pared lemon rind strips and then
serve immediately.

CHOCOLATE BLANCMANGE

SERVES 4

60ml/4 tbsp cornflour (cornstarch)
600ml/1 pint/2½ cups milk
45ml/3 tbsp sugar
50–115g/2–4oz plain (semisweet)
   chocolate, chopped
a few drops of vanilla essence (extract)
white and plain (semisweet) chocolate
   curls, to decorate

1 Rinse a 750ml/1¼ pint/3 cup fluted
mould with cold water. Mix the cornflour
to a paste with a little of the milk.

2 Bring the remaining milk to the boil,
then pour on to the cornflour mixture,
stirring constantly.

3 Pour all the milk back into the clean
pan and bring slowly to the boil over a low
heat, stirring constantly until the mixture
boils and thickens. Remove the pan from
the heat, then add the sugar, chocolate
and vanilla essence and stir until the
sauce is completely smooth, all the sugar
has dissolved and the chocolate pieces
have melted completely.

4 Pour the chocolate mixture into the
mould, cover closely with dampened
greaseproof (waxed) paper and leave in a
cool place for several hours to set.

5 To unmould the blancmange, remove
the paper and place a serving plate
upside-down on top of the mould. Hold
the plate and mould firmly and turn over.
Give a gentle but firm shake to loosen the
blancmange, then lift off the mould.
Scatter the white and plain chocolate curls
over the top and serve.

CHOCOLATE MANDARIN TRIFLE

SERVES 6–8

- 4 trifle sponges
- 14 amaretti biscuits (cookies)
- 60ml/4 tbsp Amaretto di Sarone or sweet sherry
- 8 mandarin oranges

For the Custard
- 200g/7oz plain (semisweet) chocolate, chopped into small pieces
- 30ml/2 tbsp cornflour (cornstarch)
- 30ml/2 tbsp caster (superfine) sugar
- 2 egg yolks
- 200ml/7fl oz/scant 1 cup milk
- 250g/9oz/generous 1 cup mascarpone cheese

For the Topping
- 250g/9oz/generous 1 cup mascarpone
- mandarin slices
- chocolate shapes

1 Break up the sponges and amaretti, and put in a large glass serving dish. Sprinkle with Amaretto or sherry.

2 Squeeze the juice from 2 mandarins and sprinkle into the dish. Segment the rest and put in the dish.

3 Make the custard. Melt the chocolate. In a heatproof bowl, mix the cornflour, sugar and egg yolks to a smooth paste.

4 Heat the milk in a small pan until almost boiling, then pour on to the egg yolk mixture, stirring constantly. Return to the clean pan and stir over a low heat until the custard has thickened and is smooth.

5 Stir in the mascarpone until melted, then mix in the melted chocolate. Spread over the sponge and biscuit mixture, cool, then chill well. To serve, spread the mascarpone over the custard, then decorate with mandarin slices and chocolate shapes.

COOK'S TIP

You can use canned mandarin oranges, if you prefer. Spoon about 30ml/ 2 tbsp juice over the sponges and amaretti.

CHOCOLATE PROFITEROLES

4 Beat 1 egg in a small bowl and set aside. Add the whole eggs, one at a time, to the flour mixture. Beat in just enough of the beaten egg to make a smooth, shiny dough. It should pull away and fall slowly when dropped from a spoon.

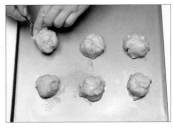

5 Using a tablespoon, put 12 mounds on the baking sheet. Bake for 25–30 minutes, until golden brown.

6 Remove the puffs from the oven and cut a small slit in the side of each one to release the steam. Return the puffs to the oven, turn off the heat and leave them to dry out, with the oven door open.

7 Remove the ice cream from the freezer and allow it to soften for about 10 minutes. Split the profiteroles in half and put a small scoop of ice cream in each. Arrange on a serving platter or on individual plates. Pour the sauce over and serve at once.

> **VARIATION**
> Fill the profiteroles with whipped cream, if you prefer. Spoon the cream into a piping (pastry) bag and fill the slit puffs, or sandwich the halved puffs with the cream.

SERVES 4-6

110g/3¾oz/scant 1 cup plain (all-purpose) flour
1.5ml/¼ tsp salt
a pinch of freshly grated nutmeg
175ml/6fl oz/¾ cup water
75g/3oz/6 tbsp unsalted (sweet) butter, cut into 6 equal pieces
3 eggs
750ml/1¼ pints/3 cups vanilla ice cream
For the Chocolate Sauce
275g/10oz plain (semisweet) chocolate, chopped into small pieces
120ml/4fl oz/½ cup warm water

1 Preheat the oven to 200°C/400°F/Gas 6. Grease a baking sheet. Sift the flour, salt and nutmeg on to a sheet of foil.

2 Make the sauce. Melt the chocolate with the water in a heatproof bowl set over a pan of barely simmering water. Stir until smooth. Keep warm until ready to serve, or reheat when required.

3 In a pan, bring the water and butter to the boil. Remove from the heat and add the dry ingredients all at once, funnelling them in from the foil. Beat with a wooden spoon for about 1 minute until well blended and the mixture starts to pull away from the sides of the pan. Set the pan over a low heat and cook the mixture for about 2 minutes, beating constantly. Then remove from the heat.

BITTER CHOCOLATE MOUSSE

SERVES 8

225g/8oz plain (semisweet) chocolate, chopped into small pieces
60ml/4 tbsp water
30ml/2 tbsp orange-flavoured liqueur or brandy
25g/1oz/2 tbsp unsalted (sweet) butter, cut into small pieces
4 eggs, separated
90ml/6 tbsp whipping cream
1.5ml/¼ tsp cream of tartar
45ml/3 tbsp caster (superfine) sugar
crème fraîche and chocolate curls, to decorate

1 Melt the chocolate with the water in a heatproof bowl set over a pan of barely simmering water, stirring until smooth. Off the heat, whisk in the liqueur or brandy and butter.

2 With a hand-held electric mixer, beat the egg yolks until thick and creamy, then beat into the melted chocolate.

3 Whip the cream until soft peaks form, then stir a spoonful into the chocolate mixture to lighten it. Fold in the remaining cream.

4 Beat the egg whites until frothy. Add the cream of tartar and beat until soft peaks form. Gradually sprinkle over the sugar. Beat until stiff and glossy.

5 Using a metal spoon, stir a quarter of the egg whites into the chocolate mixture, then gently fold in the remaining whites until they are combined. Spoon into individual dishes. Chill.

6 Spoon a little crème fraîche over each mousse and decorate with the chocolate curls.

WHITE CHOCOLATE VANILLA MOUSSE WITH DARK CHOCOLATE SAUCE

SERVES 6–8

200g/7 oz white chocolate, chopped into small pieces
2 eggs, separated
60ml/4 tbsp caster (superfine) sugar
300ml/½ pint/1¼ cups double (heavy) cream
1 sachet powdered gelatine
150ml/¼ pint/⅔ cup Greek (US strained plain) yogurt
10ml/2 tsp vanilla essence (extract)
For the Sauce
50g/2oz plain (semisweet) chocolate, chopped
30ml/2 tbsp dark rum
60ml/4 tbsp single (light) cream

1 Line a 1 litre/1¾ pint/4 cup loaf tin (pan) with clear film (plastic wrap). Melt the chocolate. Whisk the egg yolks and sugar until pale and thick, then beat in the chocolate.

2 Heat the cream until almost boiling. Off the heat, sprinkle over the powdered gelatine, stirring until completely dissolved. Pour on to the chocolate mixture. Whisk until smooth.

3 Whisk in the yogurt and vanilla. Whisk the egg whites until stiff, then fold into the mixture. Tip into the tin, level, then chill.

4 Make the sauce. Melt the chocolate with the rum and cream in a bowl set over a pan of simmering water. Leave to cool.

5 Serve the mousse in thick slices with the cooled chocolate sauce spooned around.

MANGO <u>AND</u> CHOCOLATE CREME BRULEE

SERVES 6

2 ripe mangoes, peeled, stoned (pitted)
and chopped

300ml/½ pint/1¼ cups double
(heavy) cream

300ml/½ pint/1¼ cups crème fraîche

1 vanilla pod (bean)

115g/4oz dark (bittersweet) chocolate,
chopped into small pieces

4 egg yolks

15ml/1 tbsp clear honey

90ml/6 tbsp demerara (raw) sugar, for
the topping

1 Divide the mangoes among six
flameproof dishes and set them on a
baking sheet.

2 Mix the cream, crème fraîche and
vanilla pod in a large heatproof bowl.
Place the bowl over a pan of simmering
water. Heat the cream mixture for
10 minutes. Remove the vanilla pod
and stir in the chocolate until melted and
smooth. Set aside.

3 Whisk the egg yolks and clear honey in
a heatproof bowl. Gradually whisk in the
chocolate cream. Place over the pan and
stir until the chocolate custard thickens
enough to coat the back of a wooden spoon.

4 Remove from the heat and spoon the
custard over the mangoes. Cool, then chill
in the refrigerator until set.

5 Preheat the grill (broiler) to high.
Sprinkle 15ml/1 tbsp demerara sugar
evenly over each dessert and spray lightly
with a little water. Grill briefly, as close to
the heat as possible, until the sugar melts
and caramelizes. Chill again before serving
the desserts set on plates.

WHITE CHOCOLATE PARFAIT

SERVES 10

225g/8oz white chocolate
600ml/1 pint/ 2½ cups whipping cream
120ml/4fl oz/½ cup milk
10 egg yolks
15ml/1 tbsp caster (superfine) sugar
40g/1½oz/½ cup desiccated (dry
  unsweetened shredded) coconut
120ml/4fl oz/½ cup canned sweetened
  coconut milk
150g/5oz/1¼ cups unsalted
  macadamia nuts
fresh coconut curls, to decorate

For the Chocolate Icing

225g/8oz plain (semisweet) chocolate
75g/3oz/6 tbsp butter
20ml/1 tbsp golden (light corn) syrup
175ml/6fl oz/¾ cup whipping cream

1 Carefully line the base and sides of a 1.4 litre/2⅓ pint/6 cup terrine mould with clear film (plastic wrap).

2 Chop and melt the white chocolate with 50ml/2fl oz/¼ cup of the cream using a double boiler or heatproof bowl set over a pan of simmering water. Stir continuously until the mixture is smooth. Set aside.

3 Put the milk in a pan. Add 250ml/8fl oz/1 cup of the remaining cream and bring to boiling point over a medium heat, stirring constantly.

4 Meanwhile, whisk the egg yolks and caster sugar together in a large bowl until thick and pale.

5 Add the hot cream mixture to the yolks, whisking constantly. Pour back into the pan and cook over a low heat for 2–3 minutes, stirring, until thickened.

6 Add the melted chocolate, desiccated coconut and coconut milk, then stir well and leave to cool. Whip the remaining cream in a bowl until thick, then fold into the chocolate and coconut mixture.

7 Put 475ml/16fl oz/2 cups of the parfait mixture in the prepared mould and spread evenly. Cover and freeze for about 2 hours, until just firm. Cover the remaining mixture and chill.

> **WHITE CHOCOLATE AND
> GINGER PARFAIT**
> Use sliced preserved stem ginger instead of macadamia nuts for the central layer of the parfait, and substitute syrup from the jar of ginger for the golden syrup in the icing. Leave out the coconut, if you prefer, and use sweetened condensed milk instead of the coconut milk.

8 Scatter the macadamia nuts evenly over the frozen parfait. Spoon in the remaining parfait mixture and level the surface. Cover the terrine and freeze for 6–8 hours or overnight, until the parfait is firm.

9 To make the icing, chop and melt the chocolate with the butter and syrup using a double boiler. Stir occasionally.

10 Heat the cream until just simmering, then stir into the chocolate mixture. Set aside and leave to cool until lukewarm.

11 To turn out the parfait, wrap the terrine in a hot towel and set upside-down on a plate. Lift off the terrine, then peel off the clear film. Place the parfait on a rack over a baking sheet and pour the icing evenly over the top. Working quickly, smooth the icing down the sides with a metal spatula. Leave to set slightly, then transfer to a freezer-proof plate and freeze for 3–4 hours more.

12 Remove the parfait from the freezer about 15 minutes before serving, to allow the ice cream to soften slightly. When ready to serve, cut into generous slices, using a knife dipped in hot water between each slice. Serve, decorated with coconut curls.

WHITE CHOCOLATE RASPBERRY RIPPLE ICE CREAM

RASPBERRY RIPPLE AND WHITE CHOCOLATE ICE CREAM TEAMED TOGETHER ARE AN IRRESISTIBLE COMBINATION, FULL OF FLAVOUR AND RESONANT OF SUMMER.

2 In a pan, combine the milk and 250ml/8fl oz/1 cup of the cream and bring to the boil. In a bowl beat the yolks and sugar with a hand-held mixer for 2–3 minutes until thick and creamy. Gradually pour the hot milk mixture over the yolks and return to the pan. Cook over a medium heat until the custard coats the back of a wooden spoon, stirring constantly.

3 Off the heat, stir in the white chocolate until melted. Pour the remaining cream into a large bowl. Strain in the hot custard, mix, then stir in the vanilla. Cool, then transfer the custard to an ice-cream maker and freeze according to the manufacturer's instructions.

MAKES 1 LITRE/1¾ PINTS/4 CUPS
  250ml/8fl oz/1 cup milk
  475ml/16fl oz/2 cups whipping cream
  7 egg yolks
  30ml/2 tbsp granulated sugar
  225g/8oz fine quality white chocolate,
    chopped into small pieces
  5ml/1 tsp vanilla essence (extract)
  mint sprigs, to decorate
For the Raspberry Ripple Sauce
  275g/10oz packet frozen raspberries in
    light syrup or 275g/10oz jar reduced-
    sugar raspberry preserve
  10ml/2 tsp golden (light corn) syrup
  15ml/1 tbsp lemon juice
  15ml/1 tbsp cornflour (cornstarch)
    mixed with 15ml/1 tbsp water

1 Prepare the sauce. Press the raspberries and their syrup through a sieve into a saucepan. Add the golden syrup, lemon juice and cornflour mixture. (If using preserve, omit cornflour, but add the water.) Bring to the boil, stirring often, then simmer for 1–2 minutes. Pour into a bowl and leave to cool, then chill.

4 When the mixture is frozen, but still soft, transfer one-third of the ice cream to a freezerproof bowl. Set half the raspberry sauce aside. Spoon one-third of the remainder over the ice cream. Cover with another third of the ice cream and more sauce. Repeat. With a knife or spoon, lightly marble the mixture, then cover and freeze. Allow the ice cream to soften for about 15 minutes before serving with the rest of the raspberry sauce. Decorate with the mint sprigs.

CHOCOLATE FUDGE SUNDAES

SERVES 4

4 scoops each vanilla and coffee ice cream

2 small ripe bananas

whipped cream, to serve

toasted flaked almonds, to decorate

For the Sauce

50g/2oz/⅓ cup soft light brown sugar

120ml/4fl oz/½ cup golden
(light corn) syrup

45ml/3 tbsp strong black coffee

5ml/1 tsp ground cinnamon

150g/5oz plain (semisweet) chocolate,
chopped into small pieces

75ml/3fl oz/5 tbsp whipping cream

45ml/3 tbsp coffee liqueur (optional)

1 Make the sauce. Place the brown sugar, golden syrup, coffee and ground cinnamon in a heavy pan. Bring to the boil, then boil for about 5 minutes, stirring the mixture constantly.

2 Turn off the heat and stir in the chocolate. When the chocolate has melted and the mixture is smooth, stir in the cream and the liqueur, if using. Leave the sauce to cool slightly. If made ahead, reheat the sauce gently until just warm.

3 Fill four glasses with a scoop each of vanilla and coffee ice cream.

4 Peel the bananas and slice them thinly. Scatter the sliced bananas over the ice cream. Pour the warm fudge sauce over the bananas, then top each sundae with a generous swirl of whipped cream. Sprinkle the sundaes with toasted almonds and serve at once.

CHOCOLATE ICE CREAM

SERVES 4–6

    750ml/1¼ pints/3 cups milk
    10 cm/4 in piece of vanilla pod (bean)
    4 egg yolks
    115g/4oz/½ cup granulated sugar
    225g/8oz plain (semisweet) chocolate,
      chopped into small pieces

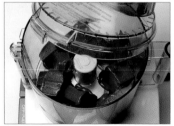

1 Heat the milk with the vanilla pod in a small pan. Take off the heat as soon as small bubbles form on the surface. Strain into a jug (pitcher) and set aside.

2 Using a wire whisk or hand-held electric mixer, beat the egg yolks in a bowl. Then gradually whisk in the sugar and continue to whisk until the mixture is pale and thick. Slowly add the milk to the egg mixture, whisking after each addition. When all the milk has been added, pour the mixture into a heatproof bowl.

3 Place the heatproof bowl over a pan of simmering water and add the chocolate. Stir over a low heat until the chocolate melts, then increase the heat slightly and continue to stir the chocolate-flavoured custard until thickened enough to coat the back of a wooden spoon lightly. Remove the custard from the heat, pour into a bowl and leave to cool, stirring from time to time to prevent a skin from forming on the surface.

4 Freeze the chocolate mixture in an ice-cream maker, following the manufacturer's instructions, or pour into a suitable container for freezing. Freeze for about 3 hours, or until set. Remove from the container and chop roughly into 7.5cm/3in pieces. Place in a food processor and chop until smooth. Return to the freezer container and freeze again. Repeat two or three times, until the ice cream is smooth and creamy.

CHOCOLATE FLAKE ICE CREAM

SERVES 6

300ml/½ pint/1¼ cups whipping
   cream, chilled
90ml/6 tbsp Greek (strained plain) yogurt
75–90ml/5–6 tbsp caster (superfine) sugar
few drops of vanilla essence (extract)
150g/5oz/10 tbsp flaked or roughly
   grated milk chocolate

COOK'S TIPS

Transfer the ice cream from the freezer
to the refrigerator for about 15
minutes before serving so that it
softens and the full flavour can be
appreciated.
   Use a metal scoop to serve the ice
cream, dipping the scoop briefly in
warm water between servings. If the
ice cream has been made in a loaf tin,
simply slice it.

1 Have ready an ice-cream maker, or use
a 600–900ml/1–1½ pint/2½–3¾ cup
freezerproof container, preferably with a
lid. Make a space in the freezer that you
can reach easily. If necessary, turn the
freezer to the coldest setting.

2 Softly whip the cream in a large bowl,
then fold in the yogurt, sugar, vanilla
essence and chocolate. Stir gently to mix
thoroughly, then transfer to the ice-cream
maker or freezer container.

3 Smooth the surface of the ice cream,
then cover and freeze. Gently stir with a
fork every 30 minutes for up to 4 hours,
until the ice cream is too hard to stir. If
using an ice-cream maker, follow the
manufacturer's instructions.

4 Serve in generous scoops, decorated
with a piece of flaked chocolate, if wished.

CHOCOLATE SORBET

SERVES 6

150g/5oz dark (bittersweet) chocolate, chopped
115g/4oz plain (semisweet) chocolate, grated
225g/8oz/1¼ cups caster (superfine) sugar
475ml/16fl oz/2 cups water
chocolate curls, to decorate

1 Put all the chocolate in a food processor, fitted with the metal blade, and process for 20–30 seconds until finely chopped.

2 Bring the sugar and water to the boil, stirring until the sugar dissolves. Boil for 2 minutes, then remove from the heat.

3 With the machine running, pour the hot syrup over the chocolate in the food processor. Process until melted.

4 Strain the chocolate mixture into a large measuring jug (pitcher) or bowl. Leave to cool, then chill, stirring occasionally. Freeze the mixture in an ice-cream maker. Alternatively, pour into a container suitable for use in the freezer, freeze until slushy, whisk until smooth, then freeze again. Whisk for a second time before the mixture hardens completely. Allow the sorbet to soften for 5–10 minutes at room temperature and serve in scoops, decorated with chocolate curls.

CHOCOLATE SORBET WITH RED FRUITS

SERVES 6

475ml/16fl oz/2 cups water
45ml/3 tbsp clear honey
115g/4oz/½ cup caster (superfine) sugar
75g/3oz/¾ cup cocoa powder
50g/2oz plain (semisweet) or dark (bittersweet) chocolate,
    chopped into small pieces
400g/14oz soft red fruits, such as raspberries, redcurrants
    or strawberries

1 Gently heat the water, honey, caster sugar and cocoa powder in a pan until the sugar has completely dissolved. Off the heat, add the chocolate and stir until melted. Leave until cool.

2 Tip into an ice-cream maker and churn until frozen. Alternatively, pour into a container suitable for use in the freezer, freeze until slushy, whisk until smooth, then freeze again. Whisk for a second time before the mixture hardens completely, and cover the container.

3 Remove from the freezer 10–15 minutes before serving, so that the sorbet softens slightly. Serve in scoops in chilled dessert bowls, with the soft fruits.

ROCKY ROAD ICE CREAM

SERVES 6

115g/4oz plain (semisweet) chocolate,
    chopped into small pieces
150ml/¼ pint/⅔ cup milk
300ml/½ pint/1¼ cups double
    (heavy) cream
115g/4oz/2 cups marshmallows,
    chopped into small pieces
115g/4oz/½ cup glacé (candied)
    cherries, chopped
50g/2oz/½ cup crumbled shortbread
    biscuits (cookies)
30ml/2 tbsp chopped walnuts

1 Melt the chocolate in the milk in a
sauce pan over a gentle heat, stirring
occasionally. Pour into a bowl and leave
to cool completely.

2 Whip the cream until it just holds its
shape. Gradually beat in the chocolate
mixture until smooth. Use an ice-cream
maker and churn until almost frozen. Or
use a suitable freezerproof container.
Freeze until ice crystals form around the
edges, then whisk with a strong hand whisk
or hand-held electric mixer until smooth.

3 Stir the rest of the ingredients into the
iced mixture, then return to the freezer
container and freeze until firm.

4 Allow the ice cream to soften at room
temperature for 15–20 minutes before
serving in scoops. Add a wafer and
chocolate sauce, if desired.

ICE CREAM BOMBES

SERVES 6

  1 litre/1¾ pints/4 cups soft-scoop
    chocolate ice cream
  475ml/16fl oz/2 cups soft-scoop
    vanilla ice cream
  50g/2oz/⅓ cup plain (semisweet)
    chocolate chips
  115g/4oz toffees
  75ml/5 tbsp double (heavy) cream

1 Divide the chocolate ice cream among
six small cups. Push it to the base and up
the sides, leaving a small hollow in the
middle. Return to the freezer. Take the
cups out again after 45 minutes and
smooth the ice cream in each into shape,
keeping the centre hollow. Freeze again.

2 Put the vanilla ice cream in a small
bowl and break it up slightly with a spoon.
Stir in the chocolate chips and use this
mixture to fill the hollows in the cups of
chocolate ice cream. Smooth the tops,
then cover with clear film (plastic wrap)
and return to the freezer overnight.

3 Melt the toffees with the cream in a
small pan over a very low heat, stirring
constantly until smooth, warm and creamy.

4 Turn the bombes out on to individual
plates and pour the toffee sauce over the
top. Serve immediately.

CHOCOLATE MINT ICE CREAM PIE

<u>SERVES 8</u>

75g/3 oz plain (semisweet)
chocolate chips
40g/1½oz butter
50g/2oz crisped rice cereal
1 litre/1¾ pints/4 cups mint chocolate-
chip ice cream
chocolate curls, to decorate

1 Line a 23cm/9in pie tin (pan) with foil. Line the base with baking parchment.

2 In a bowl set over a pan of just simmering water, melt the chocolate with the butter. When melted, remove the bowl from the heat and gently stir in the cereal.

3 Press the chocolate mixture over the base and sides of the tin, forming a 1cm/½in rim. Chill until completely hard.

4 Remove the cereal base from the tin. Peel off the foil and paper. Return the base to the pie tin.

5 Remove the ice cream from the freezer and allow it to soften for 10 minutes.

6 Spread the ice cream evenly over the cereal base. Freeze until firm. Scatter the chocolate curls over the ice cream just before serving.

SMALL CAKES AND BAKES

There's no end to the ways to use chocolate in small cakes and cookies. Start the day with a warm Brioche au Chocolat for breakfast, or treat yourself at coffee time with rich, totally indulgent Nut and Chocolate Chip Brownies or Double Chocolate Chip Muffins. Or, if you're after an elegant touch of texture to serve alongside a creamy dinner party dessert, light, crisp Chocolate Cinnamon Tuiles are the perfect choice.

CHOC-CHIP NUT BISCUITS

MAKES 36

115g/4oz/1 cup plain (all-purpose) flour
5ml/1 tsp baking powder
5ml/1 tsp salt
75g/3oz/6 tbsp butter or margarine
115g/4oz/1 cup caster (superfine) sugar
50g/2oz/⅓ cup soft light brown sugar
1 egg
5ml/1 tsp vanilla essence (extract)
115g/4oz/⅔ cup plain (semisweet) chocolate chips
50g/2oz/½ cup hazelnuts, chopped

1 Preheat the oven to 180°C/350°F/Gas 4. Grease 2 or 3 baking sheets. Sift the flour, baking powder and salt into a bowl. Set aside.

2 Cream the butter or margarine and sugars together. Beat in the egg and vanilla essence. Add the flour mixture and beat well.

3 Stir in the chocolate chips and half the hazelnuts. Drop teaspoonfuls of the mixture on to the baking sheets in 2cm/¾in mounds. Space them 5cm/2in apart to allow room for spreading.

4 Flatten each mound lightly with a wet fork. Sprinkle the remaining hazelnuts on top and press lightly into the surface. Bake for 10–12 minutes, until golden brown. Transfer the biscuits (cookies) to a wire rack to cool.

CHOC-CHIP OAT BISCUITS

MAKES 60

115g/4oz/1 cup plain (all-purpose) flour
2.5ml/½ tsp bicarbonate of soda (baking soda)
1.5ml/¼ tsp baking powder
1.5ml/¼ tsp salt
115g/4oz/1 cup butter or margarine, softened
115g/4oz/1 cup caster (superfine) sugar
75g/3oz/½ cup light brown sugar
1 egg
1.5ml/¼ tsp vanilla essence (extract)
75g/3oz/scant 1 cup rolled oats
175g/6oz/1 cup plain (semisweet) chocolate chips

1 Preheat the oven to 180°C/350°F/Gas 4. Grease 3 or 4 baking sheets. Sift the flour, bicarbonate of soda, baking powder and salt into a mixing bowl. Set the bowl aside.

2 With a hand-held electric mixer, cream the butter or margarine and sugars together in a bowl. Add the egg and vanilla essence and beat until light and fluffy.

3 Add the flour mixture and beat on low speed until thoroughly blended. Stir in the rolled oats and chocolate chips, mixing well with a wooden spoon. The dough should be crumbly.

4 Drop heaped teaspoonfuls on to the prepared baking sheets, spacing the dough about 2.5cm/1in apart. Bake in the oven for 15 minutes, until just firm around the edge but still soft to the touch in the centre. With a metal spatula, transfer the biscuits (cookies) to a wire rack and leave to cool.

CHOCOLATE-DIPPED HAZELNUT CRESCENTS

MAKES ABOUT 35

275g/10oz/2 cups plain
  (all-purpose) flour
a pinch of salt
225g/8oz/1 cup unsalted (sweet)
  butter, softened
75g/3oz/6 tbsp caster
  (superfine) sugar
15ml/1 tbsp hazelnut-flavoured liqueur
5ml/1 tsp vanilla essence (extract)
75g/3oz plain (semisweet) chocolate,
  chopped into small pieces
50g/2oz/½ cup hazelnuts, toasted and
  finely chopped
icing (confectioners') sugar, for dusting
350g/12oz plain (semisweet) chocolate,
  melted, for dipping

1 Preheat the oven to 160°C/325°F/Gas 3. Grease 2 large baking sheets. Sift the flour and salt into a bowl. Set aside. Beat the butter until creamy. Add the sugar and beat until fluffy, then beat in the liqueur and vanilla. Gently stir in the flour mixture, then the chocolate and hazelnuts.

2 With floured hands, shape the dough into 5 x 1cm/2 x ½in crescent shapes. Place on the baking sheets 5cm/2in apart. Bake for 20–25 minutes until the edges are set and the biscuits (cookies) slightly golden. Remove the biscuits from the oven and cool on the baking sheets for about 10 minutes, then transfer the biscuits to wire racks to cool completely.

3 Have the melted chocolate ready in a small bowl. Dust the biscuits lightly with icing sugar. Using a pair of kitchen tongs or your fingers, dip half of each crescent into the melted chocolate. Place the crescents on baking parchment until the chocolate has set.

CHUNKY DOUBLE CHOCOLATE COOKIES

MAKES 18–20

- 115g/4oz/½ cup unsalted (sweet) butter, softened
- 115g/4oz/⅔ cup light muscovado (brown) sugar
- 1 egg
- 5ml/1 tsp vanilla essence (extract)
- 150g/5oz/1¼ cups self-raising (self-rising) flour
- 75g/3oz/¾ cup rolled oats or ground almonds
- 115g/4Oz plain (semisweet) chocolate, roughly chopped
- 115/4oz white chocolate, roughly chopped

1 Preheat the oven to 190°C/375°F/Gas 5. Lightly grease 2 baking sheets. Cream the butter and sugar until pale and fluffy. Beat in the egg and vanilla.

2 Sift the flour over the mixture and fold in lightly with a metal spoon, then add the oats or almonds and plain and white chocolate and stir until evenly mixed.

3 Place small spoonfuls of the mixture in 18–20 rocky heaps on the baking sheets, leaving space for spreading.

4 Bake for 12–15 minutes or until the biscuits are beginning to turn pale golden. Cool for 2–3 minutes on the baking sheets, then lift on to wire racks. The biscuits will be soft at first but harden on cooling.

CHOCOLATE MARZIPAN COOKIES

MAKES ABOUT 36

200g/7oz/scant 1 cup unsalted (sweet)
  butter, softened
200g/7oz/generous 1 cup light
  muscovado (brown) sugar
1 egg, beaten
300g/11oz/2¾ cups plain
  (all-purpose) flour
60ml/4 tbsp cocoa powder
200g/7oz marzipan paste
115g/4oz white chocolate, chopped

1 Preheat the oven to 190°C/375°F/Gas 5. Lightly grease 2 large baking sheets. Using a hand-held electric mixer, cream the butter with the sugar in a mixing bowl until pale and fluffy. Add the egg and beat well.

2 Sift the flour and cocoa over the mixture. Stir in with a wooden spoon until all the flour mixture has been smoothly incorporated, then use clean hands to press the mixture together to make a fairly soft dough.

3 Using a rolling pin and keeping your touch light, roll out about half the dough on a lightly floured surface to a thickness of about 5mm/¼in. Using a 5cm/2in plain or fluted biscuit (cookie) cutter, cut out 36 rounds, re-rolling the dough as required. Wrap the remaining dough in clear film (plastic wrap) and set aside.

4 Cut the marzipan paste into 36 equal pieces. Roll into balls, flatten slightly and place one on each round of dough. Roll out the remaining dough, cut out more rounds, then place on top of the almond paste. Press the dough edges to seal.

5 Bake for 10–12 minutes, or until the cookies have risen well and are beginning to crack on the surface. Cool on the baking sheets for about 2–3 minutes, then finish cooling on a wire rack.

6 Melt the white chocolate, then either drizzle it over the cookies or use a piping (pastry) bag and quickly pipe designs.

VARIATION
Use glacé icing instead of melted white chocolate to decorate the cookies, if you prefer.

BLACK AND WHITE GINGER FLORENTINES

120ml/4fl oz/½ cup double (heavy) cream

50g/2oz/¼ cup butter

50g/2oz/¼ cup granulated sugar

30ml/2 tbsp clear honey

150g/5oz/1¼ cups flaked (sliced) almonds

40g/1½oz/6 tbsp plain (all-purpose) flour

2.5ml/½ tsp ground ginger

50g/2oz/⅓ cup diced candied orange peel

75g/3oz/½ cup diced stem ginger

50g/2oz plain (semisweet) chocolate, chopped into small pieces

150g/5oz dark (bittersweet) chocolate, chopped into small pieces

150g/5oz fine quality white chocolate, chopped into small pieces

1 Preheat the oven to 180°C/350°F/Gas 4. Lightly grease 2 large baking sheets. In a pan over a medium heat, stir the cream, butter, sugar and honey until the sugar dissolves. Bring the mixture to the boil, stirring constantly. Remove from the heat, stir in the almonds, flour and ground ginger, then the candied peel, ginger and plain chocolate.

2 Drop teaspoonfuls of the mixtur on to the prepared baking sheets at least 7.5cm/3in apart. Spread each round as thinly as possible with the back of the spoon.

3 Bake for 8–10 minutes, or until the edges are golden brown and the biscuits (cookies) are bubbling. Do not under-bake or they will be sticky, but be careful not to over-bake as they burn easily. Continue baking in batches. If you wish, use a 7.5cm/3in biscuit (cookie) cutter to neaten the edges of the florentines while they are still on the baking sheets.

4 Allow the biscuits to cool on the baking sheets for 10 minutes, until firm enough to move. Using a metal spatula, carefully lift the biscuits on to wire racks to cool completely.

5 Melt the dark chocolate in a heatproof bowl over barely simmering water. Set aside. In a separate bowl melt white chocolate the same way, stirring frequently. Remove and set aside to cool for about 5 minutes, stirring occasionally.

6 Using a small palette knife (metal spatula), spread half the florentines with the dark chocolate and half with the white chocolate. Place on a wire rack, chocolate side up. Chill for 10–15 minutes until they are set completely.

CHEWY CHOCOLATE BISCUITS

4 egg whites

350g/12oz/2½ cups icing (confectioners') sugar

115g/4oz/1 cup cocoa powder

30ml/2 tbsp plain (all-purpose) flour

5ml/1 tsp powdered instant coffee

15ml/1 tbsp water

115g/4oz/1 cup walnuts, finely chopped

1 Preheat the oven to 180°C/350°F/Gas 4. Line 2 baking sheets with baking parchment.

2 With a hand-held electric mixer, beat the egg whites until frothy. Sift the icing sugar, cocoa, flour and coffee into the egg whites. Add the water and beat gently to blend, then on high speed until the mixture thickens. Fold in the walnuts using a rubber spatula.

3 Place generous spoonfuls 2.5cm/1in apart on the baking sheets. Bake for 12–15 minutes, until firm and cracked on top but soft on the inside. Cool on wire racks.

CHOCOLATE CRACKLE-TOPS

MAKES ABOUT 38

200g/7oz dark (bittersweet) or plain
(semisweet) chocolate, chopped into
small pieces
90g/3½oz/7 tbsp unsalted (sweet) butter
115g/4oz/½ cup caster (superfine) sugar
3 eggs
5ml/1 tsp vanilla essence (extract)
200g/7oz/1¾ cups plain
(all-purpose) flour
25g/1oz/¼ cup cocoa powder
2.5ml/½ tsp baking powder
a pinch of salt
175g/6oz/1½ cups icing
(confectioners') sugar, for coating

1 Grease 2 or 3 large baking sheets. Melt
the chocolate and butter until smooth,
stirring frequently. Off the heat, stir in the
sugar until dissolved. Add the eggs one at
a time, beating well. Stir in the vanilla.

2 Sift the flour, cocoa, baking powder and
salt into a bowl. Gradually stir into the
chocolate mixture in batches to make a
soft dough. Cover in clear film (plastic
wrap). Chill for 1 hour or until firm enough
to hold its shape.

3 Preheat the oven to 160°C/325°F/Gas 3.
Place the icing sugar in a small, deep
bowl. Using a small ice-cream scoop or
teaspoon, scoop the dough into small balls
and roll between your palms.

4 Drop the balls, one at a time, into the
icing sugar and roll until heavily coated.
Remove each ball with a slotted spoon and
tap the spoon against the bowl to remove
excess sugar. Place the balls on the baking
sheets, about 4cm/1½in apart.

5 Bake the biscuits (cookies) for 10–15
minutes or until the top of each feels slightly
firm when touched with a fingertip. Leave
for 2–3 minutes, until just set. Transfer to
wire racks and leave to cool completely.

CHUNKY CHOCOLATE DROPS

MAKES ABOUT 18

- 175g/6oz dark (bittersweet) chocolate, chopped into small pieces
- 115g/4oz/½ cup unsalted (sweet) butter, diced
- 2 eggs
- 115g/4oz/½ cup granulated sugar
- 50g/2oz/⅓ cup light brown sugar
- 40g/1½oz/6 tbsp plain (all-purpose) flour
- 25g/1oz/¼ cup cocoa powder
- 5ml/1 tsp baking powder
- 10ml/2 tsp vanilla essence (extract)
- a pinch of salt
- 115g/4oz/1 cup pecan nuts, toasted and coarsely chopped
- 175g/6oz/1 cup plain (semisweet) chocolate chips
- 115g/4oz white chocolate, chopped
- 115g/4oz milk chocolate, chopped

1 Preheat the oven to 160°C/325°F/ Gas 3. Grease 2 large baking sheets. In a medium pan over a low heat, melt the chocolate and butter until smooth, stirring frequently. Remove from the heat and leave to cool slightly.

2 In a large mixing bowl, beat the eggs and sugars until pale and creamy. Pour in the chocolate mixture gradually, beating well. Beat in the flour, cocoa, baking powder and vanilla essence. Stir in the remaining ingredients.

3 Drop heaped tablespoonfuls of the mixture on to the baking sheets, 10cm/4in apart. Flatten each to a 7.5cm/3in round. (You will get only 4–6 biscuits (cookies) on each sheet.) Bake for 8–10 minutes until the tops are shiny and cracked and the edges look crisp. Do not over-bake or the biscuits will break when they are removed from the baking sheets.

4 Remove the baking sheets to wire racks to cool for 2 minutes, until the biscuits are just set, then carefully transfer them to the wire racks to cool completely. Bake the biscuits in batches and, when cool, store in an airtight container.

CHOCOLATE AMARETTI

MAKES ABOUT 24

115g/4oz/1 cup blanched
  whole almonds
115g/4oz/½ cup caster (superfine) sugar
15ml/1 tbsp cocoa powder
30ml/2 tbsp icing (confectioners') sugar
2 egg whites
a pinch of cream of tartar
5ml/1 tsp almond essence (extract)
flaked (sliced) almonds, to decorate

1 Preheat the oven to 180°C/350°F/Gas 4. Bake the almonds for 10–12 minutes, turning occasionally until golden brown. Set aside to cool. Reduce the oven temperature to 160°C/325°F/Gas 3.

2 Line a large baking sheet with baking parchment. In a food processor, process the toasted almonds with half the caster sugar until finely ground. Transfer to a bowl and stir in the cocoa powder and icing sugar. Set aside.

3 In a medium mixing bowl, beat the egg whites and cream of tartar with a hand-held electric mixer until stiff peaks form. Sprinkle in the remaining caster sugar about 15ml/1 tbsp at a time, beating well after each addition, and continue beating until glossy and stiff. Beat in the almond essence.

4 Sprinkle over the almond-sugar mixture and gently fold into the beaten egg whites until just blended. Spoon the mixture into a large piping (pastry) bag fitted with a plain 1cm/½in nozzle. Pipe 4cm/1½in rounds about 2.5cm/1in apart on the baking sheet. Press a flaked almond into the centre of each biscuit (cookie)

5 Bake the biscuits for 12–15 minutes, or until crisp. Cool on the baking sheet for 10 minutes. With a palette knife (metal spatula), transfer the biscuits to wire racks to cool completely. When cool, store in an airtight jar or biscuit tin. Serve after a dinner party with coffee, or use in trifles.

CHOCOLATE KISSES

MAKES 24

75g/3oz dark (bittersweet)
   chocolate, chopped
75g/3oz white chocolate, chopped
115g/4oz/½ cup butter, softened
115g/4oz/½ cup caster (superfine) sugar
2 eggs
225g/8oz/2 cups plain (all-purpose) flour
icing (confectioners') sugar, to decorate

1 Melt the plain and white chocolates in separate bowls and set aside to cool.

2 Beat the butter and caster sugar together until pale and fluffy. Beat in the eggs, one at a time. Sift in the flour and mix well.

3 Halve the creamed mixture and divide it between the two bowls of chocolate. Mix each chocolate in thoroughly so that each forms a dough. Knead the doughs until smooth, wrap them separately in clear film (plastic wrap) and chill for 1 hour. Preheat the oven to 190°C/375°F/Gas 5.

4 Shape slightly rounded teaspoonfuls of both doughs roughly into balls. Roll the balls between your palms to neaten them. Arrange the balls on greased baking sheets and bake for 10–12 minutes. Dust liberally with sifted icing sugar and cool on a wire rack.

MOCHA VIENNESE SWIRLS

MAKES ABOUT 20

115g/4oz plain (semisweet) chocolate, chopped into small pieces

200g/7oz/scant 1 cup unsalted (sweet) butter, softened

90ml/6 tbsp icing (confectioners') sugar

30ml/2 tbsp strong black coffee

200g/7oz/1¾ cups plain (all-purpose) flour

50g/2oz/½ cup cornflour (cornstarch)

To Decorate

about 20 blanched almonds

150g/5oz plain (semisweet) chocolate, chopped into small pieces

1 Preheat the oven to 190°C/375°F/Gas 5. Melt the chocolate in a bowl over barely simmering water. Cream the butter and icing sugar until smooth and pale. Beat in the melted chocolate, then the coffee.

2 Sift the plain flour and cornflour over the mixture. Fold in lightly and evenly to make a soft biscuit (cookie) dough.

3 Lightly grease 2 large baking sheets. Spoon the dough into a piping (pastry) bag with a large star nozzle. Pipe about 20 swirls on the baking sheets, allowing room for spreading. Keep the nozzle close to the sheet so that the swirls are flat.

4 Press an almond into the centre of each swirl. Bake for about 15 minutes, or until the biscuits are firm and starting to brown. Cool for 10 minutes on the baking sheets, then transfer to a wire rack to cool.

5 When cool, melt the chocolate and dip the base of each swirl to coat. Place on a sheet of baking parchment and leave to set completely.

CHOCOLATE MACAROONS

MAKES 24

50g/2oz plain (semisweet) chocolate,
    chopped into small pieces
115g/4oz/1 cup blanched almonds
225g/8oz/1 cup granulated sugar
3 egg whites
2.5ml/½ tsp vanilla essence (extract)
1.5ml/¼ tsp almond essence (extract)
icing (confectioners') sugar, for dusting

1 Preheat the oven to 160°C/325°F/
Gas 3. Line 2 baking sheets with
baking parchment.

CHOCOLATE PINE NUT MACAROONS

As a variation, add pine nuts. Spread
50g/2oz/⅔ cup toasted pine nuts in a
shallow dish. Press the balls of chocolate
macaroon dough into the nuts to cover
one side and bake as described above,
nut-side up.

2 Melt the chocolate using a double
boiler, or in a heatproof bowl set over
barely simmering water.

3 Grind the almonds finely in a food
processor. Transfer to a mixing bowl.

4 Add the sugar, egg whites, vanilla
essence and almond essence and stir to
blend. Stir in the chocolate. The mixture
should just hold its shape. If too soft, chill
in the refrigerator for 15 minutes.

5 Use a teaspoon and your hands to
shape the dough into walnut-size balls.
Place on the baking sheets and flatten
slightly. Brush each ball with a little water
and sift over a thin layer of icing sugar.
Bake for 10–12 minutes, until just firm.
With a metal spatula, transfer to a wire
rack to cool completely.

CHOCOLATE CINNAMON TUILES

3 In a separate bowl, mix together the cocoa and cinnamon. Stir into the larger quantity of mixture until well combined. Leaving room for spreading, drop spoonfuls of the chocolate-flavoured mixture on to the prepared baking sheets, then spread each gently with a metal spatula to make a neat round.

4 Using a small spoon, drizzle the reserved mixture over the rounds, swirling lightly to give a marbled effect.

5 Bake for 4–6 minutes, until just set. Using a metal spatula, lift each biscuit (cookie) and drape it over a rolling pin to give a curved shape as it hardens. Allow the tuiles to set, then remove them and finish cooling on a wire rack. Serve on the same day.

CHOCOLATE CUPS

Cream 150g/5oz/2⅔ cup butter with 115g/4oz/½ cup caster (superfine) sugar. Stir in 75g/3oz/1 cup rolled oats, 15ml/1 tbsp cocoa powder and 5ml/ 1 tsp vanilla essence (extract). Roll to the size of golf balls and space well on greased baking sheets. Bake at 180°C/ 350°F/Gas 4 for 12–15 minutes. Cool slightly, then drape over greased upturned glasses until cool and firm. Makes 8–10.

MAKES 12

  1 egg white
  50g/2oz/¼ cup caster
   (superfine) sugar
  30ml/2 tbsp plain (all-purpose) flour
  40g/1½oz/3 tbsp butter, melted
  15ml/1 tbsp cocoa powder
  2.5ml/½ tsp ground cinnamon

1 Preheat the oven to 200°C/400°F/Gas 6. Grease 2 large baking sheets. Whisk the egg white until softly peaking. Gradually whisk in the sugar to make a smooth, glossy mixture.

2 Sift the flour over the meringue mixture and fold in evenly without deflating the mixture. Fold in the butter. Transfer about 45ml/3 tbsp of the mixture to a small bowl and set aside.

CHOCOLATE PRETZELS

MAKES 28

150g/5oz/1¼ cups plain
(all-purpose) flour
a pinch of salt
25g/1oz/¼ cup cocoa powder
115g/4oz/½ cup butter, softened
115g/4oz/½ cup caster
(superfine) sugar
1 egg plus 1 egg white, beaten
sugar crystals, for sprinkling

1 Sift together the flour, salt and cocoa.
Set aside. Grease 2 baking sheets.

2 Cream the butter. Add the caster sugar
and beat until fluffy. Beat in the egg. Stir in
the dry ingredients. Gather the dough into
a ball and chill for 1 hour.

3 Roll the dough into 28 small balls.
Preheat the oven to 190°C/375°F/Gas 5.
Roll each ball into a rope about 25cm/
10 in long. With each rope, form a loop
with the two ends facing you. Twist the
ends and fold back on to the circle,
pressing in to make a pretzel shape.
Place on the greased baking sheets.

4 Brush the pretzels with the egg white.
Sprinkle sugar crystals over the top and
bake for 10–12 minutes until firm. Transfer
to a wire rack to cool.

CHOCOLATE FAIRY CAKES

MAKES 24

115g/4oz plain (semisweet) chocolate,
  chopped into small pieces

15ml/1 tbsp water

275g/10oz/2½ cups plain
  (all-purpose) flour

5ml/1 tsp baking powder

2.5ml/½ tsp bicarbonate of soda
  (baking soda)

pinch of salt

300g/11oz/scant 1½ cups caster
  (superfine) sugar

175g/6oz/¾ cup butter, at room
  temperature

150ml/¼ pint/⅔ cup milk

5ml/1 tsp vanilla essence (extract)

3 eggs

For the Icing

40g/1½oz/3 tbsp butter or margarine

115g/4oz/1 cup icing
  (confectioners') sugar

2.5ml/½ tsp vanilla essence (extract)

15–30ml/1–2 tbsp milk

1 Preheat the oven to 180°C/350°F/Gas 4. Grease 2 x 12-hole bun tins (cupcake pans), about 6.5cm/2¾in in diameter, Line with paper cases.

2 For the icing, soften the butter and gradually stir in the icing sugar. Add the vanilla and just enough milk to make a creamy mixture. Cover closely with clear film (plastic wrap) and set aside.

3 Melt the chocolate with the water in a heatproof bowl set over simmering water. Remove from the heat. Sift the flour, baking powder, bicarbonate of soda, salt and sugar into a large bowl. Add the chocolate mixture, butter, milk and vanilla essence.

4 With a hand-held electric mixer on medium speed, beat the mixture until smooth. Increase the speed to high and beat for 2 minutes. Add the eggs, one at a time, and beat for 1 minute after each addition. Divide the mixture evenly among the prepared bun tins.

5 Bake for 20–25 minutes or until a skewer inserted into the centre of a cake comes out clean. Cool in the tins for 10 minutes, then turn out on to a wire rack. Remove the paper cases if wished. Spread the cake tops with the icing, swirling it in the centre.

CHOCOLATE MINT-FILLED CUPCAKES

MAKES 12

225g/8oz/2 cups plain (all-purpose) flour
5ml/1 tsp bicarbonate of soda
   (baking soda)
pinch of salt
50g/2oz/½ cup cocoa powder
150g/5oz/10 tbsp unsalted (sweet)
   butter, softened
350g/12oz/1½ cups caster
   (superfine) sugar
3 eggs
5ml/1 tsp peppermint essence (extract)
250ml/8 fl oz/1 cup milk
For the Mint Cream Filling
   300ml/½ pint/1¼ cups double (heavy)
      cream or whipping cream
   5ml/1 tsp peppermint essence (extract)
For the Chocolate Mint Glaze
   175g/6oz plain (semisweet) chocolate,
      chopped into small pieces
   115g/4oz/½ cup unsalted (sweet) butter
   5ml/1 tsp peppermint essence

1 Preheat the oven to 180°C/350°F/Gas 4. Line a 12-hole bun tin (cupcake pan) with paper cases. Sift the flour, soda, salt and cocoa powder together. Set aside.

2 In a large mixing bowl, beat the butter and sugar with a hand-held electric mixer for about 3–5 minutes until light and creamy. Add the eggs, one at a time, beating well after each addition and adding a small amount of the flour mixture if the egg mixture shows signs of curdling. Beat in the peppermint essence until thoroughly mixed.

3 With the electric mixer on low, beat in the flour mixture alternately with the milk, until just blended. Spoon into the paper cases, to three-quarters full.

4 Bake for 12–15 minutes, until a skewer inserted in the centre of one of the cupcakes comes out clean.

5 Lift the cupcakes on to a wire rack to cool completely. Remove the paper cases.

6 Prepare the mint cream filling. In a small bowl, whip the cream and peppermint essence until stiff. Fit a small, plain nozzle into a piping (pastry) bag and spoon in the flavoured cream. Gently press the nozzle into the base of one of the cupcakes. Squeeze gently, releasing about 15ml/1 tbsp of the flavoured cream into the centre of the cake. Repeat with the remaining cupcakes, returning each one to the wire rack as it is filled.

7 Prepare the glaze. In a pan over a low heat, melt the chocolate and butter, stirring until smooth. Remove from the heat and stir in the peppermint essence. Cool, then spread on the cake tops.

CHOCOLATE LEMON TARTLETS

MAKES 12 TARTLETS

    1 quantity Chocolate Shortcrust Pastry
    lemon twists and melted chocolate,
      to decorate
For the Lemon Custard Sauce
    grated rind and juice of 1 lemon
    350ml/12fl oz/1½ cups milk
    6 egg yolks
    50g/2oz/½ cup caster (superfine) sugar
For the Lemon Curd Filling
    grated rind and juice of 2 lemons
    175g/6oz/¾ cup unsalted (sweet)
      butter, diced
    450g/1lb/2 cups granulated sugar
    3 eggs, lightly beaten
For the Chocolate Layer
    175ml/6fl oz/¾ cup double
      (heavy) cream
    175g/6oz dark (bittersweet) or plain
      (semisweet) chocolate, chopped
    25g/1oz/2 tbsp unsalted (sweet) butter,
      cut into pieces

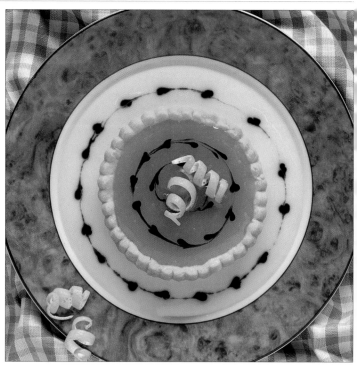

1 For the sauce, put the rind and milk in a pan. Bring to the boil then set aside for 5 minutes to infuse (steep). Strain into a clean pan and reheat gently.

2 Beat together the yolks and sugar for 2–3 minutes, until pale and thick. Beat in 250ml/8fl oz/1 cup of the hot milk.

3 Return the yolk mixture to the rest of the milk in the pan and cook gently, stirring constantly, over low heat until the mixture thickens and lightly coats the back of a spoon. Strain into a chilled bowl. Stir 30ml/2 tbsp lemon juice into the sauce. Cool, stirring occasionally, then chill.

4 Prepare the lemon curd filling. Put the lemon rind, juice, butter and sugar in the top of a double boiler. Set over simmering water and heat gently until the butter has melted and the sugar has completely dissolved. Reduce the heat to low.

5 Stir the lightly beaten eggs into the butter mixture. Cook over a low heat for 15 minutes, stirring constantly, until the mixture coats the back of a spoon.

6 Strain the lemon curd into a bowl and cover closely with clear film (plastic wrap). Leave to cool, stirring occasionally, then chill to thicken, stirring occasionally.

7 Lightly butter 12 x 7.5cm/3in tartlet tins (pans), preferably loose-based. On a floured surface, roll out the pastry to a thickness of 3mm/⅛in. Using a 10cm/4in fluted cutter, cut out 12 rounds and press into the tins. Prick the bases with a fork. Place the tins on a baking sheet and chill for 30 minutes.

8 Preheat the oven to 190°C/375°F/Gas 5. Line each pastry case (pie shell) with foil; fill with baking beans. Bake blind for 5–8 minutes. Remove the foil and beans and bake for 5 more minutes, until golden. Transfer to a wire rack to cool.

9 Prepare the chocolate layer. Bring the cream to the boil. Remove from the heat and add the chocolate all at once. Stir until melted. Beat in the butter and cool slightly. Pour the filling into each tartlet to make a layer 5mm/¼in thick. Chill for 10 minutes, or until set.

10 Remove the tartlets from the tins and spoon in a layer of lemon curd to come to the top of the pastry. Set aside, but do not chill. To serve, spoon a little lemon custard sauce on to a plate and place a tartlet in the centre. Decorate with a lemon twist. Dot the custard with melted chocolate. Draw a skewer through the chocolate to make heart motifs.

CHOCOLATE CREAM PUFFS

MAKES 12 LARGE CREAM PUFFS

115g/4oz/1 cup plain (all-purpose) flour
30ml/2 tbsp cocoa powder
250ml/8fl oz/1 cup water
2.5ml/½ tsp salt
15ml/1 tbsp granulated sugar
115g/4oz/½ cup unsalted (sweet) butter
4 eggs

For the Chocolate Pastry Cream

450ml/¾ pint/2 cups milk
6 egg yolks
115g/4oz/½ cup granulated sugar
50g/2oz/½ cup plain (all-purpose) flour
150g/5oz plain (semisweet) chocolate,
    chopped into small pieces
115ml/4fl oz/½ cup whipping cream

For the Chocolate Glaze

300ml/½ pint/1¼ cups whipping cream
50g/2oz/¼ cup unsalted (sweet) butter
225g/8oz dark (bittersweet) or plain
    (semisweet) chocolate, chopped
15ml/1 tbsp golden (light corn) syrup
5ml/1 tsp vanilla essence (extract)

1 Preheat the oven to 220°C/425°F/Gas 7. Grease 2 large baking sheets. Sift the flour and cocoa powder into a bowl. In a pan over a medium heat, bring to the boil the water, salt, sugar and butter. Remove the pan from the heat and add the flour and cocoa mixture all at once, stirring vigorously until the mixture is smooth and leaves the sides of the pan clean.

2 Return the pan to the heat to cook the choux pastry for 1 minute, beating the mixture constantly. Remove from the heat.

3 With a hand-held electric mixer, beat in the 4 whole eggs, one at a time, beating well after each addition. The mixture should be thick and shiny and just fall from a spoon. Spoon the mixture into a large piping (pastry) bag with a plain nozzle. Pipe 12 mounds about 7.5cm/3in across at least 5cm/2in apart on the baking sheet.

4 Bake for 35–40 minutes until puffed and firm. Remove the puffs. Slice off and reserve the top third of each puff; return to the oven for 5–10 minutes to dry out. Transfer to a wire rack to cool.

5 For the pastry cream, bring the milk to the boil. Beat the yolks and sugar until pale and thick. Stir in the flour. Slowly pour 250ml/8fl oz/1 cup of the hot milk into the yolks, stirring constantly. Return the yolk mixture to the remaining milk in the pan and cook, stirring, until the sauce boils for 1 minute. Remove from the heat and stir in the chocolate until smooth.

6 Strain into a bowl and cover closely with clear film (plastic wrap). Cool. Whip the cream until stiff. Fold into the pastry cream.

7 Using a large piping bag, fill each puff with pastry cream, then cover each puff with its top. Arrange the cream puffs on a large serving plate.

8 Make the glaze by heating the cream, butter, chocolate, syrup and vanilla over a low heat until melted and smooth, stirring frequently. Leave to cool for 20–30 minutes until slightly thickened. Pour a little glaze over each of the cream puffs to serve.

CHOCOLATE RASPBERRY MACAROON BARS

2 In a bowl, beat the softened butter, sugar, cocoa powder and salt with a hand-held electric mixer for about 1 minute, until creamy. Beat in the almond essence and the flour until the mixture forms a crumbly dough.

3 Turn the dough into the prepared tin and pat firmly over the base to make an even layer. Prick the dough with a fork. Bake for 20 minutes until the pastry has just set. Remove from the oven and increase the oven temperature to 190°C/375°F/Gas 5.

4 Make the topping. In a small bowl, combine the raspberry jam and the liqueur. Spread the mixture evenly over the chocolate crust, then sprinkle evenly with the chocolate chips.

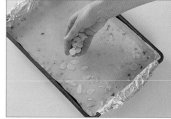

5 In a food processor fitted with a metal blade, process the almonds, egg whites, salt, sugar and almond essence until well blended and foamy. Gently pour over the jam layer, spreading evenly to the edges of the tin. Sprinkle with the almonds.

6 Bake for 20–25 minutes, until golden and puffed. Cool in the tin on a wire rack for 20 minutes or until firm. Using the foil, remove the bake from the tin and cool completely. Peel off the foil, and, using a sharp knife, cut into bars.

MAKES 16–18 BARS

115g/4oz/½ cup unsalted (sweet) butter
50g/2oz/½ cup icing (confectioners') sugar
25g/1oz/¼ cup cocoa powder
a pinch of salt
5ml/1 tsp almond essence (extract)
115g/4oz/1 cup plain (all-purpose) flour
For the Topping
150g/5oz/½ cup seedless raspberry jam
15ml/1 tbsp raspberry-flavoured liqueur
175g/6oz/1 cup mini chocolate chips
175g/6oz/1½ cups ground almonds
4 egg whites
a pinch of salt
225g/8oz/1 cup caster (superfine) sugar
2.5ml/½ tsp almond essence (extract)
50g/2oz/¼ cup flaked (sliced) almonds

1 Preheat the oven to 160°C/325°F/Gas 3. Invert a 33 x 23cm/13 x 9in baking tin (pan). Mould a sheet of foil over the tin and smooth the foil evenly around the corners. Lift off the foil and turn the tin right side up. Then line the tin with the moulded foil and grease the foil.

CHOCOLATE BUTTERSCOTCH BARS

MAKES 24

225g/8oz/2 cups plain (all-purpose) flour
2.5ml/½ tsp baking powder
150g/5oz plain (semisweet)
  chocolate, chopped
115g/4oz/½ cup unsalted (sweet)
  butter, diced
50g/2oz/⅓ cup light muscovado
  (brown) sugar
30ml/2 tbsp ground almonds

For the Topping

175g/6oz/¾ cup unsalted (sweet)
  butter, diced
115g/4oz/½ cup caster (superfine) sugar
30ml/2 tbsp golden (light corn) syrup
175ml/6fl oz/¾ cup sweetened
  condensed milk
150g/5oz/1¼ cups whole
  toasted hazelnuts
225g/8oz plain (semisweet)
  chocolate, chopped

1 Preheat the oven to 160°C/325°F/Gas 3. Grease a shallow 30 x 20cm/12 x 8in tin (pan). Sift the flour and baking powder together into a large bowl and set aside. Melt the chocolate in a heatproof bowl set over a pan of simmering water then remove from the heat.

2 Rub the butter into the flour with your fingers until the mixture resembles coarse breadcrumbs, then stir in the sugar. Gradually work in the melted chocolate and ground almonds to make a light biscuit (cookie) dough.

3 Spread the dough roughly in the tin, then use a rubber spatula to press it down evenly into the sides and the corners. Prick the surface all over with a fork and bake for 25–30 minutes until firm. Leave to cool in the tin.

4 For the topping, heat the butter, sugar, syrup and condensed milk, stirring until the butter and sugar melt. Simmer until golden, then stir in the hazelnuts. Pour over the cooked base. Leave to set.

5 Melt the chocolate for the topping in a heatproof bowl over barely simmering water. Spread evenly over the butterscotch layer, then leave to set again before cutting into bars to serve.

CHOCOLATE AND TOFFEE BARS

MAKES 32

   350g/12oz/2 cups soft light brown sugar
   450g/1lb/2 cups butter or margarine, at room temperature
   2 egg yolks
   7.5ml/1½ tsp vanilla essence (extract)
   450g/1lb/4 cups plain (all-purpose) or wholemeal (whole-wheat) flour
   2.5ml/½ tsp salt
   175g/6oz plain (semisweet) chocolate, broken into squares
   115g/4oz/1 cup walnuts or pecan nuts, chopped

1 Preheat the oven to 180°C/350°F/Gas 4. Beat the sugar and butter or margarine until light and fluffy. Beat in the egg yolks and vanilla, then stir in the flour and salt to make a soft dough.

2 Spread the dough in a greased 33 x 23 x 5cm/13 x 9 x 2in baking tin (pan). Bake for 25–30 minutes, until lightly browned but soft.

3 Quickly place the chocolate on top. Set aside until soft, then spread it out with a spatula. Sprinkle with the chopped nuts.

4 While the bake is still warm, cut it into 5 x 4cm/2 x 1½in bars, remove from the tin and leave to cool on a wire rack.

CHOCOLATE PECAN SQUARES

MAKES 16

   2 eggs
   10ml/2 tsp vanilla essence (extract)
   a pinch of salt
   175g/6oz/1½ cups pecan nuts, roughly chopped
   50g/2oz/¼ cup granulated sugar
   50g/2oz/½ cup plain (all-purpose) flour
   120ml/4fl oz/½ cup golden (light corn) syrup
   75g/3oz plain (semisweet) chocolate, chopped into small pieces
   40g/1½oz/3 tbsp unsalted (sweet) butter
   16 pecan nut halves, to decorate

1 Preheat the oven to 160°C/325°F/Gas 3. Line a 20cm/8in square baking tin (pan) with baking parchment.

2 In a bowl, whisk the eggs with the vanilla essence and salt. In another bowl, mix together the pecan nuts and flour.

3 Boil the syrup with the sugar. Off the heat, stir in the chocolate and butter until smooth. Stir in the egg mixture, then fold in the nuts and flour.

4 Pour into the tin. Bake for 35 minutes or until firm to the touch. Cool in the tin for 10 minutes before turning out on to a wire rack. Cut into 5cm/2in squares and press pecan halves into the tops while still warm. Cool completely before serving.

CHUNKY CHOCOLATE BARS

MAKES 12

350g/12oz plain (semisweet) chocolate
115g/4oz/½ cup unsalted (sweet) butter
400g/14oz can condensed milk
225g/8oz digestive biscuits (graham crackers), broken
50g/2oz/⅓ cup raisins
115g/4oz ready-to-eat dried peaches, roughly chopped
50g/2oz/½ cup hazelnuts or pecan nuts, roughly chopped

1 Line a 28 x 18cm/11 x 7in cake tin (pan) with clear film (plastic wrap). Chop and then melt the chocolate with the butter in a large heatproof bowl over a pan of simmering water. Stir until well mixed.

2 Pour the condensed milk into the chocolate and butter mixture. Beat with a wooden spoon until creamy.

3 Add the remaining ingredients and mix in well, digging deep into the bowl, until completely coated in the chocolate sauce.

4 Tip the mixture into the tin, pressing well into the corners. Leave the top craggy. Cool, then chill until set.

5 Lift the cake out of the tin using the clear film and then peel off the film. Cut into 12 bars and serve at once.

CHOCOLATE AND COCONUT SLICES

MAKES 24

175g/6oz digestive biscuits (graham crackers), crushed

50g/2oz/¼ cup caster (superfine) sugar

a pinch of salt

115g/4oz/½ cup butter or margarine, melted

75g/3oz/1 cup desiccated (dry unsweetened shredded) coconut

250g/9oz/1½ cups plain (semisweet) chocolate chips

250ml/8fl oz/1 cup sweetened condensed milk

115g/4oz/1 cup walnuts, finely chopped

1 Preheat the oven to 180°C/350°F/Gas 4. Put a baking sheet inside to heat up.

2 In a bowl, combine the crushed biscuits, sugar, salt and melted butter or margarine. Press the mixture evenly over the base of an ungreased 33 x 23cm/ 13 x 9in baking dish.

3 Sprinkle the coconut over the biscuit base, then scatter over the chocolate chips. Pour the condensed milk evenly over the chocolate. Sprinkle the chopped walnuts on top. Place on the hot baking sheet and bake for 30 minutes. Turn out on to a wire rack and leave to cool. When cold, cut into slices.

WHITE CHOCOLATE MACADAMIA SLICES

MAKES 16

150g/5oz/1¼ cups macadamia nuts,
blanched almonds or hazelnuts
400g/14oz white chocolate
115g/4oz/½ cup ready-to-eat
dried apricots
75g/3oz/6 tbsp unsalted (sweet) butter
5ml/1 tsp vanilla essence (extract)
3 eggs
150g/5oz/scant 1 cup light muscovado
(brown) sugar
115g/4oz/1 cup self-raising
(self-rising) flour

1 Preheat the oven to 190°C/375°F/Gas 5.
Grease and base-line 2 x 20cm/8in round
sandwich tins (pans).

2 Roughly chop the nuts and half the
white chocolate, making the pieces the
same size. Use scissors to cut the apricots
to similar sized pieces.

3 In a heatproof bowl over a pan of barely
simmering water, melt the remaining white
chocolate, broken into squares for ease,
with the butter. Remove from the heat and
stir in the vanilla essence.

4 Whisk the eggs and sugar together in a
mixing bowl until thickened and pale, then
pour in the melted chocolate mixture,
whisking constantly.

5 Sift the flour over the mixture and fold
it in evenly. Finally, stir in the nuts,
chopped white chocolate and chopped
dried apricots.

6 Spoon into the tins and level the tops.
Bake for 30–35 minutes or until the top is
firm and crusty. Cool in the tins before
cutting each cake into 8 slices.

CRANBERRY <u>AND</u> CHOCOLATE SQUARES

<u>MAKES 12</u>

150g/5oz/1¼ cups self-raising (self-
  rising) flour, plus extra for dusting
115g/4oz/½ cup unsalted (sweet) butter
60ml/4 tbsp cocoa powder
215g/7½oz/1¼ cups light muscovado
  (brown) sugar
2 eggs, beaten
115g/4oz/1⅓ cups cranberries
75ml/5 tbsp coarsely grated plain
  (semisweet) chocolate, for sprinkling

For the Topping

150ml/¼ pint/⅔ cup sour cream
75g/3oz/6 tbsp caster (superfine) sugar
30ml/2 tbsp self-raising (self-rising) flour
50g/2oz/4 tbsp soft margarine
1 egg, beaten
2.5ml/½ tsp vanilla essence (extract)

1 Preheat the oven to 180°C/350°F/Gas 4.
Grease a 27 x 18cm/10½ x 7in cake tin
(pan) and dust lightly with flour. Combine
the butter, cocoa powder and sugar in a
pan and stir over a low heat until melted.

2 Remove the melted mixture from the
heat and stir in the flour and eggs, beating
until thoroughly mixed.

3 Stir in the cranberries, then spread the
mixture in the tin. For the topping, mix all
the ingredients in a bowl. Beat until
smooth, then spread over the base.

4 Sprinkle with the grated chocolate and
bake for 40–45 minutes until risen and firm.
Cool for 10 minutes. Cut into 12 squares,
remove from the tin and cool on a wire rack.

NUT AND CHOCOLATE CHIP BROWNIES

MAKES 16

150g/5oz plain (semisweet) chocolate, chopped into small pieces
120ml/4fl oz/½ cup sunflower oil
215g/7½oz/1¼ cups light muscovado (brown) sugar
2 eggs
5ml/1 tsp vanilla essence (extract)
65g/2½oz/generous ½ cup self-raising (self-rising) flour
60ml/4 tbsp cocoa powder
75g/3oz/¾ cup walnuts or pecan nuts, chopped
60ml/4 tbsp milk chocolate chips

1 Preheat the oven to 180°C/350°F/Gas 4. Grease a shallow 19cm/7½in square cake tin (pan). Melt the plain chocolate in a heatproof bowl set over a pan of barely simmering water.

2 Beat the oil, sugar, eggs and vanilla together. Stir in the melted chocolate and beat well until evenly mixed and smooth. Sift in the flour and cocoa powder, and fold in thoroughly. Stir in the nuts and chocolate chips. Spread evenly into the prepared tin.

3 Bake for 30–35 minutes, or until the top is firm and crusty. Cool in the tin before cutting into squares.

LOW-FAT BROWNIES

MAKES 9

75ml/5 tbsp fat-reduced cocoa powder
15ml/1 tbsp caster sugar
75ml/5 tbsp skimmed milk
3 large bananas, mashed
175g/6oz/1 cup soft light brown sugar
5ml/1 tsp vanilla essence (extract)
5 egg whites
75g/3oz/¾ cup self-raising (self-rising) flour
75g/3oz/¾ cup oat bran
15ml/1 tbsp icing (confectioners') sugar, for dusting

1 Preheat the oven to 180°C/350°F/Gas 4. Line a 20cm/8in square cake tin (pan) with baking parchment. Blend the cocoa powder and caster sugar with the milk. Add the bananas, brown sugar and vanilla.

2 Lightly beat the egg whites. Add the chocolate mixture and continue to beat well. Sift the flour over the mixture and fold in with the oat bran. Pour the mixture into the cake tin.

3 Bake for 40 minutes or until the top is firm. Cool in the tin before cutting into squares. Dust with icing sugar before serving.

MARBLED BROWNIES

MAKES 24

225g/8oz plain (semisweet) chocolate, chopped into small pieces
75g/3oz/6 tbsp butter, diced
4 eggs
300g/11oz/1½ cups granulated sugar
150g/5oz/1¼ cups plain (all-purpose) flour
2.5ml/½ tsp salt
5ml/1 tsp baking powder
10ml/2 tsp vanilla essence (extract)
115g/4oz/1 cup walnuts, chopped
For the Plain Mixture
50g/2oz/¼ cup butter
175g/6oz/¾ cup cream cheese
75g/3oz/6 tbsp granulated sugar
2 eggs
25g/1oz/¼ cup plain (all-purpose) flour
5ml/1 tsp vanilla essence (extract)

1 Preheat the oven to 180°C/350°F/Gas 4. Line a 33 x 23cm/13 x 9in baking tin (pan) with lightly greased baking parchment.

1 Melt the chocolate and butter in a heatproof bowl set over a pan of barely simmering water, stirring constantly until smooth. Set aside to cool.

2 Meanwhile, beat the eggs until light and fluffy. Slowly add the sugar and beat until blended. Sift in the flour, salt and baking powder and fold in gently but thoroughly.

3 Stir in the cooled chocolate mixture. Add the vanilla essence and walnuts. Measure and set aside 450ml/16fl oz/ 2 cups of the chocolate mixture.

4 For the plain mixture, cream the butter and cream cheese in a bowl. Beat in the sugar, then the eggs, flour and vanilla.

5 Spread the unmeasured chocolate mixture in the prepared tin. Pour over the plain mixture. Drop spoonfuls of the reserved chocolate mixture on top.

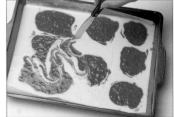

5 With a palette knife (metal spatula), swirl the mixtures to marble them. Do not blend completely. Bake for 35–45 minutes, until just set. Turn out when cool and cut into squares to serve.

WHITE CHOCOLATE BROWNIES <u>WITH</u> MILK CHOCOLATE MACADAMIA TOPPING

SERVES 12

115g/4oz/1 cup plain (all-purpose) flour

2.5ml/½ tsp baking powder

a pinch of salt

175g/6oz white chocolate, chopped

115g/4oz/½ cup caster
   (superfine) sugar

115g/4oz/½ cup unsalted (sweet)
   butter, cut into small pieces

2 eggs, lightly beaten

5ml/1 tsp vanilla essence (extract)

175g/6oz plain (semisweet) chocolate
   chips or plain chocolate chopped into
   small pieces

For the Topping

200g/7oz milk chocolate, chopped

175g/6oz/1½ cups unsalted macadamia
   nuts, chopped

1 Preheat the oven to 180°C/350°F/Gas 4. Grease a 23cm/9in springform tin (pan). Sift together the flour, baking powder and salt, then set aside.

2 Melt the white chocolate, sugar and butter over a low heat until smooth, stirring frequently. Cool slightly, then beat in the eggs and vanilla essence. Stir in the flour mixture until well blended. Stir in the chocolate chips or chopped chocolate. Spread evenly in the prepared tin.

3 Bake for 20–25 minutes, until a skewer inserted in the cake tin comes out clean. Do not over-bake. Remove the cake from the oven and place the tin on a heatproof surface.

4 Sprinkle the chopped milk chocolate evenly over the cake and return to the oven for 1 minute.

5 Remove the cake from the oven again and gently spread the softened chocolate evenly over the top. Sprinkle with the macadamia nuts and gently press them into the chocolate. Cool on a wire rack for 30 minutes, then chill, for about 1 hour, until set. Run a sharp knife around the side of the tin to loosen, then unclip the side of the springform tin and remove it carefully. Cut into thin wedges.

DOUBLE CHOCOLATE CHIP MUFFINS

MAKES 16

400g/14oz/3½ cups plain
  (all-purpose) flour
15ml/1 tbsp baking powder
30ml/2 tbsp cocoa powder, plus extra
  for dusting
115g/4oz/⅔ cup dark muscovado
  (molasses) sugar
2 eggs
150ml/¼ pint/⅔ cup sour cream
150ml/¼ pint/⅔ cup milk
60ml/4 tbsp sunflower oil
175g/6oz white chocolate
175g/6oz plain (semisweet) chocolate

1 Preheat the oven to 180°C/350°F/Gas
4. Place 16 paper muffin cases in muffin
tins or deep patty tins. Sift the flour,
baking powder and cocoa into a bowl and
stir in the sugar. Make a well in the centre.

2 In a separate bowl, beat the eggs with
the sour cream, milk and oil, then stir into
the well in the dry ingredients. Beat well,
gradually incorporating all the surrounding
flour mixture to make a thick and creamy
batter. Chop the white and plain chocolate
into small pieces and stir into the mixture.

3 Spoon the chocolate mixture into the
muffin cases, filling them almost to the
top. Bake for 25–30 minutes, until well
risen and firm to the touch. Cool on a wire
rack, then dust the muffins lightly with
cocoa powder.

CHOCOLATE WALNUT MUFFINS

MAKES 12

175g/6oz/¾ cup unsalted (sweet) butter

150g/5oz plain (semisweet)
  chocolate, chopped

200g/7oz/scant 1 cup caster
  (superfine) sugar

50g/2oz/⅓ cup soft dark brown sugar

4 eggs

5ml/1 tsp vanilla essence (extract)

1.5ml/¼ tsp almond essence (extract)

110g/3¾oz/scant 1 cup plain
  (all-purpose) flour

15ml/1 tbsp cocoa powder

115g/4oz/1 cup walnuts or pecan
  nuts, chopped

1 Preheat the oven to 180°C/350°F/Gas 4. Grease a 12-cup patty pan (muffin tin). Melt the butter and chocolate using a double boiler. Transfer to a mixing bowl.

2 Stir in the sugars. Slowly mix in the eggs, a little at a time. Add the vanilla and almond essences.

3 Sift over the flour and cocoa powder, fold in, then stir in the walnuts or pecan nuts. Fill the muffin cups almost to the top and bake for 30–35 minutes, until a skewer inserted in a muffin comes out clean but sticky. Leave to stand for 5 minutes before turning the muffins out on to a rack.

CHOCOLATE CINNAMON DOUGHNUTS

MAKES 16

500g/1¼lb/5 cups plain (all-purpose) flour
30ml/2 tbsp cocoa powder
2.5ml/½ tsp salt
1 sachet easy-blend (rapid-rise) dried yeast
300ml/½ pint/1¼ cups hand-hot milk
40g/1½oz/3 tbsp butter, melted
1 egg, beaten
115g/4oz plain (semisweet) chocolate,
  broken into 16 pieces
sunflower oil, for deep frying

For the Coating

45ml/3 tbsp caster (superfine) sugar
15ml/1 tbsp cocoa powder
5ml/1 tsp ground cinnamon

1 Sift the flour, cocoa powder and salt into a large bowl. Stir in the yeast. Make a well in the centre and add the milk, melted butter and egg. Stir, gradually incorporating the dry ingredients, to make a soft and pliable dough.

2 Knead the dough on a lightly floured work surface for about 5 minutes, until smooth and elastic. Return to the clean bowl, cover with a clean dishtowel and leave in a warm place until the dough has doubled in size.

3 Knead the dough lightly again, then divide into 16 pieces. Shape each into a round, press a piece of plain chocolate into the centre, then fold the dough over to enclose the filling, pressing firmly to make sure the edges are sealed.

4 Heat the oil for frying to 180°C/350°F, or until a cube of dried bread browns in 30–45 seconds. Deep-fry the doughnuts in batches. As each doughnut rises and turns golden brown, turn it over carefully to cook the other side. Drain on kitchen paper.

5 To coat, mix the sugar, cocoa and cinnamon in a shallow bowl. Toss the doughnuts in the mixture to coat them evenly. Pile on a plate and serve warm.

> **VARIATION**
> Instead of using a square of plain chocolate to fill each doughnut, try chocolate spread instead. Use about 5ml/1 tsp of the spread for each doughnut. Seal well before frying.

CHOCOLATE ORANGE SPONGE DROPS

MAKES ABOUT 14

- 2 eggs
- 50g/2 oz/¼ cup caster (superfine) sugar
- 2.5ml/½ tsp grated orange rind
- 50g/2oz/½ cup plain (all-purpose) flour
- 60ml/4 tbsp finely shredded orange marmalade
- 40g/1½oz plain (semisweet) chocolate, chopped

1 Preheat the oven to 200°C/400°F/Gas 6. Line 3 baking sheets with baking parchment.

2 Whisk the eggs and sugar in a bowl set over a pan of simmering water until thick and pale. Whisk off the heat until cool. Whisk in the orange rind. Sift the flour over the mixture and fold it in gently.

3 Put spoonfuls of the mixture on the baking sheets, spaced well apart. The mixture will make 28–30 drops. Bake for 8 minutes, or until golden. Allow to cool on the baking sheets for a few minutes, then use a spatula to transfer them to a wire rack to cool completely. Sandwich the biscuits (cookies) together in pairs with the marmalade.

4 Melt the chocolate in a heatproof bowl set over a pan of barely simmering water. Drizzle or pipe the chocolate over the tops of the sponge drops, then leave to set before serving.

BRIOCHES AU CHOCOLAT

MAKES 12

250g/9oz/2¼ cups strong white flour

a pinch of salt

30ml/2 tbsp caster (superfine) sugar

1 sachet easy-blend (rapid-rise) dried yeast

3 eggs, beaten, plus extra beaten egg
   for glazing

45ml/3 tbsp hand-hot milk

115g/4oz/½ cup unsalted (sweet)
   butter, diced

175g/6oz plain (semisweet) chocolate

1 Sift the flour and salt into a large mixing bowl and stir in the sugar and yeast. Make a well in the centre of the mixture and add the eggs and milk.

2 Beat the egg mixture well, gradually incorporating the dry ingredients to make a fairly soft dough. Turn out on to a floured work surface. Knead for 5 minutes, until smooth and elastic, adding a little more flour if necessary.

3 Add the butter to the dough, a few pieces at a time, kneading until each addition is absorbed before adding the next. When all the butter has been incorporated and small bubbles appear in the dough, wrap it in clear film (plastic wrap) and chill for at least 1 hour, or overnight if you intend serving the brioches for breakfast.

4 Lightly grease 12 individual brioche tins (pans) set on a baking sheet. Divide the brioche dough into 12 pieces and shape each into a smooth round. Place a chocolate square in the centre of each round. Bring up the sides of the dough and press the edges firmly together to seal; use a little beaten egg if necessary.

5 Place the brioches, with join side down, in the tins. Cover and leave in a warm place for about 30 minutes, or until doubled in size. Preheat the oven to 200°C/400°F/Gas 6.

6 Brush the brioches with beaten egg. Bake for 12–15 minutes, until well risen and golden brown. Place on wire racks and leave until they have cooled slightly. They should be served warm and can be made in advance and reheated if necessary. Do not serve straight from the oven, as the chocolate will be very hot.

COOK'S TIP

Brioches freeze very well and can be kept for up to 1 month in the freezer. Thaw at room temperature, then reheat on baking sheets in a low oven and serve warm, but not hot. For a richer variation serve with melted chocolate drizzled over the top of the brioches.

CHOCOLATE
TREATS

Chocolate truffles, nutty fudge and liqueur-
spiked moulded chocs and candies are simple
and rewarding to make, and, packed into
pretty boxes or jars, they make wonderful gifts.
For after-dinner sweet treats, Cognac and
Ginger Creams or Peppermint Chocolate
Sticks are so much more special than bought
mints. If you prefer liquid chocolate, at the end
of the day you can sink into a comfy armchair
with a warming glass of Irish Chocolate Velvet
or Mexican Hot Chocolate.

CHOCOLATE <u>AND</u> CHERRY COLETTES

FOR A SWEET SURPRISE FOR A FRIEND OR LOVER, PACK THESE PRETTY LITTLE SWEETS IN A DECORATIVE BOX.
IF FOIL CASES ARE DIFFICULT TO OBTAIN, USE DOUBLE THICKNESS PAPER SWEET CASES INSTEAD.

MAKES 18–20

- 115g/4oz dark (bittersweet)
  chocolate, chopped
- 75g/3oz white or milk
  chocolate, chopped
- 25g/1oz/2 tbsp unsalted (sweet)
  butter, melted
- 15ml/1 tbsp Kirsch or brandy
- 60ml/4 tbsp double (heavy) cream
- 18–20 maraschino cherries or
  liqueur-soaked cherries
- milk chocolate curls, to decorate

1 Melt the dark chocolate, then remove from the heat. Spoon into 18–20 foil sweet cases, spreading evenly up the sides with a small brush, then leave the cases in a cool place until the chocolate has set.

2 Melt the white or milk chocolate with the butter. Off the heat, stir in the Kirsch or brandy, then the cream. Cool until the mixture is thick enough to hold its shape.

3 Carefully peel away the paper from the chocolate cases. Place one cherry in each chocolate case. Spoon the white or milk chocolate cream mixture into a piping (pastry) bag with a small star nozzle and pipe over the cherries until the cases are full. Top each colette with a generous swirl and decorate with milk chocolate curls. Leave to set before serving.

COGNAC AND GINGER CREAMS

MAKES 18–20

> 300g/11oz dark (bittersweet) chocolate,
> 45ml/3 tbsp double (heavy) cream
> 30ml/2 tbsp cognac
> 4 pieces preserved stem ginger, finely
>   chopped, plus 15ml/1 tbsp syrup
>   from the jar
> crystallized (candied) ginger, to decorate

1 Polish the insides of 18–20 chocolate moulds carefully with cotton wool. Chop the chocolate and melt two-thirds in a heatproof bowl over a pan of barely simmering water, then spoon a little into each mould. Reserve a little of the melted chocolate for sealing the creams.

2 Using a small brush, sweep the chocolate up the sides of the moulds to coat them evenly, then invert on to a sheet of baking parchment and set aside until the chocolate has set.

CHOCOLATE MARSHMALLOW DIPS

Line a large baking sheet with baking parchment. Melt 175g/6oz plain (semisweet) or dark (bittersweet) chocolate in a heatproof bowl set over a pan of barely simmering water. Stir until smooth. Remove the pan from the heat, but leave the bowl on the bowl in place so that the chocolate does not solidify too soon. You will need 15–20 large or 30–35 small marshmallows. Using cocktail sticks (toothpicks), spear each marshmallow and coat in the chocolate. Roll in ground hazelnuts. Place on the baking sheet and chill to set. When completely set, remove the skewers. Place each marshmallow dip in a foil sweet case.

3 Melt the remaining chopped chocolate over simmering water, then stir in the cream, cognac, ginger and ginger syrup, mixing well. Then spoon into the chocolate-lined moulds. If the reserved chocolate has solidified, melt it, then spoon a little into each mould to seal.

4 Leave the chocolates in a cool place until set. To remove them from the moulds, gently press them out on to a cool surface, such as a marble slab. Decorate with small pieces of crystallized ginger. Keep the chocolates cool if not serving immediately. Do not chill.

CHOCOLATE TRUFFLES

MAKES 20 LARGE OR 30 MEDIUM TRUFFLES

250ml/8fl oz/1 cup double (heavy) cream
275g/10oz fine quality dark
   (bittersweet) or plain (semisweet)
   chocolate, chopped
40g/1½oz/3 tbsp unsalted (sweet)
   butter, cut into small pieces
45ml/3 tbsp brandy, whisky or liqueur
   of own choice
cocoa powder, for dusting (optional)
finely chopped pistachio nuts, to
   decorate (optional)
400g/14oz dark (bittersweet) chocolate,
   to decorate (optional)

1 Bring the cream to the boil. Remove from the heat and add the chocolate, all at once. Stir gently until melted. Stir in the butter until melted, then stir in the brandy, whisky or liqueur. Strain into a bowl and cool to room temperature. Cover the mixture with clear film (plastic wrap) and chill for 4 hours or overnight.

2 Line a large baking sheet with baking parchment. Using a small ice cream scoop, melon baller or spoon, scrape the mixture into 20 large balls or 30 medium, and place on the baking sheet. Dip the scoop or spoon in cold water from time to time, to prevent the mixture from sticking.

3 If dusting with cocoa powder, sift a thick layer of cocoa on to a dish or pie plate. Roll the truffles in the cocoa, rounding them between the palms of your hands. (Dust your hands with cocoa to prevent the truffles from sticking.) Do not worry if the truffles are not perfectly round, as an irregular shape looks more authentic. Alternatively, roll the truffles in very finely chopped pistachios. Chill on the paper-lined baking sheet until firm. Keep in the refrigerator for up to 10 days or freeze for up to 2 months.

4 If coating with chocolate, do not roll the truffles in cocoa, but freeze for 1 hour. For perfect results, temper the chocolate. Alternatively, simply melt it in a heatproof bowl over a pan of barely simmering water. Using a fork, dip the truffles, one at a time, into the melted chocolate, tapping the fork on the edge of the bowl to shake off any excess. Place on a baking sheet, lined with baking parchment. If the chocolate begins to thicken, reheat it gently until smooth. Chill the truffles until completely set.

MALT WHISKY TRUFFLES

MAKES 25–30

   200g/7oz dark (bittersweet)
      chocolate, chopped
   150ml/¼ pint/⅔ cup double (heavy) cream
   45ml/3 tbsp malt whisky
   115g/4oz/¾ cup icing (confectioners') sugar
   cocoa powder, for coating

1 Melt the chocolate in a heatproof bowl set over a pan of simmering water, stirring until smooth then cool slightly.

2 Using a whisk, whip the cream with the whisky in a bowl until thick enough to hold its shape.

3 Stir in the melted chocolate and icing sugar. Leave to firm up a little.

4 Dust your hands with cocoa powder and shape the mixture into bite-size balls. Coat in cocoa powder and pack into pretty boxes. Store in the refrigerator for up to 3–4 days if necessary.

TRUFFLE-FILLED EASTER EGG

MAKES 1 LARGE, HOLLOW EASTER EGG

350g/12oz plain (semisweet) couverture
chocolate, tempered, or plain, milk or
white chocolate, melted
Chocolate Truffles

1 Line a small baking sheet with baking
parchment. Using a small ladle or spoon,
pour in enough melted chocolate to coat
both halves of an Easter egg mould. Tilt
the half-moulds slowly to coat the sides
completely. Pour any excess chocolate
back into the bowl. Set the half-moulds,
open side down, on the baking sheet.
Leave for 1–2 minutes until just set.

2 Apply a second coat of chocolate and
chill for 1–3 minutes more, until set.
Repeat a third time, then replace the
moulds on the baking sheet and chill for
at least 1 hour, or until the chocolate has
set completely. (Work quickly to avoid
having to temper the chocolate again;
however, untempered chocolate can be
reheated if it hardens.)

3 To remove the set chocolate, place a
half-mould, open side up, on a board.
Carefully trim any drops of chocolate from
the edge of the mould. Gently insert the
point of a small knife between the
chocolate and the mould to break the air
lock. Repeat with the second mould.

4 Holding the mould open side down,
squeeze firmly to release the egg half.
Repeat with the other half and chill,
loosely covered. (Do not touch the
chocolate surface with your fingers, as
they will leave prints.) Reserve any melted
chocolate to reheat for "glue".

5 To assemble the egg, hold one half of
the egg with a piece of folded kitchen
paper or foil and fill with small truffles.
If necessary, use the remaining melted
chocolate as "glue". Spread a small
amount on to the rim of the egg half and,
holding the empty egg half with a piece of
kitchen paper or foil, press it on to the
filled half, making sure the rims are
aligned and carefully joined.

6 Hold for several seconds, then prop up
the egg with the folded paper or foil and
chill to set. If you like, decorate the egg
with ribbons or Easter decorations.

CHOCOLATE CHRISTMAS CUPS

MAKES ABOUT 35 CUPS

275g/10oz plain (semisweet) chocolate,
chopped into small pieces
175g/6oz cold cooked
Christmas pudding
75ml/2½fl oz/5 tbsp brandy or whisky
chocolate leaves and crystallized
(candied) cranberries, to decorate

1 Melt the chocolate and use to coat the base and sides of about 35 sweet cases. Leave to set, then repeat, reheating the melted chocolate if necessary. Leave to cool and set. Reserve the remaining chocolate. Crumble the Christmas pudding, sprinkle with brandy or whisky and leave for 30–40 minutes, until the liquor is absorbed.

2 Spoon some pudding into each cup, smoothing the top. Reheat the remaining chocolate and spoon over the top of each cup. Leave to set, then peel off the cases. Decorate with chocolate leaves and crystallized berries.

MARZIPAN LOGS

MAKES ABOUT 12

225g/8oz marzipan
115g/4oz/⅔ cup candied orange
peel, chopped
30ml/2 tbsp orange-flavoured liqueur
15ml/1 tbsp soft light brown sugar
edible gold powder
75g/3oz plain (semisweet)
chocolate, melted
gold-coated sweets

1 Knead the marzipan. Add the peel and liqueur. Set aside for 1 hour, to dry.

2 Break off small pieces of the mixture and roll into log shapes.

3 Dip the tops of half the logs in the sugar. Brush with edible gold powder.

4 Dip the rest in chocolate and press a gold-coated sweet on top of each. When set, arrange all the logs on a plate.

PEPPERMINT CHOCOLATE STICKS

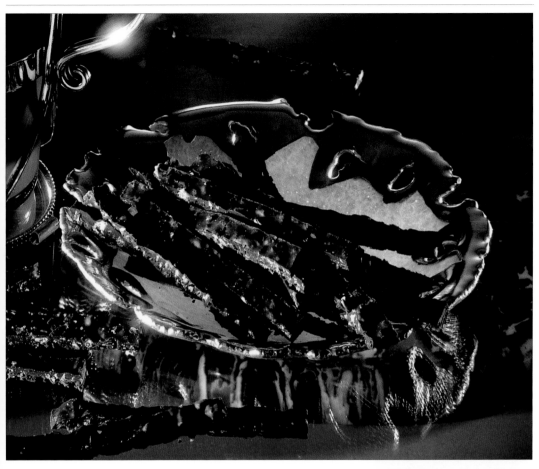

MAKES ABOUT 80

115g/4oz/½ cup granulated sugar

150ml/¼ pint/⅔ cup water

2.5ml/½ tsp peppermint essence (extract)

200g/7oz dark (bittersweet) chocolate, chopped

60ml/4 tbsp toasted desiccated (dry unsweetened shredded) coconut

1 Oil a large baking sheet. Heat the sugar and water until dissolved.

2 Boil rapidly without stirring until the syrup registers 138°C/280°F on a sugar thermometer. Off the heat, stir in the peppermint essence.

3 Pour the mixture on to the greased baking sheet and leave until set.

4 Break up the peppermint mixture into a small bowl and use the end of a rolling pin to crush it into small pieces.

5 Melt the chocolate. Off the heat, stir in the mint pieces and coconut.

6 Cut a 30 x 25cm/12 x 10in sheet of baking parchment. Spread the chocolate mixture over the parchment, leaving a narrow border all around, to make a rectangle measuring about 25 x 20cm/ 10 x 8in. Leave to set. When firm, use a sharp knife to cut into thin sticks, each about 6cm/2½in long.

CHOCOLATE ALMOND TORRONNE

MAKES ABOUT 20 SLICES

115g/4oz dark (bittersweet) chocolate,
  chopped into small pieces
50g/2oz/¼ cup unsalted (sweet) butter
1 egg white
115g/4oz/½ cup caster
  (superfine) sugar
75g/3oz/¾ cup chopped
  toasted almonds
50g/2oz/½ cup ground almonds
75ml/5 tbsp chopped candied peel
For the Coating
175g/6oz white chocolate, chopped
  into small pieces
25g/1oz/2 tbsp unsalted (sweet) butter
115g/4oz/1 cup flaked (sliced)
  almonds, toasted

1 Melt the chocolate with the butter.
Whisk the egg white and sugar until stiff.
Gradually beat in the melted chocolate
mixture, then stir in the nuts and peel.

2 Tip the mixture on to a large sheet of
baking parchment and shape into a
thick roll.

3 As the mixture cools, use the paper to
press the roll firmly into a triangular shape.
Twist the paper over the triangular roll and
chill until completely set.

4 Make the coating. Melt the white
chocolate with the butter in a heatproof
bowl over a saucepan of simmering water.
Unwrap the chocolate roll and with a clean
knife spread the white chocolate quickly
over the surface. Press the flaked almonds
in a thin even coating over the chocolate,
working quickly before the chocolate sets.

5 Chill the coated chocolate roll again
until firm, then cut the torronne into fairly
thin slices to serve. Torronne is ideal to
finish a dinner party.

DOUBLE CHOCOLATE-DIPPED FRUIT

MAKES 24 COATED PIECES

fruits – about 24 pieces (strawberries, cherries, orange segments, large seedless grapes, physalis (Cape gooseberies), kumquats, stoned (pitted) prunes, stoned dates, dried apricots, dried peaches or dried pears)

115g/4oz white chocolate, chopped

115g/4oz dark (bittersweet) or plain (semisweet) chocolate, chopped

1 Clean and prepare the fruits. Wipe the strawberries with a soft cloth or brush gently with a pastry brush. Wash firm-skinned fruits such as cherries and grapes and dry well. Peel and leave whole or cut up any other fruits being used.

2 Melt the white chocolate. Remove from the heat and cool to lukewarm (about 29°C/84°F), stirring frequently. Line a baking sheet with baking parchment. Hold the fruit by the stem or end, and at an angle. Dip two-thirds of the fruit into the chocolate. Allow the excess to drip off and place on the baking sheet. Chill for about 20 minutes until the chocolate sets.

3 Melt the dark or plain chocolate, stirring frequently until smooth.

4 Remove the chocolate from the heat and cool to just below body temperature, about 30°C/86°F. Take each white chocolate-coated fruit in turn from the baking sheet and, holding by the stem or end and at the opposite angle, dip the lower third of each piece into the dark chocolate, creating a chevron effect. Place on the baking sheet. Chill for 15 minutes or until set. Before serving, allow the fruit to stand at room temperature for 10–15 minutes to bring the flavours out.

CHOCOLATE PEPPERMINT CREAMS

1 egg white

90ml/6 tbsp double (heavy) cream

5ml/1 tsp peppermint essence (extract)

675g/1½lb/5½ cups icing (confectioners') sugar, plus extra for dusting

a few drops of green food colouring

175g/6oz plain (semisweet) chocolate, chopped

1 Beat the egg white lightly in a bowl. Mix in the cream and peppermint essence, then gradually add the icing sugar to make a firm, pliable dough. Work in 1–2 drops of green food colouring until evenly pale green.

2 On a surface dusted with icing sugar, roll out the dough to a thickness of about 1cm/½in. Stamp out 4cm/1½in rounds or squares and place on a baking sheet lined with non-stick baking parchment. Leave to dry for 8 hours, turning once.

3 Melt the chocolate in a bowl over barely simmering water. Allow to cool slightly. Spread chocolate over the top of each peppermint cream and place on fresh sheets of non-stick paper. Chill until set.

CHOCOLATE-COATED NUT BRITTLE

MAKES 20–24 PIECES

115g/4oz/1 cup mixed pecan nuts and
  whole almonds
115g/4oz/½ cup caster (superfine) sugar
60ml/4 tbsp water
200g/7oz dark (bittersweet)
  chocolate, chopped

1 Lightly grease a baking sheet. Mix the nuts, sugar and water in a heavy pan. Place over a gentle heat, stirring until all the sugar has dissolved.

2 Bring to the boil, then lower the heat to medium and cook until a rich golden brown, registering 155°C/310°F on a sugar thermometer. If you do not have a sugar thermometer, test the syrup by adding a few drops to a cup of iced water. The mixture should solidify to a very brittle mass.

CHOCOLATE-COATED HAZELNUTS
Roast about 225g/8oz/2 cups hazelnuts in the oven or under the grill (broiler). Allow to cool. Melt the chocolate in a heatproof bowl set over a pan of simmering water. Remove from the heat, but leave the bowl over the water so that the chocolate remains liquid. Have ready about 30 paper sweet cases, arranged on baking sheets. Add the roasted hazelnuts to the melted chocolate and stir to coat. Using two spoons, carefully scoop up a cluster of two or three chocolate-coated nuts. Carefully transfer the cluster to a paper sweet case. Leave the nut clusters in a cool place until set.

3 Quickly remove the pan from the heat and tip the mixture on to the prepared baking sheet, spreading it evenly. Leave until completely cold and hard.

4 Break the nut brittle into bite-sized pieces. Melt the chocolate and dip the pieces to half-coat them. Leave on a sheet of baking parchment to set.

CHOCOLATE NUT CLUSTERS

MAKES ABOUT 30

525ml/21fl oz/2½ cups double
(heavy) cream
25g/1oz/2 tbsp unsalted (sweet) butter
350ml/12fl oz/1½ cups golden (light
corn) syrup
200g/7oz/scant 1 cup granulated sugar
75g/3oz/⅓ cup light brown sugar
a pinch of salt
15ml/1 tbsp vanilla essence (extract)
350g/12oz/3 cups combination of
hazelnuts, pecan nuts, walnuts, brazil
nuts and unsalted peanuts
400g/14oz plain (semisweet) chocolate
15g/½oz/1 tbsp white vegetable fat

1 Lightly brush 2 baking sheets with vegetable oil. In a large heavy pan set over a medium heat, cook the cream, butter, golden syrup, sugars and salt together, stirring from time to time for 3 minutes, until the sugars dissolve and the butter melts.

2 Bring to the boil and continue cooking, stirring frequently, for about 1 hour, until the caramel reaches 119°C/238°F on a sugar thermometer, or until a small amount of caramel dropped into a cup of iced water forms a hard ball. Remove from the heat and plunge the base of the pan into cold water to stop cooking. Cool slightly, then stir in the vanilla essence.

3 Stir the nuts into the caramel until well coated. Using an oiled tablespoon, drop spoonfuls of nut mixture on to the prepared sheets, about 2.5cm/1in apart. If the mixture hardens, return to the heat to soften. Chill the clusters for 30 minutes until firm and cold, or leave in a cool place.

4 Using a metal spatula, transfer the clusters to a wire rack placed over a baking sheet to catch the drips. Melt the chocolate with the white vegetable fat over a low heat, stirring until smooth. Set aside to cool slightly.

5 Spoon chocolate over each cluster, being sure to cover completely.

6 Place on a clean wire rack over a baking sheet. Allow to set for 2 hours until hardened. Store in an airtight container.

CHOCOLATE FUDGE TRIANGLES

MAKES ABOUT 48 TRIANGLES

600g/1lb 5oz fine quality white
  chocolate, chopped into small pieces
375g/13oz can sweetened
  condensed milk
15ml/1 tbsp vanilla essence (extract)
7.5ml/1½ tsp lemon juice
a pinch of salt
175g/6oz/1½ cups hazelnuts or pecan
  nuts, chopped (optional)
175g/6oz plain (semisweet)
  chocolate, chopped
40g/1½oz/3 tbsp unsalted (sweet)
  butter, cut into small pieces
50g/2oz dark (bittersweet) chocolate,
  for drizzling

1 Line a 20cm/8in square baking tin
(pan) with foil. Brush the foil with oil. In a
pan set over a low heat, melt the white
chocolate and condensed milk until
smooth, stirring frequently. Off the heat,
stir in the vanilla, lemon juice and salt. Stir
in the nuts if using. Spread half the
mixture in the tin. Chill for 15 minutes.

2 In a pan over a low heat, melt the plain
chocolate and butter, stirring frequently.
Cool slightly, then pour over the white
layer. Chill for 15 minutes until set.

3 Gently reheat the remaining white
chocolate mixture and pour over the set
plain chocolate layer. Smooth the top,
then chill for 2–4 hours until set.

4 Using the foil, remove the fudge from
the pan and invert it on to a chopping
board. Lift off the foil and use a sharp
knife to cut the fudge into 24 squares. Cut
each square into two triangles. Melt the
dark chocolate in a heatproof bowl set over
a pan of barely simmering water. Cool
slightly, then drizzle over the triangles.

EASY CHOCOLATE HAZELNUT FUDGE

MAKES 16 SQUARES

150ml/¼ pint/⅔ cup evaporated
(unsweetened condensed) milk
350g/12oz/1½ cups sugar
a large pinch of salt
50g/2oz/½ cup hazelnuts, halved
350g/12oz/2 cups plain (semisweet)
chocolate chips

1 Grease a 20cm/8in square cake tin
(pan). Place the milk, sugar and salt in a
heavy pan. Bring to the boil over a medium
heat, stirring constantly. Lower the heat
and simmer gently, stirring, for 5 minutes.

2 Remove the pan from the heat and add
the hazelnuts and chocolate chips. Stir
gently until the chocolate has melted.

3 Quickly pour the fudge mixture into the
prepared tin and spread evenly. Leave to
cool and set.

4 When the fudge has set, cut into
2.5cm/1in squares. Store in an airtight
container, separating the layers with
baking parchment.

TWO-TONE FUDGE
Make the Easy Chocolate Hazelnut
Fudge and spread it in a 23cm/9in
square cake tin, to make a slightly
thinner layer than for the main recipe.
While it is cooling, make a batch of
plain fudge, substituting white
chocolate chips for the plain chocolate
chips and leaving out the hazelnuts.
Let the plain fudge cool slightly before
pouring it carefully over the dark
chocolate layer. Use a slim metal
spatula to spread the plain layer to the
corners, then set aside to set as before.
Cut into squares and store in an
airtight container.

RICH CHOCOLATE PISTACHIO FUDGE

MAKES 36

250g/9oz/1 cup granulated sugar

375g/13oz can sweetened condensed milk

50g/2oz/¼ cup unsalted (sweet) butter

5ml/1 tsp vanilla essence (extract)

115g/4oz dark (bittersweet)
  chocolate, grated

75g/3oz/¾ cup pistachio nuts

**CHOCOLATE AND
MARSHMALLOW FUDGE**

25g/1oz/2 tbsp butter

350g/12oz/1½ cups
  granulated sugar

175ml/6fl oz/¾ cup evaporated
  (unsweetened condensed) milk

a pinch of salt

115g/4oz/2 cups white mini
  marshmallows

225g/8oz/1¼ cups chocolate chips

5ml/1 tsp vanilla essence (extract)

115g/4oz/½ cup chopped walnuts
  (optional)

1 Generously grease an 18cm/7in cake tin (pan). Mix the butter, sugar, evaporated milk and salt in a heavy pan. Stir over a medium heat until the sugar has dissolved, then bring to the boil and cook for 3–5 minutes or until thickened, stirring all the time.

2 Remove the pan from the heat and beat in the marshmallows and chocolate chips until dissolved. Beat in the vanilla essence. Scrape the mixture into the prepared cake tin and press it evenly into the corners, using a metal spatula. Level the surface.

3 If using, sprinkle the walnuts over the fudge and press them into the surface. Cool, then score into squares. Chill, then cut up.

1 Grease and line a 19cm/7½in square cake tin (pan). Mix the sugar, condensed milk and butter in a heavy pan. Heat gently, stirring occasionally, until the sugar has dissolved completely and the mixture is smooth.

2 Bring the mixture to the boil, stirring occasionally, and boil until it registers 116°C/240°F on a sugar thermometer, or until a small amount of the mixture dropped into a cup of iced water forms a soft ball.

3 Remove the pan from the heat and beat in the vanilla essence, chocolate and nuts. Beat vigorously until smooth and creamy.

4 Pour the mixture into the prepared cake tin and spread evenly. Leave until just set, then mark into squares. Leave to set completely before cutting into squares and removing from the tin. Store in an airtight container in a cool place.

TRUFFLE-FILLED FILO CUPS

MAKES ABOUT 24 CUPS

3–6 sheets fresh or thawed frozen filo
  pastry, depending on size
40g/11/2 oz/3 tbsp unsalted (sweet)
  butter, melted
sugar, for sprinkling
pared strips of lemon rind, to decorate
For the Chocolate Truffle Mixture
250ml/8fl oz/1 cup double (heavy) cream
225g/8oz dark (bittersweet) or plain
  (semisweet) chocolate, chopped
50g/2oz/1/4 cup unsalted (sweet) butter,
  cut into small pieces
30ml/2 tbsp brandy or liqueur

1 Prepare the truffle mixture. In a pan
over a medium heat, bring the cream to
the boil. Remove from the heat and
add the chopped chocolate, stirring until
melted. Beat in the butter and add the
brandy or liqueur. Strain into a bowl and
chill for 1 hour until thick.

2 Preheat the oven to 200°C/400°F/Gas 6.
Grease a 12-hole bun tray (pan). Cut the
filo sheets into 6cm/2½in squares. Cover
with a damp dishtowel. Place one square
on a work surface. Brush lightly with
melted butter, turn over and brush the
other side. Sprinkle with a pinch of sugar.
Butter another square and place it over
the first at an angle. Sprinkle with sugar.
Butter a third square and place over the
first two, unevenly, so the corners form an
uneven edge. Press the layered square
into one of the holes in the bun tray.

3 Continue to fill the tray, working quickly
so that the filo does not have time to dry
out. Bake the filo cups for 4–6 minutes,
until golden. Cool for 10 minutes on the
bun tray, then carefully transfer to a wire
rack and cool completely.

4 Stir the chocolate mixture; it should be
just thick enough to pipe. Spoon the
mixture into a piping (pastry) bag with a
medium star nozzle and pipe a swirl into
each filo cup. Decorate each with tiny
strips of lemon rind.

MEXICAN HOT CHOCOLATE

SERVES 4

1 litre/1¾ pints/4 cups milk
1 cinnamon stick
2 whole cloves
115g/4oz dark (bittersweet)
  chocolate, chopped
2–3 drops of almond essence (extract)

1 Heat the milk gently with the spices until almost boiling, then stir in the chocolate until melted.

2 Strain into a blender, add the almond essence and blend on high speed for about 30 seconds until frothy. Or use a hand-held electric mixer or wire whisk.

3 Pour into warmed heatproof glasses and serve immediately.

WHITE HOT CHOCOLATE

SERVES 4

1.75 litres/3 pints/7½ cups milk
175g/6oz white chocolate, chopped
10ml/2 tsp coffee powder
10ml/2 tsp orange-flavoured liqueur
whipped cream and ground cinnamon,
  to serve

1 Heat the milk in a large heavy pan until almost boiling. Remove from the heat when bubbles form around the edge of the pan.

2 Add the white chocolate, coffee powder and orange-flavoured liqueur, if using. Stir until all the chocolate has melted and the mixture is smooth.

3 Pour the hot chocolate into four mugs. Top each with a swirl or spoonful of whipped cream and a sprinkling of ground cinnamon. Serve immediately.

ICED MINT AND CHOCOLATE COOLER

SERVES 4

60ml/4 tbsp drinking chocolate powder
400ml/14fl oz/1⅔ cups chilled milk
150ml/¼ pint/⅔ cup natural (plain) yogurt
2.5ml/½ tsp peppermint essence (extract)
4 scoops of chocolate ice cream
mint leaves and chocolate shapes, to decorate

1 Place the drinking chocolate in a small pan and stir in about 120ml/4fl oz/½ cup of the milk. Heat gently, stirring, until almost boiling, then remove the pan from the heat.

2 Pour into a heatproof bowl and whisk in the remaining milk. Add the yogurt and peppermint, and whisk again.

3 Pour the mixture into four tall glasses, filling them no more than three-quarters full. Top each drink with a scoop of ice cream. Decorate with mint leaves and chocolate shapes. Serve at once.

CHOCOLATE VANILLA COOLER
Make the drink as in the main recipe, but use single (light) cream instead of the yogurt and 5ml/1 tsp natural vanilla essence (extract) instead of the peppermint.

MOCHA COOLER
Make the drink as in the main recipe, but dissolve the chocolate in 120ml/4fl oz/½ cup strong black coffee, and reduce the milk to 300ml/½ pint/1¼ cups. Use cream instead of yogurt and leave the peppermint essence out.

IRISH CHOCOLATE VELVET

SERVES 4

250ml/8fl oz/1 cup double (heavy) cream
400ml/14fl oz/1⅔ cups milk
115g/4oz milk chocolate, chopped into small pieces
30ml/2 tbsp cocoa powder
60ml/4 tbsp Irish whiskey
whipped cream, for topping
chocolate curls, to decorate

1 Using a hand-held electric mixer, whip half the cream in a bowl until thick enough to hold its shape.

2 Heat the milk and chocolate gently, stirring, until the chocolate has melted. Whisk in the cocoa, then bring to the boil. Off the heat, stir in the remaining cream and the whiskey.

3 Pour into four warmed mugs. Top with generous spoonfuls of the whipped cream and add the curls. Serve with Peppermint Sticks, if wished.

HOT CHOCOLATE AND CHOC-TIPPED BISCUITS

SERVES 2

115g/4oz/½ cup soft margarine

15ml/3 tbsp icing (confectioners')
sugar, sifted

150g/5oz/1¼ cups plain (all-purpose) flour

few drops of vanilla essence (extract)

75g/3oz plain (semisweet)
chocolate, chopped

For the Hot Chocolate

90ml/6 tbsp drinking chocolate powder,
plus a little extra for sprinkling

30ml/2 tbsp caster (superfine) sugar,
or more according to taste

600ml/1 pint/2½ cups milk

2 large squirts of cream (optional)

1 Preheat the oven to 180°C/350°F/Gas 4 and lightly grease 2 baking sheets. For the choc-tipped biscuits (cookies), beat the margarine and icing sugar together in a bowl until very soft. Add the flour and vanilla and mix in well.

2 Put the mixture in a large piping (pastry) bag fitted with a large star nozzle. Pipe 10 neat lines, each 13cm/5in long, on the prepared baking sheets. Leave a little room between each. They will not spread much on cooking, but you will need to be able to remove them easily. Bake for 15–20 minutes, until the biscuits are pale golden brown. Allow to cool slightly before lifting on to a wire rack.

3 Put the chocolate in a heatproof bowl over a pan of barely simmering water and leave to melt. Stir until creamy, then remove the bowl of melted chocolate from the heat. Dip both ends of each biscuit in the chocolate, put back on the rack and leave to cool and set.

4 To make the drinking chocolate, put the drinking chocolate powder and the sugar in a saucepan. Add the milk and bring to the boil, whisking all the time. Divide between two tall mugs. Add more sugar if needed. Top each drink with a squirt of cream, if you like.

SAUCES, FROSTINGS <u>AND</u> ICINGS

SIMPLE BUTTERCREAM

MAKES ABOUT 350G/12OZ

   75g/3oz butter or soft margarine
   225g/8oz/1½ cups icing
   (confectioners') sugar
   5ml/1 tsp vanilla essence (extract)
   10–15ml/2–3 tsp milk

1 If using, allow the butter to come to room temperature. Sift the icing sugar. Put the butter or margarine in a bowl. Add about a quarter of the icing sugar and beat with a hand-held electric mixer until fluffy.

2 Using a metal spoon, add the remaining sifted icing sugar, a little at a time, beating well with the electric mixer after each addition. (Icing sugar is so fine that if you add too much of it at one time, it tends to fly out of the bowl.)

3 Add in 5ml/1 tsp of the milk, beating in. The mixture should be light and creamy, with a spreadable consistency. Add the vanilla essence, then more milk if necessary, but not too much, or it will be too sloppy to draw into peaks. Use as a filling and/or topping on layer cakes and cupcakes.

CHOCOLATE BUTTERCREAM

ENOUGH TO FILL A
20CM/8IN ROUND LAYER CAKE

   75g/3oz/6 tbsp unsalted (sweet) butter
   or margarine, softened
   175g/6oz/1 cup icing (confectioners') sugar
   15ml/1 tbsp cocoa powder
   2.5ml/½ tsp vanilla essence (extract)

1 Place all the ingredients in a large bowl.

2 Beat well to a smooth spreadable consistency.

VARIATIONS

Coffee Buttercream: Stir 10ml/2 tsp instant coffee into 15ml/1 tbsp boiling water. Beat into the icing instead of the milk.
Mocha Buttercream: Stir 5ml/1 tsp cocoa powder into 10ml/2 tsp boiling water. Beat into the icing. Add a little coffee essence.
Orange Buttercream: Use orange juice instead of the milk and vanilla essence, and add 10ml/2 tsp finely grated orange rind. Omit the rind if using the icing for piping.

WHITE CHOCOLATE FROSTING

ENOUGH TO COVER
A 20CM/8IN ROUND CAKE

   175g/6oz white chocolate, chopped
   75g/3oz/6 tbsp unsalted (sweet) butter
   115g/4oz/¾ cup icing
   (confectioners') sugar
   90ml/6 tbsp double (heavy) cream

1 Melt the chocolate with the butter in a heatproof bowl over a pan of barely simmering water. Remove the bowl from the heat and beat in the icing sugar, a little at a time, using a wire whisk.

2 Whip the cream in a separate bowl until it just holds its shape, then beat into the chocolate mixture. Allow the mixture to cool, stirring occasionally, until it begins to hold its shape. Use immediately.

COOK'S TIP

White chocolate frosting is a rich frosting suitable for a dark chocolate sponge without a filling. Use a metal spatula to form peaks for an attractive finish.

FUDGE FROSTING

MAKES 350G/12OZ

50g/2oz plain (semisweet) chocolate
225g/8oz/2 cups icing (confectioners')
   sugar, sifted
50g/2oz/¼ cup butter or margarine
45ml/3 tbsp single (light) cream
15ml/1 tbsp vanilla essence (extract)

COOK'S TIP
When you have covered the cake with
the frosting, use the back of a spoon or
the tines of a fork to swirl the fudge
frosting and create an attractive pattern
on the cake, but do this quickly as it
sets very fast.

1 Chop the chocolate and mix with the
icing sugar, butter or margarine, cream
and vanilla essence in a heavy pan. Stir
over a very low heat until the chocolate
and butter or margarine melt. Turn off the
heat, stir until smooth.

2 Beat the icing frequently as it cools until
it thickens sufficiently to use for spreading
or piping. Use immediately and work
quickly once it has reached the right
consistency. This is a popular frosting and
can be used for many kinds of cakes.

SATIN CHOCOLATE ICING

MAKES 225G/8OZ

150ml/¼ pint/⅔ cup double (heavy) cream
2.5ml/½ tsp instant coffee powder
175g/6oz plain (semisweet)
  chocolate, chopped

COOK'S TIP
Do not touch the icing once it has
hardened or the attractive satin
finish will be spoilt. Cakes covered
with this icing need little by way of
decoration, but half-dipped cherries
look good.

1 Put the chocolate, cream and coffee in
a small heavy pan. Place the cake to be
iced on a wire rack set over a baking
sheet or tray.

2 Place the pan over a very low heat and
stir the icing mixture continuously with a
wooden spoon until all the chocolate has
melted and the mixture is smooth and
evenly blended.

3 Remove the pan from the heat and pour
the icing over the cake at once, letting
it run down the sides slowly to coat it
completely. Spread the icing with a palette
knife or metal spatula as necessary,
working quickly before the icing has time
to thicken.

CHOCOLATE FONDANT
ENOUGH TO COVER AND DECORATE A
23CM/9IN ROUND CAKE

350g/12oz plain (semisweet)
  chocolate, chopped
60ml/4 tbsp liquid glucose
2 egg whites
900g/2lb/7 cups icing
  (confectioners') sugar

1 Melt the chocolate with the glucose
in a bowl set over simmering water,
stirring occasionally. When smooth,
remove from the heat.

2 Whisk the egg whites with a
hand-held electric mixer until soft
peaks form. Stir into the chocolate
mixture with 45ml/3 tbsp of the
icing sugar.

3 Beat the icing, gradually adding
enough icing sugar to make a
stiff paste. Wrap the fondant in
clear film (plastic wrap) if not using
at once.

DARK CHOCOLATE SAUCE

QUICK CHOCOLATE SAUCE
MAKES 225ML/8FL OZ/1 CUP

    150ml/¼ pint/⅔ cup double
      (heavy) cream
    15ml/1 tbsp caster (superfine)
      sugar
    150g/5oz plain (semisweet)
      chocolate, chopped
    30ml/2 tbsp dark rum or whisky

1 Boil the cream and sugar. Off the heat, add the chocolate and stir until melted. Stir in the rum or whisky.

2 Pour the sauce into a jar. Cool, cover and store for up to 10 days. When needed, reheat in a pan of simmering water, or remove the lid and microwave on High for 2 minutes. Stir before serving.

MAKES ABOUT 350ML/12FL OZ

    45ml/3 tbsp granulated sugar
    120ml/4fl oz/½ cup water
    175g/6oz dark (bittersweet) chocolate,
      chopped into small pieces
    25g/1oz/2 tbsp unsalted (sweet) butter
    60–90ml/4–6 tbsp single (light) cream
    2.5ml/½ tsp vanilla essence (extract)

1 Combine the sugar and water in a heavy pan. Bring to the boil over a medium heat, stirring constantly until the sugar has completely dissolved.

2 Dice the butter and add with the chocolate to the syrup, stirring with a wooden spoon, then remove the pan from the heat and continue to stir until smooth.

3 Stir in the single cream and vanilla essence. Serve the sauce warm, over vanilla ice cream, profiteroles, poached pears or crêpes.

GLOSSY CHOCOLATE SAUCE

SERVES 6

    115g/4oz/½ cup caster (superfine) sugar
    60ml/4 tbsp water
    175g/6oz plain (semisweet) chocolate,
      chopped into small pieces
    25g/1oz/2 tbsp unsalted (sweet) butter
    30ml/2 tbsp brandy or orange juice

COOK'S TIP
Any of these sauces would make a chocolate fondue, with fruit and dessert biscuits (cookies) as dippers.

1 Place the caster sugar and water in a heavy pan and heat gently, stirring occasionally with a wooden spoon until all the sugar has dissolved.

2 Stir in the chocolate until melted, then add the butter in the same way. Do not allow the sauce to boil. Stir in the brandy or orange juice and serve warm.

CHOCOLATE FUDGE SAUCE

SERVES 6

150ml/¼ pint/⅔ cup double (heavy) cream
50g/2oz/¼ cup butter
50g/2oz/¼ cup vanilla sugar
175g/6oz plain (semisweet) chocolate,
    chopped into small pieces
30ml/2 tbsp brandy

1 Heat the cream with the butter and sugar in a bowl set over a pan of barely simmering water. Stir until smooth. Cool.

2 Add the chocolate to the cream mixture. Stir over simmering water until melted and thoroughly combined.

3 Stir in the brandy a little at a time, then leave to cool to room temperature.

CHOCOLATE GANACHE
ENOUGH TO COVER A
23CM/9IN ROUND CAKE
    225g/8oz plain (semisweet)
        chocolate, chopped
    250ml/8fl oz/1 cup double
        (heavy) cream

Melt the chocolate with the cream. Leave to cool, then whisk until the mixture begins to hold its shape.

WHITE CHOCOLATE ᴬᴺᴰ ORANGE SAUCE

SERVES 6

150ml/¼ pint/⅔ cup double (heavy) cream
50g/2oz/¼ cup butter
45ml/3 tbsp caster (superfine) sugar
175g/6oz white chocolate, chopped
    into small pieces
finely grated rind of 1 orange
30ml/2 tbsp orange-flavoured liqueur

COOK'S TIP
Serve with ice cream, or with hot waffles or fresh crêpes.

1 Pour the cream into a heavy pan. Cut the butter into cubes and add it to the pan, with the sugar. Heat gently, stirring the mixture occasionally until the butter has melted.

2 Add the chocolate. Stir over a low heat until melted and thoroughly combined.

3 Stir in the orange rind, then add the liqueur a little at a time. Leave to cool.

COFFEE

*Everything you ever wanted to know about coffee you will
find here for your fascination and delight. The reference section
explores the history and cultural, political and economic
impact of coffee across the world, then examines on a
country-by-country basis the tastes and characteristics of
coffee produced today. It also explains how to grind, brew
and make the perfect cup of coffee. In the second section, there
are over 70 recipes demonstrating the wonderful versatility
of coffee in the kitchen, with delicious soufflés and meringues,
puddings, fruit and frozen desserts, and enticing cakes,
pastries and breads.*

THE HISTORY
OF COFFEE

This section traces the mysterious and conflict-ridden journey of
the coffee bean from its Ethiopian birthplace, through Arabia
and the Middle East, and on to Europe and the New World.
The crucial role of the beverage in shaping the spiritual and
social life of medieval Arabia and Turkey is examined, as is
how, later, it became irrevocably entrenched in Western cultures.
The vital role of the coffee house in political, economic and
cultural life across the world is covered, both historically and up
to the present day. There is also a section devoted to the myriad
methods of early coffee brewing and a discussion on
coffee-drinking and coffee products.

THE GENESIS OF THE BEAN

Ever since its migration from north-east Africa to Arabia many hundreds of years ago, the coffee bean has played a multifaceted role in moulding history. That short hop across the Red Sea helped alter social, political and economic life not only in Africa and the Middle East, but in mainland Europe, Britain and the Americas, too. Coffee has made the fortunes and misfortunes of many, oiled the wheels of communication, inspired creative minds, stimulated the tired, and, for countless imbibers the world over, become a daily necessity.

Myths and Mysteries

So great was the mystique ascribed to coffee, that conjecture over who invented the beverage and discovered its other properties, and how and when this was done, was intense. Different people had their pet theories and great kudos was linked to association with the so-called "discovery". As a result, in medieval Arabia and later in 17th-century Europe, stories and legends were rife.

Parched Corn or Black Broth

Those with a historical bent and a lively imagination traced the bean back to Old Testament tales, claiming that it was the same "parched corn" that Abigail gave to David, and Boaz to Ruth. Many were convinced it was the "black broth" of the Lacedaemonians, as the Spartans were then called. Petrus de Valle, a well-known Italian traveller, believed that coffee dated as far back as the Trojan war, suggesting that "the fair Helen with other ladies of Priamus's Court, used sometimes to drown the Thoughts of the Calamities she had brought upon her Family and Country, in a Pot of Coffee". Others thought that, in Homer's *Odyssey*, the substance called "nepenthes", which Helen mixed with wine and which "banishes sadness and wrath from the heart" was coffee.

Banesius, a late 18th-century writer, theorized in a treatise on coffee that since it was a medicine and most medicines were discovered by chance, the discovery of "this Liquor was as much a proof of fortuitous Experience as any of those [other medicines]".

Following this line of thought, Banesius went on to recount the ubiquitous fable of the dancing goats, in which an Arab or Ethiopian goatherd complained to the Imam of a neighbouring monastery that his flock "two or three times a week not only kept awake all night long but spent it frisking and dancing in an unusual manner". The Imam, concluding that the animals may have eaten something that was causing the reaction, went to the pasture where they danced. Here he found berries growing on shrubs, and he decided to try them himself.

Having boiled the berries in water and drunk the resulting brew, the Imam found that he was able to stay awake at night without any ill effects. Encouraged by what had been an enjoyable experience, he "enjoin'd the daily Use of it to his Monks, which, by keeping them from Sleep, made them more readily and surely attend the Devotions they were obliged to perform at Night time... It continued to keep them in perfect Health; and by this means it came to be in request throughout that whole Kingdom".

Dr James Douglas, in his scholarly work *Yemensis fructum Coféferens; or, A Description and History of the Coffee Tree* (1727), somewhat scathingly dismisses Banesius's story as having "too great an Air of Fable to be in the least depended on", stating that "those who are acquainted with the Nature of Vulgar Traditions, especially those of Eastern nations, will understand its thin credibility".

One of the many variations of the tale – this one by Sir Thomas Pope Blount – tells of how the Imam tried the coffee experiment upon "another sort of Beast, a sleepy Heavy-headed Monk". In a short time, the story goes, it had such a wonderful effect on him, that it "quite alter'd his Constitution, and hereafterwards became more quick, brisk, and airy than generally that sort of Cattle are".

Left: "Ruth on the Field of Boaz", wood engraving, from The Bible in Pictures, Leipzig, 1860 by Julius Schnorr von Carolsfeld (1794–1874).

Basic botany

Coffee comes from the fruit of an evergreen shrub, or tree, which flourishes in tropical and subtropical regions around the world. The trees produce delicate clusters of jasmine-scented blossoms, and fruit known as "cherries". Cocooned in each cherry, protected by pulp and parchment, are two coffee beans. Since approximately four thousand beans are needed to produce one pound of roasted coffee, few commodities require so much in terms of human effort.

Right: Coffea arabica, *botanical magazine, London, 1810.*

The Muslim View

The Muslims had another story which Dr Douglas describes as "still more wonderful, but equally groundless". The Muslims claimed that because of their special relationship with "Providence", and so that they would gain from so "beneficial a Liquor", the archangel Gabriel was sent to reveal to the prophet Mohammed "the Virtues and manner of preparing [coffee]."

Yet another legend tells of the dervish Omar, known for his ability to heal the sick by prayer. Exiled from his home town of Mocha to a cave in the desert and nearing starvation, Omar chewed berries from shrubs growing nearby. Finding the berries too bitter, he roasted them, hoping to improve the flavour. Obviously a man of refined palate (and surprisingly well equipped with the necessary utensils), he decided the berries now needed boiling to soften them. He drank the resulting fragrant brew and was instantly revitalized, remaining in this state for several days.

A picturesque variation of the same tale states how Omar saw a bird of marvellous plumage in a tree, where it sang an exquisitely harmonious song. When he reached out for the bird, Omar found only flowers and fruit in its place. He filled his basket with these and returned to the cave, intending to boil a few meagre herbs for dinner. However, he boiled the fruit instead and created a savoury and perfumed brown drink.

Eventually – and both variations concur with this – patients from Mocha came to the cave for medical advice. They, too, were given the drink and, since this is a legend, they were of course cured. When news of the "miracle cure" reached Mocha, Omar was invited to return in triumph and was subsequently made the patron saint of the city.

Despite the vast literature assembled by many historians, no one has ever been able to say positively how and when the plant was discovered. Its origins therefore remain shrouded in legend in which truth and imagination are inexorably entwined.

Below: 1950s' British advertisement referring to the story of the discovery of coffee's properties by goats eating the berries of a certain tree.

ODYSSEY FROM AFRICA

The coffee plant found its way from Ethiopia to Arabia sometime between AD 575 and AD 850. How it got there is not clear, but one possibility is that seeds were brought by African tribespeople as they migrated northwards from Kenya and Ethiopia to the Arabian peninsular. They were eventually driven back by spear-throwing Persians but they left behind coffee trees growing in what is now the Yemen.

Myths and Legends

Another possibility is that Arab slave traders brought the seeds back from their raids on Ethiopia; or, as is more likely, the responsibility lay with the Sufis – a mystical Islamic sect best-known for their "whirling dervishes". Classical Arabic literature endorses this, suggesting that it was a Sufi grand master, Ali ben Omar al Shadili, who brought coffee seeds to Arabia. Al Shadili had lived for a while in Ethiopia before founding a monastery in the Yemenite port of Mocha (Al Mukha). Since he later became known as the Saint of Mocha, he appears to be the same legendary Omar who discovered coffee berries while exiled in the desert, though the stories do not quite tie up.

According to Dr Douglas, a reasonably reliable account was unearthed in a collection of original manuscripts by Monsieur de Nointel, Louis IV's ambassador at the Arab ports. Written by an Arab in 1587, the document gives what was believed at the time to be the earliest account of the use of coffee and its subsequent spread through the Middle East. The author tells how the Mufti of Aden, while travelling through Persia in the mid-15th century, came upon some of his compatriots enjoying coffee. Returning to Aden in poor health, he remembered this liquor and thought it might help him recover. He sent for some, and found that it not only prevented sleep without any ill effects, but also "dissipated all manner of Heaviness and Drowsiness, and made him more bright and gay than he was wont to be".

Above: A Bedouin preparing coffee according to traditional Arabic methods.

Wishing to share the benefits with his dervishes, the Mufti gave them coffee before they embarked on their night-long prayers. He found that they, too, were able to perform "all their Exercises of religion with great Alacrity and Freedom of Mind".

Whatever the route taken and the circumstances, there is firm evidence that the first cultivated coffee trees grew in monastery gardens in the Yemen, and most Arab authorities agree that the Sufi community was probably in one way or another responsible.

From Food to Beverage

As with the discovery of the plant and its journey to Arabia, the process of development from food to hot beverage is also a matter of historical speculation.

The comments of the early European explorers and botanists indicate that the Ethiopians chewed raw coffee beans – obviously being appreciative of their stimulating effect. They also pounded ripe coffee cherries, mixed them with animal fat and moulded the resulting paste into pellets. This powerful cocktail of fat, caffeine and meat protein was a

vital source of concentrated energy, particularly valuable in times of tribal conflict when warriors were required to give their all. The cherries were probably eaten as a ripe fruit, too, since the pulp is sweet and contains caffeine.

Early records also show that a wine was made from the fermented juice of the ripe cherries. The wine was called *qahwah*, meaning "that which excites and causes the spirits to rise", a term that was eventually used for both wine and coffee. Since wine was prohibited by Mohammed, coffee was nicknamed "the wine of Araby".

It seems possible that coffee was treated as a food in Arabia, too, and only later mixed with water to make a drink. The earliest version of the beverage was probably a liquid produced by steeping a few whole hulls in cold water. Later, the hulls were roasted over an open fire, and then boiled in water for about thirty minutes until a pale yellow liquid was produced.

By about AD 1000, the drink was still a relatively crude decoction made with green coffee beans and their hulls. It was probably not until around the

Right: Illustration showing the early Arabic method of brewing coffee over an open fire.

13th century that the beans were dried before use. They were laid out in the sun, and once dry, could be stored for longer periods. After that, it was a small step to roast them over a charcoal fire.

Early Uses

Initially, coffee was consumed only as part of a religious ceremony or on the advice of a physician. Once the medical men had observed coffee's beneficial effects, more and more of them started to prescribe it. Coffee was used to treat an astounding variety of ailments, including kidney stones, gout, smallpox, measles and coughs. A late 17th-century treatise on coffee and its uses quotes the work of Prosper Alpinus, a botanist. In his book on the medicines and plants of Egypt, Alpinus writes: "It is an excellent Remedy against the stoppage of Women's Courses, and they make often use thereof, when they don't flow so fast as they desire...it is a quick and certain remedy for those Women, who not having their courses are troubled with violent pains."

He goes on to describe how coffee was made: "This Decoction they make two ways: the one with the skin or the outside of the aforesaid Grain, and the other with the very substance of the Bean. That which is made with the skin is of more force then the other...

The Grain...is put into an Iron Instrument firmly shut together with the coverlid, through this Instrument they thrust a Spit, by the means thereof they turn it before the Fire, till it shall be well roasted; after which having beaten it into a very fine Powder, you may make use thereof, in an equal proportion according to the number of people that will drink it: Viz the third part of a spoonful for each person, and put it into a glass of boyling Water, putting a little Sugar thereto: And after having let it boyl a small time, you must pour it into little dishes of porcelain or any other sort, and so let it be drunk by little and little, as hot as it can be possibly indur'd."

Bun and bunchum

The African word for the coffee plant was *bun*, which then became the Arabic *bunn*, meaning both the plant and the berry. Rhazes (AD 850–922), a doctor who lived in Persian Iraq, and a follower of Galen and Hippocrates, compiled a medical encyclopedia in which he refers to the bean as *bunchum*. His discussion of its healing properties no doubt led to the belief that coffee was known as a medicine over a thousand years ago. Similar references appear in the writings of Avicenna (AD 980–1037), another distinguished Muslim physician and philosopher.

The word "coffee", meaning the drink, is a modified form of the Turkish word *kahveh* which, in turn, is derived from the Arabic *kahwa* (or *qahwah*).

Above: Portrait of Avicenna, Muslim physician, painting c. 17th century.

THE WINE OF ARABY

Above: On the steps of a Turkish coffee house, illustration, early 19th century.

Following the example of the Mufti of Aden and his monks, religious communities throughout Arabia took up the practice of drinking coffee. Little by little, however, its use spread beyond religious confines. Aden's citizens were among the first to take up the habit. Since the Mufti was a respected authority on Muslim law and presumably would not knowingly consume an illegal substance himself, they were keen to follow his example and try this new drink themselves.

Coffee-drinking took place in the mosque where, after the monks had had their fill, the Imam offered it to others who happened to be present. Served in this ceremonious manner against a background of devout chanting, coffee-drinking was seen as a wholesome and pious activity. However, everyone who tasted coffee liked it and wanted more, and it was not long before word spread of the rewards to be reaped from visiting the mosque.

Anxious to quell the trend, religious authorities tried in vain to restrict coffee consumption. Imams and monks were allowed to imbibe, but only in conjunction with their nightly prayers; physicians were also allowed to prescribe small quantities. However, as the less spiritually inclined continued to make late-night appearances at the mosque, and doctors increasingly began to prescribe coffee for all manner of ills, it was hard to curtail its use.

Recipients in the mosque found coffee a pleasant stimulant and conducive to sociability. Before long, the beverage was sold openly in the area, attracting a motley crowd of law students, night workers and travellers. Eventually, the whole city took up the practice, not just at night but round-the-clock and in the home, too. Not surprisingly, the hot, strong coffee was particularly popular during Ramadan, when fasting is obligatory from sunrise to sunset.

Coffee Takes a Hold

The new drink quickly spread from Aden to neighbouring towns, and by about the end of the 15th century had reached the holy city of Mecca. Here, as in Aden, coffee-drinking at first centred around the dervish community at the mosque.

Before long, the citizens were also regularly drinking coffee at home and in public areas set apart for the purpose. They did so with obvious enjoyment as an Arab historian reports: "Thither Crowds of People resorted at all Hours of the Day, to enjoy the pleasure of Conversation, play at Chess and other games, dance, sing, and divert themselves all manner of ways, under the pretence of drinking Coffee."

As the centre of the Muslim world, Mecca's social and cultural practices were inevitably copied by Muslims in other major cities. Within a relatively short time, therefore, coffee-drinking took hold throughout much of Arabia, spreading west to Egypt, and north through Syria. The coffee habit was also established further by the Muslim armies who, at that time, were advancing through southern Europe, Spain and North Africa, and east to India. Wherever they went, they took coffee with them.

Coffee thus became an integral part of Middle Eastern life. So crucial was the drink to the smooth-running of society that, in many areas, marriage contracts stipulated that a husband should allow his wife as much coffee as she wanted. Failure to do so was grounds for a woman to sue for divorce.

Coffee in Persia

The coffee habit perhaps took root in Persia even before it came to Arabia. Persian warriors were said to have driven back the Ethiopians when they tried to settle in the Yemen. The Persians would have undoubtedly found to their liking the coffee cherries growing on the trees planted by the Ethiopians, and taken them back to their own country. The story of the Mufti of Aden also refers to coffee-drinking in Persia in the mid-15th century.

Coffee and religious devotion

The Muslims were convinced that the drink was a gift from Allah and were almost fanatical in their enthusiasm, as the following eulogy – or tirade – shows. Translated from the Arabic and printed, curiously, in the Transylvanian *Journal of Medicine* in the early part of the 19th century, the original is said to be the work of Sheik Abdal-Kader Anasari Djezeri Haubuli, son of Mohammed:

"O COFFEE! thou dispellest the cares of the great: thou bringest back those who wander from the paths of knowledge. Coffee is the beverage of the people of God, and the cordial of his servants who thirst for wisdom...
...Every care vanishes when the cup bearer present thee the delicious chalice. It will circulate fleetly through thy veins, and will not rankle there: if thou doubtest this, contemplate the youth and beauty of those who drink it...
...Coffee is the drink of God's people; in it is health...Whoever has seen the blissful chalice, will scorn the wine cup. Glorious drink! Thy colour is the seal of purity, and reason proclaims it genuine. Drink with confidence, and regard not the prattle of fools, who condemn without foundation..."

From very early on, most major Persian cities boasted stylish and spacious coffee houses situated in the best parts of town. These establishments had a reputation for serving coffee quickly, efficiently, and "with abundance of Respect". As a rule, the political discussions and resulting disturbances usually associated with the coffee house scene were kept low-key; it seems the clientele were more interested in hedonistic pursuits. Persian coffee houses developed a reputation for talking, music, dancing and "other things of that kind", and there are even several reports of how the government was obliged to put a stop to "the infamous practices committed there".

An English traveller tells the tale of how the wife of the Shah tactfully appointed a mullah – an expert in legal and ecclesiastical matters – to make a daily visit to a particularly crowded and popular coffee house. His job was to sit there and entertain the patrons with civilized discussion of poetry, history and law. A man of discretion, he avoided controversial political issues, and disturbances were therefore rare. The mullah became a welcome visitor.

Having seen that the scheme was a success, other coffee houses soon followed suit and employed their own mullahs and story-tellers. These newfound entertainers sat in a centrally placed high chair "from whence they make speeches and tell satirical stories, playing in the meantime with a little stick and using the same gestures as our jugglers...do in England".

Coffee in Turkey

Despite having reached neighbouring Syria, coffee-drinking was relatively slow to spread to Turkey. However, following the expansion of the Ottoman Empire and the subsequent conquest of Arab Muslims, the Turks finally took to coffee drinking with a vengeance, as an English doctor writing from Constantinople confirms: "When a Turk is sick he fasts and takes Coffa, and if that will not do, he makes his will, and thinks of no other Phisick."

New watering holes According to a 16th-century Arab writer, the first two coffee houses in Constantinople were set up in 1554 by a couple of Syrian entrepreneurs quick to spot a trend. Their premises were impressively furnished with "very neat couches and carpets, on which they received their company, which first consisted mostly of studious persons, lovers of chess,

Right: A Turkish domestic servant preparing coffee in the home.

trictrac, and other sedentary Diversions". Other equally opulent coffee shops quickly opened, sometimes to the dismay of the more pious Muslims. They were richly decorated and the clientele reclined on luxurious cushions while they were entertained with stories and poetry as well as singing and dancing by professional performers.

Despite the ever-increasing number of new establishments, the coffee houses were always crowded with people. Historians disagree as to the social standing of the clientele, some saying the coffee houses were frequented almost exclusively by "the lower orders", others claiming that they

appealed to all levels of society. As Hattox states in *The Social Life of the Coffeehouse*: "From the assumption that all classes went to coffee houses it does not of necessity follow that all classes went to the same coffee house."

The legal profession obviously found the coffee houses a useful place for networking, since the patrons of one establishment were said to consist mainly of travelling *cadhis* (judges) who were in Constantinople looking for work;

the professors of law or other sciences; as well as students coming up for graduation and eager to secure a prestigious job. Even the chief officer of the Sultan's palace and other high-ranking members were seen to drop by.

The travelling English – writers, botanists, doctors – had never seen anything like the coffee houses and wrote extensively about them. Henry Blunt in his *Voyage to the Levant* recounted with amazement: "For there upon Scaffolds half a yard high and covered with Mats, they sit crosse-legg'd after the Turkish manner, many times two or three hundred together, talking, and likely with some poor Musick passing up and down."

Sir George Sandys wrote somewhat disapprovingly: "There sit they chatting most of the day, and sip of a Drink called Coffa...in little China Dishes, as hot as they can suffer it, black it is as soot, tasting not much unlike it...which helpeth, as they say, Digestion, and procureth Alacrity. Many of the Coffa-men keeping beautiful Boys, who serve...to procure them Customers."

Coffee at home The Turks drank as much coffee at home as they consumed at the coffee house. A French traveller observed: "As much money must be spent in the private families of Constantinople for coffee as for wine at Paris". Sir Henry Blunt wrote in a letter to a friend: "For besides the innumerable store of Coffa-houses, there is not a private fire without it all day long."

Blunt went further, extolling the many therapeutic benefits of drinking coffee: "They [the Turks] all acknowledge how it freeth them from Crudities caused by ill Diet, or moist Lodging, insomuch as they using Coffa Morning and Evening, have no Consumptions which ever come of Moisture; no Lethargies in aged People; or Rickets in Children, and but few Qualms in Women with Child: But especially they hold it of singular prevention against the Stone and Gout."

Left: Large numbers gathered in the coffee houses to gossip and sip coffee.

CUSTOM AND RITUAL

Once coffee had started to lose its religious associations, coffee houses, or *qahveh khaneh*, sprang up all over the Middle East. There were also hole-in-the-wall coffee shops, and strolling vendors who heated coffee over small spirit lamps and filled the dishes of passers-by.

At the same time, coffee-drinking had become equally well established in the home. No social interaction was complete without it. Coffee was served by barbers before haircuts, by merchants before and after bargaining, at chance meetings between friends and at the most formal of banquets. European travel writers were astounded by the level of consumption. One wrote: "They drink coffee not only in their houses, but even in the publick streets as they go about their business, and sometimes three or four people, by turns, out of the same cup."

A Better Brew

By the early 16th century, whole coffee beans were roasted on special stone trays, and later on metal plates. Once roasted, the beans were boiled for thirty minutes or more, producing a strong dark liquor that was stored in vats until needed. As demand increased, however, preparation and brewing techniques improved. Coffee was freshly made with pulverized beans and boiling water. Sugar and delicious spices, such as cardamom, cinnamon and cloves, were added to improve the flavour. Although the use of roasted beans had become common practice, coffee made with the lightly roasted cherries (with the bean removed) was still highly prized in the Yemen where the coffee trees grew. Known as "Sultan's coffee", it was drunk mainly by those of the highest rank, or by visitors to whom it was served as a testimony of respect and honour.

> ### Café à la Sultane
> "*The manner of making the* Café à la Sultane *is this. They take the husks of perfectly ripe fruit, beat them, and put them in an earthen Pan over a Charcoal-Fire, keeping them constantly in motion, and only toast them until they change Colour a little. At the same time Water is set to boil in a Coffee-Pot, and when the Husks are ready, they throw in both the outer and inner Shells separately, about three times as many of the first as of the last; then boil them up in the same manner as common Coffee. The Colour of the Liquor is pretty much like that of best English Beer. The Husks must be kept in dry Places till they are used; for the least Moisture spoils the Taste of them.*"
> Dr James Douglas, 1727.

Above: A strolling street vendor of coffee, Istanbul, early 18th century.

Life in the Coffee House

As the coffee houses proliferated, so did competition for customers. The coffee house masters tried to attract clientele "not only by the goodness of their Liquor, neatness and dexterity of their Servants" but also by sumptuous surroundings and entertainment. Musicians, jugglers and dancers were employed, and puppet shows were provided as well.

When customers grew bored with what the house had to offer, and conversation began to flag, they would make their own entertainment. Poets would be asked to recite, or, if a dervish was present, he would be invited to deliver a light-hearted sermon.

Backgammon, chess and various card games were also popular. Gambling almost certainly took place, as did drug use. Coffee had become popular with opium users, and there were always two or three *narghiles* (water pipes) available for the leisurely smoking of hashish or tobacco while customers waited to be served.

The British ritual of buying rounds of drinks in pubs undoubtedly has its roots in the Turkish coffee house. If a customer saw someone he knew about to order a coffee, he would shout a single word *caba*, meaning "gratis", which indicated to the proprietor that he was not to take the man's money. The newcomer, in turn, would individually greet all those already present before taking his seat. If an older man arrived, everyone would rise in respect and the best seat would be vacated for him.

It was customary to drink coffee as hot as the mouth could bear, so it was sipped, or more probably slurped, from a small china dish – handles were to come later. Early English travellers were probably amused, or even repelled, by this strange, rather exotic habit. One wrote: "They are sometimes near an hour on one dish...and it is none of the least diversions which strangers find among them, to hear this Sipping-Musick in a publick Coffee House, where perhaps some hundreds are drinking at a time."

Above: Turkish coffee house, lithograph, 1855.

Coffee Drinking in the Home

In 16th-century Constantinople, there was no house, rich or poor, Turkish or Jewish, Greek or Armenian, where coffee was not drunk at least twice a day, and usually more often – twenty dishes a day was not uncommon. It became a custom in every home, no matter how humble, to offer coffee to visitors and it was considered unspeakably ill-mannered to refuse it. At formal banquets, guests were offered coffee immediately upon arrival, and they were plied with it continually for the duration of the feast, which could have lasted as long as eight hours.

Though coffee-drinking had become an accepted part of everyday life, it nevertheless continued to maintain its magic. The way in which coffee was served in the home was always ceremonious. There was a requisite exchange of courteous greetings, enquiries after health and family, the praising of God, and elaborate rituals, similar in complexity to those of the Japanese tea ceremony. Melon seeds and dates might be served alongside the coffee to add to the enjoyment.

Most well-to-do households kept coffee stewards, whose sole responsibility was to attend to the preparation and serving of coffee. The chief steward, known as the *Kahveghi*, had the privilege of an "apartment" – probably little more than a cupboard – situated next to the coffee hall where visitors were received. The hall was decorated with richly coloured rugs and cushions, and gleaming ornamental coffee pots. Coffee was served with great decorum on silver or painted wooden trays large enough to hold up to twenty porcelain coffee dishes. These were always half-filled, not only to prevent spillage, but so that the dish could be held with the thumb below and two fingers on the upper edge.

Very grand households also kept pages, or *Itchoglans*, who, at a nod from the head of the household, took the coffee from the stewards and, with impressive dexterity, handed it to visitors without either touching the rim, burning themselves or spilling a drop.

Above: Wealthy households had servants whose sole duty was to prepare the coffee.

Lord Byron on coffee

The Victorian poet's view of Turkish coffee comes across in this poem:
And Mocha's berry, from Arabia pure,
In small fine china cups, came in at last;
Gold cups of filigree, made to secure
the hand from burning, underneath them placed.
Cloves, cinnamon, and saffron, too, were boiled
up with the Coffee, which, I think, they spoiled.

COFFEE AND CONFLICT

When a seemingly exclusive group of people are seen to be enjoying themselves and getting a little lively, especially at night, other groups tend to feel threatened. So it was in 16th-century Arabia when the political and religious leaders could not fail to ignore the good times being had in the coffee house. As Hattox states in *The Social Life of the Coffeehouse*, the relaxed clubby atmosphere inevitably led to caffeine-induced airing of news, views and grievances concerning the state. Even worse, attendance at the mosque was in decline now that coffee could be obtained elsewhere.

The first place to experience the crackdown was the holy city of Mecca, where an assembly of muftis, lawyers and physicians declared that coffee-drinking was not only contrary to religious law but caused physical harm. The level of argument that went on demonstrates the passion that coffee aroused and the conflict it provoked amongst those anxious to be seen to be taking the politically correct line.

The Suppression of Coffee Drinking

The story goes that the Governor of Mecca was scandalized by the behaviour of a group of coffee-drinkers in the mosque who were legitimately preparing themselves for a long night of prayer. At first the Governor thought they were drinking wine, which was of course forbidden by Muslim law. Even when assured otherwise, the Governor concluded that coffee made people drunk or at least prone to acts of civil disorder, and he decided to prohibit its use. However, he first summoned a group of experts and asked for their considered opinion.

The legal experts stated that coffee houses were indeed in need of some reform, but that there was a fine line as to whether coffee beverages themselves were genuinely physically harmful, or whether they were simply a catalyst that adversely affected people's behaviour. Not wishing to take final responsibility for such a serious and delicate issue, they declared that the decision should rest with the physicians.

Two Persian brothers – practising physicians in Mecca – were summoned; it was no accident that one of them had written a book discouraging the use of coffee. Medical practice in those days was based on the concept of bodily humours, and the brothers accordingly declared that *bunn*, from which coffee was usually made, was "cold and dry" and therefore harmful to health. Another doctor present argued that *bunn* "scorched and consum'd the Phlegm", and could not possibly have the qualities attributed to it by the Persian brothers.

After protracted debate, everyone decided to play safe, and agreed that it would be prudent to declare coffee an illegal substance – as the Governor had intended all along. As a result, many of the assembled company eagerly confirmed that coffee had indeed "disordered their senses". One man inadvertently declared that when he drank coffee he experienced the same effects as wine produced – a laughter-provoking comment, as he would have had to break Muslim law in order to know. When questioned, he imprudently acknowledged he had drunk wine and was duly punished.

Right: As coffee houses grew in popularity, it was not long before the relaxed behaviour of the coffee drinkers attracted the notice of religious and political leaders.

The Mufti of Mecca, a holy man and a lawyer by profession, heatedly opposed the decision but was alone in defending the drink. Ignoring the Mufti, the Governor signed a declaration outlawing the selling or drinking of coffee both in public and in private. All stores of the seditious berry were burnt; the coffee houses were shut down and their owners pelted with the fragments of broken pots and cups.

The declaration was sent to the Sultan of Egypt, who, much to the Governor's embarrassment, was astonished to hear of the condemnation of a beverage that the whole of Cairo found wholesome and beneficial. Moreover, Cairo's doctors of law, who had much greater status than those at Mecca, found nothing illegal in the use of it. The Governor was duly reprimanded and told he could use his authority only to prevent disorders that might take place in the coffee house. Coffee-drinking, which in any case had been going on behind closed doors, was restored. A year later, the Sultan condemned the Governor to death for his crime against coffee; the two Persian physicians subsequently met the same fate.

Arguing the finer points of Islamic law in relation to coffee became increasingly bizarre and esoteric. In Constantinople, for example, religious zealots claimed vehemently that the process of roasting reduced coffee to charcoal, and to use such a base article at the table was grossly impious. The Mufti agreed and declared that coffee was illegal.

As usual, the ban was never entirely followed. People gradually reinstated coffee-drinking at home, and, having given up hope of enforcement, the officers of the law started to grant permission for coffee to be sold in private. Eventually, a less scrupulous Mufti was appointed and the coffee houses were opened again.

Next, a tax was introduced forcing Constantinople's coffee-house owners to pay an amount proportionate to business done. Despite this hefty contribution to government coffers, the

Above: The ritual of coffee drinking encompassed grinding, brewing and serving.

price of a cup of coffee remained as low as ever – a sure indication of the vast amount served.

In the years to follow, repeated attempts at suppression were made throughout the Middle East by political and religious leaders. Each time the usual string of complaints met with the usual anarchistic resistance. Lacking popular support and faced with divided opinion among the lawyers, physicians and religious experts, the attempts consistently failed. By the end of the century, coffee-drinking was a deeply rooted habit throughout the Middle East that no level of prohibition could budge.

MIGRATION OF THE TREE

Towards the end of the 16th century, reports from travellers and botanists of a strange new plant and drink began to reach Europe from the Middle East. As the reports grew in number and frequency, European merchants started to realize the potential of the new commodity. Already involved with Middle Eastern trade, the Venetians were quick to exploit this opportunity, and the first bags of coffee beans arrived in Venice from Mecca in the early 1600s.

The Arab Monopoly

Supplying coffee to the Venetians was the start of a lucrative export business for the Arabs, and one that they guarded jealously for almost a century. They went to great lengths to ensure that no bean capable of germination left the country; beans were either boiled or parched, and visitors were kept well away from the coffee plantations. Until about the end of the 17th century, the Yemen was the only centre of supply for the European coffee trade.

Dutch Enterprise

Around the time that the Venetians took delivery of their first consignment of beans, Dutch merchants began to examine the possibility of coffee cultivation and trading. They already had a considerable amount of information from the botanists, and the merchants saw no reason why the Arabs should maintain their monopoly. At the time, the Dutch were probably Europe's most proactive traders and in possession of the best merchant ships. It comes as no surprise, therefore, to learn that a Dutch merchant managed to steal a coffee plant from Mocha and bring it unharmed back to Europe.

By the middle of the century, cultivation trials had been set up in the East Indian Dutch colony of Java – hence the well-known Mocha-Java blend of bean – and by the 1690s plantations had been established in rapid succession in the neighbouring island colonies of Sumatra, Timor, Bali and Celebes. The enterprising Dutch East India Company had also begun

large-scale cultivation in Ceylon, where the plant had already been introduced by the Arabs.

The Universal Coffee Nursery

In 1706, Dutch growers in Java sent home the first crop of beans and a coffee plant, which was carefully transplanted in the Amsterdam Botanical Garden. This consignment, though small, was to play a key role in the annals of the coffee trade. Amsterdam became the trading centre for coffee grown in the Dutch colonies, and the plant produced berries from which seedlings were later taken to the New World. Dr James Douglas, an 18th-century scientist, regarded these plants as the ancestors of coffee plantations in the West, and named the Amsterdam Botanical Garden "the universal coffee nursery".

The Tree for the King

In 1714, the burgomaster of Amsterdam presented the King of France, Louis XIV, with a healthy 1.5m/5ft coffee tree

COFFEE MERCHANTS.

STEPHENS & HOPKINS BRISTOL

Above: Arab merchants strictly controlled the trade of Mocha coffee produced in the Yemen.

Above: Once Dutch traders broke the Arabian monopoly, coffee soon spread to all parts of the world. Painting by H. Vroom, 1640.

grown in the Botanical Garden. The French had not been blind to the commercial success of the Dutch, and had in fact smuggled seed from Mocha to Réunion Island off Madagascar. They had been less successful with propagation at home, however, so "The Tree", as this specimen from Amsterdam became known, was received with the utmost gratitude and respect. It was planted in the Jardin des Plantes, where a greenhouse had been especially built, and entrusted to the care of the Royal Botanist.

It was Louis XIV's secret ambition that the seeds from The Tree would be the progenitors of future coffee plantations throughout the French colonies. His wish came true, for The Tree flowered, bore fruit, and became the ancestor of most of the coffee trees presently growing in Central and South America.

Cultivation in the New World

The question as to whether it was the Dutch or the French who first introduced coffee cultivation to the New World has long been a matter of dispute. In the year following delivery of The Tree to the French, the Dutch sent coffee plants from the Amsterdam Botanical Garden to their territories in Guiana in northern South America. A short time later – the date is not certain – a French naval officer, Gabriel Mathieu de Clieu, determined to bring coffee cultivation to the New World, procured with great difficulty one or more coffee seedlings from the Jardin des Plantes. Historians disagree as to whether it was a single plant or several.

De Clieu set sail with his precious cargo to the island of Martinique, north of Guiana. The journey was long and arduous. Not only did a fellow passenger repeatedly try to destroy the

seedlings, even managing to rip off some of the leaves, but the voyage itself was fraught with danger and difficulty. There were terrifying storms, attacks by pirates, and finally the ship was becalmed for days on end. Though the water supply had almost run out, de Clieu shared his scanty ration with his precious plant. Miraculously, both survived, and the seedling was transplanted in the officer's garden. Kept under armed guard, the tree flourished and grew to maturity, and de Clieu was rewarded with his first harvest in 1726.

Fifty years later, there were nearly nineteen million coffee trees in Martinique and de Clieu's dream was well on the way to fulfilment. From the two coffee-growing centres of Martinique and Dutch Guiana, cultivation radiated throughout the West Indies and Central and South America.

ESTABLISHING PLANTATIONS

Wherever the European colonists went, they took coffee with them, though the Catholic missionaries and religious communities undoubtedly played a key role in its migration, too. With their natural interest in botany, monks were curious about the plant, and, as in the early days in the Yemen, coffee trees were often nurtured and studied in monastery gardens.

Initially, France was Europe's major supplier of coffee. The French took the plant from Martinique to the islands of Guadeloupe and Saint Domingue (now Haiti), and from 1730 onwards, cultivation spread rapidly throughout the French Antilles.

Meanwhile, coffee production had advanced into a large number of other countries. The Spanish took it to Puerto Rico and Cuba, and later to Colombia, Venezuela and westwards to the Philippines. From Dutch Guiana (now Surinam), cultivation spread to French Guiana, and from there in 1727 the Portuguese introduced it to Brazil, destined later to become the world's largest producer. In 1730, the British introduced coffee to Jamaica, where the highly prized Blue Mountain beans are still produced.

By around 1830, the Dutch colonies of Java and Sumatra were the chief suppliers of coffee to Europe. Financed by the British, India and Ceylon tried to compete, but could not budge the Dutch. In the mid-1800s, a coffee blight called *Hemileia vastatrix* swept through the whole of Asia and wiped out the supply, giving Brazil a long-awaited opportunity. Within a few years Brazil had become the world's leading coffee supplier, a position it still holds today.

The Final Stage of the Journey

By the end of the 19th century, coffee had spread both east and west in a belt lying roughly equidistant between the Tropics of Cancer and Capricorn. The Dutch, French, English, Spanish and Portuguese had between them managed to establish thriving coffee plantations in all their territories which lay within the zone.

The final stage in coffee's journey took place in the early 1900s in German East Africa (now Kenya and Tanzania). German settlers planted coffee on the slopes of Mount Kenya and Kilimanjaro – ironically only a few hundred miles from coffee's original home in Ethiopia. Coffee had completed its nine-century circumnavigation of the world.

The effect of the slave trade
The Portuguese and Dutch imported massive numbers of African slaves to Brazil and Java. Coffee production more than doubled, while it fell in other areas.

	in £m 1832	1849
Brazil	80.6	180.0
Java	40.3	100.0
French and Dutch West Indies	17.9	6.0
Venezuela	13.4	20.0

From Coffee As It Is, and As It Ought To Be. P. L. Simmonds, 1850

Above: Workers on a South American coffee plantation. Nineteenth-century engraving by F. M. Reynolds.

PLANTATIONS IN BRAZIL

In the early 1700s, Brazil had yet to start growing coffee. In 1727, when invited to help settle a boundary dispute between Dutch and French Guiana, the Brazilians were glad to mediate as it gave them a potential opportunity to procure some of Guiana's closely guarded coffee seedlings.

The story goes – and there are several versions – that Francisco de Mallo Palheta, a dashing army captain and well-known womanizer, was despatched to Guiana to arbitrate. Once there, he proceeded to ingratiate himself both with the Governor and his wife, with whom he had a brief affair. The boundary dispute resolved, the time came for Palheta to leave. The Governor's wife presented him with a bouquet as a token of thanks for his services, both political and amorous. Hidden among the flowers were cuttings of a coffee plant. Here the versions vary; some say he was openly presented with a thousand seeds and five living plants. Whatever the truth, Palheta returned to Brazil with the cuttings, seeds or plants.

Cultivation started on a small scale, mainly for local consumption. However, the plant adapted itself so well to the local topography, soil and climate that cultivation grew to an intensive scale. By 1765 the first shipments of beans had been exported to Lisbon.

Pioneer Planters

The first planters had to hack away areas of mosquito-infested jungle in sweltering heat. They not only had to plant the coffee seedlings, but, more importantly, food for themselves. Next, they had to get a roof over the heads of their family, slaves, machinery and harvests. Since the forest encroached on all sides, they were completely isolated, so the early *fazendas*, or estates, were the nuclei of human life in the rainforest.

As the taste for coffee spread among Europe's and America's expanding urban populations, the planters grew more wealthy, the *fazendas* larger and life became more comfortable. It was a time of unprecedented prosperity.

As Stanley Stein points out in *Vassouras, a Brazilian Coffee County, 1850–1900*, coffee cultivation in Brazil had a colossal impact on economic and social life. From an economic view, coffee cultivation created an unhealthy dependence on a staple crop subject to the fluctuations of a world market. The crop was also subject to the vagaries of the weather. Cold winds blowing in from the Andes brought severe frosts, and on several occasions the plantations were nearly destroyed.

Socially, coffee cultivation sired a new aristocracy – the coffee barons with their massive *fazendas* and autocratic lifestyle. It also resulted in an unprecedented influx of African slaves, which not only stratified society but also changed forever the ethnic makeup of central Brazil. However, it can be argued that the ultimate cause of these devastating changes was not the cultivation of the plant itself but the insatiable demand from Europe for the drink.

Coffee and slavery

The *haciendas* and *fazendas* – the massive estates of the Spanish and Portuguese colonies – grew on the back of slave labour. Between 1840 and 1850, more than 370,000 African slaves were openly smuggled into Brazil. Slavery was abolished in Spanish-speaking colonies by the 1850s, though it continued through to 1888 in Brazil.

Above: Coffee bean collection, painted by Francisco Miranda, 1750–1816.

THE COFFEE TRADE

Despite the Arab monopoly, coffee beans began to infiltrate Britain and mainland Europe from very early on via the botanists' pockets. By the early 17th century, coffee beans could be found in the cabinets of interested botanists throughout the continent. Small sacks of beans were also brought in by private individuals already familiar with the drink – merchants, diplomats, business people and travel writers, for example – but it was not long before coffee attracted the attention of merchants.

The First Shipments

Since Venetian merchants had long sailed the waters of the East, and were doing much business in Constantinople, it is widely accepted that they were the first to import coffee to Europe. The precise date is not known, but the first shipment of beans must have arrived in Venice around the early 1600s.

Hot on the heels of the Venetians, the Dutch started shipping coffee; trade records mention coffee beans from Mocha as early as 1616, though it seems they confined shipments to their colonies in Asia and the New World, as it was not until 1661 that The Netherlands received its first substantial consignment of beans. Coffee was also introduced very early on into Austria and Hungary, making an overland entrance via the northern extremities of the Turkish Ottoman Empire.

Following the shipping routes, coffee reached all the major European ports – Marseilles, Hamburg, Amsterdam and London – by around the middle of the 17th century, though it was some time before regular lines of supply were firmly established. It arrived in the 1660s in North America, probably via Dutch colonists in New Amsterdam (renamed New York after the British took control in 1664). A century later, coffee made the reverse journey across the Atlantic when Brazil started shipping it to Lisbon.

The Coffee Trade Evolves

In its journey from plantation to cup, coffee inevitably passed through the hands of the brokers and merchants. Coffee-trading attracted speculators and entrepreneurs right from the start, though it was a precarious business subject to cycles of boom and bust.

In the early days, supplies often erratic due to adverse weather conditions, which affected both the crop itself and the means of transport. The arrival of the next shipment was always uncertain, and when it did arrive, the merchants were forced to pay whatever the ship masters demanded. The artificial price manipulation, combined with erratic supply, forced coffee into the status of a luxury.

By post-Industrial Revolution days, shipping and the machinery associated with coffee grew more sophisticated.

Above: In some cases, merchants instructed workers to throw the coffee beans into the sea to avoid the lowering of coffee prices. Illustration, Brazil, 1932.

Telecommunications came into being, enabling crop forecasts to be sent by cable. As supply and distribution systems developed, more and more traders entered the market. Many of them formed syndicates that attempted to corner sections of the market and force prices up, and from the 1860s onwards, organized Coffee Exchanges were set up in major coffee-trading centres such as New York and Le Havre.

Coffee Auctions

Shapiro tells us in *The Story of Coffee*, that bags of coffee were sold in London at what were known as candle auctions. Bids were accepted for lots as long as a lighted candle set up in front of the auctioneer continued to flicker. Once the candle went out, the lot went to the last bidder. In the United States, before the New York Coffee and Sugar Exchange was set up, coffee merchants would roam the streets in particular

areas, taking bids and then selling the bags to the highest bidder at the end of the day.

Coffee merchants could be formidable figures. A young American, entering the trade, described them thus: "I ask you to picture those silk-hatted, frock-coated, bewhiskered and highly dignified gentlemen, whom one approached with awe and trembling knees, [they] were the importers and jobbers of coffee who carried large and assorted stocks of East Indian, Central and South American growths for sale to the wholesale grocers, and to the large traders."

Processing the Product

In 17th-century Europe and North America, coffee beans were at first sold unroasted and unground. American consumers bought green coffee by the bag or half bag, and roasted it on a pie plate in the oven, or in a frying pan over the fire. The British appeared to be

fussier; one former planter stated that "the care of roasting the beans and grinding is thought by many masters of families too delicate and important a task to be entrusted...to any servant".

The invention of the coffee mill in 1687 contributed to the beverage's widespread use, but brought with it the problem of adulteration. Because of the colour and powerful aroma of ground coffee, it was easy for unscrupulous vendors to "take it down". Among the substances used were roasted rye, grated burnt crusts, roasted acorns, sand, clay and sawdust. Even worse were the East London "liver-bakers". The same British planter complained: "They take the livers of oxen and horses, bake them and grind them into a powder, which they sell to the low-priced coffee-shopkeepers. Horse's liver coffee bears highest price." He pointed out that it could be identified by allowing coffee to cool. A thick skin then formed on the top.

Above: Roasting imported coffee beans in an English factory, black and white engraving, 1870.

COFFEE AS MEDICINE

Once in Europe, coffee beans moved first from individual botanists' cabinets to the apothecaries' shops, where they became a vital part of the pharmacopoeia used by 17th-century doctors, chemists, herbalists and even midwives.

Coffee was looked on as a medicine not only because of its high price, but perhaps because of its strong taste – a "black, nasty Hel-burnt Liquor" as one person wrote. Hahnemann, founder of homeopathy, stated firmly: "Coffee is strictly a medicinal substance...No one has failed to be disgusted for the first time he smoked tobacco. No healthy palate ever found strong coffee, without sugar, palatable on the first trial."

The doctrine of bodily humours taught by the herbalist Galen (AD 131– 200) continued to dominate European as much as Islamic medicine. The theory stated that the four humours – yellow bile, black bile, phlegm and blood – were reflected in a person's physical makeup. If the humours became too unbalanced, illness would result. In turn, each humour was linked to two physical qualities – heat, cold, moistness or dryness. Food, drink and medicines were thought to possess these qualities, and were administered to correct imbalances.

As is generally the case with coffee, there was disagreement. Some physicians claimed its qualities were cold and dry, others that they were hot and dry. Still others argued that the qualities of the coffee husks were different from those of the bean. This confusion is evident when we see the variety of ailments for which coffee was prescribed.

A somewhat tongue-in-cheek booklet, written in 1663, gives examples of "Persons, and Places of their Abode, who were cured [by coffee] when left off by the Physitians". These included "Benjamin Bad-cock [who] drank Coffee in Layden, and his Wife... remained barren four years, after which he left drinking Coffee, and in three quarters of a Year she had a goodly chopping Boy", and "Anne Marine of Rotterdam...troubled with a Corn on her upper Lip, the more it was cut, the bigger it grew, so that she at last drank Coffee, and the Corn dropt into the Dish as she held it to her Mouth".

On a more serious note, a French doctor, having collaborated with colleagues, asserted that among its many therapeutic effects coffee counteracted drunkenness and nausea, promoted the flow of urine and relieved dropsy, smallpox and gout. The French Larousse encyclopedia stated that coffee was particularly indicated for all men of letters, soldiers, sailors and workers who were staying in hot surroundings, and, strangely, for the inhabitants of those countries where cretinism was rife.

Coffee and creativity

Still more enthusiastically, Balzac in his *Treatise on Modern Stimulants* writes: "The coffee falls into your stomach, and straightaway there is a general commotion. Ideas begin to move like the battalions of the Grand Army on the battlefield when the battle takes place. Things remembered arrive at full gallop, ensign to the wind."

Above: Honoré de Balzac, French author. Painting by L. Boulanger, 1809–1867.

Coffee as a Stimulant

Certain after-effects of caffeine did not go unnoticed. One respected medical man wrote: "When I awake I have the intelligence and activity of an oyster. Immediately after our coffee, the stores of memory leap, so to speak, to our tongues; and talkativeness, haste, and the letting slip something we should not have mentioned, are often the consequence. Moderation and prudence are wholly wanting."

More positively, a Dr Thornton asserted: "A cup of Coffee strengthens and exhilarates our mental and bodily faculties; and nothing can be more refreshing either to the studious or the laborious."

Other eminent writers also wrote appreciatively of coffee's power to stimulate creativity. Balzac, Zola, Baudelaire, Victor Hugo, Molière and Voltaire were among its most ardent imbibers. Both Voltaire and Molière are quoted as replying to the remark that coffee was a slow poison: "I have drunk it upwards of fifty years, and unless it were very slow indeed, I would certainly have been dead long ago."

The effects of over-indulgence gave rise to considerable medical comment. Hahnemann refers to the "coffee disease" which results in "an unpleasant feeling of existence, a lower degree of vitality, a kind of paralysis". Other negative effects were reputedly melancholia, piles, headaches and a reduced libido.

There was concern, too, about the harmful effect coffee might have on children and nursing mothers. It was thought to be a major cause of tooth decay and rickets in children, and "a rattling of the breast" in nursing mothers.

Amongst coffee's opponents was Sinibaldi, an eminent Italian medical writer. He stated: "The commerce which we have opened with Asia and the new world, in addition to the smallpox and other diseases, has brought a new drink, which has contributed most shockingly to the destruction of our constitutions...it produces debility, alters gastric juice, disorders digestion, and often produces convulsions, palsy of the limbs and vertigo."

Above: The stimulating and invigorating properties of coffee are shown in a positive light in this advertisement from the Pan-American coffee bureau in the 1950s.

The medical debate was to continue for many years, as doctors, pursuing new avenues of insight, argued the pros and cons of coffee, claiming it to be alternatively therapeutic and detrimental to the body and mind. This debate still continues today.

Coffee and healthy skin

As a country where green tea has been the national beverage for nearly 1,000 years, Japan was understandably slow to take up coffee drinking. It was not introduced until the 19th century and even today is still a relatively undeveloped market.

As well as drinking coffee, the Japanese have adopted the slightly unusual practice of lying in the roasted coffee beans. It is thought that the coffee contains elements beneficial to healthy skin.

Right: Absorbing coffee's nutrients via the skin.

COFFEE CONSUMPTION DEVELOPS

Having escaped the confines of medicine and developed into a social activity, coffee-drinking spread through Europe during the first half of the 17th century. However, it was not until about 1650 onwards that we begin to hear more of when, how and by whom coffee was sold and drunk.

The people largely responsible for its growth were not necessarily the merchants, the aristocracy or well-healed professional travellers. As Shapiro states in *The Story of Coffee*, it was the "countless unnamed peddlers who spread through the streets of

Europe carrying on their backs the gleaming tools of their trade – coffeepots, trays, cups, spoons and sugar. These men bore the steaming, potent gospel of coffee beyond the boundaries of the East to the as yet uninitiated West".

At first, however, the new beverage fell under harsh criticism from the Catholic Church. Fanatical priests claimed – with somewhat hazy logic – that if Muslims were forbidden wine, which was sanctified by Christ, then coffee must be a substitute invented by the devil. Pope Clement VIII in the 16th

century eventually brought the dispute to an end by sampling coffee for himself and declaring it a truly Christian beverage. Once word of papal approval became known, coffee-drinking flourished freely throughout Europe.

Social Change and the Birth of the Coffee House

The reasons for coffee's swift and almost universal popularity were more complex than papal approval or mere availability. In *Drugs and Narcotics in History*, Porter and Teich suggest that the timing was also important. The period between the 17th and 19th centuries was one of profound social, cultural and intellectual change. Coffee was simply a timely adjunct; people took to it because they were ready for it.

First, there was an urge to establish some sort of private life outside the constraints of the family, and new gathering places were therefore needed. For the aristocracy the cultural life of the courts was gradually declining and this created another need for a new type of venue.

Second, the period was a time of progressive ideas – the age of Enlightenment in France, and later, the rise of the libertarian Risorgimento movement in Italy. (In hindsight, for such a time of enlightenment, the huge rise in slave labour needed to work on the coffee plantations in Brazil and the Dutch East Indies is an uncomfortable parallel development.) However, public meetings, harangues, resolutions and "the rest of the machinery of agitation" were not part of the culture. Coffee houses became the chief outlet through which public opinion could vent itself.

Third, developing alongside these changes was a growing criticism of the unwelcome effects of wine and beer. Coffee was obviously the perfect alternative as it provided a means of socializing without fear of intoxication.

In Europe, as in Turkey, the coffee house attracted clientele from all walks of life; professional and political mingled with commercial, creative and commoner. New forms of social interaction developed. Merchants

Above: Coffee vendor, Paris. Illustration by M. Engelbrecht, c. 1735.

Above: "Blowing a cloud at Offley's", interior of Offley's coffee house, c. 1820, scene of much animated discussion.

seeking an alternative to the ale-house needed a place where they could transact their business, as did the emerging financial and insurance communities. The coffee houses were also the type of place where artists and writers working in isolation could make contact with each other and the world.

When the coffee houses first opened, communication and information services – newspapers, telephones, directories and street maps, for example – were non-existent. The owner or head waiter of a coffee house therefore fulfilled yet another need by taking on the multifarious role of social arbiter, diplomat, matchmaker and message-taker. As George Mikes says in *Coffee Houses of Europe*: "[The head waiter] shared your secrets and knew them if you didn't want to share them, lent you money and lied for you when pursued by persistent creditor, kept letters for you especially those not meant for wife's eyes. Not everyone knew your private address but everyone knew which coffee house you went to."

Taxation and Duty

Aware of the potential income from mass consumption, revenue-hungry governments tried to stimulate demand by abandoning their former policy of prohibition and concentrating on taxation instead.

The English government in 1663 was quick to license coffee houses and levy an excise duty on coffee sold. Even so, compared to alcohol, coffee remained a bargain. The English coffee houses enticed huge numbers of working men from the ale-houses – a trend deemed beneficial by both wives, in the early days at least, and Government, though not by the breweries. Realizing that further taxation would reverse the trend, the Government progressively reduced the duty – each reduction marked by a huge increase in consumption.

In complete contrast, Frederick the Great of Prussia, in support of the barley growers and breweries, banned the working classes from drinking coffee and insisted they revert to drinking beer.

Coffee consumption

The figures demonstrate the rapid growth of coffee consumption in the 19th century, particularly in the United States where no import duty was charged.

	weight in millions of pounds 1832	1849
Holland and Netherlands	90.7	125.0
Germany and North of Europe	71.7	100.0
France and South of Europe	78.4	95.0
Great Britain	23.5	40.0
United States and British North American Provinces	45.9	120.0 (US) and 15.0 (BNAP)

THE COFFEE CONSUMERS

Coffee is universally popular, but there are some countries where it seems much more than just a drink. How coffee is drunk, and by whom, is part of its continuing appeal and mystique.

ITALY

Italy was the first country in Europe to import coffee commercially. The first shipments arrived in Venice in the 1600s just after citrus fruits had been introduced from the East. Vendors roamed the streets selling beverages such as lemonade, orangeade, chocolate and herbal infusions. Once coffee was available in reasonable quantities, the vendors added it to their wares, though they were still referred to as *limonáji* (lemonade sellers) rather than *caffetiéri* (coffee sellers). Coffee was immediately accepted by the Italians and became a familiar and widely used beverage.

As coffee flourished as a drink, so did the coffee houses. One of the earliest on record, situated in Leghorn (Livorno), dates back to 1651. It was mentioned by an English traveller who was intrigued by the roasting of coffee beans. He surmised "that roasting was by chance or perhaps from a debauch'd palate, as some with us love the burnt parts of broil'd meat", which also indicates that the barbecue may have had its devotees from very early on.

By the end of the century, Venice boasted several coffee houses situated around the Piazza di San Marco.

Florian's, said to be Europe's most celebrated coffee house, was opened in 1720. Venetians and the international elite flocked there to enjoy the gossip and the music from the orchestra playing on the terrace. It was patronized by famous artists and writers including Byron, Goethe and Rousseau. Perhaps because Florian's was the first coffee house to admit women, Casanova was a regular patron, too.

In Padua, a former lemonade seller opened Pedrocchi's – one of the most beautiful and flamboyantly kitsch coffee houses ever to be seen. Caffè Greco in Rome, named after its Greek owner, was patronized by the international music set – Mendelssohn, Rosetti, Liszt and Toscanini were regular visitors.

Above: "Cafe Greco in Rome", painting by Ludwig Passini, 1832–1903.

Above: Drinking coffee on the steps of the Cafe Florian, early 19th century drawing.

FRANCE

Coffee was reputedly brought to France in 1644, but it was almost fifteen years later before the beverage became popular. Consumption was at first centred around Marseilles, where it was introduced by traders who had grown used to drinking it in the Middle East.

Meanwhile, in Paris, in 1669, the Turkish ambassador Suleiman Aga brought coffee to the court of Louis XIV. The most extravagant coffee parties were held in opulent castles hired especially for the purpose. Isaac D'Israeli gives a graphic description: "On bended knee, the black slaves of the Ambassador, arrayed in the most gorgeous costumes, served the choicest Mocha coffee in tiny cups of eggshell porcelain, hot, strong and fragrant, poured out into saucers of gold and silver, placed on embroidered silk doylies, fringed with gold bullion, to the grand dames, who fluttered their fans with many grimaces, bending their piquant faces – berouged, bepowdered and bepatched – over the new and steaming beverage."

Though many of the aristocracy were quick to adopt coffee, there were some who found it distasteful. The German wife of Louis XIV's brother compared it to the Archbishop of Paris's breath; Madame de Sévigné, after an initial flirtation, rejected it as violently as she had chocolate; another nobleman would use it only as an enema, though he remarked that it did the job very well.

The Rise of the Café

The first coffee house opened in 1672 but it was little more than a bar in which sales of cognac exceeded those of coffee. Coffee houses really came into their own in 1686 when an Italian, Francisco Procopio dei Coltelli, an ambitious and astute waiter, opened Procope's. Wisely marketing itself as a lemonade shop, Procope's sumptuous decor and air of sophistication attracted a clientele keen to distance itself from the more loutish elements of the day. It was only when coffee began to outsell other beverages that the name *café* was given to the whole establishment.

Though not all the coffee houses were as elegant as Florian's – some were little more than dimly-lit back rooms – they were a melting pot of intellectual, creative and political ideas. Throughout the 18th and early 19th centuries, coffee houses opened one after the other in most major cities. By the end of the century the *bottega del caffè* had become an indispensable part of everyday life. They were the centre of information, conversation, entertainment, and even education, for all levels of society – professional, artisan, tradespeople, ladies and gentlemen of the leisured classes, intellectuals and political activists.

Coffee and the Spanish

The 17th-century Spaniards were committed chocolate drinkers, as it was their conquistadors who had "discovered" the cocoa bean in Central America. It was not until as late as the 19th century that coffee house culture began to take hold. By the early 20th century, artists and writers were frequenting coffee houses in Barcelona, Granada and Madrid. Even so, for many years chocolate still remained the drink of the traditionalists.

Procope's quickly became a literary salon frequented by eminent poets, playrights, actors and musicians. Rousseau, Diderot and Voltaire, among others, drank excessive amounts of coffee there. Later, during the French Revolution, the young Napoleon Bonaparte was also a patron.

The opening of Procope's marked the beginning of serious coffee drinking in Paris. Other coffee houses soon opened and they were not short of customers. Aux Deux Magots was another favourite haunt of the literary set; Verlaine and Rimbaud were among its patrons. Artists and intellectuals flocked to the Café de Flore nearby. The Café de la Paix was a monument to ostentatious display, attracting clientele that included royalty and poets. It was a competitive business, just as it had been for Turkish proprietors a century earlier. The owners of the newer establishments had to be resourceful in attracting customers. Entertainment was laid on – poetry reading, plays, songs and dances – and eventually food was served, too.

The objectors naturally started to make themselves heard. Feeling threatened, the wine makers, in a burst of patriotism, claimed that coffee was an enemy of France. They were joined by doctors, who up until then had shown neither misgivings nor any enthusiasm about coffee. They argued that it was the fruit of a tree desired only by goats and animals, and that drinking it burned the blood, weakened

Above: French breakfast coffee, in its traditional large bowl, and a croissant.

Above: Entertainment and coffee at the Café de la Paix, engraving from "Parisian Life" by David Carey, 1822.

the spleen and produced leanness, palsies, impotence, quiverings and distempers. Needless to say, their warnings fell mostly on deaf ears.

At home, the French were somewhat avant-garde in their coffee-drinking. They were probably unique in serving coffee not only in large bowls in which the breakfast baguette was dipped, but also *au lait* (with milk). They were the first to initiate the after-dinner coffee, which they served strong and black in tiny cups (*demi-tasse*), usually with a liqueur to aid digestion. Mrs Anne Roe, an English traveller and author, wrote around 1777: "Coffee is so much the fashion in France, especially in genteel houses, that one can scarcely finish their dinner before coffee is introduced, and they drink it scalding hot; all which conspire utterly to destroy the coats of the stomach."

Coffee and the French are beautifully summed up in this esoteric description by a 19th-century English journalist: "Coffee is to the Frenchman what tea is to the Englishman, beer to the German, *eau de vie* to the Russian, opium to the Turk, or chocolate to the

Above: Still an institution, the Café de la Paix as seen by night, 1938.

Impressions of coffee

"Black as the devil, hot as hell, pure as an angel, sweet as love." Prince Talleyrand (1754–1839), French diplomat and wit, on the ideal cup of coffee.

"The history of coffee houses, ere the invention of clubs, was that of manners, the morals and the politics of a people." Isaac D'Israeli.

"Strong coffee, and plenty, awakens me. It gives me warmth, an unusual force, a pain that is not without pleasure. I would rather suffer than be senseless." Napoleon Bonaparte, French emperor. *Painting, left, by Gérard von François, 1770–1837.*

Spaniard... The *garçon*, at your call for *demi-tasse*, has placed before you a snowy cup and saucer, three lumps of sugar, and a *petit verre*. He ventured the *petit verre*, inferring, from your ruddy English face, that you liked liqueur. Another *garçon* now appears; in his right hand is a huge silver pot, and in his left, another of the same material, uncovered: the former contains coffee – the latter, cream. You reject cream, and thereupon the *garçon* pours out the former until your cup – aye, and almost the saucer – actually overflows. There is hardly space for the three lumps, and yet you must contrive, somehow, to insert them...*Café noir*... pleases all the gustatory nerves, its savour ascends to rejoice the olfactory, and even your eye is delighted with those dark, transparent, and sparkling hues, through which your silver spoon perpetually shines. You pronounce French coffee the only coffee."

AUSTRIA

Records show that the Viennese were drinking coffee at home in the mid-1660s, though the coffee houses themselves did not open until the 1680s. The Viennese predilection for coffee was undoubtedly inspired by the Ottoman Ambassador, who set up residence for several months, bringing with him a vast retinue of servants and, of course, coffee. Coffee was served to Viennese guests, who took to the strange new drink with enthusiasm – so much so that a formal complaint was lodged by the city treasurer about the amount of wood being used for the fires needed to prepare the brew. By the time the Ambassador came to leave, the Viennese were buying beans from a trading company in the Orient and brewing coffee for themselves.

About 20 years later, in 1683, Vienna was under siege by the Turks. A Polish immigrant, Franz Kolschitzky, having something of a Turkish appearance, bravely slipped through enemy lines to carry messages between a waiting Austrian relief army and the besieged Viennese. Thanks to his heroism, the Turks were defeated and they fled in confusion, leaving behind a variety of exotic equipment. Amongst the loot were sacks of green beans, which Kolschitzky claimed for himself.

In recognition of his bravery, the city elders awarded Kolschitzky a house in which he is reputed to have opened the first of the city's many coffee houses. According to some versions of the tale he first started selling coffee beans door-to-door and then demanded the house; still other variations indicate that the honour of opening the first coffee house went to an Armenian. Whatever the truth, coffee had arrived in Vienna.

The city's coffee houses were an institution – not just a place but more a way of life. They served excellent coffee (a legendary twenty-eight different types) and provided newspapers and journals in abundance. Unique to the Viennese style were the wooden

Above: Café Sperl, Vienna, 1910.

newspaper poles, marble-topped tables and bentwood chairs that later became the hallmark of the European coffee houses.

Viennese patrons – male, naturally – were as unique as the coffee houses. As one writer put it, they shared a *Weltanschauung* – a way of looking at the world by those who do not want to look at the world at all. Another wrote

Above: Karlsplatz – the café booth built by Otto Wagner during his Secessionist period in Vienna.

Right: "The coffee boiler"
Viennese coffee house
scene with chess players,
a smoking Armenian,
and a newspaper
reader,
c. 1840.

that a hatred of fresh air and exercise was an almost universal trait, and that they were no great lovers of home life either. Many dropped by their favourite coffee house several times a day – in the morning and afternoon for a quiet read of the papers, in the evening for games or intellectual discussion.

The most famous coffee houses, such as the Griensteidl, and the Sperl, had an erudite clientele of writers, political activists and artists. Many became a stronghold of extreme views – the Griensteidl, for example, was opposed to women's emancipation. But there were also other establishments for "textile merchants, dentists, horse dealers, politicians and pickpockets".

Chicory

Although the Dutch had access to some of the best coffee in the world, they were curiously partial to chicory – the roasted and ground root of the wild endive. An English coffee planter complained it had "no other virtue than that of colouring...the water in which it is boiled or infused". Since good quality coffee was cheap, a possible reason for its use was that it tamed the effect of caffeine. Chicory later became popular in northern France, Germany and Scandinavia.

Coffee houses continued to proliferate not just in Vienna, but all over the Austrian Habsburg dominions. Those in Prague, Krakow and Budapest were as popular as any in Vienna. However, Vienna remained the "mother of coffee houses". By 1840 there were over 80 in the city, and by the end of the century the total came to an unbelievable 600.

THE NETHERLANDS

As one of the major coffee-trading nations, it is hardly surprising that the Dutch were free of the usual conflict surrounding the use of coffee. Consumption began in the home at the turn of the 16th century. By the time the first coffee houses opened in the mid-1660s, there was "hardly a house of standing where coffee is not drunk every morning". Not only the middle and upper classes, but even their servants had acquired a taste for coffee.

The coffee houses had their own unique style. Though elaborately furnished, their dark panelled walls and gleaming copperware gave them a particularly cosy atmosphere. Many were located in the financial areas, where merchants and administrators gathered to conduct business.

In some Dutch cities the coffee houses were situated in beautiful gardens. Here, patrons could enjoy a coffee under the shade of a tree while looking out onto a magnificent view. The garden cafés were particularly popular in spring when the gardens were ablaze with fruit blossoms and tulips.

SCANDINAVIA

Although the Finns now hold the world record for coffee consumption, paradoxically, Scandinavia was slow to take it up. Introduced in the 1680s, probably by the Dutch, coffee aroused hostility from early on. By 1746, a royal edict had been issued against coffee- and tea-drinking. The following year, those who continued to indulge had to pay a hefty tax, or suffer the indignity of having their crockery confiscated. Coffee-drinking was completely prohibited in 1756, though the ban was eventually lifted and huge taxes imposed instead. Sporadic attempts at suppression continued until the 1820s, when the government simply gave up.

Not much has been written about the early coffee houses, but it seems they lacked the opulence of their southern counterparts. In Oslo, they were Spartan

Individual preferences

Frederick the Great of Prussia was said to take "only seven or eight cups in the morning, and a pot of coffee in the afternoon". Made with champagne, the coffee was occasionally flavoured with a spoonful of mustard.

single-room establishments, popular with students, serving not only coffee but food to go with it – bowls of porridge, for example.

Middle-class Finns did better at home, holding large and elaborate coffee parties at which guests would drink up to five cups.

GERMANY

Coffee was introduced in 1675 to the court at Brandenburg in northern Germany by a Dutch physician. He was encouraged by Frederick William, a ruler known for his Calvinistic attitudes and temperate habits. Around the same time, the first coffee houses opened in Bremen, Hanover and Hamburg. Other cities rapidly followed suit and by the early 18th century, there were eight in Leipzig and ten or more in Berlin alone.

Coffee remained a drink of the aristocratic classes for some time. The middle and lower classes did not take to it until the early 18th century and it was even later before coffee was drunk at home.

Above: Drinking coffee in a German café, for female patrons only. Illustration 1880.

Above: A coffee house for the European wealthy classes. Print by Von August Hermann Knopp, 1856.

Since the coffee houses were a male stronghold, middle-class women set up *Kaffeekränzschen* (coffee clubs) – referred to by their uneasy husbands as *Kaffeeklatch* (coffee gossip).

In 1777, in an ill-concealed attempt to protect the breweries and to stem the flow of income to foreign dealers, Frederick the Great, rather hypocritically, issued a manifesto, part of which reads: "It is disgusting to notice the increase in the quantity of coffee used by my subjects...My people must drink beer...Many battles have been fought and won by soldiers nourished on beer; and the King does not believe that coffee-drinking soldiers can be depended upon to endure hardship or to beat his enemies..."

Coffee was prohibited to the working classes on the grounds that it caused sterility, but this simply gave rise to a lively black market trade. The King finally outlawed the roasting of beans in private homes, even appointing "coffee sniffers" to track down illicit aromas to their source. This ludicrous state of affairs was short-lived, though, and by the beginning of the 19th century, coffee had been reinstated.

Germany now took the lead in European coffee consumption. Coffee was served at mealtimes, at the *Kaffeekränzschen*, and at family get-togethers on Sunday afternoons. Coffee houses nevertheless remained no-go areas to respectable women. However, in public parks there were pavilions and special tents (*Zelte*) to which families could bring their own pre-ground coffee, and the patron simply provided hot water. The turn of the century saw the rise of another family-style institution – the café – which sold cakes as well as hot drinks. At first these *Konditorein* were used as an alternative to the coffee houses, but eventually they took over and the old-style coffee house gradually disappeared.

Coffee and music
Bach's *Coffee Cantata* (1734) is a satirical operetta that provides an insight into bourgeois attitudes. It tells of the efforts of a stern father to check his daughter's propensity for coffee-drinking by threatening to make her choose between a husband and coffee. Unperturbed, the daughter sings an aria beginning: "Ah, how sweet coffee tastes – lovelier than a thousand kisses, sweeter far than muscatel wine."

GREAT BRITAIN

The early history of coffee in Britain is substantially different from that of mainland Europe and North America. First, the coffee house era in Britain was intense but short-lived. Second, coffee-drinking at home was not a common feature. The majority of the British public, it seems, found the intricacies of roasting, grinding and brewing beyond them; pouring boiling water on tea leaves was more to their liking. That said, Britain was one of the first countries to start importing coffee.

John Evelyn's diary provides the first reliable reference in 1637, when a Turkish refugee brought coffee to

Right: An English coffee party relaxing after a parade at a military station in India, c. 1850.

Above: English coffee house, anonymous artist, 1668.

Oxford. The beverage became popular with students and dons, who sooner or later discovered that its stimulating properties were beneficial to prolonged or nocturnal study. The Oxford Coffee Club was eventually formed – later to become the Royal Society. Around 1650, a Jew named Jacob opened the first coffee house, called the Angel. Another soon appeared in London, in St Michael's Alley, Cornhill, set up by a Greek named Pasqua Rosée.

The new beverage had its opponents as well as advocates. A disgusted 17th-century commentator complained that it was "made of Old Crusts, and shreds of Leather burnt and beaten to a Powder"; another described it as "Syrup of soot and essence of old shoes". William Cobbett (1762–1835), politician, reformer and economist, was one of the few within his peer group to denounce coffee as "slops".

Coffee Houses Become Established

Nevertheless, by 1660 the London coffee houses were a deeply entrenched institution and were to remain so for the next fifty years. Even disasters such as the Great Plague (1665) and the Great Fire (1666) failed to stop their rapid spread across the city. Coffee houses became vital to the lives of anyone involved in business – meetings took place in them, deals were done, contracts signed and information exchanged. They were the birthplace of modern institutional monoliths such as The Stock Exchange, the Baltic and Lloyds Insurance. The coffee houses also provided a watering hole for artists, poets and writers, lawyers and politicians, philosophers and sages, who all had their favourite haunts. In his diary, Samuel Pepys (1633–1703) makes countless references to visits paid to this or that coffee house throughout London.

Some establishments charged an admission fee of one penny and, in return, visitors were offered the opportunity to debate current issues. These became known as "penny universities" and were centres of political and literary influence.

The coffee houses were also the strongholds of the gossipmongers, as this extract from a verbal attack on "Newsmongers' Hall" shows:
"There they can tell you what the Turk Last Sunday had to dinner;

Who last did cut De Ruyter's corns, Amongst his jovial crew...
You shall know there what fashions are, How periwigs are curled;
And for a penny you shall hear All novells in the world..."

Above: Rowdy behaviour in an English coffee house, c. late 17th century.

The Prohibition of Coffee Drinking

In 1675, fearing potential political unrest, Charles II issued a proclamation closing down the coffee houses. He already had the support of the women of London who, in a strongly worded and somewhat lewd petition, expressed their concern about the "Excessive Use of that Drying, Enfeebling LIQUOR". Claiming that it made men sexually inactive, the women, who were not allowed in the coffee houses, complained that their husbands spent idle time and money away from the home, as a result of which the "entire race was in danger of extinction". The men responded with equal vigour, stating that it was not the coffee that made them "less active in the Sports of Venus", but the "insufferable Din of your ever active Tongues".

Despite the women's support, prohibition of the coffee houses was short-lived. After vigorous petitioning by merchants and retailers, they were

reopened on strict condition that the proprietors should prevent the "reading of all scandalous papers and books and libels; and hinder every person

Above: The Great Subscription Room at Brook's Club, St James's Street, London. Painting by Rowlandson and Pugin, 1809.

Above: An English outdoor coffee stall as it would have looked c. 1860. Painting by C. Hunt, 1881.

from declaring, uttering or divulging all manner of false and scandalous reports against government or ministers". The absurdity of the stipulation was obvious, and it was soon withdrawn. Coffee houses continued to operate as usual and no more was heard of suppression.

Along with the rise in coffee's popularity, the temperance movement was starting to gain hold. Under its influence, many of the working class were starting to exchange the fireside of the ale-house for that of the coffee house. Since coffee houses were now frequented by all levels of society, there was anxiety – in some circles at least – about improper or unwelcome behaviour. Printed regulations were hung in conspicuous places (*see box*).

The Decline of Coffee Drinking

By the early 18th century, no matter how conspicuous the regulations, the atmosphere of the coffee houses changed. Many of them started to serve alcohol and attracted a different sort of clientele. As a result, the intelligentsia moved on to form literary circles, while "gentlemen" retreated to the safety of their own exclusive clubs in Pall Mall and St James's. Commercial and financial groups found it more practical and convenient to operate from offices or from new types of premises set up for professional associations. Another factor was the growth of circulating libraries in the latter half of the 18th century. Up until then, the coffee houses had been the sole supplier of newspapers and pamphlets, but now the libraries not only made available literature of all types, but also supplied English and foreign newspapers. Patrons who had once enjoyed a quiet read of the papers in the coffee house, now preferred to do it elsewhere.

Although the upper and middle classes had adopted coffee-drinking, tea was rapidly gaining in popularity. Other cafés emerged, selling other types of non-alcoholic drink, and food. By the end of the century, coffee was on the way out. Coffee's popularity would not soar again until the late 20th century.

The rules and orders of the coffee house
"First, gentry, tradesman, all are welcome thither,
And may without affront sit down together:
Pre-eminence of place none here should mind,
But take the next fit seat that he can find...
Let noise of loud disputes be quite forborne,
Nor maudlin lovers here in corners mourn,
But all be brisk, and talk, but not too much;
Of sacred things, let none presume to touch...
To keep the house more quiet and from blame,
We banish then cards, dice and every game..."

Above: A group of people enjoying cups of coffee and tea from a late-night stall at Blackfriars, London, England, 1923.

Below: The sumptuous interior of the Army and Navy Club House, London. Painting by R. K. Thomas.

NORTH AMERICA

Coffee was probably drunk from early on by the Dutch colonists in New Amsterdam (renamed New York in 1664), but the first reliable reference to its entry into North America occurs in 1668. Two years later, a license to sell coffee was issued to Dorothy Jones in Boston, and coffee houses soon opened throughout the eastern colonies.

In those hard-working days, coffee house management was looked on as women's work, though respectable women would not actually have been patrons. In complete contrast to European attitudes, the concept of whiling away idle hours in the coffee house was anathema. The coffee houses themselves lacked the clubby atmosphere of their European counterparts – the majority were closer to taverns that offered rooms to travelling workers and soldiers, and they attracted a correspondingly rowdy clientele. One of the more respectable was Boston's celebrated Green Dragon, headquarters of Revolution-plotting colonists, and in that sense did not differ greatly from coffee houses the world over.

The Boston Tea Party

Symbol of protest at the British tax on tea, the Boston Tea Party (1773), marked the acceptance of coffee as America's national beverage. Thereafter, coffee houses continued to spring up in major cities, some playing a vital role in the shaping of American history. Merchants Coffee House in New York was the scene of endless political discussion, declarations and strategic planning. Its famous rival, the Tontine, jointly owned by over 150 New York businessmen, served as a Stock Exchange, as well as occasional banqueting rooms and a record office for the arrival and departure of ships.

Like their English counterparts, habitués of the American coffee house eventually took their custom elsewhere as other social institutions evolved: business associations, gentlemen's clubs, banks and stock exchanges. The coffee house itself started to merge with taverns, hotels and restaurants.

Though the coffee house failed to maintain a stronghold, coffee itself became increasingly popular. The influx of European immigrants undoubtedly helped. The annexation of territories such as Florida and the French-speaking regions along the Mississippi, further expanded the market.

Coffee kept the pioneering spirit going – when the covered wagons set out for the west, coffee went too. It was even drunk by Native Americans, and legend has it that land was swopped for tools, rifles and bags of Java beans.

For the soldiers fighting the Mexican War and the Civil War, coffee was an essential part of their rations. They liked their coffee "hot, black and strong enough to walk by itself". It was so highly prized that the soldiers went to amazing lengths to make sure it was shared out equally. Identical piles of coffee were apparently spread out on a mat and the sergeant, with his back turned on the soldiers, would call out names at random.

By the mid-19th century coffee was firmly embedded in the lives of Americans. They were consuming a staggering 3.85 kg/8½ lb of coffee per head every year, compared to a European intake of 680g/1½lb. Coffee was drunk in town and country, by all, regardless of social standing. Coffee had become the national beverage.

Above: Colonials dressed as Indians throw British tea into Boston Harbour, heralding a rise in coffee drinking. Lithograph, 1846.

COFFEE SOCIETY TODAY

By the 1900s, coffee was still the beverage of choice in Europe and coffee house culture was firmly entrenched. Intellectuals and artists frequented the cafés in large numbers, particularly in Germany and Eastern Europe.

Coffee Drinking in Europe

In Germany, Berlin, for example, was rapidly becoming an international metropolis. Coffee houses such as the *Nollendortplatz* were regular meeting places for droves of enthusiastic young Germans, Scandinavians, Russian and Jewish émigrés who flocked there to read their plays and poems out loud. The scene attracted more and more people who simply wanted to be part of what was going on – including "young girls who style themselves as sculptresses and art experts", as one scathing male author wrote.

The coffee house scene in Vienna was equally cosmopolitan. By 1910, the city was home to countless immigrants from neighbouring Danube countries and beyond. With the exception of Paris, few European cities formed the cultural focal point for such a wide area. The coffee houses were allowed to stay open for as long as they had customers. For writers or students living in cramped and noisy lodgings, the coffee house became a second home. For the price of a cup of coffee, they could sit and read or write all day in comfort and warmth. There was no shortage of reading matter. Even in the 1900s, a licence was needed to sell newspapers in the street, so they were not so easy to come by. The coffee house, however, had most newspapers and magazines delivered directly, and thus provided a service similar to the modern public library reading room.

Budapest and Prague also boasted countless coffee houses which, in one way or another, were key to the development and growth of important artistic and literary movements. In Budapest, the Café Vigadó – though some say it was the New York – was the meeting place for the editorial board of a now-famous magazine *Nyugat* (West); Café Gresham was the haunt of a famous group of artists, dealers and experts, known in art history as the Gresham Circle. The reading of the first draft of Kafka's *Metamorphoses* took place in a back room of the Café Central in Prague.

Changes to coffee houses Though they fulfilled a vital social and cultural function, the economics of city life made it impossible for the coffee houses to continue in this way. Rising rents are not paid by allowing a person to "occupy a whole table by himself, stay there for hours for the price of a cup of coffee, insist on getting glasses of water and all the newspapers and magazines of Europe". Many of these delightful coffee houses became café-restaurants where the unique atmosphere became a thing of the past. In those that remain, the price of a cup of coffee reflects economic reality.

Above: A coffee house between the two World Wars.

Coffee in Britain

By the 1900s, the British taste for coffee had all but disappeared and tea-drinking had taken its place. Encouraged by the government, the British East India Company was importing more and more tea from Asia, and as a result, tea had become fashionable among all levels of society.

There was something of a revival of coffee house culture with the advent of grand establishments such as the Café Royal in London. Run by French proprietors, the Café Royal attracted a sophisticated clique of artists, poets and writers, including Oscar Wilde and Aubrey Beardsley, but it was a mockery of café life in Paris. People were thrown out for not being smartly dressed, and the "art" promoted was "homogenized for Mayfair drawing rooms".

With these magnificent cafés came the phenomenon of "café society" with its overtones of glamour and wealth. As American comedian Bob Hope said: "Café society is where they have mink for breakfast."

In complete contrast, coffee – if it can be called that – was also sold in dreary railway refreshment rooms and "cafés", along with sandwiches curling at the edges and ageing, stale cakes.

The Festival of Britain, in 1951, marked the end of post-war parsimony, and the start of a celebration of the bright new world of contemporary British culture. In keeping with the spirit of the times, The Coffee House opened near London's Trafalgar Square with the aim of providing not only a meeting place where coffee and light meals could be had in pleasant surroundings, but also lending wall-space to up-and-coming young artists. The Coffee House was soon followed by another establishment in nearby Haymarket. This was a gleaming shrine to contemporary design, notable for its striking ceiling-high edifice of coloured glass panels over which trickled a stream of water. Though both establishments in their intent and purpose attempted to replicate the early coffee houses, they differed wildly from their prototypes in terms of atmosphere and decor.

Above: Though the inspiration behind the revival of coffee drinking in Britain, most of the new coffee bars, such as this one in Coventry Street, London, above, contrasted dramatically with the traditional Parisian pavement café, below.

Above: The 1950s in Britain saw the rise of coffee bars open to men and women.

by others as an "emotional stabilizer". A rather patronizing article in a contemporary catering magazine stated: "Juke boxes have proven their worth by keeping young people off the streets and out of the pubs, drinking coffee and soft drinks instead of spirits. Most coffee bars have found the younger customers well behaved...more often than not they are content with talking, listening, humming or tapping their fingers...rather than getting up and 'jiving' about."

Coffee bars spread rapidly to the provinces. By 1960 there were over 2,000 of them, and at least 200 in London's West End. They were not only popular with teenagers, but also with patrons wanting light refreshment while shopping, or before and after the theatre, and, unlike their 17th-century predecessors, they were popular with most women.

Despite their lively atmosphere, the coffee bars of the 1950s and 60s gradually faded from view. Again, many became restaurants and others started selling alcohol. Eventually they had also to compete with the wine bars of the 1970s.

The 90s revival The 1990s saw something of a coffee house revival, though. The ubiquitous spread of the Internet brought with it the cybercafé, equipped with computers and coffee, where those so inclined may sit and surf the web. These places attract a particular clientele, but, just like their forebears, they fulfil a need by providing a meeting place for like-minded souls and for those who might otherwise spend their days in isolation in front of a computer screen.

The 1990s also saw the development of speciality coffee shops, selling fine single-estate beans, often equal in quality to the finest of wines, and treated as seriously. Developing alongside came a rash of modern coffee houses – the antithesis of the 50s' coffee bar – styled on minimalist lines and selling a bewildering choice of coffee from around the world. The British public have come full circle in their coffee drinking.

Gone was the warm fug of wood-panelled rooms; the modern coffee house was a "shining thing of chromium and plated glass; brilliant colour and contemporary design". This was to set the style for the years to come.

The coffee bar The end of the 1950s saw the emergence of the coffee bar, with its hissing espresso machine and youthful clientele. The first to open in London's Soho included The Moka Bar, Act One Scene One, The Two I's, Heaven and Hell and the Macabre – the latter painted entirely in black with coffins as tables. The names of these places went down in history for people

growing up in the early 1960s, for they were the birthplace of the music industry as we know it today. Music singers and groups such as Lonnie Donegan played live, and pop singer Tommy Steele began his show business career in The Two I's. Juke boxes were installed playing the latest hits.

Just like their 17th-century counterparts, these establishments provoked the same vociferous debate. It was the era of the teenager and teenage gangs, and there were invariably some caffeine-induced disturbances. While reviled by some critics, the music played was looked on

Above: Breakfast USA-style – coffee and a fruit juice while reading the paper at a roadside coffee stall, c. 1949.

Coffee Drinking in the United States

The habits of coffee drinkers in America developed quite differently from those in Europe and Britain, and the tastes and coffee drinking establishments often differed, too. For Americans travelling abroad in the late 19th and early 20th centuries, European coffee simply did not measure up to their home-brewed coffee. In *A Tramp Abroad*, Mark Twain declares: "You can get what the European hotel keeper thinks is coffee, but it resembles the real thing as hypocrisy resembles holiness. It is a feeble, characterless, uninspiring sort of stuff, and almost as undrinkable as if it had been made in an American hotel."

Conversely, Europeans travelling in North America bemoaned the lack of congenial coffee houses in which to while away the hours.

By the early 20th century, coffee imports to the United States had tripled, and annual consumption was up to 5kg/11lb per head. Consumption peaked after World War II in 1946 at 9kg/20lb a head.

The 1920s saw a number of coffee houses established in New York's Greenwich Village, the artists' traditional quarter. They became known as "Java spots" and were popular with American writers, film-makers, singers and actors, and with the many new emigrant writers and artists.

During the 1960s these coffee houses had become popular with the young. The legendary musician Bob Dylan is said to have arrived from the West at the Café Wha in Greenwich Village, and asked the manager if he could sing a few songs.

Since these decades, coffee consumption in the US has dropped from 60-70 per cent of the population to around 50 per cent. This is partly due to increased competition from other beverages and partly due to increased health consciousness, particularly among women.

Coffee in the 1990s Though the majority of Americans do their coffee-drinking at home, the 90s saw the rise in popularity of outlets such as Starbucks, selling speciality coffees. These include gourmet or single-estate coffees as well as various kinds of cappuccino, espressos and flavoured coffees. As in the United Kingdom, there is also an increasing number of cybercafés and drive-throughs, as well as coffee shops in upmarket fast-food outlets, convenience stores and bookshops.

THE ART OF BREWING COFFEE

From the moment coffee-drinking took hold, an enormous amount of ingenuity and effort went into perfecting the art of brewing. Not content with the simple act of pouring hot water over grounds and letting it sit, inventive minds in Europe and the United States managed to produce an astonishing variety of equipment – drips, filters, percolators and pressure machines, to name but a few. Edward Bramah states in his classic *Tea and Coffee*: "Between 1789 and 1921 the United States Patent Office alone recorded more than 800 devices for brewing coffee, not to mention 185 for grinders, 312 for roasters and 175 miscellaneous inventions with some bearing on coffee." Automatic vending machines were later added to the list.

The Cafetière

One of the earliest devices was the cafetière, which made its debut in France around 1685. Its use became widespread throughout the reign of Louis XV. It was no more than a simple jug (carafe) with a heating plate warmed by a spirit lamp below. It was superseded in about 1800 by the first percolator, invented by Jean Baptiste de Belloy, the Archbishop of Paris. In Belloy's cafetière, the ground coffee was held in a perforated container at the top of the pot and hot water was poured over it. The water passed through the small holes in the container and into the pot below.

Unusual Early Inventions

A few years after the invention of the cafetière, a formidable American named Benjamin Thompson, also known as Count Rumford, moved to Britain. Dissatisfied with the standard of coffee served – in those days it was subjected to lengthy boiling – he set about inventing a coffee-maker and eventually came up with the ominous-sounding Rumford Percolator. It was a great success, instantly finding a place in the annals of coffee-making history.

Just before 1820, the coffee biggin – the predecessor of the filter – became popular in England. In this device, ground coffee was placed in a flannel or muslin bag suspended from the rim of an earthenware pot. Hot water was poured over but, because of the bag, the water remained in contact with the coffee for longer, producing a different type of brew.

Brewing Coffee on a Large Scale

Up until the Industrial Revolution, there was no real need to make coffee in large quantities. However, with the growth of workshops and factories, combined with long working hours, some form of liquid refreshment was needed. Rail travel was becoming established, and with it, the evolution

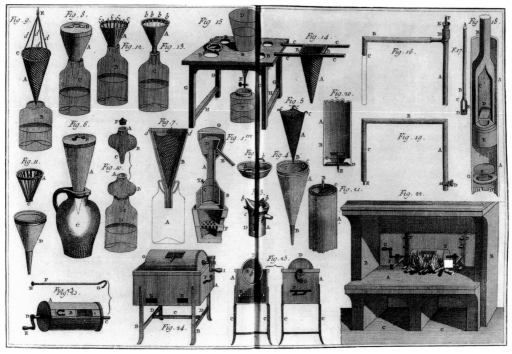

Above: Early inventions in the development of coffee brewing techniques, from the late 18th century.

Above: The Parisian Grill, London, with an Italian espresso machine, instrumental in the transformation of British drinking habits.

of the station buffet. At the same time, coffee houses, and later on hotels and restaurants, needed to find a way of producing a continuous supply of the beverage in a quick and efficient manner. We thus have the start of the development of catering equipment.

Around 1840, a Heath Robinson-like piece of apparatus appeared in Britain, invented by Robert Napier, a well-known Scottish marine engineer. The machine worked on a vacuum principle in which coffee was siphoned from a heated container through a filter and into a receiving vessel. Though not very efficient, it was to provide inspiration for later inventions capable of producing coffee in industrial quantities.

Coffee was made on a larger scale in France in a monstrous contraption which Isabella Beeton in *Modern Household Cookery* refers to as

"Loysel's hydrostatic urn". Invented in 1843 by Edward Loysel de Santais, the device worked on the principle of hydrostatic pressure in which the build-up of steam forces hot water through a valve and then down through the coffee grounds. It was a sensation at the Paris Exposition of 1855, where it supposedly produced two thousand cups of coffee an hour – presumably small cups.

The Cona

The Cona (vacuum pot) was a rather unique system that became widespread in the late 1930s. This consisted of two interconnecting toughened glass containers placed on top of each other and heated by a spirit lamp or gas or electric heater. The water in the lower container was forced into the top and drained through the coffee grounds back into the lower container.

The Espresso Machine

Perfecting Loysel's system from the previous century, the Italians went on to produce the revolutionary espresso machine that was to become so integral to Italian life. It was invented in 1948 by Achille Gaggia from Milan. These shiny hissing monsters were feared for their temperamental natures and billowing clouds of steam, but the dark, rich espresso coffee they produced was worth the time and trouble. The machines were also unique in producing a steaming hot foam of milk that transformed an espresso into a cappuccino – so called because its colour was reminiscent of the pale brown robes of the Capuchin monks. The classic cappuccino is traditionally a double espresso crowned with frothed milk and sometimes sprinkled with a powdering of rich, dark chocolate.

IN SEARCH OF THE IDEAL BREW

The majority of early coffee-drinkers in Europe made the beverage in much the same way as the Turks. Boiling water was poured on to finely ground coffee in the cup, resulting in a thick and potent brew. As coffee-brewing equipment proliferated, however, so did the nuances of national styles. Various individuals, too, had their own somewhat eccentric methods.

French Perfection

Coffee as perfected by the French was generally acknowledged among connoisseurs to be the best. Cast-iron coffee roasters and wooden coffee grinders were *de rigueur* in every household. Instead of boiling the beverage for hours, the French generally favoured the infusion method at first, before moving on to the drip-filter coffee pot and, later, the more sophisticated percolator.

Napoleon Bonaparte had his own way of brewing the perfect cup, and favoured the use of cold water. A connoisseur at the time wrote: "Put about two ounces of ground coffee for each person into a Percolator Coffee-Pot, pressing down with a ramrod, withdraw this and put on the tin covering for spreading the water over the coffee. Pour on the coffee clear cold water, and when a sufficient quantity has filtered through, plunge the jug containing the liquor into boiling water just before taking it to the table."

Some of the 19th-century coffee houses served specialities such as *mazagran*, an Algerian-style coffee extract diluted with cold water and served in a special stemmed glass. The practice of spiking coffee with alcohol also developed. William Ukers describes a unique iced coffee served in Normandy: "The man...takes half a cup of coffee, and fills the cup with Calvados, sweetened with sugar, and drinks it with seeming relish. Ice-cold coffee will almost sizzle when Calvados is poured into it. It tastes like a corkscrew, and one drink has the same effect as a crack on the head with a hammer."

Left: A classic combination – coffee with a dash of liqueur.

Above: Coffee and cream, which was a speciality of Austrian coffee houses.

Cream Lovers

Austrian coffee-drinkers favoured the French-style drip method or a pumping percolator device called the Vienna coffee machine. They were among the first to serve coffee with a cloud-like topping of whipped cream.

On entering an Austrian coffee house, it was an absurd request to simply ask for a coffee. As George Mikes points out, there was a rich choice to be had: "Strong, weak, short, long, large, medium, small, in a glass, copper pot, light brown, with milk, whipped cream, espresso...Turkish – gold, nut gold, nut brown, Kapuziner (dark) or Franciscans (lighter), with rum, whisky, with egg."

Northern Europe and Scandinavia shared the Austrian weakness for cream, though the Danes preferred their coffee black. The Dutch were particularly civilized in their manner of serving – good quality coffee was served in a pot on a tray accompanied by a pitcher of cream, a glass of water and a tiny plate with three sugar cubes.

However, in Scandinavia, the more sophisticated European brewing methods and manner of serving did not catch on. Coffee was generally boiled or stewed in a kettle and then brought to the table in a pot, or even poured straight from the kettle. The Finns were reputed to use fish skins to settle coffee grounds and clarify the brew.

Unusual Brewing Methods

British coffee in the 19th century was not always universally recommended. Despairing of procuring a good cup of coffee in Britain, one former planter concluded: "Coffee is spoiled in the burning, and sufficient care is not taken in preparing it for the table."

He goes on to deplore the "antediluvian method" of frying coffee beans with butter, declaring: "In private families, where this beverage is taken once a day, a coffee-roaster must be provided...Those who have not the facilities for roasting the berries themselves, should employ one or other of the leading coffee-roasters...who may be safely entrusted with the...berry."

Slow and steady Dr William Gregory of Aberdeen, Scotland, swore by lengthy cold water percolation requiring a laboratory-like arrangement of glass cylinders, funnels and bottles. The process took three or four days which, as he himself acknowledged, was a little tedious, stating: "It is necessary, as soon as the first portion is exhausted, to see a second in operation. In this way a supply is always to hand."

American eccentricities The Americans were particularly esoteric in their coffee-brewing habits. Boiling was the preferred technique, for ten minutes or even up to several hours. Some early recipes advised adding the white, yolk and even the crushed shell of an egg to provide richness of colour when milk was added. If fresh eggs were in short supply, an uncooked square of codfish skin was sometimes recommended. These curious techniques were reputedly popular with many American coffee lovers as late as 1880.

"Why do they always put mud in the coffee on paddle steamers?" *William Thackeray, writer and traveller, 1850.*

Advice from a 19th-century epicure

"Beat up an egg – two for a large pot – and mix it well with the coffee, till you have formed it into a ball; fill the pot with cold water, allowing room enough to put in the ingredients; let it simmer very gently for an hour, but do not think of stirring it, on any account; just before it is required, put the pot on the fire and warm it well; but as you value the true aroma, take care that it does not boil. Pour it off gently, and you will have as pure and strong an extract of the Indian berry as you desire. Use white sugar-candy in powder in preference to sugar; cream, if attainable; if not, boiled milk." Benson Hill writing in *Epicure's Almanac*.

Left: Despite the basic simplicity of the coffee-brewing procedure, variations on coffee-brewing technique are endless and ingenious. Everyone has a particular method that works best for them, as this 19th-century method for brewing coffee with eggs demonstrates.

Variations on a Theme

Coffee essence The famous Camp liquid coffee essence, in its tall square bottle, came on the market at the start of the 20th century, and is still on sale today. It was popular during both World Wars when coffee was rationed. The chicory-based essence is pre-sweetened and is traditionally made by diluting it with hot milk.

Instant coffee In 1901, the first soluble dried coffee extract was invented by Japanese-American scientist Satori Kato of Chicago. It was quick to prepare, produced no tiresome grounds to dispose of, and the flavour never varied. Among the first to use it were members of an expedition to the Arctic. With the ease of preparation, soluble coffee found a ready market during World War I, when it was widely used by American forces serving in England.

Following a request to find a good long-term solution to Brazil's coffee surpluses, Nestlé introduced "Nescafé" into Switzerland in 1938. It came on the market a year later in Britain, managing to rekindle the coffee habit there, albeit in a weakened form.

Above: Advertisement for Paterson's "Camp Coffee", 1890.

Below: Just some of the many syrups, essences and flavourings, such as vanilla and cinnamon, that are available today for adding to coffee.

Decaff In 1903, a German coffee importer named Ludwig Roselius, having received a shipment of seawater-soaked beans, gave the beans to researchers. Using a combination of steam extraction and chlorine-based solvents, they perfected a way of removing the caffeine without changing the flavour. Roselius patented the process in 1905 and began marketing caffeine-free coffee under the name Kaffee Hag. The product was introduced in the United States in 1923 as Sanka, a contraction of the French *sans caffeine*, and found a ready market of coffee drinkers anxious to limit the effects of caffeine.

Flavoured coffee In the 1970s, small coffee-roasting companies in the United States started to introduce flavoured coffee. Initially, flavourings were developed to replace those containing alcohol – Irish Cream and amaretto, for example. However, a more recent trend has been for sweeter tastes, aimed at young or first-time coffee drinkers. As a result, flavours such as tiramisu, vanilla and toffee are becoming popular. Spicy flavours – not so dissimilar to those used in 16th-century Turkey – and fruit flavours are also gaining ground. Spices such as cardamom, cinnamon, orange rind and roasted fig are among those commonly used.

Canned coffee Ready-to-drink canned coffee was first launched by the Japanese in 1969. This was partly due to the popularity of vending machines in Japan. Not surprisingly, uptake in Europe and America has been slow, but it is popular throughout Asia, where cold drinks are perhaps more welcome.

Below: Coffee in a can from Japan.

COFFEE AROUND
THE WORLD

The tropical belt girding the Earth is studded with coffee

plantations. People cultivate coffee, or at least pick the fruit

from untended trees, in more than seventy countries. In many

of these countries, the fortune and well-being of the citizens

hangs in the little red cherries of the fragile coffee tree.

In a comprehensive country-by-country analysis, the different

coffees produced around the world are discussed and described.

This section also covers all the stages, from harvesting,

processing, sorting, grading through to roasting, that are involved

in transforming the unripe green bean into the aromatic

roasted coffee bean appreciated the world over.

WHAT IS COFFEE?

The *coffea* plant is a genus of the *Rubiaceae* family. Classification of coffee plants is complicated, as there are many species, varieties and strains. The two species from which most commercial coffee comes are the *coffea arabica*, a very complex species with numerous varieties, and the *coffea canephora* species, usually called *robusta*, which is the name of its most productive variety. Other species of coffee trees include *coffea liberica*, discovered in Liberia in 1843, and *coffea dewevrei*, better known as *excelsa*, both of which have *robusta*-like qualities and are generally rather unsavoury, to say the least. Much effort has gone into the development of hybrid coffee trees, but the general consensus is that although the new strains add productivity, hardy resistance and perhaps longer life to coffee trees, the hybrid flavours are simply not as good as the old ones.

All coffee is grown in the wide tropical belt surrounding the Equator between the Tropics of Cancer and

Above: Clumps of green fruit form on the branches of the coffee tree.

Capricorn, but depending on their species and variety, the plants vary enormously in appearance. The evergreen foliage may be practically any shade in a range from yellowy-green to deep green or even bronze, and the shiny leaves are corrugated, more so for *robusta* than *arabica*. Some plants remain small shrubs, while others would tower at 18m/60ft if they were not kept pruned for ease of harvesting.

The Coffee Tree

A coffee plant, if not propagated from a cutting, begins life as a sprout issuing from a "parchment" bean that has been planted in shallow, sandy soil. As the sprout takes root, it pushes the bean out of the soil. In a few days' time the first two leaves emerge from the bean, now at the top of the tiny sprout. The old bean husk, hollow, soon falls to the ground. Next, the tiny seedling is transferred to its individual container in a nursery. For about a year, it is tended carefully and introduced to open weather as the nursery "roof" of logs or other protective covering is gradually removed; at most, a few hours per day of direct sun is all the rather temperamental coffee tree will ever want. The small plant will then be set out in the field, possibly under the protection of a banana tree's broad leaves, particularly if the plantation is located on flat terrain nearer the Equator, where the sun's rays are more direct. If the tree is

Above: One of nature's most beautiful plants: the lush foliage of the coffee tree.

Above: Lovely white coffee blossoms are similar to jasmine in looks and smell.

Above: Early morning watering at a coffee nursery in Indonesia.

planted on a mountain slope it may need no protection, as mountain-sides receive direct sun for only part of a day, and coffee trees on high plateaux often enjoy the humidity and sun-screen resulting from high-altitude cloud-cover.

For several years the tree will not produce any fruit, although it may require irrigation, pruning, weeding, spraying, fertilization and mulching. The latter two help if the soil is not the best for coffee, which thrives in the rich loam formed from volcanic ash, full of nitrogen, potash and phosphoric acid. Finally, when the tree is four to five years old, it bears its first crop. It quickly reaches its productive peak within a couple of years, but will yield fruit for a total of about twenty to twenty-five years, during which time it must be constantly tended.

All coffee trees are capable of bearing blossom, green fruit and ripe fruit simultaneously on the same branch, thus almost certainly the fruit has to be harvested by hand. There are one or two main harvests, and possibly several secondary harvests, as the growing seasons vary depending on the species and the location. A coffee plantation, therefore, is seldom without some blossoms. The flowers, which develop in clusters, are creamy white and produce a fragrance reminiscent of jasmine. The flowers last only a few days; they are soon replaced by clusters of small green berries, which then take several months to become the ripe red cherries ready for picking.

Above: Young coffee seedlings.

Coffee Species

Numerous factors affecting coffee cultivation depend very much on the species and vary considerably from country to country.

Arabica The oldest-known species of coffee tree, *arabica* is the high-grown species, cultivated on mountainous

Below: The Nicaraguan version of Maragogype beans is the world's largest coffee bean.

plateaux or volcanic slopes at optimum altitudes of 1000–2000m/3,280–6,561ft, where the annual rainfall ranges from 150–200cm/59–78in, and where mild days alternate with cool nights in a yearly average temperature range of about 15–24°C/59–75°F. *Arabica* trees flower after a rainy season, and then require up to nine months for the fruit to mature. In one year a typical arabica tree may produce less than 5kg/11lb of fruit, which processes down to about 1kg/2.2lb of actual coffee beans. Much of the *arabica* harvest around the world is "washed", or wet-processed, and the beans, which are generally larger, longer and flatter than those of *robusta*, and which contain less caffeine, produce a more delicate, acidic flavour.

Arabica coffee accounts for about 70 per cent of the world's coffee, but it is more difficult to grow, being more susceptible to disease, pests and frost, and is, not surprisingly, more expensive. Of the many varieties of *arabica*, the *typica* and *bourbon* are the most distinct and the best known, and from these have come other strains, such as *tico*, *Kent*, *mokka*, *Blue Mountain*, the Brazilian hybrid *mondo nuevo* (or *mundo novo*), *garnica* and *mibirizi*, to name only a few. Cultivars from the *mondo nuevo* variety include *villa Sarchi*, *Geisha* and *Villalobos*, and *catuai* is a hybrid of *mondo nuevo* and *caturra* (a large-beaned bourbon mutant). *Catuai's* fruit may be yellow (*amarelo*) or red (*vermelho*). *San Ramon* is another large-beaned *typica* mutant.

Maragogype The most famous *typica* mutation was first discovered in the Maragogype region of Brazil's state of Bahia. *Maragogype* trees produce the world's largest coffee beans, sometimes called "elephant" beans (not to be confused with a certain bean defect, called an "elephant ear"). *Maragogype* beans are grown in several countries and are a sought-after coffee for their smooth flavour as well as attractive appearance. Unfortunately, because their yield is low, *maragogype* trees are expensive to maintain, and at the end of their productive lives, many of the trees are being replaced with more "normal" growths.

Canephora or **robusta** The *canephora* species of coffee is very different from the *arabica*; it is as robust in taste as it is in its resistance to diseases and pests; unfortunately, in this case strong is not best, and its flavour is not as desirable as that of *arabica*. Consequently, *robusta* accounts for less than 30 per cent of world coffee production, in spite of being cheaper in price.

Robusta's commercial use is primarily in blends, where its full body is appreciated, and in soluble, or instant coffee, where the processing reduces its more obtrusive flavour. Although *robusta* trees must be pollinated or grown from cuttings, they are far easier to grow, and when many *arabica* plantations were destroyed by rust disease in the second half of the 19th century, many estates were replanted with *robusta* trees. It is now grown throughout the tropical zone, but most of the world's *robusta* comes from West and Central Africa, South-east Asia, and Brazil, where it grows in altitudes from sea-level up to 700m/2,296ft.

Robusta can withstand heavier tropical rainfalls of 300cm/118in or more, although, as with all coffee, the trees should never stand in water. Conversely, the shallow roots of *robusta* enable it to live successfully where rainfall is unpredictable or even scanty. Similarly, it survives when equatorial temperatures soar, although it is happiest at an average temperature somewhere around 24–30°C/75–86°F.

Robusta trees flower rather irregularly and take 10–11 months to go from blossom to mature cherry. The ripe cherries are generally picked by hand, except in Brazil where the flat terrain and vast spaces allow machine harvesting. *Robusta* is processed mostly by the "unwashed", or dry method, and the beans are smaller and more hump-backed than those of *arabica*; they are also often distinguished by small points at either end of the central "crack" on the bean. *Robusta* trees produce a slightly higher yield per hectare than do *arabica* trees. The most common varieties of *robusta* are *conilon* from Brazil, the *Java-Ineac, Nana, Kouilou* and *congensis.*

Other cultivars Hybridization has produced other cultivars that are propagated from cuttings rather than seeds, such as the more successful *arabusta*, developed by the French Coffee and Cocoa Institute in the 1960s and exported to many parts of the world from the Ivory Coast. The goal of most hybridization is to combine the best qualities of *arabica, robusta,* and perhaps of some of the better natural mutants, with the hope of possibly improving all. The natural *hibrido de Timor*, the dwarf *Ruiru Eleven* from Kenya, the rust-resistant *catimor*, and the *icatu* hybrids are names of some strains involved in, or resulting from, experiments in hybridization.

There are many reasons why the development of new coffee hybrids is the object of so much activity around the globe. In various cases, these efforts have pursued higher crop yields, larger beans or uniformity in bean size, better cup flavours, drought-resistant trees, adaptability to specific soil, and variants in caffeine content, to name but a few sought-after results. Almost no factors, however, present a greater challenge to coffee researchers than the two biggest enemies of the coffee plant: insects and diseases.

Above: A Javanese woman searches for the ripe fruit among the coffee tree leaves.

PESTS AND PROBLEMS

There are countless pests and diseases that regularly wreak great damage every year on coffee crops around the world. Perhaps one of the most surprising things about the fact that coffee production is the second largest industry in the world after oil, is that it is subject to such a great number of natural disasters, in the form of pests, diseases and weather patterns.

Pests

It has been estimated that there are at least 850 species of insects that regularly book tables at their favourite coffee plantations. There are those that enjoy a salad of tender green leaves, such as various leaf-miners; leaf-cutting ants; leaf-skeletonizers; thrips; countless caterpillars; and nutrition-sucking scale, which come in shades of green, white and brown, and are such messy eaters that the mucus they leave behind breeds a fungus disease called "soot". There are many mealy bugs and numerous nematodes, whose secret binges on coffee roots go unnoticed until the plants appear to suffer from nutritional problems, while stem and twig borers prefer a liquid lunch straight from the tap. The antestia bug, which attacks green cherries for preference, but will settle for buds or even twigs, is like an elegant vampire: no one knows it has supped until the pulping process exposes the darkly stained zebra-striped parchment coatings and the beans within, shrivelled, black, and decayed with the fungus that often accompanies the bug. The Mediterranean fruit fly does great damage by laying eggs in the pulp of the coffee fruit, which then becomes an all-you-can-eat buffet for the young maggots. The yellow tea mite may find itself in the wrong venue, but it stays nevertheless.

By far the most serious coffee pest is the dreaded coffee berry borer, the *broca del cafeto*, a tiny black female beetle that bores into a coffee cherry, going through the fruit pulp and penetrating the coffee bean itself, where she lays her eggs. If the bean is not totally destroyed by the voracious tunnel-making larvae, it will succumb

Above: It may look harmless, but the grasshopper preys on the coffee tree.

to the secondary rot fungus carried by the borer. Coffee berry borers were first noted in Africa in 1867, since which time they have infested every coffee-growing continent around the world, causing billions of dollars' worth of damage and devastation.

Global trends in pest control management are attempting to reduce, and hopefully ultimately replace, the use of chemical pesticides by the introduction and encouragement of natural predators and parasites of the coffee-preying pests. For example, a current International Coffee Organization project, funded by the United Nations' Common Fund for Commodities, hopes to control the coffee berry borer in at least seven member coffee-producing countries by releasing certain wasps that prey on the borer beetles.

Diseases

Unfortunately, coffee diseases have no natural predators, and although fewer in number than the hordes of coffee pests, coffee diseases are still largely chemically controlled. Although fungicides are not as ecologically harmful as pesticides and herbicides, all chemical treatments are expensive. The best control of coffee plant diseases is careful quarantine, but

that is not easy to enforce, especially given the extent of international travel. One of the worst coffee plant diseases is leaf rust (*Hemileia vastatrix*). First reported in 1861 in Africa, by 1870 it had completely wiped out the coffee industry of Ceylon, which resorted to tea-growing. The virulent leaf rust quickly spread to every continent in the

Above: Leaf rust.

coffee-growing world, although some countries have thus far been spared. It is thought that leaf rust is spread by spores being carried on the clothes of travellers from one country to another, particularly by people working in the coffee trade. It is lethal for *arabica* trees, but *robusta* is resistant to it.

A soil-inhabiting fungus causes another devastating coffee disease, tracheomycosis, also known as vascular fungus or coffee wilt disease, to which *robusta* is more susceptible than *arabica*. In fact, it was this disease that almost totally destroyed the Ivory Coast's original coffee plantations of *liberica* trees in the 1940s, after which time the Ivory Coast became a large grower of *robusta* and the developer of *arabusta*. In the Democratic Republic of Congo, coffee production has fallen consistently since 1994, due to this disease and internal tribal warfare affecting the same regions.

Another very serious disease affecting *arabica* trees is coffee berry disease (*colletotrichum coffeanum*). Also called brown blight and red blister, coffee berry disease is a fungus, first identified in Kenya in the 1920s, which may attack a coffee tree in the wake of its carrier, the antestia bug. Rain splashes can also spread residues of the disease, even those from a previous crop. The disease attacks the coffee cherries, causing maximum damage to green cherries, turning them dark with decay. Fungicidal sprays are successful in controlling coffee berry disease only to some extent, and therefore this disease is the subject of much hybridization research.

Hybridization can certainly offer hope for conquering many coffee enemies, as one variety, susceptible to a particular pest or disease, is crossed with another variety that is naturally resistant. Although crossbreeding may eventually see the disappearance of some coffee diseases (thus far what is seen is more the disappearance of flavour), there is a category of coffee enemy to which all varieties are vulnerable: these are the natural disasters that plague many coffee-growing regions.

Natural Disasters

Because of the particular climate and soil required for growing coffee, plantations are sometimes located in rather precarious positions on the slopes of volcanoes. Active or not, volcanoes exist in areas of seismic instability, as evidenced by the terrible earthquake of January 1999, which struck the Colombian coffee-growing centre of Armenia, a victim of similar devastation in 1988. Indeed, since 1972, Mexico, the Philippines, Panama, Costa Rica, Guatemala and Nicaragua have all suffered earthquake damage.

Hurricanes are endemic to the tropics, and although little coffee is grown in coastal areas, almost all tropical islands and the countries of the narrow isthmus of Central America are subject to serious tropical storms. Out of Nicaragua's 30 per cent crop loss due to Hurricane Mitch in 1998, only 10 per cent consisted of destroyed trees, mostly by mudslides; the rest was due to cherries going rotten because the roads to processing mills were impassable. Tidal waves are more infrequent than hurricanes, but can be equally devastating, as witnessed by the massive force of the wave that hit Papua New Guinea in 1998.

Less dramatic, but seemingly always present *somewhere* in countries heavily dependent on coffee crops, are more universal disasters such as droughts, famine, bad weather (such as the freak hailstorm of October 1998, in the Brazilian state of São Paulo, which went largely unnoticed by the rest of world because it destroyed *only* an estimated 100,000 bags of coffee), political disturbances if not actual revolutions, and, of course, the coffee enemy that causes chaos in coffee prices for the entire world: frost.

Frost is the bane of the Brazilian coffee crop, but it can occur in any country where the best coffee is grown in higher altitudes near the extremities of the tropical belt. Although a mild frost can sometimes be alleviated slightly with hot air machines, even one night of freezing temperatures can certainly do enormous damage to a coffee crop; a truly hard frost will completely kill the trees. Considering the years of labour and cost invested in a plantation of mature coffee trees, it must be heartbreaking to see it all come to nothing in just a few hours of cold weather.

Below: Frost destroys a Brazilian crop.

HARVESTING AND PROCESSING

Far more is done on a coffee plantation than just growing and harvesting the fruit. When coffee cherries ripen, they must be picked almost immediately, not an easy thing to time when a single tree's fruit is in various stages of maturity simultaneously. In most *arabica*-growing areas the ripe cherries will be carefully hand-picked and dropped into the picker's basket, the weight of which determines the picker's pay and, in areas of smoother terrain and shorter trees, can be as heavy as 100kg/220lb by the end of the day. The same tree will be visited on several different days as more cherries ripen.

A harvester will "strip-pick" the entire tree when the majority of its cherries are ripe, by sliding his or her fingers down the branches, causing all the cherries, ripe or not, to fall to the ground. Alternatively, a large vehicle will be driven slowly down the row of coffee trees, and its revolving arms will knock the looser, and therefore riper, fruit to

Below: Hand-pickers head out for a day's work in the mountainous regions of Java, where they use ladders to reach the tops of the trees.

Above: The process of winnowing requires the use of a large sieve-like hoop for tossing everything into the air and retaining only the cherries.

Left: A Brazilian winnower tossing the machine harvest into the air, hoping to lose all but the coffee cherries.

the ground. Harvesting machines are used primarily in Brazil, where the immense, flat terrain of the large *fazendas* (estates) allows the trees to be planted in even, widely spaced rows.

If the fruit is on the ground, it must be raked up and "winnowed" by workers who, using large meshed hoops, fling the sweepings into the air several times; twigs, leaves, cherries and dust are tossed up high, and the worker, like a juggler, catches the cherries as the lighter weight materials are blown aside. A major problem with the hand-stripping and machine methods of harvesting is that many cherries are included which are not at a point of perfect ripeness; these under- or overripe cherries must be removed by extra sorting or else they will lower the grading quality. All quality *arabicas* will be sorted several times, beginning with hand-sorting the cherries. This initial task of hand-sorting is often done by women and children.

The Coffee Cherry

The coffee fruit is called a cherry primarily because it is about the same size, shape and colour as an actual cherry. Beneath the bright red skin is the pulp, a sweet, sticky yellow substance, which becomes slimy mucilage towards the centre of the fruit, where it surrounds the coffee beans, which are actually the seeds. There are normally two beans per cherry, facing each other's flat side, like peanut halves. On the surface of the beans is a very thin, diaphanous membrane, called the silver skin. Each bean (and its silver skin) is encased in a tough, cream-coloured, protective bean-shaped shell, or jacket, called parchment or pergamino, which serves to keep the bean separate from the mucilage. Beans destined to be seed beans for growing new coffee plants must remain in their parchment if they are to sprout.

Left: Hand-sorting in Indonesia.

Above: Coffee cherries set out in the Kenyan sun to dry.

Normal coffee trees sometimes produce a few smaller-than-average cherries in which only one bean forms. This single bean, called variously a peaberry, perla or caracol, will not have a flat side; rather, it will be small and almost completely round. Sorted out and collected together, peaberries sell at a slightly higher price than do normal coffee beans from the same trees. Many people swear that the peaberry flavour is better, although it may just be that, because of the special sorting, few, if any, defective beans are able to slip through.

Processing the Cherry

The next step after harvesting is to remove the beans from the surrounding fruit pulp, which is done by either the washed (wet process) or the unwashed (dry process) method. The latter, dry processing, is the separation method, used where there is a shortage of water or equipment, or both. Because most *robusta* and much low-quality *arabica* coffee is dry-processed, many people,

experts included, wrongly assume that any dry-processed or "natural" coffee, must be inferior. On the contrary, most of Ethiopia's wonderful varied *arabicas* are dry-processed, and some of these are world-class coffees; almost all Brazilian *arabicas* are naturals, or unwashed, and there are some superbly smooth, sweet and full-bodied *Santos* beans.

Dry processing In spite of its description, dry processing begins with the washing of the newly harvested cherries, not only to clean the cherries but to implement another sorting procedure, as the floaters – defective beans due primarily to insect infestation or overripeness – are easily picked out at this stage. The cherries are then spread out to sun-dry; if on patios they are raked, and if they have been placed on matting stretched across trestles, or on some other raised platform, they are hand-turned, for about three weeks. They are protectively covered from any night condensation or rain – the unwashed process tends to be used in

drier regions anyway – and the drying process may be finished with hot-air machines. When only about 12 per cent of their moisture content remains, they are either stored in silos or are sent on for final processing at a mill or factory, which may be under government control. Here they undergo hulling, which in one operation removes all of the dried skin, pulp and parchment from the beans.

From this point the procedures are the same for both washed and unwashed beans: they are polished, screened and sorted, processes usually done with more sophisticated equipment, including electronic sorting machines; and then graded and bagged. After this the bags of green (still unroasted) beans may go into storage or they may be exported.

Wet processing This system is much more expensive, due to far greater requirements of equipment, labour, time and water. Before any fermentation can begin in the freshly picked cherries, they are immediately washed in large

Right: Pushing the pulped beans through the system of channels, which sorts them by size and weight.

tanks from which the water carries them into a system of channels. Staying in contact with the fresh-flowing water helps to loosen the outer skin, while the cherries are carried towards a depulping machine. Here they lose their skin and some of the pulp, but the flowing water takes the beans, still wearing their parchment covering and a lot of the sticky mucilage, through various screens, sieves and sluices, which further sort the beans by size and weight.

At last the beans arrive in a fermentation tank, where any remaining mucilage is broken down by natural enzymes during a 36-hour soak. The fermentation is monitored and controlled, as it must only remove the mucilage and not develop off-flavours in the beans themselves. The parchment beans, once clear of mucilage, are rinsed, drained and spread out on patios or wire-mesh platforms and left to dry in the sun.

As in the dry method, the parchment beans are raked and turned for between one and two weeks, or they may go into low-temperature drying machines until their moisture content is about 11–12 per cent. The last stages are critical because over-drying makes them brittle and they can lose quality; under-drying means vulnerability to unwanted fermentation, fungi and bacteria or bruising during subsequent hulling. Parchment beans are stored for about a month, and can be stored for several months in a controlled atmosphere. When exportation is imminent, the beans are taken to the curing mill where the parchment is removed by hulling, and the washed beans undergo the same processes as do the dry-processed beans.

Right: Once through the various stages of soaking and pulping, parchment beans are rinsed, drained and spread out to dry on large, flat patios or wire-mesh platforms.

SORTING AND GRADING

Governments of countries that export coffee usually operate or advise a department or agency that establishes a standard, regulates and monitors the coffee trade, and assesses bean quality through quality-control inspectors. In many countries the administrator is a coffee board authority; in others it is an institute, possibly under the control of the ministry of agriculture or ministry of trade and industry.

Grading Coffee

Unfortunately, there is no international standardization of coffee quality, as coffee is graded using a range of characteristics peculiar to each producing country. A sample of beans is taken from a bag, judged according to that country's standards, and the sack of beans from which the sample was taken is given a quality rating, good or bad, depending on the outcome of the assessment. The characteristics by which most coffee is graded are appearance (bean size, uniformity, colour); number of defective beans per sample; cup quality, which of course includes flavour and body; and whether the beans roast well and evenly. Because the classifications of grades and the descriptive terminology differ from country to country, and the standards of quality are only relevant within that country's range of coffees, it is not easy to interpret a coffee's true quality without some familiarization of the particular country of origin's grading system. There is at least one constant, uniform reference from country to country: all countries determine bean size with standardized screens, so the buyer doesn't have to guess how large is large or how small is small from the producer's relative point of view.

A coffee may bear an exotic regional name, and/or may be classified by the processing (washed or unwashed). It may have a descriptive title, or just an alphabetical letter or two, possibly followed by a number. For example, in certain countries where the coffee industry has been nationalized, the grading system may seem to be rather

Above: The task of sorting through the wet-processed beans is a methodical one.

uninspiring, as in Kenya, where a bag of coffee may be a washed "AA", with a number to denote one of ten cup-quality classes; yet this ordinary-sounding coffee is acknowledged by most experts to be consistently one of the world's best coffees. In India, however, a "Plantation A" – assume "washed" because an unwashed is designated "cherry" – was one of the highest qualities available, but was not in the same league as the Kenyan. India, however, has recently changed to a free market, so it remains to be seen what grading system will be used.

Most Caribbean and Central American countries indicate quality by words denoting altitude: Costa Rica's eastern regions produce LGA (low grown Atlantic), MGA (medium grown Atlantic), and HGA (high grown Atlantic), while the western slopes grow HB (hard bean), MHB (medium hard bean), GHB (good hard bean) and SHB (strictly hard bean). The harder the bean, the higher the altitude and the price! The best plantations of Costa Rica can label their own bags as well as denote the altitude, and both Costa Rica and Nicaragua also use exotic regional names. Nicaragua also indicates classifications of quality and altitude with titles like Central Bueno Lavado (MG), Central Altura for high grown, and Central Estrictamente Altura (SHG). Guatemala is a bit more obscure with its altitude designations, since the adjectives, which sound purely descriptive, indicate altitudes beginning at 700m/2,296ft and rising to 1,700m/5,577ft: Good Washed, Extra Good Washed, Prime Washed, Extra Prime Washed, Semi Hard Bean (SH), Hard Bean (HB), Fancy Hard Bean and Strictly Hard Bean (SHB).

National systems for grading Countries that have unique ways of designating different qualities of coffee include Brazil, which classifies each bag by the species of coffee, the port from which the coffee is exported (Santos, Parana, etc), and then by a defective bean

qualification: for example, NY (meaning "we are counting the defective beans the way the Americans understand it") and Standard 3 (which means an average sample of 300g/11oz would have 12 defective beans). The defects also include points for stones and twigs. Brazil's grading also includes bean size, colour, density, shape, roast potential, cup quality, processing method, crop year and lot number.

Modest Ethiopia, with some truly aristocratic, world-class coffees, is content to denote simply the processing, the name of the region of production and a grade number between 1 and 8, each of which indicates a certain number of defects. Colombia's grading is even simpler: each bag has the name of the region, and sorts by size, e.g. Excelso beans are smaller versions of the Supremo.

Indonesia has recently changed from its old Dutch system of grading. Now, R=Robusta, A=Arabica, WP=wet processed, DP=dry processed; six quality grade numbers, with 1&2 High, 3&4 Medium, 5&6 Lower grades; AP after the grade number means After Polished, and L, M and S stand for bean sizes large, medium and small. For example, R/DP Grade 2L would be a dry processed large-bean *robusta* of very high quality; A/WP Grade 3/AP would denote a medium-quality polished washed *arabica*.

The glossary overleaf lists some terms used by the coffee trade to describe particular coffee beans and their attributes. In some cases several explanations are given because, in general, there is no standardization of terms; interpretations may therefore vary or even seem to be contradictory.

Above: Professional sorters grade coffee beans by size, by painstakingly putting the beans into corresponding holes.

Grading Terminology

While the following terms may vary slightly from country to country, these are the generally accepted definitions and will give you an excellent idea of how one sample of coffee beans is differentiated from another.

Above: Black bean.

Black bean Insect-damaged; dead cherry fallen from tree pre-harvest; decomposed bean; overripe; metal contamination.

Bold bean The size falling between medium and large.

Broken Over-dried brittle beans, easily broken into pieces during hulling.

Brown bean In *arabica*, a colour denoting overripeness; over-fermentation; under-fermentation (brownish tinge); or soiled, lack of pre-washing.

Discoloured bean Any bean outside the range of normal colour (green/blue in *arabica*, khaki/brownish/yellowish in *robusta*) , indicating poor processing, with possible defective flavour.

Elephant ear Malformed cherry containing one large bean partly encircling a smaller; the two interlocking parts can separate in roast, but flavour is not impaired (East Africa).

Left: Over-fermented beans.

Elephant bean Slang name for Maragogype variety, the world's largest coffee beans; generally prized for appearance, good roast, smooth flavour; gradually dying out as financially unprofitable. Not to be confused with the malformed elephant/elephant ear bean.

Floater Underripe, or overripe bean, or brown bean that surfaces in washing – lacks density.

Foxy Off-flavour from beans either with red tinge, perhaps overripe; over-fermented (delay in pulping); yellow cherry; frost.

Hard bean Fairly mediocre *arabica* beans, indicates lower altitudes in countries where "strictly hard bean" is the best quality; not to be confused, however, with "hard" flavour.

Hull coffee Dry-processed beans before hulling has removed the surrounding dried cherries.

M'buni East African word for dry-processed (sun-dried) cherry. Also over-fruity, tart, sour flavour.

Natural bean Denotes dry-processed coffee bean.

Above: Insect-damaged beans.

Pale Yellow in colour, from immature cherries or drought-affected; will not darken satisfactorily in roast; unpleasant nutty flavour of several can spoil batch (*see* Quaker).

Parchment Protective covering or jacket (endocarp) encasing bean within the cherry, which must be intact if bean is to germinate; also "pergamino".

Parchment coffee Wet-processed beans before hulling has removed their parchment coverings.

Peaberry Also, perle, perla, caracol; small rounded bean (malformation) produced singly in a small cherry; sorted together they command a higher price than normal beans, even ones from the same trees.

Pod Beans still encased in the dried cherry after hulling, constitutes defect in sample.

Above: Pulper-nipped beans.

Pulper-nipped Bean damaged during pulping; subsequent appearance can lower quality assessment.

Quaker Similar to Pale, but not caused by immaturity, although terms are sometimes used interchangeably (*see* Pale).

Ragged Bean not fully developed due to drought.

Stinker Overripe cherry; or over-fermentation; insect- or microbe-damaged bean; bean flavour is powerfully pervasive and rotten, sour odour when crushed; undetectable by human eye, but glows under ultraviolet light of electric sorting machines; contaminates entire batch.

Strictly hard bean (SHB) Quality *arabicas* grown at highest altitudes, where density of bean concentrates flavour.

Strictly high grown (SHG) Different grading terminology for basically the same conditions as strictly hard bean.

Triage Lowest grade of coffee, never exported; left-overs; figurative factory floor sweepings.

Unwashed Dry-processed beans.

Washed Wet-processed beans.

Yellow bean In *arabica*, bean colour caused by over-drying.

COFFEE TASTING

Coffee tasting, also called "cupping", is the sensory evaluation of coffee, which assesses more than just taste; the senses of smell, taste and "feel" are all involved. Smell and taste are very dependent on each other and difficult to separate in assessment; of course, there are some coffees that will not taste as they smell, but in general the attribute of flavour can be interpreted almost as much as an aroma as a taste, and an aroma is a very good indication of the taste to follow. There are four basic tastes – salt, sweet, acid and bitter – and most specific tastes fall into one of these categories. The sense of feel involved in assessing coffee evaluates the coffee's body – its weight, fullness and texture in the mouth.

Coffee beans are regularly tasted all along the market route, though the really serious tasting is done when the coffee is graded, in its country of origin, and at a second stage when it is sold to the importing country.

Evaluating the Flavour

First, prepare the samples and equipment needed: identical cups (ideally) for each coffee to be tasted; the coffee samples and a coffee measure; another empty cup; a spoon (silver is traditional) about the size and shape of a soup spoon, or shallower; a glass of water in which to rinse the spoon between coffees; a glass of room-temperature water (or a water biscuit or cracker) for clearing the palate; a jug (pitcher) or spittoon (garboon is the specialist term); and a kettle of very hot water, just under boiling point.

• Plan to taste at least two coffees, as a frame of reference.
• Grind should be medium ("cafetière/percolator" grind). If the coffees are ground in succession in the same grinder, start with a clean grinder and wipe out the grinder between samples.
• If the tasting is a true comparison, the degree of roast should be as much the same for all samples as possible; if tasting is simply to choose a preferred coffee, taste every coffee in whatever style or roast it comes supplied. The lighter the roast, the more the true

unique flavour of the coffee is exposed; the darker the roast, the more all coffees begin to taste the same, and the easier it is to hide the flaws. In a darker roast, the coffee tastes less acidic, but since acidity is the main indicator of altitude, quality and price, it is a shame if the expensive acidity disappears in the roaster.
• Measure out the same amount of dry coffee into each cup, about 8g/1 heaped tbsp to 150ml/5fl oz/²/₃ cup water. Sniff the dry coffees. Write down any noteworthy observation about the dry smell. It is always advisable to arrange the coffees in an orderly row for tasting, placing those that may be the strongest – particularly if any *robustas* are to be tasted – at the end.
• Pour water just off the boil to the same level in each cup. Do not stir. Wait a couple of minutes, then bend over each cup and smell the surface, which is a mass of floating grounds.
• Break the crust (the grounds floating on the surface of the cup), by inserting the tasting spoon through the surface flotsam, again while bending over the cup and inhaling the aroma at very

close range. You could spoon up and smell some of the grounds and liquid from the bottom of the cup – this action will probably help to settle the grounds as much as anything.
• With the spoon, lightly skim any remaining grounds off the coffee's surface and discard into the extra empty cup. (Dipping the tasting spoon into the glass of rinsing water will get rid of any grounds left on it.)
• Get a medium-full spoonful of coffee, place it against the lips and virtually inhale it, with plenty of air and into the mouth, slurping noisily, attempting to get some of it all the way to the back of the mouth immediately. Swish it around the mouth, and after a few seconds, spit the liquid out. Make some notes for later comparison, rinse the spoon and go on to the next coffee.
• Try to taste all the coffees at the same temperature and in close conjunction with each other. As the coffees cool, go back and taste them again, as the flavours may change slightly.

Below: A professional coffee taster with the samples of brewed coffee.

Coffee Tasters' Terminology

This list may seem a little daunting, but remember that what you are looking for in a good cup of coffee is essentially body, aroma and flavour. Choose a coffee that you like and see what you can detect. Alternatively, try coffee where the taste is not as it should be, and compare it with a good brew to try to see where the differences lie.

Acidic Very desirable coffee quality, sharpness detected towards front of mouth; denotes quality and altitude; can be fruity (citrusy, lemony, berry-like, etc) or a pure tongue-tip numbing sensation (Costa Rica, Kenya, Mexico offer good examples).

Aftertaste/finish Flavour/mouthfeel remaining after coffee has left the mouth, sometimes surprisingly different from actual coffee taste.

Aromatic Coffee with intense pleasant fragrance (for example, Hawaii, Colombia, Jamaica, Sumatra).

Ashy Coffee with flavour/aroma of cold fireplace ashes.

Astringent Mouthfeel characteristic that "draws" the tongue and tissues, often apparent as after-taste.

Bitter Basic flavour sensation detected at the back of the mouth and soft-palate, often as after-taste, sometimes desirable to a limited degree (as in dark-roast, espresso). Not to be confused with acidity.

Above: The basic taste of coffee is made up of body, aroma and flavour.

Blackcurrant Flavour reminiscent of blackcurrant or berries; some acidity but with stronger undertones not found in citrusy, highly acidic coffees; not a negative term.

Body Signifies the perception of texture or weight of liquid in the mouth; thin or light body can feel watery (a few high-grown *arabicas*); full-bodied means heavy liquor, as in Sumatra, Java, and most *robustas*.

Broth-like Pleasant flavour in some lighter East African coffees similar to clear soup, like bouillon, often accompanies slightly citrusy flavour.

Burnt Carbon-type flavour and aroma, as in burnt toast; over-roasted.

Caramel Sweet flavour reminiscent of caramelized sugar, or, slightly different: candy floss (cotton candy).

Cerealy Flavour like unsweetened grain or oatmeal, sometimes found in under-roasted *robusta* coffee, bland and not particularly pleasant.

Cheesy Rather pungent flavour/aroma of slightly sour, curdled milk or cheese.

Chemical/medicinal Coffee with unnatural off-flavours, real or reminiscent of tainting.

Right: Where it all starts – with the whole roasted coffee beans.

Chocolaty Flavour reminiscent of chocolate, which can be found in various crops (some Australian, New Guinean and Ethiopian, for example).

Citrus Flavour reminiscent of citrus fruits due to high acidity; very desirable, denotes quality and high-altitude growth.

Clean Pure coffee flavour, no twists or changes in the mouth, no different after-taste (Costa Rica sometimes provides good examples).

Dirty Coffee tasting as if the beans have been rolled in dirt or soiled.

Dry A certain type of acidity and/or mouthfeel, but not, as in wine, the opposite of sweet; often accompanies light, or even delicate coffees, such as Mexican, Ethiopian and Yemeni.

Dusty Dry-earth taste and smell, exactly like dust, though not the same as dirty or earthy.

Earthy Aroma/flavour reminiscent of damp black earth, organic, mushroomy, cellar-like (can be found, for example, in some Javan or Sumatran coffees "gone wrong").

Floral Coffee beans having a very fresh, floral, heady aroma, like that of floral-scented perfume.

Fruity Flavour/aroma often found in good *arabica* coffees, reminiscent of a wide range of fruits: citrus, berries, currants, etc, always accompanied by some degree of acidity; this is usually positive, but can indicate overripeness or over-fermentation.

Gamey Unusual and interesting flavour, often found in dry-processed East African coffees (such as Ethiopian Djimmah), reminiscent of cheesy, but not sour or negative.

Grassy Green and astringent aroma with an accompanying taste like a new-mown lawn, sometimes found in coffees from Malawi and Rwanda.

Green Aroma/taste of unripe fruit or plants, as when green stems or leaves are crushed or broken; can denote under-roasting.

Hard Flavour, not to be confused with hard bean. In terms of flavour, hard signifies a brew lacking sweetness and softness.

Harsh Strong, unpleasant, sharp or "edgy" flavour; also used to describe Rio-y, iodine-like flavour.

Hidey Aroma/taste like animal hides, uncured leather, or, at best, new leather shoes.

Lemony Flavour very like mild lemon found in very acidic coffee, such as that from Kenya.

Light, mild Light-bodied coffee, pleasant low-to-medium acidity. Some Mexican, Honduran and Santo Domingan coffees exhibit these characteristics.

Malty Coffee flavour very like malted barley, sometimes in combination with chocolaty, sometimes alone.

Mellow Soft, with pleasant low acidity.

Metallic Sharpness, acidity slightly "gone wrong". Some Nicaraguan coffee, for example, can be overly metallic.

Mocha, mokka *Arabica* coffee originally named for the old port of Yemen, now also associated with Ethiopian Harrar coffee. Nothing to do with chocolate, although coffee drinks with mocha imply chocolate with coffee.

Musty Flavour of improper drying, mildew, generally undesirable.

Neutral Bland coffee, very low acidity, not derogatory, as implies no off-tastes; good for blending (often describes many ordinary Brazilian *arabicas*).

Nutty Pleasant flavour reminiscent of nuts, often peanuts (some Jamaican).

Papery A taste/aroma exactly like dry paper, slightly similar to dusty.

Phenolic Flavour/aroma so medicinal as to cause olfactory sensation reminiscent of phenol.

Rancid/rotten The flavour of a spoiled oily product, as in rancid nuts or rancid olive oil; fairly disgusting; can cause involuntary gagging.

Rio-y Iodine, inky flavour from microbe-tainted beans. Prized for traditional brewing in Turkey, Greece, Middle East.

Rounded Cup balance with no overpowering characteristic, well-balanced; can also mean pleasantly smooth, without being sharp.

Rubber Aroma/taste reminiscent of tyres, garages, often detected in certain *robustas*, for example.

Sacky Coffee tainted by improper storage, flavour/aroma of hemp, possibly damp.

Salty One of four basic tasting categories, occurs occasionally in coffee; also can denote presence of chicory in coffee blend.

Smoky Aromatic flavour of woodsmoke, very pleasant attribute sometimes found in certain coffees such as some from Guatemala and also occasionally some Indonesian *arabicas*.

Smooth Mouthfeel not sharp or astringent, pleasant, sometimes combines with winey flavour.

Soft/strictly soft Coffee with low acidity, mellow sweetness, pleasant roof-of-the-mouth easiness (possibly similar to the feel of Italian red Lambrusco wine); some Brazilian Santos, for example.

Sour Undesirable "dirty socks" flavour of over-fermentation.

Spicy Aroma/taste of spice, perhaps sweetish or peppery, found in certain coffees, such as those from Java, Zimbabwe, Guatemala; or the more erratic Yemen and Ethiopian coffees.

Stalky This gives a flavour reminiscent of dry vegetable matter or other plant material stalks.

Stinky Rotten flavour indicating possible contamination by "stinker" bean.

Sweet Pleasant, mellow, agreeable; sometimes used to describe soft coffees, but also can be found in highly acidic coffees.

Thin Term when coffee's body does not equal acidity or flavour; out-of-balance, watery, wishy-washy in mouthfeel.

Tobacco-y Aroma/flavour characteristic of unsmoked plug (chewing) tobacco.

Turpentine-y Smell or taste reminiscent of chemical, possibly phenolic-like substance.

Well-rounded, well-balanced Cup giving impression of good mix of flavour, acidity, body, and perhaps aroma.

Wild Term describing certain Ethiopian/Yemeni coffees – suggesting unusual, inconsistent, and interesting; sometimes used with spicy; also exotic, tangy, complex.

Winey Combination of slightly fruity flavour, very smooth mouthfeel and texture reminiscent of wine. Term should not be used indiscriminately to denote acidity; better reserved for coffees with genuine feel (more than taste) of wine, slightly rare but unmistakable (in some Kenyan as after-taste; found in some Ethiopian Harrars, Yemeni and various others).

Woody Flavour peculiar to either dead (indicating old crop, coffee stored too long) or green wood flavour found in certain coffees, like fresh sawdust; neither very pleasant.

Yeasty/toasty Flavour reminiscent of either yeasty (unbaked) bread, or bread lightly toasted.

Left: Roasting coffee darker can hide the less desirable characteristics of a coffee sample that may not be of the highest quality.

COFFEE-PRODUCING COUNTRIES

Today, because of increased communication and improved transportation, the world now appears very small, and almost anything is accessible to those who want it. It is, therefore, remarkable how much the coffee trade seems still to follow the old colonial routes. The explanation for this is to be found in the national coffee taste preferences established during periods when European powers supported, or exploited, their own colonies, either by using the plants indigenous to the colony, or by introducing certain crops desirable or profitable for the mother country.

If coffee, an extremely lucrative and sought-after commodity, was not native to a colony, its cultivation was often quickly encouraged and nurtured. For example, much of the coffee consumed in France today contains a surprisingly large amount of *robusta*, the coffee variety produced in those West African countries that made up much of France's empire and were, geographically – important in the days of shipping – France's nearest colonies.

Because of the activities of the British East India Company, which traded coffee among Eastern countries, but introduced tea to India and Britain, Britain drank far more tea than coffee from the mid-1700s. The British colonial acquisitions during the late 1800s and after World War I were primarily concentrated in East Africa, all *arabica*-growing regions; and, along with that from Jamaica, the coffee Britain consumed was primarily *arabica*. Even today, although many British coffee companies import *robusta*, they will seldom admit to doing so, as the overall preferred taste in Britain is for *arabica*.

Portugal, the great power in early exploration and colonization, did not retain many of its early colonies, although today it is still the main buyer for its last coffee-growing colonies, Angola and Cape Verde, which it gave up in 1975; Mozambique, also lost that year, basically stopped growing coffee when the Portuguese colonists pulled out. Portugal lost Brazil quite early on when the colony became independent in 1822, being an indirect result of Napoleon's invasion of Portugal.

North America, made up of colonies itself and a melting pot of all nations, is also a melting pot of coffee, with a wide range of coffee preferences, and also accommodating virtually all tastes.

The production figures used in the following coffee-producing country profiles are based on the information received at the time of publication.

Right: One of the best ways to familiarize yourself with the many different types of coffee available is to think about the countries that grow coffee, and to sort them into a few main coffee-growing regions. This book has grouped coffee growers into four principal regions: Africa; Central America and the Caribbean; South America; and the South Pacific and South-east Asia.

The map opposite shows all of the countries covered in the following pages, highlighting the main types of coffee grown there: arabica, robusta, a combination of these two, and the new hybridizations.

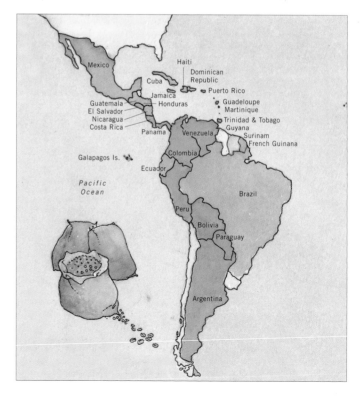

In some cases the estimated statistics given in the country profiles may differ from the information given at the back of the book, which represent the latest total figures for the 1998/99 crop year. Coffee bag figures represent a unit of 60kg/132lb of green coffee, no matter what size bag is actually used in any particular country. Also, exportable production figures may differ from those of actual exports, as green coffee can be stored for some time before shipment. The ICO expects the 1998/99 global coffee crop to be a very good harvest of about 105,241,000 bags. The statistics of coffee-producing countries who are not members of the International Coffee Organization are not included in this figure.

Right: Every year nearly 80 million bags of coffee are exported around the world.

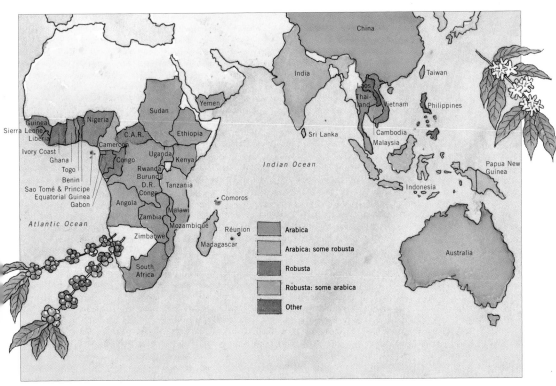

Arabica

Arabica: some robusta

Robusta

Robusta: some arabica

Other

AFRICA

As the birthplace of coffee, it is fitting that the continent of Africa produces some of the world's finest coffees. In many countries, however, social, political and economic problems make the production of coffee a difficult task.

Angola

In the 18th century Portuguese colonists began coffee cultivation in what is now the People's Republic of Angola. Although *robusta* is not generally a word associated with high quality, that is exactly what differentiates the best of Angola's *robusta* (Ambriz and Amboin) from that of other countries. The beans are uniform in size and colour, cleanly processed (mostly by the dry method), sorted and carefully graded. The *robusta* is grown on shaded trees in the northern plains, approaching the delta of the Congo River. Angola's inland plateau has a far more temperate climate than the plains, and an altitude of 1,800m/5,905ft allows some cultivation of *arabica* coffee, which is mild, unassumingly neutral, and in blending could easily substitute for an average-quality Brazilian Santos. Since the devastation of the civil war, however, it is very scarce; before the 1994 peace treaty, production sank to 33,000 bags, compared to 3.5 million bags in 1973.

Benin (formerly Dahomey)

Shaped a bit like a vertical house key, Benin can really only grow coffee in the south, its least arid zone, where many smallholders intersperse the coffee trees with palms. Although Benin's coffee – *robusta* and some *arabusta* – is too small a crop to list as a percentage of world production, it still probably exports more coffee than it grows, due to smuggling activities with Nigeria.

Burundi

Coffee brings far more income to this small land-locked African country than any other commodity. Indeed, its citizens, while appreciating the very good washed *arabica*, of which Burundi grows more than *robusta*, will consume less than one per cent, preferring the

earnings from exporting the rest, which is good quality, clean, well-graded, and has both good acidic flavour and body. However, there is some concern over future production of coffee due to tribal unrest.

Above: Burundi superior full wash, top quality green beans.

Cameroon

Cameroon is known as a producer of *robusta* coffee, although about one-third of its crop is the Blue Mountain variety of *arabica*, which is grown in the western volcanic regions. Primarily wet-processed, at one time the *arabica* coffees produced on the European plantations equalled the high-quality coffees of Central America. The *robusta* growths, first brought from Zaire, are grown now in all the provinces except in the extreme north.

Cape Verde

Cape Verde, the Windward and Leeward Islands off the extreme west coast of Africa, is not a member of the International Coffee Organization, so

no statistics are available on its current coffee production. The Portuguese, who dominated these islands from the 15th century until 1975, first planted *arabica* trees in 1790. The gradual transformation of the islands to desert, due to severe droughts, has reduced coffee growing in the volcanic soil from various heights to only the higher mountainsides, at altitudes between 500–900m/1,500–2,700ft. There is no hydroelectric power, and no irrigation is possible, so water is precious and scarce, but the humidity from the fog generated by the north-west trade winds sustains the few remaining coffee trees, which also serve as windbreaks and soil erosion deterrents. In a good year the dry-processed coffee yield may be sufficient to export, mostly to Portugal, but the islanders, coffee-drinkers themselves, actually have to resort to importing coffee, mostly from Angola, to satisfy local demand.

Central African Republic

The Central African Republic, which used to be part of French Equatorial Africa, still sells most of its coffee, a very important cash crop for the country, to France. Italy is its other main buyer. The *robusta* varieties are the usual *canephora* and the more interesting *Nana robusta*, first discovered growing wild on the banks of the Nana River in the extreme western region. The coffee is carefully classified, and consistent in quality and

Above: Cameroon robusta green beans.

roast, but because the country is land-locked, any problems in steady availability are due to transportation difficulties. The debilitating coffee disease tracheomycosis originated here.

Comoros

Between the Mozambique coast and the island of Madagascar lie four small islands that were under French control for many years. Today they make up the

Federal and Islamic Republic of the Comoros, although one of them, Mayotte, opted to remain under French territorial administration. Coffee, mostly *robusta*, is grown on Mayotte and Mohéli islands, shaded by banana and coconut trees. The quality of the hand-picked dry-processed beans is not bad, and about two-thirds of the small crop (often less than 1,000 bags) is exported. The remainder satisfies the high consumption demands of the local population, about 700,000 people.

Congo

This country of nine provinces includes a small section of Atlantic coastline and was once the middle part of French Equatorial Africa. The Equator runs across the top third of the country and its climate is basically the non-varying heat and humidity of equatorial regions. The all-*robusta* crop produced by the republic seems to be increasing. Unusually, the average-to-good coffee is not graded by size, as the beans are generally uniform, but rather by number of defective beans, of which the top grade Extra Prima has none. The cup quality is that of an average-to-good robusta, neutral and clean.

Democratic Republic of Congo

The former country of Zaire grows *robusta*, mostly of the Marchand type, but far more interesting to the specialist coffee trade is the *arabica* crop, which makes up less than 20 per cent of the harvest. These trees are grown at a very high altitude in the mountainous plateau regions of Kivu province, where the land rises towards the volcanic mountains marking the edge of the Great Rift Valley, and the lake-studded borders shared with Tanzania, Burundi, Rwanda and Uganda.

Most of the wet-processed *arabicas*, of good, bright blue or blue-green colour and consistent appearance, have remarkably few defects. At best the Kivu *arabicas* can be described as a fine,

Left: Cash cropping. In many countries the exportation of coffee provides most of the income from foreign sources.

perfect balance of good body and acidity, and the Maragogype is an extremely pleasant soft coffee.

Unfortunately, the coffee crop of the Democratic Republic of Congo has been decreasing gradually over the past decade. The larger plantations are poorly maintained, and the finest coffees, grown in a region rife with tribal warfare and tracheomycosis, must be transported through other countries on the land-locked eastern border before exportation from the Indian Ocean ports. The Kivu arabicas are thus extremely rare to find. The new Kabila regime intends to rebuild a free market economy, hopefully supportive of greater coffee production.

Equatorial Guinea

Coffee is second only to cocoa in importance for this beautiful country, which consists of five islands and a bit of continental West Africa. The coffee is mostly *robusta* and *liberica*, but *arabica* is also grown. Independence in 1968 after 190 years of Spanish rule led only to disastrous dictatorships, and today, in spite of its fertile, rich soil, Equatorial Guinea's reduced production of coffee (and cocoa) has not recovered. The country has resumed relations with Spain, buyer of almost its entire crop.

Ethiopia

The earliest accounts of coffee all refer to its being a native of this region of old Abyssinia; indeed, the coffee processed

Right: Kivu arabica beans from the Democratic Republic of Congo.

today by many Ethiopian villagers is simply picked off untended, wild bushes. Although an extremely poor country, suffering from an infrastructure destroyed by civil war and racked by periodic serious droughts, Ethiopia is a significant producer of coffee, both in quantity and quality, still managing to export some of the world's finest and most individual coffees, some of which have a very low natural caffeine content. The regions growing the best coffees are generally the Sidamo, Kaffa, Harrar and Wellega, but within each region some coffees are traditionally unwashed (naturals) and some are washed. In general, the unwashed coffees may be described as wild or gamey in flavour, not a taste to everyone's liking, but extremely interesting, if variable. At times, other terms, such as lemony, delicate, winey, floral and soft may be applied to certain Ethiopian coffees. In appearance, the beans are not only unimpressive, but may be downright off-putting, and in some cases the processing is a bit haphazard, if not careless, resulting in a maddening unpredictability. Nevertheless, these coffees are not run-of-the-mill and may represent the epitome – in other words,

as good as it gets – of coffee-tasting. Some of the best-known Ethiopian coffees are Djimmah, Ghimbi, Lekempti, Harrar (both long berry and short berry, known for their soft, winey Mocha flavour – a name stolen from the old Yemeni port of Mokka), Limu, and Yergacheffe.

Due to the unique, wonderfully delicate flavours, it is never a wise thing to dark-roast Ethiopian beans. In fact, to come across these beans dark-roasted might suggest an inferior crop for that year's production.

Gabon

The former French colony still sells much of its crop of decent, neutral *robusta* to France, and the rest to the Netherlands. Interestingly, much of Gabon's coffee is grown in the north, and as it occasionally seems to export more than it grows, there is a strong possibility that the more enterprising Equatorial Guineans, on the north-west border, smuggle beans into Gabon, where the small, mostly urban population enjoys relative prosperity due to oil-rich natural resources.

Below: Ethiopian Djimmah roasted beans.

Above: Ethiopian Sidamo grade 2 washed medium-roasted beans.

Ghana

Formerly the "Gold Coast" British colony, Ghana provides 15 per cent of the world's cocoa, which is cheaper to grow than coffee. In areas where the soil is not favourable for cocoa, however, the government encourages coffee cultivation. Although the coffee is rather nondescript *robusta*, it is bought mainly by Britain, Germany and The Netherlands.

Above: Ghanaian robusta *medium roast.*

Guinea

In 1895, the French introduced *arabica* from Tonkin to their colony, but the yield was poor; the climate and soil of this republic (since 1958) however, grows good "neutral" *robusta* in its forest shades. Unfortunately, 25 years of Marxist dictatorial rule broke many trade connections between Guinea and Western countries, and today rivalry between ethnic groups, questionable legislative elections, as well as crippling world debts, have not been conducive to re-establishing the stable trade needed to improve coffee quality or quantity. Some Guinean coffee finds its way into the Ivory Coast, its neighbour to the east.

Ivory Coast (Côte d'Ivoire)

The Ivory Coast is usually Africa's second-largest coffee producer. Thirty-three years of a stable one-man presidency, with a relatively smooth transition to another seemingly stable leader, plus monetary and defence aid from its former ruler, France, have helped to provide the stability that a long-

term, labour-intensive industry such as coffee requires. The rather average quality and its consistent and reliable supply make Ivory Coast *robusta* attractive to many coffee blenders throughout the world, although France and Italy buy much of the crop (which may include beans smuggled in from its neighbours, poor, land-locked Mali to the north, and Guinea to the west). An agricultural research centre near Abidjan recently developed *arabusta*, the most successful coffee hybrid yet produced.

Kenya

For quality rather than quantity, Kenya's high-grown, wet-processed *arabica* is one of the world's great growths. The fairly narrow range of flavours is good and consistent, probably because the Kenyan industry is strictly regulated by the Coffee Board of Kenya (Nairobi), which determines the grading of each bag of green beans, at times even blending together green beans from different plantations under the House Blend label. Those bags marked "AA" are the top quality and are sought-after by the gourmet coffee trade. Kenyan coffee is noted for its sharp, fruity, sometimes even lemony or citrus flavours, due to high acidity, and for the consistent (small, round and deep greeny-blue) appearance of the beans, be they AA, the more commonly exported AB, or the celebrated and expensive Kenyan peaberries.

Above: Kenyan peaberry green beans.

Liberia

What can be said about a country that in 1980 had 165,000 bags – though not all of it traceable to its own coffee plantations – of exportable coffee, and now produces less than 5,000? Though the quality was never particularly good, the *robusta* was usable – the USA bought most of it – which is more than could be said for the native *liberica*. There were high hopes for the *arabusta* possibilities, and a soluble-coffee factory was planned. Unfortunately, warring factions and corruption of power have led to a total economic collapse in recent years.

Madagascar

Coffee is Madagascar's most important export, although the island is the leading world producer of vanilla. A French colony until 1960, Madagascar, after 18 years of radical socialism, is now a multi-party democracy trying to re-establish its ties with Western trade and rebuild its agricultural programmes. The larger *robusta* growth is ranged along the slopes of the long eastern coastline, while the *arabica* regions are on the central plateau. Generally, the coffee, much of which is bought by France, is excellent, and there are plans to

Above: Ivory Coast robusta *grade 2.*

develop more plantations, especially as the more-than-14-million residents are enthusiastic drinkers. Part of any future plans for coffee expansion, however, is the desire to preserve the forests, home to unique species of flora and fauna.

Malawi

When Malawi (formerly Nyasaland) became independent from British rule in 1964, it spent nearly thirty years under the rule of one despot, Banda. Now, under stable multi-party rule, poverty is still endemic, but human rights, education and literacy – all conducive to the labour-intensive business of growing coffee – are iincreasing. The *arabica* coffee is grown mostly on small-holdings and processed locally in the mountainous plateaux at the extreme ends of this long, narrow country. Drought eclipses all other problems, but it is hoped that more of this excellent coffee, reminiscent of an average Kenyan, will be available for world consumption in the near future.

Above: Malawian medium-roast beans.

Mozambique

Portugal used this colony to grow tea, while its coffee-growing colony was Angola. Consequently, the *arabica* (Blue Mountain variety) grown here, supplemented by the wild *racemosa*, meets only local demands. After independence in 1975 and a 15-year civil war, Mozambique is one of the poorest countries in the world. Now, with a fragile democracy and many millions in aid pledges, there is a remote possibility that someday Mozambique could be an exporter of

good coffee once again, as it has not only the climate and soil, but also the second-largest harbour in Africa.

Nigeria

Unfortunately, there is little positive to say about this country's coffee. The mostly *robusta* crop is of poor and inconsistent quality, although Britain is one of the main buyers of its former colony's crop. Smuggling, corruption, crime, debt, pollution and aid-stopping human rights violations have helped to shrink the economy since the oil-rich boom of the 1970s, which the various military regimes sadly allowed to totally eclipse the more long-term government agricultural support.

La Réunion

Today, the main crop of this small volcanic island 805km/500 miles east of Madagascar is sugarcane. How very different from the days when coffee planting was mandatory of all free citizens, when destroying a tree exacted the death penalty, and when the monetary currency was backed by coffee! The island of Bourbon, as the French colony was then named, gave its name to the oldest, and still best, variety of *arabica* coffee, and it was from two trees brought here from Yemen in 1715 that many of the world's coffee plantations originated.

Rwanda

German and Belgian colonizers reinforced Tutsi domination here, and since a Hutu government achieved independence in 1962, there has been violent, if at times intermittent, tribal warfare. The *arabica* coffee quality is generally good, although it could be said it almost suffers from excess; the extremely rich soil, abundant rainfall, strong sun and quick growth may be the collective cause of a peculiar grassy taste sometimes found in all but the superior grade. Coffee is still very much Rwanda's primary source of income, and in spite of the warfare and pest infestations, its production is increasing. The Rwanda Coffee Board currently plans to rehabilitate 76 of the 140

Above: Freshly picked cherries show a mix of both ripe and immature fruit.

coffee-growing communes by providing fertilizers, pesticides and new high-yielding plants.

St Helena

This South Atlantic island, the only dependency still receiving British budgetary aid, was annexed by the East India Company in 1659 and began growing coffee when seeds were brought from Yemen in 1732. At some point the cultivation was abandoned, and the only remaining trees were wild.

Although at present the island's main economic activities cannot support the population, an enterprising coffee roaster in the 1980s began the revitalization of a tiny coffee industry which may soon become noted for hand-produced, totally organic, good-acidity and balanced, quality coffee.

São Tomé & Príncipe

Although cocoa brings in 90 per cent of São Tomé's export earnings, it still produces coffee, most of which is a reputedly lovely *arabica*, grown in the rich soil sloping up to the island's volcano. Since the Marxist regime, which greatly reduced coffee-growing, was replaced by a democratic constitution in 1990, the islands are seeking closer relations with various Western countries, in particular their old colonizer, Portugal, and the United States, so perhaps more of this coffee will become available on world markets.

Sierra Leone

Another sad story of a country decimated by military coups and civil war. Until as late as 1985, the *robusta* grown in this former British colony of freed slaves was some of the best of African blending coffee – FAQ (Fair Average Quality) and neutral (an important term for *robusta*) in the cup.

South Africa

For a long time South Africa has grown some good quality *arabica* coffee, cultivated from plants of the Bourbon and Blue Mountain variety, originally brought from Kenya. The region of growth is mostly that of Kwa-Zulu Natal,

which, with Southern Brazil, is one of the few regions that dares to grow coffee outside of the tropical zone. There are many reasons, however, to doubt that much of the coffee grown here will ever reach the world market: the 1996 constitution is decidedly fragile, and racial tensions and personal dangers run high; the country is heavily

populated and, indeed, has to import much of the coffee it consumes; and much of the international trading is based on lucrative mineral and mining resources. The labour-intensive coffee production and accompanying slow profit turnover do not seem encouraging to those lovers of good coffee around the world.

Above: Picked coffee cherries lose skin and pulp in wet-process pulping machines.

Above: Drying coffee cherries must be raked and turned to dry evenly and thoroughly before hulling.

Sudan

This country is blessed with high altitudes, and wild coffee, probably spread by bird and beast from Ethiopia, already grows there. However, the ambitious plans of a few years past to grow more of this excellent *arabica*, have sadly come to little. A series of problems, from civil wars, droughts, disease and starvation, through to international isolation due to concerns for human rights and terrorism, have resulted in the decimation of any coffee industry whatsoever.

Tanzania

Although Tanzania is still a very poor country, in almost every area of activity it is improving. An economic reform programme has helped to cut inflation and the budget deficit, and IMF-backed aid is helping to reorganize the agricultural sector. Coffee is Tanzania's number one crop, but where previously most of the *arabica* coffee was produced on large estates, leaving *robusta* production to the smallholders, today many smallholders with access to the equipment of a co-operative are able to grow *arabica* coffee. The washed

coffee is excellent, reminiscent of Kenyan coffee, but the acidity is less intense and the overall feel slightly milder and lighter; also the quality is not quite as consistent as that of Kenyan beans. The older bourbon variety still produces the best flavour, aroma and body. Moshi, near Mount Kilimanjaro, is a main coffee-marketing centre in an area where many smallholders grow a combined crop of coffee shaded by banana trees.

Togo

Togo's coffee story is happily different from many other former colonies in Africa. The democratic government and efficient civil service encourage and help the cultivation of the rather ordinary, but well-graded, dry-processed neutral *robusta*. It produces a fairly large harvest, considering that Togo is a very small country. Its own domestic coffee consumption is low,

Right: Tanzanian Chagga.

so it can export most of what it grows and it is happy to diversify its market, selling its coffee to various European buyers, including its former colonizer France, although the Dutch often take the bulk of the crop.

Togo maintains a good road system, and its capital is a coastal port, which can make a real difference to the success of a coffee crop. Although the country has few natural resources, its citizens, particularly the market-women of Lomé, who basically control the country's retail trade, are enterprising.

Uganda

Since 1986, President Museveni's "no-party democracy" has thus far saved Uganda from the ethnic tensions that have destroyed the economies of neighbours Rwanda and Sudan, from which thousands of refugees have poured into Uganda. Economic liberalizations have attracted aid receipts and private sector investments; the road system is under repair, and coffee production, mostly *robusta*, is high. Financial experts know that one crop providing 93 per cent of a country's export earnings is not always healthy. However, it is great news for coffee lovers, as a small percentage of tea-drinking Uganda's coffee is very good washed *arabica*, grown mostly in the Bugisu region adjoining the border with Kenya (whose coffee is very similar). Indeed, before privatization, some *arabica* beans were smuggled into Kenya for its better, unregulated prices; since privatization some *arabica* is now smuggled to avoid the Ugandan government's tax.

Above: Uganda arabica Bugisu AA green beans.

Yemen

As Arabia (Arabia Felix to the Romans), this small country gave its name to *arabica* coffee, which was introduced to the world through its ports. Lying on the eastern shores of the Red Sea, geographically it is Asian, but in reality the general coffee character is closer to those of its nearest coffee-growing neighbour, Ethiopia.

Mocha coffee Yemeni coffees are the original Mocha, taken from the name of the old port, today's Al Mukha. "Mocha"

Above: Yemeni roasted mocha 31.

coffees grown in Ethiopia (notably Harrar and Djimmah), are the impostors, although the tastes, like those of unwashed *arabicas*, may be similar to the Yemeni flavours: wild, gamey, winey, dry, delicate, varied and unpredictable, possibly with some chocolate overtones. They are, however, different coffees; the Ethiopian mochas will be cheaper, as the true Yemeni beans, even the most common (Sanani, from San`a, and Matari, from the province of Bany Matar) are quite scarce.

After Yemen sided with Iraq in the Gulf War, Saudi Arabia expelled a million Yemeni workers, whose return so burdened the government that it stopped many farm subsidies and farmers began growing the more profitable narcotic *qat* plants. Also, the political instability that resulted in a civil war in 1994 is still disruptive to the Yemen economy.

Zambia

Unlike some other African countries, Zambia's problems do not seem to be political (other than the one of bureaucratic corruption) or racial; its weakness is the fact that it is dependent

Above: Zambia green beans.

on copper for 90 per cent of its export earnings, and copper prices have fallen and Zambia's reserves are declining. Perhaps because it is land-locked and lacks a good road network, Zambia's arable land is under-utilized. At any rate, the government seems committed to market reforms, and certainly its encouragement of more cultivation of the excellent Zambian coffees is resulting in greater crops. Zambian coffee is similar in flavour to other East African *arabicas*; its lightness is particularly reminiscent of coffee from Tanzania, with whom it shares its northern border near the coffee-growing Muchinga Mountains.

Above: Zimbabwe dark-roasted beans.

Zimbabwe

Although much of land-locked Zimbabwe is a high-altitude country, rainfall is erratic and drought common, except in the mountains of the eastern region near the Mozambique border, where most of its fine washed *arabica* coffee is grown. Coffee from Zimbabwe, the best of which is found near the town of Chipinge, may not be as famous as Kenyan, but it shares many of the same cup characteristics: it is generally free from off-tastes, and has fruity acidity and good aroma; it may also have a slightly peppery flavour not found in coffee from Kenya.

Like Malawian coffee, it is sometimes recognized as a gourmet coffee by the speciality coffee trade, depending on the particular crop. Whether the government's repeated declarations to nationalize farms and plantations will ultimately affect coffee production remains to be seen.

CENTRAL AMERICA AND THE CARIBBEAN

The coffees from Central America are justly renowned for their completeness in terms of body, flavour and aroma.

Costa Rica

Many people hope to go to Heaven when they die; coffee lovers hope to go to Costa Rica. This little Central American republic enjoys the best possible conditions for growing superb coffee: a high-altitude central plateau (the Meseta Central) basking in a mild, temperate climate with good moisture and cool nights, and covering about 5,000km²/2,000 sq miles; rich volcanic-based soil; ports on two oceans; and a stable, organized, commercially oriented government. Of course, Costa Rica is not problem-free: the inaccessibility of the highest altitudes makes coffee transportation difficult and expensive, and there is always the worry of volcanic activity and the devastating

Above: A traditional Costa Rican painted cart carries the fruit picked on the plateau.

Above: Tuj San Marcos de Tarrazu green beans.

tropical storms that plague Central American existence. Costa Rica, unlike its neighbours, lost only about 90,000 bags of coffee to Hurricane Mitch.

The coffee, Costa Rica's agricultural mainstay, is all washed *arabica* – it is socially unacceptable even to mention the word *robusta* – and natives enjoy a high standard of consumption; in fact, Costa Ricans drink more than twice the amount of coffee consumed in Italy.

Quality coffee The best coffees are generally those from around the capital city of San José, and the nearby towns of Heredia and Alajuela. The Tarrazu region to the south of San José produces some superb coffees of exquisite acidity and "clean" cup liquor. Bags of beans may be labelled by the area, such as Tarrazu's Tres Rios, Dota, and San Marcos, or by owner/estate names, such as FJO Sarchi company, located on the slopes of the Poas volcano. La Minita, Windmill, Henri Tournon (HT) – whose green beans are really turquoise – are names indicative of high altitude and a sharp, tangy acidity, perhaps the most desirable attribute in a cup of coffee. Some experts shriek at the idea of drinking Costa Rican coffee any way but black; however, the sharpest acidity gives a wonderful mild flavour when the coffee is drunk with a little milk or cream.

Costa Rican coffee is almost always very fragrant, and the cup flavour is "clean" and pure. Occasionally, the body in a cup of Costa Rican coffee may err on the thin side, but the flavour is so exquisite, that a thinner liquor can be excused. Sometimes one hears of Costa Rican coffee being dark-roasted. Unless the coffee is below the usual standards, or somehow defective, such a practice should be avoided at all costs, as a darker roast destroys the lovely acidity, and the flavour loses the desired distinctive (and expensive-tasting) qualities.

Right: A dark roast spoils the acidity of Costa Rican beans.

Cuba

Since the collapse of the USSR, Cuba's mainstay in export trade, Cuba's economy has been in recession. Desperate to attract foreign capital, Cuba is allowing some outside investments in the hotel and tourist industry, a showplace for its *arabica* coffees, which are increasing in production, although sugar, of course, is still the main export crop. Cuban coffee, which has been grown since the mid-1700s, is clean and flavourful, and carefully processed and graded. It is marketed under exotic names, which in reality indicate only particular bean-size averages, the largest being Extra Turquino. Cuban coffee is lower in acidity than that of most other Caribbean coffees due to Cuba's lack of high altitudes. It is, however, pleasant in the cup and is best dark-roasted.

Dominican Republic

When Hispaniola was partitioned in 1697 between France and Spain, Spain's share was the eastern two-thirds of the island. Coffee, which has been grown here since the early 1700s, and is still traded under the Santo Domingo name, is not a major crop, but the washed *arabicas* are good. The best coffee, grown in the south-western Barahona region, is known for its acidity and full body. Slightly less acidic but very satisfying in the cup are the soft, full-bodied Bani and Ocoa coffees, from the slopes of the southern end of the central *cordillera*. Cibao are the rather

Below: Cuban Extra Turquino.

average beans. Dark-roasting accents the lovely, mellow sweetness of the Cibao, Bani and Ocoa coffee beans.

El Salvador

This poor country, small and densely populated, precariously nested on top of a seismic zone with 20 volcanoes, possesses no natural resources. Its infrastructure (roads, bridges and electricity) destroyed by eleven years of civil war, it hangs on to its fragile existence by two thin strings: coffee and international aid. With little chance to diversify, the country has relied on its wet-processed *arabica* to bring in 90 per cent of its export earnings in spite of serious attacks of rust and pests.

In October 1998, Hurricane Mitch's torrential rains figuratively washed away at least 150,000 bags of coffee, and probably more was ruined by humidity-induced fungus after the floods abated. Salvador coffee (its trade name) is grown at various levels of altitude, all of it rather high, and is graded

accordingly: the blue-green SHG is the best, with its acidy flavour, medium-to-full body and sweet overtones. "Pipil" is the brand name of a reputedly excellent organic coffee.

Guadeloupe

This little island at the northern end of the Caribbean Windward Islands is caught between wanting complete autonomy from France's Overseas Department while being almost completely dependent on French aid. In 1995, its unemployment was 26 per cent. Because banana prices are extremely unstable, it is now seeking to expand sugar production. Yet it still grows tiny amounts of what must have been a world-class coffee, described by Philippe Jobin as "one of the best 'crus' of the world...hard to replace for lovers of high class coffee". The climate, soil, workforce, expertise and resources are available, so perhaps the gourmet coffee trade could encourage Guadeloupe to bring this coffee back from virtual extinction.

Guatemala

Coffee is the first crop of Central America's largest economy, where 90 per cent of the population still live below the poverty line. The extreme inequalities in wealth and land distribution limit modernization. Coffee is grown on very large, wealthy *haciendas* (estates), and on a few thousand *fincas*, or farms, all owned mostly by *ladinos* (non-Indians), as well as on many thousand subsistence smallholdings worked by poor Indians, mostly in the highlands. Guatemala has not yet

Left: Salvador high-grown coffee, classified according to superior European Preparation standards.

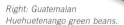

*Right: Guatemalan
Huehuetenango green beans.*

succumbed to the temptation to replace old varieties of trees, such as Bourbon, with high-yield, low-taste varieties, although the low yield per hectare is costly. There are sponsored programmes to help smallholders to minimize their costs, enabling them to continue with high-quality, low-yield trees for the gourmet market.

*Above: Guatemalan genuine Antigua
green beans.*

Types of coffee Guatemalan coffee is rated by many experts as one of the best growths in the world. Unlike the Costa Rican coffees, Guatemalans vary more from region to region, although the general flavour profile of "medium-to-full-bodied liquor, perfectly balanced with good acidity and complex smoky, spicy and chocolate tones" would fit many, if not most. Near the capital city is the famous Guatemala Antigua, the old city founded by the conquistadors and destroyed by an earthquake in 1773, which gives its name to one of Guatemala's finest coffees. Towards the north is Cobán, another city whose name represents high altitude resulting in high-quality acidity. There are numerous other regions of superb Guatemalan coffees, but Huehuetenango, in an isolated western area, is a name increasingly noted for fine acidity and unique flavours in coffees grown mostly on smallholdings.

Haiti

In the 1697 partition of Hispaniola, France received Haiti, the western third of the island. Aided by Toussaint L'Ouverture's rebellion, Haiti was free by 1804, and thus began what will soon be two hundred years of political instability. This poorest of countries, where many houses are windowless earthen huts, depends very much on coffee for much of its income.

Unfortunately, the coffee grading and classification is a confused process, and the simplest explanation is that coffee samples are graded by size of bean, altitude, cup quality, defective beans and number of stones included. The old trees, growing nearly wild, still produce lovely large bluish beans of the *typica* variety, heavy with humidity, which are often dry-processed, mostly by peasants. Sweet and mellow, these full-bodied coffees with lowish acidity – particularly the rich, winey, washed SHG beans – can be excellent, but not reliably so; they are perhaps at their best roasted medium-dark.

Most Haitian coffee is biologically pure simply because fertilizers, pesticides and fungicides are too expensive for the average Haitian grower.

Honduras

Like most other Central American countries, Honduras markets its coffees by designation of altitude. Honduras produces washed *arabicas*, clean with good acidity and flavour, possibly lacking only slightly in body – overall, a high-quality coffee, perhaps not in a gourmet class, but a worthy contributor to a blend. Hurricane Mitch caused direct losses of nearly 500,000 bags of Honduran coffee, but future production may also be affected, depending on transportation, infrastructure damage and time required for repair.

Jamaica

Few coffee-drinkers realize that Jamaica earns most of its money from, and is the world's third-largest producer of, bauxite, and that, in fact, its famous Blue Mountain coffee grows only on the eastern tip of the island, in a small area extending no further west than Kingston. The production is shared by only three parishes: St Andrew, where coffee was originally planted in 1728 by Sir Nicholas Lawes; Portland, on the northern slopes of the mountains; and the parish

*Left:
Honduran
green beans.*

of St Thomas on the south side. Other coffee-growing parts of Jamaica, which collectively would occupy an area twice the size of the Blue Mountain coffee estates and farms, actually grow about 75 per cent of Jamaica's coffee.

These other regions sell coffee bags labelled High Mountain Supreme and Prime Washed Jamaica, names

*Right:
Jamaica
Blue
Mountain
roasted beans.*

produce a cup that is an exquisite balance of nutty aroma; bright, but not overwhelming acidity; delicate sweetness; and a clean but nectar-like finish. The body may be slightly lacking in fullness, and someone who likes a hearty cup of coffee may need to use more than normal to brew a satisfying cup – another consideration when getting out your wallet at the cash till. An inferior crop, especially possible with recent years of over-production leading to possibly less careful processing, may be disappointingly mediocre and could be easily outclassed by a Costa Rican, Guatamalan, or even Cuban.

One possibility for change in the Jamaican Blue Mountain market is that while Japan has for nearly thirty years been its major purchaser, with the rest of the world scrambling to pay princely

perfectly innocent on their own, but dangerously close to Jamaica Blue Mountain in all but quality. In fact, although we speak in "bags", the real Jamaica Blue Mountain comes in barrels, and anyway, all exported Jamaican coffee is certified by the Coffee Industry Board. Even so, the unwary would-be JBM consumer is seldom safe, as when buying 200g/7oz of roasted beans (which is about all anybody can afford), they might not actually see the container the beans were shipped in. Also there are many countries that grow the Blue Mountain variety of *arabica*, and a few even have a Blue Mountain range of hills.

As more Jamaica Blue Mountain coffee is sold than that small area could possibly produce, remember Davy Crockett's motto, "Be sure you're right, then go ahead": buy 100 per cent pure Jamaica Blue Mountain coffee only from a reputable source.

Aroma and balance Jamaica Blue Mountain is only a high-quality Caribbean coffee, and as such, is subject to much the same vagaries that Mother Nature inflicts on other Caribbean coffees. A good crop will

sums for the remnants, Asia's economic crisis has plunged Japan into a terrible recession, and this could alter somewhat the distribution of the world's most expensive coffee.

Martinique

This tiny island in the middle of the Lesser Antilles, described by Columbus as "the most beautiful country in the world", was where Capt. Gabriel Mathieu de Clieu, in the 1720s, decided to plant the coffee tree "stolen" from Louis XIV's royal greenhouse. The first coffee specimen to enter the Western Hemisphere, it flourished in the rich volcanic soil of Mt Pelée's slopes and became the progenitor of the millions of coffee trees grown throughout the New World in the early colonial period.

After a hundred years of success, Martinique's coffee plantations declined, greatly hindered by the natural disasters that seem to strike Martinique, situated in "Hurricane Alley", about every five years. Today, Martinique's citizens, like those of

*Above: Jamaica
Blue Mountain
green beans.*

Above: The first stage of processing the cherries is rinsing in water.

Right: Mexican roasted beans.

Guadeloupe, receive French subsidies for their high levels of unemployment. Coffee production seems a thing of the past. The few remaining ageing trees are sporadically attended to, but as Martinique has the climate, the soil and workforce, one can only hope the situation will improve.

Mexico

Mexico, which grows some fairly average, mostly washed *arabica* coffees, classifies its crop by altitude-denoting terms similar to those of Nicaragua. Although many regions of southern Mexico grow coffee, there are some coffees which rise above the average, not only literally in altitude, but in interesting, hard-to-describe and sometimes unpredictable flavours.

In the state of Veracruz on the Gulf of Mexico, the mountainous region near Coatepec produces an excellent "altura", characterized by a light body, but with a slightly sharp, dry acidity, which sometimes has nutty or chocolate hints. The alturas of nearby Huatusco and further inland Orizaba are also fine coffees. Oaxaca, the more remote south-western state, gives its name to good coffees, including Oaxaca Pluma. Chiapas, adjoining the southern border with Guatemala, grows large amounts of *arabica* marketed under the name of Tapachula. Flavourful and particularly aromatic, and occasionally bordering on the "sour", Mexico's alturas and SHG's are not to everybody's taste, but they are very individual and never boring.

Like many Central American countries, Mexico is subject to earthquakes, particularly in the mountainous regions where the better coffees are grown. Due to its size and location, however, Mexico is not always affected simultaneously by the same problems as other Central American producers. While Honduras, El Salvador, Nicaragua, Guatemala, and Panama were all plagued by floods, rain, or heavy humidity caused by Hurricane Mitch, Mexico was in the throes of a severe six-month drought, which eventually caused the loss of about 400,000 bags.

Nicaragua

The very poor country of Nicaragua, for which coffee is the main export crop, reported crop losses of up to 30 per cent of its more than 1-million-bag-average crop after it was hit by Hurricane Mitch in October 1998. Thankfully, 20 per cent of the devastation was due to impassable roads preventing the crop reaching the processing mills, and therefore was not permanent damage. The remaining 10 per cent of the loss was direct damage when a massive mudslide from the Casita volcano destroyed entire coffee fields in the region of Matagalpa. All Nicaraguan coffees are wet-processed *arabicas* grown in fertile volcanic-based soil.

Under normal conditions, Matagalpa and the neighbouring town of Jinotega produce the best Nicaraguan coffee, of which the SHG is known for its large beans, slightly salty acidity, and medium-to-full body and good aroma. The Nicaraguan version of the Maragogype variety represents the world's largest coffee beans, although the flavour is generally not quite as universally appreciated as that of the

Above: Nicaraguan SHG medium roast.

Guatemalan Maragogype.

Panama

Panama's main coffees grow in the far western region nearest the Costa Rican border in the high-altitude slopes around the Barú volcano, where the regional names are Davíd and Boquete; the district of Chiriquí, and slightly to the east, Tole, produce notable high-grown washed *arabicas*. Café Volcán Barú is a newer gourmet coffee from the same region. The SHB Panamanian

Below: Nicaraguan Maravilla roasted coffee beans.

Above: Medium-roasted beans from Boquete, in north-western Panama.

coffees are known for their deep green colour, light body, bright but not sharp acidity, and pleasant, sweet taste; major buyers of Panama coffee are the French and the Scandinavians. The damage sustained by Panama's coffee crop from the heavy rains brought by Hurricane Mitch was about one-fifth of the 1998/1999 crop, or about 45,000 bags.

Puerto Rico

What a nice change to read about a Caribbean island revitalizing a dying coffee trade, which is exactly what Puerto Rico has been doing. Always reckoned to have been one of the world's best growths, Puerto Rico is supplier to the Vatican. A few years ago it grew less coffee as it drank more, and in 1968 stopped exporting coffee completely, as it was importing far more than it grew.

At the same time, the US minimum wage law, effective in the Associate State of Puerto Rico, ensured the Puerto Rican workforce a far higher standard of living than that enjoyed by any other Caribbean population, while attracting US industry to its "cheap" labour. As almost no struggling coffee plantations could afford to pay US minimum wages, coffee-growing was nearly a thing of the past, except for a few thousand smallholders, grouped into local cooperatives. Now, at least two of these cooperatives, Yauco, (whose "Yauco Selecto" is simply superb) and Lares, have revived coffee production by producing, in the wake of the US's demand for "specialty" [sic] coffees, high-quality beans of the grand

old varieties, carefully picked and graded. The gourmet coffees are expensive to produce but they exact high prices, which quality-seeking buyers from several foreign countries are willing to pay.

The Puerto Rican *crus*, which could be called the world's most "powerful" coffees, were always known for their intense aroma and deep, rich and amazingly sweet flavours, fully balanced by a heavy liquor; how wonderful to have them back again.

Trinidad & Tobago

These two islands, 14km/9 miles off the coast of Venezuela, grow what is called "small amounts" of *robusta* coffee, mostly for instant coffee processing; in fact, these "small amounts" make up a crop that annually exceeds the combined harvests of Liberia, Gabon, Equatorial Guinea and Benin. But

"small" is relative to the matter of income: after gaining independence from Britain in 1962, the oil-rich islands enjoyed a high level of prosperity – Trinidadians for several years had the reputation of importing more Scotch whisky per capita than any other country – while constantly increasing its oil production and refinery.

In recent years, however, world oil price movements have highlighted a need to diversify. Tobago is finally developing its tourism, as not only its beaches but also its butterfly species attract tourists. Behind the all-is-well façade, the interior of Trinidad is home to dissatisfied poverty-stricken farmers; unemployment, crime, drugs-related problems, and oil-spills are a constant threat. The day may yet come when the demanding, but satisfying, business of growing more coffee may offer an alternative to the tourist trade.

Above: Coffee tree with ripe cherries ready for picking.

SOUTH AMERICA

Brazil, as the world's largest coffee producer, dominates this region, but there are a number of countries producing superb beans worth trying.

Argentina

Argentina grows so little coffee that its production figures are difficult to obtain. The Tropic of Capricorn runs across the extreme north of the country, and the two general areas where coffee can be grown are the moderately humid and tropical north-east, where it was introduced by the Jesuits in 1729 in Misiones, and the north-west Andean provinces around Tucumán. Because of their exclusion from the tropical zone, the Argentine coffee trees, which are *arabica*, are subject to the periodic ravages of frost.

Bolivia

The Bolivian coffee crop is hand-picked, mainly washed *arabica*. Although most of it is of exportable quality, Bolivia is land-locked, and the problem is one of supply. Coffee is cultivated on about 12,000 hectares (30,000 acres), often in areas so remote that there is no way to transport the beans out during certain seasons. Also, as is the case with several South American countries, the temptation to produce coca is often too much for the inhabitants of poorer regions to resist.

Bolivian coffees tend to be slightly bitter, but, based on figures of the last several years, the coffee crop is improving in both quantity and quality, as older trees are being replaced. Perhaps Bolivia will soon be able to provide more accessible, available beans for the world market.

Brazil

Just how much is "an awful lot"? Although the quantity may vary from year to year, there is simply no other way to describe the Brazilian coffee crop, which can usually claim one-third of total global production. Unlike many other coffee-producing countries, however, who may export all of the good coffee and drink very little at home, Brazilians in one year will consume

about 12 million bags, much of it in the form of the much-beloved *cafèzinho*, the tiny cup of usually good-quality black coffee drunk by most Brazilians several times a day.

It is interesting to note that in Brazil the word for "breakfast" is *café da manhã* (morning coffee), whereas in Portugal, which in theory speaks the same language, "breakfast" is the rather less descriptive *primeiro almoço* or *pequeno almoço* (as in the French "little lunch" definition of breakfast).

Types of coffee Brazil grows both *arabica* and *robusta*, but the crop is primarily *arabica*, mostly dry-processed. With both the Equator and the Tropic of

Capricorn passing through it, the bulk of Brazil lies in the tropical zone, and around 3.2 million hectares (8 million acres) of Brazilian land is dedicated to coffee-growing. Towards the north of the country, where the climate is hotter and the terrain flatter, is where the *robusta* (conilon variety) is grown, shaded from the more direct rays of the sun.

The coffee improves towards the south of the country, where the best *arabica* is grown in higher terrain, but these plateau regions are very close to the bottom edge of the tropical zone and frost is frequently a problem, if not a major disaster. When frost warnings are reported in southern Brazil,

Above: Each bag in this Brazilian warehouse contains the annual harvest of 60 trees.

Above: Aerial view of one of the many large coffee-growing plantations in Brazil. The flat terrain suggests robusta *cultivation.*

Above: Brazilian Santos green beans.

international trade coffee prices immediately jump in anticipation of a possible shortage.

Seventeen Brazilian states grow many varieties of coffee, but there are four or five regions that dominate the exportable coffee cultivation. Brazilian beans are identified, categorized and graded by many different criteria, the first of which is the port of export. The more northerly state of Bahia, which produces some good washed *arabica* among its generally average dry-processed coffees, and small amounts of Maragogype, exports its coffee through the port of Salvador de

Bahia. The smaller state of Espírito Santo ships its rather average beans from Vitória; the large state of Minas Gerais (Sul de Minas is an excellent coffee), uses both the ports of Rio de Janeiro and the more southerly port of Santos, which is also the port for the various coffees produced in the state of São Paulo. Santos exports the "flat bean" Santos and the superior Bourbon Santos. The southernmost Brazilian coffee port is Paranagua, from which the state of Paraná ships its coffees.

Quantity or quality Brazilian *arabicas* are not usually included in the ranks of gourmet or speciality coffees. Indeed, pushed to a

general description of these enormously varying growths, most experts would say that Brazilian coffee is poor-to-average quality, low-to-moderate acidity and neutral or bland in flavour, a fairly accurate profile of most of the millions of bags exported by Brazil. Part of the problem with the quality is the fact that the sheer space in Brazil allows the

Left: Brazilian Sul de Minas medium-roasted beans.

operations of huge plantations, where the picking is not picking at all; it may be "stripping" or even machine-harvesting. In either case, the mix of fruit will include coffee cherries at wide ranges of maturation, and the odds are that no amount of later sorting will produce a

Above: Graded and sorted coffee beans are bagged, to be made ready for export.

The cup quality classifications can be mystifying: besides rather obvious terms such as "full body", "bad cup", "fair cup", and "fine cup", among others, there are more elusive terms used to describe Brazilian coffees, such as "strictly soft" and "Rio-y" (which is pronounced with a long "i", despite the fact that it comes from the state of Rio).

The term "hard" in Brazilian coffee means, as might be expected, the opposite of "soft". "Rio-y" coffee is easier to explain: this is the coffee that gives Middle Eastern coffee blends their distinctive flavour. On its own, "rio-y" coffee tastes medicinal, harsh, inky or iodine-y. The flavour is thought to be the result of certain micro-organisms and is not always present every year in crops from the same soil, although the geographic areas in which it is found have increased considerably. Shunned by most countries for being strongly defective, rio-y coffee is avidly sought by Turkey, Greece, Cyprus and most Middle Eastern countries, as well as by Denmark. Blended with Ethiopian coffee, the rio-y flavour seems to benefit from the Middle Eastern practice of boiling the coffee with sugar.

There was a time when Brazilian coffees made up 60 per cent of the world crop, and they were the standard "extenders" for almost every blend in the world; their unobtrusive character, generally good body and plenteous supply ensured that Brazilian coffee was the basis for most of the world's blended brands. It is interesting to note that the International Coffee Organization's preliminary statistics for the 1998 crop list the average "unit value" of Brazilian exports at 110.95 US cents per pound, which is extremely close to the prices of all the world's coffees averaged together: 110.05 US cents per pound. These figures mean that a blender, when considering what beans to buy in order to produce a decent flavour in an average-priced blend, must bulk out his blend with something cheaper than the average Brazilian coffee, to offset the higher prices of coffees used for better flavour.

truly homogeneous yield. Hypothetically, even the most meticulous harvesting could not make up for the lack of any really high altitudes in Brazil's topography; without the altitude there is little acidity, and the result is the bland character attributed to most of Brazil's coffees.

Of course, there are exceptions to every rule, and those who automatically dismiss Brazil from the list of the world's "gourmet" coffee producers probably have never been privy to some of the best Brazilian Santos coffees, which may not be common or easily obtainable, but do exist.

There are estates in southern Brazil where high quality is pursued intensely, and careful tending and detailed experimentation in processing have led to the production of some truly wonderful coffee – smooth, well-balanced and mellow. The best Brazilian coffee comes from young trees of the bourbon variety, whose small, rounded beans produce excellent cup qualities, fine acidity and sweetness. After the Brazilian bourbon trees have produced a few crops, the beans become larger and lose a bit of their flavour; the coffee is then described as "flat bean Santos".

be extremely difficult to harvest it any other way, given that the slopes are steep in the mountainous terrain – and the trees are usually shaded by interspersed banana trees. The climate provides plenty of moisture, so there is no irrigation or mulching required.

Above: Colombian Popayán excelso dark-roasted beans.

The central *cordillera* is the most productive region both in quantity and quality, particularly as it contains the well-known name of Medellín, one of the best-balanced coffees of Colombia, combining full-bodied heaviness with good flavour and medium acidity. Manizales, another town of the central zone, and Armenia, whose coffees are less acidic, but winey in texture with excellent aroma, in the western *cordillera*, together with Medellín, form the MAM acronym under which the majority of bags from Colombia are exported. Another central zone favourite is coffee from Libano, which in the "supremo" form is a visual delight, as its large beans roast smoothly and evenly. Popayán and San Agustín are notable coffees from the southern part of the central *cordillera*, as is coffee from the district of Nariño, very near the Ecuador border with Columbia. Nariño has the reputation of producing the cup preferred by the Vatican, (a distinction claimed equally by the island of Puerto Rico), and Starbucks, the chain of coffee speciality shops, also allegedly holds exclusive rights to the supremo beans from Nariño.

Colombia

Unfortunately, the rich soil that produces Colombia's best coffees is the result of past volcanic activity in an area of continuing subterranean instability. Although the massive earthquake that tore through the heart of Colombia's largest coffee-growing region in January 1999 miraculously did little damage to the trees themselves, farming infrastructure suffered 65 per cent damage, which could cause a drop in quality as farmers economize for necessary repairs. Whatever the outcome, Colombia will still hold its position at second place in the global statistics for coffee-growing, as its nearest rival is Vietnam, whose production of *robusta*, though still increasing, is less than half Colombia's.

Coffee-growing areas Colombia's three mountain ranges, or *cordilleras*, are really lines of Andean foothills that run from north to south, and it is on their slopes that the *arabica* coffee of Colombia is grown in altitudes ranging from 800m/2,624ft to 1,900m/6,233ft. The coffee is all hand-picked – it would

Above: Colombian "supremo" medium-roasted beans.

Colombia's eastern coffee region produces another half-dozen or so commercial coffees, of which two are better known for excellent quality: Bogotá, from the area around the capital city, is a fine coffee with a slightly lower acidity than those of the central zone; Bucamaranga, from the more northerly part of the eastern *cordillera*, has the low acid and mellow, rounded flavour of a "soft" coffee.

Flavour and aroma The old *arabica* cultivars are gradually being replaced with other more productive varieties, such as the cost-efficient "variedad Colombia", as the aged trees are removed. Developed in Colombia, this *arabica* strain is also being planted in other countries, much to the dismay of

Above: Colombian San Agustín medium-roasted beans.

discerning tasters, who find the flavour of the new variety disappointing, especially in comparison to the bourbon beans, which can be a felicitous combination of flavour, aroma, body and a golden colour when milk or cream is

added. The acidity of Colombian coffees seldom matches that of certain Kenyans and Costa Ricans, but in general Colombia produces a more balanced cup, particularly in coffees of slightly heavier body.

Colombia enjoys one advantage over all other South American countries: it can export coffee through ports on either ocean. The export crop is fairly evenly divided between the ports of Buenaventura on the Pacific, and Cartagena, Barranquilla and Santa Marta on the Atlantic. Such easy access from the plantations to international trade routes, coupled with the worldwide promotional work done by the Federation Nacional de Cafeteros de Colombia, has ensured a strong market for Colombian coffee in both North America and Europe.

Colombia also exports the highest volume of soluble (instant) coffee in the world, the expected 1998/99 figure of which is a whopping 659,000 bags' worth, mostly freeze-dried.

Ecuador

Ecuador, like Brazil, grows *arabica* as well as *robusta*; the *robustas* are unwashed, and the *arabicas* are wet- or dry-processed. The large (gigante or Galapagos classifications) *arabica* beans are heavy with humidity, but produce a thin-bodied liquor, and a slightly woody and mediocre flavour, although the aroma is good. The trees are interspersed with banana and cocoa trees for shading.

French Guiana

South America's last "colony" – a French Overseas Department – once famous for the notorious offshore penal colony of Devil's Island, is composed mostly of equatorial jungle and species-rich rainforest. The only coffee grown here now is from *robusta* trees in domestic gardens, but French Guiana had its moment of coffee glory when, through a romance of illicit passion and deception in the early 18th century, the little colony was the gateway through which the all-conquering bean first reached Brazil.

Above: Hand-picking coffee in Colombia – not an easy job in mountainous terrain.

Galapagos Islands

Gourmet coffee lovers might want to keep a look out for a coffee grown in very high altitudes on the small island of San Cristóbal. The coffee estate was established long before the islands became a national park, which banned any further agricultural development and any use of chemicals. The organically produced coffee is said to be superb, and there is scope for the production on this family-run plantation to increase.

Guyana

The Dutch founded three colonies here, Berbice, Demerara and Essequibo, which passed to Britain in 1814 and became British Guiana. Independent since 1966, Guyana produces bauxite, gold, rice, sugar and diamonds, but it still grows some coffee, primarily low-quality *liberica*, most of which is consumed locally, but may be shipped to the US for instant processing before re-importation into Guyana.

Paraguay

This country has been attempting to increase its *arabica* coffee crop for some time. As a country with no minerals, land-locked and remote, it must depend on its own agriculture for general subsistence and hope that its neighbours stay financially healthy, as its biggest exports are electricity (for which Brazil's "standing charges" sometimes represent 25 per cent of the total Paraguayan national budget) and contraband. The coffees are unwashed *arabicas*, cultivated mostly towards the eastern border where the altitude is highest, and the cup quality is unsurprisingly similar to the rather nondescript *arabicas* grown in Paraná, across the Brazilian border. All of the coffee must be taken overland through seasonally impassable terrain for shipping from the ports of Brazil, Argentina and Chile.

Peru

Coffee is one of Peru's main crops, and it provides a living for many poor families who work smallholdings in the Andean foothills. Punto, on Lake Titicaca, Cuzco and the Urubamba and Chanchamayo Valleys, and the northern provinces of Piura, San Martin, plus Cajamarca and Lambayeque, are all producing some good quality coffees, certified as organically grown, and are all areas where quality is important and improving. In general, Peruvian coffees are excellent blending coffees, as they are mild, pleasant and sweet, and occasionally some really top quality Peruvians are beginning to appear.

Suriname

Suriname was Dutch-owned from 1667, when the British swapped it for New

Above: Venezuela has been producing beans like these since 1730.

Left: Peru exports most of its washed arabicas, keeping the unwashed for internal consumption.

Amsterdam (New York), until its independence in 1975. It was through Dutch Guiana, as it was called in 1714, that coffee-growing came to South America. Today it grows only small amounts of wild-tasting *liberica*, sold to Norway.

Venezuela

The best coffees produced in this oil-rich country are those grown practically on the spine of the Andean *cordillera de Mérida*, which collectively are known as Maracaibos, as they are shipped from the port of that name. Several names of good Maracaibos include the word Táchira, the far western state; and the regions of Mérida, Trujillo and the town of Cúcuta (which is so far west it appears to be in Colombia!) also give their names to fine coffees. Other coffees are shipped under the names of the *haciendas* where they are grown. Coffee from the eastern mountains is designated as Caracas, for the proximity to the capital.

The coffee industry, having lapsed into mediocrity under government nationalization in the 1970s, is now pulling itself out of the decline, no doubt encouraged by the growing gourmet coffee market. Some of the old *haciendas* are once more the source of some lovely, if slightly unusual, coffees. Venezuelan coffees, unlike other South American growths, tend to be delicately light, if not actually thin, slightly winey, and of only moderate acidity, with a rather appealing individual aroma and flavour.

SOUTH PACIFIC AND SOUTH-EAST ASIA

This area contains some of the most enterprising coffee-producing countries.

Australia

Nearly 40 per cent of Australia lies above the Tropic of Capricorn, but much of the area in this tropical zone is not suitable for coffee cultivation: the rainfall, if adequate at all, is very variable, and the altitude conducive to producing good *arabica* is limited. Even so, at least since the 1970s *arabica* coffee has been grown in Queensland, some on a rather experimental basis; one in particular, "Skybury", hit the world stage in the early 1980s and has not looked back. Grown from the same Blue Mountain variety as the celebrated New Guinea Sigri, Skybury has received great commendations by many experts. At least its price will ensure that it doesn't suffer the same fate as that of other well-meaning Australian coffees of the 1980s: because Australians consume far more coffee than the farmers can hope to grow, any average Australian product that acquires favour with the home market will probably at some point have to be extended with imported coffee, particularly that from Papua New Guinea.

Cambodia

About forty years ago, commercial coffee plantation began in Cambodia. Soon coffee, mostly *robusta*, but a little *arabica* as well, was grown in at least five different regions of Cambodia. After the terrible events that befell Cambodia in successive years, it is difficult now to guess the state of the plantations. It is worth hoping, however, that Cambodia, like Vietnam, may have a future as a coffee-producing country once again.

China

It is known that *arabica* coffee is grown and processed in China's south-west province of Yunnan, where a very mountainous region is crossed by the Tropic of Cancer, the northern edge of the tropical belt. Here the summer temperatures are modified by higher altitudes and good rainfall, and the mild, dry winters enjoy a temperature

Left: Australian "Skybury" green beans.

range of 8–20°C/46–68°F. The Chinese government releases no figures on its coffee production, however, and because certain countries, especially Tanzania, repay debts to China in coffee beans, there is no assurance that any coffee exported from China was actually grown there. The International Coffee Organization is actively encouraging more coffee consumption in China, of which a by-product could be greater production of coffee, as the necessary growing conditions are present.

Fiji

After having had twenty-seven years of independence from Britain, Fiji rejoined the Commonwealth in 1997, having replaced its constitution with one more acceptable to the international community. At one time Fiji grew a small crop of *robusta*, which it processed by the washed method, and which was sold primarily to New Zealand. It also imported coffee for its own consumption.

The island of Vitu Levu consists of mainly mountainous terrain, including Mount Victoria (1,324m/4,344ft) and some higher places on the other smaller islands. As Fiji is attempting to further diversify its income perhaps it will be encouraged to grow more coffee.

French Polynesia

This French Overseas Territory is really a combination of 130 islands spread out over a Pacific area the size of Europe. The bourbon *arabica* is grown on various islands, each of which carries

out its own wet processing, and the coffee is then sent to Papeete, Tahiti, for hulling and grading. The islands tend to consume all that they grow and process. The large-bean coffee has been described as pleasantly mild rather than acidic, with good strength and aroma, and is therefore a well-rounded satisfying cup. Tahiti Arabica is the commercial name, but it is seldom found outside the islands that grow it.

Hawaii

Hawaii has been growing coffee since 1818, and today both the island of Kauai and the big island of Hawaii grow it, although it is the latter's coffee from the slopes of the Mauna Loa volcano in the western Kona zone that gives its name to the only coffee grown in the United States. Expert opinions on Kona coffee vary; certainly in several ways it can be compared to Jamaica Blue Mountain. Although the climate and soil are ideal, the growing area is limited, the processing is extremely careful and the appearance of the beans impeccable; it is a natural product and some crops are better than others. It is scarce and expensive, and many blends

Above: Hawaiian Kona medium-roasted coffee beans.

Above: A coffee plantation in the flat terrain of Kauai, Hawaii.

are sold as "Kona" that may contain five per cent of the genuine coffee. (The blends may, of course, be excellent, depending on the other coffees used, which are likely to be superior, but more affordable, Latin Americans.) The Hawaiian coffee industry must compete with the tourist trade for its workers, and therefore wages are extremely high, compared to those of other countries.

Flavour and aroma Hawaiian Kona differs from Jamaica Blue Mountain in many ways, although both are known for a mild, "fair" acidity, medium body and fine aroma; also, the descriptor "nutty" is sometimes applied to the flavour profiles of both. Some experts detect in Kona a spicy, cinnamon-like flavour, a quality not found in Jamaican coffee, while other experts have difficulty detecting much flavour at all.

In sheer bountiful yield, no other coffee trees on Earth can vie with the volume of fruit taken from Kona trees. The best, and surest, way to drink Hawaiian Kona is to sip it with the locals, as the best quality is kept at home. Tourists are willing to pay the normal "high dollar" price, which really is at a premium, as there are none of the normal shipping costs involved.

India

The entire economy of India is undergoing a radical change, as the government is shifting from a position of protectionism to the encouragement of totally free, global marketing. The coffee industry, which had been nationalized some time back, did little to encourage growers to improve their quality or produce coffee with individual character; same-grade beans from all regions were "blended" by the Indian Coffee Board under a uniform grading system, producing simply "Plantation A", "Plantation B", etc. As of 16 December 1998, the Indian parliament finalized a decision to allow coffee growers to sell 100 per cent of the produce on the open market. It can only be assumed that the old romantic coffee names will have true significance once more, particularly for the 40 per cent of India's crop that is *arabica*.

Above: Indian Plantation A medium-roasted beans.

Coffee-growing areas The *arabica* coffee-growing region of India is basically three states in the south-west. Mysore, which accounts for most of the *arabica*, is grown in what is now the state of Karnataka. Mysore can be described very generally as having good body, low acidity, mellow sweetness and a well-balanced strong flavour; however, it sometimes can be described as neutral, which probably reflects on those Kent-variety *arabicas*, which generally have a less distinctive flavour than the older classics like bourbon. The state of Tamil Nadu produces good *arabica*; one in particular is grown in the high altitude of the Nilgiri region in the state's west.

Above: Green beans from Mysore, India.

The most interesting *arabica* of India in both name and taste is the unwashed "Monsooned Malabar". The Malabar coast is the western shore of the entire state of Kerala. In the days of sailing, when coffee took months to reach Europe, it developed a particular taste during the voyage because of exposure to sea air and humidity; the colour also changed from green to a rather strange yellow. European consumers became fond of the enhanced body and enriched, if slightly peculiar, flavour, so when steamers shortened the sailing time, India began to "artificially" reproduce the flavour by exposing coffee for about six weeks to the humid south-west monsoon winds that begin in May or June.

These unusual coffees are not dissimilar to other "aged" coffees, such as those of Sulawesi, Java and Sumatra, and they are generally cheaper and easier to obtain.

Above: Indian Monsooned Malabar medium-roasted beans.

Above: Sumatran Lintong Grade 2 roasted beans.

Indonesia

The coffee industry provides a livelihood for around five million people living in Indonesia, and currently vies with Vietnam as the third most prolific coffee produce. Ninety per cent of its crop is ordinary *robusta*. The *arabicas*, however, are another story, and the word "ordinary" doesn't come into it; Indonesia, as the world's largest archipelago, sprawls across 5,000km/ 3,107 miles, and its 13,677 islands lie in three different time zones. It is therefore not surprising that its *arabicas*, which have far more scope for individuality than *robustas*, cover an amazing range of sometimes quirky but always interesting differences. A general description of most of the Indonesian *arabicas* would contain the words rich, full-bodied, lowish-acidity and a prolonged aftertaste, in addition to terms more specific to the individual coffees.

Sumatra There are three main islands and one or two smaller ones that together produce very nearly 100 per cent of all Indonesian coffees, *arabica* and *robusta*; Sumatra, the westernmost

Above: Sumatran Mandheling grade 2 green beans.

large island, grows 68 per cent. Much of the *arabica* is sold simply as Sumatran or Blue Sumatran; many of the Sumatran trees are newly planted in virgin, highly organic, volcanic soil, which is very fertile, and the coffees, which are only partly wet-processed, are strong and assertive.

One of the few washed coffees is the gourmet-quality Gayo Mountain, sweetly spicy and exotically herbal in character, named for its area of origin in the extreme north-western province of Aceh. Linthong, or Lintong, from northern Sumatra, is similar to, but generally not quite as consistently good as, Mandheling, from the north and the west-central regions.

Mandheling, with the deep, rich flavour and smoothness of a low-acidity coffee, merits the title "world's heaviest coffee", according to many experts. Ankola, also from the west-central region near the port of Padang, may not have quite the body of a Mandheling, but it is regarded by some connoisseurs as the world's finest unwashed *arabica*.

Above: Indonesian washed Java Jampit green beans.

Java The island of Java, which grows about 12 per cent of Indonesia's coffee, was where the Dutch began the first coffee-growing outside of Islam. Three hundred years of intensive cultivation has left Java's soil a bit depleted. After the *hemileia vastatrix* (leaf rust), infestation of the late 19th century, only the highest-grown *arabicas* survived, and those scarce growths have recently been replaced with more productive *arabica* varieties, to the detriment of the flavour. "Estate Java"

is now a wet-processed coffee, with more acidity, and less body, flavour and finish than the original Java *arabicas*, which had been known for rich smoothness, heavy body, and an earthy, mushroomy sort of flavour obtained only in unwashed coffees. There were five government-owned estates, including Jampit, Blawan and Pankur.

Above: Indonesian Sulawesi Kalossi Toraja roasted beans.

Sulawesi The third main island of *arabica* production is Sulawesi, which grows 9 per cent of all Indonesian coffee; under the Dutch, the island was called Celebes, the name under which much of the *arabica* coffee is today exported from the port of Ujung Pandang. The unwashed Kalossi coffees from the south-western region of Toraja are the true aristocrats of all Indonesian coffees. They have the heavy body and smooth texture associated with Indonesian coffees, as well as the deep earthy, mushroomy, sweetness; there is, as well, because of slightly increased acidity, a hint of fruit.

Overall, the best and most distinctive range of Indonesian coffees are those that have been aged. The coffees may be sold as "Old Government", "Old Brown" or "Old Java"; or they may simply be designated "aged" coffees, and may come from Java, Sulawesi or Sumatra. The ageing process carried out in the damp, warm climate – not the same as simply lengthy warehousing in another part of the world – lowers what acidity there may have been, enhances the sweetness and gives the already smooth, dense liquid an even heavier body. Other descriptors spring

Above: Indonesian "Old Brown" Javanese green beans.

to mind, like soft, velvety, golden and warm. In fact, an interesting suggestion is to replace the after-dinner liqueur with a small black cup of an "aged" Indonesian, particularly a Celebes Kalossi, as its concentrated, sweet, syrupy consistency is virtually liqueur without the alcohol. (And the cost is probably about the same!)

Other coffee-growing areas Other *arabica* coffees known to be excellent are those grown on Bali, Flores and Timor, although Timor stopped growing coffee after annexation by Indonesia. One can hope production will resume again soon, as it seems Indonesia is in the process of reversing the annexation of the former Portuguese colony.

There is one more type of coffee obtainable from Indonesia, which is *kopi luak*. *Kopi* is the word for coffee, and the luak is a small weasel-like animal particularly fond of coffee cherries. Villagers collect the animals' droppings and remove the hard coffee beans, which are then washed and further processed by less natural means. The flavour is exceptional and the beans command a high price.

Laos

In recent years, the strongly communist Laos People's Democratic Republic has opened up to foreign investment, as well as receiving international aid and subsidies to encourage the farmers to substitute cash crops for opium poppies. The country's most important agricultural resources are currently listed as timber and coffee. Information on the type and quality of the coffee

grown, and the regions of cultivation, is not readily available, but in the past, the Laotian climate, soil and topography allowed the production of *arabica*, *robusta* and *excelsa*, which, during the 1970s, fell to amounts that could only sustain local consumption.

Malaysia

Although Malaysia grows *arabica*, *robusta* and *excelsa*, its main coffee crop is the higher-yielding and highly unpalatable *liberica* species, grown mostly in Western Malaya. Western Malaya is also the site of a small area of *arabica* trees, which is located in the higher altitudes of the Cameron Highlands. Because of the large population of the country, local consumption generally accounts for all the coffee that can be grown. Malaysia is very

concerned with economic success, and as coffee is not as lucrative a crop as some others, such as palm oil, rubber, timber and, of course, oil and gas, it is not usually seen to be a priority crop for cultivation.

New Caledonia

This small group of islands, called Kanaky by the natives, lying 1,497km/930 miles north-east of Australia, is still a French Overseas Territory, although independence seems possible. The windward (eastern)

Below: Kopi luak comes from droppings of the luak animal, containing undigested coffee beans. The beans are collected, washed and processed – the resulting coffee is considered a rare delicacy by coffee lovers.

coast has the distinction of growing the world's best *robusta*, while the little *arabica* still grown comes from the western side of the island. The *robusta* is unusual for its type, as it is described as delicate, although the flavour of both coffees, known commercially as "Nouméa", is said to be aromatic and rich. The *arabica* is seldom exported, as the islands prefer to save the best for themselves, which they can afford to do, since New Caledonia has large deposits of nickel, accounting for 25 per cent of the world's supply.

Above: New Guinean "Y" grade roasted beans.

Papua New Guinea

It was probably extremely fortunate for all coffee lovers that coffee-growing came late to Papua New Guinea. Otherwise, the disastrous plague of *hemileia vastatrix* (leaf rust) that wiped out *arabica* plantations throughout South-east Asia and Oceania in the late 1800s, would have ensured that today Papua New Guinea would be growing mostly *robusta*, like so many other countries who replanted with resistant species at the cost of good flavour.

Much of New Guinea's *arabica* is grown, washed and further processed in varying degrees by natives of rural, and sometimes isolated, villages located in the high-altitude mountainous region that occupies so much of Papua New Guinea's landmass. These coffees are an extremely important source of revenue for Papua New Guinea, providing a living for hundreds of thousands of people, and the government provides encouragement and support by announcing, at the start of each year's crop, an ensured

minimum price it will pay for the coffee, in the event that the market price should fall unexpectedly.

Gourmet-quality coffee New Guinea coffee was cultivated from Blue Mountain variety stock, and the results make the New Guinea washed *arabicas* rather different from other coffees from this part of the world. Although New Guineas have good body and sweetness, as do many Indonesians, they also have a higher acidity closer in style to Central Americans. In short, a good New Guinea coffee can stand on its own, or be a terrific contribution to any high-quality blend, as it has literally everything to offer.

The sorting and grading, after some inconsistencies, is now regular and stringent. The top AA grade is very scarce, while about 60 per cent of beans make up the ordinary, decent Y grade. Quality names to look out for include Arona, Okapa and Sigri.

Philippines

The world's second-largest archipelago has everything it takes to grow good quality coffee in large amounts. In fact, it already grows all four of the main commercial species, *robusta*, *liberica*, *excelsa* and *arabica*, and is experimenting with hybrids. The small crop of good *arabica*, known for its full, slightly spicy flavour, is concentrated on the southern island of Mindanao.

At one time the Philippines were in fourth place for world coffee production, but that was before the terrible rust infestation that wiped out most of the *arabica* growths of South-east Asia, the Philippines included, in the late 1800s.

Above: Philippino arabica green coffee beans.

Above: Vietnamese robusta medium-roasted coffee beans.

As the *arabica* is not very acidic, and the flavour is fairly strong, this coffee works well where a darker roast is appreciated, as in after-dinner or espresso blends.

Sri Lanka

The world's greatest tea exporter, this island, which Tamils and Sinalese have cohabited in conflict for fourteen centuries, grew a lot of good *arabica* coffee, until almost the entire crop was destroyed by *hemileia vastatrix* (leaf rust) in 1870. Although tea-growing basically replaced coffee cultivation, the British colonists introduced *robusta*, which still accounts for the majority of the generally poor-quality coffee, which is sold under the name Sinhala.

Taiwan

Taiwan is known for its consumerism, and coffee is no exception. Trendy gourmet coffee houses vie for high-street prominence in Taipei. The small, good-quality, well-processed *arabica* crop, grown in the mountain region that dominates the island, is all consumed locally.

Thailand

Thailand's current coffee crop of about only a million bags is mostly *robusta*, grown primarily in the Malay Peninsula; some *arabica* is grown in the highlands of the north and north-west. Recently Thailand seems to be eager to increase its coffee cultivation, which may be due to several reasons. Any increase will help to satisfy the consumption demands of its 58.8 million population, and at the same time utilize the potentially abundant workforce of hundreds of thousands of indigenous hill people and refugees from Laos and Cambodia in virtually all rural regions of the country. It will also help to redistribute the country's wealth and population from Bangkok, one of the world's most congested cities, by developing commercial interests in more remote provinces, and help to replace the growth of opium poppies in the Golden Triangle. There is one major problem for increased coffee production, as well as for other crops: there is a major national water shortage exacerbated by a lack of water storage facilities. Deforestation has contributed to both flooding and droughts, and the massive amounts of water required to maintain numerous golf courses designed to improve the tourist industry adds to the problem.

Vanuatu

Previously the New Hebrides, this Pacific archipelago became independent from joint French and British rule in 1980. Copra and cocoa are the main exports, although coffee-growing had been introduced to the islands at the same time by the Europeans. Today, while Vanuatu, frightened by declining copra and cocoa prices, explores the possibilities of other export crops, cattle roam around the several hundred remaining *robusta* trees, which are basically untended except when the cherries are picked. The small crop is dry-processed completely by hand, loaded in 60 kg/ 132lb bags and sent to France. Although ungraded, it is described as fairly homogeneous and good.

Vietnam

As usual, the French first introduced coffee-growing to their colonies of Indo-China, but when most of the *arabica* succumbed to rust, it was replaced with *robusta*, the quality of which is fairly ordinary. What is not ordinary is the incredible growth in the Vietnamese coffee industry. After the devastation of the war, the remains of the French colonists' coffee estates were turned

into state collectives. In 1980 Vietnam was 42nd in world coffee production. In 1982 it exported 67,000 bags.

In 1988, with the imminent break-up of the Soviet Union, the Vietnamese government encouraged private enterprise, and by 1993 it exported more than three million bags of *robusta*, a figure which the 1997 crop saw more than doubled to 6.893 million bags, putting it third in world production behind Brazil and Colombia, with

Above: Though Colombia's coffee production outnumbers that of Vietnam by nearly two to one, Vietnam's rise from 42nd to 3rd place in world production rankings has been meteoric.

Indonesia close behind. And, while the coffee crop was burgeoning, so was the rice, as Vietnam became the third largest exporter after the US and Thailand. No wonder Vietnam is being billed as the next Asian "tiger".

ROASTING

Of all the processes involved with coffee, the quickest and most critical is roasting. Roasting coffee is a terrible responsibility, because in a few minutes beans that cost hundreds of people time, effort and money can be completely ruined by ignorance or carelessness. Roasting coffee is an art, and like all true art it takes years of practice before one becomes a master roaster; also, roasting is learned only by trial and error experience, and the errors may ruin many beans.

The main reason that roasting is difficult is that virtually every batch of beans is different from any other.

Above: These two samples of the same Ugandan Bugisu arabica *bean show the differences that occur during roasting, not only in colour, but also size and shape.*

In factories, a small sample of every shipment is "batch" roasted to anticipate any potential problem

that could arise in a commercial-size roast of perhaps 114kg/250lb of beans. A bright rather than a dull roast is desired, as dullness can indicate over-drying or poor processing; also, a good quality sample of beans will appear even, as a variety of colours, particularly "pales", among the coffee beans can indicate immature picking, poor sorting of cherries, and varying degrees of fermentation and drying on the plantation. Misshapen beans, broken beans, or simply an overly wide variety in bean sizes constitutes a "ragged" roast, as different-sized beans roast to different colours in the same roast.

The physical changes that occur to beans during roasting are many. The obvious changes are that the beans get bigger, gaining up to a third more of their former "green" size: this is because the decomposing carbohydrates create carbon dioxide, which literally causes the cells of the bean to expand. Meanwhile, most of the moisture remaining in the green beans after the plantation depulping, drying, storing and shipping, will be evaporated by the heat of roasting, and the beans will thus lose weight. Although moisture content can account for up to 23 per cent of green bean density, dehydration during roasting is usually kept to a maximum of about 15 per cent of the beans' weight, lest they become tasteless, brittle objects that reduce to powder at the first touch of a grinder's blade. The other very obvious physical change is that beans change colour during roasting.

Above: Sacks of different coffee samples, ready for roasting.

The Roasting Process

The most important effect of roasting beans is that the flavour is developed through the complex chemical changes caused by heat, which is the process of pyrolysis. It is estimated that a coffee bean contains more than 2,000 chemical substances, which may be broken down or changed during roasting into hundreds of "volatile aroma compounds". Various acids, oils, proteins, vitamins, sugars, starches and caffeine are altered; some are enhanced and some are diminished. In certain cases, some substances are both developed and then burned away if the roasting time is extended.

A light roast is seldom used commercially, as it shows up all the flaws inherent in beans, many of which will disappear, or at least be hidden by other flavours, in a dark roast. For example, if a coffee has the distinctive, sometimes unusual, pleasant and expensively acidic qualities of a high-grown *arabica*, it is better for it not to be dark-roasted. The darker the roast, the more uniform all coffees taste, as a truly dark roast will overwhelm the taste-buds, allowing them to perceive nothing of the coffee itself. A darker roast may sweeten some coffees, but only to a point; past a certain degree of roast all coffee becomes bitter. Also, the darker the roast, the greater the loss of acidity, that most sought-after quality.

Coffee roasters all vary in size and capacity, but the roasting process changes little from one size to another. All equipment should be preheated to a roasting temperature some minutes before the green beans are added, so all surfaces are uniformly hot. Many roasters are equipped with a revolving drum, often lined internally with curved metal strips that constantly toss the beans towards the centre of the drum. Above all, beans must be kept moving if they are to roast evenly, without burning. In fact, if a drum stops revolving while the heat is still on and the beans are hot, there is a danger of instant combustion within the drum. (The saying goes, "You're not a coffee roaster 'til you've had your first fire!")

Fine Tuning

The actual roast is a balancing act. Depending on the condition of the beans and the desired degree of roast, the beans are roasted at temperatures around 200–240°C/392–464°F, give or take about 20°C/68°F on either side. Many roasters have devices for air ventilation, which, like fan-assisted ovens, cause the beans to cook faster. As the roast goes on (in total the process will take between eight and fourteen minutes in a conventional-heat roaster), the beans retain more heat, and start to turn first yellow-green, then gold and then shades of brown. (All but the smallest drum roasters have devices allowing samples to be manually taken and returned to the drum.) The critical decision-making time is when the beans start to make popping sounds, as within seconds of this they turn dark very quickly. The drier the beans, the sooner the "popping" of pyrolysis begins; therefore, beans that are less green when unroasted, such as *robusta*, roast much quicker. Moisture-laden high-grown *arabicas* will take a bit longer to reach the same degree of roast.

The problem is deciding at what degree of roast each coffee tastes best, and the same coffee, roasted to

Above: Home roasting with a revolving drum over an outdoor fire.

different colours, will taste different. Even more complicated is the fact that the same coffee, roasted to the same colour at a higher temperature for a shorter time, will taste different if roasted at a lower temperature for a longer time. With extremes of either time or temperature, the same colour roast can produce coffee that tastes undercooked internally – cerealy or even green, or over-cooked – dried out, brittle when ground, or even burnt.

The last maddening fact of roasting is that the beans really need to be removed from the roaster immediately before the optimum colour is obtained, as they will darken in spite of cooling devices, such as revolving air-cooled trays outside the front of a drum roaster, or even the quick burst of water (quenching) of larger commercial machines, designed to stop the beans' continued cooking after they have left the drum. In later stages of roasting, beans release oils. Sometimes, even if a darker "oily" roast is not intended, the beans, if left in the roaster a fraction too long, will develop oil on their surfaces while in the cooling tray.

Types of Coffee Roasters

There are many sizes and types of coffee roasters available, ranging from factory machines, helped by sophisticated quenching devices and automatic timers, with the capacity to roast hundreds of pounds of beans, down to tiny "professional" batch roasters that roast no more than a couple of hundred grams. Some companies use "high-yield" roasters, developed in the 1970s, which "roast" beans in relatively small amounts, but in a matter of precisely timed seconds, perhaps up to two minutes, on fluidized "beds" of hot air rather than with the directly transferred heat of metal drums. Called high-yield because the beans' surface areas expand so much as to produce more coffee when ground, these roasters are not favoured by many experts, who feel that the high-yield flavour is not as fully developed and round as that produced in conventional roasters.

There are small table-top roasters for the domestic market, but they can be hard to find, and expensive when located. Many people find it a joy to

Above: Roasted coffee beans spill out of the drum into the cooling tray below.

roast small amounts of coffee in frying pans over a cooker-burner (on the stove). (Oven-roasting is not recommended mainly because it is not possible to keep the beans moving, and the roast is therefore usually very uneven and uncontrollable.) To roast coffee beans correctly, use a heavy, possibly cast-iron, frying pan, which has been warmed up. Add a single layer of beans over a low heat, increasing the heat to high as they roast, stirring constantly with a wooden spatula. In some Middle-Eastern countries whole spices such as cloves, cinnamon, cardamom, ginger, or fennel may be added, to be ground with them later. Other countries actually roast the beans in small amounts of butter or sugar, depending on the desired flavour.

When the beans are roasted to the desired colour, they must be cooled immediately, perhaps by putting them into a pre-chilled container, or onto a very cold surface. It is not advisable to grind beans for brewing immediately after roasting as the flavour will be sharp, green and sour. To achieve the desired mellowness of a good brew, do not grind until the coffee beans have had time to de-gas, preferably for a minimum of twelve hours.

Above: Checking the beans after the roasting is completed.

Degrees of Roast

As in tasters' terminology, there is no standardized definition of different degrees of roast. "Light", "medium" and "dark" are the most-used terms, but coffees are seldom truly light-roasted, and there are many perceived degrees of medium and dark. (Also, it should be noted that Turkish coffee is not dark-roasted.) A combination of various opinions results in the following possibilities:

Light This roast is used only for extremely good-quality delicate or high-grown *arabicas*. Ideal for breakfast coffees when acidic coffees are mellowed by the addition of milk or cream. The American version of this roast, "Cinnamon", is so called because it is the colour of cinnamon bark. It is high in acidity and low in body. Also sometimes called "half-city" or "New England" roast.

Medium "American roast"; or possibly "city" if slightly darker than medium. Also called "regular", "brown"; as dark as possible with no oily surfaces.

Viennese American term meaning slightly darker than medium roast. This roast is speckled with dark-brown spots, and a bit of oil on surface; also "light French", or "full city".

Dark "Spanish"; "Cuban"; there may be some oil on bean surface, "deep brown"; "French roast".

Continental Can also be referred to as "Double roast"; "High"; in America, "French roast", "New Orleans roast" and "European". With a nearly dark/bittersweet-chocolate colouring, this roast is variously described as "very dark", "dark French", "heavy" and "Italian".

Italian In America, darker than in Italy; may be called "espresso" roasts (or may not!); almost black and very oily; the predominant taste is the roast rather than the coffee. Coffee beans should never be burned black.

Even if there were universal agreement on the meaning of the above roasting terms, there would not be general consensus as to how dark certain coffees should or should not be roasted. In America, all roasts are becoming darker, probably because of the emphasis on espresso and espresso-based drinks, which are seen to be the height of sophistication. In fact, in many other countries as well, there are those who think the goal of all roasting is to make the coffee taste pleasant and balanced, even if this involves suppressing the more unique and unusual flavours. It must be remembered that dark roasts were originally designed to hide the flaws of inferior coffees, and to bring out the best in cheap blends loaded with inferior-tasting *robusta*. Surely true sophistication is to approach every coffee with an open mind, prepared to judge it on its own merits.

Light-roasted beans

Medium-roasted beans

Dark-roasted beans

Above: The enormous differences in taste between coffees are best appreciated when the beans are treated to their own best roast. Sometimes a coffee's more unusual attributes are outside the normal range of coffee tastes.

BLENDING

An ideal cup of coffee should have good aroma, good colour (if milk or cream is to be added), good body, and good tastes for whichever way the coffee will be roasted, brewed and served at any intended time of day. Out of the millions of bags of coffee processed every year, relatively few can provide the "ideal cup" criteria without a little help from their friends, the other coffees with whom they will be blended. Regarding the few that can stand alone, they will probably not provide an all-round, perfect, well-balanced cup; rather, they will have one or two particularly fine points that more than compensate for falling short on other aspects.

Balancing Flavours

Each coffee used in a blend should make its own contribution. Dark roasting hides the not-so-desirable flavours of *robustas*, and of other coffees that may happen to have lower acidity, but usually have good body, which is only enhanced by the dark roast. Conversely, many high-grown *arabicas*, while producing a sharp flavour that can dominate the overall tastes of other less acidic coffees, are "thin-in-the-cup", and lack body. With these watery *arabicas*, the solution is not to roast darker, as roasting burns off the acids that contribute to the sharp, "expensive" taste. Other coffees may be pleasantly acceptable, having no particularly distinctive quality either to recommend or condemn them; these neutrals are ideal for bulking out a blend, as their flavours are not obtrusive, nor are they lacking in body.

There are no rules or taboos in blending coffees, but the idea is to combine coffees that complement each other, not those that are similar. A good starting point, therefore, for a middle-of-the-road, any-time-of-day, well-rounded cup of coffee, would be a blend of perhaps 35 per cent high-grown *arabica* to provide the dominant flavour, 15 per cent darker-roasted *robusta* or heavier-bodied, lower-acidity coffee to provide the body, and 50 per cent of a more neutral and possibly more affordable coffee, like an average Brazilian Santos,

Above: Few coffees, on their own, can provide the perfect combination of good aroma, colour, body and taste. Blending seeks to achieve this in a consistent form.

or one of the slightly lower quality and less expensive Central American coffees. The character of this blend could be changed considerably just by altering the proportions. Also, lowering the proportions of each would allow for the addition of a small amount of a different, fourth, coffee, perhaps an unwashed *arabica*, as most "natural" *arabicas* are known for their sweetness.

All blends should be worked out in percentage weights with a taste or style in mind, whether the overall blend is to be, for example, a "fruity" blend; a "mild" breakfast coffee; a "deep, rich, syrupy" after-dinner indulgence; a naturally low-caffeine blend; a high-caffeine "pick-me-up" with lots of caffeine-rich *robusta*; or perhaps simply a strongish-flavoured coffee to provide the basis of an alcoholic coffee cocktail. If a blend is to be used often and remain consistent, the availability and affordability of each particular coffee must be considered.

Classic Combinations

A few combinations of particular coffees are so successful that they have become standards through the years. Mocha (either from Yemen or a reasonable second from Ethiopia) and

Mysore from India are the most famous coffee marriage. Mocha–Java will be a bit earthier and heavy, but still winey, and wild (or gamey) from the Mocha. A very particular Mocha–Brazil combination is that favoured by Middle-Eastern roasters for the traditional "Turkish" coffee flavour: the Brazilian coffee is the famous, or infamous, rio-y flavour. A good Brazilian Santos will smooth out an average *robusta* to make a strong, smooth blend, while a blend requiring some lightness can be illuminated by the addition of some Kenyan coffee, or a high-grown Central American. A Haiti or a Peruvian adds some decent flavour without being too expensive. An aged coffee adds sweetness, and a Colombian can add aroma as well as body and flavour.

In America, a "New Orleans Blend", and in Britain a "French Blend", neither to be confused with any degree of roast, is a blend of coffee and the roots of the chicory plant, just as a "Viennese" blend in Britain contains roasted fig or fig-seasoning ground in with the coffee. Of these two "economy" blends, the Viennese is cheaper, being the least expensive coffee blend of the average British supermarket range.

STORAGE

No matter how carefully coffee is grown, processed, blended, roasted, ground and brewed, the ultimate quality depends on one overall factor: freshness. Considering the ready availability of ground coffee, there would never be any real reason to grind coffee beans at all – except, crucially, to obtain the freshest possible taste. When coffee is roasted, carbon dioxide develops within the beans; it escapes from the coffee for several hours, and does so with a force that ruptures seams in tin cans and causes softer packages to "balloon". Many roasters, therefore, allow the roasted beans or ground coffee to stand for hours before packing. Of course, while standing, the coffee goes stale, losing its volatile aromas and absorbing tasteless oxygen.

Given the practicalities of coffee packaging (which can be vacuum-sealed tins (cans), brick packs, one-way valve-lock bags, or gas-flushed packs, all trying to let the gas out and keep the freshness in), no coffee is ever 100 per cent fresh. It's no good trying to roast, grind and brew coffee within a few minutes because, until the coffee has degassed, it will not taste good.

However, the fact is that roasted beans do retain their freshness longer than ground coffee, as there is less cell surface exposed to the air. Assuming that the roasting company and the retailer have just roasted the beans and maintained their freshness, the obvious next question is how best to store them at home.

Experts differ widely in advice on storing coffee, particularly beans. Certainly coffee can absorb odours easily, and will taste of those odours when brewed. Therefore some people advise against keeping coffee in the fridge. Others advocate using an airtight container, which will keep out oxygen, but what about the oxygen sealed inside with the beans? The solution would be to keep the surface of the beans very high in the jar, but then one could never use the beans further down in the jar.

Even the freezing of beans has its opponents, who say that after freezing, the coffee will never taste the same. Certainly, freezing darker-roasted beans, which have an oily surface, is definitely not a good idea, as the oils congeal and never regain their original consistency and distribution throughout the coffee.

Above: Coffee pods for certain espresso machines are factory produced.

The ideal solution to the problem of keeping coffee fresh is to purchase smaller amounts more frequently. In Italy, for example, many people buy small amounts, perhaps 100-200g/3½-7oz of coffee several times a week from their local coffee bar; they choose a blend of roasted beans, and the *barista* (barman) grinds them. The ground coffee is then placed in a grease-lined paper bag. Similarly, a person who shops infrequently could still maximize the freshness of the coffee by buying several smaller packs of factory-sealed coffee instead of one or two large packs, as unopened factory-sealed containers will stay fresh for many months.

Helpful hints for keeping whole beans and ground coffee as fresh as possible

• Never pour dry coffee out of one container into another, as that is deliberate exposure.

• Keep the smallest air space between the top of the coffee and the lid, or top, of the container.

• If kept in the refrigerator, seal the original bag or packet as tightly as possible around the coffee, place a clip on it or a rubber band around it, and place it in a similar-sized airtight container.

• If the beans will not be used within a couple of weeks, pack them as for the refrigerator and store in the freezer. It is not a good idea to freeze ground coffee.

• Store small amounts of freshly ground coffee in resealable bags, pressing down gently to trap as little oxygen as possible in the bag to maximize freshness.

THE ART OF COFFEE DRINKING

Many people derive as much pleasure from brewing coffee as from drinking it. For some, making coffee is a time-honoured traditional ritual, and the satisfaction is even greater with the knowledge that one is using the same equipment that yielded cups of the much-loved liquid to past generations. Other people delight in acquiring and using the latest trendy gadgets, and certainly coffee brewing and serving offer scope for constant design innovations, be they practical or aesthetic, or both. The following pages show you all you need to know to be able to select, grind and brew coffee with a range of different equipment — all part of the quest for the perfect cup.

HOME GRINDING

When purchasing a grinder, the choices may not be many, but the price range is wide, and it is best to bear in mind a particular brewing method when choosing a grinder, as the degree of grind required is dictated by this.

Hand Mills

For hundreds of years, coffee to be used at home was ground by hand with a box-type mill that held only a small amount of coffee. Anyone who uses one of these, and they are still available, realizes immediately that a greater storage capacity is not required; it takes so long to grind the beans that any ground coffee would be drunk before the little box could ever be full. Still, the hand mill can grind well, and with a surprising degree of uniformity in the particles. The grind is adjustable within a range that would qualify as "coarse", to a "medium" or even "fine", but it cannot grind fine enough for espresso. These are inexpensive, but it is an extremely time-consuming method of grinding.

Below: Hand mills have changed little for hundreds of years.

Using a hand mill

1 Rotating the lid reveals the aperture through which the beans are poured.

2 The coffee grounds, which fall into the drawer below, should be of a fairly consistent size, whether coarse, medium or fine.

Turkish Grinders

The prince of hand mills is the genuine Turkish grinder. The tall, heavy copper or brass mills are still used today throughout Turkey and other Middle Eastern countries for home grinding. The dome-like top pulls off to reveal the space where the whole beans go. The handle on the top is used to turn the mill; this detaches and fits over the grind adjustment screw, which is revealed in the middle of the cylinder when the bottom half is removed. At the end of grinding – the range of which is all degrees of "extremely fine" – the bottom part of the cylinder holds the ground coffee. Middle Eastern coffee must be ground to the consistency of talcum powder, something no other type

of domestic grinder can achieve. The difficulty in serving an authentic Middle Eastern coffee is not in getting the grind right; rather, it is in finding the right blend of coffee roasted to the right degree. (It is far easier just to buy a commercial brand, such as People's, imported from Nicosia, or Kurukahveçi, from Istanbul.)

Below: Turkish grinder.

Using a Turkish grinder

1 Remove the handle and dome top and insert the whole beans into the upper cylinder. Use the handle to adjust the grind screw to achieve the desired grind size.

2 After obtaining the desired grind consistency, replace the dome top and handle. Turn the handle to grind the beans. Remove the coffee from the bottom cylinder.

Electric Grinders

There is a wide range of electric coffee grinders available for the domestic market, most with some sort of receptacle or space for catching the ground coffee, which never needs to hold more than enough coffee for a day or two. There are two general designs for domestic grinders – those that simply cut the beans with a propeller-type blade, and those that truly grind the beans between metal discs.

Blade, or propeller, grinder The most common kind of home coffee grinder is the rotating blade, or propeller, grinder. This type, which sometimes comes as an accessory for a blender or some other food processor, is almost useless when it comes to coffee. The first problem is that it is nearly impossible to get uniformity of grind, which means that the coffee liquid will be very unevenly extracted. The larger chunks are wasted if they are too coarse for the water to penetrate; the fine powder particles will quickly saturate and yield bitterness, and can also clog a filter basket and create sediment in cups of plunger-pot coffee.

With a blade grinder it is best to grind small amounts of beans, shaking them up and down in the hope that the propellers will get to all the particles. Running the machine in short bursts will help you avoid scorching the beans by overheating. At least it is relatively easy to keep a blade-type grinder clean and avoid contamination with rancid coffee oils. With the machine unplugged, use a damp cloth or sponge to wipe the chamber and the blades. The plastic lid is washable, but must be carefully rinsed so as not to leave a soapy taste for the beans to absorb.

Below: Electric grinder.

Using an electric blade grinder

Always ensure the grinder is un-plugged when adding or removing coffee, or when cleaning.

Burr mills By far the best all-round domestic grinder is a burr mill, which is the closest thing to a commercial grinder in that two metal discs perform the grinding. The uniformity of particles is amazingly precise considering the fairly compact size of the machines. The costs vary widely among brands, but even the cheapest will do a decent job. In fact, it is probably better to invest in a good burr mill than in an expensive coffee-maker, if the object is a good cup of freshly ground coffee.

Burr mills are noisy and slow, but easy to operate, as the grind choice is made by selecting a number or degree on a knob. Manufacturers' instructions, which indicate certain settings for desired grinds, may not be entirely accurate, but once the desired grind is discovered, it is easy to get consistent results. Certain brands of burr mills are better at one range of grind, although all are adjustable. Some also have a timer, and will switch off automatically.

Never grind more coffee than will be used within a day or two. Before grinding, clear the discs of any old coffee remains, or of any coffee of a different origin or blend, by running the grinder with just a few beans of the new batch, before grinding in earnest.

For those that need an espresso grind, it is possible to buy a burr mill that specializes in very fine espresso grinds. They are precise and quick, but tend to cost more than those intended for a more general range of grinds; even so, in the espresso grinder category there are some models that can do an adequate job without requiring a bank loan. The price can be daunting, but it may be worth paying a higher price for a model with a measured espresso dose-dispenser, which makes the task of loading the filter-holder infinitely simpler and less messy, as the proper amount of coffee required is dispensed straight into the filter-holder. Espresso brewing, generally, benefits from buying proper equipment; a good grinder is just as important as the brewing machine, if not more so.

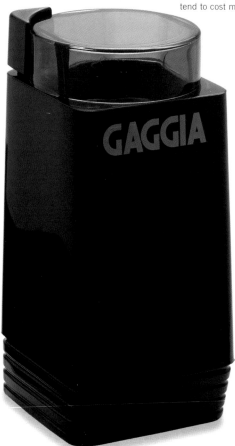

Below left and right: Two electric mills intended for espresso grind. The one on the right has a convenient dose-dispenser.

Degrees of Grind

Commercial coffee grinds vary from brand to brand. Coffee companies set and monitor coffee grinds by using mesh sieves stacked in a series with the coarsest mesh at the top. The level at which the particles of a grind stop falling, as well as the percentage of particles arrested in other sieves of the stacks, gauges not only the basic degree of grind, but also indicates the uniformity of particle size. If, for example, a coffee company wanted to check its medium-grind coffee, intended for a cafetière (press pot) or percolator, it would expect that a high percentage of particles from a sample of ground coffee would stop at Gauge 9. If too many particles were to fall too far, or perhaps never even drop through to the Gauge 9 sieve, the company would know that the grind was faulty, and that the grinder might need re-calibrating.

Also, beans grind differently depending on the degree of roast. For example, darker-roasted beans become more brittle with moisture loss and are more prone to break into various-sized pieces and powder. The grinder might need some adjustment in order to produce the same degree of grind as that obtained with a different roast.

An excellent way to determine the correct degree of grind to suit the brewing method is to obtain a small sample of commercially ground coffee. Rubbed between thumb and forefinger, the degree of grind is relatively easy to judge. Commercial grinds are specifically designated as Turkish, espresso, filter fine, and medium grinds. Grinds coarser than medium are practically non-existent commercially. They are generally used only in *al fresco* or jug (carafe) brewing, and are not very economical, since the same amount of beans ground coarsely produces less volume, less extraction and therefore less flavour than if it were ground finer.

In recent years, certain coffee companies have attempted to gain a larger share of the market by producing in-between grinds, promising consumers of filter and cafetière coffee alike that the same "omnigrind" works for both. Another grind (which defies the laws of physics) is one that supposedly satisfies the requirements of both filter and espresso machines. Not only does the production of such grinds result in the wrong extraction in one or the other of the brewing methods, it also confuses people who want to understand why coffee is ground to different degrees.

One good result of the "omnigrind" for machines requiring a fine- or a medium-ground coffee, is that it provides the perfect alternative grind for the Neapolitan flip machine and the Cona vacuum machine. Both of these methods of brewing benefit from the greater extraction rate of a near-filter grind, and the fact that the very slightly larger particles of the "omnigrind" are not as prone to fall into the coffee liquid because of the machine design.

One tip for espresso perfectionists: in Italy, to maintain the production of a perfect espresso, the barman (*barista*) will alter his grinder to produce a very slightly coarser grind on a day of high humidity.

Turkish grind

Espresso grind

Fine (filter) grind

Medium grind

Omnigrind

BEFORE BEGINNING TO BREW

A coffee lover, setting out to make the best possible coffee, or at least a very enjoyable cup of coffee, should ponder several things before investing in any equipment. He or she must first consider which type of coffee is the preferred taste. It can be anything from the rich flavour of espresso or a mellow, high-grown *arabica* blend, whose acidity is softened by a touch of cream. Perhaps a full-bodied cup, providing pleasure in both taste and stimulation, is what is required. It is important to have the freedom to experiment with all sorts of blends and roasts.

Second, the time of day and how the choice of coffee is brewed needs to be taken into account. At breakfast, when time is short, volume and caffeine content are perhaps most welcome. After dinner, however, a small cup of pure flavour is more appropriate, ensuring that both the conversation continues and the palate is cleared of any lingering flavours of the meal still clinging to the taste buds. At a quiet, reflective moment, or when seeking to unwind, slowly savouring a deep, smoky, velvety black coffee transports the mind into another place and time.

The volume and strength of the coffee should also be considered. Is a small amount of coffee likely to be drunk all at once or are several cups required immediately? Perhaps one person may want to drink several cups over an extended period. Texture, too, is important. The liquid could slip down better if it were clean and clear of sediment, or one might prefer the roughness of a brew steeped in the particles from which it comes. Weak or strong, clear or thick, morning or evening, all of the requirements of coffee can be met by one or the other method of brewing.

Ensuring Lasting Flavour

Once the brewing method is decided, the question of "to grind or not to grind, and if so, what grind is necessary?" can be answered. The ultimate question is then "Can the magic of the moment last, can the coffee be maintained as fresh as it was brewed, until it is finished?" This question is perhaps the easiest to answer because it has been discovered that hot coffee stored in a preheated vacuum flask will taste good far longer than that kept hot by any other method. Nothing lasts forever, and the fresh flavour may very gradually deteriorate, but the coffee is not being heated up and cooled down and heated up again, which is what happens to the coffee molecules in a jug (carafe) on a hotplate.

Left: From elegant serving styles to tough durability, vacuum (or insulated) jugs and flasks can provide the solution to almost any situation where coffee quality needs to be maintained for more than half an hour.

THE PRINCIPLES OF COFFEE BREWING

The beverage called coffee is the result of mixing dry coffee with water. The combination can be done by one of many methods – ranging from the very simple, with the minimum of equipment, to the use of complex machines that can be prohibitively expensive. Understanding a few facts about coffee brewing can help answer some of the questions that arise when wondering which brewing method to use.

Extracting the Flavour

A single coffee bean is an extremely complex entity, being composed of literally hundreds of substances, many of which are water-soluble. Nearly one-third of these water-soluble compounds can be removed in normal extraction processes. The goal of brewing coffee, however, is not to extract the greatest number of elements from ground coffee, because not all of them are

desirable. Expert tasters generally agree that the overall coffee flavour, which consists of colour, aroma, taste and body, is best when about 18–22 per cent of the flavour components have left the solid coffee and infused into the water. When more than 22 per cent of the extractable materials permeate into the water, over-extraction occurs and harsh flavours are added to the brew, as the last substances to leave the grounds are unpleasant and bitter.

A second technical consideration is that, even if only the best-flavoured components have been extracted from the coffee, the cup flavour can be too concentrated or too diluted, depending on how much water is used. Again, most expert tasters generally agree that a cup of coffee tastes best when the liquid consists of 98.4–98.7 per cent water and 1.3–1.6 per cent "soluble solids", the latter being what would be

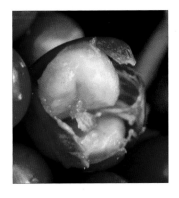

Above: From the coffee cherry spill two beans: the object of universal interest.

left if a cup of liquid coffee was reduced back to dry ingredients by an evaporation process. This ideal coffee strength is easily achieved by controlling the proportion of ground coffee to water, which for European tastes is about 50–75g/2–3oz/ per 1 litre/1¾ pints/4 cups of water. Many would consider normal strength coffee as one brewed at about 55g/10 tbsp per litre of water. Much of North America drinks a weaker cup.

The most beautiful and expensive coffee machines do not always produce the most satisfying cup of coffee, and when choosing any coffee-brewing equipment, consideration must be given to whether the design allows for a correct balance of brewing factors, as well as taking into account various safety aspects.

Water Condition

People quite often buy coffee from a particular place where they previously enjoyed an excellent cup. They take the coffee home, brew it correctly, then wonder why it doesn't taste the same. As a cup of coffee is more than 98 per cent water, the condition and taste of the water are at least as important as the coffee used, and only water from the same source will re-create an exact taste. Coffee experts tend to agree that the best water for brewing coffee is slightly hard; a few minerals will

---

Key brewing factors

Correct coffee brewing depends on a balance of several factors, and each coffee will react differently and uniquely to exactly the same balance of factors. When brewing, consider the following factors:
• The degree of grind of the ground coffee.
• The ratio of coffee to water.
• The condition of the water.
• The water temperature.
• The contact time between the coffee and the water.

Above: These two glasses show the difference in strength when coffee is made with 50g/2oz of coffee per litre, left, and when made with only 75g/3oz, right.

The importance of having the right grind

The finer the grind, the greater the surface area exposed to the water and the faster the extraction of soluble solids. Finely-ground particles of coffee are thus required for brewing methods where the contact time between the coffee and the water is shorter.

Conversely, a coarser grind will help to delay the extraction when grounds are left in the container from which the coffee will be served. A good grinder, whether manual or electric, will reduce the coffee beans to particles of a consistent size, so as to ensure an even extraction.

coffee made with distilled water would also be tasteless and would need a "pinch of salt to bring out the flavour". Wrong! Because it contains nothing to interfere with the extraction, coffee brewed with tasteless, distilled water has a very strong coffee flavour, which in the course of normal brewing, especially with a cheap blend, could easily be far too strong. Very soft water requires less coffee per brew, or a slightly coarser grind, or less contact time – any of which work to ensure that over-extraction does not occur. The old wives' habit of adding a pinch of salt may have worked not in bringing out the flavour, but rather in toning it down and modifying the flavour for the better, if the original water was very soft.

Chlorinated or other chemically treated water, or water polluted by old pipes, rust or other tastes, can affect the flavour of coffee. Filtering devices, which remove objectionable tastes, are available both in jug (carafe) form and in more permanent systems that attach to the kitchen main water pipe.

Generally, experts agree that fresh, cold water, which presumably has a higher oxygen content, makes the best coffee. Somewhat confusingly, however, it is oxygen that causes ground coffee to go stale, and it is from oxygen that vacuum flasks protect liquid coffee. Thus the need to have oxygen in the brewing water seems surprising, especially as convincing scientific explanations are rather scarce. (This calls for the challenge of a taste test: try brewing the same coffee with stale, warm water and with fresh, cold water and observe the difference.) Remember that most electric coffee-makers are equipped with thermostats which expect to start with cold water, and may not function very well if hot water is used.

Water Temperature

Water of any temperature will extract coffee, but hot water extracts faster than cold. Never pour boiling water on coffee, even on instant, as it brings out a harsh flavour. The optimum temperature range for coffee preparation is around 92–96°C/197–205°F.

Comparing water types

You can easily do a few comparative tests for yourself on the effect different types of water have on the flavour of a cup of coffee. Try different waters, such as tap and distilled, and also add a pinch of salt to some distilled water to see if salt does in fact "bring out the flavour".

Conversely, if cooler water is used, the brew will be under-extracted. When coffee is intentionally boiled, as with Turkish brewing, sweetening offsets any bitterness.

Contact Time

When ground coffee and water are combined, a certain amount of time is needed for the water to saturate the coffee grounds and extract the various soluble solids, some of which take longer than others to pass into the water. For the first few minutes of the brewing cycle, the "blend" of the flavour compounds in the liquid is changing continuously. If the contact time is to be limited, the particles must be finer for the water to penetrate them and extract the flavour compounds. If the contact time is very long, the grounds should be coarser so as to slow the rate of extraction. In certain methods of brewing, such as those in which cold water drips very slowly through coffee grounds for several hours, the resulting brew will be extremely bitter, which is to be expected with such over-extraction, but will be offset later by dilution and sweetening.

enhance the coffee flavour, hence the old custom of adding a "pinch of salt to bring out the flavour". If the brewing water is very hard, however, the calcium and magnesium ions can actually get between the water molecules and the coffee particles, interfering with the extraction process, and the resulting brew will have little flavour.

When considering the effect of soft water in brewing coffee, it is interesting to examine the softest water possible, which is distilled or de-ionized; as water it has virtually no taste, and no one would dream of making coffee with it. It could therefore be assumed that

Helpful Hints

• When using coffee equipment for the first time, follow the manufacturer's instructions. The following pages give recommended measures of coffee for each method of brewing. A good idea is to take one coffee scoop, and, having filled and weighed its capacity content, use it all the time for ease of measuring.

• If all the same equipment is to be used regularly and for the same amounts of coffee, note the number and size of the scoops of dry coffee required as well as the level of water in the measuring jug (cup). If it should happen that the first coffee brewed turns out to be weaker or stronger than preferred – all coffee is a matter of personal taste – make a note to adjust either the coffee, the water or perhaps the brewing time.

• Many coffee makers have indicators for the level of water required for a specific number of cups, but this rarely seems to correspond to the actual number of cups poured, no matter what size cup is being used. If in doubt about the ratio of coffee to water, it is far better to use more coffee than may be required; if the brew is too strong, it can be diluted after brewing. Coffee made too weak, that is, with too little dry coffee, cannot be "undone".

• Remember that coffee grounds absorb some water, so the yield of liquid coffee will always be less than the amount of water used in the brew; 600g of coffee will absorb 1.2 litres of water, which means that 1g of dry coffee will absorb 2ml of water.

• As much as possible, never reheat coffee and never use the same coffee grounds more than once.

• Any time a small amount of coffee (one or two cups) is being brewed, and the amount of coffee is not dictated by the size of the machine (as it is with the espresso pot, for example), use proportionally more dry coffee per cup. Approximately 50g coffee per litre of water is almost exactly 1oz per pint; this makes a slightly weakish "normal" brew and is a good starting point for determining preferred strength.

Above: The key to a good espresso machine is a mix of fine-tuning of the machine's pressure by the manufacturer, the skills of the roaster and blender, and the careful grinding and brewing of the barista (barman).

Some useful conversions

DRY MEASURES

28g = 1oz
440g = 1lb
5.7g coffee = 1 rounded tbsp
2.5g coffee = 1 heaped tsp
55g coffee = 10 tbsp/generous $\frac{2}{3}$ cup

LIQUID MEASURES

50ml = 2fl oz/$\frac{1}{4}$ cup
1 litre = 33fl oz/4 cups
600ml = 20fl oz/2$\frac{1}{2}$ cups

1 espresso
cup (empty) =
2$\frac{1}{2}$fl oz

Liquid
coffee for
1 espresso cup =
1$\frac{1}{2}$fl oz coffee
(about 44ml)

Below: The basic equipment for brewing coffee couldn't be simpler – a scoop, measuring jug, pan and coffee – the trick is to familiarize yourself with your equipment and what amount and type of coffee and water best suit your equipment and tastes. Whatever the brewing method, measuring the coffee and water, noting the levels of each and the resulting flavour, makes successive brews easy.

COFFEE AND HEALTH

Caffeine ($C_8H_{10}N_4O_2$) is a white, slightly bitter alkaloid, sometimes also called "theine". It is a natural ingredient in coffee, where it comprises two to three per cent of the weight of each bean, or about 60–90mg in an average cup of coffee. *Robusta* coffee has a much higher caffeine content than does *arabica*. As well as in coffee, caffeine is found in about sixty other plants, such as tea, cocoa, guarana and kola, and in products made from them, such as chocolate and cola-based soft drinks.

Because caffeine, as a stimulant of the central nervous system and cerebral circulation, imparts a feeling of energy and can often alleviate headaches, it is an ingredient in many pharmaceutical products, particularly those for headaches and colds. It is also a diuretic.

Tests have proved that caffeine increases mental alertness and the ability to concentrate, but the idea that strong coffee can offset the effects of too great a consumption of alcohol is a fallacy. Coffee does not "sober up" a truly inebriated person. Rather, it wakes one up, and as a sleepy drunk is preferable to a lively one, administering strong coffee to counter the alcohol is probably not a good idea. Also, the ensuing hangover seems to be worsened by the added complication of large doses of caffeine.

Excess Coffee

In general, too much caffeine consumption can cause palpitations, shaky hands, a feeling of anxiety and an inability to sleep. "Too much", however, varies enormously among caffeine consumers: for some people a single cup of coffee causes ill effects, while others thrive on ten cups a day. Coffee is one of the most widely researched substances on Earth, and yet scientific and medical opinions are still extremely divided. There is every reason to believe that the individual coffee drinker, exercising some degree of moderation according to his or her level of caffeine tolerance, can probably look forward to many years of "safe" coffee enjoyment.

Coffee is an acidic drink, especially if it is high-grown *arabica*, and many people who find that coffee upsets their stomach blame the caffeine content instead of the acidity. Decaffeination does not remove acidity, so drinking decaffeinated coffee is not the solution for stomach upset. Acid-neutralized coffees are difficult to find, but they are available in North America and the United Kingdom, in France (*café allégé*) and Germany (*reizarmer Kaffee*). They may not, however, be particularly tasty, as it is acidity that contributes so crucially to the flavours of high-grown *arabicas* and their blends.

Above: To many people, the difference in flavour between decaffeinated and regular coffee beans will be slight. When market research indicated a growing niche for decaffeinated coffee, better quality beans were introduced by coffee companies.

Coffee and Medical Research

It has been proven that pregnancy greatly increases the time required for a woman's body to metabolize caffeine, and, as caffeine can be transferred to a foetus (fetus), it is recommended that a pregnant woman reduce her regular coffee intake by at least 50 per cent, with greater spaces of time between cups. If concerned, eliminate all caffeine from the diet during pregnancy.

For years, many thorough and exhaustive studies have been conducted to try to link coffee consumption with cancer or heart disease, but to no avail; nor does caffeine cause high blood pressure. One study indicating a definite link between coffee and high blood cholesterol (which in itself may cause cardiovascular problems), found that cholesterol was increased only in certain subjects who drank large amounts of coffee prepared by a particular Scandinavian method of excessive boiling and steeping of coffee. Filtering the boiled coffee before consumption, however, seemed to eliminate the cholesterol-raising oils. Other tests that link boiled coffee to an increase in cholesterol have proved that it is some other substance, and not caffeine, which raises the cholesterol levels, as decaffeinated coffee – but only that which has been boiled and is consumed unfiltered – seems to contribute to higher cholesterol. Of course, if one suffers from low caffeine tolerance, is concerned about the safety of caffeine consumption, or simply wants to enjoy the taste of a late-night coffee drink without losing any sleep, a decaffeinated or even one brewed half-and-half, provides a perfectly acceptable alternative.

Decaffeinated Coffee

It is a fairly accurate statement that, although decaffeinated coffee has been produced since the early years of the 20th century, most of it was rather tasteless, at best, before about 1980. During the mid-80s, most likely due to numerous unfounded health scares about caffeine, there was an unprecedented interest in decaffeinated coffee. Almost immediately the flavour of decaffeinated coffee improved immensely, and all the major brands of supermarket coffee offered such a version. The decaffeination processes were changed very little, if at all. The Swiss Water Process, patented by

Coffex SA in 1979, needed several years to acquire a wide following, and many coffee companies are still producing decaffeinated beans that are not water-processed. So why did decaffeinated coffee start tasting good? The answer is that suddenly there was a market for it. For years only the very committed health enthusiast had drunk decaffeinated coffee, and coffee companies did not bother to use good beans for such a low-profile product. By about 1987, when decaffeinated sales represented around 25 per cent of the massive United States coffee market, coffee companies, in order to cash in on the phenomenal demand, started using higher quality beans for decaff products, and the flavour improved as quickly as the market grew.

Since caffeine is almost tasteless, except for a slight bitterness, its removal should not interfere with the coffee flavour at all, unless the decaffeination process inadvertently extracts flavour compounds as well as the caffeine. The goal of all decaff processors has been to remove only the caffeine, not the flavour. It is the quality of the beans that will ultimately determine the flavour of the coffee.

For around two hundred years it has been known that, while caffeine survives roasting, retaining its properties through temperatures as high as 240°C/475°F, it is completely vulnerable to liquid, and will pass from green (unroasted) coffee beans into any liquid in which they are soaked. Some liquids extract the caffeine faster than others.

Left: Hide the package and most people would not know from taste alone if a coffee was decaffeinated.

The Decaffeination Process

The oldest method of decaffeinating coffee is that used by Kaffee Hag, among others, in which carbon dioxide, pressurized to a supercritical nearly fluid state, is forced through steamed green beans, removing the caffeine. Many companies do not use this method simply because the equipment and facilities required are so expensive.

The most widespread method of decaffeination is soaking warmed or steamed green beans in a solution containing a chemical solvent, usually methylene chloride, which is selective in its target: all but about three per cent of the caffeine, and practically none of the flavour, passes into the solvent. The beans, rinsed and dried, go on to be roasted, and almost any trace of the solvent remaining with the beans is destroyed in the high roasting temperatures. In 1995 this method was banned in Europe because methylene chloride vapours, particularly in aerosol form, destroy the ozone layer. The United States Food and Drug Administration has limited methylene chloride residues in brewed coffee to ten parts per million, a figure that does not worry most coffee processors, who insist the actual residue is already less than one-millionth part anyway.

The slowest, and therefore most expensive, form of decaffeination is the patented Swiss Water Method, which uses only steamed beans, hot water and carbon filters to remove the caffeine. Unfortunately, some of the volatile flavour compounds also go with the caffeine, so the water is evaporated, and the remaining flavour concentrate is then sprayed on to the decaffeinated beans.

Although coffee lovers and experts alike are still convinced that decaffeination destroys the taste of coffee, many would find it extremely difficult to differentiate between a "regular" coffee and its "unleaded" ("no-lead") version. In an exhaustive tasting project carried out over a period of several weeks at the International Coffee Organization, United Kingdom, a panel of trained tasters compared three cups of coffee, each made from beans from the same crop and same plantation: one cup was coffee decaffeinated with a solvent, one was water-processed decaffeinated, and the third was regular un-decaffeinated coffee. The tests were carried out time and again, not just with one set of coffee samples, but with coffees from Kenya, Colombia and Brazil. The results showed that often tasters could not tell which cups contained decaffeinated coffee, and, further, when tasters thought they could distinguish a difference, if asked for a preference, they often preferred the taste of the chemically decaffeinated coffee to the "regular" version of the same coffee.

Anyone who loves the taste of coffee, but is concerned about the effects of caffeine, should realize that today there are some fabulous decaffeinated coffees available, particularly from specialist shops. Cover the label, hide the box, and enjoy one of the luxuries of life: a cup of good coffee.

Left: Good beans make good flavour – decaff or not.

BREWING EQUIPMENT

Considering that there are a limited number of ways that coffee and water can be combined, it is amazing how many factors there are in brewing that make a difference to the resulting coffee flavour. But then it seems rather miraculous that anyone ever thought of combining the two substances anyway. Almost certainly, the first means of brewing coffee (probably only a few steps removed from the earliest practice of chewing on the fruit) was based on boiling the beans in water, although it was probably the entire coffee cherry that was first boiled.

The Turkish method of brewing coffee soon became the common way to prepare coffee, though Europeans did not take up the same means of brewing it. The first Europeans undoubtedly boiled the coffee, but not in a device like that retained throughout the Muslim world for perhaps six hundred years. We can only wonder why Europeans and their colonial descendants have felt the need to constantly modify their coffee-makers. Museums around the world are filled with strange-looking pieces, such as beakers and tubes suspended above a flame, ceramic locomotives, complicated cylinders forcing water upwards, machines with pistons of near horse-power proportions which eke out tiny streams of coffee, cloth bags that could double as dirty socks and slow-drip devices like some form of water torture. The following brewing methods, perhaps less creative than the above, but generally more gratifying, are only some of those available to coffee lovers seeking the perfect cup.

Above: It is quite likely that very soon after coffee began to be used in Yemen, the brewing method that we today call Turkish became the common way to prepare coffee.

TURKISH IBRIK

The only real difficulty in making Turkish coffee is obtaining the right blend. The traditional Middle Eastern concoction has a very distinctive taste, due primarily to a penchant for rio-y flavoured Brazilian beans, which are usually blended with Ethiopian ones. Many people erroneously believe that Turkish coffee is dark-roasted, but the pulverized coffee is usually a reddish-brown shade, not dark at all.

The traditional brewing vessel, the *ibrik* (or Greek *briki*), is a small, long-handled copper- or brass-plated pan with a narrow neck. *Ibriks* come in different sizes, and usually each one has a tiny number underneath, which indicates how many cups it holds.

If an *ibrik* is not available, a small straight-sided pan for heating milk will do, although the coffee may not boil as easily. This is the only method that insists on breaking the "never boil coffee" rule, but as the coffee actually boils with sugar, the bitterness from boiling never affects the flavour. Adding spices to the brew further enhances the flavour.

Left: Turkish coffee is usually served with a small glass of water and/or a piece of Turkish Delight. Turkish coffee is never served with milk or cream.

Using a Turkish *ibrik*

1 Remembering the proportions for Turkish coffee is simple: one of everything for each cup the *ibrik* holds. If it is a two-cup *ibrik*, place two very heaped teaspoons of Turkish coffee in the *ibrik*. (The coffee will heap high on the spoon very easily because of its fine consistency.)

3 Lastly, using one of the tiny Turkish cups from which the coffee will be drunk, measure two cups of water into the *ibrik*. At this point possibilities for variations from the basic Turkish taste can be obtained: add cardamom pods, a cinnamon stick or aniseed to the brew.

5 When the froth rises to the top the third time, carefully remove the *ibrik* from the heat and alternate pouring the contents of the *ibrik* between the two small Turkish cups, being careful to give some of the all-important froth to each.

COOK'S TIP
Returning the *ibrik* to boil the third time ensures the roundness of flavour and thorough blending of coffee and sugar.

Below: A number on the under-side of an ibrik *indicates how many cups it holds.*

2 Next, place two very heaped teaspoons of sugar in the *ibrik*. (The sugar will not heap quite as easily as the coffee, but it really needs to be somewhere between heaped and very heaped anyway, to achieve the "medium" sweet specification favoured by most Westerners.)

4 Place the *ibrik* over a lowish heat and wait for it to boil. When the seething mixture threatens to run over the rim of the *ibrik*, quickly remove it from the heat, stir, then return to the heat. In a moment it will again start to boil over, so it must be instantly removed from the heat. Don't stir again.

ALFRESCO

This is a simple method of making coffee when no proper serving jug (carafe) is available, or when the source

Above: Alfresco coffee requires only a pan, measuring jug (cup) and strainer.

Making coffee alfresco

1 Measure the amount of cold water needed into a pan. If no measuring jug (cup) is available, use a coffee cup (multiplied by the number of cups to be served plus a little extra for absorption). Place the pan over the heat.

2 Measure out the amount of dry medium-to-coarse grind coffee needed. When the water is just beginning to boil, quickly add all the coffee to the water.

3 Immediately remove the pan from the heat, stirring well. Set aside for about 4 minutes. Strain the coffee into cups.

of heat is a cooker or even an open fire. Any blend or roast of coffee is suitable, and brew for normal strength at 55g/10 tbsp per 1 litre/33fl oz/4 cups of water.

As alfresco brewing is useful in Spartan conditions, it is possible that the correct grind of coffee – medium

if it is a commercial grind, slightly coarser if home-ground – may not always be available. If fine-grind coffee is used, shorten the brewing time to no more than 3 minutes and expect some sediment to remain in the bottom of each cup served.

JUG (CARAFE)

As with *al fresco* brewing, this infusion method is simple and requires little equipment. Any blend or roast of coffee is acceptable – though a medium grind is best, it can be a bit coarser, too.

Above: Earthenware jugs are ideal for this method of brewing coffee.

Making coffee with a jug or pot

1 Warm the jug by filling it with hot water, mentally noting the desired water level in the jug. Meanwhile, heat enough water for another jugful. Pour the first hot water out of the jug. (Measure the water capacity of the jug by pouring the water into a measuring jug.) Dry the jug and place medium-grind coffee in the base. Normal strength coffee for the jug would be about 55g/10 tbsp per 1 litre/1¾ pints/4 cups water.

2 When the water being heated is below boiling point – either just before or after it has boiled – pour the water over the coffee. Stir well, preferably with a wooden spoon, and wait about 4 minutes before straining the coffee into the cups.

COOK'S TIP
Do not try to keep jug coffee hot. If it is not to be drunk immediately, strain it into a preheated vacuum flask.

THE CAFETIÈRE (PRESS POT)

Making coffee in a cafetière (press pot) is almost exactly like making coffee in a simple jug (carafe). In fact, it is easier than using a jug in that it requires no separate strainer, and once one is accustomed to using it, it is easier to judge the correct water level. (It is not easier to clean, however.) The correct grind of coffee is medium, but if for some reason only finely ground is available, the brewing time should be reduced to no more than 3 minutes. Using a fine grind may make the plunging difficult – take care when pressing down, so that there is no danger of breaking the glass. Also, if using a fine grind, there will be more sediment in the bottom of the cup.

Cafetières, also called French presses, come in a variety of sizes, and there are various styles of "cosies" available to fit most. Although cafetière coffee cannot be kept hot, its warmth can be slightly prolonged by wrapping a cosy around it. If the coffee is not to be drunk immediately, pour it into a preheated vacuum flask directly after plunging.

There are many different sizes and brands of cafetières available, and the prices vary enormously. The more expensive ones, however, are generally better made, and the mesh sieve will last longer. In cheaper models the mesh may fray and curl around the edges, letting coffee grounds escape into the brew, and replacement meshes may not be available.

General Care and Maintenance

The cafetière is not as easy to clean as an ordinary jug because coffee grounds get trapped in the mesh and the metal disks on either side of it. These should be separated and cleaned after every use, as coffee grounds are oily and can go rancid, ruining the flavour of successive brews. When pressing the plunger down, be sure to press straight down and not at an angle, thus minimizing the risk of breaking the glass.

Above: Mesh sieves and also the strong glass jugs (carafes) can be replaced in the more expensive models, so it is worth enquiring about availability of spare parts when purchasing a cafetière (press pot).

Using a plunger pot

1 Preheat the glass cylinder by filling it with hot water. While more water is heating for brewing, pour the water from the glass cylinder into a measuring jug and calculate the amount of coffee needed, working at 55g/10 tbsp per 1 litre/1¾ pints/4 cups water.

2 Dry the glass and place the dry coffee in it. When the water for brewing is almost at boiling point (just before it boils or just after), pour it over the dry coffee.

3 Stir very well with a large metal spoon. The more freshly ground the coffee, the more it has a tendency to float and seems more resistant to saturation by the water, so stir thoroughly to incorporate all the dry coffee.

4 Prop the sieve device, with the lid above it, just inside the top of the cylinder for 4 minutes. When the brewing time is up, hold the lid down with one hand to stabilize the plunger shaft and, with the other hand, slowly push down the plunger. Serve the coffee as soon as possible.

THE NEAPOLITAN

Like the earliest large espresso machines, the Napoletana was claimed by Italians but was actually invented in France, where it is called the "café filtre", and indeed it is a form of filter machine, as the hot water, after the "flip", filters down through the ground coffee. Using a Neapolitan is a wonderful way of making a relatively small amount of coffee.

These unusual-looking pots are not particularly common, however, and well-made ones, in stainless steel, are even harder to come by, so no one quibbles about whether it's a two-cup or three-cup machine. Once a good Neapolitan is purchased, however, it should practically last forever, as long as the handle doesn't break. There are no glass parts to break, no disposable requirements to run short of, no seals or washers to wear out, and no electric coils to burn out.

Getting to Know Your Neapolitan

The trick when using this type of machine is getting the right grind, as all the aspects of brewing would indicate that the grind should be filter fine. The top and bottom of the coffee compartment, however, are both perforated, and the size of the holes

Above: Quirky and distinctive, the Neapolitan is a fun way to brew coffee.

Choosing your Neapolitan

When purchasing a Neapolitan, look for sturdy, preferably stainless steel, construction. An extremely welcome safety feature is a wooden or plastic-coated handle for holding when flipping over. The perforations in the top and bottom of the coffee basket can often vary in size from one manufacturer to the next, and generally speaking, the smaller the holes, the easier the operation of the machine, as fewer grounds will fall through and a finer grind is more desirable.

can vary depending on the nationality of the manufacturer. The coffee must therefore be somewhere between medium and fine, so if a commercial grind is used, perhaps this method is one for "omnigrind".

Ascertaining that the water is the right temperature for flipping is not always easy. Some people therefore heat the water cylinder without attaching the coffee basket or the spouted cylinder until the water is hot, and ready for flipping. If the machine (or "macchinetta", as it is sometimes called in North America) is not assembled until the water is hot, care must be taken not to burn oneself; again, a non-metal handle is strongly recommended.

Occasionally, when the "flip" is done with a particular Neapolitan model, a small stream of water may arch out of the tiny steam vent, which at this stage is now towards the bottom of the top compartment. If this happens, it is only for a second or two, as it is just a few drops that get free before the coffee basket inside blocks the hole. Having the steam vent aligned with the spout below may ensure that the drops are caught by the spout. After the coffee is brewed and served, it is a good idea to let the apparatus cool down before attempting to separate the two halves for cleaning, as they usually fit together very tightly. When cooler, they contract and are less likely to burn anyone attempting the separation.

Using a Neapolitan

1 When using the machine for the first time, measure the capacity of the unspouted cylinder. To make the coffee, fill this cylinder with water, then place the ground coffee in the coffee container, observing whether the grounds are falling through the bottom perforations; if they are, the grind is too fine and should not be used. Be generous with the coffee, especially if only one or two cups are being made; too few grounds will let the water zip through instead of holding it long enough for good extraction to take place.

3 Place the Neapolitan over a low to medium heat and wait for the water to boil. It is not always easy to tell when the water in the lower chamber starts boiling. (Of course, by the time a bit of steam comes from the hole near the top of the lower chamber, it is definitely boiling.)

5 If the spout is set fairly low in its cylinder, the brew will not need stirring, as the first cup will get good-strength coffee and serving it will mix the remainder of the brew. If the spout is higher up the cylinder, remove the top half of the apparatus and the coffee compartment and stir the pot before serving the coffee.

COOK'S TIP
Although the Neapolitan is designed to sit on a burner, do not be tempted to try to keep the coffee hot over a low heat; it never works and the flavour will be ruined.

2 If the grind is all right, place the coffee compartment on top of the pot with the water and attach the spouted top in an upside-down position. The attachment varies depending on the manufacturer, but it should lock securely.

4 Remove the machine from the heat and wait a few seconds for the water to drop to just off the boil. Flip the machine over, being careful not to touch any hot parts, and set it on a heatproof surface. The water will filter through the coffee for about three minutes, passing to the bottom cylinder, which now has a spout.

Above: Omnigrind coffee is best for Neapolitan brewing.

FILTER COFFEE MACHINES

Manual and One-Cup Filter Machines

For many years people have been letting water run through coffee grounds to extract the flavour instead of leaving the coffee to steep in the water. In a sense the electric percolator is a form of filtering, but the term "filter" (or *filtre*, as the French invented it) is understood by most people to mean some form of drip mechanism.

With filter coffee, the brew is clear and clean (although admittedly this can make the body seem thinner), and a stopwatch is no longer necessary, as the timing is all down to gravity, once the correct grind is obtained. Because the contact time between the ground coffee and the water is limited, a fine degree of grind is required for the proper amount of extraction to take place, but take care not to use too fine a grind or use too much coffee in the brew basket, lest the filter clog, causing over-extraction.

The invention of the electric drip machine about forty years ago meant that filter lovers were no longer required to stand over a filter device. However, the manual filter is cheaper to buy and maintain, easier to clean, requires less space and is far easier to control. Even its one disadvantage is actually another benefit: there is no hotplate on which to stew the coffee. The only equipment necessary is a kettle; a filter and filter paper, or a metal or synthetic filter that requires no paper; a jug for catching the liquid (a thermal jug (carafe) or vacuum flask solves the problem of keeping the brew hot); and a spoon (wooden is best) with which to stir the coffee.

Plastic filter cones or baskets come in various sizes, and it is important to have a brew basket that corresponds to the number of cups to be brewed; the

Left and above: Manual filter cups come in a variety of sizes and shapes.

Making filter coffee using a manual filter machine

1 First, preheat the jug (carafe) or flask with hot water. It helps to know the desired level of the brewed coffee in the jug, in order to assess the amount of dry coffee to be used.

A good amount for normal strength filter coffee is about 55g/10 tbsp per 1 litre/1¾ pints/4 cups, but if in doubt, use more coffee, as filter coffee can be diluted very successfully with a little hot water after the brewing is completed.

3 Give the filter a gentle shake to level out the bed of coffee; this will help to ensure even extraction.

2 While the brewing water is heating, place the filter cone or brew basket on the jug. Measure the coffee into the cone.

4 When the water has boiled, count to ten to let the temperature drop to about 95°C/203°F.

5 Pour a small amount of the water as widely as possible over the grounds just to moisten the surface, and pause a few seconds while the grounds form into a harder bed.

6 Continue slowly pouring the rest of the water over the grounds in a circular motion. If any grounds remain dry, or if the drip flow stops, stir the mixture in the filter basket.

7 When the water has all run through the grounds, remove the basket from the top of the jug, stir the coffee and serve, or seal the flask if the coffee is not to be drunk immediately.

Below: Individual-sized manual filter.

bed of coffee will be too shallow if less than 50 per cent of the basket capacity is used. A wedge-shaped filter is better for brewing smaller amounts of coffee (one to three cups) as it concentrates the grounds and provides a deeper bed of coffee to keep the water from rushing through too quickly. Flat-bottomed baskets work better for larger brews.

Commercial Products

For several years commercial coffee companies have produced individual one-cup or on-cup coffee filters. These are pre-measured, pre-packaged doses of filter coffee and a plastic holder with a lid, designed to sit on almost any-sized coffee cup or mug. Most companies offer these in both regular and decaffeinated versions. Some companies sell "sleeves" of usually ten of these filters, each designed to be disposed of entirely after using once; this seems a terrible waste of materials

and packaging and space. Other companies sell boxes supplying two plastic filter-holders and lids, and ten individually vacuum-sealed pods of coffee, which fit neatly into a recess in the filter-holder. The same company will also sell boxes of just the ten pods of coffee without the filter-holders at a cheaper price, for regular return customers who have retained the plastic filter-holders from a previous purchase.

Commercial on-cup filters are extremely easy to use, requiring only a kettle or some other source of hot water, and a cup or mug for drinking. The coffee is good, well-packaged and correctly ground, and by simply filling the filter holder with hot water as it holds the coffee pod over the cup, there is little mess to clear up. In situations where two people require two vacuum flasks – if, for example, one preferred decaffeinated coffee, or perhaps tea, to the other person's

"regular" coffee – one good vacuum flask of extremely hot water could satisfy the demands of both people with the use of one or two on-cup filters.

There are only two drawbacks to on-cup disposable filters. One is that they are more expensive than an equivalent cup of just ground coffee, but, as they eliminate the need for any equipment other than a hot water source, and as they are clean and convenient to use, the extra cost can be easily justified by many happy consumers.

The other negative aspect of on-cup commercial filters for the coffee "gourmet" is that one has very little choice or information about the origins of the coffee itself, although this aspect could be eliminated somewhat if a coffee company were to market a package containing perhaps two pods each of five different blends or coffees from five different countries of origin, with accompanying labelling.

Automatic Filter Machines

The many brands of electric filter machines vary as much in quality as they do in price, but there are a few points to consider when purchasing one. The first factor in choosing a machine is the capacity, which is critical in filter machines, as the filter cone or brew basket is of a particular size to accommodate a certain amount of coffee. Use too little coffee for the design (less than 50 per cent of the machine's capacity) and the water will rush through, not having time to extract the coffee flavour. Use too much coffee and the bed of coffee will be too deep, the water will be held too long in the basket and the coffee will be over-extracted. Even worse, brewing the full capacity of a badly designed filter machine can easily result in the water/coffee mixture overflowing the sides of the brew basket, because there is not enough headroom at the top of the brew basket. Coffee grounds swell to nearly double their original volume during brewing, especially when freshly roasted and ground.

Another consideration is whether to buy a filter machine that comes with a permanent filter, which is probably made of metal mesh coated with gold (or of some sort of synthetic mesh), or a machine that requires paper liners for the filter basket. Generally, paper filters, easily disposed of, produce a cleaner, clearer cup of coffee, than do permanent filters, but what a nuisance to discover – at an inconvenient time of day or night – a lack of filter papers. Care must be taken to keep a permanent filter clean, however – a stiff brush is recommended – as its mesh can easily become clogged with old coffee grounds, causing a rancid taste and uneven extraction.

The importance of power Possibly the most important consideration in the choice of a filter machine will be the electrical power, as the greatest complaint against filter machines is a cold cup of coffee. The machine should take no longer than six minutes total to brew coffee, and should start the brewing cycle with a burst of water, which hits the grounds at a minimum temperature of 92°C/198°F. Whatever the wattage of the available machines, the higher the power, the better.

Many filter machines offer welcome options, such as a timer, so that the machine can be loaded with coffee and water at night to produce a morning brew at a specific time. However, any filter machine can be set to brew with the kind of timer that simply plugs into an electrical socket. The option of interrupting the brewing cycle by removing the jug (carafe) from the hotplate can be very convenient, but the coffee poured from the first half of an interrupted cycle will not be evenly extracted, and may be extremely strong and rather unpleasant. The best option possible on an electric filter machine is having a thermal vacuum jug to brew into instead of a conventional glass jug and hotplate.

KRUPS
ProAroma

Right: Permanent filters, besides eliminating the need to keep buying paper filters, allow more flavour (and a tiny bit of sediment) to come through.

General Care and Maintenance

An automatic filter machine needs to be descaled regularly to prevent calcium build-up in its internal tubes that can slow down the flow of water, extending the brewing time and causing over-extraction. Calcium scale can also shorten the life of the machine. Undiluted vinegar can be just as effective as a commercial descaler in cleaning a machine if the scale build-up is not excessive.

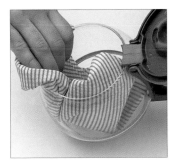

1 Keeping an electric machine clean is also important, as coffee is oily and can leave an invisible film that can turn rancid. Clean and rinse the jug (carafe) after every use.

2 Do not allow the spray head to become clogged with old coffee grounds that will spoil the flavour of successive brews, as well as cause uneven extraction. Clean regularly with a soft cloth. Also, a hotplate will heat more efficiently and evenly if it is cleaned of liquid coffee residues.

Using domestic electric filter machines

It is always best to follow the manufacturer's instructions, which can vary from model to model. Most filter machines have markers on the side of the water reservoir indicating how many cups of coffee are made by certain water levels. These cups never seem to correspond to any exact cup size, so again, a trial and error system is best when getting used to a new machine. If in doubt about the number of cups and the amount of dry coffee required, use more coffee than may be correct, in the knowledge that the stronger coffee liquid can be diluted quite easily and successfully with hot water afterwards.

1 Begin by loading the electric filter machine with cold water and a level bed of dry, fine-grind coffee, at a ratio of about 55g/10 tbsp per 1 litre/1¾ pints/4 cups water.

It is not a good idea to try to hasten the brewing process by pouring preheated water into the machine, as it has a thermostat set to operate with cooler water. The time saved will be slight at any rate.

COOK'S TIP

Never re-use coffee grounds; after one brew cycle the flavour is completely extracted and the grounds produce only a weak and bitter liquid.

2 If it is a good machine, the brewing cycle will begin with a burst of water (which a thermometer will show to be about 92–96°C/198–205°F) wetting the grounds. Look at the coffee bed in mid-brew to check that all the grounds are wet and the surface of the mixture is fairly even; if it isn't, stir it carefully.

3 When the brew is finished, stir the jug and serve. The hotplate should hold any remaining coffee at 80–85°C/176–185°F, but do not leave the jug on the hotplate longer than half an hour.

If the coffee is not to be drunk within this time, it should be stored in a preheated vacuum flask. Some machines supply jugs with funnel lids, which fill from the bottom, but by far the best optional feature of an electric filter machine is a thermal flask jug into which the coffee is brewed and which can be sealed.

MANUAL AND ELECTRIC PERCOLATORS

For many years, the "modern" means of making coffee was the percolator, which sat on a burner of the stove. It consisted of a metal jug (carafe), inside which was a central tube topped with a perforated metal brewing basket and its cover. The lid to the entire jug often had a glass knob through which coffee could be seen to be "perking".

Today's percolators are electric, but are still based on the same brewing principles: fresh, cold water in the bottom of the jug is brought to the boil, and passes up the hollow tube and out of the top, overflowing the perforated cover of the brew basket. It then filters through the dry coffee in the basket and drops back down into the bottom of the jug in the form of liquid coffee.

Contrary to the opinion of many connoisseurs, percolators can make excellent coffee, but the brewing cycle must occur only once. Better brands of electric percolators achieve this by switching to a lower heat after one cycle, which usually takes six to seven minutes. Remove the brew basket after one cycle. Even so, some, but hopefully not much, of the first coffee brewed is going to be boiled and re-passed through the grounds, which breaks all the rules. In spite of percolator brewing being basically a filter-drip method, a medium grind of coffee is required to keep potentially disastrous over-extraction to a minimum. Again the ratio of coffee to water should be about 55g/10 tbsp per 1 litre/ 1¾ pints/4 cups.

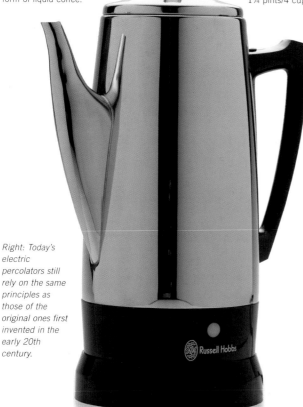

Right: Today's electric percolators still rely on the same principles as those of the original ones first invented in the early 20th century.

Russell Hobbs

As with the filter, even though the electric percolator can keep coffee warm, it is better to transfer it into a preheated vacuum flask if it is not for immediate drinking.

General Care and Maintenance

Cleaning the jug of an electric percolator is not easy, as most are not submersible, but it must be done. The invisible film left by coffee liquid can ruin the flavour of successive brews. Any surfaces touched by the grounds or the liquid should be washed with a mild detergent and well rinsed to avoid tainting future brews with a soapy taste.

CONA VACUUM POT

The vacuum pot, invented before 1840 by the Scottish engineer Robert Napier, is best known today by the name Cona, the principal manufacturer of these elegant and amazing machines. The method of brewing is actually steeping, or infusion, as the grounds are inundated by water for a few minutes before the natural law of cool-air contraction takes over and separates the grounds from the brew. The Cona company supplies not only the machines (and replacement parts) and very good instructions for operating them, but also the choice of apparatus for one of two methods of heat: a spirit lamp and an electric coil. In addition to the source of heat, the vacuum mechanism consists of a glass jug (carafe), a glass bowl, a funnel, a plug and a holder frame. A large spoon will also be needed.

This is another machine that works best when the coffee is a grind somewhere between filter fine and medium, and the best choice of commercial grinds is "omnigrind". The ratio of coffee to water is the usual 55g/10 tbsp per 1 litre/1¾ pints/4 cups, but as the machine works best at full capacity, it is not difficult to calculate, if the size of the model is known.

General Care and Maintenance

The Cona vacuum machine provides a science lesson by way of a fascinating visual experience, and it can be an interesting topic of conversation at the end of a dining table, but its greatest feat is producing an excellent pot of coffee. The disadvantages of this method of brewing are that it is definitely not fast and the delicacy and fragility of the glass parts, particularly the funnel, mean that it must be treated with great care during cleaning and handling to avoid breakage (although replacement parts are available from the Cona company).

Right: Perhaps one of the most striking designs for a domestic coffee machine, the Cona is perfect for making coffee at the table after dinner, as it is both beautiful and interesting to watch.

Using a Cona vacuum pot

1 As the glass jug (carafe) must be filled with hot water, it is quicker to heat the water in a kettle and add it to the jug. (The alternative is to let the water heat from cold in the jug, but it will take much longer, as neither the spirit lamp nor the electric coil can boil water quickly.)

2 Carefully insert the funnel plug into the funnel, place the glass bowl on top of the jug with the funnel in the water, and join the bowl and the jug by gently but firmly twisting together.

3 Light the spirit lamp or turn on the electric coil. Measure the dry coffee into the upper bowl and place the entire structure in the frame that will suspend it above the heat.

4 After the water boils, it will begin to move up the funnel into the upper bowl. When most of the water has risen, extinguish the spirit lamp or turn off the electric coil. The water will continue to rise. (Waiting a bit longer before reducing the heat will slightly prolong the brewing time, as the cooling of the air in the jug will be delayed.)

5 When enough water has risen to wet the ground coffee thoroughly, stir the mixture in the upper bowl, making sure that all the coffee is saturated. (Some water will remain below in the jug, as the funnel does not reach to the very bottom.)

6 When the temperature in the jug has dropped sufficiently, a partial vacuum will be created that will suck the liquid coffee back down into the jug, leaving the spent grounds above.

7 Very carefully detach the bowl and funnel, placing it in the hole provided over a small drip tray in the frame.

8 Serve the coffee immediately, or pour it into a preheated vacuum flask if it is not to be drunk within a few minutes of brewing.

ALL ABOUT ESPRESSO

The simplest and most accurate definition of espresso is "hot water being forced under pressure through very finely ground, dark-roasted coffee". The idea of using steam to propel the brewing water for coffee was the brainchild of a Frenchman, Louis Bernard Rabaut, in the early 1820s. Another Frenchman, Edward Loysel de Santais, used the same principle to produce a machine that could make larger amounts of coffee; he exhibited it at the Paris Exposition of 1855. In Italy, in around 1900, changes were made that enabled several individual

Below: Manual espresso pots come in a wide variety of shapes and sizes, convenient for individual use or by two or more people.

cups – instead of one large pot of coffee – to be brewed by steam pressure at a speed which gave rise to the name "espresso".

The improvements culminated in Luigi Bezzera's patented machine of 1902. Another milestone towards the perfection of the commercial espresso machine was Giovanni Achille Gaggia's use in 1948 of a spring-powered piston to increase the amount of pressure on the brewing water, so that it no longer needed to be heated to such a high temperature, potentially scalding the coffee. Eventually the spring-powered pistons gave way to electric pumps, and today's *barista*, Italian barman, needs only to press a button to harness nine bars of pressure for a few sips of pure liquid energy.

Espresso *crema*

Making espresso to compare with that of a commercial machine is sometimes still beyond the limits of those espresso devices used domestically, many of which lack the capacity to produce that indication of espresso perfection, the *crema*. This is simply the light-brown foam on the espresso surface that results from the exact combination of fresh coffee and the correct degrees of grind, water temperature and pressure.

There are also definite differences between espresso made with a manual espresso pot and that produced by an electric domestic espresso machine. It is reassuring to remember, however, that probably 90 per cent of all Italian homes are still content to rely on the simple pot, which will never show signs of any *crema*, to provide the breakfast brew, consisting of half coffee and half milk, the latter heated in a saucepan. After a marathon midday Italian meal,

the same simple pot will brew the small cups of black "caffè" (as many Italians call an espresso) which provide caffeine stimulation while the human body is trying to concentrate on digestion. (In Italy, evening coffee is often taken in a bar or restaurant.)

Making cappuccino at home

Electric home espresso machines can cost a fair amount of money and still do not guarantee a commercial-type cup of espresso, *crema* included. As for cappuccino, even if the little electric machine is capable of frothing cold milk – and not all are – the number of cups of cappuccino that can be produced in succession is directly dependent on the steam power and the price tag.

For owners of espresso pots and electric machines incapable of steaming milk, it is worth remembering that some electric machines offer accessory devices for frothing milk, and there are separate machines available that only steam and froth milk. Some of the latter are electric, and others are made to produce steam on the stove-top.

Above: For home users, there are a number of devices for frothing milk.

MANUAL ESPRESSO POTS

There are numerous manufacturers of manual espresso pots, which vary in size and materials of construction as well as in price, although most operate in exactly the same way. As an espresso pot must be used to its full capacity, buying the right size is probably the most important priority. Bear in mind that the smallest pots may not balance over an average-size gas burner, so an adapter frame may be necessary to make the pot stable.

For more than sixty years, the most popular and affordable brand has been the Moka Express, but these, unfortunately, are made of aluminium, which can interact with coffee acids, producing off-flavours, and they conduct heat so well that they can burn the coffee. More expensive and reassuringly heavier are those models made of stainless steel, but even so, a high price does not guarantee the best results. Certain stainless steel designer models are disastrous when it comes to usage, as the handles are not heat resistant and are red-hot if touched during or after brewing. The lids, as well as being too hot to touch, have no hinge and are too tight to remove easily, which is a problem if one wants to check the level of the coffee in the upper half of the pot.

Safety and Hygiene

A few safety and hygiene tips for the espresso pot include:
• Never leave an espresso pot unattended on a hot stove top.
• Never let an espresso pot remain on the heat with no water in the bottom.
• Wash the espresso pot after every use.
• Check to make sure that the rubber seal underneath the upper half does not need replacing.
• Make sure the inside of the bottom chamber is thoroughly dry before storing it.

Using a manual espresso pot

1 To make coffee in an espresso pot, fill the lower chamber with fresh water up to the bottom of the safety valve.

2 Fill the filter funnel basket with very finely ground dark-roasted coffee, using the back and edge of a spoon to eliminate any possible air pockets in the coffee and any gaps around the rim of the basket.

3 The ground coffee should always be level with the top of the basket. (The coffee should be very slightly compressed and any space in the top of the coffee basket filled; this holds the water longer in the coffee grounds and prevents the coffee being too watery.)

4 Using your finger, remove any loose coffee grounds from the outside of the basket rim, and place the coffee basket into the top of the lower chamber.

5 Very firmly screw the top half of the pot on to the bottom, keeping the bottom chamber containing the water upright, to avoid wetting the coffee grounds too soon.

6 Place the espresso pot on a low to medium heat. After the water boils, its steam will start to push the remainder of the water up the funnel and into the coffee.

7 Immediately reduce the heat to very low. (If the heat remains too high, the coffee liquid will be acidic and thin, as the water will have passed through it too quickly.)

8 When most of the water has left the lower chamber, the bubbling sound will become more and more intermittent, and it is very important to remove the pot from the heat at this time. Wait for the bubbling to ease before serving.

Above: Stove-top manual espresso.

ELECTRIC DOMESTIC ESPRESSO MACHINES

Choosing an electric espresso machine for home use is not an easy matter, as there are many brands and the price range is wide. If money is no object, a few companies that make commercial machines offer models that are nearly more commercial than domestic. Sadly, only the most serious espresso lovers can justify paying several hundred pounds for this type of machine.

Looking at machines at a more average price level, the pump machines (not the piston) are the easiest to operate, although all may take some getting used to. Also, making espresso with an electric machine is always a bit messy, so it is a good idea to opt for the added accessory of a "knock-out"

drawer as a means of clearing the filter holder of used grounds. When making a choice, consider weight and solidity an indication of strength; if the apparatus for holding the coffee filter (the "group") feels lightweight, it may reflect the flimsiness of the metal used overall. The newer thermal block machines have the advantage of being quieter, but a common complaint is that they lack pressure. However, as this is a prime consideration, a wiser choice might be to go for a noisy machine with normal boiler-generated pressure.

The machines that are made to brew only a particular pre-packaged "pod" or cartridge of espresso coffee can provide a temptingly easy solution to messy

brewing, and worrying about the roast, the blend and the grind. The machine, however, is expensive and the cost of the coffee is also very high. Also, no real espresso lover wants to be tied to drinking the same coffee day after day, denied the opportunity to experiment with other tastes.

Another relatively recent addition is the filter holder with a valve that enables even cheaper machines to produce espresso with surface *crema* and good body. This is a very desirable feature, and obviously an important factor to consider when choosing a machine. Previously, the lack of *crema* highlighted the inferiority of a smaller machine to a commercial one.

Using electric espresso machines

1 To use an electric domestic espresso machine, follow the manufacturer's instructions, which, with most machines, will incorporate the following points. Assuming that the right roast and grind are being used, place a sufficient amount of water in the reservoir and turn on the espresso machine.

2 Wait for a light to come on or go off indicating that steam is available, then decide on whether to brew one cup or two and, with the appropriate filter holder in place, use the "brew" mechanism to run some water through the filter to warm it.

3 Remove the filter holder, shaking out any water, and load it with espresso-grind coffee, allowing approximately 6g/1 tbsp per cup.

4 Press the coffee down evenly and firmly with the tamper supplied.

5 Clear any remaining coffee grounds from around the rim of the filter holder (or group). Position the filter holder under the water (brewing) aperture by holding the filter holder level, with the handle on the far left side (usually). Raise the filter holder to the brewing aperture until it feels securely in place.

6 Lock the filter holder into place by pulling the handle to the far right.

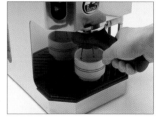

7 Place the cup(s) under the filter and press the brew button (with a valve-filter option), then open the valve by pulling the filter handle back to the left.

8 Stop the brew when the cups are slightly more than half-full (about 40ml/1½fl oz).

General Care and Maintenance

Cleaning an electric espresso machine can be tedious but it is an extremely important task that must be done regularly. A good idea is to clean the machine thoroughly each time it is turned off, if possible. A soft brush or soft cloth are suitable, but never use an abrasive cleaner or hard cloth that will scratch.

Below: Spend some time comparing the different electric espresso machines, as each machine's features can vary. It is important to keep in mind functional features, as well as appearance.

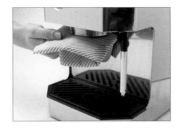

1 Keep the filter and filter holder clean and clear of any coffee grounds. Do not allow the spray head, above the filter holder lock, to become clogged with coffee grounds.

2 Empty and rinse the drip tray, where old sludge can turn into mould; the same applies to the knock-out box.

3 Get into the habit of wiping the steam nozzle after each use; a build-up of burnt milk around the nozzle is not only dirty, but it can easily cause a major clogging of the nozzle itself.

Ensuring the perfect espresso

Making slight adjustments to the grind, dosage and tamping pressure can result in the perfect cup that will take between 15–20 seconds to brew a maximum of 40ml/1½fl oz of coffee.

The appearance of the *crema* on the surface is an excellent diagnostic tool in determining why some cups of espresso are not perfect. If the *crema* is more white than brown, the coffee is under-extracted and needs either a finer grind and/or firmer tamping. If the *crema* looks burnt or is very dark in the middle, the coffee is over-extracted: perhaps the grind is too fine, the dose too large, the tamping too hard, or too much water was run through the coffee.

Espresso Types

Espresso is first a method of brewing coffee; second, it is the coffee produced by the brewing method; and third, it is a style of serving that coffee – for example, cappuccino is made with espresso coffee, but because of its milk and greater volume, it would never be called espresso.

Espresso romano This is a normal espresso served with a small piece of lemon peel. Brazil's *cafezinho*, its espresso equivalent, is also often served with a slice of lemon.

Espresso (normale) Made from 6g/1 tbsp of very finely ground dark-roasted coffee extracted by highly pressurized water heated to 93–96°C/199–204°F water, the basic cup of espresso is approximately 40–50ml/1½–2fl oz of strong black coffee served in a 75ml/2½fl oz cup.

Espresso ristretto A basic espresso served in an espresso cup, but restricted in volume to about 25ml/1fl oz. Espresso ristretto is strong because it is made from the same amount of coffee as a normal espresso but is less diluted with water.

Espresso macchiato This is a normal espresso "marked" or "stained" with about 15ml/1 tbsp of foamed milk on top.

Espresso corretto A cup of normal espresso laced with an alcoholic spirit or liqueur; a northern Italian breakfast favourite is espresso "corrected" with grappa.

Espresso doppio Two doses of espresso coffee brewed in a two-group filter holder but dispensed into one 150ml/5fl oz cup; approximately the same volume as an espresso lungo, but twice the coffee, thus twice the caffeine, with less dilution. A real jolt of energy.

Espresso con panna or espresso tazza d'oro Espresso macchiato with a touch of luxury from the addition of whipped cream instead of foamed milk.

Espresso lungo or Caffè Americano A normal serving of espresso which is lengthened with hot water after it has been brewed to a volume of about 75–95ml/2½–3½fl oz. The body of espresso lungo is like that of filter coffee, and it is usually served in a 150ml/5fl oz (small cappuccino) cup.

FLAVOURINGS AND DECORATIONS

Of many tastes that seem to be natural partners with coffee, the most obvious are the flavours of milk or cream. Depending on the drink being concocted, the choice of milk or cream is wide. A simple cup of a high-grown *arabica* coffee, medium-roasted so as not to have lost its acidity, is wonderful with a splash of milk or cream. The acidity is slightly mellowed by the alkaline milk and the delicate, subtle arabica flavour is enhanced.

Milk and Cream

Many people making espresso-based drinks eventually ask the question, "Which milk is best for frothing?" as almost everyone has difficulty learning to froth or steam milk. There is disagreement on this topic. Any milk can be frothed, but some experts advocate skimmed milk because it froths very quickly; unfortunately, it also tastes like cardboard! Other choices include homogenized and heat-treated milks. Semi-skimmed (low-fat) works adequately, but for real Italian-style flavour nothing beats pure whole milk,

such as the British "gold top", and any rich, creamy milk is superb for complementing the flavour of espresso. Experience will show that the temperature factor is perhaps as important as the fat content: the milk to be steamed should be very cold.

Whipped cream should not be used as a substitute for milk intended for steaming, but it works well as a coffee garnish. Double (heavy) cream, especially with a tablespoon of milk to lessen the risk of over-whipping, adds richness and body.

Milk heated conventionally for hot coffee drinks curdles easily. To help avoid milk separation, heat it gently and do not let it boil. Also, the inclusion of sugar in hot drinks containing potentially milk-curdling ingredients helps to stabilize the milk compounds.

Below: Whether to add milk or cream to coffee is up to the individual, and it may be worth experimenting with skimmed and semi-skimmed milks when frothing milk. Use whipped or double cream for garnishing, though not for steaming.

Frothing milk with an electric espresso machine

1 First, pour the very cold milk into a cold 500ml/1 pint metal jug (pitcher), with straight sides or sloping inwards towards the top.

2 To steam the milk, insert the steam nozzle to nearly the bottom of the jug, open the steam valve fully and rotate the nozzle around in the milk for 5–8 seconds. (The bottom of the milk jug should start to feel warm to the touch.)

3 Lower the jug until the nozzle is just below the milk surface; when the surface just begins to froth, place the nozzle slightly lower in the milk and turn the steam down. A deep purring sound signifies that the milk is steaming, and a few seconds is all that is needed for the milk to rise in volume.

4 When fine, smooth foam has just formed, close the steam valve and put the jug aside until ready to use. Cool if desired. Take care to stop frothing the milk before big airy bubbles form.

Below: Choose from a range of sugars; clockwise from back left: soft brown, demerara (raw), dark muscovado (brown), sugar cubes, cane sugar, caster (superfine) sugar.

Chocolate

In any form and any colour, chocolate provides a superb accompanying flavour for coffee, so much so that many coffee drinks include the word "mocha", which can imply a combination with chocolate. Also, as the Aztecs seem to have been the first chocolate drinkers, many coffee-chocolate recipes contain "Mexican" in their title. Powdered chocolate or cocoa powder (which is slightly bitter) can be sprinkled on top of any foamy, milky coffee surface. Chocolate syrup or melted chocolate of any type can be added to coffee to produce a happy combination. Chocolate mints or plain (semisweet) chocolate (milk, dark (bittersweet) or white) wafers make a lovely garnish, as do chocolate-covered whole coffee beans.

Sugar

Sugar is an ingredient in many coffee drinks, not only to stabilize milk, but also to offset the bitterness, which is almost always present to some degree in recipes using cold coffee. There are many types of sugar available, and a lot of people assume that one must be better for use in coffee than others.

Various sugars have different tastes depending on whether they are refined (all white sugars) or unrefined ("raw") cane sugar. Unrefined sugar has more flavour because of the molasses content, which varies from low in demerara (raw) to higher amounts in dark muscovado (molasses) and darker soft brown sugar. Other brown sugars are made from white refined sugar to which molasses is added. The truth is that, like many aspects of coffee drinking, the choice of sugar is purely a matter of taste. Caster (superfine) sugar is excellent in recipes because it is quick-dissolving.

Right: Chocolate powder and chocolate decorations.

Chunky rock sugar crystals, marketed specifically for coffee, are simply lumps of amber-coloured refined (white) sugar. Used in small cups of espresso, which is not normally brewed at a particularly high temperature, rock sugar has little chance of dissolving before the coffee is consumed, and it contributes little flavour. It could therefore be considered a waste of time, although admittedly it looks good in a sugar bowl.

Essences and Flavourings

Vanilla, in the form of syrup, powder or even vanilla sugar, goes well with coffee. A drop of vanilla essence (extract) can convert an ordinary drink into an addictive elixir.

Many people consider cinnamon, either in the natural stick form, as an essence, or more commonly as a sprinkling powder, a suitable coffee accompaniment. Sometimes coffee concoctions containing cinnamon have the word "Viennese" somewhere in their title – these are not to be confused with coffee marketed in Britain as "Viennese style", which is normal coffee bulked out with no more than 4 per cent fig or fig seasoning. The addition of fig makes the blend less expensive, as well as altering the coffee taste slightly.

The early 1980s saw a widening of flavours considered suitable coffee companions with the development of "flavoured" coffees. Just after roasting, flavour concentrates in the form of oil or powder are mixed with the hot coffee beans to produce combinations of fruit, nut and liqueur tastes in the brewed coffee. These are still very popular, particularly in North America, and perhaps also with people who prefer another taste than that of coffee. They can, however, provide a welcome change or round off a special meal. Any coffee equipment that touches a flavoured coffee must be thoroughly washed and

Left: Adding a drop of essence (extract) or a flavouring can greatly change the taste of an ordinary coffee drink.

rinsed afterwards, as the flavourings can cling persistently and influence the taste of future brews adversely.

Just as all coffee is a matter of taste, there are no hard and fast rules concerning combinations of other flavours with that of coffee. Somehow the "gourmet" coffee craze that began in the United States has led to all sorts of taste combinations, many of which are obtained by the use of simple syrups, essences or liqueurs, as well as the natural product itself. If a cold coffee recipe calls for milk or cream, as most do, a scoop of flavoured ice cream can be substituted (with amendments to the proportions, of course).

Above: Fruit and nuts make versatile flavourings and decorations.

Left: Cinnamon sticks, nutmeg, star anise and ground ginger all combine well with coffee.

as does mint, and a mint leaf with a dollop of whipped cream makes a lovely garnish.

Ginger, cardamom, cinnamon, nutmeg and cumin are spices that might be overlooked as coffee companions, but those flavours, if used in small proportions, provide a subtle difference to a coffee drink. The best way to add a ginger or nutmeg flavour is to grind small amounts of the fresh spice. A single cracked cardamom seed or a stick of cinnamon work particularly well in hot coffee drinks. A few cumin seeds or a sprinkle of ground cumin can provide a delicate undertone to a cold, milky coffee drink.

Fruit, Nuts and Spices

Fruit flavour possibilities include banana, blackcurrant, blueberry, cherry, coconut, lemon, orange, peach, pineapple, raspberry and strawberry. These can be combined with coffee in various ways, depending on the desired texture and length of the concoction. The use of a blender can provide a smooth mélange of coffee and fresh fruit. Alternatively, fruit pieces or slices can be used in the drink or as a garnish. Fruit syrups, concentrates and essences are easy ways of obtaining a coffee and fruit flavour mix.

Nuts seem to provide a more indisputably happy marriage with coffee, and the tastes of hazelnut, almond, pecan and even peanut, obtained from powders, essences (extracts), or the nuts themselves used as garnish, work very well in coffee drinks.

Caramel and maple are flavours that enhance coffee well,

Right: Alcohol and coffee have made many classic combinations.

Alcohol

Coffee and alcohol can be a delightful combination. In general, orange-based liqueurs, such as Cointreau, curaçao and orange-flavoured brandy, are wonderful coffee partners. "Normal" brandy, Armagnac, cognac, Calvados and poire each individually blend well with the flavour of coffee, as do grappa, marc and raki.

More individual tastes are achieved with Benedictine, Galliano, Kirsch, Strega, Southern Comfort, crème de menthe, Drambuie, vodka, or, of course, the classic Caribbean standard, rum. Numerous variations on the established Irish coffee are possible with Scotch whisky or American bourbon. In fact, used in the right proportions with usually quite strong coffee, there are few liqueurs or spirits that would not make a suitable addition to a coffee-based concoction.

HOT NON-ALCOHOLIC DRINKS

Be it a classic cappuccino with snowy-white frothed milk on top or a Spanish combination of coffee and molasses, there can be nothing more enjoyable than a steaming hot cup of coffee on a cold winter's day.

Cappuccino

The classic espresso and milk drink.

SERVES 2

INGREDIENTS
   120–250ml/4–8fl oz/$^{1}/_{2}$–1 cup very
      cold whole milk
   about 15g/$^{1}/_{2}$oz/2 tbsp dark-roast
      espresso finely ground coffee
   chocolate or cocoa powder (optional)

1 Pour the milk into a metal jug (pitcher) or frothing device, steam until a fine, smooth foam forms. Set aside.

2 Next, brew two cups of espresso into cappuccino or regular 150ml/6fl oz/$^{2}/_{3}$ cup coffee cups.

3 Pour the steamed milk over the coffee, holding back the froth with a spoon until last, when it can be spooned on to the surface.

4 The ideal cappuccino should be about one-third each espresso coffee, steamed milk and frothed milk. (After brewing the coffee you may need to re-steam the milk for just a moment if it has begun to "fall" or lose the froth.) If the milk has boiled or has been too aerated, throw the milk away and start again.

5 Top with a sprinkling of chocolate or cocoa powder, if using.

Caffè Latte (Café au Lait)

The is a very basic breakfast drink, as served in homes and bars throughout Italy and France. It can be made with only a manual espresso pot and a pan to heat the milk.

SERVES 2

INGREDIENTS
   2 parts espresso or very strong coffee
   6 parts boiled milk
   sugar (optional)
   steamed, frothed milk for
      topping (optional)

1 Pour the brewed coffee into glasses or large French coffee bowls. Add the hot milk and sugar, if using, and stir well.

2 Top each glass with a spoonful of steamed, frothed milk, if using.

VANILLA VARIATION

1 Pour 700ml/1¼ pints/scant 3 cups milk into a pan. Add a vanilla pod (bean) and place over a low heat until hot. Set aside to infuse for about 10 minutes, then remove the vanilla pod.

2 Mix strong coffee with 450ml/16fl oz/2 cups milk in a large heatproof jug (pitcher). Add sugar to taste.

3 Return the pan of milk to the heat and add 45ml/3 tbsp vanilla sugar. Bring to the boil, then reduce the heat. Add 115g/4 oz dark (bittersweet) chocolate. Heat until melted. Pour the chocolate milk into the jug and whisk. Serve in tall mugs.

Normandy Coffee

Normandy, like Washington State in the United States of America, is known for its apple orchards, and gives it name to many dishes made with apple juice or apple sauce. This recipe blends the flavour of apples with spices for a delicious, tangy coffee drink.

SERVES 4

INGREDIENTS
  475ml/16fl oz/2 cups strong black
    coffee (espresso strength, or
    filter/plunger brewed at 75g/3oz/
    scant 1 cup coffee per 1 litre/
    1 3/4 pints/4 cups of water)
  475ml/16fl oz/2 cups apple juice
  30ml/2 tbsp brown sugar, or to taste
  3 oranges, thinly sliced
  2 small cinnamon sticks
  a pinch of ground allspice
  a pinch of ground cloves
  4 cinnamon sticks, to serve

1 Bring all the ingredients to the boil over a medium heat, then reduce the heat and simmer for 10 minutes.

COOK'S TIP
This recipe could be made into an alcoholic drink if one-fourth of the apple juice were replaced with Calvados, added when the heat is reduced to simmer in step 1. Do not allow the Calvados to boil.

2 Strain the liquid into a preheated flask or serving jug (pitcher). Pour into cappuccino-style cups, and add a cinnamon stick to each.

Georgia 'n Ginger

This is named after the US state of Georgia, famous for its peaches.

SERVES 6

INGREDIENTS
  1 can (450–500g/1–1 1/4lb) sliced
    peaches in syrup
  750ml/1 1/4 pints/3 cups strong coffee
  120ml/4fl oz/1/2 cup whipping cream
  25ml/1 1/2 tbsp brown sugar
  1.5ml/1/4 tsp ground cinnamon
  a generous pinch of ground ginger
  grated orange rind, to decorate

1 Drain the peaches, retaining the syrup. In a blender, process half of the coffee and the peaches for 1 minute.

2 In a clean bowl, whip the cream, taking care not to overwhip.

3 Place 250ml/8fl oz/1 cup cold water, the sugar, cinnamon, ginger and peach syrup in a pan and bring to the boil over a medium heat; reduce the heat and simmer for 1 minute.

4 Add the blended peaches and the remaining coffee to the pan and stir well. Serve topped with whipped cream and decorated with grated orange rind.

Mexican Coffee

The Aztec Indians were the first known chocolate addicts, and chocolate is an ingredient in many Mexican recipes. Combined with coffee, it makes a rich, smooth drink.

SERVES 4

INGREDIENTS
30ml/2 tbsp chocolate syrup
120ml/4fl oz/½ cup whipping cream
1.5ml/¼ tsp ground cinnamon
30ml/2 tbsp brown sugar
a pinch of grated nutmeg
475ml/16fl oz/2 cups strong
   black coffee
whipped cream and cinnamon
   shavings, to decorate

1 Whip together the chocolate syrup, cream, cinnamon, sugar and nutmeg.

2 Pour the hot coffee into the mixture and stir well, before dividing among four mugs. Top with a generous dollop of whipped cream and decorate with a few shavings of cinnamon.

COOK'S TIP
This recipe can be made with filter or plunger brewed coffee using 40g/ 7 tbsp/½ cup coffee per 475ml/16fl oz/ 2 cups water.

Café de Olla

This recipe is traditionally brewed in large quantities over a wood fire in a heavy earthenware Mexican cooking pot, called an "olla".

SERVES 4

INGREDIENTS
1 litre/1¾ pints/4 cups water
150g/5oz/⅔ cup soft dark
   brown sugar
5ml/1 tsp molasses
1 small cinnamon stick
aniseeds (optional)
50g/9 tbsp/⅔ cup darker-roasted
   coffee, medium grind

1 Place the water, sugar, molasses, cinnamon and aniseeds, if using, in a pan and slowly bring to the boil.

2 Stir thoroughly to dissolve the sugar and molasses.

3 When the mixture reaches boiling point, stir in the dry coffee, remove from the heat, cover, and steep for 5 minutes. Strain into earthenware mugs and serve immediately. Add a few of the aniseeds, if you wish.

COOK'S TIP
Use a French or Viennese roast coffee, dark but not as dark as that used for espresso, so that the spice and treacle flavours aren't overwhelmed.

HOT ALCOHOLIC DRINKS

There are any number of combinations of alcohol with hot brewed coffee, some more successful than others. The following recipes include six of the classic mixes, and provide the perfect starting place for discovering your own personal favourite blends and flavours.

Jamaican Black Coffee

This delicious version of black coffee is only slightly alcoholic.

SERVES ABOUT 8

INGREDIENTS
    1 lemon and 2 oranges, finely sliced
    1.5 litres/2½ pints/6¼ cups black
      coffee (filter/plunger brewed using
      55g/10 tbsp/generous ⅔ cup coffee
      per 1 litre/1¾ pints/4 cup of water)
    45ml/3 tbsp rum
    70g/2½oz/⅓ cup caster
      (superfine) sugar
    8 lemon slices, to serve

1 Place the lemon and orange slices in a pan. Add the coffee and heat.

2 When the mixture is about to boil, pour in the rum and sugar, stirring well until the sugar has dissolved, and immediately remove from the heat.

3 While the coffee is still very hot, pour or ladle into glasses and decorate with a lemon slice.

COOK'S TIP
This recipe uses hot normal-strength coffee. Any degree of roast is suitable, but a medium-to-darker roast will allow more perception of the citrus and rum flavours than would a dark roast.

French Toddy

This is a variation of a very old French recipe – said to have been a favourite of Flaubert – to which coffee and sugar have been added.

SERVES 2

INGREDIENTS
    120ml/4fl oz/½ cup Calvados
    50ml/2fl oz/¼ cup apricot brandy
    20–30ml/4–6 tsp sugar, to taste
    300ml/½ pint/1¼ cups very strong
      coffee (filter brewed at about 45g/
      8 tbsp/generous ½ cup coffee per
      475ml/16fl oz/2 cups water)
    25ml/1½ tbsp double (heavy) cream

1 Very gently warm the Calvados and brandy together over a low heat and transfer to large balloon glasses.

2 Dissolve the sugar in the coffee and add to the liqueurs. Stir.

3 While the contents are still rotating from the stirring, pour the cream over the surface in a circular motion. Do not stir, just sip and savour.

COOK'S TIP
This French Toddy can be drunk without cream and/or with poire (pear *eau de vie*) substituted for the Calvados, if you prefer.

Café à l'Orange

This is one of numerous drink possibilities in which the flavours of orange and coffee are combined.

SERVES 4

INGREDIENTS

120ml/4fl oz/½ cup whipping cream
30ml/2 tbsp icing
 (confectioners') sugar
5ml/1 tsp grated orange rind
600ml/1 pint/2½ cups hot coffee
150ml/¼ pint/⅔ cup any orange-
 flavoured liqueur, such as Grand
 Marnier, Filfar, Cointreau, triple sec
4 orange wedges, to decorate

1 In a clean bowl, whip the cream until stiff. Fold in the icing sugar and rind.

2 Chill for 30 minutes, or until the cream mixture is firm enough to hold a wedge of orange on top.

3 Divide the black coffee equally among tall glass mugs and stir about 30ml/ 2 tbsp of the liqueur into each. Top with chilled whipped cream and decorate with an orange wedge, and pared rind if wished. Serve.

COOK'S TIP
The flavour of this drink will vary depending on which orange liqueur is used, as some are quite subtle.

Hot Mint Julep

Instead of a long cool sip on a shady Southern American veranda, here the bourbon and mint are combined with coffee to produce something comforting for colder weather as well.

SERVES 2

INGREDIENTS

120–150ml/4–5fl oz/½–⅔ cup Bourbon
30ml/2 tbsp sugar
450ml/¾ pint/scant 2 cups hot strong
 black coffee
30ml/2 tbsp double (heavy) cream
2 mint sprigs, to decorate

1 Put the Bourbon and sugar into two large warmed wine glasses. Add the hot coffee and stir to dissolve the sugar.

2 Top with cream by pouring it over the back of a spoon. Do not stir. Decorate with the mint sprigs.

VARIATION
This simple recipe can be adapted for use with any one of the many different forms of alcohol available. For example, Southern Comfort or Wild Turkey will certainly add different flavour from that of ordinary Bourbon.

Grasshopper Coffee

This drink is named after the crème de menthe flavour suggestive of a green grasshopper colour.

SERVES 2

INGREDIENTS
 dark (bittersweet) and white
  chocolate mints
 50ml/2fl oz/¼ cup crème
  de menthe
 50ml/2fl oz/¼ cup coffee liqueur,
  such as Tia Maria or Sangster's
 350ml/12fl oz /1½ cups hot
  strong coffee
 50ml/2fl oz/¼ cup whipping cream

1 Cut the dark and white chocolate mints diagonally in half.

2 Divide the two liqueurs equally between two tall, strong latte glasses. Combine well.

3 Fill each glass with the hot coffee and top with whipped cream. Decorate with the chocolate mint triangles, dividing the white and dark chocolate evenly between the drinks.

COOK'S TIP
Use strong coffee that will not taste watery or be too diluted by the liqueurs, though weaker than espresso.

Easy Café Brûlot

This is a traditional coffee drink from New Orleans, where all the ingredients except the coffee are heated by being "flamed" in a heat-proof bowl at the table; the flame is extinguished by pouring the coffee into the bowl. Except for the dramatic visual effects, this recipe achieves the same flavour with less fuss.

SERVES 3–4

INGREDIENTS
 90ml/6 tbsp brandy or rum
 50ml/2fl oz/¼ cup Cointreau or other
  orange-flavoured liqueur
 30ml/2 tbsp sugar
 6–8 cloves
 2 sticks cinnamon
 1 strip lemon peel and/or 1 strip
  orange peel
 750ml/1¼ pints/3 cups strong
  hot coffee
 cinnamon sticks and orange rind,
  to decorate (optional)

1 Gently heat the brandy or rum, liqueur, sugar, cloves, cinnamon sticks and lemon or orange peel in a large pan. Stir continuously to dissolve the sugar.

2 Pour the black coffee, brewed at about 65g/11½ tbsp/¾ cup per 1 litre/ 1¾ pints/4 cups water by the filter or cafetière method, into the mixture. (A slightly darker-roast is best, as espresso would be too overwhelming.) Stir, then ladle the mixture into coffee cups. Decorate with a cinnamon stick and orange rind, if using.

COOK'S TIP
For greater visual impact, ignite the brandy mixture just before the coffee is added. Slowly add the coffee in a continuous stream, extinguishing the flames as you do.

COLD NON-ALCOHOLIC DRINKS

Perhaps one reason for coffee's enduring popularity is its sheer versatility. Drunk cold, and mixed with a variety of flavourings, nothing could be more refreshing.

Coffee Milkshake

This is a cold coffee drink that does not require an electric blender, as any closed container used as a shaker will work equally well.

SERVES 2

INGREDIENTS

    200ml/7fl oz/scant 1 cup chilled strong coffee (about 4 generous cups of espresso, or filter/plunger brewed using 70g/12 tbsp/generous 3/4 cup coffee per 1 litre/1 3/4 pints/ 4 cups water)
    2 eggs, beaten well
    450ml/3/4 pint/scant 2 cups cold milk
    120ml/4fl oz/1/2 cup single (light) or double (heavy) cream
    15ml/1 tbsp sugar
    pinch of salt
    4 drops vanilla or almond essence (extract)
    ginger bisuits (cookies), crumbled, to decorate

1 Combine all the ingredients in a shaker or blender until well-mixed.

2 Serve at once, sprinkled with biscuit.

Coffee Frappé

Similar to a milkshake, this frappé recipe is another long, cold coffee drink that is both refreshing and uplifting.

SERVES TWO

INGREDIENTS

    450ml/3/4 pint/scant 2 cups cold strong coffee (brewed using about 80g/14 tbsp/1 cup coffee per 1 litre/1 3/4 pints/4 cups of water)
    8 drops vanilla essence (extract)
    300ml/1/2 pint/1 1/4 cups crushed ice
    60ml/4 tbsp sweetened condensed milk
    whipped cream and sliced banana, to decorate (optional)

1 Pour the cold brewed coffee into a large blender.

2 Add the vanilla essence, crushed ice and condensed milk. Blend well until a smooth texture is obtained.

3 Pour into tall, clear glasses and stir in sugar to taste. Decorate with some whipped cream and banana slices, if using.

VARIATION

There are countless variations on the classic frappé. Any of the following essences would be suitable: almond, banana, maple and peppermint.

Coffee Yogurt

This is really a variation on a "lassi", the refreshing yogurt drink of Indian restaurants. It can be made as either a sweet drink (traditionally with sugar and ground cinnamon) or salty (using salt and a little cumin).

SERVES 2

INGREDIENTS

350ml/12fl oz/1½ cups cold black coffee (filter/plunger brewed using about 65g/11½ tbsp/¾ cup coffee per 475ml/16fl oz/2 cups water)
350ml/12fl oz/1½ cups natural (plain) yogurt
20ml/4 tsp sugar
a pinch of ground cinnamon, to taste

VARIATION

For a salty version, use 5ml/1 tsp salt and a pinch of ground cumin, instead of the cinnamon, possibly with some sugar to taste, if desired.

1 Combine all the ingredients in a blender. Mix until creamy.

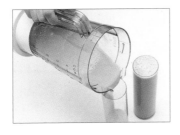

2 Serve sprinkled with cinnamon.

Chilled Coffee Caribbean

Use coffee that is not too strong; filter coffee gives a clean, clear texture.

SERVES 2

INGREDIENTS

600ml/1 pint/2½ cups strong filter coffee, cooled for about 20 minutes
½ orange and ½ lemon, thinly sliced
2 pineapple slices
sugar, to taste
1–2 drops Angostura bitters (optional)
3 ice cubes per serving
slice of orange or lemon, to decorate

1 Add the cooled coffee to the fruit slices in a large bowl.

2 Stir and chill in the freezer for about 1 hour or until very cold.

3 Remove from the freezer and stir again. Remove the fruit slices from the liquid. Add sugar to taste and stir in the bitters, if using.

4 Add three ice cubes per drink to tall glasses, or whisky tumblers, then pour over the chilled coffee drink. Decorate with a half-slice of orange or lemon on the rim or add to the drink, if preferred.

Granita di Caffè

This is basically coffee ice, or slush. It makes just over 1 litre/1¾ pints/4 cups.

SERVES 4

INGREDIENTS
　200ml/7fl oz/scant 1 cup strong
　　coffee (about 5 generous cups of
　　espresso or filter/plunger brewed
　　using 80g/14 tbsp/1 cup coffee per
　　1 litre/1¾ pints/4 cups of water)
　400ml/14fl oz/1⅔ cups water
　140g/5oz/¾ cup sugar
　2.5ml/½ tsp vanilla essence
　　(extract) (optional)
　1 egg white (optional)
　120ml/4fl oz/½ cup double (heavy)
　　cream, whipped, to decorate

1 Pour the brewed coffee into a large bowl or blender and set aside.

2 Boil half the water with the sugar, stirring to dissolve the sugar. Place in the refrigerator.

3 When the sugar syrup is cold, add it, the remaining water and the vanilla to the coffee. Stir until well blended.

4 If using, whisk the egg white and fold it into the mixture; it will make the granita much smoother.

5 Pour the mixture into a shallow freezer-proof tin (pan), such as a baking sheet, and place in the freezer.

6 About every 30 minutes, break the freezing mixture up with a fork to create the traditional grainy shaved-ice consistency. When well frozen, serve in individual cups, and top with a little whipped cream.

Coffee-chocolate Soda

This is a fun, refreshing drink that looks as good as it tastes.

SERVES 2

INGREDIENTS
　250ml/8fl oz/1 cup strong cold
　　coffee (4 espresso cups of coffee)
　60ml/4 tbsp double (heavy) cream or
　　30ml/2 tbsp evaporated (unsweetened
　　condensed) milk (optional)
　250ml/8fl oz/1 cup cold soda water
　2 scoops chocolate ice cream
　chocolate-covered coffee beans,
　　roughly chopped, to decorate

1 Pour the coffee into tall glasses. Add the cream or evaporated milk, if using.

2 Add the soda water and stir. Gently place a scoop of ice cream into the mixture. Decorate with some of the roughly chopped chocolate-covered coffee beans. Serve with a long spoon or a straw.

VARIATION

Try the soda with chocolate mint, vanilla, hazelnut or banana ice cream and sprinkle with chocolate shavings, fruit slices or some roughly chopped hazelnuts.

COLD ALCOHOLIC DRINKS

Chilled and served in pretty glasses, coffee and alcohol make delicious and simple desserts.

Coffee Egg Nog

This is a rather special coffee drink, particularly suitable for daytime summer holiday festivities.

SERVES 6–8

INGREDIENTS
   8 eggs, separated
   225g/8oz/generous 1 cup sugar
   250ml/8fl oz/1 cup cold strong
      coffee (espresso strength or filter/
      plunger brewed at 75g/13 tbsp/
      scant 1 cup coffee per 1 litre/
      1¾ pints/4 cups water)
   200ml/7fl oz/scant 1 cup whisky,
      Bourbon, rum or brandy, or
      combination of these
   220ml/7½fl oz/scant 1 cup cold
      double (heavy) cream
   120ml/4fl oz/½ cup whipped
      cream
   ground nutmeg, to decorate

1 In a clean bowl, beat the egg yolks thoroughly, then slowly add the sugar, mixing until well combined.

2 Pour into a large pan and heat gently over a low heat, stirring all the time with a wooden spoon.

3 Remove the pan from the heat, allow to cool for a few minutes, stir in the coffee and alcohol, and then slowly add the cream, stirring well.

4 Beat the egg whites until stiff and stir into the egg nog, mixing well. Pour into punch (small round) cups, top each with a small dollop of whipped cream and sprinkle nutmeg on top.

COOK'S TIP
Use a little more sugar, if necessary, to avoid the cream and alcohol separating and curdling.

African Coffee

In parts of Africa, coffee is often drunk with sweetened condensed milk. This recipe is an adaptation of an African brew with a luxurious liqueur finish.

SERVES 1

INGREDIENTS
   250ml/8fl oz/1 cup strong coffee
      (4 generous cups of espresso or
      cafetière coffee brewed using 70g/
      12 tbsp/generous ¾ cup coffee per
      1 litre/1¾ pints/4 cups of water)
   40ml/8 tsp sweetened
      condensed milk
   20ml/4 tsp crème de cacao
   ice cubes, to serve, optional

COOK'S TIP
Other chocolate- and coconut-based liqueurs, such as Malibu, work equally well in this recipe.

1 Pour the coffee, condensed milk and liqueur into a shaker and mix well.

2 Serve over ice cubes in glasses.

Caffè Vermouth

Vermouth is not an obvious choice to partner coffee, but the resulting flavour is different and sophisticated. Use a little less if unsure of the flavour.

SERVES 2

INGREDIENTS
  120ml/4fl oz/½ cup red vermouth
  60ml/4 tbsp very strong cold
    coffee (espresso strength or filter/
    plunger brewed at 75g/13 tbsp/
    scant 1 cup coffee per 1 litre/
    1¾ pints/4 cups of water)
  250ml/8fl oz/1 cup milk
  30ml/2 tbsp crushed ice
  10ml/2 tsp sugar
  coffee beans, to decorate

COOK'S TIP
This is another combination in which the milk product may have a tendency to separate in some cases. The use of a slightly higher sugar content can prevent this.

1 In a cocktail shaker, combine all the ingredients and shake well.

2 Serve immediately in cocktail glasses or glass tumblers. Decorate with a few roasted coffee beans.

VARIATION
Different flavours and textures can be obtained by varying the type of milk used, or by using a little cream instead of milk for a richer version.

Lisbon Flip Coffee

Here the coffee is not so much a main ingredient; rather it provides a flavourful undertone in an interesting and hugely satisfying cocktail.

SERVES 2

INGREDIENTS
  120ml/4fl oz/½ cup port
  45ml/3 tbsp curaçao
  20ml/4 tsp very strong coffee
  10ml/2 tsp icing (confectioner's) sugar
  2 eggs
  20ml/4 tsp condensed milk
  60ml/4 tbsp crushed ice
  grated chocolate and orange rind
    shavings, to decorate

1 Place all the ingredients in a cocktail shaker, including the crushed ice.

2 Shake vigorously, pour into cocktail glasses and serve immediately. Top with the finely grated chocolate and orange rind.

COOK'S TIPS
• To make this drink, espresso ristretto is the strength required.
• Most orange-based liqueurs, such as Grand Marnier, Cointreau, Orange Nassau and triple sec, could be used in place of the curaçao, if not available.

Coffee Colada

This coffee cocktail is a riot of bold Caribbean flavours. A jug can be made up a couple of hours in advance, then allowed to partially freeze, like a frozen margarita, before topping with plenty of whipped cream.

SERVES 4

INGREDIENTS

450ml/¾ pint/scant 2 cups cold, very strong coffee (filter or cafetière brewed using 80g/ 14 tbsp/1 cup coffee per 1 litre/ 1¾ pints/4 cups water)
50ml/2fl oz/¼ cup tequila or white rum
50ml/2fl oz/¼ cup Malibu
120ml/4fl oz/½ cup cream of coconut
2.5ml/½ tsp vanilla essence (extract)
350ml/12fl oz/1½ cups crushed ice
whipped cream and toasted coconut shavings, to decorate

1 In a blender, combine all the ingredients and blend on high.

2 Serve in tall wine glasses.

3 Decorate with whipped cream and top with toasted coconut shavings.

Coffee Cognac Cooler

This drink is unabashedly decadent – not for those counting calories!

SERVES 2

INGREDIENTS

250ml/8fl oz/1 cup cold strong darker-roast coffee
80ml/3fl oz/6 tbsp cognac or brandy
50ml/2fl oz/¼ cup coffee liqueur
50ml/2fl oz/¼ cup double (heavy) cream
10ml/2 tsp sugar
250ml/8fl oz/1 cup crushed ice
2 scoops coffee ice cream
chocolate shavings, to decorate

1 Shake or blend all the ingredients except the ice cream together.

2 Pour into tall glasses and gently add a scoop of ice cream to each. Decorate with chocolate shavings and serve with a long-handled spoon.

COOK'S TIP
The coffee liqueur can be either a cream-based one, such as Kahlua, or a non-cream based liqueur, such as Tia Maria.

THE
RECIPES

This section contains over 70 recipes presented in a beautifully illustrated step-by-step format. All the classic coffee recipes are included, such as Tiramisu, Coffee Coeurs à la Crème, Mocha Sponge Cake and Cappuccino Torte. There are also recipes for all occasions, from fruit and frozen desserts, sumptuous tortes, rich pies and pastries, and irresistible biscuits (cookies) and breads. All of the recipes demonstrate just how versatile an ingredient coffee is; it combines effortlessly with so many other flavours, such as alcohol, fruit, chocolate and cream. Always use good-quality coffee, and experiment with coffees from around the world to make each dish a delicious culinary adventure.

CREAM DESSERTS AND HOT PUDDINGS

Smooth creamy custards form the base of many cold desserts, such as Coffee Crème Caramel and Petits Pots de Cappuccino, as well as hot ones, such as Apricot Panettone Pudding. Served in tall elegant glasses, light airy mousses feature frequently among the most memorable desserts. Many are also blissfully simple — such as Coffee Cardamom Zabaglione and Chocolate and Espresso Mousse.

CLASSIC COFFEE CRÈME CARAMEL

THESE LIGHTLY SET COFFEE CUSTARDS ARE SERVED IN A POOL OF CARAMEL SAUCE. FOR A RICHER FLAVOUR, MAKE THEM WITH HALF SINGLE CREAM, HALF MILK.

SERVES 6

INGREDIENTS
    600ml/1 pint/2½ cups milk
    45ml/3 tbsp ground coffee
    50g/2oz/¼ cup caster (superfine) sugar
    4 whole eggs
    4 egg yolks
    spun sugar, to decorate (optional)
For the Caramel Sauce
    150g/5oz/¾ cup caster
       (superfine) sugar
    60ml/4 tbsp water

1 Preheat the oven to 160°C/325°F/ Gas 3. To make the caramel sauce, gently heat the sugar with the water in a small heavy pan, until the sugar has dissolved. Bring to the boil and boil rapidly until the syrup turns a rich golden brown.

5 Put the ramekins in a roasting pan and pour in enough hot water to come two-thirds of the way up the sides of the dishes. Bake for 30–35 minutes or until just set. Test by gently shaking one of the custards; it should wobble like a jelly. Remove the custards from the hot water and leave to cool.

6 Chill the coffee custards for at least 3 hours. To turn out, carefully loosen the sides with a metal spatula then invert on to serving plates. Decorate with spun sugar, if using.

COOK'S TIP
To make spun sugar, gently heat 75g/ 3oz/scant ½ cup caster (superfine) sugar, 5ml/1 tsp liquid glucose and 30ml/2 tbsp water in a heavy pan until the sugar dissolves. Boil the syrup to 160°C/325°F, then briefly dip the base of the pan into cold water. Put a sheet of baking parchment on the work surface to protect it. Holding two forks together, dip them into the syrup and flick them rapidly backwards and forwards over an oiled rolling pin. Store in an airtight container until ready to use.

2 Quickly and carefully, pour the hot syrup into six warmed 150ml/¼ pint/ ⅔ cup ramekins.

3 To make the coffee custard, heat the milk until almost boiling. Pour over the ground coffee and leave to infuse for about 5 minutes. Strain through a fine sieve into a jug (pitcher).

4 In a bowl, whisk the caster sugar, eggs and yolks until light and creamy. Whisk the coffee-flavoured milk into the egg mixture. Pour into the ramekins.

TIRAMISU

THE NAME OF THIS CLASSIC DESSERT TRANSLATES AS "PICK ME UP", WHICH IS SAID TO DERIVE FROM THE FACT THAT IT IS SO GOOD THAT IT LITERALLY MAKES YOU SWOON WHEN YOU EAT IT.

SERVES 4

INGREDIENTS

225g/8oz/1 cup mascarpone cheese
25g/1oz/¼ cup icing (confectioners')
  sugar, sifted
150ml/¼ pint/⅔ cup strong brewed
  coffee, chilled
300ml/½ pint/1¼ cups double
  (heavy) cream
45ml/3 tbsp coffee liqueur
115g/4oz sponge finger biscuits
  (cookies)
50g/2oz dark (bittersweet) or plain
  (semisweet) chocolate, grated
cocoa powder, for dusting

1 Lightly grease and line a 900g/2lb loaf tin (pan) with clear film (plastic wrap). Put the mascarpone and sugar in a large bowl and beat for 1 minute. Stir in 30ml/2 tbsp of the coffee and mix well.

2 Whip the cream with 15ml/1 tbsp of the liqueur until it forms soft peaks. Stir a spoonful into the mascarpone, then fold in the rest. Spoon half the mixture into the loaf tin and smooth the top.

3 Put the remaining strong brewed coffee and liqueur in a shallow dish just wider than the biscuits. Using half the biscuits, dip one side of each biscuit into the coffee mixture, then arrange on top of the mascarpone mixture in a single layer.

4 Spoon the rest of the mascarpone mixture over the biscuit layer and smooth the top.

5 Dip the remaining biscuits in the coffee mixture and arrange on top. Drizzle any remaining coffee mixture over the top. Cover the dish with clear film and chill for at least 4 hours. Carefully turn the tiramisu out of the loaf tin and sprinkle with grated chocolate and cocoa powder; serve cut into slices.

COOK'S TIP
Mascarpone is a silky textured, soft, thick cream cheese, originally from Lombardy, and made with cows' milk.

COFFEE CARDAMOM ZABAGLIONE

THIS WARM ITALIAN DESSERT IS USUALLY MADE WITH ITALIAN MARSALA WINE. IN THIS RECIPE COFFEE LIQUEUR IS USED ALONG WITH FRESHLY CRUSHED CARDAMOM.

SERVES 4

INGREDIENTS
4 cardamom pods
8 egg yolks
50g/2oz/4 tbsp golden caster
  (superfine) sugar
30ml/2 tbsp strong brewed coffee
50ml/2fl oz/¼ cup coffee liqueur such
  as Tia Maria, Kahlúa or Toussaint
a few roasted coffee beans, crushed,
  to decorate

1 Peel away the pale green outer husks of the cardamom pods and remove the black seeds. Crush these to a fine powder using a pestle and mortar.

2 Put the egg yolks, caster sugar and crushed cardamom seeds in a large bowl and whisk with a hand-held electric whisk for 1–2 minutes, or until the mixture is pale and creamy.

3 Gradually whisk the coffee and the liqueur into the egg yolk mixture.

4 Place the bowl over a pan of near-boiling water and continue whisking for about 10 minutes.

5 Continue whisking until the mixture is very thick and fluffy and has doubled in volume, making sure the water doesn't boil – if it does the mixture will curdle. Remove the bowl from the heat and carefully pour the zabaglione into four warmed glasses or dishes. Sprinkle with a few crushed roasted coffee beans and serve immediately.

COOK'S TIP
Cardamom is a fragrant spice from northern India. It may be bought ready-ground, but freshly crushed cardamom seeds are much sweeter.

PETITS POTS DE CAPPUCCINO

THESE VERY RICH COFFEE CUSTARDS, WITH A CREAM TOPPING AND A LIGHT DUSTING OF DRINKING CHOCOLATE POWDER, LOOK WONDERFUL PRESENTED IN FINE CHINA COFFEE CUPS.

SERVES 6–8

INGREDIENTS

   75g/3oz/1 cup roasted coffee beans
   300ml/½ pint/1¼ cups milk
   300ml/½ pint/1¼ cups single
   (light) cream
   1 whole egg, plus 4 egg yolks
   50g/2oz/4 tbsp caster (superfine) sugar
   2.5ml/½ tsp vanilla extract (essence)
For the topping
   120ml/4fl oz/½ cup whipping cream
   45ml/3 tbsp iced water
   10ml/2 tsp drinking chocolate powder

1 Preheat the oven to 160°C/325°F/ Gas 3. Put the roasted coffee beans in a pan over a low heat for about 3 minutes, shaking the pan frequently.

2 Pour the milk and cream over the beans. Heat until almost boiling; cover and leave to infuse for 30 minutes.

3 Whisk the egg, the egg yolks, sugar and vanilla together. Return the milk to boiling and pour through a sieve on to the egg mixture. Discard the beans.

4 Pour the mixture into eight 75ml/ 5 tbsp coffee cups or six 120ml/4fl oz/ ½ cup ramekins. Cover each with a small piece of foil.

5 Put in a roasting pan with hot water reaching about two-thirds of the way up the sides of the dishes. Bake them for 30–35 minutes, or until lightly set. Let cool. Chill for at least 2 hours.

6 Whisk the whipping cream and iced water until thick and frothy and spoon on top of the custards. Dust with drinking chocolate powder to serve.

COOK'S TIPS
These petits pots may also be served warm, topped with a spoonful of clotted cream. Serve straight away, with the clotted cream just starting to melt.

COFFEE AND BRANDY SYLLABUB

THIS HEAVENLY DESSERT COULDN'T BE EASIER — A FROTH OF WHIPPED COFFEE AND BRANDY CREAM TOPS JUICY GRAPES. CRISP BISCUITS PROVIDE A DELICIOUS CONTRAST.

SERVES 6

INGREDIENTS
  75g/3oz/6 tbsp soft light brown sugar
  finely grated rind of ½ orange
  120ml/4fl oz/½ cup brandy
  120ml/4fl oz/½ cup cold strong
    brewed coffee
  400ml/14fl oz/1⅔ cups double
    (heavy) cream
  225g/8oz white seedless grapes
  sugared grapes, to decorate
  crisp biscuits (cookies), to serve

COOK'S TIP
For sugared grapes, wash and dry the
fruit, then snip into small clusters. Use a
fine brush to paint lightly beaten egg white
evenly on to the grapes, then dust with
caster (superfine) sugar. Shake off any
excess sugar and leave to dry before using.

1 Put the brown sugar, orange rind and
brandy into a small bowl. Stir well, then
cover with clear film (plastic wrap) and
leave to stand for 1 hour.

2 Strain the mixture through a fine
sieve into a clean bowl. Stir in the
coffee. Slowly pour in the cream,
whisking all the time.

3 Continue whisking for 3–4 minutes,
until the mixture thickens enough to
stand in soft peaks.

4 Divide the grapes among the glasses.
Pour or spoon the syllabub over the
grapes. Chill for 1 hour, then decorate
the glasses with clusters of sugared
grapes and serve with crisp biscuits.

COFFEE JELLIES

SERVE THESE SPARKLING COFFEE JELLIES AS A LIGHT AND REFRESHING END TO A RICH MEAL.

SERVES 4

INGREDIENTS
  20ml/4 tsp powdered gelatine
  75ml/5 tbsp cold water
  600ml/1 pint/2½ cups very hot strong
    brewed coffee
  40g/1½oz/3 tbsp caster
    (superfine) sugar
For the Bay Cream
  300ml/½ pint/1¼ cups whipping cream
  15ml/1 tbsp bay-scented caster sugar
  fresh bay leaves, to decorate

VARIATION
For a creamy version of these jellies,
make the coffee with hot milk and serve
with fresh fruit instead of bay cream.

COOK'S TIP
To make bay-scented caster sugar, add
2–3 dried bay leaves to caster sugar.
Leave for at least a week before using.

1 To make the jellies, sprinkle the
gelatine over the cold water. Leave to
soak for 2–3 minutes. Add to the hot
strong brewed coffee with the sugar
and stir to dissolve.

2 Allow the coffee to cool, then pour
into four 150ml/¼ pint/⅔ cup metal
moulds. Chill in the refrigerator for
3 hours or until set.

3 To make the bay cream, lightly whisk
the cream and bay-scented caster sugar
until very soft peaks form. Spoon into a
serving bowl.

4 To serve, dip the moulds in a bowl of
hot water for a few seconds, then invert
on to individual serving plates. Serve
with the bay cream and decorate with
fresh bay leaves.

COFFEE COEUR À LA CRÈME

THESE PRETTY HEART-SHAPED CREAMS, SPECKLED WITH ESPRESSO-ROASTED COFFEE BEANS, ARE SERVED WITH A FRESH FRUIT SAUCE. USE WILD STRAWBERRIES, IF AVAILABLE, FOR THEIR WONDERFUL PERFUME.

SERVES 6

INGREDIENTS
  25g/1oz/generous ¼ cup espresso-
    roasted coffee beans
  225g/8oz/1 cup ricotta cheese or
    curd cheese
  300ml/½ pint/1¼ cups crème fraîche
  25g/1oz/2 tbsp caster (superfine) sugar
  finely grated rind of ½ orange
  2 egg whites
For the red fruit coulis
  175g/6oz/1 cup raspberries
  30ml/2 tbsp icing (confectioners')
    sugar, sifted
  115g/4oz/⅔ cup small strawberries,
    (or wild ones, if available), halved

1 Preheat the oven to 180°C/350°F/
Gas 4. Spread the espresso-roasted
coffee beans on a baking sheet and
roast for about 10 minutes. Allow to
cool, then put in a large plastic bag and
crush into tiny pieces with a rolling pin.

2 Thoroughly rinse 12 pieces of muslin
(cheesecloth) in cold water and squeeze
dry. Use to line six coeur à la crème
moulds with a double layer, allowing the
muslin to overhang the edges.

3 Press the ricotta or curd cheese
through a fine sieve into a bowl. Stir the
crème fraîche, sugar, orange rind and
crushed roasted coffee beans together.
Add to the cheese and mix well.

4 Whisk the egg whites until stiff and
fold into the mixture. Spoon into the
prepared moulds, then bring the muslin
up and over the filling. Leave in the
refrigerator overnight to drain and chill.

5 To make the red fruit coulis, put the
raspberries and icing sugar in a food
processor and blend until smooth. Push
through a fine sieve to remove the pips.
Stir in the strawberries. Chill until ready
to serve.

6 Unmould the hearts on to individual
serving plates and carefully remove the
muslin. Spoon the red fruit coulis over
before serving.

COOK'S TIP
Muslin has a fine weave that allows the
liquid from the cheese to drain through.
If you haven't got any muslin, use a new
all-purpose disposable cloth instead.

CHILLED CHOCOLATE AND ESPRESSO MOUSSE

HEADY, AROMATIC ESPRESSO COFFEE ADDS A DISTINCTIVE FLAVOUR TO THIS SMOOTH, RICH MOUSSE.
SERVE IT IN STYLISH CHOCOLATE CUPS FOR A SPECIAL OCCASION.

SERVES 4

INGREDIENTS
    225g/8oz plain (semisweet) chocolate
    45ml/3 tbsp brewed espresso
    25g/1oz/2 tbsp unsalted
        (sweet) butter
    4 eggs, separated
    mint sprigs, to decorate (optional)
    mascarpone or clotted cream,
        to serve (optional)
For the chocolate cups
    225g/8oz plain (semisweet) chocolate

1 For each chocolate cup, cut a double thickness 15cm/6in square of foil. Mould it around a small orange, leaving the edges and corners loose to make a cup shape. Remove the orange and press the base of the foil case (shell) gently on the work surface to make a flat base. Repeat to make four foil cups.

2 For the cups, break the chocolate into small pieces; place in a bowl set over very hot water. Stir occasionally until the chocolate has melted.

3 Spoon the chocolate into the foil cups, spreading it up the sides with the back of a spoon to give a ragged edge. Chill for 30 minutes or until set hard. Gently peel away the foil, starting at the top edge.

4 To make the chocolate mousse, put the plain chocolate and brewed espresso into a bowl set over a pan of hot water and melt as before. When smooth and liquid, add the unsalted butter, a little at a time. Remove the pan from the heat then stir in the egg yolks.

5 Whisk the egg whites in a bowl until stiff, but not dry, then fold into the chocolate mixture. Pour into a bowl and chill for at least 3 hours.

6 To serve, scoop the chilled mousse carefully into the chocolate cups. Add a scoop of mascarpone or clotted cream and decorate with a sprig of fresh mint, if using.

APRICOT PANETTONE PUDDING

*SLICES OF LIGHT-TEXTURED PANETTONE ARE LAYERED WITH DRIED APRICOTS AND COOKED IN A
CREAMY COFFEE CUSTARD FOR A SATISFYINGLY WARMING DESSERT.*

SERVES 4

INGREDIENTS

50g/2oz/4 tbsp unsalted (sweet)
   butter, softened
6 x 1cm/½in thick slices (about
   400g/14oz) panettone containing
   candied fruit
175g/6oz/¾ cup ready-to-eat dried
   apricots, chopped
400ml/14fl oz/1⅔ cups milk
250ml/8fl oz/1 cup double (heavy) cream
60ml/4 tbsp mild-flavoured ground
   coffee
90g/3½oz/½ cup caster (superfine) sugar
3 eggs
30ml/2 tbsp demerara (raw) sugar
pouring cream or crème fraîche,
   to serve

1 Preheat the oven to 160°C/325°F/
Gas 3. Brush a 2 litre/3½ pint/8 cup
oval baking dish with 15g/½oz/1 tbsp
of the butter. Spread the panettone with
the remaining butter and arrange in the
baking dish. Cut to fit and scatter the
apricots among and over the layers.

2 Pour the milk and cream into a pan
and heat until almost boiling. Pour the
milk mixture over the coffee and leave
to infuse for 10 minutes. Strain through
a fine sieve, discarding the coffee grounds.

3 Lightly beat the caster sugar and
eggs together, then whisk in the warm
coffee-flavoured milk. Slowly pour the
mixture over the panettone. Leave to
soak for 15 minutes.

4 Sprinkle the top of the pudding with
demerara sugar and place the dish in a
large roasting pan. Pour in enough
boiling water to come halfway up the
sides of the baking dish.

5 Bake for 40–45 minutes until the top
is golden and crusty, but the middle still
slightly wobbly. Remove from the oven,
but leave the dish in the hot water for
10 minutes. Serve warm with pouring
cream or crème fraîche.

COOK'S TIP
This recipe works equally well with plain
or chocolate-flavoured panettone.

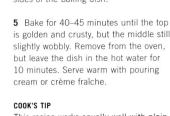

STICKY COFFEE AND GINGER PUDDING

THIS COFFEE-CAPPED FEATHER-LIGHT SPONGE IS MADE WITH BREADCRUMBS AND GROUND ALMONDS.
SERVE WITH CREAMY CUSTARD OR SCOOPS OF VANILLA ICE CREAM.

SERVES 4

INGREDIENTS
30ml/2 tbsp soft light brown sugar
25g/1oz/2 tbsp preserved stem
  ginger, chopped, plus 75ml/
  5 tbsp ginger syrup
30ml/2 tbsp mild-flavoured
  ground coffee
115g/4oz/generous ½ cup caster
  (superfine) sugar
3 eggs, separated
25g/1oz/¼ cup plain (all-purpose) flour
5ml/1 tsp ground ginger
65g/2½oz/generous 1 cup fresh
  white breadcrumbs
25g/1oz/¼ cup ground almonds

1 Preheat the oven to 180°C/350°F/
Gas 4. Grease and line the base of a
750ml/1¼ pint/3 cup ovenproof bowl,
then sprinkle in the sugar and chopped
stem ginger.

2 Put the ground coffee in a small
bowl. Heat the ginger syrup until almost
boiling; pour into the coffee. Stir well
and leave for 4 minutes. Pour through
a fine sieve into the ovenproof bowl.

3 Beat half the sugar with the egg yolks
until light and fluffy. Sift the flour and
ground ginger together and fold into the
egg yolk mixture with the breadcrumbs
and ground almonds.

4 Whisk the egg whites until stiff, then
gradually whisk in the remaining caster
sugar. Fold into the mixture, in two
batches. Spoon into the pudding basin
and smooth the top.

5 Cover the basin with a piece of
pleated greased baking parchment and
secure with string. Bake for 40 minutes,
or until the sponge is firm to the touch.
Turn out and serve immediately.

COOK'S TIP
This pudding can also be baked in a
900ml/1½ pint/3¾ cup loaf tin (pan)
and served thickly sliced.

SOUFFLÉS AND MERINGUES

Fluffy soufflés that rise to the occasion and melt-in-the-mouth meringues — these are coffee desserts to tempt your eye and your palate. The basic ingredients for meringues couldn't be simpler — just egg whites and sugar, to which coffee lends a sophisticated touch. For the perfect finish to a meal, try spicy Floating Islands, or the tropical taste of Mango and Coffee Meringue Roll.

CHILLED COFFEE AND PRALINE SOUFFLÉ

A SMOOTH COFFEE SOUFFLÉ WITH A CRUSHED PRALINE TOPPING THAT IS SPECTACULAR AND EASY.

SERVES 6

INGREDIENTS

150g/5oz/¾ cup caster
(superfine) sugar
75ml/5 tbsp water
150g/5oz/generous 1 cup blanched
almonds, plus extra for decoration
120ml/4fl oz/½ cup strong brewed
coffee, e.g. hazelnut-flavoured
15ml/1 tbsp powdered gelatine
3 eggs, separated
75g/3oz/scant ½ cup soft light
brown sugar
15ml/1 tbsp coffee liqueur, such as
Tia Maria, Kahlúa or Toussaint
150ml/¼ pint/⅔ cup double (heavy)
cream, plus to decorate (optional)

1 Cut a paper collar from a double
layer of baking parchment, 5cm/2in
deeper than a 900ml/1½ pint/3¾ cup
soufflé dish. Wrap around the dish and
tie in place with string. Chill.

2 Oil a baking sheet. Heat the caster
sugar in a small heavy pan with the
water until the sugar dissolves. Boil
rapidly until the syrup becomes pale
golden. Add the almonds and boil
until dark golden.

3 Pour the mixture on to the baking
sheet and leave to set. When hard,
transfer to a plastic bag and break into
pieces with a rolling pin. Reserve 50g/
2oz/½ cup and crush the remainder.

4 Pour half the coffee into a small bowl;
sprinkle over the gelatine. Leave to soak
for 5 minutes, then place the bowl over
a pan of hot water; stir until dissolved.

5 Put the egg yolks, soft light brown
sugar, remaining coffee and liqueur in
a bowl over a pan of simmering water.
Whisk until thick and foamy, then whisk
in the dissolved gelatine.

6 Whip the cream until soft peaks form,
then whisk the egg whites until stiff.
Fold the crushed praline into the cream,
then fold into the coffee mixture. Finally,
fold in the egg whites, in two batches.

7 Spoon into the soufflé dish and
smooth the top; chill for at least 2 hours
or until set. Put in the freezer for
15–20 minutes before serving. Remove
the paper collar by running a warmed
metal spatula between the set soufflé
and the paper. Whisk the cream for
decoration, if using, and place large
spoonfuls on top. Decorate with the
reserved praline pieces and whole
blanched almonds.

TWICE-BAKED MOCHA SOUFFLÉ

THE PERFECT WAY TO END A MEAL, THESE MINI MOCHA SOUFFLÉS CAN BE MADE UP TO THREE HOURS AHEAD, THEN REHEATED JUST BEFORE SERVING.

SERVES 6

INGREDIENTS

75g/3oz/6 tbsp unsalted (sweet)
  butter, softened
90g/3½ oz dark (bittersweet) or plain
  (semisweet) chocolate, grated
30ml/2 tbsp ground coffee
400ml/14fl oz/1⅔ cup milk
40g/1½oz/⅓ cup plain (all-purpose)
  flour, sifted
15g/½ oz/2 tbsp cocoa powder, sifted
3 eggs, separated
50g/2oz/¼ cup caster (superfine) sugar
175ml/6fl oz/¾ cup creamy chocolate
  or coffee liqueur

1 Preheat the oven to 200°C/400°F/ Gas 6. Thickly brush 6 x 150ml/¼ pint/ ⅔ cup dariole moulds or mini ovenproof bowls with 25g/1oz/2 tbsp of the butter. Coat with 50g/2oz of the grated chocolate.

2 Put the ground coffee in a small bowl. Heat the milk until almost boiling and pour over the coffee. Infuse for 4 minutes and strain, discarding the grounds.

3 Melt the remaining butter in a small pan. Stir in the flour and cocoa to make a roux. Cook for about 1 minute, then gradually add the coffee milk, stirring all the time to make a very thick sauce. Simmer for 2 minutes. Remove from the heat and stir in the egg yolks.

VARIATION
Good quality white or milk cooking chocolate can be use instead of plain, if preferred.

4 Cool for 5 minutes, then stir in the remaining chocolate. Whisk the egg whites until stiff, then gradually whisk in the sugar. Stir half into the sauce to loosen, then fold in the remainder.

5 Spoon the mixture into the moulds or bowls and place in a roasting pan. Pour in enough hot water to come two-thirds of the way up the sides of the tins.

6 Bake the soufflés for 15 minutes. Turn them out on to a baking sheet and leave to cool completely.

7 Before serving, spoon 15ml/1 tbsp chocolate or coffee liqueur over each pudding and reheat in the oven for 6–7 minutes. Serve on individual plates with the remaining liqueur poured over.

CLASSIC CHOCOLATE <u>AND</u> COFFEE ROULADE

THIS RICH CHOCOLATE ROLL SHOULD BE MADE AT LEAST 12 HOURS BEFORE SERVING, TO ALLOW IT TO SOFTEN. EXPECT THE ROULADE TO CRACK A LITTLE WHEN YOU ROLL IT UP.

SERVES 8

INGREDIENTS
    200g/7oz plain (semisweet) chocolate
    200g/7oz/1 cup caster (superfine) sugar
    7 eggs, separated
For the Filling
    300ml/½ pint/1¼ cups double
      (heavy) cream
    30ml/2 tbsp cold strong brewed coffee
    15ml/1 tbsp coffee liqueur
    60ml/4 tbsp icing (confectioners')
      sugar, for dusting
    little grated chocolate, for sprinkling

1 Preheat the oven to 180°C/350°F/ Gas 4. Grease and line a 33 x 23cm/ 13 x 9in Swiss roll tin (jelly roll pan) with baking parchment.

2 Break the chocolate into squares and melt in a bowl over a pan of barely simmering water. Remove from the heat and leave to cool for 5 minutes.

3 In a large bowl, whisk the sugar and egg yolks until light and fluffy. Stir in the melted chocolate.

4 Whisk the egg whites until stiff, but not dry, and then gently fold into the chocolate mixture.

5 Pour the chocolate mixture into the prepared tin, spreading it level with a spatula. Bake for about 25 minutes until firm. Leave the cake in the tin and cover with a cooling rack, making sure it doesn't touch the cake.

6 Cover the rack with a damp dish towel, then wrap in clear film (plastic wrap). Leave in a cool place for at least 8 hours or overnight, if possible.

7 Dust a large sheet of baking parchment with icing sugar and turn out the roulade on to it. Peel off the lining.

8 To make the filling, whip the double cream with the coffee and liqueur until soft peaks form. Spread the cream over the roulade. Starting from one of the short ends, carefully roll it up, using the paper to help.

9 Place the roulade, seam-side down, on to a serving plate; dust generously with icing sugar and sprinkle with a little grated chocolate before serving.

COOK'S TIPS
Make the roulade at least 12 hours before serving, to allow it to soften. If liked, decorate the roulade with swirls of whipped cream and chocolate coffee beans, or with clusters of raspberries and mint leaves.

MANGO AND COFFEE MERINGUE ROLL

A LIGHT AND FLUFFY ROLL OF MERINGUE IS THE IDEAL CONTRAST TO THE UNSWEETENED FILLING OF COFFEE, MASCARPONE AND JUICY RIPE MANGO.

SERVES 6–8

INGREDIENTS
  4 egg whites
  225g/8oz/generous 1 cup caster
    (superfine) sugar
For the Filling
  45ml/3 tbsp strong-flavoured
    ground coffee
  75ml/5 tbsp milk
  350g/12oz/1½ cups mascarpone
  1 ripe mango, cut into
    1cm/½in cubes

COOK'S TIP
If you like, the meringue can be sprinkled with 50g/2oz/½ cup skinned chopped hazelnuts before baking.

1 Preheat the oven to 190°C/375°F/ Gas 5. Line a 33 x 23cm/13 x 9in Swiss roll tin (jelly roll pan) with lightly greased baking parchment. Whisk the egg whites until stiff. Gradually add the sugar, whisking after each addition until thick and glossy.

2 Spoon the meringue into the prepared tin and smooth the surface. Bake for 15 minutes or until firm and golden.

3 Turn the meringue out on to a sheet of baking parchment. Remove the lining paper and leave until cold.

4 To make the filling, put the coffee in a small bowl. Heat the milk until it is nearly boiling and pour over the coffee. Leave to infuse for 4 minutes, then strain through a fine sieve, discarding the coffee grounds.

5 Beat the mascarpone until soft, then gradually beat in the coffee. Spread over the meringue, then scatter with the chopped mango.

6 Gently roll up the meringue from one of the short ends, with the help of the baking parchment. Transfer to a serving plate seam-side down. Chill for at least 30 minutes before serving.

GINGERED COFFEE MERINGUES

WHAT COULD BE MORE ENTICING THAN TO BREAK THROUGH THE COATING OF CRISP MERINGUE TO REVEAL JUST-MELTING COFFEE ICE CREAM ON A MOIST GINGER SPONGE?

SERVES 6

INGREDIENTS

   275g/10oz bought ginger cake
   600ml/1 pint/2½ cups coffee
     ice cream
   4 egg whites
   1.5ml/¼ tsp cream of tartar
   150g/5oz/¾ cup caster (superfine) sugar
   25g/1oz/2 tbsp preserved stem
     ginger, finely chopped

1 Preheat the oven to 230°C/450°F/Gas 8. Cut the ginger cake lengthways into three slices. Stamp out two rounds from each slice, using a 5cm/2in pastry (cookie) cutter, and put on a baking sheet.

2 Top each cake round with a large scoop of coffee ice cream, then place the baking sheet in the freezer for at least 30 minutes.

3 Whisk the egg whites and cream of tartar until soft peaks form. Gradually add the sugar and continue whisking until the mixture forms stiff peaks. Fold in the preserved stem ginger.

4 Carefully spoon the meringue and ginger mixture into a piping (pastry) bag fitted with a large plain nozzle.

COOK'S TIP
The ice cream is insulated in the oven by the tiny bubbles of air in the meringue, so ensure it is completely covered. Once coated, the ice cream cakes could be frozen until ready to cook.

5 Quickly pipe the meringue over the ice cream, starting from the base and working up to the top.

6 Bake in the oven for 3–4 minutes, until the outside of the meringue is crisp and lightly tinged with brown. Serve immediately.

FLOATING ISLANDS

THIS WELL-KNOWN DESSERT GETS ITS NAME FROM THE POACHED MERINGUES SURROUNDED BY A "SEA" OF CRÈME ANGLAISE. THIS VERSION IS GIVEN A TOUCH OF THE EXOTIC THROUGH THE ADDITION OF STAR ANISE AND IS SERVED WITH A RICH COFFEE SAUCE.

SERVES 6

INGREDIENTS
For the Coffee Crème Anglaise
   150ml/¼ pint/⅔ cup milk
   150ml/¼ pint/⅔ cup single (light) cream
   120ml/4fl oz/½ cup strong
    brewed coffee
   4 egg yolks
   25g/1oz/2 tbsp soft light brown sugar
   5ml/1 tsp cornflour (cornstarch)
For the Caramel Sauce
   90g/3½oz/½ cup caster
   (superfine) sugar
For the Poached Meringues
   2 egg whites
   50g/2oz/¼ cup caster (superfine) sugar
   1.5ml/¼ tsp ground star anise
   a pinch of salt

1 To make the coffee crème Anglaise, pour the milk, cream and coffee into a pan and heat to boiling point.

2 In a large bowl, whisk the egg yolks, brown sugar and cornflour together until creamy. Whisk in the hot coffee mixture, then pour the entire mixture back into the pan.

3 Heat for 1–2 minutes, stirring until the sauce thickens. Take off the heat and leave to cool, stirring occasionally. Pour back into the bowl.

COOK'S TIP
Once poached, the meringues will keep their shape for up to 2 hours.

4 Cover the bowl with clear film (plastic wrap) and place in the refrigerator.

5 For the caramel, put the sugar in a small heavy pan with 45ml/3 tbsp water and heat very gently until dissolved. Boil rapidly until the syrup turns a rich golden colour. Off the heat, carefully add 45ml/3 tbsp hot water – it will splutter. Leave to cool.

6 To make the meringues, whisk the egg whites until stiff. Combine the sugar and star anise; add to the egg whites.

7 Pour 2.5cm/1in boiling water into a large frying pan. Add the salt and bring to a gentle simmer. Shape the meringue into small ovals, using two spoons, and add to the water. Poach four or five of the meringues at a time for about 3 minutes, until firm.

8 Remove with a slotted spoon and drain on kitchen paper. Repeat with the remaining mixture.

9 To serve, spoon a little coffee crème Anglaise on to each serving plate. Float two or three "islands" on top, then drizzle with caramel sauce.

COFFEE MERINGUES WITH ROSE CREAM

THESE SUGARY MERINGUES, WITH CRUSHED ESPRESSO-ROASTED COFFEE BEANS, ARE FILLED WITH A DELICATE ROSE-SCENTED CREAM. LIGHTLY SPRINKLE ROSE PETALS FOR A ROMANTIC FINISH.

MAKES 20 PAIRS OF MERINGUES

INGREDIENTS
    25g/1oz/generous ¼ cup espresso-
      roasted coffee beans
    3 egg whites
    175g/6oz/1 cup caster (superfine) sugar
    25g/1oz/¼ cup pistachio nuts, chopped
    a few rose petals, to decorate
For the Rose Cream
    300ml/½ pint/1¼ cups double (heavy)
      cream
    15ml/1 tbsp icing (confectioners')
      sugar, sifted
    10ml/2 tsp rose water

1 Preheat the oven to 180°C/350°F/
Gas 4. Spread the coffee beans on a
baking sheet and toast for 8 minutes.
Leave to cool, then put in a plastic bag
and crush with a rolling pin.

2 Whisk the egg whites and sugar in a
bowl over a pan of hot water until thick.

3 Remove from the heat and continue
whisking until the meringue holds stiff
peaks. Whisk in the crushed beans.

4 Preheat the oven to 140°C/275°F/Gas
1. Fill a piping (pastry) bag fitted with a
large star nozzle with the mixture and
pipe 40 small swirls on to two baking
sheets lined with baking parchment.
Leave some space between each swirl.

5 Sprinkle with the pistachio nuts.
Bake the meringues for 2–2½ hours,
or until dry and crisp, swapping the
position of the baking sheets halfway
through the cooking time. Leave to cool,
then remove from the paper.

6 To make the rose cream, whip the
cream, icing sugar and rose water until
soft peaks form. Use to sandwich the
meringues together in pairs. Arrange on
a serving plate and serve scattered with
rose petals for decoration.

VARIATION
Orange flower water may be used instead
of rose water in the cream and a drop of
pink food colouring added, if you like.

COFFEE PAVLOVA WITH EXOTIC FRUITS

BOTH AUSTRALIA AND NEW ZEALAND CLAIM TO HAVE INVENTED THIS FLUFFY MERINGUE NAMED AFTER THE BALLERINA ANNA PAVLOVA. THE SECRET OF SUCCESS IS TO LEAVE THE MERINGUE IN THE OVEN UNTIL COMPLETELY COOLED, AS A SUDDEN CHANGE IN TEMPERATURE WILL MAKE IT CRACK.

SERVES 6–8

INGREDIENTS
    30ml/2 tbsp ground coffee
    30ml/2 tbsp near-boiling water
    3 egg whites
    2.5ml/½ tsp cream of tartar
    175g/6oz/1 cup caster (superfine) sugar
    5ml/1 tsp cornflour (cornstarch), sifted
For the Filling
    150ml/¼ pint/⅔ cup double (heavy)
        cream
    5ml/1 tsp vanilla orange flower water
    150ml/¼ pint/⅔ cup crème fraîche
    500g/1¼lb sliced exotic fruits, such
        as mango, papaya and kiwi
    15ml/1 tbsp icing (confectioners') sugar

4 Using a long knife or spatula, spoon the meringue mixture on to the baking sheet, spreading to an even 20cm/8in circle. Make a slight hollow in the middle. Bake in the oven for 1 hour, then turn off the heat and leave in the oven until cool.

5 Transfer the meringue to a plate, peeling off the lining. To make the filling, whip the cream with the orange flower water until soft peaks form. Fold in the crème fraîche. Spoon into the meringue. Arrange the fruits over the cream and dust with icing sugar.

1 Preheat the oven to 140°C/275°F/Gas 1. Draw a 20cm/8in circle on baking parchment. Place pencil-side down on a baking sheet.

2 Put the coffee in a small bowl and pour the hot water over. Leave to infuse for 4 minutes, then strain through a very fine sieve.

3 Whisk the egg whites with the cream of tartar until stiff, but not dry. Gradually whisk in the sugar until the meringue is stiff and shiny, then quickly whisk in the cornflour and coffee.

VARIATION
450g/1lb soft fruit, such as wild or cultivated strawberries, raspberries and blueberries, may be used instead of the exotic fruits if you wish.

FRUIT DESSERTS

*If you're looking for colour, flavour
and freshness — something a little
out of the ordinary — opt for one of
these fruit and coffee combinations.
Fruit always makes the perfect
pudding, no matter how simple or
grand the meal, but it doesn't have
to be chilled. Try steeping oranges
in a hot coffee syrup, or serve a
slice of Sticky Pear Pudding for
pure indulgence.*

Oranges in Hot Coffee Syrup

THIS RECIPE WORKS WELL WITH MOST CITRUS FRUITS; TRY PINK GRAPEFRUIT OR SWEET, PERFUMED CLEMENTINES, PEELED BUT LEFT WHOLE, FOR A CHANGE.

SERVES 6

INGREDIENTS
  6 medium oranges
  200g/7oz/1 cup sugar
  50ml/2fl oz/¼ cup cold water
  100ml/3½fl oz/scant ½ cup
    boiling water
  100ml/3½fl oz/scant ½ cup fresh
    strong brewed coffee
  50g/2oz/½ cup pistachio nuts,
    chopped (optional)

COOK'S TIP
Choose a pan in which the oranges will just fit in a single layer.

1 Finely pare the rind from one orange, shred and reserve the rind. Peel the remaining oranges. Cut each one crossways into slices, then re-form with a cocktail stick (toothpick).

2 Put the sugar and cold water in a heavy pan. Heat gently until the sugar dissolves, then bring to the boil and cook until the syrup turns pale gold.

3 Remove from the heat and carefully pour the boiling water into the pan. Return to the heat until the syrup has dissolved in the water. Stir in the coffee.

4 Add the oranges and the shredded rind to the coffee syrup. Simmer for 15–20 minutes, turning the oranges once during cooking. Sprinkle with pistachio nuts, if using, and serve hot.

Fresh Fig Compote

LIGHTLY POACHING FIGS IN A VANILLA AND COFFEE SYRUP BRINGS OUT THEIR WONDERFUL FLAVOUR.

SERVES 4–6

INGREDIENTS
  400ml/14fl oz/1⅔ cups
    brewed coffee
  115g/4oz/½ cup clear honey
  1 vanilla pod (bean)
  12 slightly underripe fresh figs
  Greek (US strained plain) yogurt,
    to serve (optional)

COOK'S TIPS
• Rinse and dry the vanilla pod; it can be used several times.
• Figs come in three main varieties – red, white and black – and all three are suitable for cooking. Naturally high in sugar, they are sweet and succulent and complement well the stronger flavours of coffee and vanilla.

1 Choose a frying pan with a lid, large enough to hold the figs in a single layer. Pour in the coffee and add the honey.

2 Split the vanilla pod lengthways and scrape the seeds into the pan. Add the vanilla pod, then bring to the boil, then boil rapidly until reduced to about 175ml/6fl oz/¾ cup. Leave to cool.

3 Wash the figs and pierce the skins several times with a sharp skewer. Cut in half and add to the syrup. Lower the heat, cover and simmer for 5 minutes. Remove the figs from the syrup with a slotted spoon and set aside to cool.

4 Strain the syrup over the figs. Allow to stand at room temperature for 1 hour before serving with yogurt, if using.

STICKY PEAR PUDDING

CLOVES ADD A DISTINCTIVE FRAGRANT FLAVOUR TO THIS HAZELNUT, PEAR AND COFFEE PUDDING.

<u>SERVES 6</u>

INGREDIENTS
 30ml/2 tbsp ground coffee,
  e.g. hazelnut-flavoured
 15ml/1 tbsp near-boiling water
 50g/2oz/½ cup toasted
  skinned hazelnuts
 4 ripe pears
 juice of ½ orange
 115g/4oz/8 tbsp butter, softened
 115g/4oz/generous ½ cup golden
  caster (superfine) sugar, plus an
  extra 15ml/1 tbsp for baking
 2 eggs, beaten
 50g/2oz/½ cup self-raising
  (self-rising) flour, sifted
 pinch of ground cloves
 8 whole cloves (optional)
 45ml/3 tbsp maple syrup
 fine strips of orange rind, to decorate
For the Orange Cream
 300ml/½ pint/1¼ cups
  whipping cream
 15ml/1 tbsp icing (confectioners')
  sugar, sifted
 finely grated rind of ½ orange

1 Preheat the oven to 180°C/350°F/
Gas 4. Lightly grease a 20cm/8in loose-
based sandwich tin (pan). Put the
ground coffee in a small bowl and pour
the water over. Leave to infuse for
4 minutes, then strain through a fine sieve.

COOK'S TIP
If you can't find ready-toasted skinned
hazelnuts, prepare your own. Toast under
a hot grill (broiler) for 3–4 minutes,
turning frequently until well browned. Rub
off the skins and cool before grinding.

2 Grind the hazelnuts in a coffee
grinder until fine. Peel, halve and core
the pears. Thinly slice across the pear
halves part of the way through. Brush
with orange juice.

3 Beat the butter and the 115g/4oz/
generous ½ cup caster sugar together
in a large bowl until very light and fluffy.
Gradually beat in the eggs, then fold in
the flour, ground cloves, hazelnuts and
coffee. Spoon the mixture into the tin
and level the surface.

4 Pat the pears dry on kitchen paper,
then arrange in the sponge mixture, flat
side down.

5 Lightly press 2 whole cloves into
each pear half, if using. Brush the
pears with 15ml/1 tbsp maple syrup.

6 Sprinkle the pears with the 15ml/
1 tbsp caster sugar. Bake for 45–50
minutes or until firm and well-risen.

7 While the sponge is cooking, make
the orange cream. Whip the cream,
icing sugar and orange rind until soft
peaks form. Spoon into a serving dish
and chill until needed.

8 Allow the sponge to cool for about
10 minutes in the tin, then remove and
place on a serving plate. Lightly brush
with the remaining maple syrup before
decorating with orange rind and serving
warm with the orange cream.

COFFEE CRÊPES WITH PEACHES AND CREAM

JUICY GOLDEN PEACHES AND CREAM CONJURE UP THE SWEET TASTE OF SUMMER. HERE THEY ARE DELICIOUS AS THE FILLING FOR THESE LIGHT COFFEE CRÊPES.

SERVES 6

INGREDIENTS

75g/3oz/⅔ cup plain (all-purpose) flour
25g/1oz/¼ cup buckwheat flour
1.5ml/¼ tsp salt
1 egg, beaten
200ml/7fl oz/scant 1 cup milk
15g/½oz/1 tbsp butter, melted
100ml/3½ oz/½ cup brewed coffee
sunflower oil, for frying
For the Filling
6 ripe peaches
300ml/½ pint/1¼ cups double
  (heavy) cream
15ml/1 tbsp Amaretto liqueur
225g/8oz/1 cup mascarpone
65g/2½oz/generous ¼ cup
  caster (superfine) sugar
30ml/2 tbsp icing (confectioners')
  sugar, for dusting

1 Sift the flours and salt into a mixing bowl. Make a well in the middle and add the egg, half the milk and the butter. Gradually beat in the flour until smooth, then the remaining milk and coffee.

2 Heat a drizzle of oil in a 15–20cm/ 6–8in crêpe pan. Pour in just enough batter to thinly cover the base of the pan. Cook for 2–3 minutes, until the underneath is golden brown, then flip over and cook the other side.

COOK'S TIP
To keep the pancakes warm while you make the rest, cover them with foil and place the plate over a pan of barely simmering water.

3 Slide the crêpe out of the pan on to a plate. Continue making crêpes until all the mixture is used, stacking and interleaving with baking parchment.

4 To make the filling, halve the peaches and remove the stones (pits). Cut into thick slices. Whip the cream and Amaretto liqueur until soft peaks form. Beat the mascarpone with the sugar until smooth. Beat 30ml/2 tbsp of the cream into the mascarpone, then fold in the remainder.

5 Spoon a little of the Amaretto cream on to one half of each pancake and top with peach slices. Gently fold the pancake over and dust with icing sugar. Serve immediately.

PLUM AND RUM BABAS

A POLISH KING THOUGHT UP THESE SPONGY YEAST CAKES AFTER HEARING THE STORY OF ALI BABA.
SOAKED IN A COFFEE AND RUM SYRUP, THEIR MIDDLES ARE FILLED WITH JUICY PLUMS.

SERVES 6

INGREDIENTS

65g/2½oz/5 tbsp unsalted (sweet)
  butter, softened
115g/4oz/1 cup strong plain
  (all-purpose) flour
pinch of salt
7.5ml/1½ tsp easy-blend (rapid-rise)
  dried yeast
25g/1oz/2 tbsp soft light brown sugar
2 eggs, beaten
45ml/3 tbsp warm milk
crème fraîche, to serve
For the Syrup
115g/4oz/½ cup granulated sugar
120ml/4fl oz/½ cup water
450g/1lb plums, halved, stoned
  (pitted) and thickly sliced
120ml/4fl oz/½ cup brewed coffee
45ml/3 tbsp dark rum

4 Cover with clear film (plastic wrap) and leave to rise for 40 minutes. Mix the remaining butter into the dough. Put the tins on a baking sheet and drop the dough into the moulds. Cover with oiled clear film and leave until the dough has almost risen to the top. Remove the film and bake for 15–20 minutes.

5 Meanwhile, make the syrup. Put 25g/1oz/2 tbsp of the sugar in a pan with the water. Add the plums and cook over a low heat until barely tender; remove with a slotted spoon. Add the remaining sugar and coffee to the pan. Heat gently until dissolved, but do not boil. Remove from the heat and stir in the rum.

6 Turn out the babas on to a wire rack and leave to cool for 5 minutes. Dunk them in the warm syrup until well soaked. Return them to the wire rack with a plate underneath to catch any drips. Leave to cool completely.

7 Put the babas on a serving plate and fill the middles with the sliced plums. Spoon a little extra syrup over each and serve with crème fraîche.

1 Preheat the oven to 190°C/375°F/Gas 5. Brush 6 x 9cm/3½in ring tins (pans) with 15g/½oz/1 tbsp butter.

2 Sift the flour and salt into a mixing bowl and stir in the yeast and soft light brown sugar.

3 Make a well in the middle and add the eggs and warm milk. Beat for about 5 minutes with a wooden spoon to make a very sticky dough that is fairly smooth and elastic.

COOK'S TIP
The babas may also be split in half horizontally, filled with whipped cream and sandwiched back together.

COCONUT AND COFFEE TRIFLE

DARK COFFEE SPONGE, LACED WITH LIQUEUR, COCONUT CUSTARD AND A COFFEE CREAM TOPPING
MAKES THIS A LAVISH DESSERT. SERVE IN A LARGE GLASS BOWL FOR MAXIMUM IMPACT.

SERVES 6–8

INGREDIENTS

For the Coffee Sponge
    45ml/3 tbsp strong ground coffee
    45ml/3 tbsp near-boiling water
    2 eggs
    50g/2oz/¼ cup soft dark brown sugar
    40g/1½oz/⅓ cup self-raising
        (self-rising) flour, sifted
    25ml/1½ tbsp hazelnut or sunflower oil
For the Coconut Custard
    400ml/14fl oz/1⅔ cup canned
        coconut milk
    3 eggs
    40g/1½oz/3 tbsp caster
        (superfine) sugar
    10ml/2 tsp cornflour (cornstarch)
For the Filling and Topping
    2 bananas
    60ml/4 tbsp coffee liqueur
    300ml/½ pint/1¼ cups double
        (heavy) cream
    30ml/2 tbsp icing (confectioners')
        sugar, sifted
    fresh coconut, to decorate

1 Preheat the oven to 160°C/325°F/
Gas 3. Grease and line an 18cm/7in
square tin with baking parchment.

2 Put the coffee in a small jug (pitcher).
Pour the hot water over and leave to
infuse for 4 minutes. Strain through a
fine sieve, discarding the grounds.

3 Whisk the eggs and soft dark brown
sugar in a large bowl until the whisk
leaves a trail when lifted.

4 Gently fold in the flour, followed by
15ml/1 tbsp of the coffee and the oil.
Spoon the mixture into the tin and bake
for 20 minutes, until firm. Turn out on
to a wire rack, remove the lining paper
and leave to cool.

5 To make the coconut custard, heat
the coconut milk in a pan until it is
almost boiling.

6 Whisk the eggs, sugar and cornflour
together until frothy. Pour into the hot
coconut milk, whisking all the time.
Heat gently, stirring, for 1–2 minutes,
until the custard thickens, but do not
boil. Set aside to cool for about 10
minutes, stirring occasionally.

7 Cut the coffee sponge into 5cm/2in
squares and arrange in the base of a
large glass bowl. Slice the bananas and
arrange on top of the sponge. Drizzle
the coffee liqueur on top. Pour the
custard over and leave until cold.

8 Whip the cream with the remaining
coffee and icing sugar until soft peaks
form. Spoon the cream over the
custard. Cover and chill for several
hours. Sprinkle with ribbons of fresh
coconut before serving.

COOK'S TIP

To make coconut ribbons, use a vegetable
peeler to cut thin ribbons from the flesh
of a fresh coconut, or buy shredded
coconut and toast until pale golden.

FLAMBÉED BANANAS WITH CARIBBEAN COFFEE SAUCE

THIS DESSERT HAS ALL THE FLAVOUR OF THE CARIBBEAN; BANANAS, DARK SUGAR, COFFEE AND RUM.

SERVES 4–6

INGREDIENTS
  6 bananas
  40g/1½oz/3 tbsp butter
  50g/2oz/¼ cup soft dark brown sugar
  50ml/2fl oz/¼ cup strong
    brewed coffee
  60ml/4 tbsp dark rum
  vanilla ice cream, to serve

1 Peel the bananas and cut in half lengthways. Melt the butter in a large frying pan over a medium heat. Add the bananas and cook for 3 minutes, turning once.

COOK'S TIP
These hot bananas taste equally good served with coconut or coffee ice cream.

2 Sprinkle the sugar over the bananas, then add the coffee. Continue cooking, stirring occasionally, for 2–3 minutes, or until the bananas are tender.

3 Pour the rum into the pan and bring to the boil. With a long match or taper, and tilting the pan, ignite the rum. As soon as the flames subside, serve the bananas with vanilla ice cream.

GRILLED NECTARINES WITH COFFEE MASCARPONE FILLING

THIS SIMPLE DESSERT IS PERFECT FOR NECTARINES THAT ARE STILL SLIGHTLY HARD, AS THEY ARE GRILLED WITH A DELICIOUS HONEY AND BUTTER GLAZE AND FILLED WITH CHILLED COFFEE CREAM.

SERVES 4

INGREDIENTS
  115g/4oz/½ cup mascarpone
  45ml/3 tbsp cold very strong
    brewed coffee
  4 nectarines
  15g/½oz/1 tbsp butter, melted
    and cooled
  45ml/3 tbsp clear honey
  pinch of mixed (apple pie) spice
  25g/1oz/¼ cup flaked (sliced)
    brazil nuts

1 Beat the mascarpone until soft. Add the coffee. Cover with clear film (plastic wrap). Chill for 20 minutes.

2 Cut the nectarines in half and remove the stones (pits). In a small bowl, mix the butter, 30ml/2 tbsp of the honey and mixed spice. Brush the spicy butter all over the cut surfaces.

3 Arrange the nectarines, cut-side up on a foil-lined grill (broiler) pan. Cook under a hot grill (broiler) for 2–3 minutes. Add the brazil nuts to the grill pan for the last minute of cooking and toast until golden.

4 Put a spoonful of the chilled cheese mixture in the centre of each hot nectarine. Drizzle with the remaining honey and sprinkle with the toasted brazil nuts before serving.

COOK'S TIP
If possible, choose a scented honey for this dessert: orange blossom and rosemary are both delicious.

VANILLA POACHED PEARS WITH FROTHY CAPPUCCINO SAUCE

VANILLA-SCENTED PEARS ARE SERVED WITH A BUBBLY ESPRESSO SAUCE AND FINISHED WITH A FAINT DUSTING OF SPICY CHOCOLATE FOR A LIGHT, ELEGANT DESSERT.

SERVES 6

INGREDIENTS
 1 vanilla pod (bean)
 150g/5oz/¾ cup granulated sugar
 400ml/14fl oz/1⅔ cups water
 6 slightly underripe pears
 juice of ½ lemon
Fro the frothy cappuccino sauce
 3 egg yolks
 25g/1oz/2 tbsp caster (superfine) sugar
 50ml/2fl oz/¼ cup brewed
  espresso coffee
 50ml/2fl oz/¼ cup single (light) cream
 10ml/2 tsp drinking chocolate powder
 2.5ml/½ tsp ground cinnamon

1 Split the vanilla pod lengtways and scrape out the seeds into a large pan. Add the split pod, sugar and water. Heat gently until the sugar has completely dissolved.

2 Meanwhile, peel and halve the pears, then rub with lemon juice. Scoop out the cores with a melon baller or teaspoon. Add the cored pears to the syrup and pour in extra water to cover.

3 Cut out a circle of baking parchment and cover the top of the pears. Bring to a light boil, cover the pan with a lid and simmer for 15 minutes, or until tender.

4 Using a slotted spoon, transfer the pears to a serving bowl. Bring the syrup to a rapid boil and cook for 15 minutes, or until reduced by half.

5 Strain over the pears and leave to cool. Cover with clear film (plastic wrap) and chill for several hours. Allow to come back to room temperature before serving.

6 To make the sauce, put the egg yolks, sugar, coffee and cream into a heatproof bowl over a pan of barely simmering water. With a balloon whisk, beat until the mixture is very thick and frothy. Remove from the heat and continue beating for 2–3 minutes.

7 Arrange the pears on individual plates and pour a little sauce over each. Mix together the drinking chocolate and cinnamon and sprinkle over the sauce. Serve immediately.

FRAGRANT FRUIT SALAD

THE SYRUP OF THIS EXOTIC FRUIT SALAD IS FLAVOURED AND SWEETENED WITH LIME AND COFFEE LIQUEUR. IT CAN BE PREPARED UP TO A DAY BEFORE SERVING.

SERVES 6

INGREDIENTS

    130g/4½oz/½ cup sugar
    thinly pared rind and juice of 1 lime
    60ml/4 tbsp coffee liqueur, such as
        Tia Maria, Kahlúa or Toussaint
    1 small pineapple
    1 mango
    1 papaya
    2 pomegranates
    2 passion fruit
    fine strips of lime peel, to decorate

1 Put the sugar and lime rind in a small pan with 150ml/¼ pint/⅔ cup water. Heat gently until the sugar dissolves, then bring to the boil and simmer for 5 minutes. Leave to cool, then strain into a large serving bowl, discarding the lime rind. Stir in the lime juice and liqueur.

2 Using a sharp knife, cut the plume and stalk end from the pineapple. Peel thickly and cut the flesh into bite-sized pieces, discarding the woody central core. Add to the bowl.

3 Cut the papaya in half and scoop out the seeds. Cut away the skin, then cut into slices. Cut the pomegranates in half and scoop out the seeds. Break into clusters and add to the bowl.

COOK'S TIP

To maximize the flavour of the fruit, allow the salad to stand at room temperature for an hour before serving.

4 Cut the mango lengthways, along each side of the stone (pit). Peel the skin off the flesh. Add with the rest of the fruit to the bowl. Stir well.

5 Halve the passion fruit and scoop out the flesh using a teaspoon. Spoon over the salad and serve, decorated with fine strips of lime peel.

CARAMELIZED APPLES

A TRADITIONAL DESSERT WITH A DIFFERENCE — BAKED APPLES BATHED IN A RICH COFFEE SYRUP.

SERVES 6

INGREDIENTS
   6 eating apples, peeled, but
      left whole
   50g/2oz/4 tbsp unsalted (sweet)
      butter, melted and cooled
   90g/3½oz/½ cup caster
      (superfine) sugar
   1.5ml/¼ tsp ground cinnamon
   90ml/6 tbsp strong brewed coffee
   whipped or clotted cream, to serve

COOK'S TIP
This recipe is equally good made with
pears, but reduce the cooking time by
10–15 minutes and use mixed spice in
place of the cinnamon.

1 Preheat the oven to 180°C/350°F/
Gas 4. Cut a thin slice from the base of
each apple to make them stable. Using
a pastry brush, thickly coat each apple
with melted butter.

2 Mix the caster sugar and cinnamon
in a shallow dish. Holding each apple
by its stalk, roll in the mixture to coat.

3 Arrange the apples in a shallow
baking dish into which they just fit,
standing upright.

4 Pour the coffee into the dish then
sprinkle over any remaining sugar
mixture. Bake the apples for 40 minutes,
basting with the coffee two or three
times. Baste a last time, then pour the
juices into a small pan. Return the
apples to the oven.

5 Boil the juices rapidly until syrupy
and reduced to about 60ml/4 tbsp. Pour
over the apples and cook for 10 more
minutes, or until the apples are tender.
Serve hot with a spoonful of cream.

SUMMER BERRIES WITH COFFEE SABAYON

*FOR A LIGHT AND DELICIOUSLY REFRESHING FINALE, SERVE A PLATTER OF FRESH SUMMER FRUITS WITH
A FLUFFY COFFEE SAUCE, WHICH HAS THE ADDED ADVANTAGE OF BEING DELIGHTFULLY EASY TO MAKE.*

SERVES 6

INGREDIENTS
   900g/2lb/6–8 cups mixed summer
      berries such as raspberries,
      blueberries and strawberries (hulled
      and halved, if large)
   5 egg yolks
   75g/3oz/scant ½ cup caster
      (superfine) sugar
   50ml/2fl oz/¼ cup brewed coffee
   30ml/2 tbsp coffee liqueur, such as
      Tia Maria, Kahlúa or Toussaint
   strawberry or mint leaves,
      to decorate (optional)
   30ml/2 tbsp icing (confectioners')
      sugar, for dusting

1 Arrange the fruit on a serving platter
and decorate with strawberry or mint
leaves, if using. Dust with icing sugar.

2 Whisk the egg yolks and caster sugar
in a bowl over a pan of simmering water
until the mixture begins to thicken.

3 Gradually add the coffee and liqueur,
pouring in a thin, continuous stream
and whisking all the time. Continue
whisking until the sauce is thick and
fluffy. Serve warm, or allow to cool,
whisking occasionally, and serve cold
with the fruit.

FROZEN DESSERTS

Frozen desserts are an ideal choice for all occasions as they can be made in advance, then stored in the freezer. In this chapter, you'll find smooth, velvety ice cream and refreshing sorbets. Some ices are only part of the dessert, such as in Dark Chocolate and Coffee Mousse Cake, a rich chocolate sponge with an ice cream centre.

CINNAMON AND COFFEE SWIRL ICE CREAM

LIGHT ICE CREAM SUBTLY SPICED WITH CINNAMON AND RIPPLED WITH A SWEET COFFEE SYRUP.

SERVES 6

INGREDIENTS
  300ml/½ pint/1¼ cups single
  (light) cream
  1 cinnamon stick
  4 egg yolks
  150g/5oz/¾ cup caster (superfine) sugar
  300ml/½ pint/1¼ cups double
  (heavy) cream
For the Coffee Syrup
  45ml/3 tbsp ground coffee
  45ml/3 tbsp near-boiling water
  90g/3½oz/½ cup caster (superfine) sugar
  50ml/2fl oz/¼ cup water

1 Pour the single cream into a pan and add the cinnamon stick. Bring to the boil, turn off the heat, cover and leave to infuse for 30 minutes. Bring back to the boil and remove the cinnamon.

2 Whisk the yolks and sugar until light. Pour the hot cream over the egg mixture, whisking. Return to the pan and stir over a low heat for about 1–2 minutes, until it thickens. Cool.

3 Whip the double cream until peaks form and fold into the custard. Pour into a container and freeze for 3 hours.

4 Meanwhile, to make the syrup, put the coffee in a bowl and pour the hot water over. Leave to infuse for 4 minutes, then strain through a sieve.

COOK'S TIP
Make sure that the cinnamon ice cream is sufficiently frozen before adding the coffee syrup.

5 Gently heat the sugar and cold water in a pan until completely dissolved. Bring to the boil and simmer gently for 5 minutes. Cool, then stir in the coffee.

6 Turn the cinnamon ice cream into a chilled bowl and briefly whisk to break down the ice crystals.

7 Spoon a third back into the container and drizzle some of the coffee syrup over. Repeat in this way until all is used.

8 Drag a skewer through the mixture a few times to achieve a marbled effect. Freeze for 4 hours, or until solid. Allow to soften slightly before serving.

TOASTED NUT <u>AND</u> COFFEE ICE CREAM <u>IN</u> BRANDY SNAP BASKETS

SCOOPS OF CRUSHED CARAMEL AND TOASTED NUT ICE CREAM ARE SERVED IN CRISP CASES, THEN DRIZZLED WITH A WARM COFFEE AND COGNAC SAUCE.

SERVES 6

INGREDIENTS
　75g/3oz/½ cup whole nuts, such as
　　blanched almonds and hazelnuts
　90g/3½oz/½ cup caster
　　(superfine) sugar
　1 vanilla pod (bean), split
　30ml/2 tbsp ground coffee
　200ml/7fl oz/scant 1 cup double
　　(heavy) cream
　300ml/½ pint/1¼ cups Greek
　　(US strained plain) yogurt
　6 brandy snap baskets, to serve
For the Coffee and Cognac Sauce
　115g/4oz/½ cup soft light brown sugar
　50ml/2fl oz/¼ cup hot water
　100ml/3½fl oz/½ cup brewed coffee
　60ml/4 tbsp cognac

2 Pour on to an oiled baking sheet to cool and harden. Crush to a fine powder. Put the vanilla, coffee and cream in a pan. Heat almost to boiling, turn off the heat, cover and infuse.

3 After 15 minutes, strain through a sieve and leave to cool. Stir the coffee cream into the yogurt with the crushed nut mixture. Transfer to a freezerproof container and freeze for 4 hours.

4 To make the sauce, heat the sugar and water in a small heavy pan over a gentle heat until melted. Simmer for 3 minutes. Cool slightly, then stir in the coffee and cognac.

5 Meanwhile, allow the ice cream to soften in the refrigerator for 15 minutes. Scoop into the brandy snap baskets and serve immediately with the warm coffee and cognac sauce.

1 Heat the nuts and caster sugar gently in a large heavy pan until the sugar caramelizes to a light golden brown..

COOK'S TIP
To make brandy snap baskets, in a bowl, gently melt 50g/2oz/4 tbsp butter, 50g/2oz/¼ cup demerara (raw) sugar and 50g/2oz/ ¼ cup golden (light corn) syrup. Stir in 50g/2oz/½ cup sifted plain (all-purpose) flour and 5ml/1 tsp brandy. Drop well-spaced teaspoons on to oiled baking sheets. Bake in a preheated oven at 160°C/325°F/Gas 3 for about 8 minutes. Cool for 1 minute, then lift with a metal spatula and mould over the base of an inverted glass.

COFFEE ICE CREAM

FRESHLY GROUND COFFEE GIVES THIS CLASSIC ICE CREAM A DISTINCTIVE AND SOPHISTICATED FLAVOUR. CHOOSE A DARK-ROASTED BEAN TO ENSURE A RICH, GLOSSY COLOUR TO THE ICE CREAM.

SERVES 8–10

INGREDIENTS
   60ml/4 tbsp dark-roasted
      ground coffee
   600ml/1 pint/2½ cups milk
   200g/7oz/scant 1 cup soft light
      brown sugar
   6 egg yolks
   475ml/16fl oz/2 cups
      whipping cream

1 Put the coffee in a jug (pitcher). Heat the milk in a pan to nearly boiling and pour over the coffee. Leave to stand for 4 minutes.

2 Meanwhile, in a large bowl, beat the sugar and egg yolks until light. Pour the milk over, whisking all the time. Strain the mixture back into the pan through a fine sieve.

3 Cook the custard over a low heat for 1–2 minutes, stirring until it coats the back of a wooden spoon. Do not boil. Pour into a shallow freezer container and leave to cool, stirring occasionally.

COOK'S TIP
If using an ice cream maker, do not whip the cream: stir it into the coffee custard before adding to the machine.

4 Freeze for about 2 hours, then tip into a bowl and whisk with a fork until smooth. Whip the cream until peaks form and fold into the frozen mixture.

5 Return to the freezer for 1 more hour, then turn out and whisk again. Finally, freeze for 3–4 hours, until solid. Transfer to the refrigerator for 20 minutes, before scooping and serving.

CAPPUCCINO CONES

PRETTY WHITE AND PLAIN CHOCOLATE CONES ARE FILLED WITH SWIRLS OF CAPPUCCINO CREAM AND TOPPED WITH A LIGHT DUSTING OF COCOA POWDER.

SERVES SIX

INGREDIENTS
   115g/4oz each good quality plain
      (semisweet) and white cooking
      chocolate
For the Cappuccino Cream
   30ml/2 tbsp ground espresso or other
      strong-flavoured coffee
   30ml/2 tbsp near-boiling water
   300ml/½ pint/1¼ cups double
      (heavy) cream
   45ml/3 tbsp icing (confectioners')
      sugar, sifted
   15ml/1 tbsp cocoa powder, for dusting

1 Cut nine 13 x 10cm/5 x 4in rectangles from baking parchment, then cut each rectangle in half diagonally to make 18 triangles. Roll up each to make a cone and secure with adhesive tape.

2 Heat the plain chocolate in a bowl over a pan of barely simmering hot water until melted. Using a small pastry brush, thickly brush the insides of half the paper cones with chocolate. Chill until set. Repeat the procedure with the white chocolate. Peel away the paper when set and keep the cones in the refrigerator until needed.

3 To make the cappuccino cream, put the coffee in a small bowl. Pour the hot water over and leave to infuse for 4 minutes, then strain through a fine sieve into a bowl. Leave to cool. Add the cream and sugar and whisk until soft peaks form. Spoon into an piping (pastry) bag fitted with a medium star nozzle.

4 Pipe the cream into the chocolate cones. Put on a baking sheet and freeze for at least 2 hours or until solid. Arrange on individual plates, allowing three cones per person and dusting with cocoa powder before serving.

COOK'S TIP
Make sure, when melting the chocolate, that the water doesn't boil or the chocolate will overheat and stiffen.

MAPLE COFFEE AND PISTACHIO BOMBES

REAL MAPLE SYRUP TASTES INFINITELY BETTER THAN THE SYNTHETIC VARIETIES AND IS WELL WORTH SEARCHING FOR. HERE IT SWEETENS THE DARK COFFEE CENTRE OF THESE PRETTY PISTACHIO BOMBES.

SERVES 6

INGREDIENTS
For the Pistachio Ice Cream
  50g/2oz/¼ cup caster (superfine) sugar
  50ml/2fl oz/¼ cup water
  175g/6oz can evaporated (unsweetened
    condensed) milk, chilled
  50g/2oz/½ cup shelled and skinned
    pistachio nuts, finely chopped
  drop of green food colouring
    (optional)
  200ml/7fl oz/scant 1 cup
    whipping cream
For the Maple Coffee Centres
  30ml/2 tbsp ground coffee
  150ml/¼ pint/⅔ cup single
    (light) cream
  50ml/2fl oz/¼ cup maple syrup
  2 egg yolks
  5ml/1 tsp cornflour (cornstarch)
  150ml/¼ pint/⅔ cup whipping cream

1 Put six 175ml/6fl oz/¾ cup mini ovenproof bowls or dariole moulds into the freezer to chill. Put the sugar and water in a heavy pan and heat gently until dissolved. Bring to the boil and simmer for 3 minutes.

2 Cool, then stir in the evaporated milk, pistachios and colouring, if using. Whip the cream until it forms soft peaks and blend into the mixture.

3 Pour the mixture into a freezerproof container and freeze for at least 2 hours. Whisk the ice cream until smooth, then freeze for a further 2 hours or until frozen, but not solid.

4 To make the centres, put the ground coffee in a jug (pitcher). Heat the single cream to nearly boiling and pour over the coffee. Leave to infuse for 4 minutes. Whisk the maple syrup, egg yolks and cornflour together. Strain the hot coffee cream over the egg mixture, whisking continuously. Return to the pan and cook gently for 1–2 minutes, until the custard thickens. Leave to cool, stirring occasionally.

5 Meanwhile, line the moulds with the ice cream, keeping the thickness as even as possible right up to the rim. Freeze until the ice cream is firm again.

6 Beat the cream until peaks form, then fold into the custard. Spoon into the middle of the moulds. Cover and freeze for 2 hours. Serve immediately.

FROSTED RASPBERRY AND COFFEE TERRINE

A WHITE CHOCOLATE AND RASPBERRY LAYER AND A CONTRASTING SMOOTH COFFEE LAYER MAKE THIS ATTRACTIVE-LOOKING DESSERT DOUBLY DELICIOUS.

SERVES 6–8

INGREDIENTS

    30ml/2 tbsp ground coffee,
      e.g. mocha orange-flavoured
    250ml/8fl oz/1 cup milk
    4 eggs, separated
    50g/2oz/¼ cup caster (superfine) sugar
    30ml/2 tbsp cornflour (cornstarch)
    150ml/¼ pint/⅔ cup double
      (heavy) cream
    150g/5oz white chocolate, chopped
    115g/4oz/⅔ cup raspberries
    shavings of white chocolate and
      cocoa powder, to decorate

1 Line a 1.5 litre/2½ pint/6¼ cup loaf tin (pan) with clear film (plastic wrap). Chill in the freezer. Put the coffee in a jug (pitcher). Heat half the milk to nearly boiling; pour over the coffee. Leave to infuse.

2 Blend the egg yolks, sugar and cornflour together in a pan and whisk in the remaining milk and the cream. Bring to the boil, stirring all the time, until thickened.

3 Divide the hot mixture between two bowls and add the white chocolate to one, stirring until melted. Strain the coffee through a fine sieve into the other bowl and mix well. Leave until cool, stirring occasionally.

COOK'S TIP
After decorating, leave the terrine to soften in the refrigerator for 20 minutes before slicing and serving.

4 Whisk two of the egg whites until stiff. Fold into the coffee custard. Spoon into the tin and freeze for 30 minutes. Whisk remaining whites and fold into the chocolate mixture with the raspberries.

5 Spoon into the tin and level before freezing for 4 hours. Turn the terrine out on to a flat serving plate and peel off the clear film. Cover with chocolate shavings and dust with cocoa powder.

COFFEE AND MINTY-LEMON SORBET

THE FLAVOURS OF FRESH MINT, SHARP LEMON AND AROMATIC COFFEE ARE COMBINED IN THIS DELICIOUS ICY SORBET. THE LEMON SHELLS ARE AN EASY, BUT PRETTY, SUMMERY DECORATIVE TOUCH.

SERVES 6

INGREDIENTS

   115g/4oz/generous ½ cup sugar
   400ml/14fl oz/1⅔ cups water
   15g/½oz fresh mint leaves
   30ml/2 tbsp coffee liqueur, such as
     Tia Maria, Kahlúa or Toussaint
   6 lemons
   1 egg white
   mint sprigs, to decorate

1 Put the sugar in a large heavy pan with the water and heat gently until dissolved, stirring occasionally. Bring to the boil, and simmer for 5 minutes.

2 Remove from the heat, add the mint leaves, stir and leave to cool. Strain into a jug (pitcher) and stir in the liqueur.

4 Pour into a freezerproof container and freeze for 3 hours. Whisk to break down the ice crystals, then freeze for 1 more hour. Whisk the egg white until stiff, then whisk into the ice. Scoop into the lemon shells and replace the lids.

3 Cut a thin slice from the base of each lemon so that they will stand upright, being careful not to cut through the pith. Cut the tops off the lemons and keep for lids. Scrape out the lemon flesh and squeeze the juice. Strain the juice into the mint and coffee syrup.

COOK'S TIP
Fresh fruit sorbets will keep in the freezer for up to 2 months, but are best eaten within days of making.

5 Place upright on a tray and freeze for 2 hours, until solid. Transfer to the refrigerator 5 minutes before serving, to soften. Decorate with sprigs of mint.

ESPRESSO GRANITA

THIS FAMOUS FROZEN ITALIAN ICE MAKES A REFRESHING FINISH TO A RICH MEAL.

SERVES 6

INGREDIENTS

   600ml/1 pint/2½ cups espresso or
     other strong-flavoured coffee, hot
   90g/3½oz/½ cup sugar
   whipped cream, to serve
     (optional)

COOK'S TIPS
• Don't whisk the granita too vigorously – it should have a rough granular texture, rather than a smooth one like a sorbet.
• After step 3, the granita can either be served at that stage or covered and stored in the freezer for up to 2 weeks.

1 Put the coffee in a bowl; stir in the sugar until dissolved. Cool, then pour into a 900ml/1½ pint/3¾ cup shallow freezer container.

2 Freeze for at least 3 hours, or until ice crystals form around the edges. Whisk with a fork, then return to the freezer for another 1 hour.

3 Whisk the mixture again with a fork and re-freeze. Repeat until the mixture is frozen and there is no liquid.

4 Transfer the granita to the refrigerator 20 minutes before serving. Break up the ice crystals with a strong fork and serve in glasses, topped with whipped cream, if you like.

ICED COFFEE MOUSSE <u>IN A</u> CHOCOLATE CASE

A PLAIN CHOCOLATE BOWL IS FILLED WITH A LIGHT, ICED COFFEE MOUSSE. IT LOOKS A DRAMATIC DESSERT, BUT IT ISN'T DIFFICULT TO MAKE.

SERVES 8

INGREDIENTS
    1 sachet powdered gelatine
    60ml/4 tbsp very strong brewed coffee
    30ml/2 tbsp coffee liqueur, such as
        Tia Maria, Kahlúa or Toussaint
    3 eggs, separated
    75g/3oz/scant ½ cup caster
        (superfine) sugar
    150ml/¼ pint/⅔ cup whipping cream,
        lightly whipped
For the Chocolate Bowl
    225g/8oz plain (semisweet) chocolate,
        chopped, plus extra for decoration

1 Grease and line a deep 18cm/7in loose-based cake tin (pan) with baking parchment.

2 Melt the chocolate in a bowl over a pan of simmering water. Using a pastry brush, brush a layer of chocolate over the base of the tin and about 7.5cm/3in up the sides, finishing with a ragged edge. Leave the chocolate to set before repeating. Put in the freezer to harden.

3 Sprinkle the gelatine over the coffee in a bowl and leave to soften for 5 minutes. Put the bowl over a pan of simmering water, stirring until dissolved. Remove from the heat and stir in the liqueur. Whisk the egg yolks and sugar in a bowl over the simmering water until thick enough to leave a trail. Remove from the pan and whisk until cool. Whisk the egg whites until stiff.

4 Pour the dissolved gelatine into the egg yolk mixture in a thin stream, stirring gently. Chill in the refrigerator for 20 minutes, or until just beginning to set, then fold in the cream, followed by the whisked egg whites.

5 Remove the chocolate case (shell) from the freezer and peel away the lining. Put it back in the tin, then pour in the mousse. Return to the freezer for at least 3 hours. To serve, remove from the tin and place on a plate. Allow to soften in the refrigerator for 40 minutes before serving. Decorate with grated chocolate. Use a knife dipped in hot water and wiped dry to cut into slices to serve.

DARK CHOCOLATE AND COFFEE MOUSSE CAKE

THIS DOUBLE TREAT WILL PROVE ABSOLUTELY IRRESISTIBLE — RICH SPONGE FILLED WITH CREAMY COFFEE MOUSSE.

SERVES 8

INGREDIENTS
    4 eggs
    115g/4oz/generous ½ cup caster
      (superfine) sugar
    75g/3oz/⅔ cup plain (all-purpose)
      flour, sifted
    25g/1oz/¼ cup cocoa powder, sifted
    60ml/4 tbsp coffee liqueur
    icing (confectioners') sugar, for dusting
For the Coffee Mousse
    30ml/2 tbsp dark-roasted ground
      coffee beans
    350ml/12fl oz/1½ cups double
      (heavy) cream
    115g/4oz/generous ½ cup
      granulated sugar
    120ml/4fl oz/½ cup water
    4 egg yolks

1 Preheat the oven to 180°C/350°F/ Gas 4. Grease and line the bases of a 20cm/8in square and a 23cm/9in round cake tin (pan) with baking parchment. Put the eggs and sugar in a bowl over a pan of hot water and whisk until thick.

2 Remove from the heat and whisk until thick enough to leave a trail when the whisk is lifted. Fold in the flour and cocoa. Pour a third of the mixture into the square tin and the rest into the round tin. Bake the square sponge for 15 minutes; the round for 30 minutes.

3 Cool on a wire rack before slicing the round cake in half horizontally. Place the bottom half back in the tin. Sprinkle with half the liqueur.

4 Trim the edges of the square sponge, cut into 4 equal strips and use to line the sides of the tin.

5 To make the mousse, put the coffee in a bowl. Heat 50ml/2fl oz/¼ cup of the cream to nearly boiling and pour over the coffee. Leave to infuse for 4 minutes, then strain through a fine sieve.

6 Gently heat the sugar and water until dissolved. Increase the heat and boil steadily until the syrup reaches 107°C/ 225°F. Cool for 5 minutes, then pour on to the egg yolks, whisking until the mixture is very thick.

7 Add the coffee cream to the remaining cream and whip until soft peaks form. Fold into the egg mixture. Spoon into the sponge case and freeze for 20 minutes. Sprinkle the remaining liqueur over the second sponge half and place on top of the mousse. Cover and freeze for 4 hours. Remove from the tin and dust with icing sugar.

COOK'S TIP
Cover the seams of the cake with swirls of piped whipped cream and decorate with chocolate coffee beans, if you like.

CAKE AND TORTE RECIPES

From simple sponges to elaborate tortes and velvety cheesecakes, these are cakes to rival any shop-bought confection. Some, such as Coffee Almond Marsala Slice, are perfect with mid-morning coffee. Others, like Coffee Chocolate Mousse Cake and Cappuccino Torte, make unforgettable dinner party desserts.

COCONUT COFFEE CAKE

COCONUT AND COFFEE ARE NATURAL PARTNERS, AS THESE LITTLE SQUARES OF ICED CAKE PROVE.

SERVES 9

INGREDIENTS
45ml/3 tbsp ground coffee
75ml/5 tbsp nearly boiling milk
25g/1oz/2 tbsp caster (superfine) sugar
175g/6oz/⅔ cup golden (light corn) syrup
75g/3oz/6 tbsp butter
40g/1½oz/½ cup desiccated (dry
  unsweetened shredded) coconut
175g/6oz/1½ cups plain (all-purpose) flour
2.5ml/½ tsp bicarbonate of soda
  (baking soda)
2 eggs, lightly beaten
For the Icing
115g/4oz/8 tbsp butter, softened
225g/8oz/2 cups icing (confectioners')
  sugar, sifted
25g/1oz/⅓ cup shredded coconut, toasted

1 Preheat the oven to 160°C/325°F/Gas 3.

2 Grease and line the base of a 20cm/8in square cake tin (pan). Put the coffee and milk in a bowl to infuse for 4 minutes, then strain through a fine sieve.

3 Heat the caster sugar, syrup, butter and desiccated coconut in a pan, stirring with a wooden spoon, until completely melted.

4 Sift the flour and soda together and stir into the mixture, along with the eggs and 45ml/3 tbsp of the coffee-flavoured milk.

5 Spoon the mixture into the prepared tin and level the top. Bake in the oven for 40–50 minutes until well-risen and firm. Leave the cake to cool in the tin for about 10 minutes, before running a knife around the edges to loosen. Turn out and cool on a wire rack.

6 To make the icing, beat the softened butter until smooth then gradually beat in the icing sugar and remaining coffee milk to give a soft consistency. Spread over the top of the cake and decorate with toasted coconut. Cut into 5cm/2in squares to serve.

VARIATION
Substitute 50g/2oz/½ cup chopped pecan nuts for the coconut and decorate the squares with pecan halves dusted with icing sugar.

MOCHA SPONGE CAKE

THE YEMENI CITY OF MOCHA WAS ONCE CONSIDERED TO BE THE COFFEE CAPITAL OF THE WORLD, AND STILL PRODUCES A COFFEE THAT TASTES A LITTLE LIKE CHOCOLATE. TODAY "MOCHA" MAY REFER TO THE VARIETY OF COFFEE, OR MEAN A COMBINATION OF COFFEE OR CHOCOLATE, AS IN THIS RECIPE.

SERVES 10

INGREDIENTS
  25ml/1½ tbsp strong ground coffee
  175ml/6fl oz/¾ cup hot milk
  115g/4oz/½ cup butter
  115g/4oz/½ cup soft light brown sugar
  1 egg, lightly beaten
  185g/6½oz/1⅔ cups self-raising
  (self-rising) flour
  5ml/1 tsp bicarbonate of soda
  (baking soda)
  60ml/4 tbsp creamy liqueur, such as
  Baileys or Irish Velvet
For the Glossy Chocolate Icing
  200g/7oz plain (semisweet) chocolate
  75g/3oz/6 tbsp unsalted (sweet)
  butter, cubed
  120ml/4fl oz/½ cup double
  (heavy) cream

1 Preheat the oven to 180°C/350°F/ Gas 4. Grease and line a 18cm/7in round cake tin (pan).

2 Put the coffee in a jug (pitcher). Pour over the milk; infuse for 4 minutes. Strain through a sieve and cool.

3 Gently melt the butter and sugar until dissolved. Pour into a bowl and cool for 2 minutes, then stir in the egg.

4 Sift the flour over and fold in. Blend the soda and coffee-flavoured milk. Stir into the mixture.

5 Pour into the tin, smooth the surface, and bake for 40 minutes, until well-risen and firm. Cool in the tin for about 10 minutes. Spoon the liqueur over the cake and leave until cold. Loosen the edges with a metal spatula and turn out on to a wire rack.

6 For the icing, chop and place the chocolate in a bowl set over a pan of barely simmering water until melted. Remove from the heat and stir in the butter and cream until smooth. Allow to cool before coating the top and sides of the cake. Leave until set.

COFFEE ALMOND MARSALA SLICE

ROASTED AND CRUSHED COFFEE BEANS ARE SPECKLED THROUGHOUT THIS DELICIOUS ALMOND CAKE, DISTINCTLY FLAVOURED WITH ITALIAN MARSALA WINE.

SERVES 10–12

INGREDIENTS
25g/1oz/⅓ cup roasted coffee beans
5 eggs, separated
175g/6oz/scant 1 cup caster
   (superfine) sugar
120ml/4fl oz/½ cup Marsala wine
75g/3oz/6 tbsp butter, melted
   and cooled
115g/4oz/1 cup ground almonds
115g/4oz/1 cup plain (all-purpose)
   flour, sifted
25g/1oz/¼ cup flaked (sliced) almonds
icing (confectioners') sugar,
   for dusting
crème fraîche, to serve

1 Preheat the oven to 180°C/350°F/
Gas 4. Grease and base-line a 23cm/
9in round loose-based tin (pan). Place
the roasted coffee beans in a large
plastic bag and crush with a rolling pin.

2 Beat the egg yolks and 115g/4oz/
generous ½ cup of the caster sugar
until very pale and thick.

3 Stir in the crushed coffee, Marsala,
butter and almonds. Sift the flour over,
then carefully fold in.

4 Whisk the egg whites until they are
stiff, then gradually incorporate the
remaining caster sugar.

5 Fold into the almond mixture, a third
at a time. Spoon into the tin and
sprinkle the top with flaked almonds.

6 Bake for 10 minutes, then reduce
the oven to 160°C/325°F/Gas 3 and
cook for a further 40 minutes, or until
a skewer inserted into the centre comes
out clean. After 5 minutes, turn out and
cool on a wire rack. Dust with icing
sugar and serve with crème fraîche.

SOUR CHERRY COFFEE LOAF

DRIED SOUR CHERRIES HAVE A WONDERFULLY CONCENTRATED FRUIT FLAVOUR AND CAN BE BOUGHT IN SUPERMARKETS AND HEALTH FOOD SHOPS.

SERVES 8

INGREDIENTS
175g/6oz/¾ cup butter, softened
175g/6oz/scant 1 cup golden caster
   (superfine) sugar
5ml/1 tsp vanilla extract (essence)
2 eggs, lightly beaten
225g/8oz/2 cups plain (all-purpose) flour
1.5ml/¼ tsp baking powder
75ml/5 tbsp strong brewed coffee
175g/6oz/1 cup dried sour cherries
For the Icing
50g/2oz/½ cup icing (confectioners')
   sugar, sifted
20ml/4 tsp strong brewed coffee

1 Preheat the oven to 180°C/350°F/
Gas 4. Grease and line a 900g/2lb loaf
tin (pan).

2 Cream the butter, sugar and vanilla
together in a bowl until fluffy. Gradually
add the eggs, mixing well after each
addition. Sift the flour and baking
powder together. Fold into the mixture
with the coffee and 115g/4oz/⅔ cup of
the sour cherries. Spoon the mixture
into the prepared tin and level the top.

3 Bake for 1¼ hours or until firm to the
touch. Cool in the tin for 5 minutes,
then turn out and cool on a wire rack.

4 To make the icing, mix together the
icing sugar and coffee and the
remaining cherries. Spoon over the top
and sides. Leave to set before slicing.

COFFEE AND MINT CREAM CAKE

GROUND ALMONDS GIVE THIS BUTTERY COFFEE SPONGE A MOIST TEXTURE AND DELICATE FLAVOUR.
IT IS SANDWICHED TOGETHER WITH A GENEROUS FILLING OF CRÈME DE MENTHE BUTTERCREAM.

SERVES 8

INGREDIENTS
  15ml/1 tbsp ground coffee
  25ml/1½ tbsp nearly boiling water
  175g/6oz/12 tbsp unsalted (sweet)
    butter, softened
  175g/6oz/scant 1 cup caster
    (superfine) sugar
  225g/8oz/2 cups self-raising
    (self-rising) flour, sifted
  50g/2oz/½ cup ground almonds
  3 eggs
  small mint sprigs, to decorate
For the Filling
  50g/2oz/4 tbsp unsalted
    (sweet) butter
  115g/4oz/1 cup icing
    (confectioners') sugar, sifted,
    plus extra for dusting
  30ml/2 tbsp crème de menthe

1 Preheat the oven to 180°C/350°F/
Gas 4. Lightly grease and base-line
two 18cm/7in sandwich tins (pans) with
baking parchment.

2 Put the coffee in a bowl and pour the
hot water over. Leave to infuse for about
4 minutes, then strain through a sieve.

3 Put the butter, sugar, flour, almonds,
eggs and coffee in a large bowl. Beat
well for 1 minute until blended. Divide
the mixture evenly between the tins and
level off. Bake for 25 minutes until well-
risen and firm to the touch. Leave in the
tins for 5 minutes, then turn out on to a
wire rack to cool.

4 To make the filling, cream the
unsalted butter, icing sugar and crème
de menthe together in a bowl until light
and fluffy.

COOK'S TIP
Make sure the butter is really soft and
creamy before starting to mix the cake.

5 Remove the lining paper from the
sponges and sandwich together with
the filling.

6 Generously dust the top with icing
sugar and place on a serving plate.
Scatter with the fresh mint leaves just
before serving.

COFFEE AND WALNUT SWISS ROLL WITH COINTREAU CREAM

COFFEE AND WALNUTS HAVE A NATURAL AFFINITY. HERE THEY APPEAR TOGETHER IN A LIGHT AND FLUFFY SPONGE ENCLOSING A SMOOTH ORANGE CREAM.

SERVES 6

INGREDIENTS
   10ml/2 tsp ground coffee
   15ml/1 tbsp nearly boiling water
   3 eggs
   75g/3oz/scant ½ cup caster (superfine)
   sugar, plus extra for dusting
   75g/3oz/⅔ cup self-raising
   (self-rising) flour
   50g/2oz/½ cup toasted walnuts,
   finely chopped
For the Cointreau Cream
   115g/4oz/generous ½ cup caster
   (superfine) sugar
   50ml/2fl oz/¼ cup cold water
   2 egg yolks
   115g/4oz/8 tbsp unsalted (sweet)
   butter, softened
   15ml/1 tbsp Cointreau

1 Preheat the oven to 200°C/400°F/ Gas 6. Grease and line a 33 x 23cm/ 13 x 9in Swiss roll tin (jelly roll pan) with non-stick baking parchment.

2 Put the coffee in a bowl and pour the hot water over. Leave to infuse for about 4 minutes, then strain through a sieve.

3 Whisk the eggs and sugar together in a large bowl until pale and thick. Sift the flour over the mixture and fold in with the coffee and walnuts. Turn into the tin and bake for 10–12 minutes, until springy to the touch.

4 Turn out on a piece of baking parchment sprinkled with caster sugar, peel off the lining paper and cool for about 2 minutes. Trim the edges then roll up from one of the short ends, with the baking parchment where the filling will be. Leave to cool.

5 To make the filling, heat the sugar in the water over a low heat until dissolved. Boil rapidly until the syrup reaches 105°C/220°F on a sugar thermometer. Pour the syrup over the egg yolks, whisking all the time, until thick and mousse-like. Gradually add the butter, then whisk in the Cointreau. Leave to cool and thicken.

6 Unroll the sponge and spread with the Cointreau cream. Re-roll and place on a serving plate seam-side down. Dust with extra caster sugar and chill in the refrigerator until ready to serve.

COOK'S TIP
Decorate the roll with swirls of piped whipped cream and walnuts, if you like.

COFFEE CHOCOLATE MOUSSE CAKE

SERVE THIS DENSE, DARK CHOCOLATE CAKE IN SMALL PORTIONS AS IT IS VERY RICH.

SERVES 6

INGREDIENTS
175g/6oz plain (semisweet) chocolate
30ml/2 tbsp strong brewed coffee
150g/5oz/10 tbsp butter, cubed
50g/2oz/¼ cup caster (superfine) sugar
3 eggs
25g/1oz/¼ cup ground almonds
about 25ml/1½ tbsp icing
  (confectioners') sugar, for dusting
For the Mascarpone and Coffee Cream
250g/9oz/generous 1 cup mascarpone
30ml/2 tbsp icing (confectioners')
  sugar, sifted
30ml/2 tbsp strong brewed coffee

1 Preheat the oven to 200°C/400°F/
Gas 6. Grease and base-line a 15cm/6in
square tin (pan).

2 Put the chocolate and coffee in a
small heavy pan and heat very gently
until melted, stirring occasionally.

3 Add the butter and sugar to the pan
and stir until dissolved. Whisk the eggs
until frothy and stir into the chocolate
mixture with the ground almonds.

4 Pour into the prepared tin, then put
in a large roasting pan and pour in
enough hot water to come two-thirds up
the cake tin. Bake for 50 minutes, or
until the top feels springy to the touch.
Leave to cool in the tin for 5 minutes,
then turn the cake out upside-down on
to a board and leave to cool.

5 Meanwhile, beat the mascarpone
with the icing sugar and coffee. Dust
the cake generously with icing sugar,
then cut into slices. Serve on individual
plates with the mascarpone and coffee
cream alongside.

COOK'S TIP
The top of this flourless cake, with its
moist mousse-like texture, will crack
slightly as it cooks.

CAPPUCCINO TORTE

*THE FAMOUS AND MUCH LOVED BEVERAGE OF FRESHLY BREWED COFFEE, WHIPPED CREAM, CHOCOLATE
AND CINNAMON IS TRANSFORMED INTO A SENSATIONAL DESSERT.*

SERVES 6–8

INGREDIENTS
75g/3oz/6 tbsp butter, melted
275g/10oz shortbread biscuits
  (cookies), crushed
1.5ml/¼ tsp ground cinnamon
25ml/1½ tbsp powdered gelatine
45ml/3 tbsp cold water
2 eggs, separated
115g/4oz/½ cup soft light
  brown sugar
115g/4oz plain (semisweet)
  chocolate, chopped
175ml/6fl oz/¾ cup brewed espresso
400ml/14fl oz/1⅔ cups
  whipping cream
chocolate curls and ground
  cinnamon, to decorate

1 Mix the butter with the biscuits and
cinnamon. Spoon into the base of a
20cm/8in loose-based tin(pan) and
press down well. Chill.

2 Sprinkle the gelatine over the cold
water. Leave to soften for 5 minutes,
then set the bowl over a pan of hot
water and stir to dissolve.

3 Whisk the egg yolks and sugar until
thick. Put the chocolate in a bowl with
the coffee and stir until melted. Add
to the egg mixture, then cook gently in
a pan for 1–2 minutes until thickened.
Stir in the gelatine. Leave until just
beginning to set, stirring occasionally.

4 Whip 150ml/¼ pint/⅔ cup of the
cream until soft peaks form. Whisk the
egg whites until stiff. Fold the cream
into the coffee mixture, followed by the
egg whites. Pour the mixture over the
biscuit base and chill for 2 hours.

5 When ready to serve, remove the torte
from the tin and transfer to a serving
plate. Whip the remaining cream and
place a dollop on top. Decorate with
chocolate curls and a little cinnamon.

BAKED COFFEE CHEESECAKE

THIS RICH, COOKED AND CHILLED CHEESECAKE, FLAVOURED WITH COFFEE AND ORANGE LIQUEUR, HAS A WONDERFULLY DENSE, VELVETY TEXTURE.

SERVES 8

INGREDIENTS
    45ml/3 tbsp nearly boiling water
    30ml/2 tbsp ground coffee
    4 eggs
    225g/8oz/generous 1 cup caster
      (superfine) sugar
    450g/1lb/2 cups cream cheese,
      at room temperature
    30ml/2 tbsp orange liqueur, such
      as Curaçao
    40g/1½oz/⅓ cup plain (all-purpose)
      flour, sifted
    300ml/½ pint/1¼ cups whipping cream
    30ml/2 tbsp icing (confectioners')
      sugar, for dusting
    single (light) cream, to serve
For the Base
    115g/4oz/1 cup plain (all-purpose) flour
    5ml/1 tsp baking powder
    75g/3oz/6 tbsp butter
    50g/2oz/¼ cup caster (superfine) sugar
    1 egg, lightly beaten
    30ml/2 tbsp cold water

1 Preheat the oven to 160°C/325°F/
Gas 3. Lightly grease and line a
20cm/8in loose-based cake tin (pan).

2 Sift the flour and baking powder into
a bowl. Rub in the butter until the
mixture resembles fine breadcrumbs.
Stir in the sugar, then add the egg and
water and mix to a dough. Press the
mixture into the base of the tin.

3 To make the filling, pour the water
over the coffee and leave to infuse for
4 minutes. Strain through a fine sieve.

4 Whisk the eggs and sugar until thick.
Using a wooden spoon, beat the cream
cheese until softened, then beat in the
liqueur, a spoonful at a time.

5 Gradually mix in the whisked eggs.
Fold in the flour. Finally, stir in the
whipping cream and coffee.

6 Pour the mixture over the base and
bake in the oven for 1½ hours. Turn off
the heat and leave in the oven to cool
with the door ajar. Chill the cheesecake
in the refrigerator for 1 hour. Dust with
icing sugar. Remove from the tin and
place on a serving plate, Serve with
single cream.

IRISH COFFEE CHEESECAKE

THE FLAVOURS OF IRISH WHISKEY, COFFEE AND GINGER GO WELL TOGETHER, BUT YOU CAN RING THE CHANGES BY USING ALMOND BISCUITS FOR THE BASE.

SERVES 8

INGREDIENTS
  45ml/3 tbsp ground coffee
  1 vanilla pod (bean)
  250ml/8fl oz/1 cup single (light) cream
  15ml/1 tbsp powdered gelatine
  45ml/3 tbsp cold water
  450g/1lb/2 cups curd cheese, at
    room temperature
  60ml/4 tbsp Irish whiskey, such as
    Millars or Irish Velvet
  115g/4oz/½ cup soft light
    brown sugar
  150ml/¼ pint/⅔ cup whipping cream
To Decorate
  150ml/¼ pint/⅔ cup whipping cream
  chocolate-covered coffee beans
  cocoa, for dusting
For the Base
  150g/5oz ginger nut biscuits
    (ginger snaps), finely crushed
  25g/1oz/¼ cup toasted almonds,
    chopped
  75g/3oz/6 tbsp butter, melted

1 To make the base, mix together the crushed gingernut biscuits, toasted almonds and melted butter and press firmly into the base of a 20cm/8in loose-based tin (pan). Chill.

2 Heat the coffee, vanilla and single cream in a pan until nearly boiling. Cover and leave to infuse for 15 minutes. Strain through a fine sieve. Sprinkle the gelatine over the water in a bowl and leave for 5 minutes. Place over a pan of simmering water until dissolved. Stir into the coffee cream.

3 Mix the curd cheese, whiskey and sugar together, then gradually blend in the coffee cream. Leave until just beginning to set.

4 Beat the whipping cream until soft peaks form, and fold into the coffee mixture. Spoon into the tin and chill for 3 hours, until set.

5 To decorate, whisk the whipping cream until soft peaks form and spread lightly over the top. Chill for at least 30 minutes, then transfer to a serving plate. Decorate with chocolate-covered coffee beans and dust with cocoa.

VARIATION
Instead of a smooth layer of cream on top of the cheesecake, pipe swirls of cream around the edge of the cake.

PIES, TARTS AND PASTRIES

The flavour and aroma of real

coffee transforms perennial family

favourites into something special,

as you'll discover when you taste a

slice of Coffee Custard Tart or

Crunchy Topped Coffee Meringue

Pie. Along with these much-loved

pies and tarts are classic pastries

from around the world.

WALNUT PIE

SWEETENED WITH COFFEE-FLAVOURED MAPLE SYRUP, THIS PIE HAS A RICH AND STICKY TEXTURE.
THE WALNUTS CAN BE REPLACED BY PECAN NUTS FOR AN AUTHENTIC AMERICAN PIE.

SERVES 8

INGREDIENTS
30ml/2 tbsp ground coffee
175ml/6 fl oz/¾ cup maple syrup
25g/1oz/2 tbsp butter, softened
175g/6oz/¾ cup soft light brown sugar
3 eggs, beaten
5ml/1 tsp vanilla essence (extract)
115g/4oz/1 cup walnut halves
vanilla ice cream, to serve
For the Pastry
150g/5oz/1¼ cups plain
   (all-purpose) flour
a pinch of salt
25g/1oz/¼ cup golden icing
   (confectioners') sugar
75g/3oz/6 tbsp butter, cubed
2 egg yolks

1 Preheat the oven to 200°C/400°F/
Gas 6. To make the pastry, sift the flour,
salt and icing sugar into a bowl. Rub in
the butter until the mixture resembles
fine breadcrumbs.

2 Add the egg yolks and mix to a
dough. Turn out and knead on a lightly
floured surface for a few seconds until
smooth. Wrap in clear film (plastic
wrap) and chill for 20 minutes.

3 Use the pastry to line a 20cm/8in
fluted flan tin (tart pan). Line with baking
parchment and baking beans; bake for
10 minutes. Remove the paper and
beans; bake for 5 minutes. Set the
pastry case (pie shell) aside. Lower
the oven to 180°C/350°F/Gas 4.

4 To make the filling, put the coffee
and maple syrup in a small pan and
heat until almost boiling. Remove from
the heat and leave until just warm.
Mix together the butter and sugar,
then gradually beat in the eggs. Strain
the maple syrup mixture through a fine
sieve into the bowl and stir in with the
vanilla essence.

5 Arrange the walnuts in the pastry
case, then carefully pour in the filling.
Bake for 30–35 minutes or until lightly
browned and firm. Serve warm with
vanilla ice cream.

MISSISSIPPI PIE

THIS AMERICAN FAVOURITE WAS NAMED AFTER THE MUDDY BANKS OF THE MISSISSIPPI RIVER. IT HAS A DENSE LAYER OF CHOCOLATE MOUSSE, TOPPED WITH A MURKY COFFEE TOFFEE LAYER AND, FLOATING ON TOP, LOTS OF LOVELY FRESHLY WHIPPED CREAM.

SERVES 8

INGREDIENTS
For the Base
    275g/10oz digestive biscuits
      (graham crackers), crushed
    150g/5oz/10 tbsp butter, melted
For the Chocolate Layer
    10ml/2 tsp powdered gelatine
    30ml/2 tbsp cold water
    175g/6oz plain (semisweet)
      chocolate, chopped
    2 eggs, separated
    150ml/¼ pint/⅔ cup double
      (heavy) cream
For the Coffee Toffee Layer
    30ml/2 tbsp ground coffee
    300ml/½ pint/1¼ cups double
      (heavy) cream
    200g/7oz/1 cup caster (superfine) sugar
    25g/1oz/4 tbsp cornflour (cornstarch)
    2 eggs, beaten
    15g/½oz/1 tbsp butter
    150ml/¼ pint/⅔ cup whipping cream
      and chocolate curls, to decorate

1 Grease a 21cm/8½in loose-based tin (pan). Mix together the biscuit crumbs and the butter and press firmly over the base and sides of the tin. Chill in the refrigerator for 30 minutes.

2 To make the chocolate layer, sprinkle the gelatine over the cold water in a large bowl and leave for 5 minutes. Then set the bowl over a pan of hot water and stir until completely dissolved. Melt the chocolate in a bowl set over a pan of barely simmering water. Remove from the heat and stir in the gelatine.

3 Blend the egg yolks and double cream together and stir into the chocolate. Whisk the egg whites and fold into the mixture. Pour into the biscuit case and chill for 2 hours.

4 To make the coffee layer, put the coffee in a bowl. Reserve 60ml/4 tbsp of cream. Heat the remaining cream to nearly boiling and pour over the coffee. Infuse for 4 minutes. Strain through a sieve back into the pan. Add the sugar and heat gently until dissolved.

5 Mix the cornflour with the reserved cream and the eggs. Add to the coffee and cream mixture and simmer gently for 2–3 minutes, stirring.

6 Stir in the butter and leave to cool for 30 minutes, stirring occasionally. Spoon over the chocolate layer. Chill in the refrigerator for 2 hours.

7 To make the topping, whip the cream until soft peaks form and spread thickly over the coffee toffee layer. Decorate with chocolate curls and chill until ready to serve.

CRUNCHY TOPPED COFFEE MERINGUE PIE

A SWEET PASTRY CASE IS FILLED WITH A COFFEE CUSTARD AND A MERINGUE TOPPING – CRISP AND GOLDEN ON THE OUTSIDE AND SOFT LIKE MARSHMALLOW UNDERNEATH.

SERVES 6–8

INGREDIENTS

For the Pastry
175g/6oz/1½ cups plain
  (all-purpose) flour
15ml/1 tbsp icing (confectioners')
  sugar
75g/3oz/6 tbsp butter
1 egg yolk
finely grated rind of ½ orange
15ml/1 tbsp orange juice

For the Filling
30ml/2 tbsp ground coffee
350ml/12fl oz/1½ cups milk
25g/1oz/4 tbsp cornflour (cornstarch)
130g/4½ oz/½ cup caster
  (superfine) sugar
4 egg yolks
15g/½ oz/1 tbsp butter

For the Meringue
3 egg whites
1.5ml/¼ tsp cream of tartar
150g/5oz/¾ cup caster
  (superfine) sugar
25g/1oz/¼ cup skinned hazelnuts
15ml/1 tbsp demerara (raw) sugar

1 For the pastry, sift the flour and icing sugar into a bowl. Rub in the butter until the mixture resembles breadcrumbs. Add the egg yolk, orange rind and juice and mix to a firm dough. Wrap in clear film (plastic wrap) and chill for 20 minutes.

2 Roll out the pastry on a lightly floured surface and use to line a 23cm/9in loose-based fluted flan tin (pan). Cover with clear film (plastic wrap) and chill for 30 minutes.

3 Preheat the oven to 200°C/400°F/ Gas 6.

COOK'S TIP
The pastry case can be made up to 36 hours in advance, but once filled and baked the pie should be eaten on the day of making.

4 Prick the pastry all over, line with baking parchment and baking beans and bake for 15 minutes, removing the paper and beans for the last 5 minutes. Lower the oven to 160°C/325°F/Gas 3.

5 To make the filling, put the coffee in a bowl. Heat 250ml/8fl oz/1 cup of the milk to nearly boiling and pour over the coffee. Leave to infuse for 4 minutes, then strain. Blend the cornflour and sugar with the remaining milk and whisk in the coffee-flavoured milk.

6 Bring the mixture to the boil, stirring until thickened. Remove from the heat.

7 Beat the egg yolks. Stir a little of the hot coffee mixture into the egg yolks, then add to the remaining coffee mixture with the butter. Cook over a low heat for 3–4 minutes, until very thick. Pour into the pastry case (pie shell).

8 To make the meringue, whisk the egg whites and cream of tartar until stiff. Whisk in the caster sugar a spoonful at a time.

9 Spoon the meringue over the filling and spread right to the edge of the pastry, swirling into peaks. Sprinkle with hazelnuts and demerara sugar and bake for 30–35 minutes, or until golden brown and crisp. Serve warm, or cool on a wire rack and serve cold.

COFFEE CUSTARD TART

A CRISP WALNUT PASTRY CASE, FLAVOURED WITH VANILLA, IS FILLED WITH A SMOOTH CREAMY COFFEE CUSTARD, BAKED UNTIL LIGHTLY SET AND TOPPED WITH CREAM.

SERVES 6–8

INGREDIENTS
1 vanilla pod (bean)
30ml/2 tbsp ground coffee
300ml/½ pint/1¼ cups single
  (light) cream
150ml/¼ pint/⅔ cup milk
2 eggs, plus 2 egg yolks
50g/2oz/¼ cup caster (superfine) sugar
icing (confectioners') sugar, for dusting
whipped double (heavy) cream, to serve

For the Pastry
175g/6oz/1½ cups plain
  (all-purpose) flour
30ml/2 tbsp icing (confectioners') sugar
115g/4oz/8 tbsp butter, cubed
75g/3oz/½ cup walnuts, finely chopped
1 egg yolk
5ml/1 tsp vanilla essence (extract)
10ml/2 tsp iced water

1 Preheat the oven to 200°C/400°F/ Gas 6. Put a baking sheet in the oven. Sift the flour and sugar into a bowl. Rub in the butter until the mixture resembles breadcrumbs. Stir in the walnuts. Mix the egg yolk, vanilla and water. Add to the dry ingredients and mix to a dough. Wrap in clear film (plastic wrap) and chill for 20 minutes.

2 Roll out the dough and use to line a deep plain or fluted 20cm/8in flan ring or tart pan; trim the edges. Chill for 20 minutes. Prick the base with a fork. Line with baking parchment and baking beans and bake on the hot baking sheet for 10 minutes. Remove the paper and beans and bake for a further 10 minutes. Lower the oven to 150°C/ 300°F/Gas 2.

3 Meanwhile, split the vanilla pod and scrape out the seeds. Put both in a pan with the coffee, cream and milk. Heat to nearly boiling, cover and infuse for 10 minutes. Whisk the eggs, egg yolks and caster sugar together.

4 Bring the cream back to boiling point and pour on to the egg mixture, stirring. Strain into the pastry case (pie shell).

5 Bake the tart for 40–45 minutes or until lightly set. Take out of the oven and leave on a wire rack to cool. Remove the tart from the tin, pipe cream rosettes around the edge and dust with icing sugar to serve.

BLUEBERRY FRANGIPANE FLAN

A TANGY LEMON PASTRY CASE IS FILLED WITH A SWEET ALMOND FILLING DOTTED WITH RIPE BLUEBERRIES. THE JAM AND LIQUEUR GLAZE ADDS AN INDULGENT FINISH.

SERVES 6

INGREDIENTS

    30ml/2 tbsp ground coffee
    45ml/3 tbsp nearly boiling milk
    50g/2oz/4 tbsp unsalted (sweet) butter
    50g/2oz/¼ cup caster (superfine) sugar
    1 egg
    115g/4oz/1 cup ground almonds
    15ml/1 tbsp plain (all-purpose)
      flour, sifted
    225g/8oz/2 cups blueberries
    30ml/2 tbsp seedless blackberry jam
    15ml/1 tbsp liqueur, such as
      Amaretto or Cointreau
    mascarpone, crème fraîche or
      sour cream, to serve
For the Pastry
    175g/6oz/1½ cups plain
      (all-purpose) flour
    115g/4oz/8 tbsp unsalted (sweet) butter
    25g/1oz/2 tbsp caster (superfine) sugar
    finely grated rind of ½ lemon
    15ml/1 tbsp chilled water

1 Preheat the oven to 190°C/375°F/ Gas 5. For the pastry, sift the flour and rub in the butter. Add the sugar and rind, then the water, and mix to a firm dough. Wrap in clear film (plastic wrap) and chill for 20 minutes.

2 Roll out the pastry on a lightly floured surface and use to line a 23cm/9in loose-based flan tin (tart pan). Line with baking parchment and baking beans and bake for 10 minutes. Remove the paper and beans and bake for a further 10 minutes. Remove from the oven.

3 Meanwhile, to make the filling, put the coffee in a bowl. Pour the milk over and leave to infuse for 4 minutes. Cream the butter and sugar until pale. Beat in the egg, then add the almonds and flour. Strain in the coffee through a fine sieve and fold in.

COOK'S TIP
This flan can also be made in individual tartlets. Use six 10cm/4in tartlet tins and bake for 25 minutes.

4 Spread the coffee mixture in the pastry case (pie shell). Scatter the blueberries over and push them down slightly into the mixture. Bake for 30 minutes, until firm, covering with foil after 20 minutes.

5 Remove from the oven and allow to cool slightly. Heat the jam and liqueur in a small pan until melted. Brush over the flan and remove from the tin. Serve warm with a scoop of mascarpone or with crème fraîche or sour cream.

TIA MARIA TRUFFLE TARTS

THE IDEAL DESSERT FOR A TEA OR COFFEE BREAK, THESE MINI COFFEE PASTRY CASES ARE FILLED WITH A CHOCOLATE LIQUEUR TRUFFLE CENTRE AND TOPPED WITH FRESH RIPE BERRIES.

SERVES 6

INGREDIENTS
  300ml/½ pint/1¼ cups double
    (heavy) cream
  225g/8oz/generous ¾ cup seedless
    bramble or raspberry jam
  150g/5oz plain (semisweet)
    chocolate, chopped
  45ml/3 tbsp Tia Maria liqueur
  450g/1lb mixed berries, such as
    raspberries, small strawberries
    or blackberries
For the Pastry
  225g/8oz/2 cups plain
    (all-purpose) flour
  15ml/1 tbsp caster (superfine) sugar
  150g/5oz/10 tbsp butter, cubed
  1 egg yolk
  30ml/2 tbsp very strong brewed
    coffee, chilled

1 Preheat the oven to 200°C/400°F/ Gas 6. Put a baking sheet in the oven. For the pastry, sift the flour and sugar, and rub in the butter. Stir in the egg yolk and coffee; mix to a stiff dough. Knead lightly on a floured surface for a few seconds until smooth. Wrap in clear film (plastic wrap) and chill.

2 Use the pastry to line six 10cm/4in fluted tartlet tins (pans). Prick the bases with a fork and line with baking parchment and baking beans. Put on the hot baking sheet and bake for 10 minutes. Remove the parchment and beans and bake for 8–10 minutes longer, until cooked. Cool on a wire rack.

3 To make the filling, slowly bring the cream and 175g/6oz/generous ½ cup of the jam to the boil, stirring continuously until dissolved.

COOK'S TIP
When making the pastry, blend the egg yolk and coffee together until well mixed to ensure an evenly coloured pastry.

4 Remove from the heat, add the chocolate and 30ml/2 tbsp of the liqueur. Stir until melted. Cool, then spoon into the pastry cases (pie shells). Chill for 40 minutes.

5 Heat the remaining jam and liqueur until smooth. Arrange the fruit on top of the tarts, then brush the jam glaze over. Chill until ready to serve.

COFFEE CREAM PROFITEROLES

CRISP-TEXTURED COFFEE CHOUX PASTRY PUFFS ARE FILLED WITH CREAM AND DRIZZLED WITH A
WHITE CHOCOLATE SAUCE. FOR THOSE WITH A SWEET TOOTH, THERE IS PLENTY OF EXTRA SAUCE.

SERVES 6

INGREDIENTS
  65g/2½oz/9 tbsp plain (all-purpose)
    white flour
  pinch of salt
  50g/2oz/4 tbsp butter
  150ml/¼ pint/⅔ cup brewed coffee
  2 eggs, lightly beaten
For the White Chocolate Sauce
  50g/2oz/¼ cup sugar
  100ml/3½fl oz/scant ½ cup water
  150g/5oz good quality white dessert
    chocolate, broken into pieces
  25g/1oz/2 tbsp unsalted (sweet) butter
  45ml/3 tbsp double (heavy) cream
  30ml/2 tbsp coffee liqueur
To Assemble
  250ml/8fl oz/1 cup double cream

1 Preheat the oven to 220°C/425°F/
Gas 7. Sift the flour and salt on to a piece
of baking parchment. Cut the butter into
pieces and put in a pan with the coffee.

2 Bring to a rolling boil, then remove
from the heat and tip in all the flour.
Beat until the mixture leaves the sides
of the pan. Leave to cool for 2 minutes.

3 Gradually add the eggs, beating well
between each addition. Spoon the
mixture into a piping (pastry) bag with a
1cm/½in plain nozzle.

4 Pipe about 24 small buns on to a
dampened baking sheet. Bake for
20 minutes, until well risen and crisp.

5 Remove the buns from the oven and
pierce the side of each with a sharp
knife to let out the steam.

6 To make the sauce, put the sugar
and water in a heavy pan and heat
gently until dissolved. Bring to the boil
and simmer for 3 minutes. Remove
from the heat. Add the chocolate and
butter, stirring until smooth. Stir in the
cream and liqueur.

7 To assemble, whip the cream until
soft peaks form. Using a piping bag, fill
the choux buns through the slits in the
sides. Arrange on plates and pour a
little of the sauce over, either warm or at
room temperature. Serve the remaining
sauce separately.

DANISH COFFEE PASTRIES

THESE FAMOUS CRISP PASTRIES REQUIRE TIME AND EFFORT, BUT THE RESULTS ARE WORTHWHILE.

MAKES 16

INGREDIENTS
  45ml/3 tbsp nearly boiling water
  30ml/2 tbsp ground coffee
  115g/4oz/½ cup caster (superfine) sugar
  40g/1½ oz/3 tbsp unsalted (sweet) butter
  1 egg yolk
  115g/4oz/1 cup ground almonds
  beaten egg, to glaze
  275g/10oz/1 cup apricot jam
  30ml/2 tbsp water
  175g/6oz/1½ cups icing
    (confectioners') sugar
  50g/2oz/½ cup flaked (sliced)
    almonds, toasted
  50g/2oz/¼ cup glacé (candied) cherries
For the Pastry
  275g/10oz/2½ cups plain
    (all-purpose) flour
  1.5ml/¼ tsp salt
  15g/½oz/1 tbsp caster (superfine) sugar
  225g/8oz/1 cup butter, softened
  10ml/2 tsp easy-blend (rapid-rise)
    dried yeast
  1 egg, beaten
  100ml/3½fl oz/scant ½ cup cold water

1 For the pastry, sift the flour, salt and sugar into a bowl. Rub in 25g/1oz/2 tbsp of the butter. Add the yeast, then the egg and water. Mix to a soft dough.

2 Lightly knead for 4-5 minutes. Wrap in plastic and chill for 15 minutes. Put the remaining butter between 2 sheets of baking parchment. Beat with a rolling pin to a 18cm/7in square. Roll out the chilled dough to a 25cm/10in square. Put the butter in the middle, as shown. Enclose it with dough.

3 Roll out the pastry to about 35cm/14in long. Turn up the bottom third of the pastry, then fold down the top third. Seal the edges together with a rolling pin. Wrap the pastry again and chill for 15 minutes.

4 Repeat the rolling and folding three more times, each time turning the pastry so that the short ends are at the top and bottom. Allow a 15-minute rest between each turn.

5 To make the filling, pour the hot water over the coffee and leave to infuse for 4 minutes. Strain through a fine sieve. Cream the sugar and butter together in a bowl. Beat in the egg yolk, ground almonds and 15ml/1 tbsp of the coffee.

6 Divide the dough and filling equally into three. Roll one dough portion to an 18 x 35cm/7 x 14in rectangle. Spread with filling and roll up from a short end. Cut into six equal slices. Roll another portion into a 25cm/10in square; cut into a 25cm/10in round, remove the trimmings and cut into six segments.

7 Put a spoonful of filling at the widest end of each triangle, then roll up towards the point into a crescent.

8 Roll out the remaining dough into a 20cm/8in square; cut into four. Put some filling into the centre of each. Make cuts from each corner almost to the centre and fold four alternate points to the centre.

9 Preheat the oven to 220°C/425°F/Gas 7. Put the pastries on greased baking sheets, spaced apart. Cover loosely with oiled clear film (plastic wrap) and leave to rise for 20 minutes, until almost doubled in size. Brush with beaten egg for glazing and bake for 15–20 minutes, until lightly browned and crisp. Cool on wire racks.

10 Put the jam in a pan with the water; bring to the boil, then sieve. Brush the jam over the warm pastries. Mix the icing sugar with the remaining coffee, adding more water if necessary to make a thick icing. Drizzle the icing over some of the pastries and decorate some with flaked almonds or chopped glacé cherries. Leave to set before serving.

GREEK FRUIT AND NUT PASTRIES

*AROMATIC SWEET PASTRY CRESCENTS, KNOWN AS "MOSHOPOUNGIA" IN GREECE, ARE PACKED WITH
CANDIED CITRUS PEEL AND WALNUTS, SOAKED IN A COFFEE SYRUP.*

MAKES 16

INGREDIENTS
   60ml/4 tbsp clear honey
   60ml/4 tbsp strong brewed coffee
   75g/3oz/½ cup mixed candied citrus
      peel, finely chopped
   175g/6oz/1 cup walnuts, chopped
   1.5ml/¼ tsp freshly grated nutmeg
   milk, to glaze
   caster (superfine) sugar,
      for sprinkling
For the Pastry
   450g/1lb/4 cups plain
      (all-purpose) flour
   2.5ml/½ tsp ground cinnamon
   2.5ml/½ tsp baking powder
   a pinch of salt
   150g/5oz/10 tbsp unsalted
      (sweet) butter
   30ml/2 tbsp caster (superfine) sugar
   1 egg
   120ml/4fl oz/½ cup chilled milk

1 Preheat the oven to 180°C/350°F/
Gas 4. To make the pastry, sift the flour,
cinnamon, baking powder and salt. Rub
in the butter until the mixture resembles
fine breadcrumbs. Stir in the sugar.
Make a central well.

2 Beat the egg and milk and add to
the well in the dry ingredients. Mix
to a soft dough. Divide it into two, wrap
and chill.

3 Meanwhile, to make the filling, mix
the honey and coffee. Add the peel,
walnuts and nutmeg. Stir well, cover
and leave to soak for at least 20 minutes.

4 Roll out a portion of dough on a
lightly floured work surface until about
3mm/⅛in thick. Stamp out rounds using
a 10cm/4in round pastry (cookie) cutter.

5 Place a heaped teaspoonful of filling
on one side of each round. Brush the
edges with a little milk, then fold over
and press the edges together to seal.
Repeat with remaining pastry until all
the filling is used.

6 Put the pastries on lightly greased
baking sheets, brush with milk and
sprinkle with caster sugar.

7 Make a steam hole in each with a
skewer. Bake for 35 minutes, or until
lightly browned. Cool on a wire rack.

BAKLAVA

TURKISH COFFEE IS BLACK, THICK, VERY SWEET AND OFTEN SPICED. HERE IT IS USED IN THIS FAMOUS PASTRY CONFECTION, TRADITIONALLY SERVED ON RELIGIOUS FESTIVAL DAYS IN TURKEY.

MAKES 16

INGREDIENTS
50g/2oz/½ cup blanched
    almonds, chopped
50g/2oz/½ cup pistachio nuts, chopped
75g/3oz/scant ½ cup caster
    (superfine) sugar
115g/4oz filo pastry
75g/3oz/6 tbsp unsalted (sweet)
    butter, melted and cooled
For the Syrup
115g/4oz/generous ½ cup caster
    (superfine) sugar
7.5cm/3in piece cinnamon stick
1 whole clove
2 cardamom pods, crushed
75ml/5 tbsp strong brewed coffee

1 Preheat the oven to 180°C/350°F/ Gas 4. Mix the nuts and sugar together. Cut the pastry to fit a tin measuring 18 x 28cm/7 x 11in. Brush the tin with a little butter. Lay a sheet of pastry in the tin and brush with melted butter.

2 Repeat with three more sheets and spread with half the nut mixture.

3 Layer up three more sheets of pastry, lightly brushing butter between the layers, then spread the remaining nut mixture over them, smoothing it over the entire surface. Top with the remaining pastry and butter. Gently press down the edges to seal.

4 With a sharp knife, mark the top into diamonds. Bake for 20–25 minutes until golden brown and crisp. Meanwhile, put the syrup ingredients in a small pan and heat gently until the sugar has dissolved. Cover with a lid and leave to infuse for 20 minutes.

5 Remove the baklava from the oven. Reheat the syrup and strain over the pastry. Leave to cool in the tin. Cut into diamonds, remove from the tin and serve.

COOK'S TIP
While assembling the baklava, keep the pile of filo pastry covered with a damp cloth to stop it drying out and becoming brittle, which makes it difficult to use.

SWEETS,
BISCUITS
AND BREADS

Few people can resist the

tantalizing display of biscuits

(cookies) and breads in the baker's

shop window, and it's easy to

re-create those delectable bakes at

home. Here, you'll find a selection

of traditional and Continental

recipes from rich and gooey truffles

to a stunning candied fruit plait.

STUFFED PRUNES

CHOCOLATE-COVERED PRUNES, SOAKED IN LIQUEUR, HIDE A MELT-IN-THE-MOUTH COFFEE FILLING.

MAKES ABOUT 30

INGREDIENTS
    225g/8oz/1 cup unstoned
        (unpitted) prunes
    50ml/2fl oz/¼ cup Armagnac
    30ml/2 tbsp ground coffee
    150ml/¼ pint/⅔ cup double
        (heavy) cream
    350g/12oz plain (semisweet)
        chocolate, chopped
    10g/¼oz/½ tbsp vegetable fat
    30ml/2 tbsp cocoa powder,
        for dusting

1 Put the unstoned prunes in a bowl and pour the Armagnac over. Stir, then cover with clear film (plastic wrap) and set aside for at least 2 hours, or until the prunes have absorbed all the liquid.

2 Make a slit along each prune to remove the stone (pit), making a hollow for the filling, but leaving the fruit intact.

3 Put the coffee and cream in a pan and heat almost to boiling point. Cover, infuse for 4 minutes, then heat again until almost boiling. Put 115g/4oz of the chocolate into a bowl and pour over the coffee cream through a sieve.

4 Stir until the chocolate has melted and the mixture is smooth. Leave to cool, until it has the consistency of softened butter.

5 Fill a piping (pastry) bag with a small plain nozzle with the chocolate mixture. Pipe into the cavities of the prunes. Chill in the refrigerator for 20 minutes.

6 Melt the remaining chocolate in a bowl over a pan of hot water. Using a fork, dip the prunes one at a time into the chocolate to give them a generous coating. Place on baking parchment to harden. Dust each with a little cocoa powder.

COFFEE CHOCOLATE TRUFFLES

BECAUSE THESE CLASSIC CHOCOLATES CONTAIN FRESH CREAM, THEY SHOULD BE STORED IN THE
REFRIGERATOR AND EATEN WITHIN A FEW DAYS.

MAKES 24

INGREDIENTS
  350g/12oz plain (semisweet) chocolate
  75ml/5 tbsp double (heavy) cream
  30ml/2 tbsp coffee liqueur, such as
    Tia Maria, Kahlúa or Toussaint
  115g/4oz good quality white
    dessert chocolate
  115g/4oz good quality milk
    dessert chocolate

1 Melt 225g/8oz of the plain chocolate
in a bowl set over a pan of barely
simmering water. Stir in the cream and
liqueur, then chill the mixture in the
refrigerator for 4 hours, until firm.

2 Divide the mixture into 24 equal
pieces and quickly roll each into a ball.
Chill for a further 1 hour, or until they
are firm again.

3 Melt the remaining plain, white and
milk chocolate in separate small bowls.
Using two forks, carefully dip eight of
the truffles, one at a time, into the
melted milk chocolate.

4 Repeat with the white and plain
chocolate. Place the truffles on a board,
covered with baking parchment or foil.
Leave to set before removing and placing
in a serving bowl or individual paper cases.

VARIATIONS
Ring the changes by adding one of the
following to the truffle mixture:
Ginger Stir in 40g/1½oz/¼ cup finely
chopped crystallized (candied) ginger.
Candied fruit Stir in 50g/2oz/⅓ cup finely
chopped candied fruit, such as pineapple
and orange.
Pistachio Stir in 25g/1oz/¼ cup chopped
skinned pistachio nuts.
Hazelnut Roll each ball of chilled
truffle mixture around a whole skinned
hazelnut.
Raisin Soak 40g/1½oz/generous ¼ cup
raisins overnight in 15ml/1 tbsp coffee
liqueur, such as Tia Maria or Kahlúa, and
stir into the truffle mixture.

CHOCOLATE AND COFFEE MINT THINS

THESE COFFEE-FLAVOURED CHOCOLATE SQUARES CONTAIN PIECES OF CRISP MINTY CARAMEL AND ARE IDEAL FOR SERVING WITH AFTER-DINNER COFFEE.

MAKES 16

INGREDIENTS
    75g/3oz/scant ½ cup sugar
    75ml/5 tbsp water
    3 drops peppermint oil
    15ml/1 tbsp strong-flavoured
        ground coffee
    75ml/5 tbsp nearly boiling double
        (heavy) cream
    225g/8oz plain (semisweet) chocolate
    10g/¼oz/½ tbsp unsalted
        (sweet) butter

COOK'S TIP
Don't chill the chocolate to set it, or it may loose its gloss and become too brittle to cut easily into neat squares.

1 Line a 18cm/7in square tin with non-stick baking parchment. Gently heat the sugar and water in a heavy pan until dissolved. Add the peppermint, and boil until a light caramel colour.

2 Pour the caramel on to an oiled baking sheet and leave to harden, then crush into small pieces.

3 Put the coffee in a small bowl and pour the hot cream over. Leave to infuse for about 4 minutes, then strain through a fine sieve. Melt the chocolate and unsalted butter in a bowl set over barely simmering water. Remove from the heat and beat in the hot coffee cream. Stir in the mint caramel.

4 Pour the mixture into the prepared tin and smooth the surface level. Leave in a cool place to set for at least 4 hours, preferably overnight.

5 Carefully turn out the chocolate on to a board and peel off the lining paper. Cut the chocolate into squares with a sharp knife and store in an airtight container until needed.

COFFEE AND HAZELNUT MACAROONS

MACAROONS ARE TRADITIONALLY MADE WITH GROUND ALMONDS. THIS RECIPE USES HAZELNUTS, WHICH ARE LIGHTLY ROASTED BEFORE GRINDING, BUT YOU CAN USE WALNUTS INSTEAD, IF PREFERRED.

MAKES 20

INGREDIENTS
    edible rice paper
    115g/4oz/⅔ cup skinned hazelnuts
    225g/8oz/generous 1 cup caster
        (superfine) sugar
    15ml/1 tbsp ground rice
    10ml/2 tsp ground coffee,
        e.g. hazelnut-flavoured
    2 egg whites
    caster (superfine) sugar,
        for sprinkling

1 Preheat the oven to 180°C/350°F/Gas 4. Line two baking sheets with rice paper. Place the skinned hazelnuts on a baking sheet and cook for 5 minutes. Cool, then process until fine.

2 Mix the ground nuts with the sugar, ground rice and coffee. Stir in the egg whites to make a fairly stiff paste.

3 Spoon into a piping (pastry) bag fitted with a 1cm/½in plain nozzle. Pipe rounds on the rice paper, leaving room to spread.

4 Sprinkle each macaroon with a little caster sugar then bake for 20 minutes, or until pale golden in colour. Transfer to a wire rack to cool. Remove excess rice paper when completely cold. Serve immediately or store in an airtight tin for up to 2–3 days.

VIENNESE WHIRLS

THESE CRISP, MELT-IN-THE-MOUTH PIPED BISCUITS ARE FILLED WITH A CREAMY COFFEE BUTTERCREAM.

MAKES 20

INGREDIENTS
175g/6oz/12 tbsp butter
50g/2oz/½ cup icing (confectioners')
 sugar
2.5ml/½ tsp vanilla essence (extract)
115g/4oz/1 cup plain (all-purpose) flour
50g/2oz/½ cup cornflour (cornstarch)
icing sugar and cocoa powder, for
 dusting
For the Filling
15ml/1 tbsp ground coffee
60ml/4 tbsp single (light) cream
75g/3oz/6 tbsp butter, softened
115g/4oz/1 cup icing sugar, sifted

1 Preheat the oven to 180°C/350°F/
Gas 4. Cream together the butter, icing
sugar and vanilla essence until light.
Sift in the flour and cornflour and mix
until smooth.

2 Using two tablespoons, spoon the
mixture into a piping (pastry) bag fitted
with a 1cm/½in fluted nozzle.

3 Pipe small rosettes well apart on
greased baking sheets. Bake in the
oven for 12–15 minutes until golden.
Transfer to a wire rack to cool.

4 For the filling, put the coffee in a
bowl. Heat the cream to nearly boiling
and pour it over. Infuse for 4 minutes,
then strain through a fine sieve.

5 Beat the butter, icing sugar and
coffee-flavoured cream until light. Use
to sandwich the halves in pairs. Dust
with icing sugar and cocoa powder.

VARIATION
For mocha Viennese whirls, substitute
25g/1oz/¼ cup cocoa powder for 25g/
1oz/¼ cup of the flour.

BLACK RUSSIAN COOKIES

THE INGREDIENTS OF THE FAMOUS COCKTAIL — COFFEE AND VODKA — FLAVOUR THESE FABULOUS COOKIES.

MAKES 16

INGREDIENTS
    30ml/2 tbsp ground espresso or other
      strong-flavoured coffee
    60ml/4 tbsp nearly boiling milk
    115g/4oz/8 tbsp butter
    115g/4oz/½ cup soft light brown sugar
    1 egg
    225g/8oz/2 cups plain (all-purpose) flour
    5ml/1 tsp baking powder
    a pinch of salt
For the Icing
    115g/4oz/1 cup icing
      (confectioners') sugar
    about 25ml/1½ tbsp vodka

1 Preheat the oven to 180°C/350°F/
Gas 4. Put the coffee in a small bowl
and pour the hot milk over. Leave to
infuse for 4 minutes, then strain
through a fine sieve and leave to cool.

2 Cream the butter and sugar together
until light and fluffy. Gradually beat in
the egg. Sift the flour, baking powder
and salt together and fold in with the
coffee-flavoured milk to make a fairly
stiff mixture.

3 Place dessertspoonfuls of the mixture
on greased baking sheets, spacing them
slightly apart to allow room for a little
spreading. Bake the cookies for about
15 minutes, until lightly browned. Cool
on a wire rack.

4 To make the icing, mix the icing
sugar and enough vodka together to
make a thick icing. Spoon into a small
paper piping (pastry) bag.

5 Snip off the end of the piping bag
and lightly drizzle the icing over the
top of each cookie. Allow the icing to
set before serving.

COFFEE AND MACADAMIA MUFFINS

THESE MUFFINS ARE DELICIOUS EATEN COLD, BUT ARE BEST SERVED STILL WARM FROM THE OVEN.

MAKES 12

INGREDIENTS
25ml/1½ tbsp ground coffee
250ml/8fl oz/1 cup milk
50g/2oz/4 tbsp butter
275g/10oz/2½ cups plain
(all-purpose) flour
10ml/2 tsp baking powder
150g/5oz/10 tbsp light muscovado
(brown) sugar
75g/3oz/½ cup macadamia nuts
1 egg, lightly beaten

1 Preheat the oven to 200°C/400°F/
Gas 6. Line a 12-hole muffin or deep-
bun tin (pan) with paper muffin cases.

2 Put the coffee in a jug (pitcher) or
bowl. Heat the milk to nearly boiling
and pour over. Leave to infuse for
4 minutes, then strain through a sieve.

3 Add the butter to the coffee-
flavoured milk mixture and stir until
melted. Leave until cold.

4 Sift the flour and baking powder into
a large mixing bowl. Stir in the sugar
and macadamia nuts. Add the egg to
the coffee-flavoured milk mixture, pour
into the dry ingredients and stir until
just combined – do not overmix.

5 Divide the coffee mixture among the
prepared muffin tins and bake for about
15 minutes until well risen and firm.
Transfer to a wire rack and serve warm
or cold.

COOK'S TIP
To cool the coffee-flavoured milk quickly,
place the jug in a large bowl of iced or
cold water.

CHUNKY WHITE CHOCOLATE AND COFFEE BROWNIES

*BROWNIES SHOULD HAVE A GOOEY TEXTURE, SO TAKE CARE NOT TO OVERCOOK THEM — WHEN READY,
THE MIXTURE WILL STILL BE SLIGHTLY SOFT UNDER THE CRUST, BUT WILL FIRM AS IT COOLS.*

MAKES 12

INGREDIENTS
25ml/1½ tbsp ground coffee
45ml/3 tbsp nearly boiling water
300g/11oz plain (semisweet)
chocolate, chopped
225g/8oz/1 cup butter
225g/8oz/1 cup caster
(superfine) sugar
3 eggs
75g/3oz/⅔ cup self-raising
(self-rising) flour, sifted
225g/8oz white chocolate, chopped

1 Preheat the oven to 190°C/375°F/
Gas 5. Grease and base-line a 18 x
28cm/7 x 11in tin (pan). Infuse the
coffee in the water for 4 minutes, then
strain through a sieve.

2 Put the plain chocolate and butter in
a bowl set over a pan of hot water and
stir occasionally until melted. Remove
from the heat and cool for 5 minutes.

3 Mix the sugar and eggs together. Stir
in the chocolate and butter mixture and
the coffee. Stir in the sifted flour.

4 Fold in the white chocolate pieces.
Pour into the prepared tin.

5 Bake for 45–50 minutes, or until firm
and the top is crusty. Leave to cool in
the tin. When completely cold, cut into
squares and remove from the tin.

PECAN TOFFEE SHORTBREAD

COFFEE SHORTBREAD IS TOPPED WITH PECAN-STUDDED TOFFEE. CORNFLOUR GIVES IT A CRUMBLY LIGHT TEXTURE, BUT ALL PLAIN FLOUR CAN BE USED, IF YOU LIKE.

MAKES 20

INGREDIENTS
   15ml/1 tbsp ground coffee
   15ml/1 tbsp nearly boiling water
   115g/4oz/8 tbsp butter, softened
   30ml/2 tbsp smooth peanut butter
   75g/3oz/scant ½ cup caster
     (superfine) sugar
   75g/3oz/⅔ cup cornflour (cornstarch)
   185g/6½oz/1⅔ cups plain
     (all-purpose) flour
For the topping
   175g/6oz/12 tbsp butter
   175g/6oz/¾ cup soft light brown sugar
   30ml/2 tbsp golden (light corn) syrup
   175g/6oz/1 cup shelled pecan nuts,
     roughly chopped

1 Preheat the oven to 180°C/350°F/ Gas 4. Lightly grease and line the base of a 18 x 28cm/7 x 11in tin (pan) with baking parchment.

2 Put the coffee in a bowl and pour the hot water over. Leave to infuse for 4 minutes, then strain through a fine sieve.

3 Cream the butter, peanut butter, sugar and coffee together until light. Sift the cornflour and flour together and mix in to make a smooth dough.

4 Press into the base of the tin and prick all over with a fork. Bake for 20 minutes. To make the topping, put the butter, sugar and syrup in a pan and heat until melted. Bring to the boil.

5 Allow to simmer for 5 minutes, then stir in the chopped nuts. Spread the topping over the base. Leave in the tin until cold, then cut into fingers. Remove from the tin and serve.

COFFEE BISCOTTI

THESE CRISP BISCUITS ARE MADE TWICE AS DELICIOUS WITH BOTH FRESHLY ROASTED GROUND COFFEE BEANS AND STRONG AROMATIC BREWED COFFEE IN THE MIXTURE.

MAKES ABOUT 30

INGREDIENTS

25g/1oz/⅓ cup espresso-roasted
  coffee beans
115g/4oz/⅔ cup blanched almonds
200g/7oz/scant 2 cups plain
  (all-purpose) flour
7.5ml/1½ tsp baking powder
1.5ml/¼ tsp salt
75g/3oz/6 tbsp unsalted (sweet)
  butter, cubed
150g/5oz/¾ cup caster (superfine) sugar
2 eggs, beaten
25–30ml/1½–2 tbsp strong
  brewed coffee
5ml/1 tsp ground cinnamon

4 Lightly knead for a few seconds until smooth and shape into two rolls about 7.5cm/3in in diameter. Place on a greased baking sheet and dust with the cinnamon. Bake for 20 minutes.

5 Using a sharp knife, cut the rolls into 4cm/1½in slices on the diagonal. Arrange the slices on the baking sheet and bake for a further 10 minutes, or until lightly browned. Cool on a rack.

1 Preheat the oven to 180°C/350°F/ Gas 4. Put the espresso coffee beans in a single layer on one side of a large baking sheet and the almonds on the other. Roast for 10 minutes. Cool.

2 In a blender or food processor, process the coffee beans until fairly fine. Tip out and set aside. Process the almonds until finely ground. Set aside.

3 Sift the flour, baking powder and salt into a bowl. Rub in the butter until the mixture resembles breadcrumbs. Stir in the sugar, ground coffee and almonds. Add the eggs and enough brewed coffee to make a fairly firm dough.

COOK'S TIP
Store the biscotti in an airtight tin (or jar) for at least a day before serving.

CAPPUCCINO PANETTONE

THIS LIGHT BREAD IS SERVED IN ITALY AS PART OF THEIR TRADITIONAL CHRISTMAS FARE.

SERVES 8

INGREDIENTS
450g/1lb/4 cups plain (all-purpose) flour
2.5ml/½ tsp salt
75g/3oz/scant ½ cup caster
  (superfine) sugar
7g/¼oz sachet easy-blend (rapid-rise)
  dried yeast
115g/4oz/8 tbsp butter
100ml/3½fl oz/scant ½ cup very hot
  strong brewed espresso coffee
100ml/3½fl oz/½ cup milk
4 egg yolks
115g/4oz/⅔ cup plain (semisweet)
  chocolate chips
beaten egg, to glaze

1 Preheat the oven to 190°C/375°F/
Gas 5. Lightly grease and line a deep
14–15cm/5½–6in cake tin (pan) with
baking parchment. Sift the flour and
salt into a large bowl. Stir in the sugar
and yeast.

2 Add the butter to the coffee and stir
until melted. Stir in the milk, then add
to the dry ingredients with the egg
yolks. Mix together to make a dough.

COOK'S TIP
Unlike commercial varieties, home-made
panettone should be eaten within a day
or two of baking.

3 Turn the dough out on to a lightly
floured surface and knead for
10 minutes, until smooth and elastic.
Knead in the chocolate chips.

4 Shape into a ball, place in the tin
and cover with oiled clear film (plastic
wrap). Leave to rise in a warm place for
1 hour or until the dough reaches the
top of the tin. Lightly brush with beaten
egg and bake for 35 minutes.

5 Lower the oven to 180°C/350°F/
Gas 4 and cover the panettone with foil
if it has browned enough. Bake for a
further 10–15 minutes, or until done.

6 Allow the panettone to cool in the tin
for 10 minutes, then transfer to a wire
rack. Remove the lining paper just
before slicing and serving.

CANDIED FRUIT BREAD

THE CENTRE OF THIS COFFEE-FLAVOURED YEASTED PLAIT CONTAINS BRIGHTLY COLOURED CANDIED FRUITS, MOISTENED BY SOAKING IN RICH COFFEE LIQUEUR.

SERVES 6–8

INGREDIENTS

175g/6oz/1 cup mixed candied fruit, such as pineapple, orange and cherries, chopped
60ml/4 tbsp coffee liqueur
30ml/2 tbsp ground coffee
100ml/3½fl oz/½ cup nearly boiling milk
225g/8oz/2 cups strong plain (all-purpose) flour
1.5ml/¼ tsp salt
25g/1oz/2 tbsp soft light brown sugar
½ x 7g/¼oz sachet easy-blend (rapid-rise) dried yeast
1 egg, beaten
50g/2oz white almond paste, grated
65g/2½oz/¼ cup apricot jam
15g/½oz/1 tbsp unsalted (sweet) butter
15ml/1 tbsp caster (superfine) sugar
15ml/1 tbsp clear honey

1 Put the candied fruit in a bowl: spoon the liqueur over. Stir to coat, then leave to soak overnight.

2 Preheat the oven to 200°C/400°F/ Gas 6. Put the coffee in a bowl; pour in the hot milk and leave until lukewarm. Strain through a fine sieve. Sift the flour and salt into a bowl; stir in the brown sugar and yeast. Make a central well, add the coffee-flavoured milk and the egg and mix to a soft dough.

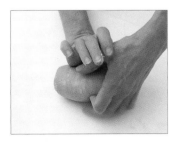

3 Knead for 10 minutes. Put the dough in a clean bowl, cover with clear film and leave to rise for 1 hour.

4 Mix the soaked fruit, almond paste and jam. Lightly knead the dough again for 1 minute, then roll out to a rectangle measuring 35 x 30cm/14 x 12in.

5 Spread the filling in a 7.5cm/3in strip lengthways down the middle to within 5cm/2in of each end. Make 14 diagonal cuts about 2cm/¾in wide in the dough either side of the filling.

6 Fold the ends of the dough up over the filling, overlapping alternate strips, Tuck in the last two strips neatly. Place on a greased baking sheet.

7 Cover with clear film (plastic wrap); leave to rise for 20 minutes. Melt the butter, sugar and honey, then brush over the braid. Bake for 20–25 minutes. Allow to cool before slicing and serving.

CHOCOLATE SUPPLIERS AROUND THE WORLD

Australia
Chocolatier Australia
224 Waterdale Road
Ivanhoe, VIC 3079
Tel: (3) 94 99 70 22

The Chocolate Box
761 Burke Road
Camberwell, VIC 3124
Tel: (3) 98 13 13 77

Darren Taylor's Handmade
Chocolates
Seet Art, 96 Oxford Street
Paddington, NSW 2021
Tel: (2) 93 61 66 17

Sweet William Chocolates
4 William Street
Paddington, NSW 2021
Tel: (2) 93 31 54 68

Simon Johnson
181 Harris Street
Pyrmont, NSW 2009
Tel: (2) 95 52 25 22

Haigh's Chocolates
Beehive Corner
2 Rundle Mall
Adelaide, SA
Tel: (8) 23 12 844

Europe
AUSTRIA
Altmann & Kühne
Graben 30, 1010 Wien
Tel: (1) 53 30 927

Demels
14 Kohlmarkt
1010 Wien
Tel: (1) 53 51 717

Hotel Imperial
Kärtner Ring 16
A-1051 Wien
Tel: (1) 50 11 03 13
Fax: (1) 50 10 355

Mirabell Salzburger Confiserie
Hauptstrasse 14-16
A-5082 Grödig
Tel: (62) 46 20 110

BELGIUM
Charlemagne
Place Jacques Brel 8
4040 Herstal
Tel: (41) 64 66 44

Godiva
Wapenstilstandstraat 5
1081 Brussels
Tel: (2) 42 21 711

Kim's Chocolates
Nieuwlandlaan 12
Industriezone B-615
B-3200 Aarschot
Tel: (16) 55 15 80

Neuhaus
Postbox 2
B-1602 Vlenzenbeek
Tel: (2) 56 82 211

Pierre Colas
2 Rue Campagne
4577 Modave
Tel: (2) 64 80 893

Wittamer
12 Place du Grand Sablon,
Grote Zavel 12
1000 Brussels
Tel: (2) 51 28 451

ENGLAND
Ackermans
9 Goldhurst Terrace
Finchley Road
London NW6 3HX
Tel: (020) 7624 2742

Charbonnel et Walker
1 The Royal Arcade
28 Old Bond Street
London W1X 4BT
Tel: (020) 7491 0939

Gerard Ronay
3 Warple Way
London W3 0RF
Tel: (020) 8730 818

Godiva
247 Regent Street
London W1
Tel: (020) 7409 0963

Grania & Sarnia
6 Sterne Street
London W12 8AD
Tel: (020) 8749 8274

Green & Black
Whole Earth Food
269 Portobello Road
London W1 1LR
Tel: (020) 7229 7545

JB Confectionery
Unit 3, The Palmerston Centre
Oxford Road, Harrow
Middlesex HA3 7RG
Tel: (020) 8863 0011

Mortimer & Bennett
33 Turnham Green Terrace
London W4 1RG
Tel: (020) 8995 4145

Rococo Chocolates
321 Kings Road
London SW3 5EP
Tel: (020) 7352 5857
Fax: (020) 7352 7360

Sara Jayne
517 Old York Road
London SW18 1TF
Tel: (020) 8874 8500

The Chocolate Society
Clay Pit Lane, Roecliffe
Near Boroughbridge
N. Yorks YO5 9LS
Tel: (01423) 322 230

The Cool Chile Company
P.O. Box 5702
London W11 2GS
Tel: (020) 7229 9360

Town & Country Chocolates
52 Oxford Road
Denham, Uxbridge
Middlesex UB9 4DH
Tel: (01895) 256 166

FRANCE
Bonnat
8 Cours Senozan
38500 Voiron
Tel: (76) 05 28 09

Christian Constant
26 Rue du Bac
75007 Paris
Tel: (47) 03 30 00

Cluizel
La Fontaine au Chocolat
101 & 210 Rue Saint Honoré
75001 Paris
Tel: (1) 42 44 11 66

Fauchon
26-30 Place de la
Madeleine
75008 Paris
Tel: (1) 47 42 60 11

Lalonde
59 Rue St Dizier
54400 Nancy
Tel: 83 53 31 57

La Maison du Chocolat
225 Rue Faubourg St Honoré
75008 Paris
Tel: (1) 42 27 39 44

Le Roux
18 Rue du Port-Maria
56170 Quiberon
Tel: 97 50 06 83

Richart Design et Chocolat
258 Bd. Saint-Germain
75007 Paris
Tel: (1) 45 55 66 00

Chocolaterie Valrhona
BP 40
26600 Tain L'Hermitage
Tel: 75 07 90 90

Weiss
18 Avenue Denfert-Rochereau
42000 St Etienne
Tel: 77 49 41 41

GERMANY
Confiserie Heinemann
Krefelder Strasse 645
41066 München-Gladbach
Tel: (2161) 6930

Dreimeister
Weststrasse 47-49
Werl Westönnen
Tel: 29 22 8 20 45

Feodora
Vertriebszentrale Bremen
Postfach 105803
D-28058 Bremen
Tel: (421) 59 90 61

Bremer Chocolade-Fabrik
Hachez Westerstrasse 32
D-28199 Bremen
Tel: (421) 59 50 64 62

Leysieffer
Benzstrasse 9
49076 Osnabrück
Tel: (541) 91 420

Stollwerck
Stollwerckstrasse 27-31
51149 Köln
Tel: (22) 03 430

Van Houten
Am Stamgleis
22844 Norderstedt
Tel: (5) 26 020

ITALY
Caffarel/Peyrano
Via Gianevello 41
10062 Luserna,

S. Giovanni (TO), Piedmont
Tel: (121) 90 10 86

Maglio Arte Dolciaria
73024 Maglio
La Via Gioacchino, Toma 4
Tel: (836) 25 723

Majani
Via Lunga 19/C
Crespellano (BO)
Tel: 51 96 91 57

Perugina
Nestlé Italiana
Via Pievaiola, San Sisto, PGIT
Tel: (75) 52 761

SPAIN
Blanxart
Tambor del Bruc 13
08970 Sant Joan Despi
Barcelona
Tel: (3) 373 3761

Ludomar
Ciudad de la Asunción 58,
08030 Barcelona
Tel: (72) 203 662

Ramón Roca
Mercaders 6
17004 Gerona
Tel: (72) 203 662

Chocolates Valor
Pianista Gonzalo Soriano 13
Villajoyosa
Tel: (6) 589 050

SWITZERLAND
Lindt & Sprüngli
Seestrasse 204
CH-8802 Kilchberg
Tel: (1) 71 62 233

Sprüngli
Bahnhofstrasse 21
8022 Zurich
Tel: (1) 21 15 777

THE NETHERLANDS
Bensdorp
Heerenstraat 51, Postbus 4
1400 AA Bussum
Tel: (35) 69 74 911

Gerkens Cacao
Veerdijk 82, Postbus 82

1530 AB Wormer
Tel: (35) 69 74 911

Cacao De Zaan
Stationsstraat 76
Postbus 2
1540 AA Koog aan de Zaan
Tel: (75) 62 83 601

Droste
PO Box 5,
8170AA Vaassen
Tel: (578) 57 82 00

USA
Dilettante Chocolates
416 Broadway
Seattle, WA 98102
Tel: (206) 328 1530

Fran's
2805 East Madison,
Seattle, WA 98122-4020
Tel: (206) 322 0233

Ghirardelli
900 North Point Street
San Francisco, CA 94109
Tel: (415) 474 1414

Joseph Schmidt Confections
3489 16th Street
San Francisco, CA 9411
Tel: (415) 861 8682

Richard Donnelly Fine
Chocolates
1509 Mission Street
Santa Cruz, CA 95060
Tel: (408) 458 4214

Moonstruck Chocolatier
6663 SW BVTN
Hillsdale Highway, STE194
Portland, OR 97225
Tel: (503) 283 8843

COFFEE SUPPLIERS AROUND THE WORLD

Australia
Coffee suppliers:
Arabicas Coffee Australia
Pty Ltd
136 Mason St
Mareeba, QLD 4880
Tel: (07) 4092 4101

Aromas Pty Ltd
427 Montague Rd
West End, QLD 4101
Tel: (07) 3846 2594

Aromas Tea and Coffee
Merchants
191 Margaret St
Toowoomba, QLD 4350
Tel: (07) 4632 4533

Australian Estate Coffee
Direct Mail Order
Tel: (1800) 043 611

Exporters:
Web: www.australiancoffee-
exporters.com.au
Email: sales@australiancoffee-
exporters.com.au
7 Lena Close
Clifton Beach,
QLD 4879
Tel: (07) 40 553315

Skybury Coffee Estate
Atherton Tablelands, QLD
Tel: (07) 4093 2194

Coffee tree supplier:
Coffee Pot Nursery
179 Tintenbar Road
Tintenbar, NSW 2478
Tel: (02) 6687 8430

Coffee equipment suppliers:
Coffee & Tea Supplies of W.A.
93 Pavers Circle
Malaga, WA 6090
Tel: (08) 9248 1500
Fax: (08) 9248 1499

Segafredo Zanetti Australia
Pty Ltd
4 Huntley St
Alexandria, 2015 NSW
Tel: (02) 9310 3664
Fax: (02) 9310 3751
Email:segafred@ozemail.com.au

Tasman Coffee Company
Pty Ltd
Depot Road
Mornington,
7018 TAS
Tel: (03) 6245 9330
Fax: (03) 6245 9331

The Short Black Company
25 Burwood Rd
Hawthorn, 3122 VIC
Tel: (03) 9818 0667
Fax: (03) 9819 0843

Art Deco Coffee Repairs
& Sales
123 Holden St
Ashfield, 2131 NSW
Tel: 0412 45 5994

Auto Cappuccino Machines
6 South Boulivard
Tea Tree Gully, 5091 SA
Tel: (08) 8264 7751

Belaroma
75 Kenneth Rd
Manly Vale, 2093 NSW
Tel: (02) 9948 0221

Classic Coffee Company Cairns
126 Sheridan St
Cairns, 4870 QLD
Tel: (07) 4051 8966

Five Star Gourmet
Foods Sydney
13 Willoughby Road
Crows Nest, NSW 2065
Tel: (02) 9438 5666

Coffee houses and cafés:
Grinder's Coffee House
1 Taylor St
Darlinghurst, NSW 2010
Tel: (02) 9360 3255
www.grinderscoffee.com.au

Forsyth Coffee
284 Willoughby Road
Naremburn, NSW 2065
Tel: (02) 9906 7388
www.netorder.com.au/forsyth/
coffee

La Buvette
Shop 2, 65 Macleay Street
Potts Point, NSW 2011
Tel: 02 9358 5113

Caffee e'Cucina
581 Chapel Street
South Yarra, VIC 3141
Tel: (03) 9827 4139
Fax: (03) 9826 8355

Internet Sites:
Coffee from Oz Coffee
www.ozcoffee.com.au

Coast Roast Coffee Co,
Cairns QLD Australia
www.coastroast.com.au

Boema
www.boema.com.au/
CoffeeRecipes.htm

Kona Coffee Company
www.kona.com.au

Bay Coffee Roasters
Neutral Bay
www.baycoffee.com.au/

Europe
Coffee suppliers, cafés and
organizations:

AUSTRIA
Café Central
Palais Ferstel
Herrengasse and Strauchgasse
Vienna
Tel: (1) 53 33 76 30

Café Museum
Friedrichstrasse 6
Vienna
Tel: (1) 586 52 02

Café Sacher
Philharmonikerstrasse 4
Vienna
Tel: (1) 512 14 87

Demel's
Kohlmarkt 14
Vienna
Tel: (1) 53 51 71 70

BELGIUM
Cafés Knopes
Grand Place 24
6700 Aron
Tel: (63) 22 7407

Corica
49 rue du Marché aux Puces
1000 Brussels
Tel: (2) 511 88 52

CZECH REPUBLIC
Café Savoy
Vitezna, 1
Prague,

ENGLAND
Algerian Coffee Stores
52 Old Compton St
London W1V 6PB
Tel: (020) 7437 2480

Aroma
273 Regent Street
London W1
Tel: (020) 7495 4911

Bar Italia
22 Frith Street
London W1
Tel: (020) 7437 4520

Café Mezzo
100 Wardour Street
London W1
Tel: (020) 7314 4000

Café Minema
43 Knightsbridge
London SW1
Tel: (020) 7201 1618

Café Nero
43 Frith Street
London W1V 5CE
Tel: (020) 7434 3887

Coffee Republic
2 South Molton Street
London W1
Tel: (020) 7629 4567

The Drury Tea and Coffee
Company
37 Drury Lane
London WC2B 5RR
Tel: (020) 7836 2607

Fern's Coffee Specialists and
Tea Merchants
27 Rathbone Place
Oxford Street
London W1P 2EP
Tel: (020) 7636 2237

Fortnum & Mason
181 Piccadilly
London W1A 1ER
Tel: (020) 7734 8040

Harrods
Knightsbridge
London SW1X 7XL
Tel: (020) 7730 1234

Harvey Nichols
Knightsbridge
London SW1
Tel: (020) 7235 5000

H.R. Higgins
79 Duke Street

London W11M 6AS
Tel: (020) 7629 3913

International Coffee
Organization
22 Berners Street
London W1P 4DD
Tel: (020) 7580 8591

Maison Bertaux
28 Greek Street
London W1V 5LL
Tel: (020) 7437 6007

The Monmouth Coffee Company
27 Monmouth Street
London WC2H 9DD
Tel: (020) 7836 5272

Pret à Manger
Head office:
Old Mitre Court
43 Fleet Street
London EC4Y 1BT
Tel: (020) 7827 6300

Seattle Coffee Company
Head office:
51/54 Long Acre,
London WC2 9JR
Tel: (020) 7836 2100

Selfridges
400 Oxford Street
London W1A 1AB
Tel: (020) 7629 1234

Wilkinson's Tea and Coffee
Merchants
5 Lobster Lane
Norwich NR2 1DQ
Tel: (01603) 625121
Fax: (01603) 789016

Wittard of Chelsea
Head Office:
Union Court,
22 Union Road
London SW4 6JQ
Tel: (020) 7627 8885

FRANCE:
Brûlerie de L'Odeon
6 rue de Crébillon
75006 Paris
Tel: (01) 43 26 39 32

Café Beaubourg
45 rue Saint-Merri
75004 Paris
Tel: (01) 48 87 63 96

Cafés Estrella
34 rue Saint-Sulpice
75006 Paris
Tel: (01) 46 33 16 37

Café de Flore
172 boulevard Saint-Germain
75006 Paris
Tel: (01) 45 48 55 26

Café de La Paix
Place de l'Opera
75009 Paris
Tel: (01) 40 07 30 20

Café Richelieu
Place Carrousel
75001 Paris
Tel: (01) 47 03 99 68

Couleur Café
34 rue de Ponthieu
75008 Paris
Tel: (01) 42 56 00 15

Les Deux Magots
6 place Saint-Germain-des-Prés
75006 Paris
Tel: (01) 45 48 55 25

La Grande Épicerie de Paris
(Le Bon Marché)
38 rue de Sèvres
75007 Paris
Tel: (01) 44 39 81 00

Cathy et Pascal Guraud
21 Boulevard de Reuilly
75012 Paris
Tel: (01) 43 43 39 27

Lapeyronie
3 rue Brantôme
75003 Paris
Tel: (01) 40 27 97 57

Verlet
256 rue Saint-Honoré
75001 Paris
Tel: (01) 42 60 67 39

Whittard of Chelsea
22 rue de Buci
75006 Paris

GERMANY
Café Einstein
Kurfürstendamm 58
Berlin
Tel: (30) 261 50 96

Eduscho
Head office:
Lloydstrasse 4
28217 Bremen
Tel: (421) 3 89 30

Alois Dallmayr
Dienerstrasse 14–15
80331 Munich
Tel: (89) 21 35 0

Eilles
Residenzstrasse 13
80333 Munich
Tel: (89) 22 61 84

ITALY
Caffè Tazza D'Oro
Via degli Orfani 84
Rome
Tel (6) 6678 97 92

Caffè Florian
Piazza San Marco 56–59
Venice
Tel: (41) 528 53 38

Caffè Paskowski
Piazza della Republica
Florence
Tel: (55) 21 02 36

Caffè Perocchi
Via Otto Febbraio 15
Padua
Tel: (49) 876 25 76

Caffè Ristorante Torino
Piazza San Carlo 204
Turin
Tel: (11) 547 356

Caffè Rivoire
Piazza della Signoria 4R
Florence
Tel: (55) 21 44 12

Caffè San Carlo
Piazza San Carlo 156
Turin
Tel: (11) 561 77 48

Caffè degli Specchi
Piazza Unità d'Italia 7
Trieste
Tel: (40) 36 57 77

Caffè Tommaseo
Riva Tre Novembre 5
Trieste
Tel: (40) 36 57 77

Sant'Eustachio
Piazza Sant'Eustachio 82
Rome
Tel: (6) 688 02 048

New Zealand
Coffee roasters and suppliers:
Allpress Espresso Coffee
Roasters
Tel: (09) 358 3121

Altura Coffee Company Ltd
3/11 Colway Place
Auckland
Tel:(09) 443 4111

Atomic Coffee Roasters
420 New North Road
Kingsland
Tel: 846 5883

Burton Hollis Coffee
6 Mepai Place
Auckland
Tel: (09) 277 6375

Chiasso Coffee Co. Ltd
71b Lake Road
Devonport, Auckland
Tel: (09) 445 1816

Columbus Coffee
Head Office:
43 High Street
Auckland
Tel: (09) 309 2845

Robert Harris Coffee &
Equipment
Direct mail order
Tel: (0800) 426 3333

Santos Coffee Roasting Co. Ltd
14 Adelaide Street
P.O. Box 91-723
Freeman's Bay, Auckland
Tel: (09) 309 8977
email: santos@xtra.co.nz

Starbucks Coffee
305 Parnell Road
Auckland
Tel: (09) 336 1599

Sweet Inspirations
143 Williamson Ave
Auckland
Tel: (09) 378 7261

Vinotica
Unit D
3 Henry Rose Place
Albany, Auckland
Tel: (09) 415 5942

Vittoria Coffee and Equipment
Cntarella Bros Pty Ltd
8 Goodman Place
Onehunga
Tel: (09) 622 2409

United States
Coffee roasters and suppliers:
Ancora Coffee Roasters
112 King Street
Madison, WI 53703
Tel: (800) 666 4869

Armeno Coffee Roasters, Ltd
75 Otis Street
Northborough, MA 01532
Tel: (800) ARMENO-1

Bainbridge Coffee Company
584 Winslow Way East
Bainbridge Island, WA 98110
Tel: (888) 472 6333

Bean Central
2817 West End Avenue
Nashville, TN 37200
1800 JAVA BEAN

Beans and Machines
1121 First Avenue
Seattle, WA 98100

Bunn Coffee Service Inc.
51 Alpha Plaza
Hicksville, NY 11801
Tel: (800) 542 0566

Caribou Coffee
55 West Monroe
Chicago, IL 60602
Tel: (888) 227 4268
www.caribou-coffee.com

Coffee Concepts
10836 Grissom
Suite 110
Dallas, TX 75229
Tel: (972) 241 1618
www.coffeeconcepts.com

The Coffee Mill Roastery
161 East Franklin Street
Chapel Hill, NC 27514
Tel: (919) 929 1727
www.coffeeroastery.com

Daybreak Coffee Roasters, Inc.
2377 Main Street
Glastonbury, CT 06033
Tel: (860) 657 4466
www.daybreakcoffee.com

Greene Brothers Specialty
Coffee Roasters
313 High Street
Hackettstown, NJ 07840
Tel: (888) 665 2626

The Kona Coffee Council
P.O. Box 2077
Kealakekua, HI 96750
www.kona-coffee-council.com

Maui Coffee Roasters
444 Hana Highway
Kahului, Maui, HI 96732
Tel: (800) 645 2877
www.nicbeans@maui.net

The Original San Juan Coffee
Roasting Company
18 Cannery Landing
Friday Harbor, WA 98250
Tel: (800) 624 4119

Ozzies Coffee & Tea
57 Seventh Avenue
Brooklyn, NY 11215
Tel: (888) 699 4371
www.ozziescoffee.com

Peet's Coffee & Tea
P.O. Box 12509
Berkeley, CA 94712-3509
Tel: (800) 999 2132
www.peets.com

Roast Your Own
P.O. Box 198
Genoa, NY 13071
Tel: (800) 784 7117

Royal Blend Coffee Company
P.O. Box 7066
Bend, OR 97708
Tel: (541) 388 8164
www.royalblend.com

San Francisco Bay Gourmet
Coffee
1933 Davis Street, Suite 308
San Leandro, CA 94577
Tel: (800) 732 2948

Spinelli Coffee Company 495
Barneveld Avenue
San Francisco, CA 94124
Tel: (800) 421 5282
Fax: (415) 821 7199

Starbucks
Consumer Relations
P.O. Box 3717
Seattle, WA 98124 3717
Tel: (206) 447 1575 x2900
www.starbucks.com

Wilderness Coffee Company
13541 Grove Drive North
Maple Grove, MN 55311
Tel: (612) 420 4830

INDEX

ACKNOWLEDGEMENTS

Thanks to the following companies for supplying chocolates for photography: Ackermans, Alfred Ritter, Bendicks (Mayfair) Ltd, Charbonnel et Walker, The Cool Chile Company, The Chocolate Society, Richard Donnelly, Feodora Chocolate, Ghirardelli Chocolate Company, Grania & Sarni, Green and Black, The Jenks Group, JB Confectionery, Leonidas, Lessiters, Nestlé Rowntree Ltd, Parsons Trading Ltd, Perugina, Richart Design et Chocolat, Rococo, Ryne Quality Confectionery, Joseph Schmidt, Town & Country Chocolates, Trustin.

Thanks also to Stefano Raimondi of the Italian Trade Centre, Patrizia De Vito of the Associazione Industrie Dolciarie in Rome, Elaine Ashton of Grania and Sarnia, Dan Mortimer of Mortimer and Bennet, David Lyle of Town and Country Chocolates and John Bacon of JB Confectionery. Christine McFadden is particularly indebted to the late Sophie Coe, and her husband Michael Coe, for their book *The True*

History of Chocolate, and to Chantal Coady for *The Chocolate Companion*.

The publishers would like to thank the following people for their generous assistance with the preparation of the *Coffee* section: Tony Higgins of H.R. Higgins Ltd., London; Mehmet Kurukaveçi of Istanbul; Frank Neale; Celcius Lodder, Martin Wattam and the library staff of the International Coffee Organization, Coffee Information Centre, London. The following companies provided helpful assistance, equipment and coffee bean

samples: Algerian Coffee Company; Andronicus; Bramah Tea and Coffee Museum; Ecom; Fairfax Kitchens; Gala Tea and Coffee company; Heals Café, Tottenham Court Road London, UK; Master Roasts; Monmouth Coffee Company and The Priory Tea and Coffee Company.

PICTURE ACKNOWLEDGEMENTS
All pictures in the *Chocolate* section are by Don Last, except for the following: pp13br, 14br, 23b, 28b, 57tr **AKG Photographic Library**; 22r, 23, 24t, 24bl, 26br, 27r, 30b, 56bl, 56br **Bridgeman Art**

Library; p29b **Mansell Collection**; pp15t, 31t, 32t, 34br, 53br **Public Records Office**; pp12l, 13l, 14, 19t, 20tl, 20tr, 24r, 29l, 29tr, 29tl, 30b, 33br, 54br, 55l, 57br 64tl, 65l **Visual Arts Library**. Other pictures supplied courtesy of **Bendick's (Mayfair) Ltd**: p20bl, **Cadburys Ltd**: pp32bl; 50b; 51bl; 56tr. **Fran's**: p58. **Godiva**: pp43bl; 54t. **Nestlé Rowntree Ltd**: pp31b; 40br; 42tr; 42l, **Rococo**: 21bl.

All pictures in the *Coffee* section are by William Lingwood, Louisa Dare and Janine Hosegood, except for the following: pp267b, 285, 309 **Advertising Archives**; pp266, 267t, 270, 284, 288, 289, 291, 292t, 293, 294b, 295, 300, 301, 302, 305 **AKG Photographic Library**; p280, 283 **Bridgeman Art Library**; pp268, 292, 351t, 356b, 372t **Cephas**; pp268t, 268b, 273, 274, 275 **Charmet**; pp277, 279, 281, 282, 286, 290b, 296t, 296b, 298t, 299b **E.T. Archive**; pp278, 299t, 302, 303, 304, 306 **Hulton Getty**; pp287, 298b **Museum of London**; p297 **Lloyds**.